AF228413

The Labors of a Godly and Learned Divine
WILLIAM PERKINS

The Labors of a Godly and Learned Divine
WILLIAM PERKINS

Including Previously Unpublished Sermons

MATTHEW N. PAYNE

J. STEPHEN YUILLE

REFORMATION HERITAGE BOOKS
Grand Rapids, Michigan

The Labors of a Godly and Learned Divine, William Perkins
© 2022 by Matthew N. Payne and J. Stephen Yuille

Reformation Heritage Books
3070 29th St. SE
Grand Rapids, MI 49512
616-977-0889
orders@heritagebooks.org
www.heritagebooks.org

Printed in the United States of America
22 23 24 25 26 27/10 9 8 7 6 5 4 3 2 1

Library of Congress Cataloging-in-Publication Data

Names: Payne, Matthew N., author. | Yuille, J. Stephen, 1968- author.
Title: The labors of a godly and learned divine, William Perkins : including
    previously unpublished sermons / Matthew N. Payne, J. Stephen Yuille.
Description: Grand Rapids, Michigan : Reformation Heritage Books, [2022] |
    Includes bibliographical references and index.
Identifiers: LCCN 2022024778 (print) | LCCN 2022024779 (ebook) |
    ISBN 9781601789471 (hardcover) | ISBN 9781601789488 (epub)
Subjects: LCSH: Perkins, William, 1558–1602. | Perkins, William, 1558-1602—
    Sermons.
Classification: LCC BX9339.P43 P39 2022 (print) | LCC BX9339.P43 (ebook) |
    DDC 285/.9092 [B]—dc23/eng/20220711
LC record available at https://lccn.loc.gov/2022024778
LC ebook record available at https://lccn.loc.gov/2022024779

For additional Reformed literature, request a free book list from Reformation Heritage Books at the above regular or e-mail address.

Contents

Preface

Reformation Heritage Books (RHB) has published William Perkins's *Works* in a ten-volume set (2012–2020). The present work cites this set and follows the same editing and formatting guidelines. Spelling and capitalization conform to modern American standards. The old forms ("thou dost") are changed to the modern equivalent ("you do"), except in Scripture quotations and references to God. Punctuation has also been modernized in some cases, removing unnecessary commas and changing colons to periods when they indicate a full stop. However, the original words are left intact, not changed into modern synonyms, and the original word order is retained even when it differs from modern syntax. Pronouns are capitalized when referring to God. Some archaic terms and obscure references are explained in the editor's footnotes. As was common in his day, Perkins did not use quotation marks to distinguish a direct quotation from an indirect quotation, summary, or paraphrase, but simply put all citations in italics (as he also did with proper names). We have removed such italics and followed the general principle of placing citations in quotation marks even if they may not be direct or exact quotations. Perkins generally quoted the Geneva Bible, but rather than conforming his quotations to any translation of Scripture, we have left them in his words. Scripture references in the margins are brought into the text and enclosed in square brackets. Parenthetical Scripture references are abbreviated and punctuated according to the modern custom (as in Rom. 8:1), sometimes corrected and sometimes moved to the end of the clause instead of its beginning. Other notes from the margins are placed in footnotes and labeled "In the margin." References to original publications have also been supplemented by reference to the RHB editions in brackets wherever possible. Titles to original publications in footnotes are partial; complete bibliographical information for every known edition of Perkins's various works can be found in appendix 3.

Manuscript (MS) sources have likewise had spelling modernized, and contracted words have been expanded. Illegible words, whether due to damaged manuscripts or unreadable script, have been marked with "<…>" and the reason for their illegibility is footnoted in most cases. If the text has been provided from Perkins's published *Works*, it is included in < >. Where words or phrases were unintentionally duplicated by the transcriber, they have been removed from the main text. Original references to "Canticles" have been updated to "Song of Songs" to match modern conventions. Latin phrases have been translated alongside the original, except where the original MS provides its own translation immediately afterward.

We are grateful to Dr. Tyler Flatt (assistant professor of humanities, Boyce College, Louisville, KY) for his assistance with the Latin translation. We are also grateful to the following institutions for their permission to publish our transcriptions of manuscript material in their keeping. To the Senate House Library, University of London, for undertaking the digitization of MS187, "Commonplace book including notes on espionage."[1] To the Master and Fellows of Pembroke College, Cambridge, for permission to publish material from MS LCII.164, "Chaderton Lecture Notes."[2] To the Syndics of Cambridge University Library for permission to publish material from MS Add.8563, "William Perkins: Sermons."[3] To the Yorkshire County Records Office for Hutton family MS ZAZ 75.[4] Lastly, to the British Library for undertaking digitization of Harley MS976, "Notes on Sermons by Michael Foster."[5]

---

1. University of London, Senate House Library, MS187, "Commonplace Book including Notes on Espionage."

2. Cambridge, Pembroke College, MS LCII.164, "Chaderton Lecture Notes."

3. Cambridge University Library, Department of Manuscripts and University Archives, MS Add.8563, "William Perkins: Sermons."

4. North Yorkshire County Record Office, Book of Theological Manuscript, Hutton family MS ZAZ 75.

5. British Library, Harley MS 976, "Notes on Sermons by Michael Foster."

Overview of Documents

This book consists of seven chapters. Chapter 1 examines the history of the publication of William Perkins's literary corpus, which culminated in three volumes in 1608–1609, and a final corrected edition in 1631. This essay is followed by various original documents which provide insight into the process by which Perkins's works were collected, edited, and printed. Chapter 2 reproduces a sermon of Perkins's which has remained out of print since its brief appearance in 1604. Chapters 3–6 reproduce material from four manuscript sources which has never before been published, mainly consisting of various of Perkins's sermons as heard and transcribed by his peers and students. Each chapter consists of an essay, analyzing the origin of the manuscript and introducing its contents, followed by a full transcription of the sermons. Those sermons which were eventually included in a published treatise are identified by their title, thereby distinguishing them from previously unpublished sermons (namely, Genesis 2:18–24, 1 Samuel 1:9–13, John 3:16, Acts 2:16–17, Romans 4:25, 1 Corinthians 11:28, and 2 Corinthians 4:3–4). Chapter 7 consists of James Montagu's sermon preached at Perkins's funeral, prefaced with an introductory essay. Appendix 1 reproduces a notice prefixed to his Exposition of the Lord's Prayer, explaining its corrections of an unauthorized edition published by a third party. Appendix 2 sets three sources of Perkins's sermons on Jude 3–4 alongside one another, offering the reader opportunity to evaluate the accuracy of notes taken down at his sermons. Appendix 3 offers a comprehensive catalogue of early-modern editions of Perkins's works, both English and foreign language editions.

Master Perkins's Prayer before His Sermons

1. Publishing Perkins's Works
   The Last Will & Testament, 1602
   Announcement 1: Advertisement to Printers & Publishers, 1603
   Announcement 2: Printer to the Reader, 1603
   Announcement 3: Editor's Preface, *The First Part of the Cases of Conscience*, 1604

Genesis 2:24 (sermon 7)
Genesis 2:24 (sermon 8)
Genesis 2:24 (sermon 9)
Genesis 2:24 (sermon 10)
Genesis 2:24 (sermon 11)

Genesis 8:21   } cf. *A Treatise of Man's Imaginations*

Acts 2:16–17

Revelation 18:4 (sermon 1)
Revelation 18:4 (sermon 2)   } cf. *A Reformed Catholic*

Jude 3 (sermon 1)
Jude 4 (sermon 2)
Jude 4 (sermon 3)
Jude 4 (sermon 4)
Jude 4 (sermon 5)
Jude 5 (sermon 6)
Jude 5 (sermon 7)   cf. *A Commentary upon the Whole Epistle of Jude*
Jude 6 (sermon 8)
Jude 6 (sermon 9)
Jude 7 (sermon 10)
Jude 8 (sermon 11)
Jude 8 (sermon 12)
Jude 8 (sermon 13)
Jude 8–9 (sermon 14)

Exodus 22:18 (sermon 1)
Exodus 22:18 (sermon 2)   } cf. *The Damned Art of Witchcraft*
Exodus 22:18 (sermon 3)

Matthew 5:27

Isaiah 50:4   } cf. *Cases of Conscience*

Matthew 23:37–38   } cf. *God's Free Grace & Man's Free Will*

7. Funeral Sermon for William Perkins
    On the Occasion of the Death of William Perkins

Appendix 1: Perkins's Preface, *Exposition of the Lord's Prayer* (1592)
Appendix 2: Perkins's Sermons on Jude 3–4 (Three Sources Compared)
Appendix 3: Catalogue of Editions of Perkins's Works

Master Perkins's Prayer before His Sermons[1]

O Almighty Lord God, most merciful and loving Father in Jesus Christ, we are here assembled before Thy glorious Majesty to be partakers of Thy heavenly Word, which of Thine infinite goodness and mercy Thou hast ordained to be the ordinary means to work our salvation.

We beseech Thee, therefore, most merciful Father, to bless every one of us in the hearing and the speaking of Thy holy Word. Good Lord, open our blind eyes, that we may be able to understand it.

And whereas our hearts are full of hardness, full of sin, full of manifold rebellions, good Lord, soften our hard hearts, grant that Thy holy Word may be the two-edged sword of the Spirit to cut down sin and corruption in us, and make us new creatures in Jesus Christ.

And whereas we are troubled with many impediments in hearing of Thy Word, as wandering imagination in our hearts, suggestions of Satan, and the dullness of our own flesh, good Lord, remove these impediments and give us, everyone, grace to hear Thy Word in fear and reverence as in Thy presence, and to receive the same not as from man but as from Jesus Christ.

And when we have heard Thy Word, grant that it may be not the savor of death to our deeper condemnation but the savor of life to our eternal comfort and salvation. For this cause, write the same in every one of our hearts and transform us into the obedience of the same in our life and conversation.

And because Satan is a deadly enemy to the ministry of Thy Word, good Lord, confound Satan. Dissolve in every one of us the cursed works of the devil. Work Thine own good works. Show Thyself more merciful in blessing of Thy Word than Satan is or can be malicious in hindering of the same.

Hear us, we beseech Thee, in these requests, and grant these graces to every one of us, not for our own merits (for unto us belong nothing but eternal shame and confusion for our sins) but for the merits of Thy dear son Jesus Christ, in whom Thou art well pleased.

To whom with Thee and the Holy Spirit be given of every one of us all praise, honor, and glory, both now and forevermore.

Amen.

---

1. William Perkins, *A Comfort for the Feeble Minded* (bound with *Satans Sophistrie*), ed. Robert Hill (London: Printed by Richard Field for E. Edgar, 1604), 158–60.

Chapter 1

Publishing Perkins's Works

On October 16, 1602, recognizing that he was "weak in body," William Perkins prepared his last will and testament.[1] He would die six days later. Expectedly, he made provision in his will for his beloved wife (Timothie), his children, parents, siblings, and "the poor people" of St. Andrews parish in Cambridge. He entrusted the sale of his house, garden, and orchard to his loving friends: Edmund Barwell (master of Christ's College),[2] James Montagu (master of Sydney Sussex College),[3] Laurence Chaderton (master of Emmanuel College),[4]

---

1. See Perkins's Last Will and Testament.

2. Edmund Barwell was educated (BA, MA, BD) at Christ's College, Cambridge. He was fellow of Christ's from 1570 to 1581, and then master until his death in 1609. He was also rector of Toft, Cambridgeshire, beginning in 1584. John Venn, *Alumni Cantabrigienses: A Biographical List of All Known Students, Graduates, and Holders of Office at the University of Cambridge from the Earliest Times to 1900*, part 1, *From the Earliest Times to 1751* (Cambridge: Cambridge University Press, 1927), 1:101.

3. James Montagu (c. 1568–1618) was a student at Christ's College, Cambridge, beginning in 1585, where he came under the influence of Perkins, who was a fellow (1584–1594). Montagu received his doctor of divinity in 1598 by special grace and served as the founding master of Sidney Sussex College, Cambridge (1596–1608). Montagu preached at Perkins's funeral at Christ's College in 1602. He went on to became dean of Lichfield (1603–1604), dean of Worcester (1604–1608), bishop of Bath and Wells (1608–1616), and finally bishop of Winchester (1616–1618). Venn, *Alumni Cantabrigienses*, pt. 1, vol. 3, p. 201; P. E. McCullough, "Montagu, James (1568–1618)," in *Oxford Dictionary of National Biography* (Oxford: Oxford University Press, 2004; online ed., January 2008); British Library, Harley MS 976, "Notes on Sermons by Michael Foster," 2r.

4. Laurence Chaderton (1536–1640) studied at Christ's College, Cambridge, beginning in about 1562, then served as a fellow from 1568 until 1577, when he relinquished his fellowship to get married. He became lecturer at St. Clements, Cambridge, at about this time, holding the post for about fifty years. Chaderton became the first master of Emmanuel College, Cambridge (1584–1622). Together Chaderton and Perkins were among the most prominent voices of the late Elizabethan Cambridge Puritan circle, and their names are often associated in student notebooks and other records of the period. Chaderton went on to be one of the four divines who championed the Puritan cause at the Hampton Court Conference in 1604, and he was also among the translators of the KJV Bible. Venn, *Alumni Cantabrigienses*, pt. 1, vol. 1, p. 313; Patrick Collinson, "Chaderton, Laurence (1536?–1640)," in *Oxford Dictionary of National Biography* (Oxford: Oxford University Press, 2004). See also Joel R. Beeke, "Laurence Chaderton: His Life and Ecclesiology,"

Richard Foxcroft (master of arts),[5] Thomas Cropley (master of arts),[6] and Nathaniel Cradock (his brother-in-law).[7] Perkins appointed his wife as sole executor, while designating Cropley and Cradock as supervisors to counsel and aid her in the operating of his will.

It fell to these assignees to decide what to do with Perkins's many sermons and treatises. Prior to his death, he had published numerous works, but additional unpublished works were in his study and in the possession of his friends. Some of these had been prepared for the press by Perkins prior to his death, while others had been copied by students and colleagues who had heard him preach.[8] The responsibility for publishing this material was entrusted by his assignees to "learned men in Cambridge."[9] The core members of this group entered Cambridge in 1588/1589, experiencing Perkins's ministry as impressionable undergraduates as his star rose to its apex in the early 1590s. By 1609, they had issued three volumes containing thirty-eight treatises.

Volume 1

In 1603, Perkins's long-term publisher, John Legate,[10] compiled into one volume most of the works that Perkins had published in his lifetime.[11] They included

A Treatise Tending unto a Declaration Whether a Man Be in the Estate of Damnation or Salvation (1590)

Puritan Reformed Journal 8, no. 1 (2016): 110–28; and Peter Lake, *Moderate Puritans and the Elizabethan Church* (Cambridge: Cambridge University Press, 1982), 1–15, 25–54, 243–61.

5. Richard Foxcroft (d. 1609) was a graduate of St. John's College, Cambridge. He attained a fellowship there in 1577, the year in which Perkins first entered Christ's College. Venn, *Alumni Cantabrigienses*, pt. 1, vol. 2, p. 170.

6. Thomas Cropley (d. 1609) was a graduate of Clare College, Cambridge. His procession through degrees aligned with Perkins: matriculation (1577), BA (1580/1581), and MA (1584), indicating a possible early peer friendship. Venn, *Alumni Cantabrigienses*, pt. 1, vol. 1, p. 424.

7. Nathaniel Cradock was a Cambridge landowner and the brother of Perkins's wife, Timothie.

8. See Announcement 2.

9. See Announcement 2.

10. John Legate (c. 1562–c. 1620) was the printer for Cambridge University—the oldest publishing house in the world, established by royal charter in 1534. David McKitterick, "Legate, John (c. 1562–1620/21)," in *Oxford Dictionary of National Biography* (Oxford: Oxford University Press, 2004; online ed., January 2008). "Legate's principal author, his best seller, was the 'learned, pious, and painful,' William Perkins." M. H. Black, *Cambridge University Press, 1584–1984* (Cambridge: Cambridge University Press, 1984), 55. Legate, along with Perkins's assignees, was an enthusiastic advocate of the careful preservation of Perkins's works. His personal devotion to Perkins's legacy evidently extended beyond commercial interests. See Announcements 1, 2, and 7. On the tensions between John Legate and other Cambridge and London printers, see David McKitterick, *A History of Cambridge University Press*, vol. 1, *Printing and the Book Trade in Cambridge, 1534–1698* (Cambridge: Cambridge University Press, 1992), 109–35.

11. See Announcement 2. For a complete list of editions of Perkins's works, see appendix 3.

The Foundation of Christian Religion (1590)

An Exposition of the Lord's Prayer (1592)

A Golden Chain (trans. Robert Hill[12]) (1592)

A Case of Conscience (1592)

A Direction for the Government of the Tongue (1593)

Two Treatises: Of the Nature and Practice of Repentance; Of the Combat of the Flesh and Spirit (1593)

A Salve for a Sick Man (or *The Right Manner of Dying Well*) (1595)

An Exposition of the Symbol or Creed of the Apostles (1595)

A Discourse of Conscience (1596)

A Declaration of the True Manner of Knowing Christ Crucified (1596)

A Grain of Mustard Seed (1597)

A Reformed Catholic (1597)

A Warning against Idolatry of the Last Times (1601)

How to Live and That Well (1601)

The True Gain (1601)

A Treatise of God's Free Grace and Man's Free Will (1601)

A Treatise of the Vocations or Callings of Men (ed. Thomas Pickering[13]) (1603)

---

12. Robert Hill (d. 1623) was educated at Christ's College, Cambridge (1581–1588), before being admitted as a fellow of St. John's College in 1588, which he held until 1608/1609. Early in his St. John's fellowship, Hill was commissioned by Perkins to translate his *Armilla Aurea* (1590) into English in two successive revised editions (*A Golden Chain*, 1591, 1592). After Perkins's death he published two volumes of Perkins's sermons on Matthew 4:1–11: William Perkins, *Satans Sophistrie Answered by Our Saviour Christ*, ed. Robert Hill (London: Richard Field, 1604); and William Perkins, *Lectures upon the Three First Chapters of the Revelation*, ed. Robert Hill (London: Richard Field, 1604). These volumes did not meet with the approval of Perkins's assignees and were soon afterward revised by Thomas Pierson (see below). Hill went on to hold several preaching posts in London. He would author several theological and pastoral works and continued his editorial and translation efforts, publishing works by Richard Greenham (c. 1540–1594), Girolamo Zanchi (1516–1590), Samuel Hieron (1572–1617), and William Bucanus (d. 1603). Venn, *Alumni Cantabrigienses*, pt. 1, vol. 2, p. 373; J. F. Merritt, "Hill, Robert (d. 1623)," in *Oxford Dictionary of National Biography* (Oxford: Oxford University Press, 2004; online ed., January 2008). For more on Hill, see J. F. Merritt, "The Pastoral Tightrope: A Puritan Pedagogue in Jacobean London," in *Politics, Religion and Popularity in Early Stuart Britain: Essays in Honour of Conrad Russell*, ed. Thomas Cogswell, Richard Cust, and Peter Lake (Cambridge: Cambridge University Press, 2002), 143–61.

13. Thomas Pickering (d. 1625) was a graduate of Emmanuel College, Cambridge. He entered the college in 1588 and was appointed a fellow in 1596. While at Cambridge, Pickering finalized Perkins's preparation of *A Treatise of the Vocations* for the press before undertaking the far larger task of preparing *The Whole Treatise of the Cases of Conscience* for publication in two installments (1604, 1606). See Announcements 3 and 4. He then served as vicar of Finchingfield, Essex, from 1606 until his death in 1625. During the early years of that appointment, he prepared two more of

The last, *A Treatise of the Vocations*, was published a few months after Perkins's death, but Legate included it in his compilation because Perkins himself had prepared it for the press.[14]

Volume 2

In 1608 Legate republished his volume of Perkins's works. He informed his readers of his intent to produce a second volume consisting of many other treatises from Perkins's own collection.[15] It appeared the following year and included

> *A Commentary upon the Five First Chapters of the Epistle to the Galatians* (ed. Ralph Cudworth[16]) (1604)

> *Hepieikia; or, A Treatise of Christian Equity and Moderation* (ed. William Crashawe[17]) (1604)

Perkins's works for publication: *A Discourse of the Damned Art of Witchcraft* (1608) and an English translation of Perkins's Latin manuscript treatise, *Christian Oeconomie* (1609). Venn, *Alumni Cantabrigienses*, pt. 1, vol. 3, p. 360.

14. See Announcement 1, which was published with *A Treatise of Vocations* (1603). The foreword indicates that the final manuscript was edited by "T. P." William Perkins, *A Treatise of the Vocations, or, Callings of Men* (Cambridge: John Legate, 1603), 4r. This almost certainly refers to Thomas Pickering, who was prominently involved in editing various works of Perkins's during this period. The other potential candidate with those initials, Thomas Pierson, had not yet arrived back in Cambridge from his post in Weaverham. Note: the RHB edition of this foreword contains a typo, making it Perkins's own preface ("W. P."), though it speaks of him in the third person as recently deceased (RHB 10:35).

15. See Announcement 7.

16. Ralph Cudworth (c. 1572–1624) was a graduate of Emmanuel College, Cambridge, entering the college in 1588 and holding a fellowship there until 1609. He went on to serve as minister at St. Andrews, Cambridge; as rector of Aller, Somerset (1610–1624); and as a chaplain to James I. He is not to be confused with his son of the same name (1617–1688), the influential Cambridge Platonist whose legacy would be at odds with that of his father. Venn, *Alumni Cantabrigienses*, pt. 1, vol. 1, p. 431; David A. Pailin, "Cudworth, Ralph (1617–1688)," in *Oxford Dictionary of National Biography* (Oxford: Oxford University Press, 2004; online ed., January 2008).

17. William Crashawe (1572–1626) was a graduate of St. John's College, Cambridge, entering in 1588 and becoming a fellow in 1594. He served as a minister in his native county of Yorkshire from 1599 to 1605 before obtaining the post of preacher to Inner and Middle Temples in London in 1605. Crashawe would take on a central role in the publication of Perkins's complete works. See Announcement 5. During this period, he personally brought several of Perkins's works to print: *Hepieikia; or, A Treatise of Christian Equity and Moderation* (1604), *The Calling of the Ministry* (1605), *A Faithful and Plain Exposition upon the First Two Verses of the Second Chapter of Zephaniah* (1605), *A Commentary upon the Eleventh Chapter to the Hebrews* (with Thomas Pierson, 1607), and the republication of *A Fruitful Dialogue concerning the End of the World* (1609). He went on to become vicar of St. Mary, Whitechapel, London, in 1618, which post he held until his death in 1626. Venn, *Alumni Cantabrigienses*, pt. 1, vol. 1, p. 414; W. H. Kelliher, "Crashawe, William (bap. 1572, d.1625/6)," in *Oxford Dictionary of National Biography* (Oxford: Oxford University Press, 2004; online ed., October 2009).

The Whole Treatise of the Cases of Conscience: Book 1 (1604), *Books 2 & 3* (ed. Thomas Pickering) (1606)

A Treatise of the Manner and Order of Predestination (trans. Francis Cacot[18] and Thomas Tuke[19]) (1606; orig. 1598)

The Art of Prophesying (trans. Thomas Tuke) (1607; orig. 1592)

A Harmony of the Old and New Testaments (1609; orig. 1598)

A Treatise of Man's Imaginations (ed. Thomas Pierson[20]) (1607)

The Problem of the Forged Catholicism (1609; orig. 1604)

Perkins had prepared his commentary on Galatians prior to his death. According to Ralph Cudworth, he wrote it "upon mature deliberation after his sermons...with his own hand." Cudworth claims to have but polished a

---

18. Francis Cacot was a graduate of Corpus Christi College, Cambridge, entering the college in 1593 and receiving his MA in 1601. He was headmaster of Rochester School (1601–1608), during which time he and Thomas Tuke translated Perkins's *De Praedestinationis Modo et Ordine* (1598) into English. Cacot went on to serve as the rector of Woldham, Kent, for nearly fifty years (1607–1656). Venn, *Alumni Cantabrigienses*, pt. 1, vol. 1, p. 279.

19. Thomas Tuke (1580/81–1657) was a graduate of Christ's College, Cambridge, entering the college in 1599 and receiving his MA in 1603. After graduation he appears to have sought preferment in Kent. During this period, he translated into English Perkins's *Prophetica* (1592) and *De Praedestinationis Modo et Ordine* (1598, with Francis Cacot). Both were published in 1606. Tuke went on to serve as the long-standing vicar of St. Olave, Jewry (1617–1657). He authored several theological and pastoral works. Venn, *Alumni Cantabrigienses*, pt. 1, vol. 4, p. 271; J. F. Merritt, "Tuke, Thomas (1580/81–1657)," in *Oxford Dictionary of National Biography* (Oxford: Oxford University Press, 2004; online ed., January 2008).

20. Thomas Pierson (c. 1573–1633) was a graduate of Emmanuel College, Cambridge, entering in 1589 and receiving his MA in 1597. Pierson returned to his native county in 1599, serving as lecturer at Northwich and then Weaverham for about two years each. In 1603, he was recalled to Cambridge by Perkins's assignees to revise Hill's publications of Perkins's sermons on Matthew 4:1–11 (*The Combat between Christ and the Devil Displayed*, 1606) and Revelation 1–3 (*An Exposition upon the First Three Chapters of Revelation*, 1606). See Announcement 6. He also edited Perkins's *A Treatise of Man's Imaginations* (1607) and his sermons on Hebrews 11 (*A Commentary upon the Eleventh Chapter to the Hebrews*, with William Crashawe, 1607) and Matthew 5–7 (*An Exposition upon Christ's Sermon in the Mount*, 1609). During this time Pierson was employed as household chaplain to Oliver St. John in Bedfordshire. Pierson saw the publication of Perkins's works through to its completion in 1609 (Announcement 8). He went on to become rector of Brampton Bryan, Herefordshire, in 1612, serving there until his death in 1633. Venn, *Alumni Cantabrigienses*, pt. 1, vol. 3, p. 332; Jacqueline Eales, "Pierson, Thomas (c. 1573–1633)," in *Oxford Dictionary of National Biography* (Oxford: Oxford University Press, 2004; online ed., January 2008). On Pierson's further significance, see Jacqueline Eales, "Thomas Pierson and the Transmission of the Moderate Puritan Tradition," *Midland History* 20, no. 1 (1995): 75–102.

few phrases of "doubtful construction."[21] As for *Cases of Conscience*,[22] Thomas Pickering states that the original copy was "perused by the author himself before his death."[23] This work was in a state of near completion at the point of Perkins's death.[24]

Three of the works, *A Treatise of the Manner and Order of Predestination*, *The Art of Prophesying*, and *A Harmony of the Old and New Testaments*, were published by Perkins in Latin before his death as *De Praedestinationis Modo et Ordine* (1598), *Prophetica* (1592), and *Specimen Digesti* (1598). They were excluded from Legate's first volume because they had not yet been translated into English. *The Problem of the Forged Catholicism* was first published in Latin in 1604 as *Problema de Romanae Fidei Ementito Catholicismo*. Prior to his death, Perkins had entrusted the manuscript of this work to Samuel Ward[25] in order that he might bring it for publication.[26] It was then translated into English for inclusion in the second volume of Perkins's collected works. No translators are identified for the 1609 English texts of *A Harmony of the Old and New Testaments* or *The Problem of the Forged Catholicism*.

Perkins's *A Treatise of Man's Imagination* stands apart from the aforementioned six works (along with those in volume 1) because he had not prepared it for publication prior to his death. It consists of sermons, copied by those who heard him. The editor, Thomas Pierson, states, "I had the author's own draft of

---

21. "To the Reader," in William Perkins, *A Commentary or Exposition upon the First Five Chapters of the Epistle to the Galatians* (Cambridge: John Legate, 1604). Cudworth authored commentary on Galatians 6 to complement Perkins's treatment of the first five chapters of the epistle (Perkins, *First Five Chapters of the Epistle to the Galatians*, 477–662 [RHB 2:395–575]).

22. See Announcement 3.

23. See Announcement 4.

24. Book 3 treats the virtues of prudence, clemency, temperance, liberality, and justice. Perkins intended to complete the work with a treatment of fortitude. William Perkins, *The Whole Treatise of the Cases of Conscience* (Cambridge: John Legate, 1606), 474.

25. Samuel Ward (1572–1643) was a student at Christ's College, Cambridge, from 1588 to 1595, thus aligning his formative years with the bulk of Perkins's time as a fellow there (1584–1594). Both Perkins and James Montagu helped Ward with his college debts during this time, and Ward expresses his deep admiration for Perkins in his personal diary. Ward became a fellow of nearby Emmanuel College, Cambridge, in 1595 and went on to become a long-serving master of Sidney Sussex College, Cambridge (1610–1643). He later served as one of the English delegates to the Synod of Dort. Venn, *Alumni Cantabrigienses*, pt. 1, vol. 4, p. 334; Margo Todd, "Ward, Samuel (1572–1643)," in *Oxford Dictionary of National Biography* (Oxford: Oxford University Press, 2004; online ed., January 2008). For more on Ward's relationship with Perkins, see William B. Patterson, *William Perkins and the Making of Protestant England* (Oxford: Oxford University Press, 2014), 197–98.

26. In his preface, Ward writes, "Since he was hastening to death, he handed over to me a book to be printed for the public good" ("Quem mihi libellum, cùm ad superos properaret, publico bono excudendum tradidit"). William Perkins, *Guilielmi Perkinsi Problema de Romanæ Fidei Ementito Catholicismo* (Cambridge: John Legate, 1604), 2v.

the platform of it; beside two perfect copies of all his sermons."[27] The same is true of *A Treatise of Christian Equity*. Its editor, William Crashawe, notes that the work consists of what Perkins had "delivered…in a few lectures,"[28] adding that it is one of "the jewels which the Lord from [Perkins's] mouth, gave us to keep, and not for our own, but for the common good."

Volume 3

These "jewels" take center stage in the third volume of Perkins's works, which also appeared in 1609. Following "the advice of grave and learned men," Legate was determined to maintain the distinction "between those books which the author himself vet[ted] [while] living by his own care, not only in penning but likewise in the correcting of the same [and] did set forth, and those others which are *posthumi*, that is, born after his death, gathered and collected by others."[29] For the most part, these *posthumi* works constitute the third volume.

A Resolution to the Countrymen (1585)

The Combat between Christ and the Devil Displayed (ed. Thomas Pierson) (1606; original ed. Robert Hill, 1604)

An Exposition upon the First Three Chapters of Revelation (ed. Thomas Pierson) (1606; original ed. Robert Hill, 1604)

The Calling of the Ministry (ed. William Crashawe) (1605)

An Exhortation to Repentance (ed. William Crashawe) (1605)

An Exposition upon the Whole Epistle of Jude (ed. Thomas Taylor[30]) (1606)

A Commentary upon the Eleventh Chapter to the Hebrews (ed. William Crashawe and Thomas Pierson) (1607)

An Exposition upon Christ's Sermon in the Mount (ed. Thomas Pierson) (1608)

---

27. "To the Reader," in William Perkins, *A Treatise of Man's Imaginations* (Cambridge: John Legate, 1607), 5r (RHB 9:185).

28. "To the Reader," in William Perkins, *Hepieikia; or, A Treatise of Christian Equity and Moderation* (Cambridge: John Legate, 1604), 5v–6v (RHB 10:363).

29. See Announcement 7.

30. Thomas Taylor (1576–1632) was a graduate of Christ's College, Cambridge, entering in 1592, going on to hold a fellowship (1599–1604), and serving as Wentworth Hebrew lecturer (1601–1604). He edited Perkins's *An Exposition upon the Whole Epistle of Jude* (1606). Taylor's career was marked by trouble stemming from his outspoken advocacy of Reformed theology and ministry against the upsurge in anti-Calvinism during his day. He went on to serve as minister of St. Mary Aldermanbury, London, from 1625 until his death in 1632. Venn, *Alumni Cantabrigienses*, pt. 1, vol. 4, p. 209; J. Sears McGee, "Taylor, Thomas (1576–1632)," in *Oxford Dictionary of National Biography* (Oxford: Oxford University Press, 2004; online ed., January 2008).

A Discourse of the Damned Art of Witchcraft (ed. Thomas Pickering)
(1608)

*Christian Oeconomie; or, The Right Manner of Erecting and Ordering a
Family* (trans. and ed. Thomas Pickering) (1609)

A Fruitful Dialogue concerning the End of the World (ed. William
Crashawe) (1587)

The title page of *Christian Oeconomie* indicates that Perkins first penned it in
Latin, though it is noteworthy that he gave related lectures in English during
the last few years of his career.[31] The text included in volume 3 is Thomas Pickering's English translation of Perkins's original Latin manuscript.[32] *A Fruitful
Dialogue concerning the End of the World* first appeared in *Four Godly Treatises*
(1587),[33] an early edition of what would become Perkins's *A Treatise Tending unto a Declaration* (1590).[34] The latter work would consist of eight short
treatises, including three of the earlier "four godly treatises." In the process of
preparing *A Treatise Tending unto a Declaration*, Perkins left *A Fruitful Dialogue* behind, likely because the contemporary dispute it specifically addressed
had passed.[35] Similarly, Perkins originally published *A Resolution to the Countryman* in 1585 as the second part of a treatise titled *Four Great Liars*, which
had only immediate contemporary relevance.[36] However, the editors recognized the lasting value of *A Resolution to the Countryman* and included it in
Perkins's works, now apart from *Four Great Liars*. Notably, Perkins's two early

---

31. William Perkins, *Christian Oeconomie; or, The Right Manner of Erecting and Ordering
a Family* (London: Felix Kingston, 1609). See the three sermons on Genesis 2:18 (Hutton MS)
below. As lecturer, Perkins was supported by "the free contributions of his congregation, aided
by gifts from gentlemen in the neighborhood, of whom Mr. Wendy of Haslingfield was chief."
Charles Cooper and Thompson Cooper, *Athenae Cantabrigienses*, vol. 2, *1586–1609* (Cambridge:
Deighton, Bell & Co., 1861), 335. For more on the Puritan lectureships, see Paul Sever, *The Puritan Lectureships: The Politics of Religious Dissent, 1560–1662* (Stanford, Calif.: Stanford University
Press, 1970).

32. The original Latin MS is no longer extant. How it came into Pickering's possession is
unknown. It is not listed among the works found in Perkins's study by his assignees (Announcement 5).

33. William Perkins, *Four Godly Treatises, Very Necessary to Be Considered of All Christians*
(London: J. Wolfe, 1587).

34. William Perkins, *A Treatise Tending unto a Declaration Whether a Man Be in the Estate of
Damnation or in the Estate of Grace* (London: R. Robinson, 1590).

35. The dialogue between a Christian and a Worldling addresses the problem that many
believed that the world would end in 1588 (RHB 6:455–56).

36. *Four Great Liars* was a side-by-side comparison of four contemporary astrological
almanacs. Placing these alongside one another was intended to show how such works blatantly
contradicted one another. William Perkins, *Four Great Liars…Also, a Resolution to the Countryman…* (London: Robert Waldegrave, 1585).

Latin polemical treatises on memory were also left out of his collected works, probably due to their more esoteric subject matter.[37]

The remaining eight treatises comprising volume 3 were copies made by hearers of Perkins's original sermons and lectures. These copies were "diligently perused" by men of "sufficiency and integrity" in preparation for publication.[38] For example, Robert Hill claims to have "heard divers of the sermons" that constitute *The Combat between Christ and the Devil Displayed*.[39] William Crashawe states on the title page of *The Calling of the Ministry* that its contents were "delivered publicly in the university of Cambridge" and "taken from his mouth."[40] Perkins preached the content of *A Faithful and Plain Exposition upon the First Two Verses of the Second Chapter of Zephaniah* at Stourbridge Fair in Cambridge in 1593.[41] Crashawe was present at the delivery of those two sermons and declares that they were "taken with this hand of mine from his own mouth."[42] Thomas Pierson mentions that *An Exposition upon Christ's Sermon in the Mount* was "taken out of mine and other's notes."[43] Thomas Pickering indicates that *A Discourse on the Damned Art of Witchcraft* was "framed and delivered by M. William Perkins in his ordinary course of preaching."[44]

Controversy

The publication of Perkins's works was not without controversy. Even early in his career, there were some who published works in his name without his knowledge or consent. In 1592 he references "a book of late published in London under this title, *Perkins upon the Lord's Prayer*," and declares that it was

---

37. G. P. Cantabrigiensis, *Antidisconus Accessit Libellus* (London: Henry Middleton, 1584); G. P. Cantabrigiensis, *Libellus de Memoria* (London: Robert Waldegrave, 1584). These works were recently translated into English for the first time as *The Antidicson* (RHB 6:476–521) and *A Handbook of Memory Recall* (RHB 6:523–58). The same view on memory is applied to preaching in *The Art of Prophesying* (RHB 10:348).

38. See Announcement 5.

39. "Epistle Dedicatory," in William Perkins, *Satans Sophistrie Answered by Our Saviour Christ* (London: Richard Field for E. Edgar, 1604), 7v (RHB 1:83).

40. William Perkins, *Of the Calling of the Ministerie Two Treatises, Discribing the Duties and Dignities of That Calling. Delivered Publickly in the Uniuersitie of Cambridge, by Maister Perkins. Taken Then from His Mouth...* (London: I. R. Roberts for William Welby, 1605) (RHB 10:195).

41. Stourbridge Fair was an annual market fair held on Stourbridge Common, Cambridge. It attracted many visitors from outside Cambridge and thus offered local preachers such as Perkins an opportunity to address a broader cross-section of the English people than was usually possible.

42. "To the Reader," in William Perkins, *An Exhortation to Repentance* (London: Thomas Creede, 1605), 4v (RHB 9:83).

43. "To the Reader," in William Perkins, *A Godly and Learned Exposition of Christs Sermon in the Mount* (Cambridge: Thomas Brooke & Cantrell Legge, 1608), 4v (RHB 1:171).

44. William Perkins, *A Discourse of the Damned Art of Witchcraft...Framed and Delivered by M. William Perkins in His Ordinary Course of Preaching...* (Cambridge: Cantrel Legge, 1608).

"faulty both in the matter and manner of writing." Evidently, someone had attended Perkins's catechetical lectures on the Lord's Prayer and published the work based on their personal notes. Perkins was essentially forced to revise material for publication that he had never intended to put in print.[45]

Perkins's reputation was such that this problem only intensified after his death with the publication of *The Practice of Faith* (1602/3) and *The Reformation of Covetousness* (1603). These were both unauthorized and deeply flawed works, produced out of "rude and confused notes" and without adequate concern for accurately presenting Perkins's teaching.[46]

The responsibility of publishing Perkins's works had fallen to his assignees. Within a few months of his death, publisher John Legate issued an advertisement on their behalf addressed to all printers and publishers, warning that some men had presumed to undertake the publication of Perkins's works without the knowledge or consent of his friends.[47] Two years later they included an additional announcement in *The Calling of the Ministry* and *An Exhortation to Repentance*,[48] appealing directly "to all such as have any copies of the works of Master Perkins or intend to [bring] any of them [to] the press."[49] Their appeal was again necessitated by the publication of several of Perkins's works without the consent of his assignees, which had resulted in imperfect publications. Moreover, it had defrauded Perkins's wife and children "of their private benefit, to whom in all equity and conscience, it does principally appertain."[50]

This controversy was likely precipitated by Robert Hill's 1604 publication of *Satan's Sophistry* and *An Exposition upon the First Three Chapters of Revelation*. Two years later, both were revised by Thomas Pierson under the instructions of Perkins's executors.[51] Hill was no outsider to the publication of Perkins's work. In 1590 Perkins had appointed him to translate the celebrated *A Golden Chain*

---

45. See appendix 1.

46. See Announcement 1.

47. See Announcement 1.

48. The title pages for each of these two treatises state that they contain "a preface…touching the publishing of Master Perkins's works and a catalogue of all such particulars thereof, as are to be expected."

49. See Announcement 5.

50. See Announcement 5. Fuller notes that as lecturer at St. Andrews the Great, Perkins had a modest income, though many children to feed. Thomas Fuller, *Abel Redevivus: or, The Dead Yet Speaking. The Lives and Deaths of the Modern Divines* (London: Printed by Thomas Brudenell for John Stafford, 1651), 435.

51. William Perkins, *Satans Sophistrie Answered by Our Sauiour Christ*, ed. Robert Hill (London: Richard Field, 1604); William Perkins, *The Combat betweene Christ and the Divell Displayed* (London: Melchisedech Bradwood, 1606), 3r (RHB 1:76); William Perkins, *Lectures upon the Three First Chapters of the Revelation* (London: Richard Field, 1604); William Perkins, *Lectures upon the Three First Chapters of the Revelation* (London: Adam Islip, 1606), 3r (RHB 4:303–4).

into English.[52] While this likely explains Hill's personal sense of authorization regarding the posthumous publication of Perkins's sermons, his efforts were not in accordance with the wishes of Perkins's assignees. In his republication of *Satan's Sophistry*, Pierson remarks, "The view hereof has formerly been presented to your Honors by Master Robert Hill, bachelor of divinity, under this title, *Satan's Sophistry answered by our Savior Christ*. And now at the entreaty of M. Perkins's executors, I have published it again, yet under a new title, and more large almost by one third part."[53]

In his republication of *An Exposition upon the First Three Chapters of Revelation*, Pierson was even more pointed in his remarks. He expresses his hesitancy in censuring "those things wherein others have gone before" but claims that "the executors of the dead" will answer for his "discharge."[54] He does not question Robert Hill's motive in publishing this work without the approval of Perkins's executors, assuming that he "intended the glory of God in the good of his church, and the credit of the reverend author."[55] While acknowledging that his revised edition might prove "prejudicial" to Hill's "good estimation," he believes it was necessitated by the inadequacy of Hill's edition. According to Pierson, in the second publication, "the author's meaning [is] truly cleared, his method rectified, many repetitions omitted, and the matter (specially toward the latter end) somewhat enlarged." In addition, "the small gain of this revised work was truly returned to the right owners thereof"—that is, Perkins's wife and children. Hill, for his part, at this point willingly ensured that proceeds from his own edition of the book went to Perkins's family. He then left management of further publication of Perkins's works to his assignees.[56]

---

52. Hill writes, "I was twenty years acquainted with him; I at his request made the first-fruits of his labors to speak English [Margin: *The Golden Chain*]." William Perkins, "Dedicatorie," in *Satans Sophistrie Answered by Our Saviour Christ* (London: Richard Field, 1604), 7v (RHB 1:83). William Perkins, *A Golden Chaine, or the Description of Theologie*, trans. Robert Hill (London: Edward Alde, 1591); William Perkins, *A Golden Chaine, or the Description of Theologie…The Second Edition, Much Enlarged, with a Table at the Ende*, trans. Robert Hill (Cambridge: John Legate, 1592).

53. William Perkins, *The Combat betweene Christ and the Divell Displayed* (London: Melchisedech Bradwood, 1606), 3v.

54. See Announcement 6.

55. Pierson includes this marginal note: "See his [i.e., Hill's] preface toward the end." William Perkins, *Lectures upon the Three First Chapters of the Revelation* (1606), 4r (RHB 4:303). Hill's preface is cited in the next footnote. It is noteworthy that Hill's preface of 1604 is included in Pierson's 1606 revision to indicate Hill's cooperation.

56. Hill writes, "I have published of his now two discourses, and I only did it, that these his labors might not perish. I have no benefit by them but exceeding great pains. And since I understand that his other labors are in the hands of his friends, to make benefit for his children, I will ease myself of the like labor, and be a means that they may have the benefit of the future impressions of this book." William Perkins, *Lectures upon the Three First Chapters of the*

In an advertisement in 1609, Pierson announced that the third volume represents "the consummation and finishing of the long-expected labors of our godly and learned divine, M. W. Perkins."[57] Pierson concluded by encouraging those who "have unprinted copies in their hands, to use them for their own private benefit." He also states that the assignees had obtained a "general inhibition out of his majesty's court of high commission, prohibiting the publishing of any of [Perkins's] works without their consent."[58] No previously unpublished work of Perkins's ever appeared after this date until the publication of the present volume.[59]

Thus, in the wake of Perkins's death, significant efforts were taken to ensure that his work was thoroughly edited, that the best manuscript sources available were used and were ably and accurately printed by authorized publishers, and that the proceeds of his work would benefit his family. Some of this might appear overly protective of Perkins's legacy. However, it is fair to say that his assignees, editors, and authorized publishers (led by John Legate) carried out the posthumous production of his works in a way that reflected his own practice. Perkins's preface to his *Exposition of the Lord's Prayer* reveals an author acutely concerned that his ideas are presented clearly, accurately, and in their entirety. Likewise, throughout his career he made a habit of personally revising and correcting imperfections in first editions of various of his works.[60] In sum, we may conclude that Perkins would likely have approved of the process

---

Revelation (1604), 3v–4r (RHB 4:301); William Perkins, *Lectures upon the Three First Chapters of the Revelation* (1606), 3r. Hill went on to produce an edition of *A Golden Chain* structuring as a dialogue (1612).

57. See Announcement 8.

58. See Announcement 8.

59. There are two apparent exceptions, though both are erroneously attributed to Perkins (see appendix 3). The first was *Deaths Knell: or, The Sicke Mans Passing-Bell* (London: M. Trundle, 1628). This work was reprinted no fewer than six times. However, Perkins was not the author of this work. While the 1628 edition is stated as being the ninth edition, there is no evidence that it existed before this time, and its contents differ markedly from Perkins's other works, both in style and content. See Ian Green, *Print and Protestantism in Early Modern England* (Oxford: Oxford University Press, 2000), 479–80. Another work erroneously attributed to Perkins first appeared anonymously during his lifetime: *Nova et Expedita via Comparandæ Linguæ Latinæ* (London: Printed for John Legate, c. 1590). This work was reprinted in 1644 by Thomas Harper and confidently attributed to Perkins. The most likely explanation is that Harper sought to bolster interest in the work through association with Perkins's name. He might have believed that its original publication by John Legate supported this attribution. However, Perkins had not established a record of publication with Legate at that time. His first Legate work, *Armilla Aurea*, only appeared in the same year as *Nova et Expedita*, and Perkins had more established publishing histories with other publishers. *Nova et Expedita* is an unremarkable humanist manual of advice and exercises on eloquence. There is nothing about its contents that testify to Perkinsian authorship.

60. Besides the *Lord's Prayer* revision (1592), Perkins personally revised and corrected his *Treatise Tending unto a Declaration* (1591), *Creed* (1596), *Grain of Mustard Seed* (1603), and the

by which his work was posthumously published under the supervision of his friends.[61]

Manuscript Sources

This brief account of the publication of Perkins's works raises two important questions that the present volume seeks to address.

First, were all of Perkins's works published? In his advertisement at the beginning of the third volume of 1609,[62] Pierson acknowledges that they were not. Perkins's assignees had previously indicated that they would publish expositions of Psalms 32 and 110, the *Confutation of Canisius*, and other sermons.[63] However, they had subsequently decided against it because these works belonged to "the first fruit" of Perkins's labors.[64] If Perkins had intended them for the press, they reasoned, "he would no doubt have revived [them] long since, as he did some other things, which then he handled and published for your good." Moreover, in their estimation, the subject matter of these works is more fully treated at other points in Perkins's published works.[65]

The mention of "other sermons" implies the possibility that unpublished sermons of Perkins still exist. Indeed, notes taken down by hearers of his previously unpublished sermons survive in several manuscript notebooks. The present volume publishes more than twenty sermons that have never previously appeared in print, covering Genesis 2:18–24; 1 Samuel 1:9–13; John 3:16; Acts 2:16–17; Romans 4:25; 1 Corinthians 11:28; and 2 Corinthians 4:3–4.

Second, what impact did the editorial process have on the form and content of Perkins's *posthumi* works? This is a more complicated question and requires a multifaceted answer.

---

original Latin version of *The Art of Prophesying* (*Prophetica*) (1592). He was also likely involved in correcting *Two Treatises* (1597). See appendix 3 for full publication details.

61. The extensive translation and publication of Perkins's works into other languages falls outside the scope of this essay. However, it is notable that Thomas Draxe (d. 1618), another of Perkins's students from Christ's College, Cambridge, translated many of Perkins's works into Latin, including *The Whole Treatise of the Cases of Conscience* (1609), *The Damned Art of Witchcraft* (1610), *A Direction for the Government of the Tongue* (1613), and *Two Treatises* (1615) (see appendix 3). Draxe entered Cambridge in 1588 and earned his BA in about 1595. He would serve as vicar of Colwich, Lincolnshire (1613–1615) and Dovercourt, Essex (1615–1619). Draxe was the author of several theological works. Venn, *Alumni Cantabrigienses*, pt. 1, vol. 2, p. 66; Stephen Wright, "Draxe, Thomas (d. 1618/19)," in *Oxford Dictionary of National Biography* (Oxford: Oxford University Press, 2004; online ed., September 2004).

62. See Announcement 8.

63. See Announcement 5.

64. See Announcement 8.

65. See Announcement 8. The same likely applies to the sermon on Revelation 14:8, published by Robert Hill but subsequently excluded from republication. See discussion below.

When Perkins died, he left behind a large amount of material that he was not given opportunity to edit himself. As discussed above, Perkins's editors were eager to publish these sermons and treatises based on notes taken down by themselves and others; however, this task faced significant challenges. In the preface to *An Exposition upon the Whole Epistle of Jude*, Thomas Taylor mentions that Perkins "was wont to transcribe out of the notes of some of his hearers, the hand and marrow of things more largely in public delivered, explaining the points which were more obscure, and with a second hand polishing and perfecting things so explained."[66] That is, Perkins did not preach from a full manuscript, so when it came to publishing material originating in lectures and sermons, he revised the notes taken down by others as the basis of what would be published.[67] Without Perkins himself present to perform this task of polishing, editing, and filling in the gaps of what others had taken down, it fell to his editors to imitate his method as best they could in his absence.

Perkins's editors amply testify to the challenges this process entailed. Crashawe and Pierson acknowledge that *A Commentary upon the Eleventh Chapter to the Hebrews* "is much obscured for lack of the refining hand of the godly author himself."[68] Likewise, Thomas Taylor, in his preface to *Exposition on the Whole Epistle of Jude*, reflects that it is to be "bewailed" that Perkins did not edit his own sermons, admitting that his posthumously edited works at times fail to represent his mind accurately or to preserve his forms of expression. Such an undertaking involved a compromise in which these editors accepted that their preservation of Perkins's work would be flawed but that even imperfect results were far better than these works being lost to the church entirely.[69] This was John Legate's reason for distinguishing between works

---

66. "To the Reader," in William Perkins, *A Godlie and Learned Exposition upon the Whole Epistle of Jude* (London: Felix Kyngston, 1606), 6r (RHB 4:9–10).

67. This was likely the process used in the publication of homiletical treatises such as *A Salve for a Sick Man* (1595), *A Declaration of the True Manner of Knowing Christ Crucified* (1596), *The True Gain* (1601), and *How to Live and That Well* (1601). See Joseph A. Pipa, "William Perkins and the Development of Puritan Preaching" (PhD diss., Westminster Theological Seminary, 1985), 104–5. On Perkins's approach to sermon preparation and delivery, see Pipa and Yuille's discussion in "Preface," RHB 10:xviii.

68. "The Epistle Dedicatory," in *A Cloud of Faithful Witnesses, Leading to the Heavenly Canaan* (London: Humfrey Lownes, 1607), 3v (RHB 3:2).

69. Taylor states, "It is not now to be wished, but bewailed rather, that all his works were not finished by him before his own course, seeing the orphan writings of the learned published by others are commonly less polished. For sometimes the author's mind is not taken, and sometimes his matter is mistaken. Other times his form is inverted, and not seldom either his own elegancies and proprieties, 'which are like goads' [Eccl. 12:11], are neglected, or something besides his own is injuriously inserted. But yet the Lord, having loosed him from his labors, the Christian care of his executors commends itself to the church herein, that before it should be deprived of any part of his pains so profitably employed, desirous they are to communicate them, if not altogether in such

published during Perkins's lifetime and *posthumi*. Perkins's posthumous editors could not help but distort his literary legacy, a fact with which they were never entirely comfortable.

But in what ways did the editorial task impact the form and content of Perkins's *posthumi* works? Given that most of the manuscript evidence was either collected and suppressed by his assignees (Announcement 8) or else subsequently lost, historians have had few sources on which to investigate this question. The present volume offers precisely the kind of evidence needed to peer behind the editorial curtain erected by the authorized editions of Perkins's posthumously published works. In addition to material that has never been published in any form, the present volume contains transcriptions of more than thirty manuscripts taken from sermons that eventually became parts of published works—namely, *A Treatise on Vocations, An Exposition upon the Whole Epistle of Jude, A Commentary upon the Eleventh Chapter to the Hebrews, An Exposition upon Christ's Sermon in the Mount, A Discourse of the Damned Art of Witchcraft, A Treatise on Man's Imaginations, A Reformed Catholic,* and *Cases of Conscience.* Comparison of these manuscript notes with published editions sheds light on the editorial process by providing additional textual witness to Perkins's original delivery of this material. Such material also aids in the difficult task of dating and tracing the development of Perkins's work.

Perkins's treatment of Jude 3–4 offers a useful case study of how his works were posthumously edited. We now have three witnesses to Perkins's original delivery of that material—namely, the notes of Sidney Sussex student James Tomlin; those of the notetaker responsible for the Hutton MS; and Thomas Taylor, who edited the authorized publication. These three sources have been laid alongside one another for comparison in appendix 2. Comparison indeed reveals differences of expression and occasional modest expansion for the purpose of explanation. It also reveals that Taylor omitted small amounts of material that Perkins originally delivered, partly to make the published text flow continuously. However, the striking similarity between these sources bears witness to Taylor's able and faithful editorial work, his own lament of its inadequacies notwithstanding.[70]

---

exact manner as they would, yet as perfectly as they can, contented rather to hazard the due regard of the author himself, by committing unto his scholars' hands the publishing of his labors, than that the church should want them by their holding and hiding them with themselves." Thomas Taylor, "To the Christian Reader." Cited from RHB 4:9. The original text can be found in Perkins, *A Godlie and Learned Exposition upon the Whole Epistle of Jude* (London: Felix Kyngston, 1606), 5r–6v. On this point Taylor's foreword is worth reading in full.

70. Pipa's claim that Perkins's sermons "were greatly altered as they were prepared for press" is overstating the matter. Pipa, "William Perkins and the Development of Puritan Preaching," 105.

These manuscripts also shed light on the delivery of the series. Taylor's published edition is formatted as a continuous commentary, though the title page reveals that the material was originally delivered in sixty-six sermons. The Hutton MS demonstrates that the material on Jude 3–4 was originally delivered in five sermons, from which the breakdown of the rest of the series can be reasonably extrapolated.[71]

The most striking point demonstrated by these three sources is their structural similarity. It has long been recognized that Perkins employed Ramist methodology to structure his work.[72] Readers of Perkins will be familiar with the characteristically Ramist structural diagrams, dividing subjects into topics and subtopics—a structure that Perkins often communicated verbally by listing his division of subjects before expounding them in order. These manuscripts demonstrate not only that Perkins was committed to Ramist methodology but that his hearers had ears to hear that Ramist structure. For example, the enormous Ramist chart mapping the structure of the entirety of the epistle of Jude might be taken as the editor's own addition.[73] In fact, Taylor was merely making the logic of Perkins's exposition visually explicit. This is supported by the sections of this chart being materially present in the notebooks of those who heard the sermon.[74] In short, these manuscript sermons demonstrate that Perkins and his educated hearers were engaged in Ramist discourse, in which both speaker and hearer had common methodological expectations. Hearers listened for expected structural markers as the preacher spoke, making it the focus of their notetaking and memorization of sermons. This explains the structural similarity between the three texts on Jude 3–4. Leaving aside the specific wording, all faithfully reproduce the same structure of points and subpoints. Ramist hearers listened for structure, and it was a core concern of their notetaking efforts. This makes further sense of Taylor's concern that, while the substance of Perkins's

---

71. Perkins, *Exposition upon the Whole Epistle of Jude*, title page. Indeed, even in the absence of the title page specifying that it originally consisted of sixty-six sermons, after dividing the relevant section of Taylor's published edition into the five sermon units provided by the Hutton MS, by extrapolation one would conclude that the series consisted of approximately sixty-five sermons.

72. Donald K. McKim, *Ramism in William Perkins' Theology* (New York: Peter Lang, 1987); Donald K. McKim, "William Perkins's Use of Ramism as an Exegetical Tool," in William Perkins, *A Commentary on Hebrews 11 (1609 edition). With Introductory Essays*, ed. John H. Augustine (New York: Pilgrim Press, 1991), 32–45.

73. Perkins, *Exposition upon the Whole Epistle of Jude*, 1r (RHB 4:13–18). Other examples could be cited, for example: William Perkins, *A Godly and Learned Exposition or Commentarie upon the Three First Chapters of the Revelation* (London: Adam Islip, 1606), 6v (RHB 4:305–6). Note: the RHB editions do not reproduce the structural lines.

74. For example, Tomlin's notebook (MS Add.8563, "William Perkins: Sermons," 7r–v, 12r–v, 17v, 23v, 28v). These diagrams are preserved in the transcription text below.

work could be reproduced from the best manuscript copies, particular points and forms of expression were far less likely to be recoverable without Perkins's assistance. Perkins's manuscript sermons witness to the widespread influence of Ramist methodology in his Cambridge circle and its importance for understanding their intellectual context.[75]

Finally, the texts published in the present volume engage a long-standing problem in Perkins scholarship—namely, the recovery of his voice as preacher. Given that Perkins was a highly renowned preacher in his day, it is striking to realize that we do not have access to his sermons in their original genre. "None of his sermons were published as sermons but were altered into other genres, such as topical or expository treatises, commentaries, or lectures."[76] This process of transforming sermons into treatises was supervised by Perkins in his lifetime and then by his editors posthumously, as illustrated by texts published in the present volume. For example, a sermon on Matthew 23:37 became the beginning of *God's Free Grace* (1601), a series of sermons on Exodus 22:18 became *The Damned Art of Witchcraft* (1608), and so on. Even his volumes of biblical exposition were transformed into something approximating devotional biblical commentary rather than remaining sermons as such.[77] For all the riches of Perkins's work that remain available today (not least through the labors of his posthumous editors), what remains elusive is the vibrant voice of late-Elizabethan England's most famous preacher, whose passion and rhetorical skill his biographers lauded.[78]

---

75. Some scholars have sought to minimize the importance of Ramism in Perkins's work: Peter Marshall, "William Perkins, A Ramist Theologian?," *Baptist Review of Theology* 7, no. 1–2 (1997): 49–68; David M. Barbee, "A Reformed Catholike: William Perkins' Use of the Church Fathers" (unpublished PhD diss., University of Pennsylvania, 2013), 5–7, 80–82, 247n137. On Ramist methodology, see Simon J. G. Burton, *Ramism and the Reformation of Method: The Franciscan Legacy in Early Modernity* (Oxford: Oxford University Press, forthcoming).

76. James Thomas Ford, "Preaching in the Reformed Tradition," in *Preachers and People in the Reformations and Early Modern Period* (Leiden: Brill, 2001), 78. Also see Pipa, "William Perkins and the Development of Puritan Preaching," 104; Andrew S. Ballitch, *The Gloss and the Text: William Perkins on Interpreting Scripture with Scripture* (Bellingham: Lexham Press, 2020), 83n35.

77. This is even true of the Galatians commentary, which Perkins effectively edited himself. William Perkins, *A Commentary or Exposition upon the First Five Chapters of the Epistle to the Galatians* (Cambridge: John Legate, 1604), 5v (RHB 2:12).

78. For example, Thomas Fuller reports, "He would pronounce the word *Damn* with such an emphasis as left a doleful Echo in his auditors ears a good while after. And when Catechist of Christ's College [Cambridge], in expounding the Commandments [he] applied them so home [as] able almost to make his hearers hearts fall down and hairs to stand upright. But in his older age he altered his voice, and remitted much of his former rigidness, often professing that to preach mercy was that proper office of the Ministers of the Gospel." Thomas Fuller, *The Holy State* (Cambridge: Printed by Roger Daniel for John Williams, 1642), 90.

The present volume goes some way to recovering a sense of Perkins the preacher. Occasionally, as one reads the texts contained in this volume, the unmistakable rhythm of a preacher's rhetoric emerges from roughly set down notes, in passages likely taken down verbatim by aspiring young preachers, no doubt desiring to emulate the godly and learned Master Perkins.

> "Some have very secure hearts, they never think of their sin, never of the judgment for it, never think to give an account for their sin, never think of hellfire, and therefore never humble themselves inwardly, because they perform outward obedience."

> "We know Scripture to be Scripture by Scripture, not by the tradition of the church, for who yet craves it, shall find [in] the Lord the answer and the life of it to be most excellent. We are then still to reverence this Scripture and hold it to be perfect: that is perfect in its end, perfect in its answers, perfect in this life. And in defense of this doctrine, we are to stand and die."

Last Will & Testament, 1602

Perkins's will, 1602.[1]

In the name of God Almighty, [on] the sixteenth day of October in the year of our Lord Christ, 1602.

I, William Perkins of Cambridge in the Diocese of Ely, being weak in body yet of good and perfect remembrance (thanks be to God, therefor) do make and ordain this my last will and testament in form following.

First, I commend my soul into the hands of God in Christ hoping assuredly to die in the faith which I have confessed and preached. And my body I commit to the earth to be buried in Christian burial at the discretion of my executor.

Also, I bequeath to the poor people of the parish of St. Andrews in Cambridge where I now dwell £40 to be distributed among them at the discretion of the overseers of the poor of that parish.

Also, I bequeath to my worshipful and loving friends, Mr. Edmund Barwell and James Montagu, doctors of divinity; Mr. Laurence Chaderton (master of Emmanuel College); Richard Foxcroft and Thomas Cropley, masters of arts; and my loving brother-in-law Nathaniel Craddock all the messuage[2] or tenement wherein now dwell together with the houses, and yard, and garden, and orchard adjoining, or thereunto belonging with all and singular the appurtenances all which are situated in the town and bounds of Cambridge aforesaid: to have and to hold the said messuage or tenement with the houses, yard, garden, and orchard adjoining, or thereunto belonging with all and singular the appurtenances to the said Edmund Barwell, James Montagu, Laurence Chaderton, Richard Foxcroft, Thomas Cropley, and Nathaniel Craddock the heirs and assignees forever to the only use and behoof[3] of the said Edmund Barwell, James Montagu, Laurence Chaderton, Richard Foxcroft, Thomas Cropley, and Nathaniel Craddock, their heirs and assignees forever. Notwithstanding, I do request and desire that they, the said Edmund, James, Laurence, Richard,

---

1. "Original Wills, 1600–1603" (Cambridge University Library, Archives, VCCt Wills 4). A copy also exists in "Will Register 1602–1658" (Cambridge University Library, Archives, VCCt Wills 3).

2. *Messuage*: a dwelling house with smaller buildings and land assigned to its use.

3. *Behoof*: advantage or benefit.

Thomas, and Nathaniel, or the survivors of them, within two years after my decease would sell the said messuage or tenement, houses, yard, garden, with all and singular the appurtenances for the best worth thereof in money at their discretion, and that all the money thereof made may be divided in to the three equal parts.

One of which three parts I will to be delivered, paid, or assured unto Timothie, my beloved wife, and I will the other two parts be paid or assured unto and among all my children equally, as well those which are now unborn as those which are now living. And in case my wife should die before such sale be made then I will that all the money aforesaid shall be divided, delivered, or assured unto all my said children as well now unborn as born and now living, equally at the discretion of the said Edmund, James, Laurence, Richard, Thomas, and Nathaniel, or the survivors of them.

Item. I will that the price and value of all my moveable goods and chattels whatsoever be divided into seven parts. Two parts whereof, or of the goods or chattels themselves, I bequeath unto the said Timothie, my wife. And the five other parts, or the fifth part of the other goods or chattels themselves, I give and bequeath to all my children unborn and born to be divided equally among them, and to be paid or delivered to them at their several ages of one and twenty years, or day of marriage, whichever of the said two times shall first and next happen to come and be.

Item. My will is that if any of my said children shall depart this life before they shall have received their said legacy or legacies, that the other survivors or survivor of them shall have their part of the legacy, and a portion of the part or parts deceased equally divided among them, and to be paid to the said survivors or survivor at the times afore limited for the receipt of their proper first legacies consecutively.

Item. My will is that if my wife shall depart this life before the said proved this my will, that then all my said goods and chattels, or the price or value thereof, shall be equally divided and paid or delivered unto all my said children as aforesaid, at the days and times above limited.

Item. I ordain and make the said Timothie my wife sole operative of this my last will and testament. And in case she departs this life and does never prove this my will, then I ordain and make Nathaniel Cradock aforesaid sole executer of the same.

Item. I request my loving friends Nathaniel Cradock and Thomas Cropley to be supervisors of this my last will, and to counsel and aid my wife in the operating of the same, and I give to either of them £5.

Item. I give to my father Thomas Perkins and my mother Anna Perkins £10 a piece, and to any of my own brethren and sisters £5 a piece, and to Richard Love (apothecary) £5,[4] and to my sister-in-law Katherine Cradock £5.

Item. I give to my son-in-law John Hinde my English Bible.[5]

And this I publish to be my last will and testament, written in three leaves of paper to which I have subscribed my name and sealed them altogether in the presence of Thomas Miller of St. Andrews parish (tailor) and of Anthony Harrison.[6]

William Perkins

---

4. Perkins appeared to have befriended the Cambridge apothecary Richard Love (d. 1605). Love's son, then five years old, would go on to become head of Corpus Christi College, Cambridge, in 1632. E. T. Bradley, rev. S. L. Sadler, "Love, Richard (1596–1661)," in *Oxford Dictionary of National Biography* (Oxford: Oxford University Press, 2004; online ed., October 2009). Perkins's views on the lawful use of medicine appear in *A Salve for a Sick Man* (RHB 10:438–42); cf. *A Golden Chain* (RHB 6:84–85, 123). For further discussion, see Norman Gevitz, "Practical Divinity and Medical Ethics: Lawful versus Unlawful Medicine in the Writings of William Perkins (1558–1602)," *Journal of the History of Medicine and Allied Sciences* 68, no. 2 (2012): 198–226.

5. While there were several Cambridge alumni by the name of "John Hinde," none is a likely candidate for Perkins's son-in-law (cf. Venn, *Alumni Cantabrigienses*, pt. 1, vol. 2, p. 376). Rather, John Hinde appears to have been a son of Perkins's wife, Timothie Hinde, from a previous marriage. In the early modern period "son-in-law" could refer to what we today call a "step-son," and it was common for men of Perkins's convictions to marry widows and to provide for their orphaned children. This answers the difficult question of how Perkins could have had a "son-in-law" after only seven years of marriage. It also proves untenable Breward's suggestion that John Hinde was the husband of an alleged illegitimate daughter of Perkins, fathered during his "wild" undergraduate years. Perkins subsequently enjoyed a high-profile career in Cambridge as a Christ's College fellow, renowned preacher, and best-selling author, all of which would likely have been hindered if such a scandal were true. "Introduction," in *The Works of William Perkins*, ed. Ian Breward (Appleford: The Sutton Courtney Press, 1970), 6.

6. Venn lists two Anthony Harrisons as the possible witness. The first was born in 1563 and was a close contemporary of Perkins. He began at King's College in 1579/80 (two years after Perkins enrolled at Christ's), and he served as rector of Catfield Norfolk beginning in 1609. The second enrolled as a student at St. John's College in 1587, and he was ordained to the ministry in 1595/96. Venn, *Alumni Cantabrigienses*, pt. 1, vol. 2, p. 314.

Announcement 1

Advertisement to Printers & Publishers (John Legate, 1603)[1]

An advertisement to the reader and to all printers and publishers
of M. Perkins's books.

It is a speech uttered by the wise man in his Proverbs, worthy [of] your due
observation (Christian Reader), that he who sends a message by the hand of
a fool is as he who cuts off his feet or drinks some hurtful thing (Prov. 26:6).
By the fool, Solomon means anyone who undertakes a business on behalf of
another without advice or due consideration either of the weight of the thing
itself or of the party to whom it belongs. By the cutting off [of] the feet, [he
means] the want of wit, skill, and dexterity, for the carriage and conveyance of
the business in [a] good and seemly manner. And [the phrase] "the drinking
of a noisome thing" imports not only the grief but also the hurt and prejudice
that grows unto him whose affairs are either not at all or very ill dispatched by
so foolish and witless a messenger. Now this may be gathered out of Solomon's
parable: that it is a shameful disgrace unto a man to put the hand unto any
work, either committed unto him by another or undertaken of his own head,
and not to go through it with credit and commendation. Again, that a business
unadvisedly begun and unskillfully followed is as a message sent by the hand
of a fool, who must needs bewray his folly and mar the fashion of the message,
which, besides the imputation of his own want of wit, makes greatly to the
impeachment of the author's credit.

To these and such like footless messengers may not unfitly be compared
some publishers and printers of men's works in these days. Upon a greedy
desire of a little gain, [they] are willing to run into a greater inconvenience by
doing manifest injury to the authors, and justly incurring the certain loss of
their own credit and good name. Not to insist in generalities: it is not unknown
unto you (Good Reader) what an open wrong has been done by this sort of
men unto that worthy servant of God, the writer of this book lately deceased,

---

1. Reproduced from RHB 10:37–39. For the original, see William Perkins, *A Treatise of the
Vocations, or, Callings of Men, with the Sorts and Kinds of Them, and the Right Use Thereof* (Cambridge: John Legate, 1603), 4v–6v.

in the publishing of two treatises under his name. One [is] entitled *The Practice of Faith*,[2] the other *The Reformation of Covetousness*.[3]

First, the writers of these books have very boldly presumed to undertake this work without the knowledge or consent of the author's friends, not once considering what better copies might elsewhere be had, far more agreeable to his own style, and consequently more beneficial to the church. [This is] a plain argument that they wanted wit and common reason, either to conceive or carry a message of so great importance.

Second, to speak the best of their books, especially the latter, they are but rude and confused notes, some taken perhaps from the author's mouth, others foisted in by whole pages, which (upon my knowledge) he never delivered. [They are] all scraped up together by some hungry scribe, not upon conscience of crediting the author or furthering the reader but in a covetous humor to get money of the printer as needy as themselves.

Third, let appeal be made unto the judgment of a reader but meanly grounded in knowledge, whether *The Reformation of Covetousness* (as they term it) is not for method, interpretation, collection, and application, in the most places, unlearnedly, imperfectly, disorderly, and ridiculously penned. I spare to point at the particulars (though it might easily have been done to the shame and disgrace of the writers) because there is hope upon this item; they may be better advised hereafter.

As for the versifier, who writes before it, *In Memoriam Perkins*,[4] whose also the epistle is, though he has subscribed to the verses only, as to the worthier work, besides that he bewrays his want of judgment in other matters in being so willing to premise his letter to so sweet a piece of service. He may be well assured that both the name and the works of that holy man have sufficiently commended themselves unto the church of God, and therefore need not to be set forth by a man whose commendation is rather a blemish than an honor and whose life and profession deserve neither just praise nor honest report. Now, if it seems strange unto any that men should be so shamefully overseen, discrediting themselves and dishonoring the dead by these base and shameless enterprises, they may remember that the like injury was done unto him not many years before his death in the setting forth of an exposition upon the Lord's Prayer under his name without his consent or knowledge.[5] And, there-

---

2. This work is no longer extant.

3. William Perkins, *The Reformation of Covetousness. Written upon the 6. Chapter of Matthew, from the 19. Verse to the End of the Said Chapter* (London: Thomas Creede, 1603).

4. Perkins, *Reformation of Covetousnesse*, 1r.

5. See appendix 1.

fore, it is no marvel that persons ill-disposed do now proclaim their folly to the world after his death, who did so palpably bewray it while he lived.

Considering, then, both the wrong offered even to the ashes of that holy man and the abuse of godly and religious people by such ungodly and wicked practices, it was thought expedient to advertise the Christian Reader, and all printers and publishers of books, that there are sundry copies in the hands of M. Perkins's assigns, some prepared for the press by himself, whereof this present treatise is one, and others hereafter to be published as occasion shall serve upon the view of some learned men here in Cambridge. Withal, wishing those who are well affected, and do desire still to enjoy the benefit of his labors, not to suffer themselves to be abused in such sort as lately they have been by ruder copies, divulged hand over head by ignorant and unlettered persons, but rather to hearken after those which shall be set forth upon better warrant as occasion shall serve. In the meantime, use this in hand for your better directions, in the calling wherein you are placed by God, and finding good thereby give praise unto Him in your heart, who has vouchsafed to His church in these latter days so worthy an instrument of His glory.

Farewell

Announcement 2

Printer to the Reader (John Legate, 1603)[1]

I here present unto your view, Christian Reader, those books compiled into one sum which this worthy man of God first delivered by word of mouth unto his auditors, afterward published by handwriting unto all, willing to profit both by tongue and pen, both at home and abroad, both alive and dead, endeavoring as Saint Paul speaks, "to become unto all, that he might gain some unto Christ" [1 Cor. 9:22]. Other writings there are of his besides these, unseen as yet by the eyes of the world, which so soon as they shall come unto my hands I purpose not to wrap up in a napkin and bury them within the walls of my own house but [to] set them like a candle upon the table, or rather as a beacon on a hill, to direct ignorant passengers to their heavenly country. I know nothing can be so well meant or sincerely purposed but that the malicious construction of some (like infected eyes that infected colors) will be ready to poison it and to pervert it. Yet if ever any other work set forth by any other man was of force to purchase the love of such as are froward, or to deserve the entertainment and free passport of the indifferent, or if ever any was mighty enough to shake off the censures and snarlings of the humorous,[2] as the great apostle did the viper from his hand, I suppose (without any offense let it be spoken) this worthy man is no whit inferior unto them. But some perhaps will rather expect the printing of those works yet unpublished, which I mentioned before, then set upon this as but a moitie[3] of the whole. Let them understand that the printing of those (when it shall please God to give leave that they be printed) shall be nothing prejudicial to the entireness and absoluteness of this work. For each of them I determine shall be printed by themselves nothing ever hereafter added to this, which is grown already greater than I looked for. Thus, in short, desirous to fulfill the desire of that blessed spirit who now reigns in bliss with the holy spirits

---

1. William Perkins, *The Works of That Famous and Worthy Minister of Christ in the Universitie of Cambridge, M. W. Perkins: Gathered into One Volume, and Newly Corrected according to His Owne Copies* (Cambridge: John Legate, 1603), 3r.

2. *Humorous*: those given to poor behavior due to the disproportion of bodily fluids ("humors"). Behind the use of this term is the faculty-humoral understanding of human physiology that was broadly accepted from antiquity right up to the modern period with the emergence of germ theory.

3. *Moitie* (French): half.

and saints of God, desirous also to further your virtuous endeavors whosoever you are, courteous reader, that willingly delight herein, by publishing these his works, which long exemplified by his life he has now sealed with his death to the end that even the children yet unborn may reap the fruit and benefit of him unknown, I commit you to the protection of the Almighty.

Announcement 3

Editor's Preface, The First Part of the Cases of Conscience
(Thomas Pickering, 1604)[1]

To the godly and well affected reader whosoever,

It was not my purpose (Christian Reader) at the first to have sent abroad only one part of the *Cases of Conscience* without the rest; but that I was moved thereunto, partly upon the importunity of some of the author's friends and partly because I desired to satisfy your expectations in a thing which I persuade myself has been long expected. Upon which two motives I have now commended unto you this first part, promising by the grace of God, ere it be long, to add the second and the third so far as the author proceeded in this treatise before his death. And although I could have wished this labor had been undertaken by others better able to perform it than myself, yet being well acquainted with the copy, which is mine own, and knowing it to have been perused by the author himself before his death, I was the more encouraged to bestow my pains for your good in that behalf. If in reading thereof you find either anything amiss or yourself not fully satisfied in the particulars, then remember that the author himself is gone, who might have brought the work to perfection if God had pleased to prolong his days upon the earth. And withal consider that it were better for you to accept of these his labors as they are now imparted to you than by the suppressing of them to be deprived of so great a benefit. And thus, hoping of your kind acceptance of my pains for your behoof, I commend you to God and to the word of His grace.

June 28, 1604
T. P.[2]

---

1. William Perkins, *The First Part of the Cases of Conscience Wherein Specially, Three Maine Questions concerning Man* (Cambridge: John Legate, 1604), 7v.
2. Thomas Pickering.

Announcement 4

Editor's Preface, The Whole Treatise of the Cases of Conscience
(Thomas Pickering, 1606)[1]

I do now at length offer unto your view (Christian Reader) the whole treatise of case divinity, so far as the author proceeded in the delivery thereof before his death. If you have been longer held in expectation thereof than either you desired or was meet, I must entreat your favorable interpretation of my forbearance, partly in regard of many private distractions and sundry occurrents wherewith I was detained from this duty and partly also in respect of my desire to publish it in such sort to your contentment, that it might afterward require no further filing or furbishing by secondary corrections. Wherein, notwithstanding my endeavor to the contrary, my hope has been in part prejudiced by reason of some faults escaped in the printing, through want of careful attendance on the press in my necessary absence. The principal I have noted in a table before the first book, and the other of lesser moment I commend to your private pardon.

Touching the treatise itself, I have dealt as faithfully as I could, keeping close to the preacher's own words, without any material addition, detraction, or amplification. His method remains the same in the body of the discourse, not admitting the least alteration. Only it was thought convenient to distinguish it into books according to the several distinct parts: the books into chapters, the chapters that were most capable of divisions, into sections. And my meaning therein was to help the memory of the reader and to avoid tediousness, the daughter of longsome discourses.

Now, if in the perusing you either find anything amiss or yourself haply not fully satisfied in particular, then remember what is the lot of learned men's works which are *scripta posthuma[2]* (whereof these latter times have yielded many examples), to be left, after a sort, naked and imperfect, when the authors themselves are gone, who might have brought them to perfection. Consider again that in regard of the weight of this worthy argument, it is much better kindly and thankfully to accept and enjoy these labors, howsoever imparted,

---

1. Reproduced from RHB 8:103–4. For the original, see William Perkins, *The Whole Treatise of the Cases of Conscience Distinguished into Three Bookes* (Cambridge: John Legate, 1606), 8r–v.
2. Posthumous writings.

than by their suppressing to be wholly deprived of such a benefit. And withal rest with me in hope that as [he] himself has first traced the way, and walked by the banks of this main sea, so others upon this occasion will be encouraged to attempt the like course or at least to enlarge this work by addition of more particulars. Meanwhile, not doubting of your Christian acceptance of my pains for your good, I commend them to your love, yourself unto God and the word of His grace.

Emmanuel College, November 28, 1606
Yours in Christ Jesus,
Thomas Pickering

Announcement 5

Editor's Call for Manuscripts (William Crashawe, 1605)[1]

To the Christian Reader, and especially to all such as have any copies of the works of Master Perkins or intend to [bring] any of them [to] the press.

For as much as there has been lately signification made of divers of Master Perkins's works hereafter to be printed in an epistle to the reader promised before the treatise of *Callings*,[2] and that signification, being but general, might peradventure give occasion to some to set out some particulars (without the consent of Master Perkins's assignees) as imperfectly as are these two books, entitled *The Reformation of Covetousness* and *The Practice of Faith*, justly and truly (for ought that I see) censured in the aforesaid epistle. It is, therefore, now thought good to mention the particular treatises and works of his, which shall hereafter (if God will) be published for the benefit of God's church. I do, therefore, hereby make known to all, whom it any way may concern, that there were found in the study of the deceased, and are in the hands of his executors (or assignees) and preparing for the press,

1. His expositions on the epistle to the Galatians
2. On the epistle of Jude
3. His book of the Cases of Conscience
4. His treatises: (1) Of Witchcraft. (2) Of Callings

All these he had perused himself and made them ready for the press, according to which copies by himself so corrected some of them already are, and the rest will be published in due time. And hereupon we desire all men who have copies of them not to offer that wrong to that worthy man of God as to publish any of their own, seeing the copies hereof which are to be printed are of his own correcting. But rather if they can help to make any of them more

---

1. Reproduced from RHB 9:87–88 (also 10:201–2). The original was prefaced to multiple works: William Perkins, *Of the Calling of the Ministerie Two Treatises, Discribing the Duties and Dignities of That Calling* (London: I. R. Roberts, 1605), 6r–8r; William Perkins, *M. Perkins, His Exhortation to Repentance, out of Zephaniah: Preached in 2. Sermons in Sturbridge Faire. Together with Two Treatises of the Duties and Dignitie of the Ministrie* (London: Thomas Creed, 1605), 10r–12v; William Perkins, *M. Perkins, His Exhortation to Repentance, out of Zephaniah Preached in 2. Sermons in Sturbridge Faire* (London: T. Creede for William Welby, 1606), 4r–v.
2. Announcement 1.

perfect by their copies, they may therein do a good work to the benefit of many and much comfort to themselves.

And further, I do hereby make known that I have in my hands at this present of his works, taken from his mouth with my own hand, hereafter (if God will) to be published, with the allowance of our church and for the benefit of his children, these particulars:

1. His expositions or Readings on Psalm 101
2. On Psalm 32
3. On Hebrews 11
4. On Revelation 1–3
5. On Matthew 5–7
6. His confutation of Canisius, his little Popish Catechism[3]
7. His treatises:
    (1) Of Imaginations, out of Genesis 8:2
    (2) Of Temptations, out of Matthew 4
    (3) Of Christian Equity, out of Philippians 4:3
    (4) Of the Callings of the Ministry, out of two places of Scripture
    (5) Of Repentance, out of Zephaniah 2:1

Besides many other particular sermons, and short discourses made upon several and special occasions, of all which some are already published by others and some by myself. And all the rest that remain, as they are the jewels of God's church, so did I willingly dedicate them to the public and general good, judging it were a foul sin in me, or any other, to impropriate to our sins or our own private use the labors of this or any other learned man, which are in my opinion parts of the treasury of the militant church. And as it were wrong to the church if I should conceal them, so doubtless were it to him and his children if I should publish them for mine own alone and not for their benefit. If I do, I think it may be justly said unto me, or whosoever does so, "Your money perish with you." And what herein I have said for myself, I know I may boldly and safely say for his executors or assignees, who have or had in their hands any of those which were found in his study. In the publishing of all which, as we do intend to deal truly with the Christian reader, and not to commit anything to the press which has not either been written or corrected by the author himself, or faithfully penned according to the truest copies, taken from his own mouth, and since by others of sufficiency and integrity diligently perused. Some purpose to refer

---

3. Peter Canisius, *A Catechism or Short Instruction of Christian Religion Drawn Out of the Scriptures and Ancient Doctors* (Paris: Peter Hyry, 1588). Peter Canisius (1521–1597) was an influential Dutch Roman Catholic priest of the Jesuit order. His catechetical works were highly influential in the promotion of Roman Catholic theology in opposition to Protestantism, particularly in Germany.

them to the benefit of the author's wife and children, as much as may be, wishing that upon this caveat men would not be so hasty (as some have been) to commend to the world their imperfect notes, upon a base desire of a little gain, both to hinder the common good of the church and to defraud the said parties of their private benefit, to whom in all equity and conscience it does principally appertain. And desiring all who have any perfect copies of such as are in my own hands, that they would either help me with theirs or rather take mine to help them. That by our joint power and our forces laid together, the walls of this worthy building may go up the fairer and the faster. And so I commend them all to God's blessing who endeavor to commend themselves and their labors to God and to His church.

Your brother in the Lord,
W. C.[4]

---

4. William Crashawe.

Announcement 6

Editor's Preface, Revelation *(Thomas Pierson, 1606)[1]*

I am not ignorant (Good Reader) how ungrateful a thing it is to deal by way of censure or reformation in those things wherein others have gone before; and many times for the smart that follows do men beshrow their own fingers. Yet the warrant of a good calling will breed peace in his conscience, that herein shall endeavor the observance of these rules of love, to wit, judge the best of that which is done [1 Cor. 13:5],[2] and refer his own pains to the glory of God in the good of others.[3] Hereto I aim in this second edition of this book. For my calling to this work, when my accusers stand forth, the executors of the dead shall answer for my discharge. And for my endeavor to do good, the small gain of this revised work was truly returned to the right owners thereof. If you therefore return glory to God for good received to your soul, in this behalf I have my desire. Here only rests the doubt, how this second edition should not be prejudicial to his good estimation that published the former. I answer, well enough: for I hope he intended the glory of God in the good of His church[4] and the credit of the reverend author of this work. Now if any addition be brought hereunto, his intent is furthered, and wherein then can he be grieved? If one man should help poor orphans to some lands or living, he would not think himself wronged by another that should enlarge their just claims or settle their possession in a better tenure. So I trust it fairs in this work, where you shall find upon your diligent view in some doubtful things[5] the author's meaning truly cleared, his method rectified, many repetitions omitted, and the matter (specially toward the latter end) somewhat enlarged. If anything be dissonant to the author's judgment in his live works (which I hope you will not perceive),

---

1. William Perkins, *A Godly and Learned Exposition or Commentarie upon the Three First Chapters of the Revelation* (London: Adam Islip for Cuthbert Burbie, 1606), 6r (RHB 4:303–4). This was first published by Robert Hill (1604), revised by Thomas Pierson under instruction by Perkins's assignees in 1606, and then revised again by Pierson in 1607. This announcement is from the 1606 edition. William Perkins, *A Godly and Learned Exposition or Commentarie upon the Three First Chapters of the Revelation* (London: Adam Islip, 1606).

2. In the margin: "Love thinketh not evil."

3. In the margin: "It seeketh not her own things."

4. In the margin. "See his preface toward the end." This refers to William Perkins, *Lectures upon the Three First Chapters of the Revelation* (London: Adam Islip, 1606), 4r (RHB 4:301).

5. In the margin: "As touching the images of the Trinity. Pag. 53. Col. 1." Cf. RHB 4:385.

rather charge the fault on me through ignorance or misunderstanding than entertain in your heart the least conceit of wavering levity in so godly, learned, and judicious a divine, who has so well deserved of your love, if you love the truth. Thus, craving your favorable acceptance of my helping hand, to do you good, I end with him, that is the beginning and the end: "Let him that hath an ear hear what the Spirit saith unto the churches."

Yours in Him, who is Lord of all,
T. P.[6]

---

6. Thomas Pickering.

Announcement 7

Printer's Preface, Works *(John Legate, 1608)[1]*

The Printer to the Reader.

I suppose it altogether needless (Christian Reader) by commending M. William Perkins, the author of this book, to woo your holy affection, which himself in his lifetime by his Christian conversation has wooed you, or since his death, the never-dying memory of his excellent knowledge, his great humility, his sound religion, his fervent zeal, his painful labors in the church of God do most justly challenge at your hands. Only in one word I dare be bold to say of him, as in times past Nazianzen spoke of Athanasius.[2] His life was a good definition of a true minister and preacher of the gospel. And as needless were it (if not injurious) by praising of his learned and godly writings to think to incline your better judgment, which in so holy a subject (as is the body of divinity and principles of religion) I dare not suspect to be unsettled. And in so easy a method and familiar a style which he used in them both, I am sure can hardly miscarry. Such is his love to all, that as for the matter of his doctrine, he contends and satisfies the most learned, so for the matter of his delivering the same, he condescends to the capacity of the meanest of God's children. Such then do I here once more present unto you M. Perkins's *Works.* Read them diligently and judge of them freely. I doubt not but in your most exact censure you will conspire with those learned men who, for the profitable instruction they contain (if not in all yet in the most [important] points of Christianity) for the more common good of the church of God, have deemed them worthy their godly labors in translating them into diverse languages, as into Latin, Dutch, Spanish, etc., a thing not ordinarily observed in other writings of these our times.

---

1. William Perkins. *The Workes of That Famous and Worthy Minister of Christ in the Universitie of Cambridge, Mr. W. Perkins. The First Volume: Newly Corrected according to His Owne Copies* (Cambridge: John Legate, 1608), 2r. The preface was lightly revised in 1612, and that version appears in subsequent editions.

2. Gregory of Nazianzus (329–390) delivered a celebrated oration on Athanasius (c. 296–373). See "On the Great Athanasius, Bishop of Alexandria," (Oration 21) in *Nicene and Post-Nicene Fathers, Second Series,* ed. Philip Schaff and Henry Wace (Buffalo, N.Y.: Christian Literature Publishing, 1894), 7:269–80.

Concerning this new edition, if you ask why I have not added those other treatises of his which have been published since the former impression, I answer, it is not done without the advice of grave and learned men in two respects. First, to set a difference (as indeed there is great odds) between those books which the author himself vet[ted] [while] living by his own care, not only in penning but likewise in the correcting of the same [and] did set forth, and those others which are *posthumi*, that is, born after his death, gathered and collected by others. Such as are these following:

1. Upon three chapters of Revelation[3]
2. Satan's Sophistrie[4]
3. Upon the epistle of Jude[5]
4. The Dignity of the Ministry[6]
5. Upon the eleventh chapter of the Hebrews[7]
6. Upon three chapters of Saint Matthew's gospel[8]

Secondly, because I have remaining by me so many other treatises in diverse prints and forms of the same author's own collection which I purpose (by God's permission) to set forth as will amount to a second volume equal to this, if not bigger.[9]

In the meantime, I could with those who have an interest in those after-births agree likewise to draw them into one volume so that they that take delight in M. Perkins his writings might with less labor of their own attain to

---

3. William Perkins, *A Godly and Learned Exposition or Commentarie upon the Three First Chapters of the Revelation*, ed. Thomas Pierson (London: Adam Islip, 1606). A third revised edition had been published in 1607.

4. This is the title of the original work edited by Robert Hill (1604). The revised edition, edited by Thomas Pierson, was available at this time and titled *The Combat betweene Christ and the Divell Displayed*, ed. Thomas Pierson (London: Melchisedech Bradwood, 1606). Legate may be using the former title here to reinforce his point about the relative deficiencies of posthumously edited works.

5. William Perkins, *A Godlie and Learned Exposition upon the Whole Epistle of Jude*, ed. Thomas Taylor (London: Felix Kyngston, 1606).

6. William Perkins, *Of the Calling of the Ministerie Two Treatises, Discribing the Duties and Dignities of That Calling*, ed. William Crashawe (London: I. R. Roberts, 1605).

7. William Perkins, *A Cloud of Faithfull Witnesses, Leading to the Heavenly Canaan: or A Commentarie upon the 11. Chapter to the Hebrewes*, ed. William Crashawe and Thomas Pierson (London: Humfrey Lownes, 1607).

8. William Perkins, *A Godly and Learned Exposition of Christs Sermon in the Mount*, ed. Thomas Pierson (Cambridge: Thomas Brooke and Cantrell Legge, 1608).

9. Released the following year: William Perkins, *The Workes of That Famous and Worthy Minister of Christ in the Universitie of Cambridge, M. William Perkins. The Second Volume* (Cambridge: John Legate, 1609).

the complete body of his labors,[10] it being also more convenient for their use to have them rather compacted in one volume than scattered into diverse parcels of diverse forms. Thus, with promise to make all possible expedition in setting forth the second volume of his works, I commend this to your diligent reading, my endeavors to your charitable construction, and us both to the blessing and holy protection of almighty God.

From Cambridge, this 6th of September, 1608

---

10. The beginning of the 1612 version of this sentence was revised as follows: "In the meantime, what herefore I have wished concerning such as have the interest in those after-births, viz. that they would agree likewise to draw them into one volume…" William Perkins, *The Workes of That Famous and Worthy Minister of Christ in the Universitie of Cambridge, Mr. W. Perkins. The First Volume: Newly Corrected according to His Owne Copies* (Cambridge: John Legate, 1608), 2r.

Announcement 8

Advertisement of Completion (Thomas Pierson, 1609)[1]

An Advertisement to the Christian Reader, concerning the works
of M. W. Perkins.

Because the title of this book (Good Reader) imports a consummation and
finishing of the long-expected labors of our godly and learned divine, M. W.
Perkins, and yet in this catalogue prefixed, beside the two former volumes, you
want[2] some particulars that heretofore were promised, as his *Exposition* of the
32nd and 110th Psalms, the *Confutation of Canisius' Catechism*, with other *Sermons*, I thought good to acquaint you with some reasons whereby his executors
have been persuaded to make a final stay and suppressing of them.[3]

First, they were of the first fruit of his labors, which if he had intended for
the press, he would no doubt have revived long since, as he did some other
things, which then he handled and published for your good.

Second, beside that the church of God enjoys the benefit of other
men's labors of the same kind[4] (whereto our reverend author had due

---

1. William Perkins, *The Workes of That Famous and Worthy Minister of Christ in the University of Cambridge, M. W. Perkins. The Third and Last Volume. Newly Corrected and Amended*, 2nd
ed. (Cambridge: Cantrell Legge, 1609), 5r–v.

2. *Want*: lack.

3. See Announcement 5.

4. In the margin: "Sadeel Mornay on the 32nd Psalm; Sohnius on the 110th Psalm; Pezehus,
Confutation of Canisius Catechisme." "Sadeel" was the pen name of Antoine de Chandieu (1534–
1591), a French Reformed theologian whose career primarily centered on Paris and Geneva.
Antoine de Chandieu, *Moste Excellent Meditations vppon the xxxii. Psalme, Written in Latin by
That Godly Lerned Divine Antonie Sadel, and Nowe Newly Translated into English, for All Those
Which Love to Reade the Comfortable Doctrine of Remission of Sinnes. By VV.VV. Student* (London: Thomas Dawson for Tobie Cooke and Thomas Man, 1579). This was published in Latin the
previous year: A. Sadeele Theopsaltes, *Meditationes in Psalmum XXXII* (Lausanne: François Le
Preux, 1578). George Sohnius (1551–1589) was professor of divinity at the University of Marburg,
then briefly at Heidelberg. George Sohn, *Explicatio Psalmi CX, in Operum Georgii Sohnii Sacrae
Theologiæ Doctoris,* 3 vols. (Herborn: Christoph Corvin, 1591–1592), 3:1–69. Christoph Pezel
(1539–1604) was a German Philippist-Lutheran theologian who wrote a refutation of Canisius's
catechism: Christophoro Pezelio, *Pars Prima Refutationis Catechismi Jesuitarum Utriusque: Tum
Parvi Illius, Quo in Scholis Puerilibus Utuntur ad Teneræ Iuventutis Animos Imbuendos Erroribus, Superstitione, & Idololatria Religionis Pontificiæ: Tum Alterius Prolixioris, Quem Catechesin*

respect[5]), the truth is that the most material points contained in these suppressed lectures are more largely and exactly handled in his *Works* already published. To instance in some, the whole argument of the 110th Psalm, to use our author's own division, contains either Christ's kingdom or His priesthood, both [of] which points you shall find particularly handled in the *Golden Chain* (ch. 18)[6] and more at large in the *Creed* (His kingdom in these words, "He sits at the right hand of God,"[7] and his priesthood in handling Christ's sacrifice).[8] And for the 32nd Psalm, the points of largest discourse are the knowledge of remission of sin, with assurance of salvation, upon the first verse, which is far more fully discussed in the *Treatise of Conscience*,[9] *Cases of Conscience*,[10] and *Reformed Catholic*.[11] And upon the second verse, the point of justification by imputed righteousness, and not by works, which to your full content are cleared in the *Golden Chain*,[12] *Reformed Catholic*,[13] beside many other places, which I purposely omit. And for the confutation of Canisius, what material point of controversy can be expected, which is not either in his *Golden Chain, Reformed Catholic, Idolatry of the Last Times, Treatise of God's Free Grace and Man's Free Will*, or in his *Problem*?[14] No, I am persuaded it would not be any difficult thing to note out in particular the several points of these forenamed sermons in some one place or other of his published works, whereby it is plain that the suppressing of them is neither prejudicial to the author or to the reader.

These things well considered, and withal the great quantity and price whereto his works are already risen, I hope you will approve of their advice who deliberately wished their final stay. It may be some will think it unmeet that anything of this reverend divine should be suppressed, but let such consider well what the beloved apostle says of the blessed works of our Savior Christ,

---

Austriacam Vocant, Cuius Velut Epitome seu Compendium Parvus Ille Catechismus Videri Potest: In Schola Bremensi (Harnisius, 1599).

5. In the margin: "See his advertisement to the Reader, before his exposition of the Lord's Prayer, in the end." See appendix 1.

6. Perkins, *Golden Chain*, RHB 6:54–64.

7. Perkins, *Creed*, RHB 5:270–82.

8. Perkins, *Creed*, RHB 5:201–10.

9. Perkins, *Discourse of Conscience*, RHB 8:61–82.

10. Perkins, *Whole Treatise of the Cases of Conscience*, RHB 8:153–60 (bk. 1, ch. 6: "Of the Second Main Question: Touching Assurance of Salvation").

11. Perkins, *Reformed Catholic*, RHB 7:25–33 ("The Third Point: Certainty of Salvation").

12. Perkins, *Golden Chain*, RHB 6:181–85, 220–41 (chs. 37 and 51).

13. Perkins, *Reformed Catholic*, RHB 7:34–50 ("The Fourth Point: Touching the Justification of a Sinner").

14. These works are located in RHB as follows: *A Golden Chain* (vol. 6), *A Reformed Catholic* (vol. 7), *A Warning against the Idolatry of the Last Times* (vol. 7), *A Treatise on God's Free Grace and Man's Free Will* (vol. 6), and *The Problem of Forged Catholicism* (vol. 7).

to wit, that many of them, yes, the greatest number of them were omitted, and those things only written which were necessary for the ground and confirmation of our faith.[15] There needs no application, seeing our times are more like to suffer with abundance than starve for want of printed books. Wherefore I hope this may suffice, to persuade those that have unprinted copies in their hands, to use them for their own private benefit. But if any rest not satisfied herewith, I would yet entreat thus much of them: that before they put hand to work for the press, they would acquaint Master Perkins's executors with their reasons that move them thereunto; from whom I doubt not but they shall receive either sufficient satisfaction for their stay or good leave to proceed in their intended course. Which thing I do the rather advise, because the executors have a general inhibition out of his Majesty's Court of High Commission, prohibiting the publishing of any of his works without their consent.

Now the God of all grace, who is Lord of the harvest, send forth daily such faithful workmen and bless these and their labors for the beauty and wealth of Zion. Amen.

September 1, 1609

Yours in Christ Jesus,
Thomas Pierson

---

15. John 20:25, 30–31.

Chapter 2

Robert Hill Transcription

The following sermon was included as an appendix to the first edition of Perkins's Revelation sermons, edited by Robert Hill.[1] It did not subsequently appear in print and was omitted from Perkins's collected works. It seems likely that it was excluded by Perkins's executors because much of its content is treated more fully elsewhere.[2]

Hill states that the sermon was "preached long since" by Perkins. Indeed, the title page of the volume indicates that it was "penned at the request of… Ambrose, Earle of Warwicke." Given that Ambrose Dudley, Earl of Warwick, died in 1590,[3] the sermon must have been delivered at some point in the 1580s, most likely during Perkins's Christ College fellowship, locating the sermon sometime between 1584 and 1590. Dudley was an enthusiastic supporter of Puritan clergy, which is in keeping with his presence at one of Perkins's sermons.[4]

The sermon appears to have been delivered before a learned audience: it features long and complex sentences and unapologetically offers Latin patristic quotations in support of its arguments. The sermon is a follow-up to a previous sermon on Psalm 122 (no longer extant) that Perkins had delivered before the

---

1. William Perkins, *Lectures upon the Three First Chapters of the Revelation: Preached in Cambridge Anno Dom. 1595. by Master William Perkins, and Now Published for the Benefite of This Church, by Robert Hill Bachelor in Divinitie. To Which Is Added an Excellent Sermon, Penned at the Request of That Noble and Wise Councellor, Ambrose, Earle of Warwicke: In Which Is Proved That Rome Is Babylon, and That Babylon Is Fallen*, ed. Robert Hill (London: Printed by Richard Field for Cuthbert Burbie, 1604), 341–73.

2. See Announcement 8. Perkins included many of the points made in this sermon in his *A Reformed Catholic* (1597) and *Forged Catholicism* (1604). It is understandable that Pierson did not explicitly note the exclusion of this sermon in Announcement 8 (1609) since that would have drawn attention to Robert Hill's edition of the Revelation commentary (1604), which his own edition (1606, 1607) was intended to replace.

3. Simon Adams, "Dudley, Ambrose, Earl of Warwick (c. 1530–1590)," in *Oxford Dictionary of National Biography* (Oxford: Oxford University Press, 2004; online ed., January 2008).

4. Adams, "Dudley, Ambrose, earl of Warwick"; Collinson, *Elizabethan Puritan Movement*, 166–67, 189.

same audience. It expounded the nature of the church in its flourishing state. It seems likely that these sermons were delivered in Christ's College chapel services, a setting in which Perkins would have shared occasional preaching duties with other fellows and learned guests.

The sermon centers on the standard Protestant claim that the Roman Catholic Church is the Babylon of which Scripture warns and that the pope is the antichrist. Such had long been the claim of Protestant Reformers, including Luther, Calvin, Knox, and Cranmer, and this view was widely held in Elizabethan England. Indeed, the sitting archbishop of Canterbury, John Whitgift, had defended the proposition that "the pope is antichrist" in order to take his doctorate in 1567.[5] Perkins's own circle of moderate Puritans in Cambridge was particularly vocal on this theme, with notable voices including William Whitaker, Laurence Chaderton, William Fulke, and Robert Some.[6]

In this sermon Perkins sets out to defend his thesis from Scripture and from patristic authors, including Irenaeus, Tertullian, Chrysostom, Jerome, and Augustine. He reasons that such authors cannot be dismissed as having the polemical motives that modern Protestants had in making this claim, yet here they plainly agreed with the Protestants. The burden of this sermon, and indeed of all of Perkins's polemical engagement with Roman Catholicism, was not the demonization of foreign ecclesiastical and political powers but a sincere warning to all English people that the Roman religion represented a persistent threat to the spiritual and temporal well-being of all people and therefore must be completely and entirely repudiated.

---

5. William Joseph Shiels, "Whitgift, John (1530/31?–1604)," in *Oxford Dictionary of National Biography* (Oxford: Oxford University Press, 2004; online ed., January 2008).

6. Peter Lake, *Moderate Puritans and the Elizabethan Church* (Cambridge: Cambridge University Press, 1982), 55–76; Peter Lake, "The Significance of the Elizabethan Identification of the Pope as Antichrist," *The Journal of Ecclesiastical History* 31, no. 2 (1980): 161–78. For an excellent overview of Perkins's place amid Reformation polemical engagement with Roman Catholicism, see Shawn D. Wright and Andrew S. Ballitch, "Preface to Volume 7 of William Perkins's *Works*," in RHB 7:xi–xxxv.

Revelation 14:8

An excellent sermon plainly proving that Rome is Babylon and that Babylon is fallen. Preached long since by a famous divine and added as a commentary to the hardest part of the Revelation.

"She is fallen, she is fallen, even Babylon that great City: for of the wine of the fury of her fornication she has made all Nations to drink." (Rev. 14:8)

The holy evangelist Saint Luke, in the fourth chapter of his gospel, records that on a time when our Savior came into the synagogue at Nazareth to read as His custom was, there was delivered to Him a book containing the prophecy of the prophet Isaiah. Which, after He had opened, at the first He found the place where it was written in these words: "The Spirit of the Lord is upon me, because he hath anointed me that I should preach the gospel to the poor. He hath sent me that I should heal the broken in heart, that I should preach deliverance to the captives and sight to the blind, that I should set at liberty them that are bruised, and to preach the acceptable year of the Lord."[1] Then, after He had closed the book and delivered it to the minister, He sat down to preach, and the eyes of all them that were in the congregation were bent upon Him. Then He opened His mouth and spoke unto them these words: "This day is this Scripture fulfilled in your ears," and they all gave Him testimony that it was so.[2] In like manner may I say, concerning this place of Scripture which I have read unto you, In your eyes and ears is this Scripture this day fulfilled. And I pray God you may all likewise bear witness with me that it is so.

The last time that I spoke in this auditory, I entreated of the flourishing and prosperous estate of Jerusalem, which is the church of God, set forth in the 122nd Psalm; and, therefore, good order now requires that I should speak of the decay and overthrow of the enemy of Jerusalem, which is Babylon, the see and church of antichrist. And for that purpose, principally, have I chosen this text of Scripture to speak of, that by the one we might be enflamed with love of the true church of Christ and by the other be moved to the hatred of that false church of antichrist. Now, this text of Scripture ("She is fallen, she is

---

1. Luke 4:16–19; Isa. 61:1–2.
2. Luke 4:21–22.

fallen, even Babylon that great city, for of the wine of the fury of her fornication she hath given all nations to drink"[3]) offers me three special things to be considered: first, what Babylon is; second, what is become of her; and, third, what is the cause of her heavy decay. In the first part, by the assistance of God, I shall plainly show and prove that Babylon is Rome; in the second, that Babylon or Rome by the just judgment of God is fallen, yea, she is fallen; in the last, the reason of this so sharp sentence of God against her, because she has deceived all the world with drunkenness and whoredom.

Preface

Within the compass of these three propositions, I will keep myself in all my discourse, saving that by your favor, forasmuch as this is the middle voice of three angels that speak in this chapter, for a preface I will use the voice of the first angel, of whose preaching this my text is a consequent. And in the stead of a conclusion, I will touch the voice of the third angel, which is a consequent of this the middle angel's voice. Concerning the preface, it shall be this in few words. After that Saint John had described the preservation and unity of the church of God in Christ their head, even in the midst of the fury of antichrist, under the figure of the Lamb standing on Mount Zion with 144,000 of His chaste worshipers. Next, he declares that God would bring the same again into the sight of the world by preaching of the gospel and the overthrow of the kingdom of antichrist. Wherefore he sends an angel flying in the midst of heaven, or between heaven and earth, bringing with him an everlasting gospel and preaching that all men should fear God and give glory to His name, for the time of His judgment was at hand, and that they should worship Him that made heaven and earth and all things that are in them. A very angelical sermon indeed, and an everlasting gospel is that, howsoever the enemies charge it with novelty, that teaches to fear God, to give glory to His name, and to worship Him only that is the Creator of heaven and earth. And a consequent of that gospel is this sermon of the angel: "She is fallen, she is fallen, even Babylon that great city." For wheresoever men are taught to fear God aright, to give all glory to Him alone, and to worship none other but Him that made heaven and earth and all things in them contained, there must needs follow a great fall and overthrow of Babylon, and babylonical religion, which teaches the contrary. Wherefore if we love the peace of Jerusalem, to the overthrow of this her great adversary, let us embrace this everlasting gospel, that we fear God, glorify God, and worship God alone. Again, if we hate Babylon with a perfect hatred (as we ought to do and therefore would seek her utter ruin and decay), let us procure

---

3. Rev. 14:8.

that this gospel may be preached, that men may learn to fear, honor, and serve God only, and then undoubtedly Babylon shall fall; she shall fall, I say, she can stand no longer. Let this suffice, therefore, for a preface.

What Babylon Is

Now, we have to consider what Babylon is. I have undertaken to prove that Babylon here spoken of is Rome. But first I must admonish you how I understand Rome. And that is not only for a certain place in Italy, compassed about with walls and furnished with buildings as other cities are, but for that authority, government, and preeminence which is challenged by means of that city, or for the Roman Empire which is claimed by prerogative of the same city. And so is Babylon taken in the Scripture, and namely in this prophecy. For in the eleventh chapter of this Revelation, the same great city is called also Sodom and Egypt, where our Lord was crucified: Sodom, for the great abomination and filthiness therein maintained, and Egypt, because it keeps the people of God in miserable bondage and slavery as Egypt under Pharaoh did of old. Whereby it is manifest that the great city is to be taken for that tyranny, government, and preeminence, as I said, which is challenged in the right of that great city; and so is the regiment and governance of the Roman antichrist, depending upon the prerogative of his see, which is Rome. Now if any will contend that Babylon must be taken in the proper sense, for a city in Chaldea only, as though we should look for the see of antichrist out of the East (as the papists for thirty or forty years ago devised a fable, that was renewed also in Queen Mary's days, of a monstrous child which should be born at Babylon, which they would have men suppose to be antichrist), he may be flatly convicted of great ignorance when the angel in the seventeenth chapter of this prophecy testifies that her name is Babylon in a mystery,[4] as in the eleventh chapter that she is spiritually called Sodom and Egypt, not in respect of situation of the place but in similitude and likeness of conditions.[5]

Wherefore it remains that (according to my promise) I prove Babylon here mentioned to be Rome. The greatest controversy that this day troubles the world is where the true church of God should be, the papists making great brags that it is on their side, and we affirm that it is on our side. This controversy will soon be cut off and brought to an end if it may be shown that Babylon is Rome, for then Rome cannot be the church of Christ, but the church of antichrist. And, therefore, it stands me upon to bring very good and substantial proofs to maintain this my assertion, that Babylon is Rome. But what proofs may be counted

---

4. Rev. 17:5.
5. Rev. 11:8.

sufficient? Is not the authority of Holy Scripture, and the testimony of ancient doctors of the church, good and substantial proofs? Therefore, if authority of Scriptures be a good and substantial proof, you shall have Scriptures; if consent of ancient writers in the same sentence be of any value, you shall have plenty.

And first beginning with Scriptures, I will not allege such places as be hard and dark to understand but such as be plain, evident, and manifest and can receive no other interpretation to satisfy the judgment of any reasonable man. I omit, therefore, so many figures as in this Revelation do not very obscurely signify, but even directly point at and paint out that anti-Christian church. For although they do so aptly and fitly agree thereto (as a man might easily judge they were made even for the same purpose), yet because they might be wrested to some other meaning if manifest places did not withstand, I will leave all advantage that I might take of them and hold me only at this time to those plain and evident demonstrations which with no equity nor conscience can admit any other interpretation. Only I will here note that forasmuch as all figures, types, and colors contained in this book may so conveniently be applied to Rome as though they had been properly appointed to describe her (as they were indeed), it is great prejudice against Rome, although no plainer proofs might be brought. But when so plain arguments are brought forth that without too much impudency cannot be avoided, and all other figures and dark speeches agree accordingly, it is a manifest conjunction that Rome is none other but this Babylon.

But to begin with these plain places (as I have promised), the first shall be out of the eleventh chapter of this Revelation, the place before alleged, where it is declared that God in all times, yea, in the greatest persecution, would maintain His church and reserve at the least two witnesses which should testify of His truth in spite of antichrist and his adherents.[6] Which although the monstrous beast that arises out of the bottomless pit should murder and slay, yet God should restore them to life again, continually stirring up a sufficient number to bear witness of His name and doctrine. In that chapter I say is contained that when the beast had murdered them, he should envy them the honor of burial and so their bodies should lie in the street or marketplace of that great city, which is spiritually called Sodom and Egypt, where our Lord was crucified. Declaring thereby that as Rome had slain and crucified the head, so should Rome persecute the members. And in the same city where their Lord was murdered, the servants should be persecuted.

But here a man would think that I was impudent to affirm that our Savior Christ was crucified at Rome, whom all the world knows to have suffered death

---

6. Rev. 11:3–13.

at Jerusalem. But you must call to remembrance that at the first I gave warning that I did not understand Rome for the topography of Rome—that is, so much ground only as is compassed within the walls of that city—but for the regiment, governance, and prerogative that is claimed, by reason of that city or monarchy, whereof Rome is the head. And then I shall easily prove that Christ was crucified at Rome.

For by whom was He condemned? Was it not by Pilate the deputy or lieutenant of the Roman Empire? For what cause or crime was He adjudged to die? Was it not for treason pretended to be committed against the Roman Empire? With what kind of execution was He put to death? Was it not such as was usual by the laws of the Romans for such heinous offenses as were unjustly laid to His charge? Finally, was not the place wherein He suffered within the circuit of the Roman Empire? May I not then justly affirm that He was crucified at Rome, when by the Roman judge He was condemned for a crime against the Roman state, and executed by a kind of death appointed by the Roman laws, and in a place of the Roman dominion? As for the Jews, they had at that time no authority to put any man to death, as they confess themselves when Pilate bade them take Him and judge Him according to their own law, meaning they should decree some light punishment against Him. They answered: "It is not lawful for us to judge him to die."[7] As touching the cause, although they accused Him of blasphemy in that He made Himself the Son of God, yet could He not be condemned for that because Pilate would admit no accusation but such as contained a crime against the Roman laws. And as for the death of the cross, it is manifest to be proper to the Romans, for the Jews would have stoned Him, if they might have condemned Him for blasphemy, according to the law of Moses. And that the angel in that place by no means can understand Jerusalem, it is manifest by these reasons. First, that he calls it "that great city," which term could never be spoken of Jerusalem. Also, he calls it Sodom and Egypt, which was the see of the monstrous beast antichrist, which in other places is often called Babylon, whereas no man ever did imagine that Jerusalem should be called Sodom, Egypt, or Babylon. Add hereunto that Jerusalem, the place where Christ suffered, was utterly destroyed in Saint John's time, whereby it is evident that by this great city, spiritually called Babylon, Sodom, and Egypt, is meant none other but the Roman Empire, which crucified the head and should also bring forth to put any man to death. And he has deserved the monstrous beast antichrist, which should torment and afflict the members, which began with [the] murder of the Lord and should continue, till it were destroyed, in murdering of the servants. And by this plain text, which cannot be wrested to

---

7. John 18:31.

any other sense, this great city of Babylon, where Christ was crucified, is proved to be Rome and the authority, rule, and power of the Roman city.

The second plain and evident proof which I will use at this time shall be taken out of the thirteenth chapter of this Revelation, where that evil shaped beast is described, which is the head of the persecuting malignant church, having seven heads and ten horns, and is the same which afterward in the seventeenth chapter bears the great whore Babylon, the mother of all abominations of the earth.[8] Who so therefore will compare these things that are written in this book, concerning the description of that monstrous beast, with those things that the prophet Daniel, in the seventh chapter of his prophecy, describes of the four beasts, and specially of the fourth, which all men confess to be the Roman Empire.[9] Except he be too much blinded with frowardness and perverse affection, he must needs acknowledge that this beast which John paints out is the same that Daniel sets out, which containing in it the cruelty of the leopard, the bear, and the lion, which were the former monarchies, is unlike to them all and therefore is the fourth empire, which all the world acknowledge to be the monarchy of Rome. What should I speak of the number of the horns, equal in both, and generally of all other parts of their description, which is set forth so like and almost with the same words, both of the one and of the other, that it were mere madness to imagine that this beast which John describes should be any other than that Daniel had so long before portraited. Then if the beast in Daniel's description does signify the fourth kingdom, as the angel expounds it, which no man will deny to be the Roman monarchy, the same monstrous beast being here painted out in this Revelation with the same shape, colors, and conditions must needs signify the Roman Empire. And so, Babylon by this reason also is proved to be Rome.

The third argument or proof is taken out of the seventeenth chapter of this Revelation, and the ninth verse, where the angel expounding to Saint John the mystery of the beast with the seven heads declares in very plain words that the seven heads do signify seven hills, whereon the woman sits.[10] Now seeing it is evident that the woman signifies a great city, we must see where we can find a great City built upon seven hills. And that, by the interpretation of the angel, is Babylon, the see of antichrist. And if we seek throughout the whole world, where shall we find a great city built upon seven hills but that great city in Italy? Which all writers poets, historians, cosmographers with one consent do confess to be Rome, which is built upon seven hills whose names are these: Palatine, Capitoline, Aventine, Esquiline, Viminal, Quirinal, and Caelian. This

---

8. Rev. 13:1–9; 17:1–6.

9. Dan. 7:1–8.

10. Rev. 17:9. Cf. *Reformed Catholic*, RHB 7:10–12.

is so plain a notation of Rome to be Babylon, built on seven hills, that the angel could not more plainly have expressed Rome, though he had named her. Nay, this is a more evident and certain description of Rome to be the see of Antichrist than if in plain words he had said, "Babylon is Rome." For it might be that some other city, than that here was meant, might have the name of Rome, but no other city could have this notation, to be built on seven hills. For Constantinople was afterward called new Rome, but Constantinople was not built upon seven hills like unto old Rome. Therefore, this is a plain and manifest circumlocution of Rome, which with no reason can receive any other exposition.

For what boy going to the grammar school and reading in Virgil's *Georgics* this verse, *Septem quae una sibi muro circundedit arces*, "That city (says Virgil) which has compassed seven hills within her walls,"[11] what boy, I say, in the grammar school does not understand this to be meant of the city of Rome, although the poet in that place does not once name Rome? With what face, therefore, will any man deny that the angel here means any other city by this periphrasis and circumlocution than Rome? For if any will be so froward to except that the word of "hills" is not taken in the proper sense, but figuratively and metaphorically for some other thing, as some would seem to interpret seven hills in this place for seven kingdoms, he shall plainly be convinced by these reasons. First, it were absurd that the angel should repeat one thing twice, for in the next clause he shows that the seven heads do signify kingdoms also, but specially we must remember that this is an interpretation of the angel which must either be plain and easy to be understood or it deserves not the name of an interpretation. Therefore, if the angel offering to expound the mystery of the seven heads gives this exposition that they signify seven hills, if hills be not taken in their proper sense, to what purpose serves this exposition? For if the name of hills has need of another exposition, he had been as good to have left the name of heads unexpounded. And as for the interpretation of hills to signify kings, [it] is more obscure, dark, and far-fetched than that heads should represent kings, for it is more apt by metaphor to call a king a head than to call him a hill. Therefore, except we will say that the interpretation of the angel is vain, yea, more dark than the thing that is expounded by him, we must needs confess that hills are taken in their proper sense for hills, and then the city built upon seven hills without all controversy is the city of Rome.

The fourth and last proof that I will take out of the Holy Scripture is the last verse of the same seventeenth chapter, which is yet a more plain description of Rome, if anything can be more plain than that has been already spoken. For there the angel in plain words expounds that the woman, which Saint John saw,

---

11. Virgil, *Georgics*, bk. 2, line 535.

which was the great whore Babylon, is that great city which has dominion over the kings of the earth.[12] What brazen face is so impudent to deny that Rome was that great city which had dominion over the kings of the earth at that time when this was spoken? Or what other city had dominion over the kings of the earth in Saint John's time but Rome? Who is, therefore, so froward and untoward that he will not acknowledge Babylon here to be plainly called Rome? If I should name the chief city of England, who would not understand London? If I should speak of the chief city of France, who would not conceive Paris? And when the angel named the chief city of the world, who could be ignorant, living in that time, or knowing the history of that time, that he understood it of the city of Rome, which was the see of the empire, and from whence we should look that antichrist should come, according to the former prophecies? For it is a shame in this place to fly unto allegories and further expositions of this angelical interpretation, which as I said before, if it be not clear, plain, and easy to be understood, deserves not the name of an exposition, as when one knows one unknown thing is expounded by another as much or more unknown, it is vain, superfluous, and ridiculous. Wherefore, whom any bonds of reason will hold in, they must be satisfied with the exposition of the angel that Babylon is Rome. For seeing it was necessary for the church of God to know as well the place where antichrist should sit as to be instructed of his craft and cruelty, our Savior Christ, the author of this Revelation, would not suffer His congregation to be ignorant thereof, but sent His angel plainly to interpret and expound the vision of the great whore, that the church being thoroughly admonished of her wickedness and instructed perfectly to know her might more easily take heed of her, fly from her, and abhor her. So that, according to my promise, I have sufficiently proved by authority of Holy Scriptures this first proposition which I took in hand, that Babylon is Rome.

But because some are of such obstinate and willful frowardness that nothing will satisfy them, but they will still grudge and repine, carp, and object against my interpretations of Holy Scriptures (for the texts they cannot deny), I wish them that are such, if they like not these expositions which I have brought to the defacing of antichrist and his religion, that then they admit and reverence those expositions which their own authors bring for the maintenance of the pope's authority and his religion. Of which sort are these. God (says Moses in Genesis) made two great lights, the sun to rule the day and the moon to govern the night.[13] That is, says the famous interpreter, God ordained the pope and the emperor to rule the world. By the sun is meant the pope and by the moon

---

12. Rev. 17:18.
13. Gen. 1:16.

the emperor. And look how much greater and more glorious the sun is than the moon, so much greater and more glorious is the pope than the emperor. And not content with this, he counts by arithmetic how much greater the sun is in quantity than the moon, by proportion that it has to the earth, and so by many parts he concludes that the pope is greater than the emperor.[14] But here a man might help him, what by geometry and what by arithmetic, for whereas the sun is 166 times greater than the earth, and the earth 39 times greater than the moon (as is proved by mathematical demonstration), the pope should be 6,474 times greater than the emperor. This is one noble exposition that is set forth to advance the dignity of the pope and his kingdom.

Another like to this is upon the words of the apostles, which answered unto our Savior Christ, when He commanded him that had no sword to sell his coat and buy one, signifying the great danger that was at hand: "Lord (say they) here are two swords."[15] These swords (says the glosser) are the civil and ecclesiastical power which remained in Peter, and therefore his successor the pope has preeminence of both.[16] No doubt a worthy interpretation, and that agrees well with the text and does the pope great worship. Again, Saint Paul says to the Corinthians, "The spiritual man judges all things, and he himself is judged of none" (1 Cor. 2).[17] This spiritual man, says the interpreter, is the pope, which is judge of all the world and may not be controlled of any man, no though he draw with him innumerable souls into hell fire, there to be tormented with the devil and him forevermore. Yet no man must be so bold as to find fault with him or to say, *Domine, quid ita facis?* "Lord, why do you so?" Is not this a handsome exposition? Yea, I promise you, even like unto this other: *Statuimus ut Clerici nec comam nutriant, nec barbam radant*, "We decree (says the canon of an ancient council) that the clergy shall neither wear long hair nor shave their beards."[18] The glosser finding this canon to be so clean contrary unto the custom of the popish clergy, who used to wear long hair and to shave their beards, thought he would draw it, at the least if it would not come by fair

---

14. This basic analogy was widely used among medieval advocates for papal political supremacy, most notably in a letter of Pope Innocent III (November 3, 1198). Perkins appears to refer specifically to Henry of Susa, or "Hostiensis" (d. 1271), who argued on the basis of the analogy that the pope has exactly 7,644 ½ times the authority of the emperor (Hostiensis, *Summa Aurea Super Titulis Decretalium*). While Perkins ridicules the analogy, he cannot help himself but correct Hostiensis's calculation. See Anthony Cassell, "'Luna est Ecclesia': Dante and the 'Two Great Lights,'" *Dante Studies* 119 (2001): 1–4, 19.

15. Luke 22:38.

16. Perkins is here engaging with the papal bull *Unam Sanctum* (1302), promulgated by Pope Boniface VIII (c. 1230–1303).

17. Verse 15.

18. Fourth Council of Carthage, canon 44.

means, to maintain the laudable custom of the popish clergy, and by exposition of one word he makes the whole canon to serve his turn. Therefore, *Statuimus* (says he) which is, we decree, to be expounded for *abrogamus*, which is, we disannul or abrogate, and so the sense afterward falls out very plain for the popish priests thus: we disannul that priests should go without long hair or unshaven beards. A right cunning interpretation, and proper for the place, and such in effect are all those that serve for the maintenance of the pope's authority and the religion of popery. Therefore, he that is of so sharp judgment that he will mislike and refuse those plain expositions which I have brought of the places before alleged and except against them as enforced, constrained, and far-fetched, let him like of praise, magnify, and admire these interpretations which are sought to uphold and establish the pope's throne and religion as rightly, faithfully, and truly collected. *Atque idem jungat Vulpes, et mulgeat Hireos*, and by as good reason let him join for his plough not oxes but foxes, and milk for his pail not she goats but he goats, as the poet says.[19]

Now that I have proved Babylon to be Rome by authority of Scripture, it follows that I must show for the same the consent of ancient doctors. And as in my former probation I touched only such places as did plainly, directly, and manifestly set forth my purpose, so in this behalf I will deal with the doctors. Not such as they are wont to allege against us names indeed of great and reverent antiquity, but works of mere falsehood and forgery, bewraying their authors not to be such as they are fathered upon but such as out of the body of blindness and superstition of much later time have begotten them. Such are the decretal epistles of the old bishops of Rome, Linus, Clemens, Anacletus, etc.[20] Of which, Clemens writing to Saint James forsooth in his second epistle, charges him very earnestly that the pixe[21] be cleanly kept, so that there appear no mice dung or any other filthiness among the fragments of the body of Christ, with many other like apostolical commandments.[22] The impudence of whose authors appears notably in this, that whereas they were ignorant buzzards that could not write true Latin, they would ascribe their counterfeit epistles to so learned fathers, as though at that time when women and children spoke Latin naturally as their mother tongue, the bishops were so unlearned that they did write so barbarously and were not able to utter their mind in true Latin.

But leaving those delicates for such as long after them, I will use no authority for this purpose but such as they cannot refuse, but that that is ancient,

---

19. Aesop's fables.

20. The "decretal epistles" of these alleged first-century popes were actually ninth-century forgeries.

21. *Pixe* (*pyx*): a small container used to hold the bread of the Eucharist.

22. Psuedo-Clemens, *Second Epistle to James*. See Perkins, *Forged Catholicism*, RHB 7:178.

catholic, and authentical. I will begin therefore with Irenaeus, one of the most ancient and authentical writers that the church has, who in the fifth book of his *Treatise against all Heresies*, speaking of the see of antichrist, upon the last verse of the 13th chapter of this Revelation,[23] where it is said that the number of the beasts name is six hundred, sixty and six, shows that the opinion of many in his time was that seeing this name λατεινος, which is in English "the Latin man" or "Roman," in the numeral Greek letters contains this number, that antichrist must be sought at Rome. His words are these: *Sed et λατεινος nomen sexcentorum sexaginta sex numerorum, etc. et valde verisimile est, quoniam verissimum regnum hoc habet vocabulum. Latini enim sunt qui nunc regnant.* "Also (says he) this name *LATEINOS*, containing the number of 666 is thought to be the name of antichrist. And it is very like so to be, for that which most undoubtedly is a kingdom has that name. For they be Latins which now do reign."[24]

You see by this testimony of Irenaeus that this prophecy of old time was understood of Rome and that the number of the beast's name is to be found in one that bears rule at Rome. If this exposition or explication of the beast's name had been devised by Luther, Zwingli, or Calvin it might have been suspected as a thing imagined of spite and envy against the Church of Rome. But when it is brought forth by so ancient a doctor, which lived not many years after this revelation was given, as he himself says that it was but a little before his time under Domitian the Emperor, which died thirteen hundred years before Luther was born, we must needs judge it both to be very ancient and void of all partiality. Wherefore I will pass over divers other applications of that number to other names which nevertheless hit Babylon home, because they have been sought out of late by such as bear ill will unto Rome. For I think this is sufficient with all reasonable men of equal judgment to prove that this is no new opinion to seek the see of antichrist at Rome. They themselves to prove their doctrine catholic allege authority of eleven or twelve hundred years antiquity. Behold, this opinion is thirteen or fourteen hundred years old, that antichrist should be a Roman and that the see of his tyranny should be at Rome.

The second witness of this assertion that Babylon is Rome is Tertullian, a very ancient writer also, who in plain words affirms that Babylon signifies Rome, in the third book against Marcion, which denied that Christ had a true body. Wherefore Tertullian used this reason against him: that thing which has a figure of it must be a thing of truth. And so, discoursing of many things figured and the figures of them, comes to these words: *Sic et Babylon apud Johannem nostrum, Romana urbis figuram portat, perinde et magna, et regno superbae, et*

---

23. Rev. 13:18.

24. Irenaeus, *Against Heresies*, bk. 5, ch. 30.3. See Perkins, *Warning against Idolatry*, RHB 7:468.

sanctorum debellatricis;[25] that is to say, "Even so does Babylon (in the Apocalypse of our Saint John) bear the figure of the city of Rome, which is altogether as great, and as proud in reign, and as great a persecutor of the saints, as Babylon was." You see, therefore, most clearly and plainly that Tertullian with all his learning could not interpret these things that be written in this revelation concerning Babylon to be applied to any other city than Rome. And he is also a witness void of all partiality or affection to either part of them that strive in our days, for he departed near about fourteen hundred years before our time. Why should he not then be credited in this case?

Well, next unto him I will join Chrysostom, in his commentary upon the second epistle to the Thessalonians, the second chapter, in his fourth homily. Whereas Saint Paul, speaking of the manifestation of antichrist, says they knew what was the stay that he was not presently revealed. But when that stay is taken away, he should be revealed in his due time. Chrysostom expounds this stay to be the Roman Empire, which must give place unto antichrist, that like as the Persians came in place of the Chaldeans, the Grecians in place of the Persians, and the Romans in place of the Grecians, even so antichrist should invade the empire of the Romans. *Vacantem imperii principatum invadet, et tentabit ad se rapere hominum et Dei imperium,* "Antichrist (says he) shall invade the vacant principality of the Empire and shall assay to draw unto himself the empires both of God and men."[26] And is it not manifest that the papacy grew and took increase by the decay of the empire, and at the fall of the monarchy, [and] challenged full possession of all dominion, both spiritual and temporal?

Of the same judgment is Saint Jerome writing upon the same place of Paul, unto Algasia, in the eleventh question, whose words are these: *Nec vult apertè dicere Romanum imperium destruendum, quod ipsi qui imperant aeternum putant, unde secundum Apocalypsim Iohannis in fronte purpuratae meretricis scriptum est nomen blasphemiae, id est Romae aeternae, etc.*[27] That is, "Neither will he openly say that the Roman Empire should be destroyed, which they that govern it think to be everlasting. Wherefore according to the Revelation of Saint John, in the forehead of the purple whore there is written a name of blasphemy, which is, Rome everlasting." Lo, here another witness of good antiquity and sufficient credit, which not only agrees plainly with Chrysostom that antichrist should take possession of the Roman Empire when it should be decayed in the emperors but also most plainly agreeing with Tertullian, calls

---

25. Tertullian, *Against Marcion*, bk. 3, ch. 13.

26. Chrysostom, *Homilies on Second Thessalonians*, Homily 4 (on 2 Thessalonians 2:6–9).

27. Jerome, Letter to Algasia. See *Sancti Eusebii Hieronymi Epistulae*, ed. Isidorus Hilberg (New York: Johnson, 1970), 3:1–55. Jerome's letter answered a series of questions previously asked by Algasia.

that babylonical strumpet, which is described in the seventeenth chapter of this Apocalypse, that purple whore of Rome, and the name of blasphemy to be Rome everlasting, as though he had heard the pope brag of the eternity of his see, which he says is the rock, against which the gates of hell cannot prevail. But he is foully beguiled, for Rome the see of his popedom is by Saint Jerome's judgment that Babylon of whom the angel preached, that howsoever she boasts of her eternity, "She is fallen, she is fallen, even Babylon that great city, and never shall rise again."[28]

They cry out against us that we rail and speak contumeliously of the holy see of the pope when we call Rome the whore of Babylon, but when the old doctors (to whose judgment they themselves appeal from the authority of the Scriptures) fear not so plainly in their writings to paint out the babylonical strumpet in her right colors, and in flat words to say she is Rome, the mother of all abomination, and the see of antichrist, why should we be blamed for saying as we are taught by them? And especially of those men that make so great vaunts that the judgment of the fathers is altogether on their side by whom they offer to be tried, when they dare not abide the judgment of the Scriptures?

Again, consider I pray you: if the old doctors before antichrist were openly revealed did understand by the Scriptures that he should sit at Rome, what think you would they have said and written if they had lived in these days and known and seen all that was prophesied to be fulfilled in him? With what confidence, suppose you, would they have inveighed against him? With how open mouths would they have cried out upon him? At least wise do you not think in your conscience that when they had considered the authority of the pope and his wholesome doctrine, they would have changed their minds and recanted their writings against Rome and repented that ever they had called her the purple whore of Babylon, seeing she is the holy mother Church of Rome, the see of the most holy father the pope, the head of the same church?

I must needs say thus much in your behalf (O you papists) as ill as I love you, that if Jerome, Tertullian, and the rest of the doctors did so account of Rome as you affirm of them, they were much to blame to defame her with such odious names as to call her the whore of Babylon, which must needs make her vehemently suspected to be the church of antichrist and not of Christ. For what papist in these days dares says that which Jerome said, that Rome is that purple harlot Babylon, which Saint John speaks of in the Apocalypse? The same Jerome in his 13th book of commentaries of the prophecy of Isaiah, upon the 47th chapter, writes in this manner: *Licet ex eo quod juxta 70. scriptum est θυγάτης βαβυλωιος, id est, filia Babylonis, non ipsam Babylonem quidam,*

---

28. Rev. 18:2.

sed Romanam vrbem interpretantur, quae in Apocalypsi Johannis et Epist. Petri Babylon specialiter appellatur, etc.[29] That is to say, "For as much as the seventy interpreters write not the daughter Babylon but the daughter of Babylon, some do interpret thereof not Babylon in Chaldea but the city of Rome, which in the Revelation of Saint John and the Epistle of Peter is specially called Babylon." Note that Jerome in this place accounted Rome to be Babylon the younger, daughter of Babylon the elder. And, secondly, that this was not his opinion only but the consent of many others in his time, and namely, of such as used to interpret the prophet Isaiah. Thirdly and especially, consider that he affirms Rome in the Apocalypse to be especially called Babylon. So that Babylon in the Apocalypse, by his judgment, can be understood for nothing else but Rome because Rome is there specially figured by Babylon. What means Jerome so often to beat in this nail, that Babylon is Rome? If it had slipped out of his pen but once, he might have been pardoned for his oversight, but when he has never done writing that Rome is Babylon, why should we account him any longer for a Catholic?

For in his preface unto the book of Didymus, *De Spiritu Sancto*, which he translated out of Greek into Latin, writing to Paulinianus, he utters these words: *Cùm in Babylone versarer, et purpuratae Meretricis essem Colonus, et jure Quiritum viverem, etc,*[30] "Of late (says he) when I was in Babylon, and was an inhabitant of the purple harlot, and lived after the laws of the Romans, I thought to intreat somewhat of the Holy Spirit." What needed Jerome in this place so odiously and contumeliously to call Rome by the name of Babylon but that he could never consider Rome otherwise but to be the see appointed for antichrist? For in other places where he interprets the Scriptures and prophecies concerning antichrist, we may less marvel if he interprets Babylon for Rome because no reason could lead him to expound it otherwise. But here talking pleasantly with his friend, what necessity compelled him to use such descriptions of Rome but that this persuasion was so deeply graven in his mind that Babylon is Rome that neither in earnest nor jest he could forget it, but is always harping upon it as though he thought scorn to call Rome by any other name, than that he had learned in the Scriptures to be Babylon and the purple harlot? For in like manner writing to Marcella, a virtuous gentlewoman of Rome, whom he allured to forsake Rome, and to dwell near unto him in Bethlehem, one special reason that he uses to persuade her is this: that as Bethlehem whither he would have her to repair is situated in the holy land and the place

---

29. Jerome, *Commentary on Isaiah*, bk. 13.

30. Didymus's *De Spiritu Sancto* (*On the Holy Spirit*) survived only in Jerome's Latin translation, *Didymi Libro de Spiritu Sancto* (c. 385). Jerome's prologue was addressed to Paulinianus, his younger brother.

consecrated to the birth of Christ, so Rome where she desired to remain was the babylonical harlot, according to the Revelation of Saint John, appointed for the birth of antichrist, which there should arise and exercise his tyranny and from thence should deceive the whole world with his wicked wiles.[31]

But who so will read the works of Jerome may find yet more places in which he is bold to call Rome Babylon, the very see of antichrist. Whereby it is apparent that it is no new or strange matter to seek antichrist at Rome, when such old doctors of the church so commonly in commentaries, epistles, and other writings do teach us that Rome is Babylon and the Scripture affirms that Babylon is the see of antichrist. But let us leave Saint Jerome and see what others say of the same matter.

Saint Ambrose, writing a commentary upon the Revelation of Saint John, is of the same judgment.[32] Of the authority of the work I will move no question at this time, seeing it is commended to us by Cuthbert Tunstall,[33] late bishop of Durham, who found it in an old library and first set it in print under the name of that great Saint Ambrose and is willing that men should so think of it. It is good authority, I say, against the papists, being commended by so Catholic a prelate, and because they are wont to receive whatsoever coming under the name of an old doctor, though it be never so unlike his writing, and cry out upon us for rejecting at our pleasure the works of ancient doctors that make against our doctrine, as though we rejected any without cause or they refused none for any cause. Whereas Pigius their great patron blushed not to reject the report of two general councils, the fifth and sixth of Constantinople, which are commended to us by public faith of the Church of Constantinople, because in the one Pope Honorius is condemned and accursed for a heretic and in neither of both the pope's legates could have the highest place according to the request of their ambitious master.[34] But as for this Ambrose, if he were not Ambrose of Milan, yet is it apparent by the style that he was some ancient writer of the Latin church, and he throughout this prophecy interprets Babylon to be Rome and antichrist to be sought nowhere but at Rome. Primasius, also a very ancient

---

31. Jerome, Letter 46 (to Marcella), 12.

32. Ambrose Autpert, *Expositio in Apocalypsim* (*Exposition of John's Apocalypse*). As Perkins indicates, this work was often attributed to the more famous Ambrose of Milan (c. 340–397). In fact, it was by Ambrose Autpert (d. 784). Perkins here accepts the erroneous attribution for the sake of the argument.

33. Cuthbert Tunstall (1474–1559) was successively bishop of London (1522–1530) and Durham (1530–1559). He never embraced Protestantism and remained Roman Catholic, managing to navigate the changing policies of Henry VIII, Edward VI, Mary I, and Elizabeth I while suffering only relatively minor personal difficulty.

34. Albert Pighius (1490–1542) was a Dutch Roman Catholic theologian, mathematician, and astronomer.

writer who likewise comments upon the Apocalypse, expounds these prophecies of antichrist to be fulfilled in the Roman Empire and of the city of Rome.[35]

Saint Augustine in his learned work *De Civitate Dei*, not once or twice, but oftentimes, is bold to call Rome Babylon, and Babylon Rome, as in his sixteenth book and seventh chapter he calls Rome another Babylon in the west. And in his eighth book and second chapter he calls Babylon of Chaldea the first Rome, and Rome of Italy the second Babylon, willing men to consider that in the beginning of the city of God (which was the church in Abraham's time) the first Rome (that was eastern Babylon her enemy) was built in Chaldea, and about the same time that the first Babylon was destroyed, lest the city of God should lack her enemy, the second Babylon (which is Rome in Italy) was erected. It is a strange matter that the same city which is the professed enemy of the city of God should be the mother of all religion and the very city of God itself. O Augustine, you were not well advised to make the city of Rome an enemy to the city of God, that Rome should be the same to the church of God that Babylon of old was to Jerusalem! The same Augustine in the 22nd chapter of the 18th book calls Rome another Babylon and daughter of the first Babylon. And in the 27th chapter he calls Rome western Babylon.[36]

By these (and other testimonies of old writers that might be brought but for tediousness) I suppose it is sufficiently proved that Babylon, in this my text spoken of, is Rome and that we should not seek antichrist to proceed from any other place than from Rome. But what need I trouble myself to seek further testimonial for confirmation of this matter that Babylon is Rome than of the papists themselves? Which affirm that Saint Peter in his epistle, where he sends salutations from the church gathered in Babylon, by Babylon understands Rome.[37] And they learn it of Jeronime, which in the life of Saint Mark does so expound it. So greedy they are to find a place in Scripture where Peter should be said to have been at Rome that they are content to acknowledge Babylon in the Scripture to be understood of Rome.

And thus, I have performed, I trust sufficiently, that which I took in hand to prove, both by the authority of Holy Scripture in plain and manifest texts and by consent of many ancient writers, yea, by the confession of the papists themselves, that Babylon in the Scripture is taken for Rome. And thus much for the first part, in which, because I have been over long, I will be shorter in that which remains.

---

35. Primasius, *Commentarius in Apocalypsin* (*Commentary on the Apocalypse*). Primasius (d. c. 560) was bishop of Hadrumetum, in Tunisia.

36. Augustine, *De Civitate Dei* (*On the City of God*), bk. 16, ch. 7; bk. 18, chs. 22 and 27.

37. 1 Peter 5:13.

What Has Become of Babylon

In the second part I promised to declare how Babylon, which is Rome, is fallen, according to the prophecy of this angel: "She is fallen," says the angel, "she is fallen." He repeats the word of falling for two causes. First, to declare the certainty of her decay, that howsoever she seemed to flourish and triumph, as though she should never have fallen or come to ruin, yet God, for her wickedness most righteously, and for the comfort of His church most mercifully, had decreed undoubtedly that she should fall when that time was once come which in His most wise and well-ordered counsel was appointed for her destruction. Secondly, he repeats twice that she is fallen to show that she should have an unrecoverable fall. She should not fall as other cities which have risen again, but she should fall without all hope of recovery, never to be restored again. Therefore, in the eighteenth chapter, a mighty angel takes up a great millstone and throws it into the sea, saying, "With such violence shall Babylon that great city be thrown down, and never be seen any more."[38] So that, as it is impossible for a great millstone, thrown with great force by a mighty angel into the bottom of the sea, to rise up again and swim above the water, so impossible is it that Babylon when she is at the lowest of her fall should ever be set up again. And in the nineteenth chapter it is said, "That the smoke of her burning ascended up for ever and ever."[39] Also of her utter desolation, descriptions are made in the eighteenth chapter, where it is said that Babylon is made a dwelling place of devils, a cage of unclean birds, according to the prophecy of Isaiah concerning old Babylon, that ziim and ohim (which be sprites and goblins) shall walk in her palaces, screeching owls[40] and ostriches shall cry in her houses, apes and satyrs shall dance in her beautiful buildings.[41] No voice of men shall be heard in her, no sound of a mill shall be heard, no light of a candle shall be seen, but perpetual solitude and sorrow shall dwell there for evermore.[42] Therefore, says the angel, "she is fallen, she is fallen," that is, she is destroyed and never shall be repaired.

But if we will better understand how she is fallen, we must consider more distinctly wherein she is fallen. First, in wealth and riches she has sustained a great fall. Consider how many kingdoms and states of the world have renounced her obedience, and all those have withdrawn great rents, revenues, and commodities that in times past were addicted to the maintenance of Babylon, the Church of Rome; a great fall without peradventure and that will never be

---

38. Rev. 18:21.
39. Rev. 19:3.
40. Original: Scrichowles.
41. Rev. 18:2; Isa. 13:21, Geneva Bible.
42. Rev. 18:11–19.

recovered. Remember so many abbeys, monasteries, nunneries, friaries, hospitals, chantries, churches, and chapels now overthrown and made even with the ground. All lands, jewels, ornaments, and great treasures that belonged unto them clean taken away from them, and you will confess with me that Rome in riches has a great fall. Yea, if you would see with your eyes a manifest example of God's judgment against Babylon, behold those evil favored ruins and heaps of monasteries that were sometimes gorgeous and sumptuous buildings. The same end remains all that pomp and pride of Babylon not yet altogether beaten down, but even now in falling. For the mouth of the Lord has spoken it, and His immutable counsel has decreed it, and He has sent an angel to proclaim it.

Some wish perchance that monasteries had stood still and been converted to better uses, but undoubtedly the providence of God so ordered all things that His curse which was upon them might be executed and the prophecies that were concerning them might be fulfilled, that they might be a monument of His wrath unto all the posterity, the beginning of the fall of Babylon, and an example of the destruction of all the rest that should follow soon after. Who would ever have thought that so great riches, treasures, and revenues should so suddenly be overthrown, destroyed, and come to nothing? Therefore, it is manifest that the wealth and worldly substance, whereby the pride, voluptuousness, and intemperance of riotous Rome was maintained and grown to an intolerable excess, is greatly diminished, sore decayed, and has a foul fall, and shortly shall have a final fall.

Well, Babylon is not fallen only in wealth and riches but also in power and authority. For the kings of the earth which sometimes were subject to that monstrous beast have now shaken off the yoke of her servitude and withdrawn the obedience of all their subjects from her. Yea, the most part of the ten horns, which sometime gave over their power and authority unto the beast, which were all the kings and potentates that acknowledged the pope for their supreme head and sovereign lord, do now hate and abhor the harlot of Rome and shall make her desolate by withdrawing their subjects from her obedience, and naked by spoiling her of her treasures, and shall eat her flesh for pure hatred and burn her with fire. For great is the Lord which judges her. So that she which before at her pleasure might command all princes to begin war, to cease from war, to defend her quarrels, to annoy her enemies now is glad to flatter a few seduced princes to take her part, that she be not utterly forsaken of all men, or else to practice by treason and treachery, suborning rogues and vagabonds to stir up tumults among the rude people, to trouble godly estates and commonwealths that despise her dominion, but without all hope ever to recover her ancient tyranny.

Her thunderbolts of excommunication, which were sometimes terrible to all men, are now feared of no man. What though she retains her proud and presumptuous stomach, and will do while her breath lasts, to pronounce sentence of deprivation against princes that abhor her wickedness? Her impudent arrogance is not so much detested of many as laughed to scorn of all. Her proctors and privy practicers, though they change themselves like Proteus[43] into ever so unlikely shapes, are espied in every corner. For God Himself reveals their pretenses and will not suffer her to prevail any longer. So that in power and authority Babylon is fallen and falls daily more and more into utter contempt with all men until she be utterly consumed and brought to nothing, which will not be long before it come to pass. For this sentence that God has pronounced against her, and begun also to execute, cannot be changed or much longer deferred.

But especially and chiefly Babylon is fallen in credit of her doctrine. For besides so many princes and estates of Christendom that by public authority have received the gospel and utterly abolished all babylonical doctrine, even in the midst of her tyranny and persecution great multitudes daily are lightened with the bright beams of the gospel. That for all inquisitions, imprisonments, exquisite torments, and cruel burnings, they never a whit diminish, but rather increase, as God has provided that the blood of the martyrs should be the seed of the church.[44] And they are more than obstinate if they do not acknowledge that this matter is governed from God above. For if it had been of men, it must needs have decayed before this time and have come to naught, as Gamaliel said of the doctrine of the apostles.[45] Therefore, in fighting against it, they show themselves but after the manner of the old giants, to make war against God. Or, as it is contained in this prophecy, that antichrist should gather together the princes of the earth to make battle against Him that sits upon the white horse, whose name is the Word of God, but all to their utter confusion and destruction.[46] For the Word of God must conquer and prevail in the last age, and antichrist must be consumed by the spirit of the mouth of Christ, which is His holy Word, and utterly abolished by the glorious brightness of His coming to judgment, as Saint Paul testifies in the second chapter of the second epistle to the Thessalonians.[47] Therefore, it is vain that they seek to underprop the doctrine of Babylon by cruelty and tyranny, for all will not serve, seeing the

---

43. Proteus was an ancient Greek sea god, whose nature was ever changing and shifting as the waters of the sea themselves.

44. This often repeated saying comes from Tertullian, *Apologeticus*.

45. Acts 5:35–39.

46. Rev. 19:19.

47. 2 Thess. 2:8.

time of her final fall approaches, and now already our Savior Christ with the spirit of His mouth has wasted and consumed a great part of that credit and estimation, in which the doctrine of Babylon of long time has triumphed. And it is our part to pray that her credit may daily more and more decrease, that the kingdom of Christ may be perfectly established among us and the kingdom of antichrist overthrown, even from the foundations, that no superfluous relics of babylonical religion may remain where the church of Christ is in building, but that the doctrine of Babylon may fall altogether.

Thus, I have declared that Babylon in wealth and substance, in power and authority, in credit and estimation of her doctrine is fallen, and that without hope of recovery. For her credit is cracked, not only among her enemies the Protestants but even among her best friends and greatest arch-papists. For I suppose there is none in the world so blind, so superstitious, so devoutly addicted in all points of popish idolatry and superstition as they were thirty or forty years past. Although they close their eyes ever so obstinately against the light of God's Word, yet some effect of the beams of force will pierce even through their eyelids. And that they themselves cannot dissemble, although they would never so fain, but that they have been deceived with gross errors and shameful superstitions—their pardons, their pilgrimages, their legends—who is now so blind that sees not how the world has been seduced by them? And the simplicity of the people abused to satisfy their unsatiable covetousness?

As for the greatest patrons of popery that be learned, they cannot deny but that great errors have been received and taught for truth. Yea, the pope himself has acknowledged that many errors have crept into the church—yea, even into the Mass—but the reformation of them pertain to him alone and the general council. But what hope of reformation is to be looked for at their hands, let it be seen in the decrees of the last Council of Trent.[48] What little mise those great mountains in so many years' travel have brought forth? In forty or fifty years' consultation [were] two great matters reformed: one for pardoners not to be common peddlers, another for the communion in both kinds to those that desire it, so they confess it were as good in one kind and agree with them in all other points of popery. Yet all was not well, they confess by their correction. And as for the greatest pillars and proctors they have, if they be pressed near, [they] acknowledge a great deal more. As one that landed lately at Yarmouth before witness of good credit testified,[49] that if he might be satisfied in two points, concerning the pope's supremacy and the real presence, for other matters he would not greatly strive. So that I will conclude that Babylon is fallen in

---

48. The final session of the Council of Trent was in 1563.
49. Jesuit missionaries landed in Yarmouth, Norfolk, in 1580.

riches, in power, in credit of doctrine, not only with Protestants but even with papists themselves.

But now I know what will be objected against me, that I have travailed all in vain to prove that Babylon is fallen and that Babylon is Rome, and that I have abused the texts of Scripture and sentences of old doctors to prove the same. For whatsoever is contained either in the Scripture or in the writings of the ancient doctors to prove that Babylon is Rome is to be understood of Rome under the heathen emperors, and not under the popes, and that all this while I have wrested the Scriptures and enforced the doctors to affirm that which they never thought of. Indeed, I will confess that some prophecies contained in this Revelation were fulfilled in the heathen emperors and that the heathen empire was an introduction unto antichrist. But that antichrist, the great enemy of the church of Christ and which is principally called antichrist, could not be any of the heathen monarchy I will make it manifest by plain demonstrations. And first, I will retain this principle sufficiently proved before that Rome is the see of antichrist and that by authority of Scriptures and consent of ancient writers we can seek him nowhere but in the Roman Empire.

And now the controversy rests in this, whether the heathen emperor or the pope be he.

First, Saint Paul in the second chapter of the second epistle to the Thessalonians, speaking purposefully of antichrist, says expressly that he shall sit in the temple of God, which is the church of Christ.[50] But it is manifest that the heathen emperors did not sit in the church of God; therefore, the heathen emperor is not this antichrist. And by the same reason it is manifest that Muhammad[51] is not that especial antichrist because he sits without the temple of God, as there be divers that would have these things to be understood of Muhammad or Ottoman.[52] But it is as clear as the sun at noon day, for as much as neither the heathen emperors, nor Muhammad, nor Ottoman sits in the temple or church of God, that none of them is that great antichrist of whom the prophecies of the Scripture are to be expounded.

And whereas some of them interpret the abomination of desolation whereof Christ speaks to be meant of antichrist, or at leastwise to be a sign of him, that cannot be understood of the heathen emperors or any other that is without the church, for that stands in the holy place which is the temple and signifies the church. Now, the pope sits in the midst of the temple of God and

---

50. 2 Thess. 2:4.

51. The original uses the archaic *Mahomet* throughout. This has been updated here.

52. Osman I (d. 1323/24), was the founder of the Ottoman Empire, which existed until the beginning of World War I. In Perkins's day, it was at the peak of its power and proclaimed itself to be the Islamic Caliphate.

boasts himself to be God, challenging to himself such authority as is proper only to God and usurping such honor as is peculiar only to God. Therefore, not in the heathen emperors but in the popes is this prophecy accomplished.

Another reason to prove that antichrist (which in this Revelation is foreshown to come into the world) cannot be understood to be the heathen emperors is taken out of the seventeenth chapter of the same book. For there the angel interpreting to Saint John the mystery of the beast that bears the harlot, which has seven heads, signifying seven hills, he declares also that they signify seven kings, or principal estates, or forms of regiment, for so the name of king is often taken in the prophets and specially in Daniel, at which prophecy Saint John borrows many phrases. Of these seven heads, five (he says) were fallen, the sixth was then presently in authority, and the seventh was not yet come, which seventh was the monstrous beast antichrist, that was both the seventh and the eighth.[53] Now it is evident that this could not be understood of the heathen emperors, for Nero the first persecuting paynim[54] was come and gone, and Domitian, another persecutor (by whose tyranny Saint John was banished into the Isle of Patmos, where he saw and received this Revelation), was then in authority. So that of the monarchy or tyranny of heathen emperors this could not be understood, and of the Christian emperors no man will expound it, so that it must needs be turned over to the pope, for it can rest in no place else, and being referred unto him, all the rest have a very apt exposition.

For the city of Rome, and the dominions thereof, have had seven principal states or forms of regiment: the first state of kings, the second of consuls, the third of *Decemviri*,[55] the fourth of dictators, the fifth of *Triumviri*,[56] the sixth of caesars or emperors, and the seventh of popes. Now, five of these states or forms of regiment were fallen and abolished in Saint John's time; the sixth, which was the emperors, in his time was in place; and the seventh, which is the popes, was not yet come, which was the very beast itself, the Roman Empire revived and raised up from the bottomless pit of hell into the usurped tyranny of the pope. And this is that beast that sometimes was of wonderful great power and glory in the days of Augustus, and some other of his successors, but then much decayed, as if it had not been, although in some sort it were, but should be restored in the usurped authority of the pope that claims all the world to be his diocese, which power comes not from God but from the prince of pride, out

---

53. Rev. 17:9–11.

54. *Paynim*: a non-Christian.

55. Literally "ten men." In the Roman Republic the *Decemviri* was an official commission made up of ten men.

56. Literally "three men." In the Roman Republic the *Triumviri* was a special administrative commission made up of three men.

of the bottomless pit. But chiefly let us consider that the beast, although he be but one, yet in the account he stands for two, for he is that seventh head and the eighth also. And remember that the pope challenges double authority, namely, the power of both the swords, the spiritual and temporal. So that in this exposition all things agree most aptly.

Again, it is manifest in the Scriptures that antichrist should deceive the world with false doctrine under pretense and color of true religion, and therefore so oftentimes the Scripture warns men that they be not seduced by him, which were needless if any open professed enemy of Christ should be that antichrist. For there is no likelihood that a heathen man, a Jew, or a Turk should deceive any multitude of true Christians, but he that under the pretense of the name of Christ seeks most of all to deface the honor of Christ, he is a subtle adversary and the very spirit of antichrist, as Saint John also in his epistle does testify. For in the second chapter, speaking of those antichrists which were the forerunners of the great antichrist, he shows that they went out from the church. And in the fourth chapter he calls them false prophets and teaches men how to know the spirit of antichrist: he that denies Jesus to be Christ, he that denies that Jesus Christ is come in the flesh, that is, he that derogates anything from the honor of Jesus to be Christ and in His flesh to have performed the full work of man's redemption, as the pope does most blasphemously, he is antichrist, and who so teaches any such doctrine speaks by the spirit of antichrist. For the testimony of Jesus is the spirit of prophecy.[57] Seeing, therefore, that Saint John accounts antichrist for one that is gone from the church and for a false prophet, it is clear that antichrist is no heathen emperor, which was never of the church, nor yet a false prophet that took upon him to teach in the church. The same may be said of Mohammed, who never professed himself to be a Christian nor yet a prophet in the church of Christ, pretending to uphold the religion of Christ, but an open enemy of the gospel and of our Savior Christ, altogether without the church. By these arguments I doubt not but all men may see that, seeing Babylon is Rome and that the head of Babylon is antichrist, he cannot be any of the heathen emperors, but even the pope himself. And, therefore, I conclude according to my text that Rome is fallen if Babylon be fallen.

The Cause of Babylon's Fall
Now remains the last part that I promised to entreat of, namely, the cause of God's so severe judgment against Babylon that He has decreed her utter overthrow and destruction, which the angel comprehends in these words, "Because

---

57. 1 John 2:18–19, 22; 4:1–3.

she has made all nations drunk with the wine of the fury of her fornication."[58] That is, she has deceived all the world with false doctrine, which he compares unto two kinds of vices whereby men are so deceived that they lose all their right judgment: drunkenness and fornication. For as these two vices do allure men to commit them by coveting of vain delectation that is in them, even so Babylon has enticed all men like another circe,[59] to drink of the cup of her delectable errors and to commit most filthy fornication with her idolatrous religion. For of all other religions, to the carnal man none is so pleasant as popery is, in which be so many kinds of satisfaction to be obtained, both in this life and after men be dead, that there is no greater security for a hypocrite to sleep in than in the fair promises of popery. And that causes so many willingly to embrace it and so loath to depart from it because they would still continue without check of true doctrine, which calls men to repentance and amendment of life or else threatens eternal damnation. For howsoever it pleases them to charge the doctrine of the gospel with cause of security,[60] it may easily be seen by comparison of it with the doctrine of popery, whether [it] is cause of security: that which teaches no satisfaction but one for them that be penitent in this life, or theirs that has so many ways to merit rewards and to satisfy for sins, not only while men live in the world but also for them that are already gone out of it. And there is no wine so sweet to the taste of a carnal man as that which makes him drunk with opinion of his own righteousness, as it is the nature of strong wine to make very cowards think themselves to be valiant champions. And such is the cup of popish doctrine, containing merits and satisfactions.

Again, when we consider that antichrist should make men drunk with his erroneous doctrine, we marvel less how men could be so blinded and infatuated that they could not see and perceive such gross errors and manifest untruths as are in popery. For as they that are overcome with the strength of wine have lost the right use both of their wit and of their senses, even so they that are drunk with the heretical doctrine of papistry do grope in the clear light of the sun and see not their own deformity, though all the world beside cries out of them. In like manner, they that be overcome with the dishonest love of harlots, they have their reason so imprisoned in corrupt affection and foolish fantasy that they are at liberty neither to see their own folly nor to admit any wise and godly counsel. So it fares with those that the babylonical circe, the Church of Rome, has allured by her enchantments to commit spiritual fornication with her. They cannot abide to hear the voice of them that call them out of that damnable estate, so highly they please themselves in their own misery, as if they were in

---

58. Rev. 18:3.
59. *Circe*: an enchantress.
60. That is, presumption of salvation, as opposed to a Spirit-wrought assurance.

case of perfect felicity. This is the effect of their drunkenness, this is the effect of their fornication, and this is the just judgment of God, that they which have shut up their ears from hearing the truth should be deceived with strong delusions that they might believe lies.

Furthermore, by the names of these vices, the angel comprehends all other vices that follow drunkenness and incontinency. For these crimes go not unaccompanied, for where either of them is, commonly both will be, and they have either of them and both together, their train to wait upon them. And all these we see to have overflowed in Rome the western Babylon, as she herself, though she has a brazen forehead and be past all shame, cannot deny altogether. And because of these so great and heinous enormities, the just sentence of God pronounced here by the angel is come upon her, that she is now in her fall and decay as she was once in her ruffe and glory. But this especially is to be noted: that the angel here says that she should deceive all nations with the fury of her fornication. For this is the great universality that they make so great brags of and would have it to be a certain note and mark of the Catholic Church to be universal. Behold, the angel says here in plain words that all nations should drink of the wine of the fury of her fornication. Where is then the universal consent and unity of all nations in religion that makes a true religion? And yet universality and unity be two great pillars of the Church of Rome. And for my part, I do not envy her those marks which she challenges of universality and unity (although we might stand in law with her for them), but let her peaceably enjoy them, for they may help to prove her to be the false church of antichrist, but they cannot make her to be the true church of Christ. We see plainly that Babylon has here universality and unity, for she makes all nations to drink of the furious wine of her fornication, but the church of Christ (as He Himself says) is a small flock, and Himself by Simeon is said to be a sign of contradiction, a mark that is gainsaid of most men.

And here also is answered one great mighty objection wherewith they think to choke us: that seeing the church of Christ is the spouse of Christ, how could it be that Christ should forsake His spouse and suffer her to continue in damnable errors so many hundred years? Why, Christ Himself declares that the deceits and errors of false prophets should be so great that if it were possible the very elect should be deceived;[61] yea, there should be such a miserable dispersion that scarce two true professors of His name should remain together in one place,[62] and yet the holy band of unity should be in the head, which is our Savior Christ, for wheresoever the carcass is, thither the eagles would be

---

61. Matt. 24:24.
62. Matt. 24:40.

gathered.[63] And Saint Paul in manifest words declares that the second coming of Christ should not be before there were a general apostasy (that is, a departure from the true faith and religion of Christ) and that the son of perdition, antichrist, were openly showed.[64] And in this Revelation how often is it said that antichrist should deceive all the world, all nations, people and tongues, and that the church of Christ should be driven into the wilderness, out of the sight of the world, and there remain a space, until she should be brought again to light and open knowledge of all men?[65] As it is come to pass this day, God's name be therefore everlastingly praised.

Conclusion

But because I have occupied long time, I will draw to an end. For by that I have said, I trust it does sufficiently appear that God, according to His righteous judgment, has determined utterly to overthrow Babylon because she has deceived all nations with the wine of the fury of her fornication. And now it rests only that I speak a word or two of the voice of the third angel, which is a consequent of this my text and serves very aptly for the conclusion of my sermon.

The third angel followed, crying with a loud voice, saying, "If any man shall worship the beast, or his image, or receive his mark on his forehead or in his hand; or shall acknowledge any obedience or reference to him as willing to drink of the cup of Babylon's fornication, the same shall drink of the wine of the fury of God's wrath which is poured forth unmingled into the great cup of God's anger, and they shall be tormented with fire and brimstone before the Lamb and his holy angels, and the smoke of their torments shall ascend for evermore, and they shall have no rest day nor night from extreme torments that worship the beast or shew any reverence unto Antichrist."[66] The effect is in few words: that horrible, intolerable, and eternal torments remain for all them that now (especially when Babylon is now discovered) will have anything to do with her damnable errors and pernicious doctrine. For howsoever ignorance before her fall though it were inexcusable yet seemed to diminish the greatness of the crime, now that her wickedness is openly displayed, no pretense can save men from the extremity of God's wrath if they will still obstinately continue in her heresies.

Let us therefore pray unto Almighty God instantly that all men in their vocation may seek the utter overthrow and destruction of Babylon, that princes

---

63. Luke 17:37.
64. 2 Thess. 2:3.
65. Rev. 12:6.
66. Rev. 14:9–11.

and magistrates may according to the prophecies of them hate her with a perfect hatred and utterly abolish whatsoever belongs to her, that they may reward her as she has rewarded us and give her double punishment according to her works, and in the cup of affliction that she has poured forth for us they may pour forth double as much to her. And look how much she has glorified herself and lived in wantonness (which was without measure) so much [that] they may bestow upon her of sorrow and torments. That preachers and ministers of God's Word may plainly and without dissimulation or halting discover her wickedness and earnestly to urge whatsoever has yet need of perfect reformation. That all subjects may continue in holy obedience, first to God and then to their prince, to the advancing of the honor and glory of God, through Jesus Christ: to whom with the Holy Spirit be all honor, glory, power, and dominion, both now and ever. Amen.

Chapter 3

Senate House Commonplace Book

Perkins's two sermons on John 3:16 were recorded in a small commonplace book along with another eight sermons, all of which were delivered between 1588 and 1589.[1] The book is catalogued in relation to its political significance since it contains instructions given by Robert Devereux, Second Earl of Essex, to three English intelligence agents working in Europe.[2] The material in the book was produced by several hands; however, all ten sermons are in the same hand, though not the various marginal notes scattered throughout.[3] Many of the sermons appear to have been copied secondhand, and we cannot assume that this transcription of Perkins's sermons was taken down firsthand. The sermons contain two sections of Latin. The first is a brief reflection attributed to Laurence Chaderton. The second contains three apparently unrelated notes taken from material delivered by Perkins—the first on speech, the second a brief commentary on Genesis 1:3, and the last a theological reflection on providence from John 19:19–20. The transcriber thus appears to have filled a randomly selected page in his manuscript book with Latin material taken from Perkins that he deemed useful.

---

1. University of London, Senate House Library, MS187, "Commonplace book including notes on espionage." The ten sermons fill pp. 1–149. Perkins's two sermons transcribed here are from pp. 104–34, including an unnumbered page of Latin text between pages 130 and 131. The sermon immediately preceding Perkins's is dated 1588/1589, and the one following 1589. A commonplace book was a kind of scrapbook in which students would keep quotes, letters, poems, sermons, and so on. Perkins himself gave brief instruction on the right use of commonplace books in *The Art of Prophesying* (RHB 10:302). On commonplace books in Perkins's circle, see Kenneth Parker and Eric J. Carlson, *"Practical Divinity": The Works and Life of Revd Richard Greenham* (Aldershot: Ashgate, 1998), 37–57.

2. See discussion in Paul E. J. Hammer, "Essex and Europe: Evidence from Confidential Instructions by the Earl of Essex, 1595–1596," *English Historical Review* 111, no. 441 (1996): 357–81.

3. Gateway to Early Modern Manuscripts, GEMMS-MANUSCRIPT-000741, "Commonplace Book including Notes on Espionage," accessed March 29, 2021, https://gemms.itercommunity.org /view_record.php?table=manuscript&id=741.

The transcriptions are occasionally messy and unpolished. No attempt has been made to correct everything in our transcription of the text. Some sentences contain errors, and occasionally the reader will need to work out for themselves what Perkins intended.[4] However, his overall communicative intent remains reasonably straightforward throughout.

The two sermons on John 3:16, along with that on Revelation 14:8, are the earliest extant examples of Perkins's preaching and the only examples of his preaching prior to the 1590s.[5] This dearth of extant early homiletical material is most likely due to two factors. First, Perkins had not yet risen to the prominence he enjoyed after the publication of *A Golden Chain* (Latin, 1590; English, 1591), so his earlier work was less likely to be of interest to notetaking students before that time. Furthermore, editors of Perkins's posthumously published works were mostly young men who had entered Cambridge at around the same time that these sermons were delivered. When they came to publish Perkins's works, they prioritized publishing based on notes taken down firsthand by themselves and trusted friends, which severely limited their access to homiletical material delivered by Perkins prior to this time.[6]

These sermons are also virtually unique among Perkins's extant sermons in that they were evidently delivered to a learned, clerical audience.[7] Nowhere else among Perkins's sermons do we find such frequent use of Latin phrases and scholastic terminology. Indeed, Perkins's seminal work on preaching, *The Art of Prophesying* (1592), championed a plain style of preaching, arguing that preachers must not make displays of learning from the pulpit. The preacher must instead set forth the truths of Scripture as plainly and accessibly as possible, to the benefit of learned and unlearned hearers alike.[8] It is striking, therefore, that Perkins's two sermons on John 3:16 make unencumbered use of "Greek and Latin phrases and quirks," which would be a blatant contradiction of his own advice if they were not given to an audience who could edifyingly engage with such material. In contrast, the bulk of Perkins's extant sermons were delivered at the parish church of St. Andrews the Great before mixed audiences. All these sermons bear the characteristics of the method Perkins set

---

4. Perkins's seventeenth-century editors likewise describe wrestling with this problem. See the introduction of this book.

5. Several of Perkins's published tracts had their beginnings in early sermons, though many dates remain unknown, and the material was often substantially reworked. See, for example, the material discussed in the Hutton MS below.

6. See the introduction of this book.

7. Perkins's sermon on 1 Corinthians 11:28 (Hutton MS, below) also has something of this character, though in a less thoroughgoing manner.

8. Perkins, *Art of Prophesying*, RHB 10:349–50.

forth and are highly accessible.[9] As Thomas Fuller stated, "His sermons were not so plain but that the piously learned did admire them, nor so learned but that the plain did understand them."[10] Perkins's sermons on John 3:16, therefore, offer unique insight into his use of a decidedly academic mode of address that can be taken as representative of a significant amount of material which he would have delivered to the residents of Cambridge colleges (especially during his fellowship, 1584–1594) but has not survived. It is noteworthy that these two sermons retain Perkins's characteristic clarity of presentation, affective tone, and practical concern for the edification of his listeners. This is recognizably Perkins's voice speaking.

The implied audience of the sermon suggests that Perkins originally delivered these sermons at a "prophesying" meeting. Such gatherings typically involved a gathering of clergy, possibly with some lay listeners in attendance, who would listen to sermons by exemplary preachers among them. Prophesying meetings might be moderated by more senior clergy, and reflections and discussions of the sermons would follow. The goal was the mutual edification of ministers and providing examples for the development of younger aspiring preachers.

This practice would prove controversial to Queen Elizabeth, who suspected subversive motives behind such practices. Indeed, her opposition to the "prophesyings" ultimately led to the suspension from office of the archbishop of Canterbury, Edmund Grindal, from 1577 until his death in 1583.[11] For reform-minded clergy, including Grindal and Perkins's circle of Cambridge Puritans, the promotion of preaching belonged to the nonnegotiable essence of what it meant for England to be a Reformed nation. How could one hope for the genuine conversion of the English people unless competent preachers were raised up to fill English pulpits?

Perkins's engagement with Laurence Chaderton's "question" in his first sermon suggests that Chaderton, as a senior member of the Cambridge Puritan circle, moderated the meeting at which Perkins preached. Chaderton lived a long and influential life (1536–1640) and has fittingly been described as "the

---

9. For a discussion of Perkins's interpretive method in his published sermons, see Andrew Ballitch, *The Gloss and the Text: William Perkins on Interpreting Scripture with Scripture*, Studies in Historical and Systematic Theology (Bellingham: Lexham Press, 2020), 74–126.

10. Thomas Fuller, *The Holy State* (Cambridge: Printed by Roger Daniel for John Williams, 1642), 89–90.

11. On the prophesying meetings, see Patrick Collinson, *The Elizabethan Puritan Movement* (London: Methuen, 1967), 168–90. On the Grindal affair, see Patrick Collinson, *Archbishop Grindal: 1519–1583. The Struggle for a Reformed Church* (London: Jonathan Cape, 1979), 233–52. For an excellent introduction to the latter, see Lee Gatiss, *Edmund Grindal: The Preacher's Archbishop* (London: Latimer Trust, 2013).

pope of Cambridge puritanism."[12] He was personally influential in Perkins's early development while at Christ's College and served as the founding master at Emmanuel College (1584–1622). The two men shared deep affinities of theological conviction and pastoral priority.

Perkins's apparent involvement in a prophesying meeting is unsurprising, though these sermons are the only direct evidence of it. The very title of his book, *The Art of Prophesying*, is more than suggestive. Furthermore, Chaderton and Perkins were both also present at a "classis meeting" concerning the Presbyterian book of discipline in 1589. While the two practices were not identical, the lines between them were blurry. The participants in prophesyings and the more developed Presbyterian classis meetings naturally overlapped given their common interest in further reform and revitalization of biblical Christianity in England. Indeed, Collinson argues that "the prophesying was the *classis* in embryo."[13] Perkins was no Presbyterian; however, his circle of reform-minded clergymen naturally included a range of Puritan concerns.[14] An emphasis on the importance of preaching was one of the main things that united Puritans of every kind.

The sermons themselves yield some insight into the context in which they were delivered. They were really two parts of one long sermon, with each part handling two of its four overall points. The first was given in the morning immediately prior to the Lord's Supper and directed its hearers regarding the right reception of the sacrament. The second sermon was given in the afternoon of the same day.[15] The first sermon also explicitly answers a question posed by Laurence Chaderton, apparently earlier in the same meeting. It is possible that Chaderton (and perhaps other gathered clergy) had reflected on John 3:16 prior to Perkins's own sermon, as was common in such meetings.

The sermon expounds God's saving love in Christ in four points, framed according to language derived from Ephesians 3:18. Perkins sets out to impress on his hearers the sheer breathtaking magnitude of God's love: its height, depth, breadth, and length. The sermons also appeal to the theology of the early church fathers, particularly Augustine of Hippo (354–430). However, they most notably bear marks of the influence of Bernard of Clairvaux (1090–1153),

---

12. Collinson, *Elizabethan Puritan Movement*, 125.

13. Collinson, *Elizabethan Puritan Movement*, 179.

14. Lake describes the position and party to which Perkins belonged as "moderate Puritanism" and profiles several of its key representatives in Perkins's circle. Lake, *Moderate Puritans*, 10.

15. The first sermon begins with reference to the Lord's Supper. The second is introduced as being on "the same day afterward" and refers back to what Perkins had discussed "in the morning."

both in their explicit appeal to his description of God's love and in their use of spousal imagery and their overall affective character.[16]

Perkins's first sermon begins by describing the nature of God's love itself. This love is entirely unmotivated by anything outside God's own being, and it flows toward the most undeserving and wicked recipients. God loves His world as His creation, yet sin has so corrupted God's creation as to render it the most unworthy and unlikely object of His love. Yet He extends His love to us, our sin and corruption notwithstanding. Perkins discusses several potential motivating factors for God's love, demolishing them one by one by appeal to Scripture. In sum, the Bible reveals a God possessed of a pure love, entirely undiluted by factors outside itself, and rightly regarded as the exclusive cause of our salvation.

Second, Perkins examines the depth of God's love, which is no mere affection or ineffective well-wishing but rather a love that brings healing and restoration with it by means of Jesus Christ. Mankind enjoys expressions of God's love in His many good gifts of creation, yet the sheer depth of His love is only fully expressed in sending His Son for our salvation. Perkins reflects on the fact that for human parents to lose a son is an unspeakable loss. The fact that God Himself would willingly lose His only son for us demonstrates a depth of love beyond which our tongues can possibly express. There simply can be no deeper love than that which God extends to us in Christ.

The afternoon sermon takes up the breadth and extent of God, turning the focus from God Himself to the notion that God's love lays claim on all people and the eternal implications of that love. The "breadth" of God's love describes the universal scope of the offer of the gospel: God's promises are to "whosoever believes." Aspects of Perkins's discussion here might seem counterintuitive given the Reformed tradition's common emphasis on "particular" or "limited atonement"—that is, that the extent of Christ's saving work is delimited to God's chosen elect people. Perkins famously set out a double-predestinarian soteriological scheme in his *A Golden Chain* (1590), which entailed that Christ's atoning work would effect salvation only for those whom God sovereignly elected. Nevertheless, Perkins also affirmed that Christ's saving work

---

16. David Barbee profiles Perkins's citations of extrabiblical sources, demonstrating that Augustine is by far the most cited theologian in Perkins's writings. Bernard of Clairvaux is the most cited nonpatristic source and is a significant influence on his thought. See David M. Barbee, "A Reformed Catholike: William Perkins's Use of the Church Fathers" (unpublished PhD diss., University of Pennsylvania, 2013), 162–64. Perkins was particularly familiar with Bernard's sermons on Song of Songs (or Canticles). For a preliminary consideration of the influence of mysticism on Perkins's theology, see Randall J. Pederson, "Richard Greenham and William Perkins," in *Protestants and Mysticism in Reformation Europe*, St. Andrews Studies in Reformation History, ed. Ronald K. Rittgers and Vincent Evener (Leiden: Brill, 2019), 258–63.

was "sufficient to have redeemed a thousand thousand worlds of sinners," though it would only be savingly applied to the elect.[17] For Perkins, these underlying theological principles came to expression in the universal call of God's promises in the gospel. As Perkins stated in *A Golden Chain*, "The evangelical promises are indefinite and do exclude no man, unless peradventure any man do exclude himself."[18] Here Perkins expands on this point, emphasizing the gospel's demand that all people believe that Christ came to save them particularly and that all would be saved if only they believed. Contrary to many Reformed accounts of the doctrines of grace, Perkins's predestinarian scheme incorporated both a genuinely universal gospel invitation to all sinners and something close to what has been described as "hypothetical universalism," wherein Christ's atoning work is sufficient for all but effective only for the elect.[19] Perkins concludes this point by delimiting the effective scope of Christ's saving work to all who are truly "in Him."

---

17. Perkins, *Manner and Order of Predestination*, RHB 6:288; cf. Perkins, *Golden Chain*, RHB 6:48, 250–51.

18. Perkins, *Golden Chain*, RHB 6:197.

19. See further discussion on the extent of the atonement in the introduction to the Tomlin MS (below). Whereas older scholarship tended to erroneously label all forms of hypothetical universalism as "Amyraldian," more recent scholarship recognizes that there were a variety of hypothetical universalist understandings of the atonement within the Reformed tradition that predate Moïse Amyraut (1596–1664). See especially Richard A. Muller, "Diversity in the Reformed Tradition: A Historiographical Introduction," in *Drawn into Controversie: Reformed Theological Diversity and Debates within Seventeenth-Century British Puritanism*, Reformed Historical Theology 17, ed. Herman J. Selderhuis (Göttengen: Vandenhoeck & Ruprecht, 2011), 1–30; Richard A. Muller, *Calvin and the Reformed Tradition: On the Work of Christ and the Order of Salvation* (Grand Rapids: Baker, 2012), 70–106; David L. Allen, *The Extent of the Atonement: A Historical and Critical Review* (Nashville: B&H Academic, 2016), 35–253. Hypothetical universalism was common among Perkins's English contemporaries and near contemporaries. See especially Michael J. Lynch, *John Davenant's Hypothetical Universalism: A Defense of Catholic and Reformed Orthodoxy*, Oxford Studies in Historical Theology (Oxford: Oxford University Press, 2021); Michael J. Lynch, "Richard Hooker and the Development of English Hypothetical Universalism," in *Richard Hooker and Reformed Orthodoxy*, ed. W. Bradford Littlejohn and Scott N. Kindred-Barnes, Reformed Historical Theology 40 (Göttingen: Vandenhoeck & Ruprecht, 2017), 273–93; Jonathan D. Moore, *English Hypothetical Universalism: John Preston and the Softening of Reformed Orthodoxy* (Grand Rapids: Eerdmans, 2007); Jonathan D. Moore, "The Extent of the Atonement: English Hypothetical Universalism versus Particular Redemption," in Selderhuis, *Drawn into Controversie*, 124–61; Richard Snoddy, *The Soteriology of James Ussher: The Act and Object of Saving Faith*, Oxford Studies in Historical Theology (Oxford: Oxford University Press, 2014). This theme has also been explored in relation to key early modern Reformed creedal statements. See Lee Gatiss, "Shades of Opinion within a Generic Calvinism: The Particular Redemption Debate at the Westminster Assembly," *Reformed Theological Review* 69, no. 2 (2010): 101–18; Lee Gatiss, "A Deceptive Clarity? Particular Redemption in the Westminster Standards," *Reformed Theological Review* 69, no. 3 (2010): 180–96; Lee Gatiss, "The Synod of Dort and Definite Atonement," in *From Heaven He Came and Sought Her: Definite Atonement in Historical, Biblical, Theological,*

Finally, the extent of God's love refers to its eternal duration, a love ever new and unending. While death is a confronting prospect and might even occur for the sake of witness to Christ who has conquered it, in Him it has been transformed from perishing to a transition into a better state. When the nature of this eternal life is rightly perceived, one cannot help but seek it.

---

and Pastoral Perspective, ed. David Gibson and Jonathan Gibson (Wheaton, Ill.: Crossway, 2013), 143–63; Anthony Milton, *The British Delegation and the Synod of Dort (1618–1619)*, Church of England Record Society 13 (Suffolk: Boydell Press, 2005). On the historical pedigree of the TULIP acronym (popularly and erroneously understood as defining the boundaries of Calvinistic orthodoxy), see Kenneth Stewart, *Ten Myths about Calvinism: Recovering the Breadth of the Reformed Tradition* (Downers Grove, Ill.: InterVarsity, 2011); and Muller, *Calvin and the Reformed Tradition*, 51–69. On Perkins's views on the extent of the atonement, see his first sermon on Romans 4:25 (below) and the introductory discussion.

John 3:16 (Morning)

"So God loved the world that he gave his only begotten Son." (John 3:16)

Eusebius notes that the servants of God in the primitive church usually made a distinction in the reading of the gospel, for some part of it they called *euangelium magnum*, the great gospel, and some part they named *euangelium parum*, the little gospel. The great gospel they accounted the former evangelists because the history of Christ, His miracles, and the other actions of wonder were in them described, which in the strict use of the word can hardly be allowed the name of the gospel. The other, the little gospel, [is] the short or summary description of those things that comprehend our salvation. All [of] which diversely declared are (as it were) compounded [and] shut up in this verse, and whatsoever can be uttered concerning them may hither be referred.

This may very well serve to stir up our attention and diligent regard to that which shall be spoken when we know the whole mystery of our salvation is in this verse contained. When in the fourth verse of this chapter, Nicodemus, considering the high nature of God and looking on the low and base condition of the state of man, asks of Christ a question, How it is possible for man to enter into the kingdom of heaven, Christ teaches him how it is possible many ways, but for all gives this as the great and main resolution: "So God loved the world that he gave his only begotten Son," to this end, "that whosoever believeth in him should not perish but have life everlasting." So that by this love, notwithstanding the inequality between God and mankind, it is possible.

Therefore, in regard of this action, we come now to celebrate the communion of the body of Christ. Considering the great penalty which is due to the unworthy receiver,[1] it may cause the weak hands of the sinner to hang down and the weak knees to halt (Heb. 12:12), [to] turn aside from receiving, because he cannot conceive how it is possible that he should be a worthy receiver and so enter into heaven. Let him look on the banner which the church hangs forth,

---

1. Perkins draws the language of "worthy reception" from the English confession of faith, the Thirty-Nine Articles of Religion (1563, 1571), which states regarding the sacraments, "in such only as worthily receive the same have they a wholesome effect or operation: but they that receive them unworthily purchase to themselves damnation, as Saint Paul saith" (article 25; cf. 1 Cor. 11:29).

which is the love of God the Father and Christ His Son (Song 2:4), that as soon as he hears that the banner of love is displayed, his heart may be comforted, his hands and feet strengthened, to appear unto so great a benefit. Because as it is, seeing God so loved the world "that he spared not his only begotten Son but gave him for us, how shall he not with him give us all things" (Rom. 8:32), so also, He who has performed this love will also bestow on us His grace, that our receiving shall be to life everlasting.

Structure

And in these respects, I made choice of this Scripture for this present [occasion]. In the handling thereof, according to the observation of the fathers of the primitive church, so will we, following their steps, observe four points. First, the love of God which is the fountain of living water (Gen. 2:13). The second, His liberality, the humanity of Christ, that He gave His only begotten Son, the difference whereinto this fountain of living water flows. The third, the conduit pipe which conveys the water out of the cistern in those words, "that whosoever believeth on him," faith having to his[2] ears the audible word and to his eyes the visible word, the sacrament, which faith the fathers call *conductus gratiae*, the conduit of the living water. The fourth, the rivers of water that flow from this fountain (John 7:38), the one, that he shall not perish, the other, that he shall have life everlasting.

Or, if he like better to follow some other division, let him take this: the first, the love of God; the second, His liberality in offering His Son; the third, out of Hosea 2:19, the spousal[3] of Christ; the fourth, the church's jointure,[4] the avoiding of hell, the enjoyment of heaven. These favors are the complete and full vow of that which God in His love promises, Christ in His obedience effects, faith believes, [and] hope hopes for. Therefore, that counsel which Saint Paul gives, that he would [that] we should search out the height, depth, breadth, and length of the love of God (Eph. 3:18), is here offered. For the height upward is the love or good pleasure of God. The depth downward [is] the humanity or incarnation of Christ. He gave Him[self] for us, whereby He descended to the earth, nay, even "to the lowest parts of the earth" (Eph. 4:9). The breadth [is] all who believe. And the length [is] life everlasting, eternity, eternal life by faith obtained, by the love of God, loving us before all beginning to the adopted in Christ Jesus (Eph. 1:5); [it] is the height, depth, length, and breadth of God's love. A bar to all curious questions that may be moved in predestination. Therefore, whatsoever we receive, Christ merits and the love of God occasioned.

---

2. Perkins often uses the third-person singular *his* instead of the third-person neuter *its*.

3. That is, the betrothal of Christ to the church.

4. *Jointure*: the material provision made for a wife after the death of her husband.

The Height of God's Love: The Good Pleasure of God

The first motion [is] the love of God, and Christ the end of this love, so that if our mind fancy any grace from Christ, it must ascend to the fountain: the love of God. Now, if anything moved from ourselves to draw this love from God, then it could rather be called *redamant*, God loved us again, than *amavit*, [God] loved us first. And if there were any desert on our part, then the giving of His Son should not be *dedit*, a gift, but *redidit*, a recompense or reward. But God loved us without any cause proceeding from us and gave us His Son without any desert of ours, so that all the glory might be ascribed unto His name. This Saint Bernard does most excellently express in the words *tantus*, *tantillos*, *tales*, *tantum prior gratis*, that is, so great a God to love so base persons, nay, *tales*, so wicked persons, and *tantum*, with such a measure of love, and *prior*, first before we loved Him, and even *gratis*, without any desert of ours, is a love unspeakable.

This *prior*, that He loved us first, is expressed in 1 John 4:10, "In this is love, not that we loved him, but that he loved us and sent his Son." And the other, *gratis*, [in] Romans 3:24, "Being justified freely without any desert of ours." So that salvation is neither *reditio*, a restoring or requital of our deserts, nor *venditio*, a porte-sale.[5] Neither is the cause of our salvation *redamatio*, a reloving or recompense for love, but it is a loving first and a gift without cause proceeding from us (1 John 4:10). All [of] which must be referred to this love, according as the fathers read *ante lucifer genui tu*; that is, My love adopted you in Christ to be given for you before the morning star, nay, when there was yet no morning star.

Now, seeing love is called a chain, we are to consider the parts that be coupled together by this chain, and they be two: the first, God, [and] the other, the world. God drawn out of heaven to the world, humbled (Phil. 2:8), and the world carried into heaven, according to Christ, seeing *cum exaltatus fuero*, "When I shall be exalted I will draw all men unto me" [John 12:32]. As Saint Bernard says, this love called God out of heaven and called man into heaven, made God propitious unto man and reconciled man to God.

Concerning God, it is certain no error can grow but we may easily be deceived in the term "world," and therefore we must see what is meant thereby. For if God loved the world, why may not we love the world too? And if God loves the world, why do we find fault with worldly men for embracing this present world? Therefore, lest we be deceived by this error, we are to know how the Scripture understands this word "world," and that is [in] two manner of ways. The one, as it is in Genesis 1:31, "God saw all that he had made, and

---

5. *Porte-sale*: "An open sale of wares." James Orchard Halliwell, *A Dictionary of Archaic and Provincial Words: Obsolete Phrases, Proverbs, and Ancient Customs, from the Fourteenth Century* (London: John Russell Smith, 1847), 2:638.

it was good," that is, this world comprehends the whole frame and compass of those creatures. The other, [as in] Galatians 4:1, where Saint Paul calls it an "evil world," expounding Genesis 6, that God repented Him of His works. Because, as Saint Peter speaks, there is in it corruption through lust (1 Peter 4:2), so that this corruption through lust is also called the "world."

Now, God loves the creature because it is His workmanship. And man [loves] the vanity of the creature, nor a man because he is a man, but because he is rich or honorable or possessed with some kind of vanity. But the love of God is far otherwise, who loves the creature because it is His creature and therefore seeks the delivery thereof. When we, therefore, say that God so loved the world, it is true of the whole creation. But, seeing this benefit, mentioned in the last verse, is straitened to mankind, we have no warrant to speak of the whole, nay, neither of man as he is *compendium mundi*, a summary or short verse of the creation, in his soul of the creation, in his soul of the celestial essence in his body of his earthly and temporary constitution. Now, as he is, as the heathen man said, *Hōson temporis et eternitatis*, the *hoson*[6] of time and eternity, of the eternity in the mortality of his soul, of time in the mortality of his body. Now, as he is the master, or county Palatine of the earth,[7] which being destroyed the rest are scattered accordingly. For his sake the waters destroyed (Gen. 6:7), even as his restoring shall be the restoring of the whole earth (Rom. 5:21). We say, therefore, that His love extends to all as it is [in] Psalm 36:6, but so that, "Oh thou preserver of men" (Job 7:20), of whom it is said, God is said to be *philanthropos*, "a lover of men" (Titus 3:4), so that He loves the world, mankind [being] His creature.

Now, seeing the word "world" is explained, so that no error can grow, that may let us to come to the verse and consider of the love itself. David says, "Oh Lord, what is man?" [Ps. 8:4]. And Job [asks], "What is man, that thou magnifieth him, and set thy heart upon him?" (Job 7:17). And we shall see that this is a part of the angel's song, "Good will to men" [Luke 2:14]. In this love appeared that God sent His only begotten Son (1 John 4:9). All which doubt will be acquitted if we consider the indignity of man upon whom so great love is bestowed.

There are diverse judgments of love proceeding from the party beloved. Therefore, when the thistle of Lebanon sent to the cedar in Lebanon, to give him his daughter in marriage, it was such an indignity [that] the wild beasts in the forest came and trod down this thistle (2 Kings 14:9). That is, in all love there must be an equality between the parties beloved. Now, seeing there is

---

6. *Hoson* (Greek: ὅσον): so long, signifying duration.
7. *County Palatine*: an area ruled by a nobleman.

greater difference between God and us than is between a thistle and a cedar, judge you what cause of love there can be from us, why God should set His heart on us. Now, this is not perceived nor seen because, though aspiring is noted in every one, yet humiliation or abasing is not regarded. Yet, seeing God is said to humble Himself and to become man, this is one degree of *sic dilexit*, He so loved us; that is, He loved us indeed a strange and unusual love.

A second cause of love is beauty of itself of sufficient commendation and judgment to love. It is said of God that His eyes are pure eyes, and so pure that [they] can behold no wickedness (Hab. 1:13). Why then, if God's eyes be so pure, and the world so wicked, there is little likelihood of love. And, therefore, the church, before she be washed and purified, is said to be full of wrinkles and spots (Eph. 5:26). Why then, surely there is little beauty to procure love, but a great deal of deformity to effect hatred, little sin as spots and great sin as wrinkles, to discover deformity. So that, having neither beauty nor favor, no marvel if there be no love. And yet, then to love is another degree of *sic dilexit*, so He loved so strongly and so wonderfully.

Now, there be no outward beauty, yet perhaps there are some inward virtues to set love on fire, as charity, modesty, etc. No, surely not so much neither, for in Numbers 15:39 God says they go a whoring [after] their own heart and after their own eyes. And, beloved, this is the continual cry of all the prophets, as appears [in] Isaiah 50:1, and therefore there are continual bills of discontent. Why then, if there be neither equality nor beauty nor charity, but that she is base deformed and also a strumpet. For God to love such a people is another degree of "God so loved" the world.

Well yet it may be that God reaps some profit or gain by loving the world. [But] if we look, we shall see that the church has that given her and pity that she is wretched, miserable, poor, blind, and naked (Rev. 3:17). Hither from such a one there is no reason to hope for gain or profit.

All these, being great degrees of love, yet I think the last is the greatest of all. For though none of these motives of love before rehearsed be in the church, yet we see divers times that sinners love sinners (Matt. 5:46). And that consideration to them is *magnes amores*, "the loadstone of love."

Or, it may be the world loved God, and so God loved the world again, and then that way there may be some provocation. But we shall find *cum nondum nati essent*, "before they were born," God loved <...>, that then there could be nothing from those beloved to cause love (Rom. 9:11). This affection of God toward man is very evident, for being created and having transgressed, and for his transgression ready to be cast out of paradise, God does not pronounce the curse before He has published the promise (Gen. 3:19). And then, in [Genesis] six, [He] repented Him because of the wickedness of man, that He had created him. Yet, in [Genesis] nine He gives him the rainbow in the heavens as the seal of His love and favor.

The world, nevertheless, makes small account of His love and is content with Esau to sell it for a mess of pottage (Heb. 12:16), for any trifle. And, whereas in reason a man should have sought, first God is willing to seek man to offer him His love. Which, being offered, there is no reason it should be refused, and yet it is despised (Luke 7:30). The consideration of this is the stopping of the mouth of the world because "I will call her beloved which was not beloved" (Rom. 9:25). Though that fall out to be true, which Saint Paul says, he proved true in his own experience, "The more I love you, the less I am beloved of you" (2 Cor. 12:15).

There was then nothing in us that we might be loved, and we were not worthy to be beloved, serving the lusts of the world (Titus 3:3). Yet, this notwithstanding, we see God stands (as it were) in a pitiful case. "How shall I give thee up, Ephraim? How shall I deliver thee, Israel?" (Hos. 11:8). That is, "I am pressed by your wickedness to do that which of all others I am most unwilling to do, for indeed my nature is not to destroy but to love." And, therefore, God says, "My heart is turned and My repenting are rolled together; that is, in regards of My love toward you, I am content to cloud and wrap up all My repenting to punish you, and to unfold My love unto you." This then shall be for the first, which is the height of the love of God. For God loved us with a pure love, a love not mixed with any outward provocation from us because it might be *pura dilectio*, "a sincere love," so that no praise might return to mankind, but all glory be ascribed to the love of God.

The Depth of God's Love: The Incarnation of Christ

The second which He gave, and that is the depth of God's love, which may be called *crestotes*,[8] a bounteous love, rather than a bare love, because it is barren but brings forth *in eum* with it. And this kind of love the world likes well of us: "Isaac loved Esau because he saw venison was in his mouth" (Gen. 25:28). And so, the Jews say to Christ, *Amat gentem nostram*, "he loves our nation," *et edificat nobis synagogam*, "and has built us a synagogue" [Luke 7:5]. There is a real love nary the love which the world performs, [which] is that which Saint James so much complains of: "You warm themselves, and fill your bellies, but in the meantime, you give nothing" (James 2:16). And this Saint John calls *amor lingue*,[9] holy water of the tongue (2 John 3:18).

---

8. Greek: χρηστότης. Cf. Rom. 2:4; 3:12; 11:22.

9. *Amor lingue*: love of language.

This is far from God, whose love is not as the Levite, who came by [and] looked on him and went his way (Luke 10:32), but it is a Samaritan's love which appears in verse 34, which bound up his wounds and poured in oil and wine. For if it were nothing else but a washing (which it was not), it might be called a compassion but no love. But this love of God brings somewhat[10] with it, it is a dative,[11] even as God says, "I will set thee as a seal upon my hand, and as a signet upon my arm" (Song 8:6). That is, He will not only bear an affection from the heart, but His arm shall concur to the manifesting of this love. It shall be outward and visible as well as inward and in the heart; that is, there shall be of God's love an epiphany or appearance.

Now, as there is no epiphany of our faith, so there is no epiphany of our love. If you ask concerning the gifts of God, they are unspeakable, yet for some taste of them. God made His covenant with Noah to destroy the earth no more by water (Gen. 9:12). And God has set bars and doors to stay the proud waters of the sea (Job 38:10–11). These be two great gifts. The beasts seek not their prey in the day, lest they should devour us (Ps. 104:21–23). For man he has not made as fishes without a ruler, so that the lesser should be a prey to the greater. And for our enemies God has His hook in their nostrils to pull them back (Hab. 1:14–15). And against the plague devouring, therefore, and ten thousand He makes his angel to slay (Isa. 37:36). And [He] has also His sun and His rainbow for comfort and fruitful seasons. And this last we most of all long after well. In bestowing these blessings, He may be said so to love.

Yet all this is not the depth of the love of God. But in this—that He so loved that He gave His only begotten Son—is comprehended this depth of the love of God. And if the other benefit before mentioned be compared with this benefit, they are but as shadows. For indeed this is the substance. There be two respects which cause a gift to be acceptable. The one, the mind of the giver, and therefore a small gift of a friend is better than a great gift of an enemy. And Christ in the gospel affirms that the poor widow, who had but two mites, and yet offered them, put into the treasury more than all the rich men because they gave of their surplus and she of her poverty all she had [Mark 12:41–44]. So that the mind of the giver manifests the greatness of the gift.

The second respect is in the gift itself, according as Christ says, *si scires donim dei*, "If thou knewest the gift of God" (John 4:10). Indeed, we do not know this gift of God, and that is the reason we set so little by it. Which gift, howsoever we account it, in itself is so great that it is unspeakable and cannot be uttered (2 Cor. 9:15). Let us, therefore, a while consider this gift, for we shall

---

10. Perkins uses *somewhat* in an archaic sense, meaning "something."

11. The dative case (e.g., in Latin or Greek) indicates the indirect object of an action.

see whom God gives this gift. He does not only give all, but if it were possible more than all.

The old Hebrews note that Adam, when he gave names to all creatures, upon the <…> of the frame of the world, named it a named thing. But when he had a son, he named him Cain, "possession," meaning that, though before he was lord of the whole earth, yet he had no possession nor riches till he had a son. And that which he enjoyed before was but roundness[12] as he should have enjoyed around <…>.

Abraham was of this opinion. For though God said unto him, "Fear not Abraham, I am thy buckler and thy exceeding reward," alas, says Abraham, "What is all this that thou wilt give me, seeing I am childless and have no son to inherit?" (Gen. 15:2). Meaning that all this that God promised him was nothing in comparison of a son.

Jacob expressed the same assertion. For though Joseph sent to Jacob wagons to bring him down and asses laden with the best things of Egypt for a present, yet when Jacob heard and was persuaded that Joseph his son was alive, "It is enough," says he, "I will now go down and see him" (Gen. 45:28). Meaning that this was enough that Joseph did live, in estimation and regard whereof all the presents were nothing. All these show the special love of God in giving His Son, in comparison of whom all things in the world are nothing. For if God had planted that natural love in beasts, that "the lion and lioness love their whelps" (Nah. 2:12), and "the dragons draw out the breast and give suck to their young" (Lam. 4:3), it cannot be but God has reserved a great love to Himself toward His Son. And, therefore, God, who gave to us His Son, has in Him given us more than if He had given the whole world.

The text adds a further degree of love than if He had said "he whom he gave is his Son"; that is, He was not only His Son, but He was His only begotten Son. If He lost Him, He lost all. Hereupon Origen says well that "though one has many sons, yet he would be loath to lose any of them." And if he were asked the question, with which he would part, he could give no answer. And, therefore, we see, though Jacob had twelve sons, yet when news was brought him that some wild beast had devoured Joseph, it so struck him to the heart that all his sons and daughters rose up to comfort him, and he would not be comforted (Gen. 37:35). But it must needs be, for otherwise where one is but one because there be many, and when one is all and that one is lost, so then there can be no comfort.

And this consideration likewise does a greatness to the love of God. For that was the reason of David's aggrievance, seeing his neighbor had but one

______

12. Perkins appears to be using the term "roundness" in the sense of "fullness."

sheep and he took it, "He shall surely die" (2 Sam. 12:5). And the ground of Christ's amplification in the gospel, that the widow's two mites were more than all the rest of the treasures because she gave all she had (Mark 12:41–44). And so, God loved the world that He gave His Son. This is also another *sic dilexit*, so He loved.

To this so says Chrysostom, "Put what you will and it fit well"; that is, God loved us wonderfully, so unspeakably, so unthinkably, so inexpressibly. Paul expresses this love with a word of great emphasis or signification, which word is "abound" (Rom. 5:20). But this is more than abounding; that is, it is unbound love. When a thing is full, we say it is full. When [it is] more than full, we say abundant. When more than that, [we say] superabundant. Now, though sin has super-abounded, yet the love of God has more than abounded; that is, the love of God is greater than sin. So likewise, 1 Timothy 1:14, "exceeding abundant," that is, a *pleonasmus* of love, a love more than more exceeding. Which emphasis of words, though one tongue will not bear, yet the matter itself is such as will bear all the words which the heart of man can conceive and the tongue of man utter.

We see that Jacob loved Benjamin so dearly that he would not let him go down into Egypt, though it were to redeem his brother Simeon out of prison (Gen. 42:38). Well, it may be we can endure to see our son need but never able to see him bleed. And, therefore, Zipporah, when she was to see her son circumcised, though that wound was not deadly, but curable, yet what a rail she kept and repeats, "Oh bloody husband" (Ex. 4:25). But when the case is so hard that he must not only need but bleed his heart blood, that case is intolerable. [He will] never suffer him to be killed. As we see in 1 Kings 3:26, the honest harlot, when she saw that her child must be slain and divided, her bowels yearned within her, and she had rather let the other harlot have it; rather, it should live with a stepmother than be slain.

Yet so, God loved so He has given Him *thusia*,[13] an oblation or sacrifice; that is, He gave Him not only to be slain but even to be quartered and shambled out, as we see beasts in the shambles.[14] He gave Him forth to be *filius hominus*, "the Son of man," and then to be a servant, *filius perditionis*, "the Son of destruction," even to be within the curse of God for sin. Here is the depth of the love of God. He descended to the lowest part of the earth so that the depth of His love might be manifest.

If God loves the world, how comes it to pass that He can[not] keep it from perishing, except His Son die for to save it? The case stood so that He could not,

---

13. θυσία (Greek): sacrifice or offering.
14. *Shambles*: slaughterhouse.

and therefore He bought it so dear. And this observation is another increase of the love of God. For because of that sentence, "In that day thou eat of the tree, thou shalt die the death" (Gen. 2:17), the wrath of God challenged a contract with man, and so made a divorce between the love of God and mankind, so that [by] this divorce, being abridged, God could not bestow any benefit or blessing upon man. Therefore, the Son must come and fight it out before He can restore man again to the love of God, so that the mercy of God may be triumphing over justice (James 2:13). Which cannot be before justice be laid flat on the ground and killed, which cannot be before the sentence, which strengthened and aided is disannulled. And this is mercy and victory over justice, for Christ must win His church, as David did win Michal with a hundred foreskins of the Philistines (1 Sam. 18:25). And He must do as Jacob did for Rachel. He must serve for her (Gen. 29:18). So must Christ be crushed to death, so that by death overcoming death He may by His resurrection triumph over His enemies.

So, we see here by it also the love of God receives another increase so that if it comes to this narrow issue, why their God will lose the world and keep His Son or save the world and give His Son, God does rather choose to give His Son even to the death than the world shall not be redeemed. This is, therefore, an answer to Master Chaderton.[15] His question—that the love of God to man and the salvation of His church is so dear and precious in His sight that it exceeds the love He bears toward His Son, that He chooses rather to forbear to love His Son than to forbear to save His church—[is] accorded right as Christ testifies that God loved them as He loved Him (John 17:23).

This is a great comfort, for if it be thought a sign and testimony of love to give one thing for another, to require one <...> testifies a courtesy as dear as the other, and yet in this there is an equality. And if the world were equal to His Son, why then God had some reason to love the world because, though He lost His Son to redeem the world, yet His loss was recompensed. "Can a mother forget her child and not have compassion of the son of her womb?" (Isa. 49:15). That is, "My love to the church passes all parents' love, for though the mother could, yet I can never, and, therefore, My love is much greater." And this love is not only greater than the mother's, but it is greater than Himself. For if David says, truly as no doubt he did when he heard of the death of his ungracious imp: "O my son Absalom, O my son Absalom, would God I had died for thee" (2 Sam. 18:33), that is to say, "I could be content for all your ungraciousness to have redeemed your death by my life," we must need imagine that the Son of God was by infinite degree dearer to His Father when He had never in His life

---

15. In the original: "Mr. Chadermus." The reference appears to be to Laurance Chaderton, master of Emmanuel College. Latin notes attributed to him appear on p. 123 of the manuscript.

offended, and that if it had been possible God could Himself have been content to have suffered death to have saved His Son.

Therefore, we see the prophet is not content with this word, "love," prophesying of the delight of the church, but calls it "the zeal of the Lord" (Isa. 9:7).[16] And Saint Paul calls it "the great love" of God passing and exceeding all of His other loves (Eph. 2:4). So that, by this we see the height and the depth of this *sic dilexit*, "so God loved." This is then the comfort of those that be penitent, that He is a banner of love hung forth to call them to approach. And come none, that is, God is content to give His Son, the Holy Spirit willing to move the Son to give Himself. And then, the Son says, "A body haste thou required" (Ps. 40:6). *In ecce veni*, "Behold I come to do thy will, oh Lord" [Ps. 40:6–8; Heb. 10:5].

And, therefore, the repentant, if they say with Nicodemus, "how can this be?" [John 3:4], here they may see how it is possible. And as this comfort is great, that God so loved the world that He gave His only begotten Son, and in giving of Him has given us all things with Him (Rom. 8:32), so the due regard hereof must cause us to make this use of it, that it be a stirring us up, that it be [im]possible to prevent God in His love because *fervens est*, He is of ironlike constitution. If he does not love God, yet God will not love for Himself, following the counsel of Saint Augustine that, seeing we cannot love God as we ought, yet let us love Him as well as we can. Because in that love which is as much we can, there is nothing wanting. And this is the conclusion of all. And as love was the beginning of the promise, so it was the end of the commandment proceeding from a good conscience and faith unfeigned.

---

16. The MS erroneously cites Isa. 9:6.

John 3:16 (Afternoon)

the same day afterward

To the end that, "Whosoever believeth in him should not perish but have life everlasting."

Hitherto weighing the love of God to the gift that He gave, Christ Jesus the Savior of the world, that which we have heard already is cause of admiration and wonder. This that follows is matter of use and profit unto ourselves. For as the love was great, and from so great love proceeds so great a gift, so in this sentence is set down the great fruit that is enjoyed by [means of] so great a gift—that is, our Savior Christ, who is here given, is not only a precious pearl for admiration to our eyes (Matt. 13:45), though so He be, but also as He often resembles Himself. He is bread to strengthen the heart (John 6:32); that is, He appropriates unto Him[self] this prerogative: to be life unto the soul. And this is manifest in the first word, that God did not only love but so loved that He gave, and so gave to this end, that everyone who "believeth should not perish but have life everlasting."

It is said of God in this verse that He gave His Son that "whosoever believeth should not perish." It is said of Christ that He came into the world to save sinners (1 Tim. 1:15). So that, the end of the counsel of God was that none should perish, and the end of the coming of Christ was to this purpose, that sinners should be saved. So that, here is not only love, but as it is, He so loved that He gave Himself and that *propter nos*, "for us" (Eph. 5:2). Though the consideration of this be [a] matter of great comfort, that He gave Himself for us, yet that is of more consolation to the soul of every believer, "he loved me and gave himself for me" (Gal. 2:20), so that whosoever does not make this use of the love of God and of the gift, Christ Jesus, does despise and set lightly the end of the counsel of the love of God in giving His Son and does try and make void the end of the coming of Christ, which was to this end, "that whosoever believeth should not perish but have life everlasting." As in the morning we saw the height of the love of God in this word, "so God loved," and the depth in that "he gave his Son," now in this part of the verse, let us see the breadth and the length of it.

The Breadth of God's Love: All Who Believe

The breadth, *omnis*, "whosoever"; that is, the love is as broad as everyone, but then this "whosoever" has a qualification annexed unto it, that is, *qui credit*, "he that believeth." And this, "he that believeth," is also strengthened with this, *in eum*, "in him." So that, we see everything in this little gospel is of great importance.

The length of this love is as broad as from the east to the west (Ps. 103:12), even as broad as the world is and as large as *omnis*, "whosoever," is. So great is the extension of His mercy, you have then this joined: "he that believeth shall be saved" (Mark 16:16), and *quorum remiseritis peccata*, "whose sins soever you remit," and *quemque*, "what sins soever ye remit they shall be remitted" (John 20:23). That "whosoever believeth shall not perish but have life everlasting," in consideration that all who believe, or everyone who believes, shall be saved.

The ancient fathers have reduced this to four heads, to wit: (1) ages, (2) nations, (3) conditions of man, and (4) from men to sinners. And, therefore, whatsoever stood before the flood or after the flood, in the law or gospel, stood by faith. By faith Abel, Enoch; by faith Noah (Heb. 11:4–7). And as their seed: Abraham by faith, and David by faith, and all that stand, stand by faith, so that there was not any ever saved out of this standing.

And as ages stood, so likewise stood nations. "For there is no difference between the Jew and the Gentile" (Rom. 10:12). But as the Gentile is now saved, so was the Jew before. And as the Jew before, so is the Gentile now, "by faith did not perish but have life everlasting."

And so must we say of the conditions and estates of men. When the jailor asked what he must do to be saved, this only is propounded: "Believe[1] in the Lord Jesus" (Acts 16:31). And as this was the means to save the jailor, so there is no other condition allotted to King Agrippa, though he sits in his chair of estate, but this: "Believest thou the prophets?" (Acts 26:27). That is, all estates and callings are shut up in this *omnis*, "whosoever."

And, lastly, sinners have no other means of forgiveness of their sins but this too, that if sinners will be saved, they must believe that Christ Jesus came to save them, *quorum ego primus*, "of whom I am the chief" (1 Tim. 1:15). That is, there be lower forms of sinning, and sinners sitting in the higher forms, sinners offending in the great and monstrous sin, and sinners that [are] touched with so great abuses, but that if they be sinners, they must believe that Christ came to save them.

And, indeed, this is a worthy saying, and by all means to be received, that salvation is not an enclosure, as the devil wants to persuade, that He gave His

---

1. The term is "before" in the original.

Son for some, and not for others, not for all. And, therefore, Saint Jude calls it, "the common salvation" (Jude 3) and adds that it was needful for him so to write because else some might have been thought to have been curbed. And, therefore, at the beginning Christ will not plant Himself in a garden, but chooses rather to be *flos campi*, "the flower of the field" (Song 2:1), because now He may be gathered of everyone. And Christ, that He might sanctify the people with His blood suffered without the gate upon the mount Golgotha, because if [He] had suffered within the city, the Jews might have kept the Gentiles out. And because both Jew and Gentile might have benefit by His suffering, therefore He chooses to suffer without the city (Heb. 13:12). This, therefore, we see, that the knowledge of the breadth of the love of God is preeminent.

The second thing to be considered is the qualification in those words, *qui credit*, "he that believeth," as in the morning. Because God *sic dilexit*, "so loved," therefore there was no merit. So, we see how much God loved, *propter mundum*, "for the world," the price of His love, His Son, and *organon per quod*, "the instrument to convey this love," *qui cred*, "he that believeth." That which saves is everyone's mouth: "the word of faith" (Rom. 10:8). The seal of this righteousness by faith [is] the sacrament (Rom. 4:11), so that he who believes the word preached to the ears of faith and believes the sacrament offered to the eyes of faith shall not perish but have life everlasting.[2]

Has God said to His church *sponsabo te mihi*, "I will marry thee to me in righteousness and in judgment" (Hos. 2:19)—that is, in my only begotten Son, and in mercy and compassion, that is, "so God loved the world." Now, as righteousness and mercy are that which God performs of His part, so likewise God says, "I will marry thee to me in faith"; that is, that we must perform our part. Now, the want of this faith makes the divorce and separation. Therefore, at the preaching of Paul "some believed" and "some believed not" (Acts 28:24) because "all have not faith" (2 Thess. 3:2). For if everyone had faith, everyone

---

2. At this point in the manuscript (p. 123) there are two notes in Latin, written upside down at the bottom of the page. These appear unrelated to Perkins's sermon, though they were possibly taken down on the occasion on which these sermons were given. They are translated as follows: "Otho the Emperor (according to Tacitus) on death in this manner: 'death is only distinguished from oblivion or glory among those who come afterwards'" [the citation is a paraphrase of Tacitus, *Histories* 1:21, likely from memory]. Original: "Otho Imperator apud Tacitum. de morte in hunc morem / Mors destinguitur tantum oblivione vel gloria inter posteros." The second note is attributed to Laurence Chaderton in the margin ("Mr Chad."). It is as follows: "The minister of God is a servant. But it is not for any one member of the church to be served as the body of which Christ is the head, even if there are certain offices which are owed to some member. For [this office] serves to that glorious end and magnificent salvation, namely of others." Original: Minister dei est servus. Sed cui inservi. ecclesia ut corpori cuius / Christus est caput non uni alicui membro tame[t] si quædam muniae / sunt quae cuilibet etiam membro debentur. Servit autem ad quem / finem <u>s</u> gloriosum illum quidem & magnifiam salutem [quod] aliorum."

should be saved. Here we see then the cutting away of some. For though they dealt unkindly with God in the first covenant of the will, in this second covenant [He] adds this, to believe "that God is true" (John 3:33), which is their seal which they add to this covenant. And by not believing [they] make God a liar (1 John 5:10).

It is enough that whoever refuses to do is worthy of all torment, seeing the former point runs thus: "God so loved the world that he gave his only begotten Son." Why does He not say that whosoever loves should not perish but have life everlasting? What should mean the altering of the phrase? Truly, beloved, he who loves as the commandment of the other covenant and "that shall love the Lord thy God with all thy heart" (Deut. 6:5), and the touch of this love was that they "love me and keep my commandments" (John 14:15), this was too hot. Now, love is said to be the fulfilling of the law (Rom. 13:10). And if we could have loved, then we might have been crossed that "so God loved the world that he gave his only begotten Son." Therefore, because we could not perform the first, therefore God so loved that He has given another commandment. For seeing the former was too severe, therefore He has put out that, and in that stead has given a mild one, only to add our seal to this second covenant, that God is true and by believing in Him not make Him a liar.

This may be thought a good, easy way to heaven, but it will not appear so when we have heard what it is that is here added, that "whosoever believeth." It is commanded to mark diligently; that is, we must have an earnest regard to hear that which is spoken to us (Luke 9:44). Now a great part hear so negligently and without regard, as if it were a matter of no account what was uttered. If anyone be to learn an occupation, we do commonly persuade him to observe diligently what is taught him because it is that which hereafter must be his living. Therefore, regarding eternal life, there is a great reason that we should hear with great attention that which is taught us. And as the word commanded them that were bitten with the fiery serpents, to look earnestly upon the brazen serpent, so must we give diligent heed to that which shall be declared concerning eternal life.

And as we fail in the first commonly, we fail in the second that we may know now because we have no *cognoscimus*, "knowledge" (John 10:38). The second [failure], therefore, [is that] we have not *credimus*. The third [failure], we believe for it is not [that] we should believe before we know. For if we must assent, we must know to what to assent, for to assent is *ultimus actus fidei*, "the last work of faith," for as Christ says, "Amen, the faithful and true witness" (Rev. 3:14). In Christ all the promises are "amen" (2 Cor. 1:20). So likewise must we say "amen" also. Then, said James, "Oh Lord, that as all these promises of life eternal are amen in Christ, so to this must we add our seal to amen."[3] So be it, O Lord.

But what if we hear negligently, live ignorantly, and nourish infidelity in our hearts, that we say not "amen" to the promises of God? Why yet if we say within, "Lord, I believe, help thou me my unbelief" (Mark 9:24), though incredulity possess my soul so that I cannot believe in the measure which is required, yet, "oh Lord, help thou my unbelief," it is enough, for in Luke 12:47, that servant which will not be beaten must either do his master's will or, if he cannot do it, he must yet prepare himself to do it. And then it is not only true in callings but in all other graces. Of the Spirit a man shall be recompensed according to that he has and not according to that he has not.

This distinction that is farther added, in believing of Him, cuts off two counterfeit faiths, which are embraced in the world: the one, the heretical faith; the other, the faith of the carnal professor. And this belief in Him can abide neither. For the heretical faith is not sound (Titus 1:13) and, therefore, believes not *in eum*, "in Him." But they are enticed with the devil in seducing of Eve, "Ye shall be as gods." So [are] they, in deceiving themselves that they have in themselves sufficient matter of truth and confidence, and therefore there is no reason they should carry themselves out of themselves to believe *in eum*.

It has ever been a desire of man to find cause in himself to move the love of God toward him. And, therefore, [some think], though God chooses the people of Israel to be a peculiar nation to Himself, yet He had reason for what He did, for they were [a] populous goodly nation. Nay, says God, "Not because you were more in number but because I loved you, and for the oath sake I swore to your fathers" (Deut. 7:7–8). Yet though they were fewest in number, [some think], in righteousness and good nature [they] exceeded all the inhabitants of the earth, and therefore that respect might cause the love of God. No, surely, that was no cause. "For thou art a stiff-necked people." But that the Lord might perform the word which He swore to the fathers, therefore He has loved you. Therefore, we see that "God so loved" can abide no cause of love in us and that "he gave" admits no desert in us and "believe *in eum*" excludes any confidence or trust in *illos*, "in themselves."

It was not a judgment in God because of our works *praevisa*, "before seen." And it was no merit to cause God by way of sale to give His Son. And therefore, he that will have any interest in Christ must confess and believe that "God loved" proves Christ was given freely and that there is nothing but "*in eum*." So, by this "*in eum*" the heretical faith is confuted.

---

3. This appears to be drawn from 2 Corinthians 1:20–22, not from James.

Now, as badly as it sided with the heretical faith, so badly shall we see it again with the carnal faith. Religion is not a stooping or a sitting still, but it is a moving or stirring forward. "We dwell in him and he in us" (1 John 4:13). Of this there is resembling in the sacraments, for by baptism we are buried with Him and by the Supper Christ dwells in us. Yet all they that have *fidem sce fidem*, "a faith sitting still," not a faith working through charity (Gal. 5:6) but a faith keeping continual holidays, a faith that does not allow laws but makes frustrate and void the law (Gal. 2:21), this faith is not *in eum* and therefore not allowable.

For Christ, when He went to Jerusalem, had His face toward it. And we have our faces toward the world and our backs toward Jerusalem, so that our faith may very well be called, *aversa fides*, "a faith turned clean backward." And you shall be that in Hebrews 10:39, [where] Saint Paul uses a word which will not unfitly warrant this opinion, for there he names *pistis hupostata*,[4] "a faith drawing backward" or "a backsliding faith," looking clean away, not toward God, not toward Jerusalem, but fixed fast upon the world and the vanity thereof. For they believe a God but yet live as if God were ever at their backs, never afore them. Well, this *in eum* cuts off this carnal faith too and so can abide neither the heretical faith to admit confidence in ourselves nor the carnal faith to believe God, but to live as if there were no God.

The Length of God's Love: Everlasting Life

Now, this that follows admits a double division; that is, we receive two things from Christ. The one [is] the forgiveness of our sins. The other [is] the gift of life. The one [is] a paying of our debt. The other [is] a voluntary reward. The one [is] a pardon. The other [is] a restoring or rather indeed [giving] a better thing because now we are sure we shall never fail, though if Adam had stood yet he had a nature subject to falling. The one [is] in that he was given to death for us. The other [is] in that he rose again for our justification. By the first, His death, a pardon from perishing. By the other, His resurrection, a largesse or gift of eternal life. And so, out of His only begotten Son these two branches spring as out of one root.

There was no reason Christ should come to cause perishing, for that was Moses's office, because by original sin from our parents, and by reason of actual sin from ourselves continual transgressions [of] the law, and therefore there was need of continual forgiveness and this forgiveness to be renewed by seals and sacrifices of their deity. Therefore, Moses's offering being the sin offering, there was reason Christ's offering should be the offering of pardon or forgiveness.

---

4. Perkins is referencing the Greek text: "πίστεως…ὑποστείληται" (Heb. 10:38).

And so He was resembled before by the serpent, curing all those who were stung with the fiery serpent, that looking on Him they should not perish.

So, when anyone feels his conscience cited[5] by his transgression, or indeed if it be our thoughts with that sting of the serpent, which above all other stings, *morte moriens*, "thou shalt die the death," because he who keeps not the law is thereby guilty of the law. And, therefore, *statutum est omnibus sensorum mori*, "there is a statute for this, that one must once die," and by virtue of this opt out of the first death, the person which in this statute is delivered unto eternal death. When any man <...> himself thus strong, would he not think you give the whole world, though he had loved it before never so well for this *non peries*, "thou shalt not perish." Indeed, the true *nequa qua moriens*, "thou shalt not die," not that *nequa qua moriens*, "thou shalt not die," which the devil persuades while we are a sinning, but that which the truth itself promises, "thou shalt not die," the "thou" is the fruit of this not perishing.

It is a great shaking of faith when one who serves Christ is taken tardy in his first speech, for he says, "they shall not perish," and we see Stephen stoned and James lose his head, and only because they believed in Him. For if they would not have believed in Him, they might have escaped. And they only perished for this *in eum*, in Him. And, therefore, this must be looked into, for indeed faith is a shield (Eph. 6:16),[6] which has this property, as the fathers of the Greek church very well note from the custom of the Greeks in their plays, who when they delivered the shield to the champion with the shield, they added this, *aut hunc aut super hunc*, either be sure to keep yourself safe under this or else you shall be brought home upon this. And their shield was so great that they were carried upon them, being dead, as upon coffins. And so is our faith a shield when upon [it] we are diverse times brought home to be buried.

Why the case standing thus, we must see what is the answer thereunto. In this answer we will use Saint Paul's distinction in 2 Corinthians 4:9, "We are cast down, we perish not." That is, as Saint Augustine well expounds it, *aliud est perire aliud est transire*, "it is one thing to perish, it is another thing to pass from one condition or estate to another." And, therefore, Christ, passing to death, was not called *interitus*, "a perishing," but *transitus*, "a passing over." And Simeon, when he saw Christ, having been assured before by prophecy that he should not see death till he had seen the Lord, says, *nunc dimittis servum tuum in pace*, "Now, let thy servant depart in peace" [Luke 2:29]. He does not say, "Lord, now let thy servant perish."

---

5. Perkins likely uses the term "cited" in the sense of "excited."

6. The original erroneously cited Ephesians 6:10.

And when our friends, who have been long with us, depart from us to their new home, we do not think them perish[ed]. No more must we think of this departing, for though in the harvest the sickle comes to cut down the wheat, indeed the wheat perishes, but the corn is carried into the garner. And the sickle that in the vintage cuts down the grapes, it is truly[7] said that the husks which are cast out to the swine perishes, but the wine pressed out is reserved to a good use. And the axe that hews down the trees, the trees which serve for beams in princes' palaces or in the temple of God, cannot be said to perish, but those indeed which serve for fuel and are to be burned, they utterly perish.

De lingua & sermone ex concione W. Perkinsi

Ad linguae moderationem duo veniunt consideranda & quando loquendum & quando silendum. In loquendo duo etiam & sermonis subjectum & ratio Subjectum triplex triplicem offert considerationem

1. De deo loquendum est reverenter atque hinc cavenda omnis inanis nominis eius usurpatio non solum in iuramentis quibus utuntur prophani sed vel in vehementioribus affirmationibus quomodo saepe labuntur etiam relligiosi ut cum dicant Deus itane etc.

2. De aliis parce praesertim in vituperis[8] ad quae nisi vocati accedere nullomodo debemus. Id est maioris mali vitandi gratia ut si huic conducat ab huius commercio absterreri etc.

3. De nobis moderate im[m]o revera nisi sit ad gloriam dei omnino in laudem nostri vocem imittere non debemus.

Ratio loquendi huiusmodi est ut gratia sermoni nostro assideat sua vita[e][9] vir[-][?][10] ne cuiquam iustam offensionem pareamos Atque hic mendacia excluduntur vel officiosa quali non licet vel salutem totius Reipub[licae] lucrifacere.

Silendum nisi cum loqui iuvat cedendum etiam sermonis vitiosi ta[e?] dire[11] melioribus & saepius audiendum quam loquendum Quorsum aliter

---

7. This is the last word on p. 130 prior to the unnumbered page of Latin text, translated below.

8. This appears to be an error, as there is no word with precisely this form (putatively *vituperum), but the sense (in vituperando) is clear.

9. There is an obvious abbreviation mark after the *a*. Elsewhere on the page, it always abbreviates an *e*, so here it is possibly *vitae*.

10. A possible abbreviation of *videlicet*.

11. Possibly *taediare*.

lingua a natura faucibus tanquam saepimento obsessa aut velut ensis in vagina reconditus quem stringere nullo modo oportet nisi cum opus est.

Hinc duae & aures & manus uni linguae sociantur ut scilicet bis tantum & audiamus & faciamus quantum loquamur.

[Commentary Lecture on Genesis 1:3]

Gen 1:3 dixit deus esto Lux. Lux est actus seu qualitas effecta ab igne elementari in corpore perspicuo quatenus perspicuum est sedes aeris. 1. corporis elementaris perspicui inferior ignis superior est igitur aeris παθος το φωτισθεναι quod lucem accipit. ἔργον sive opus φωτίζειν praebere lucem, idque secundum facultates utriusque elementi [/] quia naturale ignis est esse φωτιστικον[,] aeris δεκτικον του φωτος. nam opt. Damascen[us] lib 2 cap 5 *fid. orthodoxae.* ignis unum est ex elementis 4 luce[12] & quod supra reliqua omnia elementa fertur urens simul & illustrans. quae verba ille ex Nysseno contraxit ut pleraque omnia Huic Junius

[Perkins's Theological Reflection on John 19:19–20]

Quod sacra biblia debeant in multas linguas transferri non obscure indicare videtur providentia divina per illam inscriptionem in christi crucem non solum factam sed defensam & stabilitam per pilatum invitis Judæis in eius honorem quem ille ipse morimandaret quod pilatus non a se fecit sed compulsu divino ut cum aliæ inscriptiones notarent factum & dehonestarent reum christus etiam inscriptione glorificatus est vel maxime perkins Notavit primum contra papistas qui scripturas nolunt in nota lingua prodire.

On the Tongue and on Speaking, from the Lecture of W[illiam] Perkins

Two things should be considered on the topic of taming the tongue: when to speak and when to stay silent. In speaking, there are also two things we should consider: the subject of the address and its method.[13] A threefold subject presents a threefold treatment:[14]

---

12. This term is unclear. The third letter should be *o* when compared to others, but the word cannot be *luoe*. Another possibility is that it is an inadvertently closed *c*. But *luce* does not seem to fit the syntax.

13. That is, content and form.

14. As the student represents it here, Perkins's lecture itself exemplifies the rule just stated: that the structure of the discourse should mirror the parts of the topic discussed. Here Perkins evidently outlined a "three-fold subject" (how to speak about God, others, and ourselves) in three corresponding points or divisions.

1. Concerning God, one must speak *reverently*,[15] and thus every empty abuse of His name must be avoided, not only in oaths used by the profane but also in very strong affirmations of the type that even religious people often let slip, as when they say, "Lord! Is that so?" etc.

2. Concerning others, one must speak *sparingly*, especially in censuring, which we should by no means undertake unless called upon to do so— that is, for the sake of preventing a greater evil (for example, when it may benefit someone to be warned away from associating with another, etc.).

3. Concerning oneself, one must speak *modestly*—though rather, in fact, unless it be to the glory of God, we should abstain altogether from uttering a word in our own praise.

This method of speaking is designed to lend grace to our speech <…>, lest we give anyone just cause to be offended. In this, lies are out of bounds, whether they condone some kind of impropriety or whether they secure the safety of the whole commonwealth.

One must be silent except when speaking is beneficial. One must defer to those who are better <…> even if their speech is full of errors, and listen more often than talk. Why else did nature confine the tongue in the throat, as though it were hemmed in by a wall, or like a sword sheathed in a scabbard, whence it should scarcely be drawn except in time of need?

This is why two ears and two hands share one tongue—surely so that we might listen and act twice as much as we speak.

[Commentary on Genesis 1:3]

"God said, 'Let there be light…'" (Gen. 1:3). Light is a movement or property produced by elemental fire in the transparent body,[16] as far as its transparency extends. The air is lower than the transparent elemental body; fire is higher, therefore, than air.[17] The παθος, "effect," [is expressed by] το φωτισθεναι, "being illuminated," denoting that which receives light; the ἔργον, or "action," [is expressed by] φωτίζειν, "to illuminate," to give forth light—that is, according to the abilities of each of the two elements, since it is natural for fire to be φωτιστικον, "light-generating," and for air to be δεκτικον του φωτος, "light-receiving." For the noble Damascene, in book 2, chapter 5 of his *Exposition of the Orthodox Faith* [says], fire is one of the four elements, <…> and that which

---

15. Each point is structured around an adverbial characterization of the manner in which one must speak—namely, of (1) God *reverently*, (2) others *sparingly*, and (3) ourselves *moderately*.

16. Presumably the ether is meant (in the Ptolemaic model of the universe then still dominant, the fiery sphere above the spheres of air, water, and earth, in descending order).

17. The syntax is compressed and uncertain here and in the following lines.

moves above all the other elements, both burning and illuminating at the same time.[18] He has drawn these words (and nearly everything else) from Gregory of Nyssa. With this Junius [agrees].[19]

[Perkins's Theological Reflection on John 19:19–20]

That sacred Scripture should be translated into many languages seems to be pointed out plainly by divine providence, through the famous inscription on the cross of Christ which was not only made but defended and confirmed by Pilate—though the Jews opposed it—in honor of the very man whose execution Pilate himself was ordering, since Pilate did not do this of his own accord but at divine instigation, so that though such inscriptions generally indicated the crime [of the person crucified] and dishonored the guilty, by the inscription on his cross, Christ was glorified to the greatest possible extent. Perkins noted this chiefly in opposition to the papists, who do not want the Scriptures to be available in the vernacular.[20]

---

18. "Our God Himself, whom we glorify as three in one, created the heaven and the earth and all that they contain [Psalm 146:6], and brought all things out of nothing into being: some He made out of no pre-existing basis of matter, such as heaven, earth, air, fire, water: and the rest out of these elements that He had created, such as living creatures, plants, seeds. For these are made up of earth, and water, and air, and fire, at the bidding of the Creator." John of Damascus, *The Orthodox Faith*, 2:5, cited from "John of Damascus. Exposition of the Orthodox Faith," in *Nicene and Post-Nicene Fathers, Second Series*, trans. S. D. F. Salmond, ed. Philip Schaff (Charles Scribner's Sons, 1899), 9:21. See also 2:6 (p. 22): "The element, then, that is lightest and most inclined to soar upwards is fire, and hence they hold that its position is immediately after the heaven, and they call it ether, and after it comes the lower air. But earth and water, which are heavier and have more of a downward tendency, are suspended in the centre. Therefore, taking them in the reverse order, we have in the lowest situation earth and water: but water is lighter than earth, and hence is more easily set in motion: above these on all hands, like a covering, is the circle of air, and all round the air is the circle of ether, and outside air is the circle of the heaven."

19. Perkins appears to be referring to a 1589 volume by Junius (Franciscus Junius, *Protoktisia, Seu Creationis a Deo Factae, et in Ea Prioris Adami ex Creatione Integri & ex Lapsu Corrupti, Historia.* [bound with] *Confutatio Argumentorum XXII, Quae Olim a Simplicio in Sacram Mosis Historiam de Creatione, Fuerunt Proposita, & Hoc Nostro Seculo ab Hominibus Prophanis Atheisque Recocta Imperitis Obtruduntur* [Heidelberg: Hieronymus Commelinus, 1589]). Junius discusses Genesis 1:3 along the same lines as Perkins and with reference to John of Damascus, Gregory of Nyssa, and others (see esp. *Protoktisia*, 8–12; *Confutatio*, 5–6). The dating of this volume indicates that Perkins delivered this material in a lecture post-dating the 1588 sermon (i.e., between 1589 and 1594, when he resigned his fellowship).

20. That is, to be translated into the vernacular languages of Europe from the Latin of the Vulgate. Here the transcriber appears to add his own reflective comment to what he heard from Perkins.

So then, we are to think of the death of [the] wicked who are as chaff tossed with the wind, and as the husks of grapes devoured by the swine, and as wood reserved for the fire, that they utterly perish. But not so of the godly, who are as the corn gathered into the barns by the angels and as the cedars of the house of God. Saint Paul teaches us what to call the death of the righteous and the death of the wicked. The death of the righteous is as the bestowing of money of a careful and wise husbandman who always employs it to gain and advantage, so that the death of the children of God is a "gain," as Saint Paul calls it (Phil. 1:21), an advantage that is a passing from death to life. But the death of the wicked is as the money which an antichrist spends, which is altogether lost, and so they perish everlastingly.

The last thing is the reminder [that] if they be cut down, then here is the reward or recompense. They have life everlasting according as I told you. Here is death their advantage (Phil. 1:21). If indeed the love of God, in that He loved the world, in His liberality, in that He gave His Son, did only free us from perishing, it might well be called a compassion, but no gift. But here Christ is given first and life in the second place. Christ says, *volo ubi ego sum illi sint*, "I will that wherever I am they be also" (John 17:24), and that "they be one even as we are one" (John 17:22).

And, indeed, this is true love. For so it is defined by the schoolmen that love is *affectus unionis*, "an affection of unity," that those whom we love may not be only where we are, but be as we be.

So here we see that where before we did exchange a short life for an eternal death, then He made *palmares dies meos*, "my days a span long" (Ps. 39:5). There is the short life. The worm within to sting the soul dies not, and the fire without to torment the body goes not out (Mark 9:44). There is the everlasting death. This case being known before will cause the love of God, coming to remedy this, to be the better known.

Now, *hodie mecum eris in paradiso*, "today thou shalt be with me in paradise" [Luke 23:43]. There is the short death and then comes in this verse *vita eterna*, "life everlasting forever." Not giving life as the brazen serpent which helped them that were stung by the fiery serpents by that stinging, and yet those same persons a little while after died of some ague[21] or some other disease. Nor as the manna in the wilderness, of the which they who did eat are dead long ago (John 6), but indeed these be but shadows and Christ the truth. The life that Christ gives is a true life, which shall never perish. And, indeed, our life is nothing but as the heathen man said, *vivitur et peritur*, "live and perish," being as water spilt upon the ground, like unto an hourglass when it is run out.

---

21. *Ague*: a fever or shivering illness.

And, therefore, Christ wishes the people that they should not labor for the meat that perishes (John 6). That is, the meat that nourishes this natural life is perishing meat, and therefore it cannot but beget perishing life. Well though this be such a life, yet it perishes, etc.: perished if it be not visited with drinks, fed with meat, clothed with raiment. And when this cost is bestowed upon it, yet it perishes too. I say, though it be such a life, yet if any had that prerogative that Isaiah had to add fifteen years more to Hezekiah's life [2 Kings 20:6], this privilege of prolonging would be bought at a dear rate. For we see Naaman the Assyrian takes a long journey to pursue this transitory life (2 Kings 5:9). And not only are we content to travel far, but we willingly receive at the hands of the physician Colocynthis.[22]

When the children of the prophets had eaten, they cried death was in the pottage[23] (2 Kings 4:40). So that, besides our great journeys, we are willing to suffer many things of the physician, yea though it come to the spending of all our substance (Mark 5:26). Nay, we stay not here, but go to Beelzebub to save our lives. Alas, if when we have done this, we have lengthened our life, why then through very tediousness life itself is bitter and grievous unto us.[24] And if we be but crossed of our purposes we will say, as Rebekah said, "I am over weary of my life" (Gen. 27:46).

So then, considering the shortness and irksomeness of life, our condemnation must needs be just if we refuse life everlasting when it is offered. And this is here offered, that instead of perishing we shall have life everlasting, which manifests the length of the love of God. For the height of His love was the bosom of His Father, and the depth even to the burial of Christ, and the breadth to everyone who believes, and the length to life everlasting, and as the love of God be given and endures, so does our faith, receiving the end of that faith, the salvation of our souls (1 Peter 1:9).

Now last, these two, both our faith in the earth and the love of God in the heaven, are joined together, the gift of God is eternal life by faith in Christ Jesus (Rom. 6:23). And when the love of God begins the sentence, there life eternal ends the sentence. A blessed beginning and a happy end, which blessed end, if we believe in Christ, may be the end of us all.

---

22. *Colocynthis*: a medicinal herb.
23. *Pottage*: soup or stew.
24. The original cites John 10:1, but Perkins's point appears to be drawn from Ecclesiastes 2:17.

Chapter 4

Laurence Chaderton Manuscript

This manuscript notebook contains a range of material, including biblical exposition, commonplace notes, and transcriptions of studies written by various theologians, ranging from church fathers to John Calvin.[1] Its most notable contents are extensive notes taken during lectures delivered between 1590 to 1592 by Laurence Chaderton, master of Emmanuel College, Cambridge.[2] The volume also includes about a dozen additional sermons and expository lectures transcribed from the back of the book. While the majority of these also appear to be by Chaderton, one small section is headed with Perkins's name.[3] Here there are notes on three expository lectures delivered by Perkins: on 1 Samuel 1:9–13, 2 Corinthians 4:3–4, and Hebrews 11:7. There is also a brief exposition of Ecclesiastes 12:1–7 immediately afterward; however, this appears not to be by Perkins and is therefore not included in the present volume.[4] The placement of this material immediately before a dated sermon by Chaderton implies that they were delivered in January 1590.[5] The inclusion of Perkins's teaching here provides further evidence of his close association with Chaderton, not least in the perception of the students who revered the teaching of these two renowned Cambridge theologians.

It is unsurprising that the material in this book was never published given the stated priority of the executors of Perkins's will to publish only his mature, polished work. The three expositions included here move through the biblical text phrase by phrase, offering brief explanation and application. They appear

---

1. Cambridge, Pembroke College, MS LCII.164, "Chaderton Lecture Notes," 186v–184r. The transcription published here made substantial use of Ian Breward's transcription included in his doctoral dissertation ("Life & Theology of William Perkins" [PhD diss., University of Manchester, 1963], appendix 3, xxxviii–lii), though our transcription differs from his in some places.

2. "Chaderton Lecture Notes," 1r–28r, 183v; cf. 28v–43.

3. "Mr Perkins's" (186v). The references for Perkins's sermons (from the back of the book) are 1 Samuel 1:9 (186v–r), 2 Corinthians 4:3–4 (186v–185r), and Hebrews 11:7 (185v–184r).

4. Breward suggests that it was by Chaderton ("Life & Theology of William Perkins," appendix 3, ln1).

5. The sermon following is noted as "1 Feb 1590, Mr C[haderton]" (183v).

to have been delivered by Perkins to students, possibly at Emmanuel College by Chaderton's invitation.

The first works through 1 Samuel 1:9–13, Hannah's prayer for a child and the priest Eli's reaction to it. Perkins draws several parallels between that incident and contemporary Christian practice. Most notably, Perkins reads Eli's presence at the temple door as functionally equivalent of his view of the godly minister who eagerly watches the people coming for prayer, eager to help those who have doubts or other matters of conscience to resolve.[6] Perkins's exposition hits some characteristically "Perkinsian" notes of application, including his view on the ministry, right hearing of the Word, vows, and private prayer. This exhibits Perkins's noted ability to move quickly from textual observation to broader matters of doctrine and application.

The second sermon, on 2 Corinthians 4:3–4, deals with the spiritual blindness of unregenerate people to the gospel. Perkins's treatment of the subject reflects his theological commitment to "total depravity," meaning that sinners cannot respond to Christ without God's prior enabling grace. It also displays his sensitivity to the pastoral challenges this entails. Thus, while such spiritual blindness is "a dangerous and probable note of a reprobate" that all should be wary of, Perkins also asserts that those in such a state may yet come to saving faith.[7] Such a sign of reprobation is perhaps most acutely observed in the way individuals engage with sermons. Do they twist Scripture to suit their own inclinations? Do they avoid sermons altogether? Perkins links this to the doctrine of the "keys" (Matt. 16:19), whereby ministers have the solemn duty of executing the ministry of the Word, and the practices of "spiritual jurisdiction," including exhortation, excommunication, absolution of sins, and evaluation of the spiritual state of individuals.[8] This leads Perkins to one of characteristic emphases—namely, that all people seek to "make their election sure" through pursuing sanctification and ensuring that their hearts are set on God (cf. 2 Peter 1:10). There is a great danger that many will be deceived by Satan into being satisfied with mere outward profession without genuine conversion.

The third sermon, on Hebrews 11:7, is not to be confused with Perkins's material on that passage in his major expository series on Hebrews 11. Perkins

---

6. On the minister's role in treating cases of conscience, see especially *The Whole Treatise of the Cases of Conscience* (RHB 8:95–440; esp. 115–17); and *The Calling of the Ministry* (RHB 10:195–280, esp. 203–10, 223–25). See also *A Case of Conscience* (RHB 8:595–638).

7. This practical approach to identifying reprobation as a state to move out of is reflected in the lengthy title of his early work, *A Treatise Tending unto a Declaration, Whether a Man Be in the Estate of Damnation, or in the Estate of Grace: and if He Be in the First, Howe Hee May in Time Come out of It…* (1590).

8. Perkins, *Revelation*, RHB 4:567–73. Cf. *Galatians*, RHB 2:15, 42; *Jude*, RHB 4:68–70; *Calling of the Ministry*, RHB 10:223–25.

preached through Hebrews 11 in about 1595–1596 as part of his lectureship at St. Andrews the Great,[9] whereas the exposition included here was delivered in 1590. While there are some similarities, whatever material Perkins reused in his later sermon was so substantially reworked and expanded as to be considered an entirely different piece of work. The present lecture also contains some points of theological interest that are not present in Perkins's published exposition, such as the relationship between divine acts and the particular persons of the Trinity and the qualitative differences between the illuminations of the devil and the illumination of God.[10] Perkins emphasizes the providence of God in caring for Noah, the nature of Noah's faith in trusting God's promises, and Noah's stance of fear and obedience in response to God's commands and judgments. Perkins emphasizes that, whether in Noah's day or his own, the presence of the means of grace among a people not only calls them to repentance but magnifies their just condemnation if they willfully persist in rejecting God's offer.

---

9. The dating of the Hebrews 11 series is mainly established by two factors. (1) It references Perkins's previous exposition of the Apostles' Creed, published in 1595 (*Exposition of the Creed*, RHB 5:1–416). There Perkins had set out the doctrine of faith, from which "it follows in order… to lay down also the practice of faith," which is outlined in his exposition of Hebrews 11 (*Hebrews 11*, RHB 3:5). Thus, the Hebrews 11 sermons were most likely delivered in 1595 or later. (2) The sermons were originally heard by both William Crashawe and Thomas Pierson, who edited the published sermons, meaning that they were originally delivered prior to 1599, when Pierson departed Cambridge for a lectureship in Northwich.

10. Perkins treats the latter point in *A Discourse of the Damned Art of Witchcraft* (RHB 9:316–18).

1 Samuel 1:9–13

"Then Hannah rose up…" [v. 9]. The sum of these words is this: that when as Elkanah with his two wives came up to Siloah, where the tabernacle of the Lord was, for to pray there, Peninnah reproached Hannah because she was barren, and therefore she rose up for to pray unto the Lord that He would deliver her of this reproach.[1]

For the explanation of this, we must know that after they had offered sacrifice to the Lord, they made a feast. Of this we may read in chapter 13 of this book. This custom was also retained in the New Testament, as in 1 Corinthians 11, that as when they had sacrificed, they constituted a feast, showing thereby their willfulness. And so here, this cheerfulness is not in doing their service to God, [so] there is a great curse upon them. To apply that to ourselves, there is, God be thanked, the administration of the Word and sacraments among us, but there wants this alacrity. And why? Because that in this service we join hand with the world. But the Lord abhors this manner of dealing, when as they will seek to please both the world and God [Rom. 3].

"And Eli the priest sat upon…" [v. 9]. The temple here may breed some difficulty [in] how it should be understood, since there was no temple at that time. But by the word may be understood the tabernacle or any place of prayer. In these words, we are to observe certain points of doctrine. Whereas it is said that Eli sat upon a stool by the post of the temple, we are to follow his example that as he remained continually before the door of the temple that he might view those that thither came to prayer, and might resolve them of any doubt or question which they should frame, so the ministers must continually [be] resident at their charge, that they may be ready to dissolve the doubts of their consciences, for they must needs be resolved as soon as Satan does move them or else he will get more liberty in them. And, therefore, the minister ought to be resident to remove them.

"And she was troubled in mind, and she was reproached, and therefore she was humbled in mind" [v. 10]. There are two points of doctrine. First, that afflictions, whether they are inward or outward, are especial means in God's servants to stir up the good graces of God in us, and therefore the freedom of

---

1. The original MS runs continuously without breaks. The paragraph breaks have been included.

a troubled conscience is a great judgment upon any people. The second point is this: in all trouble to seek help at the Lord and pray to Him. But this is not so among us. But as it was with Ahaziah who, after he fell out of the window,[2] he sent to Beelzebub the god of Akron to know whether he should live or die, and not to the true God, and so it is among us, that many do forsake the true God in their troubles and look to the armies of the devil for help.

"And she vowed to the Lord…" [v. 11]. Hannah not only pray[ed] to the Lord, but she also made a vow unto Him. And the people of God have one general vow to the obedience of God. The vow of the New Testament is baptism, the vows of the Old Testament are ceremonial works. And now is to be considered four circumstances.[3] First, it is part of God's service, because in the New Testament He has not bound us to any vow. Second, it must be in our power to do it. Third, it must be according to our profession and baptism. Fourth, it must be according to the will of God. The vows of the Church of Rome, they are contrary to the Word of God, as the vow of poverty and singleness.

"If thou wilt look on me thine handmaid…" [v. 11]. This is an example for all fathers and mothers if they have male children. Those that have the best wits they ought to consecrate them to the Lord. Why does the Lord give to your child then forwardness, but to the end you give it to Him again? But this is clean contrary to the world, for they will first serve the world, and then if they have anyone who is lame or impotent they will set him to the school and will vow him to the Lord. There is nothing so vile or of so base account among the common people as to be a "priest," as they call them. But it is a blessed calling, and it is here said they be given unto the Lord, and therefore they have great honor thereby.

"There shall no razor come of his head…" [v. 11]. This does signify that he should be a Nazarite. This was a ceremony among the old Jews, that they would not cut their hair. And as the Nazarite was, as it were, separated from the people, so our Savior Christ; He was called a Nazarite in that He was separate from sins. Though we come to the church and to sermons and yet are after the world, we must not think that we are Christians. But we must be Nazarites; we must sever ourselves from the world if we will become good Christians.

"And as she continued praying…" [vv. 12–13]. Here are two points of doctrine. The first is of Eli, that he did mistake her in her prayer, imagining her to be drunk, which sin was counted a very great sin, even among the Gentiles.[4] And is it not so with us? For what will they say if they see one profess the Word of God? By and by they will say he is a hypocrite. The false witnesses of Christ

---

2. 2 Kings 1:2–4.

3. In the margin: Vow 4. That is, the four circumstances of a vow.

4. Rom. 1:29.

are called false witnesses and yet they repeat the very same words that Christ did, even only for mistaking the words. Therefore, we must, if we can, expound the words of all men and also of the wicked in the better part. The second point of doctrine is that her lips moved only, where we are taught when we are to pray privately, before that how we are to behave ourselves. She only gives a sign of prayer.

"Hannah poured forth her soul…" [v. 13]. Many people will say the Lord's Prayer by rote only, not knowing the meaning of the words. But their prayers are abominable to the Lord, for we ought to pour forth our souls before the Lord. This is a proper note of God's service, to pour forth their souls.

"If the gospel be hidden from any of you, it is hidden from those that perish" [2 Cor. 4:3]. In the former verse, Paul makes manifest the truth by his preaching, and it was plainly taught unto the people. Now, lest it should be objected that because it was so plainly taught, therefore all might understand it, he says here that it is hidden to none but to those who perish. And in the fourth verse, he sets down the cause why the Corinthians were so blind, namely, that it was because the devil had blinded their eyes.

"If the gospel be hid…" The first doctrine that we learn here is this: that the not receiving of the gospel is a note of a reprobate.[1] This doctrine, therefore, is not devised by man, but set down here by the Holy Spirit.[2] The Holy Spirit does not set down this for a certain note, but for a dangerous and probable note of a reprobate—as such a sign that may be recovered.

Now, to apply this to ourselves. The doctrine of the gospel has been preached in this place a great while, and therefore let this warn the hearers to receive the gospel, lest they bear in them the sign of a castaway. Some among us run away to hear the Word, but then they must have it framed according to their own affections. But as it cuts them on their sins, then they rebel against the minister. They have not yet taken on them the yoke of our Savior Christ.

And, therefore, if there are any thus affected, they are in a dangerous case. And, therefore, ignorance and rebellion and loathing of the Word of God, they are great signs and tokens of reprobates. And they who flout and jeer at the gospel, they carry great and dangerous tokens of castaways. So that these four sorts of men may be hearers of the Word and yet they carry the notes of reprobates.[3] For if the gospel is preached and not received, their end is corruption. If you should see the tokens[4] of plague upon you, you would shiver and quake at them, though they may make but an end of this life.[5] And, therefore, if you see these tokens upon you, which are able to carry you to hell, how much more ought you to tremble?

The second doctrine is that a minister may judge according unto God's

---

1. In the margin: Of reprobates.
2. Original: "Ghost." This term has been changed to "Spirit" throughout this volume.
3. In the margin: Four notes of reprobates.
4. *Tokens*: signs, symptoms.
5. In the margin: A simile.

Word.[6] The proof is manifest in this place and in 1 Corinthians 14:25. And we may see in Matthew 16 that there the keys of heaven are committed to Peter to bind and loose, and therefore the minister has power to bind and loose. And he must show the people that they are under the law of damnation. Yea, and he has the power to bind them up as faggots to hell fire if they repent not. The ignorant accuse the minister because he judges the people, but he may be bold to judge them so far as the Word of God affords.

The third doctrine that we are here to learn is that there are certain men that shall perish.

And fourth, the enemies of the gospel are ordained to judgment. And, therefore, let us make use of this. First, by considerations. We are to fear and tremble. Paul says, "Be not high minded, but fear" [Rom. 11:20]. And David says, "My flesh trembleth, O Lord, for fear of thy judgments" [Ps. 119:120]. And the prophet says, "Lord when I consider thy judgments, there is molteness in my bones" [Hab. 3:16]. The second use is that with all diligence we make our election sure. Many consider their little dangers, but few this greatest evil of all, that you are in dangerous condemnation. Are you sure that you are the child of God? Take heed, for you are in a dangerous case, for you cannot assure yourself of your election except you be sanctified.

"In whom the God of this world…" [Eph. 2].[7] He is called the god of this world not because he is so indeed but because men have made him so. How is this? Look on whom they bestow their hearts, there is their God. But yet, they will say, we serve the true God. Yet the disposition of their hearts is led away by the devil. Wicked they are [who] put their affiance in the devil, and those who seek for counsel to them, and so they make him their god. Others are said to have their hearts led away by the devil, but not so directly. They are said to make their belly their god,[8] and the devil is the cause of this. Paul calls those "idolaters" who make their riches their god,[9] for they have more care of them than of the true God. The devil, therefore, is their god, because he is the cause of it. And, therefore, whosoever bestows his heart on anything but on the true God, he makes the devil his god.

Now, let us apply it to ourselves. Every Sabbath day, we come to hear God's Word, yet we may have the devil for our god, and therefore you must look how your heart is affected. And if it is not most upon God, then Satan is your god. Satan will let God have the show, but he will keep the heart. Satan is he that is [the] aggressor when he lies at the point of death. Be not corrupted. Surely, he was but an open professor, otherwise the devil would have raged over him.

---

6. In the margin: Minister may judge.
7. In the margin: Satan the god of this world.
8. Phil. 3:19.
9. Eph. 5:5.

Hebrews 11:7

"By faith Noah being warned of God etc." In the beginning of this chapter, the Holy Spirit has set down the doctrine of faith—that it was a demonstration of things not seen, of the which He has brought many examples, among which He brings in this of Noah.

The meaning of this verse if you will know you may read the sixth and seventh chapters of Genesis, for this does contain a brief sum of the same. In this place we are to consider five points: (1) God admonished Noah; (2) Noah believed God; (3) he was moved with fear; (4) in showing his obedience, he built the ark and that for two uses: first, for to save his family, second, to condemn the world; [and] (5) he is made heir of righteousness by faith.

He was admonished of the Lord but how, for then the Word was not written, but among the three persons. The Son, who is the second person, has the execution of every action, and therefore the second person did illuminate his mind. But how did He this?[1] The Lord conveyed His Word into the hearts of His servants three manner of ways—by voice, by dreams, [and] by vision. By some of these three means He revealed His counsel to Noah.

But some may ask how shall we know this, for it may be he was deluded? The devil, though he does strangely delude many, yet he cannot give them gifts to execute it. But the case was otherwise with Noah. So, this is a plain difference between the illuminations of the devil and the illuminations of God.

In the second place, we are to consider what it was that he revealed.[2] It was a thing not yet seen. He revealed this unto him 120 years before it should come to pass. And we see here that the Lord, He was no less provident to keep and preserve His church than He was to foretell them of this danger, for He bolted the door on the outside. And, therefore, though that His church be ever[3] so small in number and His enemies ever so many, yet the Lord will always be provident of His church. The example is that he believed things not yet seen. This is the surety of any faith when as we do believe the thing that is not yet seen. In the order of nature we must not believe anything but that whereof we have experience.[4] But it is clean otherwise in the Lord's matters, for first we

---

1. In the margin: Revelation in two manner of ways.
2. This should likely read "believed." See outline above.
3. Original: "never." This term has been changed to "ever" throughout this volume.
4. In the margin: Faith.

must believe that God's promises are sure, then we shall have experience afterward. And, therefore, though you see the devil, as it were, to buffet you, and God so stand against you as an enemy, yet you must believe God's promises to be firm.

The third point was how he was moved with a reverend fear. He was shaken with a fear as though the judgment was at hand. Let us apply this to ourselves, for very few are so touched that they fear the judgments of God. But we must learn that when we hear God's judgments, that then we fear as though they were present (Hab. 3:16). As David says, "Lord, my flesh trembles for fear of thy judgments" (Ps. 119:120).

The fourth part is that he built the ark. Here we must note in Noah a pliable heart to work and to the obedience of God. Though he was mocked of the world, yet he proceeded in his duty. We know all our duties and, therefore, we must say, "Lord give us grace to do that which You command, and command what You will." For whatsoever the Lord commands, that we must do though we lose our lives for it.

To what end did Noah build the ark? For two causes. First, to save his family, and not only to save them from the flood but also to save their souls. And, therefore, this teaches every master of a household to have care of the same, not only of the food but also of their souls. For in that family where the master has no regard of the souls of his family, the hog is far better than their child. For the hog, when it dies, it has then an end of the misery wherein it lived, but when the child dies, that is but a beginning of the misery.

The second thing is that by it he might condemn the world two ways. Of the first by his obedience. Second, by his ministry. His obedience condemned the world in that they scorned. As it is said [in] Luke 11, that [the] Queen of [the] South shall condemn the Jews, and also the Ninevites should condemn them because of their obedience.

Now to apply this. There are some among us that, when they hear the Word of God, they are obedient to the same. Yet there be the greatest sort which will not obey it but will mock it. But let them know that the obedient shall rise up in judgment against them to condemn them.

Second, he condemned the world by his ministry. The administration of the sacrament is a great means of the ministry. So, this building of the ark was a part of the ministry of Noah, for he called them to repentance by his preaching, but they mocked thereat. And every speech that he gave upon the word was a sermon to call them to repentance. Nevertheless, they would not believe. The preaching of the Word, if it be not received, says Saint Paul, the world thereby shall be condemned (Rom. 2:16).

Now, to apply this to ourselves. You have heard the Word of God out of this place plentifully, and have you not yet left your sins behind? Behold, so many sermons as you have heard preached, so many indictments shall be given up against you at God's judgment seat. And, therefore, if you have not been obedient unto it, it had been better for you that you had lived in Turkey. Eli's sons, they would not obey their father, because the Lord would destroy them (1 Sam. 2:25). And, therefore, if you will not obey, it is an awful sign that the Lord will condemn you. This also goes to the minister himself, for if he preaches the Word, and obey it not, he writes so many indictments against his own self.

"He was made heir of righteousness by faith," that is, by the righteousness of Christ. In the world we magnify a man if he be an heir to a man of great wealth, but the Holy Spirit, He magnifies Noah here, for that he was made the heir of righteousness by faith.

Chapter 5

James Tomlin Manuscript

This manuscript notebook was that of James Tomlin, a student Sidney-Sussex College, Cambridge.[1] Tomlin enrolled in 1598, completing his BA in 1605 and his MA in 1608. Tomlin represents a typical example of a pious Cambridge Puritan during this period. Such men generally belonged to Sidney-Sussex, Emmanuel, or Christ's College and shared the theological and pastoral priorities of Perkins, Chaderton, and their circle. Tomlin, along with many other students of his ilk, would pursue a career as a parish minister, bringing the proclamation of biblical and Reformed doctrine to the English people. Tomlin served as rector of Scaldwell, Northamptonshire from 1611 until his death in 1617.[2]

The transcriptions in Tomlin's notebook are dated from his first year as an undergraduate. It exclusively contains material taught by Perkins and consists of three pairs of sermons: two on Romans 4:25, two on Jude 3–4, and two on prayer. The Jude sermons were part of an expository series on the entire epistle, which would later be published in its entirety (see the introduction to this volume).[3] However, the rest of the material in this book has not previously appeared in print.

Tomlin's notebook was bound after transcription and does not appear in order of its composition. Perkins delivered the prayer sermons on St. Luke's and St. Andrew's days 1598, and the Romans sermons in 1599. The Jude sermons wedged between them appear to have been transcribed at around the same time.[4]

---

1. Cambridge University Library, Department of Manuscripts and University Archives, William Perkins: Sermons, MS Add.8563, "William Perkins: Sermons." Contents: Romans 4:25 (2r–9r), Jude 3–4 (9v–24v), prayer (24v–31v). Tomlin wrote his own name on the title pages of the latter two sermon pairs (9v, 24v). The handwriting is consistent throughout the volume.

2. Venn, *Alumni Cantabrigienses*, pt. 1, vol. 4, p. 248.

3. Perkins, *Jude*, RHB 4:1–285.

4. These sermons are also independently transcribed in the Hutton MS, discussed below. If Perkins preached Jude and Galatians consecutively, then he delivered the entirety of his Jude series prior to 1600, from which time he spent three years lecturing on Galatians, a series that remained incomplete at his death in 1602 (cf. Perkins, *Galatians*, RHB 2:11).

The transcriptions were taken down with care, and each pair of sermons is headed by a title page stylized with simple line drawings. Tomlin's careful transcription and binding together of this material shows that he deeply valued Perkins's teaching. He also understood Perkins's distinctly Ramist ordering of material, accurately transcribing the structural hierarchy of what Perkins verbally communicated at several points.[5] However, Tomlin's transcriptions reflect not only his undergraduate zeal but his undergraduate lack of knowledge. He frequently provides incorrect Bible citations, makes occasional factual errors (such as confusing Gnostics with Arians), and practices his newfound Latin skills in the margins.[6] In some ways Tomlin's notebook is an example of the kind of flawed notetaking that Perkins's editors were adamant should not be used as a basis for publication.

The location at which the Romans sermons were originally delivered is not specified. Given Perkins's relationship to Tomlin's college, Sidney-Sussex, it is possible that these sermons were delivered there.[7] Each of these two sermons expounds one half of Romans 4:25. The first continues from an earlier exposition on Christ's death for sinners that is no longer extant. It begins by considering the justice of God with respect to the death of Jesus. It discusses the fact that death has a different meaning with respect to the godly, for whom it is not a punishment or curse but the beginning of life. Furthermore, God continues to chastise his children with difficulties in this life for their spiritual well-being and to expose religious hypocrites.

Perkins then turns to a discussion of the extent of the atonement. He asserts that Christ's death redeemed only the elect from their sins since Christ's priestly intercession is limited to them, and only those united to Christ partake of His benefits. Perkins's position here might appear to depart from that expressed in his *Manner and Order of Predestination*, published only the year prior to the delivery of this sermon.[8] Both texts relate a saying that describes the

---

5. Ramist structural diagrams appear throughout Tomlin's notebook (7r–v, 12r–v, 17v, 23v, 28v). See the introduction to this volume.

6. Tomlin annotated a torn page on both sides with "*lacerata papyrus*." Latin: "torn paper" (18r–v).

7. The master of Sidney-Sussex, James Montagu (c. 1568–1618), preached at Perkins's funeral. Like Chaderton's Emmanuel College, Montagu's Sidney-Sussex was founded as a distinctly Puritan college devoted to the raising up of godly preachers for England. Perkins's active involvement in Sidney-Sussex College is also suggested by the college's possession of one of the two portraits of Perkins painted during or just after his own lifetime (G176), the other hanging in his own Christ's College (Senior Combination Room). On the Sidney-Sussex portrait, see J. W. Goodison, *Catalogue of the Portraits in Christ's, Clare and Sidney Sussex Colleges* (Cambridge: Cambridge Antiquarian Records Society, 1985), 32, 84.

8. Compare also Perkins's second sermon on John 3:16 (above), and the introductory discussion.

saving potency of Christ's blood in terms of whether it could save "a thousand" or even "a thousand thousand" worlds. Whereas Perkins previously affirmed that Christ's blood does possess such saving potency, the Romans 4:25 sermon repudiates a very similar saying as a "foolish and frivolous, vain and vacant… proverb." The distinction here is a fine one, but the present text does not formally contradict what he published the previous year. There Perkins asserted that the blood of Christ was "in itself" of infinite saving potency, though Christ was sent to die specifically "for us few despicable wretches," that is, the elect.[9] In the present sermon Perkins reacts to the notion that "one drop" of Christ's blood (i.e., the least amount of punishment) could atone for all sin. On the one hand, this would make the enormity of the punishment that Christ underwent on the cross unnecessary and needlessly cruel. On the other hand, Christ's atoning work on the cross must not be understood as involving the infliction of punishment on Christ for the sins of the reprobate. Their sins remain unforgiven, and they will be justly punished for those sins in hell. If Christ had suffered the punishment due for the sins of the reprobate, then God could again be charged with unjust treatment of His own Son, punishing Him beyond saving necessity. In sum, for Perkins the blood of Christ is of infinite saving potency, but the punishment inflicted on Him on the cross was the precise, measurable amount of punishment due for the sum of the of the sins of the elect. Or, stated differently, for Perkins the atonement is of *infinite intrinsic sufficiency* and yet only of *particular extrinsic sufficiency*; that is, it is for the elect alone, since Christ did not actually pay the penalty for the sins of all people.[10] Here Perkins's view amounts to little more than holding fast to Peter Lombard's classic formulation that the work of Christ is sufficient for all yet efficient only for the elect.[11]

Finally, this sermon rejects the literal descent of Christ into hell as a Roman Catholic doctrine. The proper interpretation of the descent had been a perennial issue among theologians of the medieval through the Reformation period and indeed in Perkins's own day.[12] Perkins's position—that Christ had

---

9. Perkins, *Manner and Order of Predestination*, RHB 6:288.

10. See Moore, *English Hypothetical Universalism*, 38–42; cf. Allen, *Extent of the Atonement*, 126–28.

11. Peter Lombard, *Sentences* 3:20.5.1 (Peter Lombard, *The Sentences: Book 3: On the Incarnation of the Word*, trans. Giulio Silano, MST45 [Toronto: PIMS, 2008], 86). See discussion in Lynch, *John Davenant's Hypothetical Universalism*, esp. 58–61. Other useful surveys on the extent of the atonement among early modern Reformed theologians include Allen, *Extent of the Atonement*, 35–253; and G. Michael Thomas, *The Extent of the Atonement: A Dilemma for Reformed Theology from Calvin to the Consensus* (Carlisle, U.K.: Paternoster, 1997).

12. Karl Tamburr, *The Harrowing of Hell in Medieval England* (Cambridge: D. S. Brewer, 2007); Dewey D. Wallace, "Puritan and Anglican: The Interpretation of Christ's Descent into Hell in Elizabethan Theology," *Archive for Reformation History* 69 (1978): 248–87; Peter Marshall, "The

"descended not locally into hell"—had already been expressed in print in his *Exposition of the Apostles' Creed*, which had attracted criticism amid the Cambridge predestinarian debates of 1595.[13] What was primarily at stake here was the sufficiency of Christ's work on the cross to save.[14]

The second sermon on Romans 4:25 takes up the resurrection of Christ. Perkins argues that Christ's resurrection was necessary both for the eternal life of His own incarnate person as well as for the eternal life of all united to Him. At the present time Christ alone is ascended, as it were, above the waters of this world, yet His life extends to His members, who put to death their sin and live Christ's new life by virtue of their union with Him. As such, Perkins emphasizes that the resurrection is a profoundly practical doctrine, summoning Christ's people to live regenerate life and calling us to focus our minds on heavenly matters and to bring both the regenerate way of life and meditation upon it into the rhythms of our daily work.

Whereas the Jude material in Tomlin's volume is described as "sermons preached" at St. Andrews the Great, the prayer material was "delivered by manner of catechism" at the same location.[15] Perkins's catechetical instruction on prayer borrows from material that had likely been recently delivered in a sermon on Matthew 5:44 as part of his ongoing exposition on the Sermon on the Mount (Matthew 5–7).[16] It thus appears that Perkins made a practice of reusing material from his expository sermons as content for his catechetical lectures at other times. The catechetical form of this material includes some content not in the sermon, most notably a quotation from Augustine. Perkins's first catechetical sermon on prayer argues that Christians ought to pray positively for all people, longing for the salvation even of the worst enemies of the gospel. Christians must only pray against God's enemies conditionally and as an abstract category rather than against particular persons. This aligns with Perkins's

---

Reformation of Hell? Protestant and Catholic Infernalisms in England, c. 1560–1640," *The Journal of Ecclesiastical History* 61, no. 2 (2010): 279–98.

13. Perkins, *Creed*, RHB 5:229–36; Cambridge, Trinity College, MS B/14/9. "A Collection of Papers Relating to the Quinquarticular Controversy," 34. Useful, though flawed, discussions of the Cambridge predestinarian disputes include H. C. Porter, *Reformation and Reaction in Tudor Cambridge* (Cambridge: Cambridge University Press, 1958), 314–75; and David Hoyle, *Reformation and Religious Identity in Cambridge, 1590–1644* (Cambridge: Cambridge University Press, 2004), 71–87. On Perkins's contribution, see Mark R. Shaw, "William Perkins and the New Pelagians: Another Look at the Cambridge Predestination Controversy of the 1590s," *Westminster Theological Journal* 58, no. 2 (1996): 267–301.

14. For an overview of diverging Reformed interpretations of the descent of Christ among early modern Reformed theologians, see Samuel D. Renihan, *Crux, Mors, Inferi: A Primer and Reader on Christ's Descent* (self-published, 2021), 103–206.

15. "William Perkins: Sermons," 9v, 24v.

16. Perkins, *Sermon on the Mount*, RHB 1:378–80.

pastoral theology, wherein nobody is ever to conclude that they themselves nor anyone else is reprobate, but all are to continue to seek Christ through the means of grace so long as they live.[17] While the Bible contains examples of the prophetic condemnation of particular reprobate persons in prayer (here "incurable" enemies), such prophetic knowledge is uncommon in the post-apostolic age. In its absence, all Christian prayer against God's enemies must reflect both the possibility that enemies of the gospel may by God's grace yet repent and be saved, and the reality that God's sovereign election stands behind who will ultimately respond. Thus, Christians are to pray in a different manner than that modeled by David and other Old Testament believers.

The second catechetical sermon addresses outward circumstances of prayer. Perkins notes that he had discussed inward prayer previously. This suggests that the two sermons in Tomlin's book were part of a longer catechetical series but that Tomlin only attended the two "holy days" on which these two addresses were delivered. In the second sermon Perkins uses a short section of his published *Exposition of the Lord's Prayer* (1592) as a framework on which to expand.[18] Perkins is concerned to promote an approach to the manner of outward prayer that expresses its inward, spiritual nature. He defends the use of written prayers, which in England amounted to defending the use of the Book of Common Prayer. Perkins regarded such liturgical material as an edifying means to frame sound, biblical prayers to God. Likewise, Perkins urges that outward gestures be used which fittingly express the inward stance of prayer, but he also urges conformity to local church practice for the sake of order. He distinguishes this Protestant approach to prayer from the Roman Catholic view in terms of Christian freedom in adiaphora, or "things indifferent" (Rom. 14:1). Whereas Roman Catholicism treats matters of time and place as matters of great spiritual significance, Perkins treats such matters as things that Christians are to use for the purposes of edification and maintenance of good order.

---

17. Perkins, *Golden Chain*, RHB 6:263.
18. Perkins, *Exposition of the Lord's Prayer*, RHB 5:467–68.

Romans 4:25

(Sermon 1)

"Who was delivered up unto death for our sins…"

There remains somewhat to be spoken of further concerning the death of Christ and of the persons for whom He died.[1]

The Death of Christ

We have heard that Christ Jesus our Savior fulfilled all righteousness and also suffered death for sinners as a ransom for their sins. Now it seems hard on God's side that He should exact any punishment at His Son's hand for sin, who had kept the law, and therefore sin (being the cause), being taken away, death (being the effect of sin) must needs also be taken away, *sublata causa tollitur effectus*.[2] And, for this cause, God might be thought to deal unjustly with His Son. For the unfolding of this objection we must know the true meaning of the word "death" and how the godly are said [to] die. The godly are not truly said [to] die when they depart out of this life, and that for these reasons.[3]

First, attending to Scripture phrases, we find this epithet "dying" or "death" attributed to some and not to others. In the catalogue of all the ancient progeny of Cain before the flood, we see in every case this epithet of dying attributed to everyone, saying, "He lived so long, and then he died" (Gen. 4). And always mention is made of their death. But come to the generations of Shem after the flood, behold there is no mention of their death but [that] "he lived so many years, and begat sons and daughters" [Gen. 10], because they trusted in the promised seed. So that their death was not attributed unto them because they trusted in the promised seed who should redeem them from their sins.

Furthermore, in all the New Testament we never hear of death attributed to any but commonly by this phrase, "He sleepeth (or is dissolved)." The one is commonly our Savior Christ's saying at the death of any. "'The maid is not dead but sleepeth,' and the multitude laughed him to scorn" (Matt. 8). "He told Mary,

---

1. The title page specifies the date 1599.

2. "Upon removal of the cause, the effect is removed."

3. This discussion is similar to that which is found elsewhere in Perkins's published works. See, for example, Perkins, *Treatise of Christian Equity and Moderation*, RHB 10:394.

saying, 'Thy brother Lazarus sleepeth.' Then said she, 'Lord, if he sleepeth, he shall do well enough'" (John 11).[4] [But] He meant this of his natural death, of the dissolution of the soul from the body. Paul also says, "These that sleep in Christ…" (1 Cor. 15:18).[5] He also says the word "dissolved," saying, "I greatly desire to be dissolved" [Phil. 1:23].

Second, the godly are not truly said to die in God's estimation. For as God esteems of any, so they are indeed to be accounted. Now, God esteems not of the dissolution of the bodies of His servants as a death, that is, as in any way hurtful. And, therefore, it is not truly a death in His estimation. Because that then it is rather a life, for then in pureness of their souls they come nearer to participate of the glory of God. For it is so far from being a death that it is the very way—yea, the beginning—of immortality and society with God and His holy angels.

Third, they are said to die in regard of the nature of death, that it is not any way executable[6] to them, seeing Christ Jesus has taken away the sting thereof. For death, being a wage for sin, a due reward, recompense, and stipendium[7] for the same, by Christ was taken away, and therefore death is no punishment but is as a humble bee that buzzes but can do no harm at all unto them.

To prove that death is in no wise[8] accursed, executable, or hurtful, but rather profitable and necessary for the children of God, the testimonies of their own mouths, as also the prayers that they have made for the same, do evidently declare it. Paul does pray for it, saying, "O how greatly do I desire to be dissolved" [Phil. 1:23]. Elijah in like manner prayed for death (1 Kings 19).

> Paul prayed for death.
> It is a sin to pray for a curse.
> Therefore, death is not a curse.[9]

Then it may very well be objected that if death is in no wise executable to the righteous, how comes it to pass that God's children have as many crosses and calamities as the wicked, yea, sometimes in greater abundance they sustain sickness and adversity? We must know that these afflictions, which God lays upon them, are not properly punishments for their sin but castigations or trials.

First, it is a sign of a fatherly love and affection toward them. For a good father will chasten his child, as the apostle Paul says, "He scourgeth every son

---

4. Perkins (or the transcriber) seems to have confused the details of this story. The exchange was between Christ and His disciples, not Mary (John 11:12).

5. The original erroneously cited verse 21.

6. *Executable*: hateful, deplorable, detestable.

7. *Stipendium*: payment.

8. *In no wise*: never.

9. This is a syllogism.

he receiveth" (Heb. 12). And, therefore, they who live here without adversity, it is a sign that they are not the true elect of God. They are bastards (as Paul in the forecited place tells [Heb. 12:8]) and not sons; neither are they likely to have any part of the inheritance with Christ Jesus.

Second, God will not bring up His children so cockeringly,[10] but He will chasten them to make a trial of their faith and patience in adversity, and that their love and obedience to Him and His laws might be tried in the cross affairs and calamities of this life. <...>[11] according to the proverb that between friends is observable, *amicus certus in re incerta cernitur*, "a friend is tried in a doubtful matter." Even so, adversity tries the children of God, who are His and who are not.

Third, it argues God's continual love and [the] tender affection He bears to His, in that He chastens them here in this life temporally, that they might not with the wicked be punished in the life to come eternally. And He chastens them for the commodity[12] of their souls, so that they are (as it were) kept in awe and daily exercised, that they might more and more grow in fear and reverence of His majesty. Whereas contrariwise the wicked, feeding and grazing on pleasures and delights, never tamed and kept under by any cross and adversity, wax fat like an ox against the day of slaughter.

The chastisements and punishments that God lays upon any in this life are for two causes. (1) To discover some notable virtue or point of faith and obedience, which would otherwise be kept secret. (2) To boult[13] out some unstable hypocrisy, frailty, or hidden sin, which otherwise would have been kept close, to the deceiving of many.

An example of the former [cause] we have in Paul, etc. A singular pattern of faith we have in Abraham, worthy of perpetual remembrance, who was commanded a hard piece of service by God, who (with his wife being barren) obtained, and long waited, for a son according to God's[14] promise, yea, and such a son in whom all the nations of the earth should be blessed, in whom consisted his salvation, namely, of him and his seed (Gen. 17). And yet, this son was by God's commandment [to] be slain for a sacrifice to Him, a hard service, and yet in being willing and ready to do the same, his excellent faith and obedience was made manifest to all generations, to his commendation.

And so, Job [is] a notable pattern of patience, not long after Abraham, whom God committed for his strong faith into Satan's power, to punish his

---

10. *Cockering*: to pamper, spoil, coddle.
11. The MS is torn at the corner, making this term illegible.
12. *Commodity*: advantage.
13. *Boult*: sift.
14. The term is "the" in the MS, but it is corrected in a marginal note: "God's."

body, only not to take away his life. "Hast thou not tried my servant Job, a just man that feareth me" [Job 1:8]. "Now touch him and see if he will not blaspheme thee to thy face" [Job 1:11]. Satan punished [Job] most grievously, and [he was] turned loose to the devil, yet he could not prevail. And though the devil had his whole swing at him, yet notable was his faith and constancy, that he trusted in God—yea, he says, "Although he should slay me yet will I trust in him" [Job 13:15]. And again, "I know my redeemer liveth…" [Job 19:25]. Which constancy of his, if it had not been put in trial, it would never have been supposed to be so great as indeed it was. I might speak of David, etc.

As for the other [cause], we have a most notable example to prove it, of a most notorious reprobate and hypocrite as ever was, who had so secretly and subtly couched his hypocrisy that all the world could not have found it out, for he was among the Twelve: Judas, the disciple of Christ, a minister of the Word, one who wrought miracles with the rest of the disciples, the purse bearer, one that (it seemed) He trusted unto; and yet, his tratorism[15] and hypocrisy was such that for the covetousness of gaining a few silver plates[16] he betrayed his Master and Lord, Christ Jesus (Matt. 27). And so, for gaining worldly pelf,[17] he lost eternal life and ended miserably his wretched life.

Now, therefore, we see that Christ suffered dearly that punishment due to mankind, which they had deserved for their own sins, and also perfectly kept the law, that by His keeping thereof, through faith, they might by imputation be said to fulfill the former, adding their endeavor thereunto, and that He died that He might free all His children from the curse and malediction of death, so that whereas to the wicked it is most miserable and the beginning of eternal punishment, to them it is made most comfortable, even the beginning of joy and heavenly felicity.

The Persons for Whom Christ Died[18]

Now, we come to speak of the persons who are saved, which by this text seems to be general. Also, many other places [affirm] His blood is shed for all. And His mercy is mentioned: "He would not the death of one sinner…" [Ezek. 18:23]. [But] another place of Scripture has "Many are called but few chosen" [Matt. 22:14]. "He will set the sheep on his right hand, and the goats on his left hand" [Matt. 25:33]. And, therefore, we see the Scripture says a controversy against itself: while one speaks general and another particular.

---

15. *Tratorism*: spirit of betrayal.
16. *Plates*: coins.
17. *Pelf*: money that is gained in a dishonest way.
18. The MS introduces this section with the quotation "For us."

But we must know that Christ Jesus has not redeemed all persons in general with His precious blood, but only such and so many as His father has of eternal decree elected to salvation before the foundation of the earth was laid, and in time called to the light of His glorious gospel. Proof of it [is found in] John 16, where [is] our Savior's holy prayer, made to His Father a little before His deprehension.[19] He prays, saying, "Father, I pray not for all, but those only which thou hast given me" [John 17:9]. The syllogistical argument here out arises:

> Those which Christ prayed for, He paid for.
> But He prayed not for all.
> Therefore, He paid not for all.

Furthermore, to prove the same, we may gather it from the essential differences of the Godhead. (1) Internal, concerning the deity: the Father [is] unbegotten, the Son begotten, the Holy Spirit proceeding from them both. (2) External, in regard of every proper work of the person. The work of creation [is] proper to the Father, the work of redemption to the Son, [and the work] of sanctification to the Holy Spirit. Now, in respect of every several work, as namely in respect of redemption, it cannot be called a redemption but in regard of some who are in bondage.

Again, a great inconvenience would ensue if it were true that Christ redeemed all or, at least wise, died for all, for then everyone who is saved might have thanked himself for his salvation and not Christ, since He did as much for the most vile and ungodly person as He did for him.

We will clear it by a comparison. As truly as Adam did naturally receive all, and made them culpable of damnation, to whom he was a root unto, even so truly Christ saves all who are ingrafted into Him—that is to say, so many, and no more, as He is a root unto. And abiding in the lively root, Christ, there cannot possibly be any condemnation; but all those branches bearing out of the stock shall have sap. But those that grow and remain in the old stock [of] Adam, all whom he nourishes and is a root unto, are blighted and dead branches, apt to [bear] no fruit, but only serve for the fire. For such boughs, for such dead sprigs,[20] I mean such reprobates and obstinate persons; Christ shed not His blood to save them.

But it seems to be a hard case that God will not suffer His Son to die for all, that is, that His death should not be of meritorious sufficiency for all. Concerning such secrets, we must not be too curious in searching into God's works, but so much as His Word declares of them. Yet, for the answering hereof, we must

---

19. *Deprehension*: arrest.
20. *Sprig*: twig or stem.

know that the intent of God was to have none saved but those whom in His eternal wisdom and counsel He had from all eternity elected. And so, He did not elect all, but some, because He knew everything and the state and condition of every man before he was conceived. And, therefore, He knowing who will believe and who will not, He ordained a punishment for His Son that should be sufficient to answer the deserts[21] of all the elect and no more. And, therefore, not one sinner more, which He has not died for, can be saved. Foolish and frivolous, vain and vacant, is that common proverb: *One drop of Christ's blood is able to save one thousand worlds.* If it were so, why was He not slain,[22] or why did He suffer such great torments as He did?

And this saying is utterly false, for if He had died for all sinners, good and bad, He must of necessity have suffered greater tortures than He did. Again, if He had suffered for all, He might very well argue[23] His Father of injustice toward Him, to require more punishment at His hand than was needful. For not one drop of His blood shall be lost, but it shall be available and effectual to those for whom it was shed. Neither is one drop shed in vain, but [that] it shall effect His proper working to the salvation of him or them whom, [by] God's unsearchable knowledge, are appointed thus. And so, a measurable punishment is inflicted upon Him.

Let us not perversely censure God, but refer all things to His love and His knowledge, and not dispute why He refuses some and chooses [others] but rather acknowledge His mercy and love to us above all others, and give Him greater thanks, and be careful to walk before Him in obedience, in that He vouchsafes to receive us, passing over many worthier than ourselves. Let us, therefore, walking in the light, walk worthy of that light, lest He come and remove the candlestick out of [its] place, lest He takes away the means from us, by reason of our ingratitude. For if He had saved all people, where had been vessel of glory? Where had been His justice made manifest? And, therefore, He ordains some to be vessels of wrath and some of honor, and yet both so set for His glory. As an earthly prince has both vessels for the table, which are vessels of honor, and he has other vessels for his chamber and for a base use, and yet both do serve for the setting forth of the prince's dignity, so our God will be honored not only by the righteous but the wicked. Even the devils in hell shall be instruments of His glory in justice.

---

21. *Deserts*: deserved punishment.

22. This seems to be a double negative, likely a typographical error on the part of the transcriber.

23. *Argue*: accuse.

But here seems to be a breach[24] in the chain. All the evangelists, although they do largely entreat of the death and burial of Christ, in what tomb and where it was that He was laid in, etc., but there is no mention made of His descension[25] into hell as our creed seems to import, which shows that He descended not locally into hell (as the papists affirm and there out the damnable doctrine of purgatory) but that by hell is meant the hellish torment and extreme anguish suffered.

---

24. *Breach*: gap, break, rupture.
25. *Descension*: descent.

Romans 4:25

(Sermon 2)

"And is risen again for our justification…"

Now comes to be considered the resurrection of Christ, wherein I pretermit[1] severally to speak of the circumstances which are themselves [the] same with the former, and because that brevity requires haste, and the selfsame offer themselves again, it shall be more necessary to prove.

First, we must recount the text which seems to make a breach in the Scripture, in that it is said He rose again for our justification, whereas we are justified by His death properly. And this seems to be against the whole tenor of the Scriptures. We must consider two things in Christ whereby we are justified: (1) His passion, the effect whereof is His satisfaction, [and] (2) the merit and efficacy of His passion, which is intercession. He does the one as a priest [and] the other as a mediator.

The satisfaction must be applied to God, when He both fulfilled the law for us and also for our sins suffered death to this end, that He might bring us into favor with God again, and so by His death satisfying God ensure we come to have access to God the Father and are through Christ justified before God by faith.

By the merit and efficacy of His passion, whereby He prays to the Father that all the actions He did, whether in His life in fulfilling the law or in death for our sins, might be ascribed and imputed to our justification. And this for the understanding of the text: that all the things He did as a Savior for man—birth, miracles, doctrines, death, resurrection, and ascension—might be imputed to their justification.

The Necessity of Christ's Resurrection

Now, let us come to the necessity of His resurrection and see what comfort it will bring to our souls. First, His resurrection was needful in regard of Himself as He was man. For if He had not been, it might have been thought He had not been the Messiah and true Savior of the world and had been overcome by death. For, seeing all His lifetime He was so bare and contemptible in person,

---

1. *Pretermit*: omit.

much more it might have been affirmed of Him to be not the true Messiah. And, for this cause, by rising out of the grave the third day, by the power of His body, He revealed and manifested Himself to be the Redeemer and one of an extraordinary office. Second, it was necessary that He should arise in regard of His Godhead. For hereby He sufficiently showed Himself to be the only begotten Son of God, that as the people said, "Did ever any man open the eyes of the blind?" (John 9), so it might be said again, "Did ever any man arise out of the grave?" And so, by coming out of the grave, rolling away the stone from the tomb by the strength of His body, it might be credibly reported, "Truly, this is God."

There is a threefold resurrection. When a man rises by the power of:

his own body			Christ		time past
God a Judge	} which is	{	the wicked	}	
Christ a Redeemer			the godly		to come

The first is past, which was proper to Christ alone, who (as I said) by the power of His body rose out of the grave.

The wicked, etc., shall arise from the earth by the power of God, a Judge and Avenger. For He will suddenly with the sound of [a] trump raise up their bodies to their former vigor and beauty to receive the fearful doom and sentence pronounced: "Depart ye cursed…" [Matt. 25:41]. Woeful and accursed shall their rising be.

The righteous shall[2] arise also by a power, but it is by the virtue of their elder brother, Christ Jesus. Their resurrection shall be comfortable, seeing they have their Savior to be their Judge to acquit and free them from all ill by His death, shed blood, and resurrection, and to make them partakers of His kingdom, to be heirs with Him of His glory and kingdom. Then shall He wipe away all tears from their eyes and crown them with endless glory.

Now we have seen how needful Christ's resurrection is:

		Himself in His	{	1 Godhood
In regard of	{			2 manhood
		us His members		

That by His resurrection we may assure ourselves that we shall rise with Him (as immediately before) follows.

---

2. Original: that.

The End of Christ's Resurrection

Now, seeing we have seen the necessity, let us see the ends of His resurrection.

Christ rose again for { Himself to glorify His { 1. Godhead / 2. manhood } / the commodity of His members { 3. generally / 4. particularly }

In regard of His manhood, that it might be glorious, which before throughout all His life was bare and humble, so that all His life was nothing but a death (as it were) and a humiliation of His person until His death, and then was He in that most base estate. But in His resurrection, in the very instant thereof, He became glorious in majesty which He was forced to hold their eyes, that they should not see the glory of His person, then all the former weaknesses and frailties were put off from Him, then His body took strength upward in bliss and agility in the air, to mount up into heaven to God His Father.[3]

In regard of His Godhead, that He might be again with the majesty and strength of the Godhead which was before eclipsed by reason of the manifold infirmities of His manhood.

The second end is in regard of us, His true members of one body, He Himself being the head; lively branches of one tree, He being the root; that as He is ascended, so all His are ascended already with Him, though not substantially and bodily yet spiritually; that being members beneath are united to Him, the head above. For although in body they live in earth yet their conversation[4] is in heaven. A man who swims has his head and neck above the water, and all the other parts beneath, yet these members beneath the water have the same agility which the head has in swimming. As the head goes forward, so do all the other parts of the body. So Christians, the members, have the virtue of the resurrection of Christ, who is above, and do arise with Him by mortifying and crucifying their sins and daily rising to newness of life.

[Christ rose again] in regards of every particular member, and that in these respects. First, that He might impute the virtue or fruits of His resurrection, namely, His sanctification, to every one of His members in particular. Second, that as sure as Christ overcame death, hell, and damnation for sinners, so surely it might be sealed to the soul of every Christian, that death, hell, and damnation eternally shall have no power over them. Third, that every true Christian might be infallibly persuaded of his resurrection, which the Sadducees and like enemies scoffed at, and the apostle does by many forcible arguments persuade

---

3. In the margin: *Credere surcum* ("believe thoroughly").
4. *Conversation*: fellowship.

(1 Cor. 15). God labored in the law to persuade His people of the certainty thereof and by the ceremony of the scapegoat (Lev. 16:8), which should be laid in the wood and presently run away from the altar into the forest, never any man seeing him, signifying that God's elect shall rise again by the virtue and power of Christ's resurrection, who overcame death and is ascended into heaven to prepare a place for them.

So the people came to Elisha, saying, "Knowest thou not that thy master shall be taken from thee this day?" (2 Kings 2:5). "Yea, I know, hold ye your peace." [He] signified by his affirmative speech that he had a sure faith in the promised seed, that he also should at last arise by the sight of his master's ascension.

Application

Now we are to make some use and application of this doctrine of Christ's resurrection.

First, the resurrection of Christ ought to make us have a progress in our souls answerable to the same. He has overcome death and has raised His body out of His grave; much more ought we to be stirred up to raise our souls up from sin to holiness of life, putting off [the] old Adam and putting on the new man, Christ Jesus (as the apostle says [Eph. 4:24; Col. 3:10]), washing away the corruption of the flesh and putting on the armor of faith. For the dead bones of Elisha, being buried, awoke up, and prophesied, when the bones of a man were cast into the same grave.[5] Much more ought our dull minds be stirred up to a holy life. Shall the apostles, men of inferior knowledge, be able to convince at one sermon one thousand souls [Acts 2:41], and shall not ministers now by greater knowledge and many privileges be able to raise up into a holy life? Can they raise up the lame to feet, the blind to sight, the dead to life, and shall not ministers now be able to raise up the dead in soul to the light by the glorious gospel?

Second, another lesson or use is the same which the apostle Paul teaches: "If Christ be risen seek the things that are above" [Col. 3:1] and "not to walk any longer in darkness" [Eph. 5:8]. If our minds are full of vain thoughts, our mouths of fruitless speeches, and our hands full of wicked actions, it is a sign that as yet we have not tasted of the sweetness and comfort of His resurrection. Therefore, if we reap profit by the resurrection of our Savior, we shall find ourselves somewhat prone and ready in spirit to walk as becomes Christians in our several callings. In the law, every anointing had a special spiritual grace answerable unto the function and office whereto he was anointed, resembled

---

5. Perkins (or the transcriber) seems to have confused the details of this story. It was the dead man (not Elisha) who arose from the grave (2 Kings 13:21).

by the pouring of the oil, as David when he was taken from the sheep to be anointed king. It taught him to bear a noble and princelike mind. Even so, Samuel, the anointing of him as prophet, taught him to be distracted from all earthly matters and walk as a true messenger of God.

Even so ought every man in his vocation, whatsoever it be, to behave himself so in the same that it may as means to provoke him to set forth God's glory, which may be done in two manner of ways. (1) If he makes the same the means to his living and in the same show his love to God by that love and compassion he shows to his neighbor. (2) If he makes all the several actions thereof to be means to raise him up to higher cogitations,[6] as the husbandman, whose sowing of the corn into the good ground resembles that sowing of God's Word into man's fleshly heart (to take root and bring forth fruit) by the minister, etc.

And so shall we take profit from Christ's resurrection.

---

6. *Cogitations*: thoughts.

Two sermons preached of Master W. Perkins concerning prayer
delivered in manner of catechism upon the holy days,
the one preached upon Saint Luke's day,
the other upon Saint Andrew's day
in the year 1595. Gathered from him by James Tomlin.

Sermons preached at Cambridge in St. Andrew's Church by Master Perkins
taken out of the epistle of the holy Apostle Jude, verses 3 & 4.[1]

"He that will save his life shall lose it, & he that
loseth it for my sake shall save it"
(Matthew 10:[39]).

Written by James Tomlin

---

1. The MS title page lists verses 2, 3, and 4, but 4 is crossed out. It appears that Tomlin ought to have crossed out 2 since no sermons on that verse appear in his book.

<h1 style="text-align:center">Jude 3</h1>

(Sermon 1)

Then if it be a precious treasure, then we must be "swift to hear," as the apostle James says, and "slow to wrath."[2] We must cheerfully hear the same and be very greedy to receive the prize and profit thereof.

Again, if it be a treasure, we must hide it in our hearts, for a treasure, we know, is not fit to be cast up and down, but it must have a fit place to be hid in, and the place and secret chamber and coffer wherein this treasure must be [is] in our hearts, so that we are happy if we can say with David, "I have hid thy word in my heart that I might not sin against thee" (Ps. 119).[3]

We shall hide [it] in our heart by these three means: (1) when we have a care to embrace it and hear it preached, (2) [when we] remember it daily to lay it up and meditate on it, [and] (3) when we apply all our affections to it and put in practice in our lives and conversations.

If it be a treasure, it must bring true honor and delight, prosperity, riches; even so does this treasure. While the ark was in the house of Obed-Edom, he prospered, and all his family.[4] To this end, he does exhort the paint[ing of] wisdom before our eyes, which wisdom is nothing but the Word of God, saying, "It is better than gold, or precious stone" (Prov. 3:14). And truly this treasure makes this our land flow over with prosperity and peace, for forty years of true faith is the cause of so many heavenly, spiritual, earthly, and temporal blessings. Let us, therefore, having the same, keep it secretly in our hearts, that our profit and joy (as the prophet says [in] Psalm 4)[5] might be full. Then shall our wealth still increase.

Now, the second point is this, namely, that the saints only are keep[er]s of this faith. First, [it] is a notable mark to know that true church of God by. And by this we may discern that true church from the counterfeit, [namely], that the true servants of God they have their part chiefly and principally in this treasure of God their Father. This was the chiefest honor of the Jews above the Gentiles, above all other nations, which they kept: the ark, the law, the statutes,

---

2. James 1:19.
3. Verse 11.
4. 2 Sam. 6:11.
5. Verses 6–8.

the excellent treasures of God (Rom. 3).[6] So, this is now our credit, our joy, our comfort, our honor. "Come to the tents of the shepherds, my spouse, my love, where I am" (Song 1:7), says the bridegroom Christ Jesus to His sister and spouse, the church. And by this we maintain the wholesome doctrine of the prophets and apostles in very substance. So are we keepers of the faith.

Second, in that we are keepers of this heavenly treasure, we must learn two doctrines. First, to praise and magnify the name of God, acknowledging His fatherly love to us above all other nations. "He hath not dealt so with every nation."[7] Second, it stands us upon (seeing we are stewards and keep[er]s of the treasure) to be so diligent in keeping and using the same, that we may never be displaced, and others put in our room. For that is the office of a keeper, to be daily circumspect and daily exercised in keeping the same.

"Once given to the saints." God gives His faith once. This "once" may be understood two ways. First, once for all, that He never needs to give it any more to the saints, wherein we learn divers necessary and wholesome instructions. The chief whereof is that there is no alteration of the divine words of God, and that all the visions, all the precepts and traditions of man in matters of religion, more than the Word of God has or allows, are mere superstition and idolatry, yea are all vain and frivolous additions of the brain of man. And to such there is heavy sentence pronounced: "Whosoever shall add anything, etc." (Rev. 22).[8] Wherein we see the pureness and perfection of the Word of God in its own nature, but which we are so blockish that we cannot well understand the same.

Again, it may be understood "once for all" in regard of God's [grace],[9] that that it being once lost it will never be received again (Heb. 6).[10] But it is not meant of some frailness and weakness whereby man may revolt from the same for a time and give occasion of offense, but of such revolting and backsliding as is of willful stubbornness and unbelief, whereby we make a shipwreck of faith.

First, this serves, therefore, to admonish us to take heed of apostasy and backsliding from this faith which now we embrace, for this is so dangerous that, once it being lost, it can never be recovered again.

Second, not only so, but also to take heed even of the least declination and sliding in religion, which is a means of the former, and a first step and degree to apostasy.

---

6. Verse 2. See also Rom. 9:4–5.
7. Ps. 147:20. The MS erroneously cites Psalm 139.
8. Verse 18.
9. The MS reads "man."
10. Verses 4–6.

Third, we are forewarned [in] 2 Peter 2 not to call in question and deliberate and doubt of the ground of our religion, but hold it steadfastly.[11] James says, "A wavering minded man, (meaning [in] matters of religion) is as a ship tossed up and down with waves."[12] And the doubt and deliberation concerning the grounds of our religion is dangerous and is a second step to apostasy.

Fourth, we are charged to be continually exercised in the Scriptures, that we may become strong men in Christ, that no illusions, no persuasions of the enemy, the papists, or anything for life and death may be able to remove us from the faith once received. And, therefore, "Search the Scriptures," says Christ (John 5).[13] "His delight is the law of the Lord and thus is he exercised day and night," which is continually said the Psalms (Ps. 1).[14] This is a means to be freed from the former evils.

The third point of the true church is to fight manfully for the faith once received. The persons that fight are the saints: all Christians in general. The battle that they must fight is specifically not by sword, bill,[15] and mattock,[16] but by the shield of faith, the helmet and buckler of constancy.[17] The enemies against whom [they must fight] are the wicked deceivers spoken in the next verse and in our times antichrists.

The manner how we must fight is diverse.

We must fight by	⎧	doctrine	1
	⎨	confession	2
	⎩	example	3
		prayer	4

First, by doctrine or obedience, everyone in his calling and place is a prophet, [and] is commanded to teach not only those committed to his charge, as children and his family, but among others [to] teach and defend the grounds of religion against whosoever. "Your sons and daughters shall prophesy" (Joel 2).[18] And this belongs principally to masters and superiors. Their servants must teach their masters also in the Word of life.

Second, one must confess and profess the true faith always before all persons and in all places. "He that is ashamed of me (says Christ) before men, him

---

11. Verse 21.
12. James 1:6.
13. Verse 39.
14. Verse 2.
15. *Bill*: a polearm weapon, like a halberd.
16. *Mattock*: a hand tool, like a pickaxe.
17. Eph. 6:16–17.
18. Verse 28.

will I be ashamed of in the kingdom of heaven."[19] "Hold out (says Paul) your faith before all persons in humility of heart."[20] And this confession is needful, if place so requires, in the people of God that they must not be afraid to profess the truth before princes, before tyrants. "I will confess your name before kings. I will sing of thee among the nations," says David (Ps. 57).[21]

Third, we must fight for the maintenance of our religion by prayer. "Pray to the Father (says Christ to His disciples and so to all Christians) that he will thrust forth laborers into the harvest" (Matt. 11).[22]

Fourth, we must not only profess ourselves to be Christians, but we manifest the same by our good example and pattern of life, "that men seeing our good works (may be more encouraged, etc.) and glorify our Father who is in heaven."[23] "That we may shine as stars in the sky."[24] Then shall our doctrine and manner and conversation of life be acceptable to God and liked and praised of others.

Let us, therefore, fight with Rome and antichrists whosoever for the maintenance of the pure treasure of God's truth. Let the death hold it out, that we may be accounted good stewards.

---

19. Luke 9:26.
20. Phil. 2:16.
21. Verse 9.
22. Matt. 9:38.
23. Matt. 5:16.
24. Phil. 2:15.

Jude 4

(Sermon 2)

"For there are certain men crept in[1] which were before of old ordained to this condemnation:[2] ungodly men they are,[3] which turn the grace of our God into wantonness,[4] and deny God the one Lord and our Lord Jesus"[5] (Jude 4).[6]

In this verse is propounded the whole sum of the epistle, wherein he confirms his exhortation in the former verse by a reason taken from the condition of the adversary against whom they should fight.

And this concerns us now as well as yourselves to whom Jude wrote in those days, for now there are secret enemies without, like men going among the sheep in lamb's clothing, but within are ravening wolves seeking cunningly and secretly to undermine the true doctrine and religion which here in England we profess.

The reason is set forth by a description of these men.

They are described by their	hypocrisy: "certain men crept in"	1
	eternal condition, "ordained to this, etc."	2
	religion, "ungodly men they are"	3
	doctrine, "turn the grace of God, etc."	4
	lives, "deny the Lord God and our Lord, etc."	5

The First Point

First, their hypocrisy is seen in this, that they cunningly winded themselves into the fellowship of God's people, making a show of zeal to God, when thereby they sought nothing else but [to] undermine and (if it could be possible) to deface the same.

Under their hypocrisy here lays two things to their charge: first, their dissimulation; second, their usurpation. Their dissimulation in that they made a show of religion, under a color of society, with the righteous, to overthrow the same (Matt. 13:25).

---

1. In the margin: Hypocrisy.
2. In the margin: Their estate.
3. In the margin: Their religion.
4. In the margin: Their doctrine.
5. In the margin: Their lives.
6. The MS erroneously labels this sermon as "Jude 3."

Wherein we see the crafti[ness] of Satan together with his malice, that he raises up enemies of all sorts, as in the primitive church, <...>, atheists, wicked men mingled with the godly that he might overthrow their faith (this is <...> and will be not the end of the word), his subtleness and timing joined together with his malice against the righteous.

But let us not be offended when we see this in the true church of God, that the wicked are here mingled with the godly, for it must be so in this life in the church militant, which by daily exercise and daily strife, by doctrine and life, which I said before, the faith of His people might be put in use for their trial. And we must know this, that the wicked persons and seducers are nothing else but instruments the devil uses to supplant true religion. Although the papists affirm that they be members of church, they be members of Satan, dead members annoying all the whole body.

Again, they set down by their hypocrisy, usurping of office, and function of the ministry, they thrust themselves into public government, and teaching of the church, and so they pester and fill the church with a most damnable doctrine, giving instead of wine, vinegar to the people; instead of nutmeg, gall; instead of honey, poison; and so they think by bring[ing] strife in the church, to overturn the whole ground of pure religion. Mark herein a further degree of Satan's subtlety, thinking if he can dissolve the head, the whole body will be dead. And, therefore, in setting over them in authority such seducers they will quickly be led away unto error, usurping their authority, thrusting themselves into the bosom of the church without any calling thereunto, which none can lawfully do but those that are called unto the ministry. And so, no calling, no preaching, and that for these reasons.

First, because the minister is not his own, but the messenger of God, and an ambassador must come in the name of his prince, so must God's ambassadors. And how should they go in the name of their prince, the high and mighty God, to take upon them such a weighty office unless they be sent and are made with gifts and graces answerable thereto?

Second, he that teaches publicly must defend what he teaches and, therefore, he must pray to God for the assistance of His Spirit, which none can presume to crave, neither can he have any assurance in his conscience that he shall obtain, unless he is called unto that weighty office.

Third, the people must account him as God's own messenger, and that the word which he speaks is from God, which they cannot do unless they acknowledge that he has a calling thereto. Neither is he God's messenger if he has no calling thereto.

Therefore, to know who are usurpers of high offices, civil and ecclesiastical, which creep into the office, they are these sorts: (1) they that have no calling thereunto, (2) they that procure it by friendship, [and] (3) [they that procure it] by money.

All these and most of this sort are said to creep into their office, and they are such as commonly by their doctrine or their lives do annoy God's flock.

The Second Point

Their eternal estate and condition before God: "which were of old ordained to this condemnation."

The plain meaning hereof is this: which were before all times before the foundation of the earth was laid registers billed or enrolled to this judgment, namely, to trouble the church and so consequently to procure their own damnation.

In these words is set down the eternal estate of those men, that they are written in God's book [and] what manner of men they should be. To prove this the Scripture is plentiful. (1) There are some that be books of the providence of God, as says the psalmist, "In thy book were all things written of thee which were in time accomplished" (Ps. 139). (2) Other books that the Scripture mentions which be books of God's judgments (Dan. 9; Rev. 22).[7] (3) There are some called books of records, or books of men's names (Phil. 4:3). Our Savior said, "Rejoice rather that your names are written in the books of life" (Luke 10).[8]

But we must not imagine that there are any material books wherein He should inscribe with pen and ink, but as in all the course of the Scripture, the Holy Spirit speaks metaphorically according to our sense, as when He says, "The Lord walked in the garden at the cool of the day" (Gen. 6),[9] and in the delivering of the Israelites from the bondage in Egypt "with a mighty hand and an outstretched arm."[10] And in Exodus, Moses saw His back part, as though God was a man like us in substance and matter.[11] But by these metaphors, taken from man, our dull and senseless nature may be more effectually drawn to consideration of the thing that is spoken of.

Then, the lesson we learn out of this [is] God's knowledge and understanding of all things indicating and disposing thereof, which the Scripture calls by the name of a steward who writes all things in a book are many.

First, we learn that in regard of God there is no chance, fate, or fortune (as the heathen <...> on) but everything is done by His will. And this is the

---

7. These are erroneous Scripture references. The intended references appear to be Daniel 7:9–10 and Revelation 20:12. Cf. Perkins, *Jude*, 4:96.

8. Verse 20.

9. The Scripture reference is erroneous. Genesis 3:8 was intended.

10. Deut. 4:34, 5:15, 7:19, etc.

11. Ex. 33:23.

foolishness of man, that when anything good or ill come to them, the cause whereof is hidden from, they ascribe it presently to fortune and never look up to God that sent the same.

Second, there is nothing [that] comes to pass but by the will and ordination of God. Yea, even that which is done against His will, yet it is His will that it should be so.[12] So it is true He wills the thing that is evil, and yet He wills it not, for He wills not the action or thing itself, but He wills the being thereof.[13]

Here we are to consider a little a special point of religion concerning election and reprobation, that God has from the beginning of the world ordained some to be vessels [of] wrath and some to be vessels of honor. Concerning eternal reprobation, we find it proved by the Scripture in many places. "God hath not ordained you to wrath" (1 Peter 3:8).[14] Romans 1:28; 9:22; 2 Thessalonians 2:12; 1 Timothy 2:20;[15] 2 Peter 2:12. If in the foresaid place of Paul (Rom. 9:22), where God is compared to a potter who makes some vessels of the selfsame mold to be vile and contemptable for dishonor, others to be vessels meet for the table, even so says He, "I have loved Jacob and hated Esau," that is, "in My everlasting decree and counsel."

Objection. Then, if it be so that God does from all eternity refuse some as well as choose some others, then He deals unjustly in that simply He ordains some to salvation and others to damnation absolutely.

Answer. We must not adjudicate and prescribe any justice or injustice to our Creator. "Shall we, the vessel, say to the potter, 'why hast thou made me thus?'"[16] Because that our judgments are altogether corrupt, we must give care to the will of God. For He, being high and mighty, and all the scope of salvation and reprobation in His knowledge, therefore He knowing what their estate will be before they be conceived, and seeing He is not the cause thereof anyway, how should it be accorded injustice in Him?

Further, secondly, God refuses men in order. He observes degrees. He vouchsafes His grace to all, but He vouchsafes the riches of His grace to some. And in that regard, He passes by some part of mankind and leaves them to themselves in His justice, and then they sin, and then consequently for sin their condemnation is just. For He ordains not condemnation simply, but *præcedente causa*,[17] and therefore sin before is not the cause of damnation. And so,

---

12. In the margin: Objection.
13. In the margin: Answer.
14. The correct reference is 1 Thessalonians 5:9.
15. The intended reference appears to be 2 Timothy 2:20.
16. Rom. 9:20.
17. *Præcedente causa* (Latin): antecedent cause.

God, being the Creator and Potter, who will argue[18] Him of injustice in doing with His own what He will?

Then, we must make a double use of the same. First, we are taught to humble ourselves under the hand of God and go on in the course of our salvation with fear and trembling as the apostle says, "Be [not high minded but fear]" (Rom. 11).[19] Secondly, we must not be offended when we hear or see the gospel of Christ oppugned and resisted by the wicked, because they all are not appointed to be the heirs of salvation with Christ.

Objection. But again, this seems to breed security in the hearts of man. If election and reprobation of everyone is set down by God before their conception, then it may seem hard on God's side. They may say that God is the cause thereof, and if a man ever so strive in the way of religion, if he be ordained to destruction, all is nothing, and if a man is ever so lewd, if he be willed to salvation, he shall be saved.

Answer. I deny that, for (firstly) it is not possible that the godly should be at all times so void of God's Spirit to be so vain and wicked as once to think of any such thing; although their frailties often break forth, yet [they] have the power by God's Spirit with the same to arise again. But the wicked are contrarily so prone to wickedness only, it is a death to them to do good because they have not the Spirit of sanctification which works faith in them, as the godly have. And, therefore, without the Spirit, and without faith wrought in them by the Spirit, they cannot possibly have any sense of God's love to them, and so they cannot follow that which is acceptable. And thereupon they fall into sin, and so consequently for sin they are condemned. So, the one is as naturally prone to sin, as the other is by God's Spirit to holiness.

Secondly, again (to make it more clear and to confound those papists that would have God to be the cause of the salvation and damnation of all) it cannot be so, for God places all in a particular church, where His Word, will, and sacraments are indifferently offered to all. All are made partakers of His grace. They may take the water and refuse the fire, they may believe and be saved, [or] they may be obstinate and condemned. Now then, God offering His grace to all, He would not the death of the sinner. And in another place, "O, that my people would have obeyed my voice. All my prophets have I sent to turn them to me but they would not."[20] And in another place, this is the speech of the Israelites to God's prophet: "We will not walk in thy ways; we will not come into it" (Jer. 5).[21] Now, if man will not receive God's grace when it is offered unto

---

18. I.e., accuse.

19. Verse 20.

20. In the margin: Psalm 81.

21. The correct reference is Jeremiah 6:16.

him, the fault is in himself, and who will say otherwise but that he is worthy of his condemnation? Offer a sick man health, and if he would[22] not gladly receive the means being offered, he is worthy to be sick still. Alas, we are all sick of one disease. Shall we despise to be saved? Shall we refuse to be partakers of health by the publishing of the gospel? When Christ cried, "Come to me you that are weary laden, I will ease you,"[23] will we not come? We are worthy by our judgment to have our burden redoubled upon us if we refuse such comfortable tidings.

Third, and here appears the wisdom of the Holy Spirit in that He shows men as well of destruction as salvation to deter and drive them from sin. For if salvation should be made so general abounding to all, and yet God should be full of mercy, where should then His justice appear? So, He must be a God of justice as well as of mercy, and His justice must also be manifested to keep the godly in awe and to <…> them from sin, as also if it will profit no way <…> to make the wicked inexcusable, who neither will be bended to obedience with mercy, nor yet by justice [be] deterred from sin. And, therefore, He tells them of their condition.

"Of old times," which is before the foundation of heaven and earth were laid. Now the proper and true cause of God's decrees is not of the creature, but of Himself, because His counsel was before the creature was made when His eternal counsel has registered every man's estate before the world was made. "I have loved Jacob and hated Esau" (Rom. 9:13),[24] namely, before they were conceived. He tells them that they are chosen in God to be heirs with Him together with His Son of His glory (Eph. 1).[25] And so much briefly concerning this doctrine in which occasion offered itself to our meditation in this text.

The Third Point

The third reason is taken from their religion, or rather their want of religion, in these words, "ungodly men they are."

Ungodliness is a sin much spoken of but not so well known. Therefore, we will set it down as briefly but substantially as we can. It is a grievous sin, a capital offense, a mother sin of all, even of those seven deadly sins, as the papists and also the old ethnics[26] as Horace, etc., have averred[27] of. It is grounded and rooted in the bottom of the heart, so it is a secret sin, because it is not discerned

---

22. In the MS, the term "would" is underlined and "will" is written above it.
23. Matt. 11:28.
24. The original erroneously cited verse 11.
25. Verse 11.
26. Ethnics: ethicists.
27. In the margin: "1. book of epistle 1. ep."

of man, such a hypocritical and subtle sin it is. It is a spiritual sin, for it is not only against the second table but principally against the first. It respects God and not man, for it is such a sin that it seeks to rob God of His true honor and worship due to Him.

Ungodliness has three main properties: (1) it denies the honor due unto God, (2) it gives that which is due to God to others, and (3) it gives God due honor but not in a due manner.

For the first, it causes the ungodly men by not acknowledging God and the Godhead, which is to deny His excellent attributes as mercy, justice, wisdom, and providence, when occasion is offered. "The fool has said in his heart there is no god" (Ps. 14:1), that is, the wicked who in their heart acknowledge not the grace and providence of God. The second way is by not subjecting his conscience, heart, will, and affections to the written Word of God. Such as are disobedient and study such as say, "We will not walk in your ways, depart from us" (Job 21:14). We will not suffer every will to be yoked to God's law, *libertas quoniam placam*. We will live as we list. The Jews say, "We will not have this man to rule over us" (Luke 19). But says Christ, "Bring these my enemies (such traitors) and slay them before my face."[28] Third, when they lift not up their [hearts] by invocation, neither pray to Him for such things they lack, or give some thanks for such benefits which they have received. This property is set upon three heads. "He calls not upon God, which is brutish and swinish behavior, to receive with all greediness the mast under the trees, and never look up from where they come" (Ps. 14:4). *Brutum*.[29]

The second property is to take away the honor of the Creator and give [it] to the creature, which is when a man displaces and dispossesses himself of God's honor and sets all his will and affection on some other adjunct. Therefore, the covetous man is called an idolater because he makes the eyes his god, and instead of Him sets up an idol in his heart. So says Paul, "Men in the last times shall be lovers of pleasures more than of God" (2 Tim. 3).[30] And this sin is far too manifest in these our days.

Third, the last kind is more secret than the two former, for all the sin lies hidden in the heart, and by the outward appearance they seem to be very religious but yet their hearts are full of sin. This is a hypocritical sin. It has godliness in show but not the power of godliness. They have a double-eye and a double-heart, and our Savior admonishes all His to beware of the leaven of the Pharisees, namely, their double-heart, and exhorts [us] to have a single eye.

---

28. Luke 19:14, 27.

29. *Brutum* (Latin): brutish.

30. Verses 1–5.

Therefore, ungodliness is an inborn sin of the heart which seeks to deprive God of His honor.[31] It is a dangerous sin, for if the heart be once tainted therewith, the whole body will sin when occasion is offered. This sin comes from the heart. The profane heart is the cause of this sin. The Jews knowing God would not know Him (Rom. 1).[32] Abraham said, "There is no fear of God in this place" (Gen. 13),[33] and consequently he thought that all manner of ungodliness reigned in that place. Now, that [un]godliness is a sin especially against [God], besides the testimonies, the notation or name thereof tells us plainly.

The use that we are to make of it is:

First, by how much more secret it is, by so much the more must we labor by prayer, and endeavor in ourselves daily to discern the same in ourselves, for it [is] a sin subject to all, even the godly in some manner. And when we have found it, to bewail the same, and crave pardon, and to pray for God's Spirit to aid us, that we might daily fight against it, to keep it under.

We are liars if we say this sin be not rife in these days, even among us professing Christianity. We may flatter ourselves that we follow some exercises, we are conversant in God's Word, we receive the sacraments, but what of it? Let us look to our lives; let us look into our hearts. For the political laws of the law bind us to outward obedience. Some never call themselves to account for their sin, but still lay in the cradle of security. Some are filled with the things of this world, neglecting their soul's health. Many are in subjection to the form of worship, but few to the substance. They cannot break[34] to have themselves and all their actions squared by God's law. So more need have we to beware this sin in ourselves and others.

Second, we must follow the rule of Saint Paul (1 Tim. 4), namely, to exercise ourselves no more in the works of darkness but to be clothed with the armor of light [and] to exercise our hearts in the duties of godliness by two means of ways.[35] First, we must prepare ourselves to make a good beginning and proceeding. Therefore, we must learn first to acknowledge God's providence over all things, whereunto knowledge must first be enjoined. The Gentiles, they knew not God, or they could not acknowledge the true God. And so consequently, instead of the true God, they worshipped idols. Then, where there is not knowledge, there is no acknowledgment; and where there is [no] confession, there is no godliness. Second, we must [worship] God in Spirit and truth

---

31. In the margin: The definition of godliness.
32. Verses 21, 24.
33. The intended reference is Genesis 20:11.
34. Bear?
35. Tomlin appears to conflate 1 Timothy 4:7 with Ephesians 5:11; 6:11–18.

as Christ says.[36] Romans 1, "To worship God in my spirit," says [this] chapter, [verse] 9,[37] [meaning] when a man by grace can worship God in soul and outward affection.

This inward worship of God stands in:
- faith, which respects God in His three most notable attributes, to acknowledge His
  - mercy
  - providence
  - presence
- actions of faith, which are two
  - subjection to God's
    - judgment
    - words
    - pleasure
  - Elevation of the heart to God by
    - prayer
    - thanksgiving

First, seeing we speak of God here contrary to the sin afore spoken of, in this inward worship which belongs to Him especially is twofold, namely, (1) faith [and] (2) the actions of faith.

Faith in God is chiefly divided into three heads. We must believe and be steadfastly assured of (1) His mercy in forgiving and forbearing us for ourselves; (2) His providence in His fatherly care and protection over us, even over our bodies in feeding and clothing us, etc.; [and] (3) His presence, wheresoever we be He sees us and whatsoever we do. He is ready, therefore, to hear us when we pray unto Him, and of this must we be always assured.

The first serves to comfort us and encourage us to ask pardon in the sight of our sins. His providence ought to move us to thanksgiving. His presence serves to comfort us in the good duties in our calling. Yet though we merit not, yet He sees us and forgets us not, but for His mercy's sake rewards us. Second, it serves to deter and provoke[38] us from sin to well doing, seeing he is everywhere always to see our doings. He is *altivides*,[39] He is θεός ἀπὸ τὸ θεείν[40] because He sees and rewards the wicked according to his evil.

Second, the actions of faith are twofold.

[First,] subjection, which is three[fold]. (1) A subjection to His judgments, which is when we by grace are subject before Him, in the sight of our sins accusing ourselves, and for Christ's sake craving pardon for the same. (2) A willing subjection of the heart and affection to the will of God in His written Word by obedience, when we do lay up to our profit the Word of God, the

---

36. The intended reference is John 4:24.

37. Verse 11.

38. In the margin: stir us up.

39. In the margin: One who sees from heaven.

40. In the margin: God (according to the Greeks), because He is so swift that He is in every place at once.

means of salvation, in our hearts, bringing forth the fruits thereof. (3) When we submit ourselves to God's pleasure. And this His pleasure concerning us is not known till the event of it, when we submit our wills to God's will in all things, though they be contrary to our wills and expectation, as Abraham (Gen. 12 and 22). And these be true examples of a humble subjection of a Christian.[41]

The second fruit of faith[42] is elevation: lifting up the heart to God to ask such as we need in body or soul, and to give Him thanks for the benefits we have received. And this is true worship due to God. This is true godliness.

The reasons why we should thus follow after godliness are principally three, set down by the apostle Saint Paul. (1) "Godliness is great gain" (1 Tim. 6).[43] If we will thrive here on earth and live an acceptable and a good life, if we will be rich and full of worldly wealth,[44] let us *ascultare pietatē*.[45] (2) "It has the promises of this life and a better life."[46] Because then if we follow after godliness, we shall not only be rich, but rich in God. We shall obtain His favor and love, which is better than riches, yea, and lastly everlasting felicity in Christ. (3) "Concerning the last judgment, when all things must be dissolved" (2 Peter 3).[47] Now, because we know not the hour of this dissolution, let us *colere pietatē*,[48] "be godly," and then shall we be taught to wait for His coming and then shall we live soberly and justly in this present evil world, to be heirs of an everlasting kingdom. Amen.

The Fourth Point

"Which turn the grace of our God into wantonness" [Jude 4]. This has two points: (1) the vice here condemned [and] (2) the virtue contrary to the vice commanded.

First, we must know the meaning of this word "grace." By it is understood the grace of God to salvation to every believer, namely, that gospel of Christ Jesus, because it is the doctrine of grace for the remission of sins by Christ, by which we are made heirs of glory.

Second, by the word "wantonness" is no[t] meant the particular sin, [but] a provocation to the lust of the flesh, the sum of incontinency (Rom. 7). But it

---

41. At the bottom of the page in the MS, the following is written around the torn corner: "*lacerata papyrus*." This is Latin for "torn paper."

42. I.e., the second action of faith. See above.

43. Verse 5.

44. In the margin: Follow after God and live.

45. *ascultare pietatē* (Latin): listen to piety.

46. This is a combination of 1 Timothy 4:8 and 6:6–7.

47. Verse 12.

48. *colere pietatē* (Latin): cultivate piety.

seems to be taken more generally, as namely a free liberty to sin against God when a man gives himself liberty and license to sin.[49]

Third, this vocable[50] "turn" signifies in the original very forcibly, as namely to displace the grace of God, to misconstrue the word and the doctrines of the whole Scripture according to their own fancies, so that it may be most pleasing to their lust.

As namely, seeing God, to the comfort and encouragement of His children, in well doing does make a large treatise, even whereof His mercy, and thereupon, seeing He is so merciful, these deceivers presume with confidence to give themselves liberty and will to sin against God, as some gathered from Paul's doctrine, "to do good that evil might come thereon" (Rom. 3:8).[51] Peter (from whom as by the doctrine and manner of phrase it appears Jude gathered this example) said as here, "Men under pretense of godliness crept in, teaching men to live according to their lusts" (2 Peter).[52]

And Christ's name has been generally used in the old ages. Simon Magus and his disciples taught men that they might lawfully commit fornication and adultery, which is most abominable. The Gnostics also, as Eusebius,[53] etc., taught the people to sin grossly against God, against the first and second table. And now, in these flourishing times of the gospel, this sin dies not, but is renewed again afresh, especially in [the following] sort of men.

First, the libertines of this age teach men to be enemies to the law of grace, because we are under grace (say they) and the law can take no hold of us. We are not so bound to keep the law but live as we list. We owe no obedience thereto, seeing Christ for us has fulfilled it.

Second, the Anabaptists who because they find it written in God's Word, "I will pour out my Spirit upon all flesh" (Joel 2),[54] "Plenty of grace shall be as long as the moon endures" (Ps. 92),[55] therefore they make the magistracy to be void and that there need be no oaths, etc. And thus, they play upon God's grace, presuming to give liberty to have all masters, whereas if this were not, there could be no society among us.

Third, the present Roman Church [first] is an enemy to Christian liberty, and they turn God's grace into wantonness. For God has given a gift to His

---

49. At the bottom of the page in the MS, the following is written around the torn corner: "*lacerataque charta.*" Latin: "torn paper."

50. *Vocable*: word.

51. In the margin: Christian liberty.

52. 2 Peter 2:18–19.

53. This should read "Eunomius," the fourth-century Arian. Tomlin has conflated Gnostics and Arians here.

54. Verse 28.

55. The intended reference is Psalm 72:7.

ministers for the profit of His church by the keys, and they add them as a means of profaneness and covetousness. For by that they set up a new priesthood and sacrifice. They offer every day sacrifice for the sins of the people. And so, they seek to abolish the sacrifice of Christ Jesus, who once for all offered His body for the ransom of many. Secondly, by the same he challenges rights over all nations. All princes and people must be in subjection to him. They must kneel down, and kiss his toes, and lead his horses in his progress. Thirdly, again (to pass many others) he makes the keys to be means of vice and filthiness, for thereby he sells pardon at their pleasure, and this their licentious liberty is most abominable.

Second, again, their religion is most wicked, for it serves wholly to nourish sin and uncleanness, and makes both carnal and sensible libertines. And all their service to God is but a bodily and corporal service, as (1) in fasting they must eat no flesh and white meat, but spiced wine, etc., they do account lawful, and of this sort is their ceremonial religion. (2) It makes men proud and insolent that they may by their good works merit salvation. (3) It makes them presumptuous, for they affirm that they have of nature free will to do of themselves what good they will by the light help of the Spirit, whereas the very will is of God. (4) That they can fully satisfy God's wrath by their own suffering for their sins, whereas indeed there is no name in heaven or earth whereby we can be saved but by Christ Jesus.[56] (5) Most notoriously, by their damnable doctrine, they say that all authority of life and death eternal is in the pope's hand, and that if they die, not having repented for their sins, they may go into purgatory, and therefore [by] a little bodily purification they may earn[57] eternal life. (6) The pope tolerates communion stews[58] and harlots, flat forbidden in the seventh commandment, and in all the law.[59] (8) Again, their religion makes a man, when he is ready to give up the ghost, despair that then they are ready to fly to God. For they doubt whether they shall be saved or not, whereas the godly, they are sure and certain of their salvation. And though when a Christian gave Machiavellian (a chief doctrine among the papists) counsel: flee to God to hope on Him, and cast away all merit, etc.[60] "Yea (said he desperately), you may tell me now of this, but tell not any of the rest of my brethren." And therefore, we see the very end of their doctrine, that desperately and despairingly

---

56. Acts 4:12.

57. In the margin: Obtain.

58. *Stew*: brothel.

59. There is no point 7.

60. *Machiavellian counsel*: a reference to Niccolò Machiavelli (1496–1527) and his unscrupulous approach to self-interested power politics, as primarily expressed in *The Prince* (1513). Perkins associates Machiavellian philosophy with Roman Catholicism and nominal Protestantism in several places in his works. See *Revelation 1–3*, RHB 4:518; *Discourse of Conscience*, RHB 8:50; *Cases of Conscience*, RHB 8:370; and *Treatise of Man's Imaginations*, RHB 9:205.

they end their lives. (9) A most palpable note whereby they turn God's grace into wantonness is this: that they bind certain degrees of men to continency to abstain from matrimony, and so some that have not the gift of continence fall into the most filthy sin, to the great dishonor of God.

The fourth sort of those that abuse the grace of God are among ourselves, and especially in five sorts of persons.

First, they that turn the decree of God concerning eternal election and reprobation into a sin saying that if they be ordained to salvation, they shall be [saved], and contrarily those that be predestinated to confusion shall be confused, and so they promise liberty of living unto themselves.

Second, youth who being young and lusty, strong of body, and wanton, do defer the time of their repentance till they be old, gathering from the place of Isaiah, "At what time soever a sinner repents, etc., he shall be saved."[61] And if they say, "If we can but an hour before our death repent it is sufficient," and so they promise themselves to sinning, abusing the long-suffering of God. The preacher says, "Because God defers his plagues they will go on in their wickedness,"[62] but cries to them, saying, "Remember thy creator in the days of thy youth" (Eccl. 12).[63]

A third sort are such prodigal epicures of this world, which are of [three] sorts. (1) Such as be too prodigal in spending the blessing of God on others, either for praise of men or in sign of love. (2) Such as spend away their substance in gaming. (3) Such as make away all by riotness[64] excess of wantonness in eating and drinking like filthy gluttons whose belly is their God, and so at length come to beggary or thievery.

Fourth, profane and worldly persons such as make no difference of days, and will indeed keep no Sabbath (I mean spiritual rest upon the Sabbath) but turn the Sabbath, which should be a day of holiness, to profaneness in speeches and actions by unlawful pleasures and delights.

Fifth, a last sort are such as mock the ground of religion: sin and wickedness such as the apostle speaks of, "who do evil that good may ensue."[65]

Those all, which we have spoken of, do most palpably translate the grace of God [and] make it the ground of their sin.

Thus far have we spoken of the vice forbidden. Now comes the second part of this point to be spoken, namely, the virtue that we must do contrary to the

---

61. The intended reference appears to be Ezekiel 33:14–16.
62. Eccl. 8:11.
63. Verse 1.
64. Riotous?
65. Rom. 3:8.

former vice. Which is that we make a good use of the grace of God any ways bestowed upon us, which we shall do if we apply it to a good end.

The end of God's grace is that we might be thankful to God for the same, which is proved by these reasons.

First, by the Scriptures, "He delivered us from our enemies, wherefore? That we might serve him in holiness all the days of our life."[66] Romans 6:10. "The grace of God hath appeared teaching us to deny the works of the flesh and to live righteously and soberly in this present evil world" (Titus 2).[67]

Second, the end of our election is that we might be holy. The end of our calling was that we might be holy. "As I am holy," says Christ, "so be you holy."[68] Sanctification, the end of it [is] to free us from bondage. Faith purifies the heart. Hope to purify the affections. The end of love to make men obedient to the command.

Third, another reason may be drawn from our Savior. He is a mediator between God and us, first, by the merit of His death and passion to forgive our sin [and] to reconcile us again; second, by the efficacy of His resurrection, namely, to raise us from sin to holiness in Him. The end and scope of all is to allure us, first, to thankfulness; second, to be obedient and holy in our vocations; third, to move us to amendment of life. Therefore, with Paul we must learn this doctrine: in all things to submit ourselves to God's Word, "I beseech you by the mercy of God, offer[69] up your bodies and souls as an acceptable sacrifice to God."[70]

Fourth, another end is that we take heed we sin no more, that we may hold our bodies and souls in awe before Him, endeavoring to walk before Him unblameably. Therefore, to conclude, the sum of all is

Thankfulness
Obedience

And the one must show forth the other: our thankfulness must [be] showed to Him throughout the whole course of our lives by walking in His precepts.[71] *Res essentiales.*[72]

Now more nearly to the text ("the grace of our God"). Out of these words a notable point of doctrine,[73] the several parts whereof are three: (1) how God

---

66. Luke 1:74–75.
67. Verse 11.
68. Cf. Lev. 19:2; 1 Peter 1:16.
69. In the margin: Present.
70. Rom. 12:1.
71. In the margin: *mutuæ* (Latin): exchange.
72. *res essentials* (Latin): essential things.
73. In the margin: Three grounds.

comes to be our God,[74] (2) what we ought to do to have God to be our God, [and] (3) the weight and moment of this ground, in that we have God the God of heaven to be our God.

For the first ground, we must know that God became our God not by any desert of us but by His gracious covenant made unto us in His gospel, wherein He publishes remission of sins and mercy and grace through Christ Jesus. He says to the Israelites, "I will make a new covenant" (Jer. 31),[75] and He sets down the tenor of the covenant, "I will write my law in their hearts. And they shall be my people and I will be their God" (verse 33). And of this covenant between Him and us, He is said to be our God.

Second, now the covenant standing thus on His side, we must learn what we must do on our part, that this covenant may be kept, that God may be our God. We must also make a league and covenant with God, for in every covenant there is a double consent, a mutual consent of both parties. And in this regard, on our side God will be our God. Now His covenant is specified in His Word. The dispensation of the gospel is as sure a bond as if He Himself should now speak to us from heaven. The second consent is of us, which consent, if it be mutual, there be two degrees of the same. First, outward in profession when we profess the worship of God by receiving the seals of our faith as the sacraments.[76] And this the hypocrite may do. Therefore, this outward degree is somewhat [of value], but it is not sufficient but only distinguishes them in show from Turks, etc. But the second degree is needful, which is inward. This mutual consent is [three]fold.[77] (1) When a man does by grace acknowledge himself to be a miserable sinner, a vile wretch in the sight of God. (2) When he humbles himself before God in the consideration thereof, laying open his nakedness and seeking by all means to be reconciled to God. (3) When he promises and strives with himself never to commit the same again and endeavors by all means possible to live in obedience and holiness before him.[78]

Thus is the covenant mutually consented, and thus God vouchsafes to be called our God when by grace we walk obediently before Him. And thus is the virtue of the covenant, [namely, that] we may call Him our God.

The third thing is the benefit of this league. To say truly, by the virtue of the covenant, that God is our God is the greatest comfort that a mortal man can have in this life. This was or might have been the greatest joy of Israel: "I

---

74. In the margin: May be said to be.

75. Verse 31.

76. In the margin: The covenant.

77. Tomlin did not note the number of points here, but simply left a space before "fold." He likely intended to complete it later.

78. There are parentheses around points 1–3. In the margin: inward conditions.

am thy God." "I am the Lord thy God" (Ex. 20).[79] And to the comfort of His church, God always rehearses this ground: "I am the God of Abraham, Isaac, and Jacob."[80] And our Savior Christ, when the agony and passion was in the greatest measure upon Him, stayed His manhood in this saying: "My God! My God! Why hast thou forsaken me?"[81] David in all afflictions stayed himself on his God: "O my God, I cry unto thee daily."[82] And David, being in a narrow strait, stayed himself assuredly in God's protection, saying, "My God is at hand to deliver us."[83] Yea, this the foundation of our comfort, that by the virtue of this covenant our bodies at the last day shall arise to be glorified with God in heaven.

The use of this doctrine is twofold:

First, this is a good ground of faith, namely, to provoke us always to engraft the knowledge hereof in our hearts, and also never to doubt and distrust a whit of His help in things we go about, or His mercy when we are in misery, sickness, or danger, but always rely on Him to our comfort: "He is my God, therefore will he have a care for me."[84]

Second, this is a notable ground of obedience. "He is our God, we are the sheep of his pasture" (Ps. 95).[85] The whole scope of the 50th Psalm is to assure the Israelites that God is their God, and so that they should walk obediently and uprightly before Him. And if we be thus persuaded and have this grounded in our heart, it is impossible that we should sin again against God. David confessing of himself, "I have put my trust in thee O Lord" (Ps. 31), and the ground thereof follows, "I said thou art my God."[86] So that the ground of all spiritual worship is this: to be assured of exceeding mercy and fatherly providence of God to sinners in vouchsafing to be called their God. Thus much for the fourth point.

The Fifth Point

"And deny God the only Lord and our Lord Jesus Christ." The last point in this verse of these seducers is their manners, which is set down by their sin in denying not only God but Christ Jesus the Redeemer of mankind.

Here we must consider the meaning of the text, namely, the true and significant meaning of the words, namely, these, "God the only Lord and our Lord Jesus Christ." There are sundry opinions hereof. Some read it thus: "God the Lord, etc."

---

79. Verse 2.
80. E.g., Acts 7:32.
81. Matt. 27:46, cf. Ps. 22:1.
82. Ps. 22:2.
83. 1 Sam. 30:6.
84. 1 Peter 5:7?
85. Verse 7.
86. Verse 14.

Others: "God the only ruler, which is Jesus Christ." Others have: "The Lord God, etc." But as the variety hereof, in sense they come all together, and because this epistle was borrowed from Peter, as it is evident by the style and phrase, and these words are, "Who denied the Lord who bought them" (2 Peter 3),[87] and so I hold that the most significant, that by the "Lord and our Lord Jesus Christ" is nothing but a synonym of words given to Christ our Lord to the excellency of His office of mediatorship, which they deny. And, therefore, I read it thus (as it is in effect), "and deny God the only ruler which is our Lord Jesus Christ."

The meaning of the word "deny."

To deny Christ is in this place to renounce Christ, to forsake Him in their deeds, and to make His death void as much as in them lays. We must understand these words to receive their ground from the redemption of Christ, which office of His they denied, that is renounced and acknowledged not.[88]

Objection. But here rests an objection: how should they be redeemed by Christ and yet ordained to judgment?

Answer. We must know that they were [not] redeemed, neither was the blood of Christ shed for them, neither have they any part therein, namely, by the decree and will of God. For whatsoever He wills in grace that He <…>, and says that He does, and so because Peter said they "denied him that bought them," we must know that they were bought by the counsel and decree of God.[89] And it is our part to judge every one redeemed of God, although they be utter enemies for those reasons, expressed before in the catechism concerning imputation. And indeed, all that profess Christ we must judge for the redeemed in regard of their profession. These professed Christians were but yet denied Him by their deeds. As they denied Him to be their only ruler but they acknowledge Him to be the redeemer as appears [in] Titus 3.[90] And that they are redeemed by Him and yet they do derogate much from the godhead of Christ.

To make their sin more odious he adds very excellent titles to Him whom they denied, as namely (1) that [He] is our ruler and governor, so much the word "Lord" signifies, [and] (2) in that it is said "the only Lord," which serves to put a difference between all idol gods. In the same is not excluded the Holy Spirit, but all three also are included and comprehended in the word "Lord," for all the actions done by one person are mutually done by one Godhead, "only ruler which is Christ."

---

87. The intended reference is 2 Peter 2:1.

88. In the margin: 1 Peter 3. Denied him that bought them. The intended reference is 2 Peter 2:1.

89. This appears to assert the opposite of the published version. Cf. Perkins, *Jude*, RHB 4:107.

90. The intended reference is Titus 1:16.

This is an excellent place to prove the Godhead of Christ, in that He is called "the only ruler," which He is called in respect of His church, which He is head of. And He governs it in two manners of ways. First, by His death before all times a lamb slain from the beginning of the world, He is Lord over the church. Second, by the right of redemption, in that He took upon Him the nature of man to be abased in all things and according to His manhood to suffer death for the redemption of sinners, and thus may He rightly challenge superiority and lordship over His church which thus He redeemed.

But, first, let us look further into their sin, how they may be said and wherein to deny Christ Jesus. First, they deny Him secretly and inwardly in their hearts by not acknowledging Him to be Lord and ruler over.

These enemies deny Christ {
  inwardly, in that they deny the { Godhead / power of the Godhead
  outwardly, by their { deeds / whole conversation

They deny him, first, concerning His lordship, for they will be content to be accounted His servants and that they were redeemed by Him. But they cannot brook Him to be their Lord to rule them, and thus they wear his livery[91] but they will not be His servants.

Secondly, they deny the power of His Godhead by which He is their Lord by His Spirit to write His laws in their hearts. And this they refuse. They would have Christ to redeem them, but they will not have Him their Lord. They will make His death of endless merit, able to blot out all their sins, and yet they cannot away Him to be their teacher, to be taught by Him, and so they make Christ a packhorse to carry away their sins. Thus, they will have His death, but they will none of the merit and efficacy of His death. Much like to the old Pharisees, "We will not have this man to rule over us." But what says He, therefore, "Bring these mine enemies, and slay them before my face."[92] "If you would presume to apply My death to yourselves, and yet disdain to have Me your Lord and ruler, your teacher, and your master, I will none of you, I will not own you to be My servant, neither have you any part or portion in Mine inheritance, neither have you any profit by My death and passion."

Now to the second point, which is outward, wherein they show themselves to be enemies to Christ Jesus, namely, in their deeds and conversation, in that they give themselves liberty to sin, to do what they list, yet worship Him and come to His table, and make fain show of religion. And yet, in their lives and

---

91. *Livery*: clothing.
92. Luke 19:14, 27.

deeds they deny Him and behave themselves as subtle thieves to get away the hearts of the people by giving themselves liberty to their own lusts. And all their worship is nothing but from their teeth and outward, and this lip service they give to Him only.

Now, to make an application of both these together, these are sins very general among Christians. For they will obey the form but none of the substance, they will come to the church and they be conversant in God's service, and yet when they are absent, they be extortioners, drunkards, idolaters, etc. And thus, they embrace Christ, but yet they refuse Him as their lives and conversations plainly testify. "If you love me keep my commandments."[93] But they will love Christ, and yet they will none of His precepts. They will not have Him to be their Lord and ruler.

We are taught, therefore, the contrary: to acknowledge Christ Jesus to be our Lord and ruler, and to show forth the same by being obedient unto Him, to be taught by Him to hold Him as our Savior, so our Lord equal with God in the deity. "Come to me (says He) all ye that are weary and laden, and I will refresh you" (Matt. 11).[94] But how not as these adversaries take Him as a redeemer but will do nothing in sign of His love and thankfulness they owe to Him, says He in the next verse, "Take up my cross and follow me or else I know you not. I own you, depart ye cursed."[95] These Christ teaches of, others shall allege, "Lord have we not taught in thy name?" "No, depart from me."[96] And this shall be their portion.

Let us, therefore, both honor Him [as] a father, obey Him as a prince, fight under His banner as faithful soldiers to their captain against the world, sin, Satan, and authorities. As loving and good servants, submit ourselves willingly to His precepts as godly people, under their minister be content to be taught by hunger and thirst for His Word of salvation of our souls. Then shall we at last be imputed worthy of His kingdom, to which He brings us for His mercy's sake. Amen.

---

93. John 14:15.

94. Verse 28.

95. While this is not unrelated to Matthew 11:29, it is a combination of Matthew 16:24 and 7:23.

96. Matt. 7:22–23.

Prayer

(Sermon 1): Prayer and Enemies

Prayer is a special means which God has ordained and left to His church, whereby every one of His servants may with boldness and confidence come to Him and crave of Him such things as they stand in need of in their bodies and souls, as they are bound in conscience to do. Prayer is made not only for ourselves but for others also, yea, even for our enemies and such as hate us, as our Savior Christ says (Matt. 5:44).[1] Among which we are to consider whether we are to pray also against our enemies.

For the answer hereof, we must make certain distinctions of enemies and causes. All enemies are of two sorts, either public or private.

Public enemies are such as are enemies to God and to Christians, to Christ in His members, to God's Word, and enemies to the professors thereof, as is the pope and papacy, Antichrist and all his anti-Christian laws, who are chief and capital enemies against Christ and against His doctrine and against this pure religion.

Private enemies are such as are enemies to some particular man for some special cause, for which their malice and rancor is shown toward the person with whom they are offended. Of these there are two sorts: some who are enemies unto man only and some [who are] enemies to man and in man mediately and secondarily to God Himself. Such [a] one was Saul to David, who was both a public enemy and also a private enemy to David, seeking always his destruction, notwithstanding it was God's purpose and intent to give the imperial government and regal power over His people, the Israelites, unto him.

Public enemies (of whom I spoke in the first place) are also twofold, either curable or incurable.

Curable enemies are such as, being public enemies to God and so also man in cruel persecution, in a hardened and steadfast and resolute purpose of doing God service in beheading His saints, as Christ prophesied of [Matt. 5:11; 10:22], or in more milder sort are enemies in detesting, reviling, and condemning this holy religion and worship of God, are notwithstanding by the secret and unsearchable will of God ordained before all worlds to salvation, who in time shall be converted to the marvelous light of the gospel. Thus was our father

---

1. The MS erroneously cites Matthew 6.

Abraham converted to God, though a long time he lived in an idolatrous country. So also was Paul, whose cruelty (Acts 11) is notably expressed in that he made havoc of Christians, etc., and yet was made at the end an excellent vessel to set forth the glory of God, as his life and doctrine in the Scriptures records (Acts 9, 11).

Incurable enemies are such as God has of His justice given up to the hardness of their heart, to the obedience of their own lusts, who are most cruel enemies to Christ in His doctrine and in His members, who are incurable, vessels of vengeance, as the apostle Jude speaks [Jude 4], who will continue their malice and cruelty against God and godly men as long as they have any being, as Judas, against whom David prays [Ps. 36], also Pharaoh [Ex.], Saul [1 Sam.], and many others.

Now for these both, curable and incurable enemies, we are to pray, as the Word of God by precept and pattern abundantly prove: "Bless them that curse you: do good to them that hate you" [Matt. 5].

The same person, our Savior, prayed for His enemies, the Jews, who crucified Him. How greatly did He weep [and] how bitterly did He mourn for them and their future ruin, which they for their sins brought on them, saying, "O Jerusalem, Jerusalem, that killeth the prophets and stones them! How often would I have gathered thee…even as a hen gathereth her chickens together: but thou wouldest not" [Matt. 23:37]. In like manner, Stephen, an excellent pattern of piety, who, being stoned of the Jews, at the last gasp cried, saying, "My Lord, lay not this sin to their charge" [Acts 7]. How often and how greatly did David mourn for Saul, though he had been his deadly enemy? But what of this? The Scripture is plentiful hereof.

Now we come to consider a little of deprecations[2] concerning our enemies, whether it is lawful and simply good to pray sometimes against our enemies.

For the answer hereof, it is simply lawful but yet in sundry respects. All prayers against our enemies are made either against their persons or practices. Against the practices and deeds of our enemies (namely, such enemies as are enemies to God also, as well as to man, as before I declared) we ought all to pray, but not against their persons. As, for example, we are bound, all of us who detest the pope and all his doctrine, to pray against his doctrine and evil practice, that he might be converted (if it were possible) to the true faith; but in no case [are we to pray] against his person. This prayer is made by the church, "Lord, regard their threatenings" [Acts 4:29], and not, "Lord, reward them in general." Then should they have sinned. And Christ sharply rebuked John and James, who desired that fire might be sent down from heaven to burn up their

---

2. *Deprecation*: disapproval.

enemies, as Elijah did [2 Kings 1:10], "Ye know not," says He, "of what spirit ye are" [Luke 9:55].

But here we are to meet with an objection: seeing we are commanded to pray for our enemies, why did David in sundry places pray against his enemies [Ps. 109], and Elisha cursed the little children whom presently bears devoured [2 Kings 2:23–25]? These persons, and many others recorded at large in the Scriptures, prayed against their enemies. Ergo, is it lawful for us so to do?

No, *vivunt legibus non exemplis*, "men live by laws and not by examples," as Augustine says. But these men did it by way of prophecy. God in His exquisite wisdom revealed unto them the state and condition of those persons to come, that they are vessels of wrath, appointed to destruction, and that their malice and hatred were perpetual and incurable, and [that they] would be enemies to the church continually. And, therefore, they prayed [to] God to confound even their persons, so that the church might be freed from their tyranny and wickedness. This gift of divination or prophecy is very rare now, and therefore, because we cannot tell which are curable enemies and which [are] not, we must not in any case pray against their persons, but refer the knowledge of it to God who knows only their future end. And [we may] not with David use deprecation against their persons, for God may suddenly in some convert them, and then should our prayers be void and sinful.

But if any man finds in himself these things, as David did, he may boldly pray against their persons. First, if we have extraordinary gifts, as namely the foresaid gift of prophecy or discerning into the life and future behavior of our adversaries whosoever. Second, if we have good affections in the same, as if we are moved with a fervent zeal of God's glory, we may with Paul pray against the very persons of our enemies: "Alexander the coppersmith hath done me much evil. The Lord reward him according to his doings" [2 Tim. 4:14]. And thus, the apostle, being endued with a fervency of God's Spirit, in godly zeal foreseeing his perpetual enmity against the same, used imprecation. And so of many others.

Now ordinary persons have but ordinary gifts, and every good thing they have is imperfect and mingled with innumerable corruptions and imperfections. And instead of zeal and pure and godly anger, they would soon fall into anger and malice or vengeance, and so pour out most abominable curses to the dishonor of God. And, for this cause, we must, instead of praying with David, "Lord, confound them: And for thy mercy slay mine enemies" [Ps. 40:14; 143:12], pray and say, "Lord, convert them to Your truth if they belong unto You; if not confound them," praying for them conditionally. Or else pray, "Lord, confound their evil desires, turn their privy nets and snares, which lay to catch Your saints, be of Your mercy turned to the safeguard of Your people." Then shall our supplications be acceptable in the ears of God.

Seeing as we may not use such prayers, we must know next what use we are then to make of such places in the Scriptures, whether the persons of God's enemies are prayed against, whether in reading, singing, or hearing such prayers we may lawfully, as of other Scriptures, give attendance and inward affection to them.

In reading, singing, or hearing such prayers, we must use them only as prophecies against our foes if they continue in their former wickedness. Whereas they are made to some particular person, we must use them as general prayers against all the incurable enemies of God, referring the knowledge of them to the Lord.

Prayer

(Sermon 2): Outward Prayer

Now it remains [to] speak briefly of outward prayer (for prayer is both inward and outward, of deprecation as part of inward prayer we have spoken of).[1] Outward prayer is that whereby we do, to the expressing [of] inward affection of the heart, [use] some outward and visible gesture of the body.

In outward prayer we must conceive apart these circumstances. The

- voice
- gesture } in oper.[2]
- place where
- time when } <...>

The Voice in Prayer

Concerning the voice, sometimes it may be used and sometimes not, for prayer is either public or private.

Public prayer is that which is used in the congregation and assembly of God's children. Now in this public prayer there is always required a plain form of words to be used with utterance and distinction, with a plain and sensible voice and form of words.

First, because God is <...> and the mouth of the people is the minister,[3] and so [he] prays wherewith as with one consent they join themselves inwardly to him in prayer to God, and also in voice when [in] the prayer to say "Amen," which cannot be unless there is a sensible voice and a form of words used.

Second, because God is a Spirit and will be served in spirit and truth, not only with the soul and spirit but with all inward and outward faculties of soul and body, even the voice must be used to set forth God's glory. James says we must worship God with the tongue [James 3:9], out of which I gather this syllogistical argument:

> The body of men, and every faculty and part thereof,
>> must set forth God's praise.
> The voice is a part of the body.

---

1. Perkins also speaks to the difference between "private" and "public" prayer in *Sermon on the Mount*, RHB 1:410–11.

2. In operation.

3. For similar content, but different phrasing, see *Lord's Prayer*, RHB 5:467.

Therefore, the voice must be used to set forth His praise.

But in private places made by private persons, the voice is not always simply necessary, and yet [may be] profitable. Profitable always because it serves to stir up the mind and affections of the heart to a deep consideration of the thing prayed for. And the voice oftentimes helps the zeal and force in prayer, even by the elevation and lifting up of the words.

Yet in regard of the conscience, the voice is not always requisite and necessary, and also concerning [some] public place wherein privately that prayer might be made, for a man may pray at all times and in all places privately, namely, by lifting up his heart to God, and yet [he] uses no words at all. And to avoid scorn of the worlding, etc., that [are] bereft of sense,[4] vocal prayer should be most ridiculous and absurd, and might be an occasion of dishonor of God, and therefore the preacher teaches to use wisdom in all things.

Examples of this private prayer are many. We may see Moses who prayed for the Israelites, who had procured to themselves God's wrath. He offered no words, yet the Lord said, "Why cryest thou unto me?" [Ex. 14:15]. So Hannah, who was barren, yet prayed to God for a child in the sight of Eli, and yet offered no form of words at all, but only her lips moved in so much [as] God's priest supposed that she was drunk [1 Sam. 1:13].[5] Even so, our Savior Christ in the garden. Paul records that the Spirit prays for the elect with sighs and groans that cannot be expressed [Rom. 8:26]. And in another place, [he] says, "Pray continually" [1 Thess. 5:17], which is not meant of vocal prayer but of the lifting up the heart, which may be done at all times and in all places.

Thus, we see that vocal prayer is needful in some causes and [at] some times more than [at] other [times], though always profitable.

Now we will see whether it is lawful to use set prayers or to read some prayer in a book.[6] Briefly to answer, I affirm that it is lawful, though many hold it unlawful. For as all the psalms of David (or with some and most)[7] are nothing else but prayers, [they] should be altogether superfluous and not to be used. And then those also in other places, which the Holy Spirit provided, and all the psalms that are to be sung until the end of the world should be of none effect. And so most places of the Scripture, which standeth fast for <…> should be abolished. But reading of prayer is good, lawful, and needful, and that for these reasons: First, for the helping of a man's memory, that he may know what to pray for and in what manner. Second, for the helping of his judgment and

---

4. The MS says, "that bereave sense."
5. The MS erroneously cites 1 Kings 1, whereas 1 Samuel 1:13 was intended.
6. Perkins also speaks to the issue of "reading prayers" in *Lord's Prayer*, RHB 5:468.
7. These words seem to be out of place.

understanding, that by reading a prayer rightly framed and according to God's Word he may learn in time to frame one like to it. For man's nature is so prone to earth [and] to sin, etc., that he cannot easily be drawn to the consideration of heavenly[8] things. And again, a man had need be well endued with wit and wisdom when he comes to pray to God, his heavenly Father.

Objection and answer. Therefore, to confute this objection of them who say [that] to read a prayer in a book or to use a common and special form of prayer is to tie the Holy Spirit to form. The gifts of God are weak in us and we had need to have means to increase them in us, and this serves greatly to increase God's holy Spirit in us, and not to bind the Holy Spirit to any usual forms.

Thus much for the voice.

The Gesture in Prayer

The second thing to be considered in outward prayer is the gesture of the body. Concerning the which we are to know that God in His Word has prescribed no particular gestures to be used, yet the Word of God has given us a certain use of gestures so far forth as that may serve to stir up the inward affections of the mind to a greater and deep consideration of the thing we pray for.

Gestures are lawful if they are comely, modest, and holy, that is, tending to a holy use as all ought to do, for they serve to show the humility of the mind.

There are sundry kinds of gestures necessary for the stirring up [of] the mind, but the Word of God does not strictly tie us to any gestures, only the practice of all the saints before us, the prophets and people of God, who have used divers gestures in prayer, as falling down, bending the body, bowing the knees, lifting up and spreading abroad the hands. The very angels, in token of baseness and humility in the presence of God, use to cover their feet with their wings, and they are more excellent creatures than we. And, therefore, it is a sign of stubbornness and carelessness of God's worship when the body is [un]-bended[9] in the sight of God. For yea, true humility in a Christian will move both the body and soul and all the faculties of both, and their zeal and affection in prayer will appear by their outward carriage and behavior of the body.

In those times we must follow the common gesture of the church and place where we live and only for comeliness' sake.

And thus for the use of gestures in public prayer.

In private prayer, there is more liberty for us when we are in God's presence with ourselves, no man with us. We may use any gesture which we think will most lively express or stir up the hearty affection [of] our soul.

---

8. The MS says "earthly" things, a typographical error on the part of the transcriber.
9. The MS says "bended," whereas the opposite appears to have been intended.

One thing in prayer, that [the] ancient worthy Tertullian condemns as an irreverent and impious gesture in prayer, is sitting to pray to God. But religion stands not with outward gestures. Any gesture whatsoever is needful and meet to be used with modesty in private prayer. For sometimes the time and place will constrain a man to use some extraordinary gesture, and yet it may be acceptable to God.

The Place of Prayer

Now to the third circumstance: where we must pray. For the place, we must know that one place is not any more acceptable than another in regard of holiness, but all are alike; no, not [even] the church [is] more acceptable than any other place. For this is the privilege of the New Testament, that any place to serve God in is pleasing unto Him if the prayer is made in humility, else even in the church the prayer is rejected of God, for one place is not more sanctified and holy than another.

But for order's sake, and for mutual society and edification, public prayer must [be] made in [a] public place appointed for the purpose, as namely the church, but for conscience's sake in any place as the time requires.

The papists are deadly enemies to this rule, for they tie themselves only to hallowed places, at the temple only is the place for prayer. They gather their custom by the Scriptures. David, being banished by Saul, mourned to be in the temple worshiping God. Daniel prayed three times a day and looked forth of his window toward Jerusalem when he was with Nebuchadnezzar. And so, the temple is the place where we must pray only. But in this they show their absurdity and error, for in those days God's church was tied to Jerusalem, but since the separation wall was broken since the death of Christ, salvation was published to the Gentiles. God's church is everywhere dispersed. Neither are we tied to one place. His ark was with the Israelites, His will, His Word, His prophets, His promise to hear them; but now these are more largely diffused abroad, all the types and circumstances being taken away. The church, according to our belief, is universal.

Again, they say the church must needs be the only place for prayer because the sacraments are only administered there. To the answer hereof, I say that it is not in prayer as in the sacraments, for they are received by a multitude and by the minister breaking the bread to them; but a man may pray [by] himself. And again, they affirm that the church is more holy than any place because the sacraments are administered there. Indeed, the church is made for God's worship, that it might be fit for the same, but there is no holiness included in the material church. And concerning the receiving of the sacraments alone as they are received,[10] the church is not [in] any way sanctified thereby. Therefore, their error is gross and absurd.

The Time of Prayer

Concerning the which briefly I answer that there are two kinds of prayer commenced unto us in God's Word. One is called sudden prayer, which is the lifting up of the heart to God upon some present occasion whereby every day and hour man may lift up his heart unto God. The apostle Paul says, "Pray always," which is meant of continual prayer.

I also note prayer is lawful for four causes. First, the glory of God must be the scope of all our actions. And, therefore, in everything we go about, we must pray for His aid, which we must do inwardly from the heart. Second, because we are subject to many frailties in so much [as] there is no good that can proceed from us, and so we had need continually lift [up] our heart to Him for help. Third, because Satan, as a roving lion, looks continually to catch us from the good and to bring us into his snares. Fourth, faith is necessary for everyone who will be saved. Whatsoever is done without faith is sin, says the apostle [Rom. 14:23]. And faith is increased especially by those means.

The second kind of prayer is solemn prayer, which is public and private. Now for public prayer, as also for private, God has prescribed no time but in different occasions, [as] need is, either may be made in regard of conscience. And when time of troubles, adversity, or sickness is upon a congregation for order's sake and for religion's sake, they may pray at any time. In regard of conscience religion requires times [and] public places, that the moment is according to the discretion of the minister.

They of Rome use hours for divine service: (1) the hour before day, (2) the seventh hour, (3) the ninth hour, (4) the twelfth hour, (5) the <...> hour after sunsetting. And they bind all to observe these hours, and it is a mortal sin to neglect them. And again, they bind the priests only to these canonical hours. Third, that one day [serves] for another, and if the hours are not duly kept today, tomorrow will serve. And they will change the forms of service for the afternoon. And thus is their religion in every circumstance most dangerous.

---

10. I.e., received alone in the absence of faith.

Chapter 6

The Hutton Manuscript

The Hutton manuscript is a 354-page book containing sermons transcribed in the closing years of the sixteenth century.[1] More than half of the volume consists of forty-one sermons delivered by William Perkins.[2] There are an additional thirty-five sermons, including five by Laurence Chaderton, and individual sermons by George Estey, Roger Fenton, John Blyth, Thomas Bolton, Robert Spalding, and others.[3] The transcriber evidently listened eagerly to a range of Cambridge preachers, though clearly preferred Perkins's teaching.

This manuscript has been erroneously attributed to Matthew Hutton

---

1. North Yorkshire County Record Office, Hutton of Marske family archive—Papers of Archbishop Matthew Hutton, MS ZAZ 75.

2. Perkins's sermons in the Hutton MS, in order with page references, are as follows. Numbers in square brackets number sermons in a single series: 1 Cor. 7:20 [1] (pp. 1–3), 1 Cor. 7:20 [2] (pp. 4–6), 1 Cor. 7:20 [3] (pp. 6–8), 1 Cor. 7:20 [4] (pp. 8–10), 1 Cor. 11:28 [1] (pp. 11–13), Gen. 2:18 [1] (pp. 13–15), Gen. 8:21 [1] (pp. 16–21), Gen. 2:18 [2] (pp. 21–24), Acts 2:16–17 (pp. 24–28), Jude 3 [1] (pp. 29–32), Matt. 25:35 (pp. 32–37), 1 Cor. 11:28 [2] (pp. 37–40), Rev. 18:4 [1] (pp. 41–44), Gen. 2:18 [3] (pp. 44–49), Gen. 2:19–20 [4] (pp. 49–55), Gen. 2:21–22 [5] (pp. 56–60), Gen. 2:23–24 [6] (pp. 60–66), Gen. 2:24 [7] (pp. 66–71), Gen. 2:24 [8] (pp. 72–76), Gen. 2:24 [9] (pp. 76–81), Gen. 2:24 [10] (pp. 81–86), Gen. 2:24 [11] (pp. 87–90), Jude 3 [1] (pp. 146–50), Jude 4 [2] (pp. 150–57), Jude 4 [3] (pp. 157–61), Jude 4 [4–5] (pp. 162–68), Jude 4 [6] (pp. 175–79), Jude 5 [7] (pp. 179–84), Jude 5 [8] (pp. 184–87), Jude 6 [9] (pp. 187–91), Jude 6 [10] (pp. 191–95), Jude 7 [11–12] (pp. 195–202), Jude 8 [13] (pp. 202–5), Jude 8 [14] (pp. 205–10), Jude 8 [15] (pp. 210–14), Jude 8–9 [16] (pp. 214–20). Sermons transcribed from the back of the volume: Ex. 22:28 [1] (pp. 354–52), Ex. 22:28 [2] (pp. 352–50), Ex. 22:28 [3] (pp. 349–47), Rev. 18:4 [2] (pp. 282–76), Isa. 50:4 (pp. 248–44), Matt. 23:37 (pp. 244–42).

3. The Chaderton sermons are part of a series on John's gospel. The present MS includes notes from the sermons on John 14:28 (pp. 102–8), 14:30 (pp. 108–14), 15:21 (pp. 121–25), and two on 16:11 (pp. 125–38, 138–41). On Chaderton, see the introduction to this volume.

Estey on James 2:14 (pp. 114–18). George Estey (1560/61–1601) was a fellow of Gonville and Caius Colleges, Cambridge (1584–1600), and vicar of St. Mary, Bury St. Edmunds (1598–1601). At Cambridge he served as Greek lecturer (1592) and then Hebrew lecturer (1594–1597). Estey's views aligned with those of Perkins's in disputes on predestination and on the descent of Christ, and Estey was involved in controversy on both subjects. He was the author of several expository and catechetical works. Venn, *Alumni Cantabrigienses*, pt. 1, vol. 2, p. 106; Stephen Wright, "Estye, George (1560/61–1601)," in *Oxford Dictionary of National Biography* (Oxford: Oxford University Press, 2004; online ed., January 2008).

(1529–1606) and his eldest son, Timothy Hutton of Marske (1569–1629). While Matthew Hutton was at Cambridge in a variety of capacities from 1546 to 1567, he was serving as bishop of Durham (1589–1595) and then archbishop of York (1595–1606) during the period in which these sermons and lectures were given.[4] Matthew Hutton's two sons briefly studied in Cambridge; however, both departed to pursue careers in law. Hutton's older son, Timothy Hutton of Marske, studied at Trinity beginning in 1588 but was admitted to Gray's Inn, London, in 1590.[5] A more plausible option is the younger Hutton son, Thomas Hutton of Nether Poppleton (1581–1620), who was admitted as a fellow-commoner at Queen's College in 1597 before being admitted to Gray's Inn, London, in 1599. If Perkins delivered his sermon on Jude 3 in 1598/1599 (as attested by Tomlin), then he had likely taught on Jude 9 by October that year when Thomas Hutton would have been departing for London. This is precisely where the notebook (read forward) ends.[6] Such a possibility cannot be proven

---

Fenton on Matthew 6:25 (pp. 142–45). Roger Fenton (d. 1615/16) was a graduate and fellow of Pembroke College, Cambridge (1590), then preacher at Gray's Inn, London (1598). He went on to be the rector of St. Stephen, Walbrook (1601–1616) and of St. Benet Sherehog (1603–1606), vicar of Chigwell, Essex (1606–1616), and prebendary of St. Paul's Cathedral, London (1609–1616). Venn, *Alumni Cantabrigienses*, pt. 1, vol. 2, p. 131.

Blyth on Hosea 6:12 (pp. 169–73). John Blyth (d. 1617) was a graduate and fellow of Peterhouse College, Cambridge (1587), before serving as vicar of Impington, Cambridgeshire (1588–1617). Venn, *Alumni Cantabrigienses*, pt. 1, vol. 1, p. 171.

Bolton's brief notes on Exodus (p. 174). Thomas Bolton was a fellow of Trinity College, Cambridge, beginning in 1585 and vicar of nearby Trumpington (1592–1594). He later moved to Yorkshire to serve as vicar of Kirkby-cum-Masham. Venn, *Alumni Cantabrigienses*, pt. 1, vol. 1, p. 176.

Spalding's brief notes on Ezekiel 8:14 (p. 174). The "Mr. Spaton" who delivered this address at St. Mary's, Cambridge, was most likely Robert Spalding (d. 1626), a graduate of St. John's, Cambridge. He was a fellow beginning in 1593 and went on to become regius professor of Hebrew (1605–1607). He later became rector of Edburton, Sussex (1606–1626), and of Slaugham (1616–1626), and he was employed in the translation of the KJV Bible. Venn, *Alumni Cantabrigienses*, pt. 1, vol. 4, p. 126.

Due to issues of legibility and/or use of shorthand, it is not possible to identify the subjects of all attributions in the volume. Most notably, it is unclear who delivered the series of fifteen sermons on Matthew 25:26–26:28 (from back: pp. 347–284). However, these sermons so differ from Perkins's style that he can be ruled out as the preacher.

4. Venn, *Alumni Cantabrigienses*, pt. 1, vol. 2, p. 442. Claire Cross, "Hutton, Matthew (1529?–1606)," in *Oxford Dictionary of National Biography* (Oxford: Oxford University Press, 2004; online ed., September 2004).

5. Venn, *Alumni Cantabrigienses*, pt. 1, vol. 2, p. 443.

6. Other factors also argue for this dating. For example, Thomas Pierson departed Cambridge for Northwich in 1599, and he was present for the entire series on Genesis 8:21. "To the Reader," in William Perkins, *A Treatise of Man's Imaginations* (Cambridge: John Legate, 1607), 5r (RHB 9:185). It is also striking that the Hutton MS contains no transcriptions of Perkins's Galatians sermons, which were "the substance of three years lectures upon the Lord's Day" up until his

and faces other challenges of chronology, though it makes sense of the association of this text with the Hutton name.[7] Whatever the precise origins of this MS, it is clear from its contents that it belonged to a student who identified with the Chaderton-Perkins circle of Cambridge Puritans and that it contains material delivered between 1596 and 1600.[8]

The pages at both ends of the Hutton MS are so significantly damaged that it is difficult to make sense of the text without providing additional words to the transcription.[9] Most biblical references in the Hutton MS come from the Geneva Bible with little variation in wording; however, as with the Tomlin MS, many of the biblical references provided by the transcriber are incorrect, and he appears to be a relative newcomer to Latin.[10]

The Hutton MS appears to offer a cross-section of Perkins's ministry at the turn of the century, showing him teaching a range of material concurrently. His eleven sermons on Genesis 2:18–24 are interrupted by treatments of Genesis 8:21, Acts 2:16–17, 1 Corinthians 11:28, and Revelation 18:4. The Genesis and Revelation sermons were themselves parts of ongoing series. Likewise, his two addresses on 1 Corinthians 11:28 are separated by other material, and his two catechetical lectures on Revelation 18:4 are transcribed at different ends of the book. All of this supports the notion that Perkins was a hard-working and much sought-after lecturer, engaging in a range of preaching, lecturing, and catechetical ministries in Cambridge.

The four sermons on 1 Corinthians 7:20 were part of a longer series delivered by Perkins, most likely in 1595 or 1596.[11] When he died in 1602, he was in the process of preparing this material for publication as *A Treatise of*

---

death, meaning that they were delivered from circa 1600 until Perkins's death in October 1602. "To the Courteous Reader," in Perkins, *Galatians*, 4v.

7. Assuming that the association of this notebook with the Hutton name is sound, it is worth noting that there were several other Huttons in Cambridge during this period. Anthony Hutton was admitted to Queen's in 1599 and then at Gray's Inn in 1601, though he was from a different Hutton family (son of Sir William Hutton of Penrith). Jeremy Hutton was at Trinity College (1589–1596). Samuel Hutton, possibly a nephew of Matthew Hutton, was at Trinity College (c. 1593–1603). Venn, *Alumni Cantabrigienses*, pt. 1, vol. 2, p. 442–43.

8. Lake similarly attributes it to a student of St. John's, Cambridge, sometime in the 1590s. *Moderate Puritans*, 344.

9. When necessary, the missing text is marked <...> and its location in the RHB edition is footnoted.

10. At the end of the fourth sermon in the Jude series, the transcriber writes, "*verte tria folia*" (Latin: "Turn the three leaves") to indicate where the next sermon in the series was located. This playful use of simple Latin phrases seems to indicate a student making eager use of newfound Latin skills.

11. Based on the relative dating of subsequent material in the MS.

Vocations.[12] The sermons included here are in two continuous pairs, with probably one or two sermons missing between the second and third sermons.[13] Despite the limitation of the manuscript being particularly damaged at the location of these transcriptions, this material suggests that Perkins engaged in significant revision of these sermons for publication as a treatise.

Perkins's two sermons on 1 Corinthians 11:28 appear nowhere else in his work. The first promotes the characteristic Reformation emphasis on partaking both elements of the Lord's Supper, both bread and wine, by all communicants.[14] Perkins emphasizes that all Christians are to partake regularly of the Lord's Supper, treating it as the food by which they will persevere in faith to the end.[15] However, for this sacrament to be of any use to them, they must partake of it rightly, that is, by faith and its accompanying virtues.[16] The first sermon's use of untranslated Latin terms indicates that it was probably delivered to an educated university audience, presumably at one of the "Puritan" colleges dominated by Perkins's circle.[17] Its content implies that it was likely delivered immediately before the Lord's Supper was administered at a chapel service.[18] The second sermon reads as a continuation of the first; however, there is a significant amount of intervening material in the manuscript between the two, indicating that it was probably delivered to the same audience as the first, though on a later occasion. Here Perkins expands on the seven points on right reception that he listed in the first.

---

12. The material is included throughout *Treatise on the Vocations*, RHB 10:31–108. For a discussion of its publication, see the introduction to this volume.

13. These four transcribed sermons roughly cover RHB 10:57–62, 62–70, 81–86, 88–91.

14. This view is enshrined in England's doctrinal statement, the Thirty-Nine Articles of Religion (1563, 1571), article 30.

15. See further Matthew N. Payne, "'Is It Not Dangerous to Say a Person May Fall from Grace?': The Doctrine of Perseverance in Reformation Anglican Theology," *The Global Anglican*, forthcoming.

16. Again, Perkins's exposition ought to be read against the background of England's doctrinal statement, the Thirty-Nine Articles of Religion (1563, 1571), esp. articles 28–29.

17. That is, most likely Christ's College, Emmanuel College, or the new Sidney-Sussex College, Cambridge. On Perkins's view on clarity in sermons and its implications for the audience, see the introduction to the Senate House Commonplace Book MS (above). It is also noteworthy that, according to Ames, Perkins's practice was never to use the Book of Common Prayer in his voluntarily attended lectures at St. Andrews the Great. William Ames, *A Second Manuduction, for Mr Robinson* ([Amsterdam], 1615), 29. This makes it appear more likely that these sermons were delivered at ordinary liturgical services, whether in college or parish, which was the only authorized form in which the Lord's Supper was administered.

18. The Book of Common Prayer (1559), in "The order for the administration of the Lord's Supper or Holy Communion" specifies that a homily or sermon be delivered briefly before the Lord's Supper is administered.

Perkins's eleven sermons on Genesis 2:18–24 were part of an ongoing series of expository lectures that overlap with the content of his posthumously published *Christian Oeconomie* (1609). The published work was Thomas Pickering's translation of a Latin manuscript penned by Perkins, presumably intended by him for publication. These sermons engage many of the same issues but do not bear a straightforward relationship to the published treatise. Whereas the treatise is a systematic treatment of its subject matter, the sermons are homiletical in character, proceeding through the biblical text sequentially while expounding the exegetical, theological, and practical issues arising from the text. These sermons also include material that is not present in the published treatise.[19] Perkins's characteristic concern for the pastoral issues faced by ordinary parishioners is on full display as he engages a range of common questions and case studies. The first sermon transcribed here is not the first in the series. It considers the second marriage office common to both husband and wife—namely, to win one another to Christ. In the second sermon, Perkins describes the way married persons might transgress their marriage office by failing to seek Christ with their spouse, and he discusses the third office of marriage—namely, that married persons ought to please one another. The third sermon expounds the common office of preservation, meaning husband and wife mutually protect and provide for one another. These three sermons are from Genesis 2:18.

The series then engages the creation of Eve (Gen. 2:19–23) and stresses that the creational origins of man and woman speak to the way in which they ought to relate to one another and to any children that God gives them (sermons 4–6). One noteworthy topic raised is that of naming, which Perkins treats as an aspect of the authority given to the man (sermon 4). However, Perkins also emphasizes that names need to be grounded in the created reality, as a reflection of what its object is. This is also why Perkins connects naming to memory, a subject on which he debated in print early in his career.[20] These subjects of naming, of right perception of nature, and of memory are all grounded in Perkins's metaphysically realist understanding of creation and his commitment to Ramism.[21] In short, for Perkins, language has an objective relation to created nature rather than an arbitrary and voluntaristic relation, as commonly held among modern Westerners. The implication is that, for Perkins, the practice

---

19. For comparison, the subject matter of these sermons—namely, the common and particular offices of both parties in a marriage—are treated in *Oeconomie*, RHB 10:161–75.

20. For Perkins's views on memory, see *Antidicson* (RHB 6:476–521) and *Handbook of Memory Recall* (RHB 6:523–58). His view is briefly stated and applied to preaching in *Art of Prophesying* (RHB 10:348).

21. Discussing this subject here goes beyond the scope of introducing these texts, except to say that work remains to be done on Perkins's views in these areas. On naming, see also *Creed* (RHB 5:102–3; 8:243).

of naming is to be conducted with due care and wise judgment. Finally, the series then expounds the offices and duties of each party specifically, first of the wife (sermons 7–9) and then of the husband (sermons 10–11), again engaging a range of practical questions and cases.

Perkins's sermon on Genesis 8:21 was part of a series of sermons, which became the basis of *A Treatise of Man's Imagination* (1607).[22] Its editor, Thomas Pierson, reveals that the published work was produced on the basis of Perkins's own draft outline and three different sets of firsthand notes taken down by hearers of the sermons, including his own.[23] This sermon is an additional witness to that series and covers parts of what became chapters 3 and 4 of the published work, though treating its subject matter far more briefly.

In his previously unpublished sermon on Acts 2:16–17, Perkins describes God's gift of the Spirit to all Christians. The Spirit leads believers to depend on Scripture, await Christ's coming, and exhibit fruit in their lives. Perkins relates Pentecost to the marks of the true church, while expressing a cessationist view of predictive prophecy, arguing that it was a sign of the true church in the apostolic period but not afterward.[24]

The two lectures headed by the text of Revelation 18:4 ("Come out of her my people") were part of a series that would develop into the treatise *A Reformed Catholic* (1597). Specifically, the first lecture corresponds to the treatise's chapter on assurance (ch. 4) and the second with its chapter on the Lord's Supper (ch. 11).[25] The published treatise is introduced with an exposition of the same biblical text, in which Perkins defends the common Reformed view that the pope is the antichrist and the Church of Rome has become Babylon through descent into heresy, and therefore whoever would be saved must depart from her.[26] This work represents part of Perkins's increased level of engagement with Roman Catholicism after the Cambridge predestinarian dispute of 1595.[27]

---

22. This sermon was the basis for part of chapters 3–4 in *Treatise of Man's Imaginations* (cf. RHB 9:211–19). That it belongs to an ongoing series is clear from its opening line.

23. "To the Reader," in William Perkins, *A Treatise of Man's Imaginations* (Cambridge: John Legate, 1607), 5r (RHB 9:185).

24. Cf. *Galatians* (RHB 2:158). On Perkins's primary use of the term "prophecy," see *Art of Prophesying* (RHB 10:289–90).

25. Perkins, *Reformed Catholic*, RHB 7:28–30, 93–99. The published treatise retains marks of its homiletical origins. Not only does it begin with a biblical text which frames all that follows, but the preface ends with the kind of anticipatory marker more reminiscent of speech than written prose: "The first point wherewith I mean to begin shall be the point of free will, though it be not the principal" (RHB 7:12).

26. Perkins, *Reformed Catholic*, RHB 7:9–12.

27. These disputes produced the Lambeth Articles (1595). The primary antagonist of these disputes, William Barrett, fled England and converted to Roman Catholicism in 1597. See Porter, *Reformation and Reaction in Tudor Cambridge*, 344–90.

Several works from this period reflect Perkins's concern that many English people were shifting Rome-ward in a number of interconnected ways, including *A Reformed Catholic* (1597), *The Manner and Order of Predestination* (Latin, 1598), and *God's Free Grace* (1601), as well in his choices of late-career series of biblical exposition such as *Jude* (c. 1598–1599) and *Galatians* (c. 1599–1602).[28]

The placement of these lectures in the Hutton MS provides further evidence as to how they ought to be dated. The two lectures are separated in the Hutton MS, one amid material reading from the front of the book and the other amid material reading from the back. That they clearly belong to the same series implies relative dates for surrounding material. Thus, the Exodus 22:18 sermons, given before the second Revelation 18:4 sermon, appear to have been delivered at around the same time, probably in 1596.[29] This implies that in the same year, and perhaps simultaneously, Perkins delivered lecture series on Revelation 18:4 (*A Reformed Catholic*), Genesis 2:18–24 (*Treatise of Vocations*), and Exodus 22:18 (*The Damned Art of Witchcraft*), all in addition to his regular expository sermon series on the Lord's Day.[30] This level of productivity was not unusual for Puritan preachers; however, Perkins proved especially adept at transforming the fruits of his various lecturing efforts into best-selling treatises.

The fourteen consecutive sermons, covering Jude 3–9, represent the longest series published in this volume. They were delivered in 1598/1599, most likely as Perkins's lectures each Sunday at St. Andrews the Great Church, Cambridge. Perkins emphasizes the danger that "seducers" present to the church, whether separatists, antinomians, or papists. The series exemplifies Perkins's sensitivity to the ways in which theological, political, social, and ethical errors are interconnected: errors in one of these areas often have powerful implications for the others.

The three sermons on Exodus 22:18 represent the beginnings of a series that became *The Damned Art of Witchcraft* (1608).[31] The transcriber began taking down this series from the back of the book, perhaps with the intention of

---

28. Galatians had been a Protestant commonplace since Luther's seminal treatment of the epistle in 1535, offering an emphatic biblical basis for the doctrine of justification by faith alone. Perkins's Jude series repeatedly warns of "seducers" in the church.

29. It appears that the transcriber took the Exodus 22:18 sermons down in the back of the book in order to transcribe concurrently Perkins's sermons on Genesis 2:19–24 from the front without breaking up either series.

30. During this period, Perkins's Sunday sermons were most likely on Hebrews 11 or Matthew 4:1–11. Both series were later published. See the introduction to this volume.

31. This material is included in the first three chapters of *Damned Art of Witchcraft* (9:307–14).

recording the entire series; however, this was abandoned after three sermons.[32] The transcriber appears to have missed the second lecture but heard the first, third, and fourth,[33] the scope of which was subsequently developed into the first three chapters of the published treatise. As with the transcriptions at the front of the MS, these pages are badly damaged and much of the text has been supplemented here; however, the flow of this series and its relationship to the published work is clear.

The sermon on Matthew 5:27 is the same as that heard by Thomas Pierson and posthumously published in Perkins's *Sermon on the Mount* (1608).[34] It was delivered as a Lord's Day lecture, probably in 1597.

The sermon on Isaiah 50:4 has a similar relationship to the posthumously published *The Whole Treatise of Cases of Conscience* (1606) as the sermons on Revelation 18:4 have to *A Reformed Catholic*. In both cases, Perkins treated a biblical text as emblematic for his systematic engagement with a complicated subject. Both consisted of a series of lectures under the title of one biblical verse, which later became a published treatise with a new title. *The Whole Treatise of Cases of Conscience* is Perkins's directory on case divinity—that is, the pastor's role of assisting people struggling with matters of conscience and faithful decision-making. Isaiah 50:4 sums up this role as possessing a "tongue of the learned" by which the well-trained minister is able to "speak a word in season to him that is weary."[35] The present sermon is part of Perkins's treatment of "man as he stands in relation to God" (book 2), here specifically focusing on how to spiritually benefit from hearing sermons.[36] Perkins lectured through this series through the turn of the century and had almost completed it when he died in 1602.[37]

The transcription of the sermon on Matthew 23:37 represents the latest material transcribed in the manuscript, most likely being delivered in 1599 or 1600. This biblical text was one of a handful of texts on which predestinarian debates raged in the late-Elizabethan period and thus represented a fitting

---

32. It is followed by notes on a series of fifteen sermons by an unspecified preacher, covering Matthew 25:26–26:28. The transcriber was evidently less interested in Perkins's work during this period (circa 1597), during which time the bulk of sermons by other preachers were taken down. The transcriber's interest in Perkins was evidently renewed with the Jude series.

33. RHB 9:307–13, 322–31, 332–39.

34. Perkins, *Sermon on the Mount* (RHB 1:285–89).

35. Cf. *Whole Treatise* (RHB 8:115–16); *Art of Prophesying* (RHB 10:329); *Sermon on the Mount* (RHB 1:731–32).

36. *Whole Treatise*, bk. 2, ch. 7 (RHB 8:271–74).

37. Perkins had not delivered all the series' content when he died. Cf. the introduction to this volume.

point of entry into those issues.[38] The present lecture would become the opening section of *A Treatise of God's Free Grace and Man's Free Will* (1601), in which Perkins expounded the subjects of human willing accord to the Augustinian taxonomy of the "four states of man" (created, fallen, redeemed, glorified) and the relationship between divine and human willing in terms of primary and secondary causality.[39] The series likely consisted of about thirteen lectures in total.[40] Here, as throughout his ministry, Perkins sought to uphold the reality of man's responsibility to respond to God through the means of grace that he had made available to them while also strenuously defending the fact of God's sovereign will in all things, particularly in His gracious saving acts.

---

38. See discussion in Moore, *English Hypothetical Universalism*, 55–68.

39. See Richard Muller's recent treatment of Perkins's treatise in its intellectual context: *Grace and Freedom: William Perkins and the Early Modern Reformed Understanding of Free Choice and Divine Grace* (Oxford: Oxford University Press, 2020). Cf. RHB 6:405.

40. The present lecture corresponds to RHB 6:391–95. By deduction of length there were some twelve additional lectures.

1 Corinthians 7:20

(Sermon 1)

"Let everyone abide in that calling wherein he was called." (1 Cor. 7:20)[1]

> We have heard of...
> and we proceeded...
> we considered certain...
> a calling. Secondly, that he...
> much we have handled.

<The practice of> a particular calling must be <joined to that of the general> calling of a Christian, as <before described. It is not sufficient that a man> only be a Christian in general, <but he must show this in his particular calling. As> particularly in magistracy, <he must be a Christian in bearing the sword,> and the schoolmaster, not only in the church, but <he must show himself to be a Christian in his office of teaching.> So in a word must everyone in his <particular calling show his general calling.> Personal calling severed from the <foresaid general calling is nothing else> but profaneness, and so the general calling <without the practice of some particular calling is> nothing but religion without form.[2]

<Scripture> teaches everyone to try his own life <and calling. Neglecting> this rule causes great disorder <in society and the church.> In general calling hearing of the <Word and receiving> of sacraments is good, but this is <all out of order without obedience> in particular [calling]. For howsoever a man <resolves himself that all is well in> himself, that is, performing these duties <in their general callings>, yet they are to know that as yet their case <is that of a hypocrite>. For unless that man repents in the day of judgment, it shall be better with many others than with him. So, this is the first use of this rule.

Secondly, it serves to <teach a man what is> a reformed life, when he shall know first what is his personal calling, and then join the same with his general. This must be <put> in practice of everyone who would he assured

---

1. Much of the content is missing from the MS because the page is torn. This content has been supplied from *Treatise of Vocations*, RHB 10:57–59.

2. This is possibly a transcription error on the part of the transcriber. The published version uses the term "form" for the negative rather than the positive: "nothing else but the form of godliness without the power thereof" (*Treatise of Vocations*, RHB 10:58).

of his salvation. He must join both callings together, for if we only hear the Word of God without particular practice, the more we hear it the greater is our condemnation.

<Our> personal callings must <give place to our general calling,> when they cannot <both stand together.>³ For example, a servant <is bound to his master. But his> master, a papist, <threatens> death to his servant unless <he hears Mass, which leads to his> servant departing. The question <is whether> he may lawfully depart or no. The <answer is that> he may because in general calling <the servant is bound> to God, then to his master. For man <is bound first> to God, then to man under God. Thus <much of the> rules in personal callings.

Now personal <callings are> of two sorts. They serve to number up <the foundation> (as it were) of every society. Second, they <serve for the> good estate of a society, some serve to <preserve> the life, some the health of man, some for <outward peace,> some for the attiring of the parts of the body, <and such> like. And to these heads are all callings <referred.> Thus much of the kinds.

Now we are to see how every man may in good manner use these personal <callings> ordinarily, for the learning of this point is of great <moment.> By every man's good use of his calling, his works are made good works. In every work are three duties required: first, that it be done in obedience; second, in conscience; [and] third, for the glory of God. Now, these three duties concur in a man's calling, that the value of the work does not disgrace the worker. For if he does it in these three duties, it is a good work. As if a shepherd does but his duty in discharging his office, it is as acceptable to God as the calling of a prince. Now if this is so, then we see there is cause why everyone should know the use of his calling. For this are four things required: first, a good choice of a calling; second, a good entrance into it; third, a good continuance; [and] fourth, an honest learning of it.

For the first, <in the choice of our calling, we must> remember three rules.⁴ <First, we are to choose a lawful calling> (Eph. 4:28). This rule <means that a man is to> perform his calling <in faith.> That he has a good <and honest> calling he must <choose a> calling that serves to <uphold the church and> the commonwealth and <is grounded upon> the moral law. And <if it is> a hindrance to those, it is <an unlawful calling.>

---

3. Much of the content is missing from the MS because the page is torn. This content has been supplied from *Treatise of Vocations*, RHB 10:59–60.

4. Much of the content is missing from the MS because the page is torn. This content has been supplied from *Treatise of Vocations*, RHB 10:61–62.

<The second rule> in choice is that he must <choose a fit calling. This> rule is as necessary as the <former. When men are out of their proper calling, it is like> to the body when the members are <out of place> in these states. For this choice <of a fit calling, there are> two sorts of men: men[5] and <children. Men are> to choose for themselves. That <they may make a fit choice,> they are to consider, first, his affections and, second, his gifts.> For his affections, what he likes <best, and, for his gifts,> what he is fittest for. And this is his <…> in every calling whether a man's affections <…> and his gifts withal, that is his calling <…>.[6] Some will say that men are partial of their <inclination and gifts.> We answer that then they are to be guided <by the help of others.>

Now, concerning children, we must know that their governors are to choose callings for them. That they may do this, first, every parent must consider the inclination of the child; secondly, the gifts of him. For the first, every child is naturally inclined unto something. Concerning their gifts, they are seen either in the body or mind. Those who <possess> gifts of the mind are to be applied to such callings. *Objection.* How shall we know those who are inclined to learning? *Answer.* That is seen in their labor and such like.

And thus much of this point.

---

5. I.e., adults.

6. It is difficult to ascertain from the published version how this sentence is to be completed.

1 Corinthians 7:20

(Sermon 2)

"Let everyone abide in that calling wherein he was called." (1 Cor. 7:20)[1]

<To know> what is the right use of <our particular calling, there> are requisite four things. Of <…> <…>[2] entered into part of the second <rule in choosing a particular> calling. Here we showed how <particular callings are> chosen for men and children, that <is, according to their> affections and gifts. Their gifts <are of> the body and of the mind. Those of bodily <gifts are suited> to callings wrought by the body, <and those of the> mind to the contrary. We added that there <are two understandings,> active and passive, in children, so <the active> are to be applied to learning.

Secondly, we <…> a good entrance into a calling, that we showed <how> a man called can say God placed him there: <first,> when he brings gifts fit for it; secondly, when <he is> fully set apart by men. Here we laid open a <serious> disorder, the buying of offices as of ecclesiastical <offices,> and hitherto we proceeded before.

We are further <to> consider the manner of entrance. If this is true that <a man> enters aright, who performs the forenamed duty, <we> are necessarily to answer to the question of the Church of Rome to our church touching the calling of ministers. This we answer [in] two ways. First, that the first preachers of the gospel had particular callings. They were priests and then they were called solemnly. But against this they object that these practices were all severed because they were bound to be obedient to the Church of Rome. The answer is that their oath only bound them to the catholic and apostolic church, not to the Romish church. Secondly, we answer that many of them had their calling extraordinarily, which is manifest because God calls [in] three ways. First, by His own voice, as Abraham, Moses, Paul, and His apostles. Second, by the ministry of creatures as Elisha and Aaron and the Eunuch. Third, He calls by instinct. By calling, Phillip was but a deacon and had no vocation by

---

1. Much of the content is missing from the MS as the page is torn. This content has been supplied from *Treatise of Vocations*, RHB 10:62–64.

2. It is difficult to ascertain from the published version how this sentence is to be completed.

the apostles, yet he preached in Samaria (Acts 8:14). When the church was then dispersed thither, the men of Cyrene preached the gospel (Acts 11:20).

Now whereas the church <...>[3] we answer that there were <men extraordinarily called.[4] Some will say that this> lays open a way for <heretics and deceivers. We answer> that there are notes whereby <we may discern an extraordinary> calling that is by time for <...>.[5] <First, extraordinary calling never has a place> but when ordinary calling <fails. There are two special times: first, in the grounding of the church, <and, secondly, in the restoring of the> same.

The second note is his doctrine, <which must be the very doctrine of Christ and the apostles.> <When Christ was demanded> by what authority He did things, <He answered by asking them about the> baptism of John (Luke 20:4). He shows that <...>[6] it is good. Christ says <we shall know false prophets by> their fruits (Matt. 7:15). For those whom God <called to the restoring of the gospel, He gave> them integrity of life to adorn their <doctrine.>

<The third note> is that whom God calls extraordinarily, <He does furnish with gifts above> ordinary gifts to maintain their <extraordinary calling. We find this to be> very true as in other so in Luther, <whom God notably armed with boldness.>

We may easily discern men from God <from startups in our age.> By these notes we shall know who are called <extraordinarily of God. It is> manifest that those first fathers were called <in the last age. Against this> the papists do so object. Against this the <papists> object that they could not be so called because <they did not> confirm the calling by miracles. *Answer.* <In this> age God's Word needs not to be confirmed by miracles. <Secondly,> everyone who was so called by God did not work <miracles.> Thirdly, the gift of working miracles may be <given to> the enemies of God, as well as the gift of prophesying. And this is shown in Deuteronomy 13:2.

And thus much of this question of theirs answered.

Now, touching the manner of entrance, it may be asked what the man should do if he enters into his call unlawfully. *Answer.* He is to repent and perform the duties of his calling with a good conscience, and to look for an approbation from God and man, and so continue in his calling.

---

3. It is difficult to ascertain from the published version how this sentence is to be completed. It appears to be related to the Roman Catholic Church's refusal to recognize the extraordinary calling of Protestant Reformers such as Luther and Calvin.

4. Much of the content is missing from the MS as the page is torn. The content has been supplied from *Treatise of Vocations*, RHB 10:67–68.

5. It is difficult to ascertain from the published version how this sentence is to be completed.

6. It is difficult to ascertain from the published version how this sentence is to be completed.

Now, here is to be answered another objection touching the calling of ministers. Some avouch that they are not ministers; we <answer> the contrary. Their reason is because preachers <have no good and lawful entrance into their> callings. *Answer*. Let that be granted (which notwithstanding <no man in good conscience can think>), yet there may be preachers in England, the after acceptance of God and men make supply of their entrance. That they have this acceptance appears because, first, God gives them sufficient gifts; secondly, He gives them reformed lives; [and] thirdly, He makes them instruments to convert many souls to Him (1 Cor. 9:2). <It is> manifest that God gives <approbation> to the ministers of England. <…> the parts of man, we shall <…> they likewise give their approbation.[7]

<Touching the manner of entrance,> another point is to be considered: <whether a man> may sue to enter into a calling.[8] The <answer> is set down sufficiently. Paul <says> it is lawful for a man to desire an office (1 Tim. 3:1). <There are> desires unlawful, as to desire it for <greed and pleasure,> not for honor. But to desire it for conscience, <there is no offense.> Now if this may be done with good <conscience,> then their duty, who are brought up in <it, is> to show themselves ready to practice <the duty> of ministry to the glory of God. Therefore this <is needful,> that men enabled thereunto betake them<selves> to private study, and not show themselves <unfit> to benefit the church of God. The Holy Spirit condemns desires of entering into callings for <lucre> and ambition, but there are other degrees of calling <for> good conscience sake which are not condemned.

---

7. It is difficult to ascertain from the published version how this sentence is to be completed.

8. Much of the content is missing from the MS because the page is torn. The content has been supplied from *Treatise of Vocations*, RHB 10:70.

1 Corinthians 7:20

(Sermon 3)

"Let everyone abide in that calling wherein he was called." (1 Cor. 7:20)

Having spoken before of the choice of calling, we came to speak of the practice of calling. We have spoken last of all of the sanctification of the works of calling. That is done by the Word and prayer. Here we give directions touching the life of calling, that is, in avoiding certain vices and performing contrary virtues.

The first vice is covetousness, by which all men abuse their calling. The manner to avoid this is twofold. [The] first [is] to restrain his affections. It is like the sea: if it is suffered to transcend its bounds, it will overcome the whole man. For [the] restraining of these, there are two rules.

The first is set down [in] Hebrews 13:5, which is contentation.[1] A notable example of this unto us all is Paul: "I have learned to be poor and rich and to be content" (Phil. 4:11). He signifies that it is a harder matter to do this than men think. For so this is a notable example <to be content in every estate> in which God has placed us. <For our parts, these> duties are required. First, to <see a particular providence> of God over us in every estate. <In all things that come to pass> God cares for them and shuts up <…>, contrary to these the blind world sees <no providence or goodness in> them. This, therefore, we must learn to perform <…> as content with Paul. Of this we have an <example in Job. Secondly,> that we may be content, we must labor to say, "God is my portion" [Ps. 16:5]. Now, when a man can <…> him in this life, he will be content with any <estate, whatever> it be. For he who has God has all good <things.>

<Second, for the restraining> of the earthly man's affections, he must seek <for no more but things that are> necessary in this life. For to seek for <abundance is not lawful…> no that which is sufficient. <In Scripture we see that we may> pray for daily bread and not for abundance <Prov. 30:8; Matt. 6:11>. It is a sin for men to desire to be rich, that <they might have more> than things convenient. In gathering <the manna,> they gathered more or less, everyone had his gomer (Ex. 16:17). The king must not seek for too much, that is, <more> than will maintain his own kingdom [Deut. 17:16–17].

---

1. Much of the content is missing from the MS because the page is torn. The content has been supplied from *Treatise of Vocations*, RHB 10:81–85.

And such <is the duty> of every one of us. We may seek for things necessary, <but> abundance we may not. A master of a family may <seek for as> much as will maintain him and his lent,[2] not for so <much as> will maintain two men in their estate and calling. Now, <…> to see what is convenient for everyone, this must not be done by the affection of covetous men, but by the judgment of godly and prudent men. As in the manner of attire, we must look unto the example of such men. Again, we must <…> be this, that the same condition is for every man according to their high or low estate.

[3]Against this the covetous man will first object that the blessings of God are to be sought for, but riches are the blessings of God. *Answer.* We must distinguish of these blessings. There are some simply called blessings, and these are all to be sought for. <And there are blessings in respect,> and among these are riches. <We may seek> for them, if we know <that they> themselves are good. But <they are no> more than a sword in a mad man's <hand>. <If we can say> that, in seeking of them, God blesses <them to us,> they are good. By that argument <we understand that> they are not therefore good because God blesses <them and> bestows them upon wicked men also.

<Second, he objects that> God has promised plenty to the righteous <man, and therefore we may seek riches. I> answer [in] two ways. First, that that is to be <understood of things> necessary. Second, for as much as it is to be <taken for temporal> blessings, it must be understood <with exception of cross and chastisement>, that is this, if God sees them good for us.

<Third, he objects> that everyone must do good to the church <and commonwealth, and therefore may> lawfully seek for them. *Answer.* That he <must indeed do good> to his ability, not beyond the same.

<Fourthly, he objects> that the children of God have <abounded with riches>, as Abraham, Lot, and David. *Answer.* We must <note that> they had it not of their own getting, but by <the> blessing of God. If God bestows them on us, they are not be refused, yet men must not labor for abundance. So, this must be remembered for <the restraining of> our affections, that we must always be content.

---

2. The meaning of this term is unclear. The published edition says "family." *Treatise of Vocations*, RHB 10:84.

3. Much of the content is missing from the MS because the page is torn. The content has been supplied from *Treatise of Vocations*, RHB 10:85–86.

1 Corinthians 7:20

(Sermon 4)

"Let everyone abide in that calling wherein he was called." (1 Cor. 7:20)

The last point handled was how everyone must sanctify the works of his calling. The means is the Word, which presents what we shall do. This teaches us for this purpose two things. First, to avoid certain vices. These are two: covetousness and injustice. Of the first we have spoken. Now we are to speak of the second, namely, injustice.

Injustice is that which hinders everyone's calling. Of this we have an example in Zacchaeus (Luke 19:8). And this spreads itself over the callings of men as much as covetousness. This appears in all callings, as first in princes, for this is their manner, not to content themselves with their own kingdoms but to assault others likewise and therefore shed whole rivers of blood for [the] attaining of their purpose.

This appears in the Turk and Spaniard.[1] And to these do inferior callings answer also, as in magistrates in accepting of persons and the minister in not preaching the Word to the people. In the calling of the lawyer there is taking of bribes, in the physician by ministering physic <which is> still to the destroying of the patient. In the calling of <merchant and tradesman> there is lying, swearing, foreswearing, fraud, and all <sorts> of injustice; as in the landlord in raising of rents. <In the husbandman> in selling of common grain and corn there is greediness. In the calling of the printer likewise there is <injustice> in publishing of unchaste libels and books to the <…>. In the calling of the bookseller likewise, as in selling <of truth> as well of heresies as of truth. This <does> greatly annoy the church, and so in whole <we> shall hardly find one that undermines not another, so that we may say with Micah, "Everyone hunteth his brother" (Mic. 7:2).

These things are so manifest that all men see them, yet which unjust man wants not his excuse, which is this: If <he> will live in the world, he must do as the most do, else <there is no> living in the world. We answer that those who are the children of God must do as Paul bids them. They must carry themselves as lights among a perverse generation (Phil. 2:15). But others, more shameless,

---

1. Much of the content is missing from the MS because the page is torn. The content has been supplied from *Treatise of Vocations*, RHB 10:88–90.

blush not to pretend the doing of our Savior Christ, in sending for the colt and the ass (Matt. 21:3). But we must know that He did that as Lord and having authority. And, therefore, in that action He inclined the owner's heart to let them go.

Then, to end this point, every man must learn to amend his calling and to carry himself upright in the same. To persuade us in this are many reasons. First, God's commandment: "Defraud no man" (1 Thess. 4:6; Titus 2:12). So then, never a one of us must decline from this commandment. Secondly, we must consider that as long as we practice injustice, all our worshipping of God is abominable. Thirdly, the practice of injustice incurs the curse of God. "Know ye not that the unrighteous shall not enter into the kingdom of God, neither fornicators, nor idolaters, nor adulterers, nor wantonness, nor ungrateful, nor thieves, nor covetous men, nor drunkards, nor revilers, nor extortioners shall inherit the kingdom of God" (1 Cor. 6:9–10). Then it stands everyone in hand to cast away all works of injustice, for it is a bar to keep us from the kingdom of heaven. Lastly, Paul says he endeavored in all things to please the Lord (2 Cor. 5:11). The reason is because one day we must stand at the bar of God's judgment to give account of our doing and then <all> our doings be discovered.

Thus much of the vice of injustice, and thus much of both the vices.

<We come now> to speak of the virtues which the Word of God requires of us.[2] They are especially two: faith and love. By faith I mean not a justifying faith, but that whereby we are <firmly> resolved that the works of our callings are good <before God>. Noah[3] built an ark by faith, that there is that faith which we understand in this place, and without this faith no man can please God in his particular calling. That everyone may have this faith, he must have a particular word; that word is either a commandment or a promise. The commandment is some word for the allowing of his calling. The promise is whereby God has promised to bless his calling. And whosoever has not both these cannot do the works of his calling in faith.

Here then we must learn this duty, to do the duties of his calling in faith; for this he must have both God's promise and his commandment, or else he cannot please God. Now, if any man thinks this strange, he must consider the dealing of the world. Men bind themselves to some trade by whatever laws to their master. Then we must not think it much to bind ourselves to our calling by God's law and commandment. And when men bind themselves by God's commandment, it makes them perform his works in obedience, and if by promise then it makes them know that God is with them. And when he joins both together, it eases the crosses of their callings.

---

2. Much of the content is missing from the MS because the page is torn. The content has been supplied from *Treatise of Vocations*, RHB 10:91.

3. The MS erroneously states "Abraham."

1 Corinthians 11:28

(Sermon 1)

"Let a man examine himself, and so let him eat of this bread and drink of this cup." [1 Cor. 11:28]

In these words, we are to consider two things: first, a precept, and second, a limitation of the precept.[1] The precept is set down with [these words]: "Let a man examine himself, etc." The limitation [of this precept] is contained in these words: "and so let him eat of this bread [and] cup."

By the precept we are enjoined not only to <…> <…> <…>[2] but to take bread, and not only to take bread but [to eat] it also, and not only to take and eat bread but to take the cup and drink it. By which we may learn that he <…> <…> <…>, and not to eat and drink is given to every[one] <…> <…> he will eat or not, for he which eats not is <…> <…> <…> of the Lord as he who eats, and he who <…> <…> <…> eats not. But as for the eating of this bread and drinking of this cup in this place, it is not so given to our disposition to do it and to refuse it, for of this bread and cup we are commanded in this place by the authority of God to eat and drink.

If Paul had in this place said, as he did a little before, "I think it good that you eat of this bread and drink of this cup," we were to blame if we would not follow his exhortation. Much more then, we are to blame if we do not follow his commandment, which he sets down in express words, saying, "Let a man eat of this bread and drink of this cup."

When Moses, in Exodus 18, was counseled by Jethro, his father-in-law, to take seventy of the elders of the people, Moses regarded his counsel and did as his father-in-law willed him. Shall Moses then follow the counsel of Jethro, and shall not we follow the counsel of Saint Paul? But that which is more, Saint Paul in this place *non suadet*,[3] as did Jethro, *sed iubet*.[4] And, therefore, if we do not

---

1. For more on Perkins's thoughts on preparation for receiving the sacrament, see *Hebrews*, RHB 3:306–7; *Foundation of Faith*, RHB 5:482–509; and *Golden Chain*, RHB 6:167–69. He expounds 1 Corinthians 11:28 specifically in *Whole Treatise of Cases of Conscience*, RHB 8:294–300.

2. Some words are illegible in the MS because the page is torn.

3. "does not advise."

4. "but commands."

follow his commandment, *periclitamur*,[5] and though we need not always follow counsels but may neglect persuasions, yet we must not neglect the commandment of him who has power over us to command us, unless we will undergo great danger.

But perhaps some will say to Paul, as the scribes and Pharisees said to our Savior Christ [in] Luke 10:25.[6] But to learn this, our Savior in Luke 22:19[7] commands us to eat, and therefore we must not think that Paul gives this commandment from himself.

Therefore, we may note that this negligence in refusing to come to the Lord's Supper, being invited not only by the apostles but also by Christ Himself, is a point of great ingratitude. And, therefore, whosoever refuses to come and call to mind the death of Christ is not worthy to be partakers of the benefits thereof. [Secondly, he who] refuses to come and eat of this bread and drink of this cup does refuse to fight under the banner <...>[8] his captain, whereas in eating we promise to fight <...>. Thirdly, he who refuses this Supper refuses <...> <...> with God. Fourthly, by not eating we put away <...> memory of Christ's death. Fifthly, we do <...> <...> diminish the promise of God from us. Sixthly, by refusing it we separate ourselves from the communion of Christ and His saints. Lastly, we put ourselves in great danger, for there is the food as well of the soul as of the body, and he who refuses the food of the soul is worthy to perish and starve because he will not eat the food which should <...> him when it is offered.

But some will say, "I have eaten of this once or twice already." But this is not sufficient, for as the body ought often [to] be fed with corporeal food, so ought the soul often to be nourished with spiritual food, and thereby to be sustained unto eternal life.

Thus much of the precept.

Now let us come to the limitation of the precept in these words: "And so let him eat of this bread and drink of this cup." Here we must mark that all stands not in eating but in the manner of eating, for we must not only eat but we must eat *so*. Cain offered [a] sacrifice to the Lord, as well as Abel, yet it was not accepted because he did not so offer it as did Abel. The Pharisee prayed, as well as the publican, yet because he did not so pray as the publican did, his prayer was not heard. There were many who cast more into the treasury than the widow, yet because they did not so cast it in, it was not so well accepted

---

5. "we are in danger."

6. "And, behold, a certain lawyer stood up, and tempted him, saying, Master, what shall I do to inherit eternal life?"

7. Original: Luke 11:22, a typographical error.

8. Some words are illegible in the MS because the page is torn.

whereas hers was. Simon Magus was baptized, as well as Simon, the brother of Andrew, yet he wanted the fruits of baptism. Judas, who betrayed Christ, received the sacrament, as well as the other disciples. Therefore, as it is [stated in] Proverbs 20:4, Ecclesiastes 4:17, Matthew [26:26] so must we eat of this bread and drink of this cup.[9]

It is not sufficient to eat, but we must eat <…> <…>[10] ought we to eat. Saint Paul says we must examine ourselves, but this is too generally. Therefore, if we would <…> <…> of it we must, first, eat it faithfully. Secondly, we must eat it penitently. Thirdly, we must eat it <…>. Fourthly, we must eat it in love and charity. Fifthly, we must eat it willingly. Sixthly, we must do it thankfully, for we are thanking God for it. Seventhly, and lastly, we must examine ourselves whether all these things be in us, whether we have knowledge, faith, penitence, willingness, love and charity, and thankfulness unto God—all which are necessarily required in every one of us.

---

9. The intended references appear to be Proverbs 31:4, Ecclesiastes 9:7, and Matthew 26:26. There are multiple statements of drinking in both Proverbs and Ecclesiastes that could have been intended.

10. Some words are illegible in the MS because the page is torn.

1 Corinthians 11:28

(Sermon 2)

"Let a man examine himself, and so let him eat of this bread and drink of this cup." [1 Cor. 11:28][1]

We have considered these words, a precept and a limitation of the first. We have spoken [of the first], and we are come to the limitation in these words "but so let him eat." The Pharisee praised as well as the publican, but because he did not so pray it was not accepted. Cain sacrificed as well as Abel, but because he did not so sacrifice, his sacrifice was not accepted. Therefore, our Savior says, "When you pray, pray after this manner."[2] And as Saint James wills us to receive the Word, but how wills he us to receive it, <…> with humility and meekness.[3]

Now we are to consider how we must eat. We must do it worthily, but this is to your call, more especially we must do it after those seven words. First, we must eat of it with knowledge. Secondly, we must eat it faithfully. Thirdly, we must eat it with repentance of our sins. Fourthly, we must eat of this supper with love toward our brethren. Fifthly, we must eat it willingly. Sixthly, we must eat it thankfully. Lastly, we must afterward examine ourselves.

Now we will speak of those seven points in order. First, we [are] to eat of this bread and drink of the cup with understanding and knowledge, and not to eat of it ignorantly, for as in the old law they which did eat ignorantly must pay a fine for it, so they which eat of this bread ignorantly will perhaps pay a greater fine for it than they are able to bear. In baptism this is not so required because some which are children have no discretion. But those which are of discretion are not to be baptized ignorantly. By this we learn that children and men and fools are not to be admitted to this sacrament of the Lord's Supper.[4]

Now to the second, faith, which is that we must eat of this faithfully, although we have never so much knowledge, yet if we bring not faith with us when we come to eat of these, we cannot receive it aright; therefore, after knowledge we must seek faith, for as it is in the [epistle to the] Romans, without

---

1. The MS states 1 Corinthians 11:18. This is a typographical error on the part of the transcriber.

2. Matt. 6:5–15.

3. James 1:21.

4. The MS states, "to to be admitted" instead of "not to." This is a typographical error on the part of the transcriber.

faith it is impossible to please God.[5] It was a custom not to eat meat before they wash their hands. And so now shall the Pharisees be so careful to eat of bread without washing of hands, and shall we make no bones[6] to come to eat of this bread and drink of this cup with polluted and defiled hands and mouths? But to proceed as we must bind faith to knowledge, so to faith we must join repentance, for with what mouth you eat of this bread and drink of this cup which do represent His departure, without repentance. Wherefore let all which will come to this sacrament, let them purge their hearts and ask forgiveness for those sins. Now let not this remembrance of those sins be an occasion to withdraw or forgo to come to this sacrament. Now as we must join repentance to faith, so [to] repentance we must join brotherly love, laying aside therefore all anger, all malice and rending, let us eat of this sacrament. Let not, says Saint Paul, the sun go down upon your wrath.[7] So then to come to this sacrament, we must first put away all anger, hatred, and slander. In this <…> there is no difference of bread nor wine, no difference of servitors, but all we can <…>, and there is the <…> <…> and the <…> which all receive.

Now in the fifth place, we are not to come negligently or unwillingly, we are not to come for fear of danger of the law, but we are to come willingly to eat of this; even as the Lord does receive a cheerful giver, so does He love a cheerful comer to this Supper. We must have a desire to eat of it.

Now in the sixth place, we are to eat of it thankfully. He, says Saint Paul, who eats thankfully, he eats unto the Lord. Therefore, when we eat of this Supper thankfully, we eat unto the Lord. But if we do not eat thankfully after the receiving of it in thanks, then does the eating of the same do us no good because we eat and drink our own condemnation. This eating of the sacrament does bring unto us many other benefits, and therefore it is good reason we should be thankful.

Lastly, we must, after the receiving of the Supper, we must examine ourselves, and for this cause does Saint Paul bring in his exhortation in this place, saying, "Let a man therefore examine himself and so let him eat of this bread and drink of this cup."[8]

---

5. The reference to Romans is incorrect. See Hebrews 11:6.

6. *No bones*: without a doubt.

7. Eph. 4:26.

8. 1 Cor. 11:28. The MS is signed "M Bidingsly." This name does not appear in Venn's catalogue of Cambridge alumni and thus appears not to have been a Cambridge student.

Genesis 2:18

(Sermon 1)

"Also the Lord God said, It is not good that man should be himself alone. I will make him a help meet for him." (Gen. 2:18)

We have begun to speak of the duty of married persons, the knowledge whereof was noted out in human society. We have also shown what it is to be a help and what that help is which is to be offered to the husband by the wife. We have also entered into the offices of marriage, first defining the same offices and dividing them into two sorts: first, those that are common to both, and second, those that belong to them separately.[1]

For the first sort, we have spoken of the first office, that is, cohabitation, which we have proved to be an office of making common to both persons, answering all the objections against it, and annexed an exhortation unto it, both concerning those which are married and also [those] who purpose to marry.

The second common office is that they must have a care to win one another to Christ. This is such an office of marriage which is common to both equally, for the husband is as well bound to win the wife as the wife to win the husband. This point is manifest out of the Scripture: "Ye are bought with a price, be ye not therefore servants of men" [1 Cor. 7:23], that is, in any matter of faith deny obedience to any man. Here we may this reason: if there be equal power between the servant and the master, the much more there is equal power between the husband and the wife. So that, if the question be the husband and the wife, we see that the power and office between both is equal, so that neither the wife is to usurp <…> <…>[2] above the husband, nor the husband upon <…> <…> <…> Lord has spoken it. But because the <…> <…> <…> in this life will deny the good doctrine of God, we will confirm from this by the Scriptures. The Lord says by Malachi that He has instituted marriage to make a holy seed [Mal. 2:15]. If God, therefore, joined man together that they should make a holy seed, they must first have a care to win themselves to Christ. For if the root is sour, what

---

1. The MS says, "severedly."
2. Some of the words are illegible in the MS because the page is torn.

shall the branches be? If the parents are wicked, what shall the children do but tread in their parents' steps?

But because express Scriptures will not convince the judgment of man, we will add testimonies out of the same. [In] 1 Corinthians 7, the question being asked whether a Christian, marrying a wife and infidel, should for her infidelity depart from her, Paul answers "no" because (says he) who knows whether the husband, being religious, may win the wife, being an infidel [1 Cor. 7:8–16], thereby noting that married persons are bound to win one another to Christ. The same also teaches Saint Peter: "Let the wives likewise be subject to their husbands, that even they, who obey not the word, may even without the word be won by the conversation of their wives" (1 Peter 3:1). Noting thereby it is advice common to both parties to win and convert one another to Christ.

Now we come to the objections made against this point. First, it is objected: What if they are both infidels? How can they win one another? *Answer.* If it is so, they cannot. But that does not exempt the duty. For we cannot fulfill all the law of God, yet we are bound to fulfill the same. So, though they cannot win one another, yet they are bound to do it, for this inability comes from themselves. For at the first, God created Adam perfect, but by his own fault he fell and by this corruption condemned all to inability.

Secondly, what if the husband is religious and the wife an infidel? *Answer.* In such a case they are not to be separated, but he is gently to labor that he may win her. But what if she will separate herself from her husband? *Answer.* The magistrate is to provide for that.[3] But what if the magistrate will allow her separation? *Answer.* The brother is no longer bound to <…> after her.

Thirdly, it is the property of ministers to <…>; therefore, it belongs not to wives or husbands. *Answer.* It is indeed principally the duty of ministers publicly and secretly so far as their calling will suffer, but yet it is <…> all men and so of married persons in their <…> callings.

Fourth, if the wife is religious, laboring to win her husband, being an infidel, and he being of <…> judgment will not agree with her, what <…> <…>[4] there be between those two? Therefore, this office which <…> contention is not an office of marriage. *Answer.* True it is that there arises contention, but what contention is it not acceptable to God? Read Luke 12:51, "Think ye," says Christ, "I am come to bring peace. I tell you nay, but rather debacle." But though it be acceptable to God in regard of him not making this contention, yet woe be to the man who is the cause of this contention.

---

3. I.e., such a case is to be referred to the magistrate.
4. Some of the words are illegible in the MS because the page is torn.

Now follow the means whereby they must labor to win one another. First, they must labor by godliness and entreaty, not rigorously and cruelly, but even handling one another as their own flesh. Secondly, by performing all the offices of married men, for if the wife, while she labors to win the husband, neglects her own duty, she shall hardly convince her husband. Thirdly, they must be patient of injuries and patiently suffer injuries which are offered of either without revenge either in word or deed, knowing that the sufferers of injuries shall be rewarded with eternal life; especially this must be done in the wife when her husband offers injuries. Fourthly, they must labor to effect this by their good life and conversation, for it is incredible what fruit the good and evil life of a man will bring forth in another. And for this it is that Saint Paul says, "he that will not hear the law, let him regard [his] good life and conversation."[5] These are the means which married persons are to use to win one another to Christ.

---

5. While Paul says something similar in 1 Corinthians 7:16, the intended reference appears to be 1 Peter 3:1.

Genesis 2:18

(Sermon 2)

"Also the Lord God said, It is not good that man should be himself alone. I will make him a help meet for him." (Gen. 2:18)

Now we are to show who are the breakers of this duty of marriage, and then who are the observers of the same.

For the first, all married persons who have little care of the uniting of one another to Christ are breakers of this office. Those, firstly, when they speak unto one another talk of earthly conditions as of lascivious fares, those who never mention Christ in their talk are guilty of the breach of this office. Secondly, those who, though they sometimes speak of Christ, faith, or salvation, yet when they do, they do it negligently, are breakers of this office. Thirdly, those who, though they can for a time diligently talk of these things, yet if they see no fruit, presently leave off, are transgressors of this office of marriage. Fourthly, they break this office who do not perform the duties which belong unto them in regard of marriage. For when the husband sees his wife to omit the duties which she owes to him, how can he persuade himself that she will be dutiful to her brother and neighbor, and if she cannot perform her duty to her brother and neighbor, he cannot think that she will humbly perform her duty to God, seeing it is written, "He that will not love his brother whom he seeth, how will he believe God whom he never saw?" [1 John 4:20]. Fifthly, they break this duty who do not labor to lead a chaste and pure[1] life, both before God and man, living in faith, peace, and unity. Sixthly, those break this office who will be impatient of injuries, even they who will give word for word and check for check.

Hence, we may see who are the breakers of this office. They must, before they come together, have this intent to unite each other to the Lord and make thereof a holy seed. They must also be patient of injuries, leading their life unblamable before God. Such were Abraham and Sarah, and Joseph and Mary.

The third common office is that they must please one another, that is, they must come together, pleasing one another in honesty, And this is common to them, for it belongs to brethren and neighbors, much more to man and wife

---

1. The MS says "unpure." This is a typographical error on the part of the transcriber.

whose connection is nearer. Paul commands this [in] 1 Corinthians 7, "Let the husband give unto the wife due benevolence, likewise also the wife unto the husband. The wife hath not power over her own body but the husband, neither the husband over his body but his wife" [1 Cor. 7:3–4]. Which place, though some would restrain to the bed chamber, yet such is it generally to be taken, seeing due benevolence signifies due good will. I see not why any should restrain it from the general signification. Also, this duty is commended by Saint Peter, saying, "Likewise, ye husbands, dwell with them according of knowledge, giving honor unto the woman, as unto the weaker vessel, even as they which are heirs together of the grace of life, that your prayers be not interrupted" (1 Peter 3:7). What does he else mean when he commands honor to the woman as to the weaker vessel but that the husband should study to please her because she is the weaker vessel? Whereas he says, "As those that are heirs together of the grace of life," he notes that they should live here so pleasingly and peacefully that they may be fellow heirs of the grace of life. What else wills he when he says that "your prayers be not interrupted," noting that living displeasing one another their prayers are interrupted, and pleasing one another they are accepted of God.

Secondly, we read in this chapter that God binds man to cleave to his wife, that is, only to please his wife. A notable example of this we have in David in 2 Samuel: "And when he [was] dancing before the altar to praise and glorify God thereby, Michal (his wife) came and rebuked him. And not only rebuked but also mocked and derided him for that act, saying, 'How glorious was the king of Israel this day, which was uncovered today in the eyes of his maidens, his servants, as a fool and vain man uncovers himself.' David, for all this, gave her no churlish or crooked answer, but very mildly said, 'It was before the Lord'" [2 Sam. 6:14–21]. Here the husband sought not to displease his wife, though she mocked him. Hence, I gather that if in this cause of mocking, David did not seek to displease his wife, surely in higher matters he would not have given a more rigorous answer. Therefore, see how necessarily this office is enjoined to married persons, and this point is the more necessary; because if a man cannot use his wife, how will he use other men?[2]

Third, this office is declared [in] Proverbs 31, where he, speaking of a good wife, says, "She shall do him good, not evil, all the days of his life." And in the same chapter he brings in the husband, commending the wife for her good done unto him, setting forth praise very emphatically in these words: "There are many daughters which have done well, but thou dost surmount them all" [Prov. 31:29]. So that, we see this duty necessarily imposed to married persons.

---

2. *Use*: treat someone rightly.

Genesis 2:18

(Sermon 3)

"It is not good that a man should be alone. I will make a help meet for him."
(Gen. 2:18)

For [the] better understanding of this verse concerning making a help meet for man, we have entered to speak of the duties of marriage which are necessarily required of married persons. And we have spoken of the offices common one toward another and also of mutual fellowship one toward another. Now we are come to the duty which is common to both parties for the mutual preserving one of the other.

[If] this mutual preservation often be necessary in other things, then much more is it necessary in this duty of married persons, which is the mother of all. Therefore, it is to be known what this preservation is. It is that mutual offer of married persons whereby they are mutually bound to preserve the health and life one of the other. By which description appears both not only the commodity and comfort but also the necessity thereof, for what can be more necessary than the preservation of life? For if the health of either of them is turned into sickness, we see what a grief it is to the other, so that if the life and health of either of them is comfortable to the other, it must needs be that the want of health must needs be sorrowful. Also, this necessity appears because it procures wonderful comfort not only to themselves but also to their posterity. Therefore, we see how necessary the duty of this preservation is.

Now it follows to teach wherein it consists. It consists in two things: in protection and provision. Touching the first, it is nothing else but a necessary duty whereby both parties' bodies are safely [to] be kept, and this seems to be equal to both. Examples of this the Scripture affords divers and teaches how willing married persons have done [this]. [In] Genesis 20 we shall see how willing Abraham and Sarah were to preserve the health and life one of another.[1] The same means of preservation was used of Isaac and Rebekah in the 26th [chapter] of that book. In the 19th [chapter] of [1] Samuel, Michal, understanding that her father would kill David, did let David down by a window in the

---

1. The MS originally had "Gen. 20" but 20 was crossed out and replaced with 12. The original reference to Genesis 20 was correct.

nighttime, and so he was preserved, both life and limb. By these examples we see how necessarily this duty of protection is required. Saint Paul shows it to be so necessary that he gives it out in this <…>, "No man hateth his own flesh but nourisheth the same" [Eph. 5:29]. Let us, therefore, acknowledge this duty and stir up our hearts to perform the same. What shall we say to them that they live in one place and themselves in another's place a long time? It is surely nothing else but a denial of this mutual protection one of another.

Now we must learn by what means this duty is to be offered, namely, by the married persons touching one another's health as their own flesh. Secondly, they must put on the gift of fortitude which will <…> them to the performing of this duty, for unless we be encouraged thereunto, these will both fail in this duty. Lastly, we must be willing to be partakers of our yokefellows when they are in greatest danger.

The second point is provision. This is nothing but that preservation whereby those things are provided which are necessary for the preservation of life and health. In Exodus we are not only commanded to provide for our own wives but also for those which are taken to our wives.[2] [In] Genesis 18 Abraham put in practice this duty when he hastened to make ready three cakes of fine flour,[3] thereby showing that it was not only necessary for him to provide for himself but also for Sarah his wife and those which there were to be <…> of him. Those that go not about by the gifts which are in them to provide one for the other, those I say are not worthy, as the apostle said, for to eat.[4]

But you will say: what must they provide? I answer: necessary food [and] comely apparel. Those things are fit for married persons, and [those] that cannot provide those things are unfit to marriage. These things therefore are to be provided not superfluously in them, but so much as shall be necessary. Solomon says the diligent hand builds the house and the slothful hand pulls down the house [Prov. 14:1]. By this we see that everyone ought to labor to help and relieve others, and none ought to be idle. For idleness is the mother of all poverty and beggars and all sin and wickedness. And those that are the tolerators of idleness, those are the nurses and upholders of all sin and wickedness, and of all beggaring. Cursed is that man which will not endeavor to labor for his wife, and cursed is that woman which will not labor for her husband. This duty is assured, first, by the virtue of prudence. For the fool, says Solomon, that wants prudence, he wants all things necessary for preserving there all. Secondly, it is preserved by diligence, for they must use diligence to preserve that be able of one another.

---

2. Ex. 21:10?
3. Gen. 18:6.
4. 2 Thess. 3:7–10.

The last duty is the careful avoiding of all offenses which are incident unto this state of marriage, for there is <...> but there are many scandals and offenses which shall befall the same. The last duty is that there be a mutual desire to avoid offenses which may befall each other. Therefore, that both persons should avoid those offenses, they must leave first what those things be that fall out between man and wife, and avoid the same. Now if any ask what those things be, I answer that they be the omission of those duties before named. Secondly, they must leave what are those offenses that are not of themselves [offenses] but that notwithstanding procure mislike one of the other, and labor to amend the same.

"So the Lord God formed of the earth every beast of the field and every fowl of the heaven, and brought them unto the man to see how he would call them. For howsoever the man named the living creature, so was the name thereof. The man therefore gave names unto all cattle, and to the fowl of the heaven and to every beast of the field, but for Adam found he not an help meet for him." (Gen. 2:19–20)

We have taught out of the former verse the holy and necessary offices belonging equally unto the husband and the wife, the which we noted because the Lord said He found some imperfection in man and would therefore make a help meet for him. Now because the woman is a sufficient help for man, we have justly spoken of all those helps which the woman does afford to the man. Now it follows that we should go forward in the text of Moses, who although he should presently now set down the creation of woman yet the Holy Spirit thinks meet to work a digression in these two verses, wherein it is declared that God did bring unto man all the fowls of the air and the creatures of the earth to see what name he would give to each one in their kind. The occasion of this digression is double. First, to see the excellency of those things which God had given unto man. The second is to know by what authority man does take upon him[self] to give a name unto the woman. The parts of this digression are two: first, the acts of God contained in the 19th verse; secondly, of the act of man in verse 20. Concerning the act of God, it is double, for it is said that God made the fowls of the air and creatures of the earth, and secondly did bring them unto man.

"So the Lord God formed." In these words we see Moses does remember[1] us of things which the Lord had done before, so calling to remembrance the creation of the beasts of the earth and the fowls of the air. Why does he, else but [to] command us both to be reminded of God's creation of those things, and [to] command us to make use of the same? For seeing those things were created to man's use, it behooves [us] not only to remember the creation but also [to] make profit and use [it] to ourselves. Where is it said that these were made of

---

1. I.e., remind.

the earth, it may be asked how this agrees with the 20th [verse] of the former chapter, where it appears that the fowls were made of the water. *Answer*. Here it is not flatly said that the fowls were made of the earth, and therefore that which is there expressly said is to be holden for truth. Thus much of the first act.

Now it follows, "and brought them unto the man." There we see that the Lord, when He had made those creatures, brought them unto the man. In His bringing of the creatures we must first consider the time when God brought them; also the place whither He brought them; thirdly, the manner after which He brought them; and, lastly, the end for which He brought them.

Concerning the time wherein He brought them, it is evident that He brought them in the innocency of man before when he had sinned. Here then we must stay and believe that this action of the Lord in bringing these creatures unto man was in man's innocency.

Concerning the place whither, it is evident that it was the place of paradise where the Lord had placed a man, a place full of all pleasure and delight. And thither the Lord brought all the beasts of the field and the fowls of the air, that Adam might ascribe to them names whereby they might be called, the which could not be done without great meditation of Adam. So that by this we see that in the innocency of man, the Lord would not have him to be idle either in respect of bodily labor, because of tilling of the garden, neither in respect of meditation of mind, because he was to give to every creature a name. Whereby it might be known, therefore, by this let us all learn to avoid all idleness, both of body and of meditation of mind.

Concerning the manner of bringing them, it is set down here where he says the Lord caused the creatures to come unto man. The which manner of bringing them is set down generally, and therefore we will only speak of the general bringing [of] them and not of any particular bringing of them. By this generally bringing, therefore, we must only believe a general bringing of them, for happy is that man which bradest[2] himself unto the Lord. True it is that the Lord did bring them, but then if He brought them either by His word or any other way, it is frivolous to inquire.

Concerning the end, it is here set down that He brought them to man to see how fit and convenient names he could invent for every beast of the field and every fowl of the air. This end teaches us divers things, for by this we learn by what authority man does take upon him[self] to give names to those that belong unto us, namely, by the authority of God. But we must not take too much liberty in this, for though we may give names to those that are in subjection unto us, we must not give names or titles unto God, for God only gives

---

2. *Bradest*: brade. The brade was a thin wire nail.

names and titles unto Himself. For it is not for man to give names unto Him, because He is of a power far above man's capacity.

Secondly, God giving to Adam a power to name those creatures, He does thereby give him a power and predominance over them. For he that has power to give names to anything, to him is given the dominion and preeminence over that thing. Against this in our time [is the] great offense in giving of names to beasts or to dogs. True it is that we may give names, but such names we must give as are meet and convenient. Such in this is a greater sin of man in giving of nicknames either to their children or others which are under their preeminence. "Howsoever the man names those creatures," so the naming there we see that it pleases God to rest in the name which Adam would give to those creatures.

Now follows the second action, namely, the act of man in these words: "The man therefore gave names unto all called and to the fowl of the heaven, and to every beast of the field." What the Lord did we have heard. Now man for his part gives to all those creatures names. By this means the Lord makes trial of man's wit, the which appears to be very excellent, for it is the point of a very great wit to give so diverse and sundry names. Secondly, it did manifest a wonderful profoundness of judgment in Adam in that he could discern of the nature of every one of them. Thirdly, it does manifest a singular and large memory. For after that he had named aforesaid names, he must remember every one of them lest he give to diverse of them the same name. And, therefore, it appears that there was no imperfection in his memory. Lastly, it showed his wisdom in that he did name them in their order, and his knowledge and that he did know the nature and the difference of every one of these creatures in that he could give unto everyone names which could describe their natures. Now then, the Lord did take experiences of the gifts in Adam, so surely will he take experience in us, and of every gift which he has given us. Let us then learn not to give names unadvisedly either to our cattle, to our servants, or to our children, or to any that are under us, but let us learn to give names to them with wisdom and judgment so that afterward, in the life to come, we may not be called to account for the same.

Genesis 2:21–22

(Sermon 5)

"Therefore the Lord God caused a heavy sleep to fall upon the man, and he slept: and he took one of his ribs, and closed up the flesh instead thereof. And the rib which the Lord had taken from the man, made he a woman and brought her to the man." (Gen. 2:21–22)

Now Moses comes to set down the manner how the woman was created in these two verses, to the end that man might not only know the matter whereof [he] himself was made but that he might know the matter whereof the woman was made, [and] that knowing himself and the woman he might the better give all dutiful obedience unto God. We shall easily know this creation if we see these actions of God: first, the Lord cast Adam into a sleep; secondly, [He] took out of his body a rib; thirdly, [He] did close up the flesh; fourthly, [He] did make that rib a woman; and, lastly, [He] did bring it unto man. These are the doctrines which are taught us in these words, of which in order.

First, it is said there "for the Lord God caused." In which words Moses teaches us that the woman had the same Creator which the man had, namely, Jehovah the Lord. The which Moses does teach man to put him in mind how he should judge of the woman, and that she had the same Creator which he had, and therefore [he] cannot enter into any mislike of her. Secondly, remembering that they had but one Creator, it must need stir up their hearts to mutual love one of another. Thirdly, remembering that the same Lord God was their creator, how should this memory any way hurt them? Nay, why should it not rather stir them up to honor their Creator? How, I say, should they not be moved to magnify the infiniteness of their Creator? And those duties, beloved, did no more belong to Adam and Eve than they do us.

The first action of the Lord is with words: "The Lord God caused a heavy sleep upon man." This sleep seems to be no natural sleep upon natural causes. For, first of all, it fell upon him [on] the first day, and therefore could not be weary of any labor. Again, this sleep is called a "heavy sleep" to teach us that it was no natural sleep, but a heavy sleep. Thirdly, it is said that this sleep came not from Adam or from the weariness of his body, but that the Lord cast it upon Adam, which does most manifestly show that it was no natural sleep. For this cause then, we see Adam was brought into a heavy sleep, and in that it is said that Adam slept to teach us that it was a new sleep. We are not to inquire where Adam slept or how long he slept, for it does not please God to reveal the same, and therefore we are not to search into it. And this much of the first action of God.

The second action is in the words "and he took one of his ribs," where we see that the Lord Himself took one of his ribs. *Question.* But why did He not take two or more ribs? *Answer.* Because He knew one rib to be sufficient to make the woman. *Question.* How or by what means did He take out the rib? *Answer.* It is great curiosity to search this out. But you will say: "I cannot conceive and comprehend how He could do it." What then, will not you therefore believe it because you cannot comprehend the same? If God should do nothing but that which the wise can conceive, how could God be omnipotent? Although therefore the Lord has not expressed the manner after which He has taken the rib out of man, yet let not us search into it, but let us be content with it in that God has said it. Certain it is that God took this rib out of the man. The end why [from] that location, it shall appear in the proper place. Some inquire why God did rather take a rib of man rather than some other part of man, but that is curious[ity].

The third action is "and closed up the flesh." As it pleased the Lord to take out the rib, so it pleased the same Lord to close up the flesh again. The which He did, first, because Adam being created in God's image, God would not have any deformity appear in his body. Secondly, God did close it up to revive and restore that comeliness in that part of the body of Adam which was as if no rib was taken out. Thirdly, the Lord did this not only to restore that glory which was working but also to restore straight of that part of the body out of which the rib was taken. And for this cause, it pleased God to use this action of closing up the flesh. And herein the Lord does let Adam and us see His love toward mankind in that He willed no want and defect in our creation. If then there be any defect in ourselves, the fault is in us.

The fourth action follows in the next verse: "And the rib which the Lord had taken from the man, made he a woman." Here it is said the Lord made the rib a woman. The matter whereof woman was made was a rib, and this teaches man not to mislike the woman. For if he mislikes the woman he must need mislike himself since she was made of part of himself. Again, the woman remembering she was made of part of man, she must think herself bound to afford to man all such help as she can. And, secondly, she must needs think herself to be inferior unto her husband and therefore must avoid all contention.

The last action is "and brought her unto man." You see the Lord was pleased to cast Adam into a sleep to take out one of his ribs, to close up the flesh, to make it a woman. And now, He brings up the woman to his face that he might give her a name as he did to the other creatures. And all this He did to make man a help meet for him. This does teach parents, which have children, to provide for them, and to provide for their daughters, sons, and to the sons, daughters, and not only so to provide [these] for them but afterward to bring them unto them.[1]

---

1. I.e., parents are to arrange marriage partners for their children.

Genesis 2:23–24

(Sermon 6)

"Then the man said, this now is bone of my bone, and flesh of my flesh. She shall be called woman because she was taken out of man. Therefore shall man leave his father and his mother and shall cleave to his wife." (Gen. 2:23–24)

After that Moses had showed how God created the woman and also how the Lord did bring her to man that they might be joined together in holy matrimony, now he sets down how the woman was entertained of man. For in these two verses man does deliver, both in the presence of God and the woman, that doctrine which concerns the creation of woman in the 23rd verse and the doctrine of the holy matrimony in the next verse. For the creation of woman, which is contained in this verse, we are first to consider who speaks this doctrine, and, secondly, the doctrine itself. The speaker is Adam. The doctrine is concerning the creation of woman.

First, when it is said, "then the man said," we are to understand the man, Adam, for now it pleased God to have waked Adam out of his sleep. When then he was awakened, he uttered these words. So, seeing it was spoken of Adam in his innocency, it appears that he could not deceive the woman with any false doctrine, and therefore we know that the doctrine following is sound and true.

Objection. How came Adam to the knowledge of this doctrine, that woman was bone of his bone, being then asleep when she was taken out of him? *Answer.* Not through any knowledge of himself but by the revelation of God, who thought it good rather to reveal it by His Spirit than any other way. It was necessary that Adam should know her creation, that he might know what was the root of man's posterity. Again, by knowing woman's creation he was enabled to discern rightly to love her and <...> her all the days of his life. Thirdly, that he might teach the same unto others as he does tell to the woman, "This is bone of my bone and flesh of my flesh." As if he should say, "One of my own ribs, being taken out of me by my Creator, is fashioned unto a creation like unto myself. Yea, her natural bone is my natural bone, and my natural flesh is her natural flesh." But some say God took a bone only and no flesh at all, and therefore Adam would not say this truly. But this we see by experience is not likely, for what rib is so natural that has no flesh upon it?

This affirms [a] singular doctrine. For if they be one by nature, then they ought to have one and the same judgment and ought to agree together without any dissension or discord. Secondly if they so are by nature, they ought to have one and the same affection toward the other. Their affections then must not be separated but joined. Thirdly, seeing the perfection consisted not in the union of one but in the union of two, it ought to move both of them to seek to maintain this perfection of two. And this surely is the law of nature. For this end, therefore, Adam does teach this to the woman to glorify God thereby, and, secondly, to stir up themselves to mutual love one of another. And as this was necessary in Adam and Eve, so is it necessarily required of us. But some will say that we do not see it now to fall out so. I answer that that is by reason of the twofoldness of man,[1] who will not be directed by the ordinance of God but follow their own desires and <...>.

Now follows, "She shall be called woman." Here we see Adam does according to his power give the woman a name. And surely he gives her a very wise name. For whereas the Lord gave the man the name of *ish*,[2] he called the name of woman *isha*,[3] because she was taken out of man. As if he should say, "Seeing God has given to me the name of 'man,' because the woman was taken out of me, I call her by the same manner." Likewise, the woman receiving this name does yield subjection and superiority to man and acknowledges herself bound to man (as it were), to one from whom she has her being and essence.

Secondly, man taking upon him this practice and duty to give to the woman a name, it appears to whom it belongs to give names to children and <...>, namely, it belongs to man to give them, for we see by the law of nature that woman did not give herself a name, neither did God give her a name, but gave power to man to give a name. Therefore, let us acknowledge it to be given to man only to give names to children that so they might yield to obedience both to man and also to his wife.

Now in the end Adam rendered a reason of his act in giving a name because, says he, she was taken out of man. By which we learn that though it be in the power of man to name his child, yet he is not to give what name he will, but such a name as he can render a reason for. For if Adam did so in his innocency, then much more is it required of us now in this time. If this care ought to be had in giving of names, then surely those are to be condemned which give heathen names or such names as shall shame the power of those that are named.

---

1. I.e., man is flesh and spirit. See Perkins's treatment of this theme in *Combat of the Flesh and Spirit*, RHB 9:169–80.

2. Hebrew (אִישׁ, "ish"): man.

3. Hebrew (אִשָּׁה, "isha"): woman.

The next verse follows: "Therefore shall man leave his father and his mother and cleave to his wife." Now let us see what Adam speaks of the holy office of marriage. Whose words these be there is some contention. Some say they are Adam's words; others say they are God's; others that they are Moses's words. But seeing neither form nor verse neither did doctrine cause be no as a hint that at doctrine.[4]

"Therefore shall a man leave father and mother." *Question.* This seems to be a very hard thing that children should leave their parents. *Answer.* They are not simply to leave their parents, but by way of comparison. If he must either leave his father or his wife, he is to leave his father and to cleave to his wife. Otherwise, he is not to leave his parents, but to live [with] them, to provide [for] them, yet as the Holy Spirit here teaches, that the duty toward the wife is to be preferred before the duty toward the parents.

"He shall cleave unto his wife"; that is, he shall love her so well that he shall prefer [her] above all others, because she is bone of his bone and flesh of his flesh.

---

4. This sentence is difficult to read. Perkins seems to be saying that these differences of interpretation have no significant doctrinal implications.

Genesis 2:24

(Sermon 7)

"Therefore shall man leave his father and his mother and cleave to his wife, and they shall be one flesh. And they were both naked, the man and his wife, and were not ashamed." (Gen. 2:24–25)

Of the first part of this verse we have spoken already. Now, in the latter end of this verse the Holy Spirit commands that the man should cleave unto his wife. In which words we see God requires both of the husband and wife particular duties, which they ought to perform the one unto the other, and not to any other. Therefore, at this time we are to speak of those proper offices which pertain to the married estate. Of the common offices we have sufficiently before spoken. That, therefore, we may see what be all the proper offices, let us mark how they shall be taught unto us out of this sentence now.

First of all, this proper office is that office which God has commanded one of them only, for we read of those offices commanded to the husband which are not commanded to the wife, and also that some offices are commanded to the wife which are not commanded to the husband. Also, we see that God created man for one end and woman for another end. Then this proper office is either the wife's office or the husband's.

The wife's office is to show herself obedient to her husband, so that she is bound to perform those offices which are <…> of God. Now the first office which God does enjoin the wife is the office of subjection. But to know this the better, it shall not be amiss to stand upon subjection and show what subjection is in general, and then to come to that which is proper to the wife. Subjection then is that whereby everyone voluntarily puts himself under a superior power as God has commanded. That this is so upon appears by the [epistle to the] Romans [13:1], where the apostle would have every person in the world submit himself to a superior power. And the apostle says further that he that does deign to submit himself shall be condemned both body and soul.[1] So now, seeing what subjection is, namely, a putting under a superior power, we must learn that this subjection is necessary. Thus much in general of subjection.

---

1. Rom. 13:2.

Now we come to the subjection belonging to the wife. *Question.* Why do you speak first of the wife before the offices of husband? *Answer.* This order is often observed in the Scripture, namely, to set down first the duty of the inferior, as the duty of children before their parents, and the duties of the wife before the duties of the husband. Secondly, we see it stands with the law of nature, that the question being of duties begun, the inferior should begin to do his duty. Thirdly, it is in the hand of the superior to reward the inferior for doing his duty, and therefore good reason that the inferior should begin to do his duty. *Question.* Now if it be asked that seeing subjection belongs to children and servants as well as to wives, what difference is there between this subjection? *Answer.* The subjection of children and servants is more straight[2] than the subjection of wives. Secondly, in the subjection of children and servants there is no equality at all, but in this subjection of wives there is equality. Thirdly, the other subjection is temporary, for though a man be a servant yet is he not always a servant, but the subjection of the wife is continual. Lastly, the subjection of others is begun and *conducunted* by man, but the subjection of wives is begun and *conducunted* of God Himself, and therefore they ought to continue the same.[3]

Now let us see what the wife's subjection is, namely, it is that whereby the wife is bound voluntarily to acknowledge her husband to be her lord. That she ought to do this appears by the Scriptures. [In] Ephesians 5:22–24 the Holy Spirit says, "Wives subject yourselves unto your husbands as to the Lord," and thereof renders as a reason in the 23rd verse, and in the 24th verse concludes the same with an exhortation. Also, it is there said the wife must be subject to her husband in all things, not in some things, because her subjection is perpetual.

"Wives subject yourselves to your husbands as is comely to the Lord" (Col. 3:18). Saint Paul in the third chapter of his third epistle does largely handle this point. By which it is plain that this office of subjection does necessarily belong to everyone and that she cannot be exempted from the same by any potentate in the world. This may be proved also by divers reasons. Firstly, this subjection was the ordinance of God. [In] Genesis 3, where the Lord coming to the woman after her fall, in the 16th verse He says that her will should be subject to her husband and he shall rule over her. Secondly, the church of God is propounded unto woman for an example. Thirdly, if this be not given, it cannot but be offensive to God and unprofitable to the married persons. [In] Hebrews 13 the people of God are commanded to be obedient to those that are set over them. Even so it may be said of wives. Lastly, if this subjection be denied, what

---

2. *Straight*: entire, comprehensive.

3. *Conducunt* (Latin): undertaken by.

can the husband have to reward and commend her? And, therefore, this is necessarily required to be performed.

Now she must acknowledge her husband to be her head. And this appears in the [First Epistle to the] Corinthians: "I would have you know that God is the head of Christ, and Christ the head of his church, and the man the head of his wife" [1 Cor. 11:3]. And of this the apostle renders reasons: first, because woman was made of man and not man of woman; and, secondly, woman was made for man and not man for woman; and, lastly, the woman is the glory of man as man is the glory of God. So, seeing she is the glory of man, she ought to acknowledge his preeminence above herself. *Question*. Saint Paul in the Corinthians speaks not of man and wife, but of man and woman in general, and the proper eminence [of] one above the other. *Answer*. That is true, and therefore that does the more confirm this doctrine, and therefore everyone ought to put this in practice all the days of their lives.

Genesis 2:24

(Sermon 8)

"Therefore shall man leave his father and his mother and cleave to his wife, and they shall be one flesh." (Gen. 2:24)

We have set down the wife's office, which does properly belong to the wife alone, and also have showed the difference between the wife's subjection and the subjection of other creatures, and have also showed what the wife's subjection is. Now it remains to show that the wife ought to do her duty in all things.

If this subjection did respect either the will or the commandment of the husband, then for some causes this subjection might sometimes be omitted. But if it does increase the headship and power of the husband, it cannot be that this subjection can by any means be neglected. "No power but is of God, no superiority but is of God," and therefore God does command everyone to be subject to the superior power "not for fear of punishment, but for conscience sake" (Rom. 13:1–5). So now, we have taught what is that subjection of the wife, namely, to acknowledge her husband to be her superior in all things.

Some think that the wives need not to perform this subjection to their husbands in all things. They say, "What if the husband be an idiot or a fool? Shall the wife be subject to him in all things?" That, they say, is very absurd. But we answer that this is answered in the [First Epistle to the] Corinthians, when it is said that the woman is bound to the husband as long as she lives, so that this duty is not to be broken when the Lord takes away the reason and will from the man wherewith he was before endowed. Secondly, they say, "What if the husband be a weak person and unable to perform the duties which belong to him?" To this I answer, firstly, demanding whether he was such a one when they were joined together? If it be so, then the parents of that woman may disjoin them, otherwise they are not to be separated. Thirdly, they say, "What if the husband abuses his authority? Shall the wife acknowledge her subjection to him?" *Answer.* Assuredly, for the neglect of the ordinance of God cannot give liberty to break the commandment of God. There is no cause that can free any from performing this duty of subjection.

By this we may see who be they that perform the duty, namely, those that acknowledge themselves to be bound to do this by the commandment of God.

Secondly, those that do it willingly. Thirdly, those that do well in all <...> in <...> things.

And by this also we may see who are the breakers of this, namely, those that themselves will be rulers and guides over their husbands. But how can the wives yield any subjection to God Himself which they will not to their husband? Secondly, those that though they do not rule their husbands, yet will be equal unto their husbands, but these also do greatly sin against God. Thirdly, those do break this office that, though they be contented that their husbands should rule under them, yet they cannot abide that their husbands should always govern them. Fourthly, those do offend that do think they ought not be ruled by their husbands in all things. Lastly, those do break this office which do itself in word deride it, or in deed neglect it, or anyways abuse it. Seeing then the keepers of this do purchase the favor of God and the breakers of this do purchase the curse of God, it becomes every woman to perform this duty to her husband as to God Himself.

Now the second office of the wife follows, which is obedience. The office of obedience respects the will and commandment of man, and in this the wife has more liberty than in the other. *Objection.* What is this obedience? *Answer.* It is reverent usage of the husband's government with which he ought to be well pleased. That this obedience is to be yielded to the husband, it is sufficiently shown before out of the authority of the Scriptures. Then this is a reverence using of the husband it is evident by the third [chapter] of [the first epistle of] Peter, the six first verses [1 Peter 3:1–6], where the apostle does also render a reason of it, by which place it does most evidently appear that her subjection must be a reverent using of her husband.

The next thing to be considered is that the husband ought to be content and well pleased. That he ought to be so appears because God is well pleased with this obedience. If God then be contented, how can man but be contented with it? Lastly, this is such an obedience as is commanded of God, and, therefore, cursed is that husband which is not content with it.

But some wives will say, "My husband does not like of this my obedience." *Answer.* What, though some be so profane, must the wife then leave doing this duty? God forbid, for she may not neglect that duty which God has laid upon her for the perverseness of her husband. *Objection.* When the husband cannot like of this subjection, what ought the wife to do? *Answer.* Let her continue in this obedience, and it may be God will bless her obedience, that He will bring her husband to the well liking of this her obedience. Thus much of the work of obedience. Now it remains [to consider] wherein it consists, but of this another time.

Genesis 2:24

(Sermon 9)

"Therefore shall a man leave his father and mother and cleave to his wife, and they shall be one flesh." (Gen. 2:24)

We have already spoken of the proper offices of wives and especially the office of subjection. Now it remains to speak of the will of the husband. If then the husband wills anything contrary to the law of God, therein the will of the husband is not to be obeyed of the wife, for to obey the will of her husband in all things she is not command[ed] by the law of God, for it is a thing indifferent.

The first thing to be regarded in wives obeying the husband's will is to obey his will in those things which are lawful. Again, there be some things indifferent in their own nature, wherein the ministers of God ought to deal. And those things are altogether out of the husband's regiment. And, therefore, we are to know that the husband's will reaches not to all things but only to those which fall within the regiment of [the] married estate. Though, therefore, he says that the wife's obedience belongs to the husband's will, we must understand it only of those things that fall within the compass of the husband's authority.

Now this obedience consists in three points: first, in a careful satisfying her husband; secondly, in doing his commandment; [and,] thirdly, in particular[ly] enduring the injurious dealing of her husband. Touching the first, it is evident of the 1st [epistle] of the Corinthians [chapter] 7.[1] Again, seeing the wife is to obey her husband, why should she not have a desire to satisfy her husband's will? And if this be not performed, so that the wife does not perform her duty, it cannot be but there shall be great contention. And as the wife is to have special care to obey her husband, so the husband is to have a special care to command all those things which are agreeable to God's commandment.

The second point is the doing of his commandment. It is not sufficient to have a desire to satisfy, but she must perform his commandment. That she must do thus appears not only by the authority of Scripture but also by the light of the law of nature, as appears by the first chapter of the book of Esther, where the light of nature did make them to make a decree that every husband should

---

1. Verses 1–5.

rule his wife.[2] And surely reason does teach this, for what a confusion were it that this authority should be equally given to two, it could not be that that family should be well ruled. *Objection.* What if the husband commands that which God does forbid? Shall she do that which her husband commands? *Answer.* God forbid, for every wife has both a spiritual husband and an earthly husband. Now that which the spiritual husband commands, she is to perform though both father, mother, magistrate, or whosoever does forbid it.

That this is so appears by the Scripture. [In] Daniel 6, where Daniel would not object [to] the commandment of the king, but according to the commandment of his God set open his window toward Jerusalem and prayed every day.[3] The same also we read in the New Testament. [In] Acts 4, where when the rulers commanded the apostles not to speak in the name of Jesus, Peter and John stood up and said, "whether it be better to obey God or man, judge you" [Acts 4:19], teaching us thereby that there is due unto the Lord an absolute obedience not only of the body but of body and soul. And, therefore, when the Lord commands anything, no man ought to dare to give a contrary commandment, for if any husband be then so bold to command anything contrary to the law of God, the wife is not to obey him. *Objection.* What if she do doubt of the commandment of her husband? *Answer.* If her husband's commandment be in things indifferent, she is to obey him if it belong to the married estate. But this is always to be remembered, that if in things indifferent the wife cannot obey the will of her husband without the breach of her own conscience, then she is to be pardoned. As, for example, if the wife be contented to have religion where before she has been a papist, and if she doubt whether it be lawful to eat meat on Fridays or fasting days, and if the husband commands her to eat, here the wife is to be permitted until her conscience be satisfied.

The third point is patient enduring the injurious dealing of their husband, and this is no less necessary than the other, because it cannot be but in this society there shall be trouble. For many times the husbands will not only correct their wives with equity but above measure. And sometimes they will not only correct their <…> demeanors but the well doing of their wives. Now you will say, "What is the wife in this case to do?" The Holy Spirit has said that she is patiently to suffer the injurious doing of her husband, for it is better to suffer for well doing than for ill doing. But there be few wives which do this, for they will give one word for another. But this is not to obey her husband but a challenging power over her husband, which is contrary to the law of nature.

---

2. Verses 16–20.

3. Verse 10.

There be two other duties which belong to the wife. The third duty of the wife is love, whereby the wife loves her husband. Paul, in the [first epistle to the] Corinthians, commands wives not only to obey their husbands but also to love them.[4]

The last duty is <...> and converse of the husband. "But the conversation of the wife be pure" (1 Peter 3:1–2).[5] Here the wife must be careful to avoid two extremes. The first is servile fear. She must not serve by constraint. The other extreme is audacity. She must not to be bold, but there must be mediocrity.[6] Those do sin against this that do dare speak as foul words before their husband as any other man, and also those that do despise their husband. And those do not offend this which do obey their husband for conscience's sake, and which for their husband's sake will be drawn nearer unto the service of God.

---

4. 1 Cor. 7:34.
5. The original erroneously cited 1 Peter 1:2.
6. *Mediocrity*: moderation.

Genesis 2:24

(Sermon 10)

"Therefore shall man leave his father and mother and cleave to his wife, and they shall be one flesh." (Gen. 2:24)

We have spoken of that duty which appertains to married persons, teaching what that office is. Of the proper office to the wife, we have spoken. Now it remains to speak of that office which pertains to the husband alone. As the Lord is said to be the God of wisdom, so has He assigned to all several persons sundry offices, that all things might be ruled in good order. Now, let us see what is the husband's office. It is that which properly and previously belonged unto him. So whatsoever office is proper to the husband, this he is bound to perform.

The first and principal office is to rule and govern his wife, for as obedience and subjection do beseem the wife so governed, and direction do beseem the husband, so then the principal office of the husband is to govern his wife. And this office is far harder than the office of subjection because to this there are required greater gifts and more gifts than the offices of obedience and subjection. The greater care ought every man to have to learn those gifts, to put this in practice. This is that office of the husband by which he must govern his wife as his own flesh. As the natural government of the body rests in the head, and so as the head governs all the other parts so it is <...> of is led of any parts of the body, even so it ought to be in this government of the husband. God ordained this not only before the fall of man, but also after his fall (Gen. 3:16). And this office appears by the light of nature, as appears in the book of Esther, where king Ahashueroth commands that every man should rule in his own house.[1] "Let not the wife rule but let them be subject" (1 Cor. 14).[2] "I permit not a woman to teach in the church nor to usurp authority over the man" (1 Tim. 2:12). So then, the principal office of the husband is to govern his wife as his own flesh, from which he may not exempt himself.

Now for the performance of this, four especial graces are required. The first is knowledge and wisdom, which is not only proper to the husband but to all in place of government, for he that wants wisdom, his government shall be a

---

1. Est. 1:16–20.
2. Verse 34.

government of disgrace, not of grace. [See] 1 Peter 3:7, where it is required that they should dwell with their wives as men of wisdom and knowledge. *Objection.* What knowledge is required of the husband? *Answer.* First, the knowledge of God, thus the knowledge of himself,[3] of his wife, [and] of the government of the same. And this knowledge is very necessary. Thus, those that have not learned this, if they be unmarried, they are unfit to marry; if they be married, they are to desire and seek to learn.

The second thing required is justice. He must not only govern wisely, but he must govern justly, for the man must not do the wife any wrong, withdrawing anything from her which is meet. And this duty the husband is always to practice, for justice does make the government unreprovable.

The third grace is that the husband should govern his wife according to piety and godliness, for he must sanctify his government with faith, which makes his government not overly acceptable to his wife and others, but it makes [it] acceptable to God. He must then use this government in faith, in conscience, in piety, and in godliness, for if the conversation of the wife ought to be in piety, then must the husband devote his government according to his piety and godliness.

The fourth thing is that he should order his government in love. He must govern in meekness and gentleness. And why so? Because it is his own flesh that he must govern, and therefore he must govern it in love. Some think that they may govern tyrannously over their wives, but this is far from Christian government, and therefore everyone must desire to govern his wife gently and in love and meekness. Thus much of the first duty in general.

The second office of the husband is to instruct his wife, being ignorant, not only in the fear of God but in other things. For it belongs to him to have power and wisdom and teach his wife. [In] Genesis 18 the Lord says He will reveal His counsel to Abraham because He knows he will teach his family. "If the woman will learn any things, let her ask her husband at home" (1 Cor. 14). If the wife is commanded to ask her husband, is not the husband commanded to teach his wife? If this office belongs to the master, then much more does it belong to the husband, seeing there upon to be far greater laws between them than between the master and the servant. The man is to teach his wife what is the state of everyone, teaching her what was the first estate of man, what it is now, and what it shall be.[4]

---

3. Cf. Perkins, *Golden Chain*, RHB 6:11.

4. This is a condensed summary of Augustine's fourfold state of man as created, fallen, redeemed, and glorified. Perkins expounds this framework at length in *God's Free Grace and Man's Free Will*, RHB 6:385–443.

After which the man has included her in that knowledge of God, then he is to teach her the proper duties which belong to her to perform to him. Then he is to instruct her in the duties of mothers, showing her what duty children owe to their mothers. And when he has done this then he has performed his duty.

Now, as the husband is to do this, so he is to do it in a holy manner, namely, to sanctify it with prayer unto God, instructing her both in religion and also in other things which belong to the wife to know. The man must also instruct his wife by exhortation, exhorting her to that which is good and dehorting[5] her from that which is evil. And he must adjoin thereto comforts and consolations, that the wife may be encouraged to perform her duty. And he must also do it lovingly, that she may have occasion to love him and receive him, so that this society may be a happy society and that they may live mutually together all the days of their lives.

---

5. *Dehort*: dissuade, the opposite of exhort.

Genesis 2:24
(Sermon 11)

"And he shall cleave to his wife: and they shall be one flesh." (Gen. 2:24)

We have taught the offices which pertain to the state of marriage, those which are proper to the wife, and have begun to speak of those which are proper to the husband and have taught that his government ought to be ruled according to knowledge and wisdom. The second office consisted in the teaching and instruction of the wife, and that the husband is to do this we have proved by the Word of God. Now it remains to speak of the other offices which properly do belong to the husband.

The third office then is to direct his wife in her ways. For to whom the Lord has assigned superiority, to him He has assigned direction. For this cause, the husband ought to give the wife direction and teach her wherein she ought to walk. That the husband ought to do this appears not only by the light of reason but also by the law of God, for the law of God commands that the inferiors ought to be governed of the superiors. Now, because the wives are not willing to follow the direction of their husband, therefore the husband is not only to give out a direction but to persuade and exhort his wife to follow that good direction which God has prescribed to them both.

Now, when some wives will not be persuaded by any request, the Lord has in this case given to the husband not only power to request it but He has also given him power to command, for if the husband does so rule his wife as Christ does rule His church, then so the husband has power to command his wife. But there must be wisdom and discretion used. For he must be careful and diligent to use those cautions [so] that he does not command her those things which God does forbid and that he does not forbid those things which the Lord commands.

The husband, first then, must take heed that his commandments be of things which are only indifferent, and not only in things indifferent but also things which fall within the compass of the married estate. Secondly, the husband's commandment must be such as the wife has received gifts both of health and strength to <…> the same, for if he commands that which the wife has not received strength or health to perform, his commandment is an unmerciful commandment. Thirdly, the husband must take heed that his commandment be given out in a fitting and in a discreet manner, for if it be not given out so, surely the wife is not bound to perform it. Fourthly, the husband's commandment must not desire to command the conscience or the spirit or soul of his wife, for therein none have authority to command, judge, accuse, or excuse but God the Father of the spirit.[1] The husband's commandment then reaches only to the outward action, not to the spirit. Fifthly, the husband's commandment must be such as touches to the wife's bettering, not to her hurt.

Now follows the four duties of the husband, which consist in the rewarding the good demeanor of the wife. For the husband is not only to give out this commandment but also, when he sees it obeyed, then he is to cherish and to reward this Christian obedience of his wife. If Christ do reward the good obedience of His church, how much more ought the husband to reward the Christian obedience of his wife? And the doing of this will be a singular encouragement to his wife.

Question. Wherewithal shall the husband reward the wife? *Answer.* He shall reward her by commending and praising her for her well doing. Secondly, the husband is to reward her not only with praise but also with a loving acceptation, accepting that in good part which is done of the wife. Thirdly, they are to reward the well doing of their wives with gifts according to their power and ability. Lastly, he must reward her by rendering to her mutual goodwill, which if it be performed it cannot be that there should arise so great and so many contentions and strifes in this estate.

The last duty which pertains to man is admonition. For some women there are which will do nothing without admonition. That this duty belongs to the man appears evidently by the Scripture, where they are commanded to admonish.[2] Take Job. When his wife was impatient, what said he? "Am I God that I should give children?" When he was in marvelous brokenness, his wife came unto him giving him not good counsel, [he replied] "you speak as a fool."[3] Ashumeth does not only correct his wife in word but in deed, taking from her the honor of a queen and giving it to another more worthy of it.[4]

---

1. The term "spirit" refers to the means through which the Father commands—namely, the inward human spirit. It is unlikely to be a reference to the Holy Spirit in this context. For Perkins's definition of the conscience in the terms used here, see *Discourse of Conscience*, RHB 8:6–9.

2. Perkins appears to have Ephesians 5 in mind here.

3. Job 2:9–10.

4. Est. 1.

Genesis 8:21

"For the imagination of man's heart is evil even from his youth." (Gen. 8:21)

Now let us come to speak of the thought "God will not be merciful unto me." This thought was in our first parents when they looked upon the fruit of the tree and saw it [was] beautiful. Secondly, after that beholding of the fruit, it entered into the mind of Eve after this manner: "It may be God will not regard me, or this commandment which God gave me is not true." And then she sinned and regarded the devil. All the very first entrance of the fall was this very thought.

[In] Psalm 31:22 this thought takes hold in the heart of His servant David: "I said in my heart, I am cut off from the favor of God." This is the thought of David. [In] Psalm 116 the very same thought took hold of him, for he says in the eleventh verse, "I said in my heart all men are liars."[1]

By all these examples it is evident that this is a natural thought in the mind of man to think "God will not regard me."

Now we must first consider the time when this thought takes place in the heart of man. It does not come in the heart of man at all times, but in the time of affliction and temptation. This thought humbled righteous Job, for he says, "God will not help and nor regard me."[2] But he is <…>, and this Job says in his affliction. And David says, "God will not regard me."[3] And there is no man but in affliction is troubled with thoughts of distrust. Indeed, in prosperity a man may be troubled with thoughts of presumption, but in time of adversity those thoughts of prosperity <…> him peace <…> in the heart be the thoughts of <…>.

The second point is the danger God will <…>[4] regard me, says he, this is a great <…>, as appears by the signs thereof, <…> these thoughts arise also of spiration <…> <…> <…> avouch that God has so <…> them, and this often <…> the minds of those that are repentant.

---

1. In the MS, the transcriber begins another example but crosses it out: "Our Savior where he was walking on the waters…." Presumably, he gave up trying to write this down, which suggests that these are not complete notes of Perkins's address.

2. Job 30:20.

3. In the margin: Ps. 77.

4. Some of the words are illegible in the MS because the page is torn.

Thirdly, this thought does weaken the foundation of our salvation, for the foundation of our salvation stands in the promises of God. But now this thought weakens the promise and is an enemy to faith, for this thought says, "God will not be merciful to me." So that, where this thought reigns, there is no faith.

Now, since often is such dangers, we are to be admonished to use good means to repress this thought, that it prevails not. The means are these then: preaching the Word, baptism, and the Lord's Supper.

For the first, it is a special means ordained of God to fulfill His promises and therefore most contrary to this that he should say, "God will not be merciful to me." If God should say to any man that "I belong to you," he would believe. Now when the minister says this, it is as if God Himself should say to us, "I belong to you."

The second means is baptism, which is a notable means. If any prince gives a man a pardon and puts the person's name to the pardon, he will not doubt of his pardon. Even so, God in baptism does put in our names thereby to assure us of our salvation.

Thirdly, the bread and the wine, given of God as to the hand of every man to be as pledges of particular mercies.

And these are the means. And thus much of the thought.

Now we come to speak of the thoughts of men's hearts against their neighbors. To find out these we must have regard to other commandments and the second table. They are all spiritual because they do not only forbid wicked actions but also all particular wicked thoughts. They which are forbidden are of two sorts: those without comfort and those with comfort.

Those without comfort are forbidden in the tenth commandment. Now those which are with comfort are those which a base man practices. They are forbidden in the fifth, sixth, seventh, eighth, ninth, and tenth commandment.

They may be reduced to five heads. The first is a thought of dishonor, that is, that which tends to the contempt of the person of our neighbor. And of this we may have an example that all men think with[in] themselves as thus: "Such and such persons are persons of contempt in regard of me." And this thought was in the Pharisee who, when he prayed, said, "Lord, I thank thee that I am not as this publican." Here we see the most zealous Pharisee, though himself also base in respect of himself. And this every man thinks within himself: "Such and such men are but base persons in regard of me." [In] Philippians, the apostle Paul says we must always think better of other men than ourselves.[5]

---

5. Phil. 2:3.

Now here we may see what is the heart of man: it is nothing but proud and presumptuous fare, and this is the thought of dishonor from which proceeds all contempt, hatred, mockings, and deridings.

Now how may we repress this thought, we must see. As Job did. "Behold," said he, "I am vile" [Job 40:4]. We must [see,] as Job, to the vileness of our hearts, and when we do this we may repress those thoughts.

The second is a thought of murder, which is a thought whereby a man ponders any murder to his neighbor. God does <…>, "Thou sayest not, 'I will not <…> the poor which the Lord lets out.'" That such is, although it is in the heart of man, and his thought rules in this age. A second thought of murder is in God's church, and that is such: I will do mischief to those who worship God. And this is the thought of every natural man. And this appears by the saying of Christ: "For my name's sake you shall be hated of all men." And that the thought is in all the world appears in that the church of God has always some persecuted, and for from the beginning there has been persecution in the church of God. And if everyone would look into his own heart and should see that he had this heart to show all the mischief he could to those that worshiped.

Now some may say, all men do not work mischief against the church of God, for Nebuchadnezzar showed favor to Daniel. I answer: It is true that he did, but God then did get favor for Daniel, not Nebuchadnezzar, for he wrought all the mischief he could against the church.

There are other thoughts, namely, the thought of adultery, which tend to the [act of] adultery.

The fourth kind of thought is the thought whereby one man intends to steal from his neighbor. The first thought is a thought of disgrace whereby a man tends to work another's disgrace, and this is forbidden in the ninth commandment.

[In] 1 Samuel 17, Jesse sends David to his brothers to carry victuals to his brothers, [who] say, "I know thy pride, thou comest to see the battle."[6] [In] Acts 2, when the disciples spoke with strange tongues, the Jews said, "These men are drunk."[7] And this is common which reigns in all naturally, to think that ill done which is well done, and when it is bad to think it worse.

Now we come to consider when these thoughts arise in the heart of man. I answer: when occasion is given, then commonly arises the thought, either of dishonor, adultery, disgrace, or any other, for whatsoever the thought is, it is according to the occasion.

---

6. Verse 28.
7. Verse 13.

The second point is in whom those thoughts are. I answer: they are naturally in all men, yea, and <…> <…> those thoughts abound in every man naturally. Now by this we may see what a miserable mass of corruption the heart of man is. For howsoever a man does outwardly order his life, yet if God does not reign in his heart, his heart is a fountain of all wretchedness and corruption.

Acts 2:16–17

"But this is that which was spoken by the prophet Joel: And it shall be in the last days, saith God, I will pour out my Spirit upon all flesh, and your sons and your daughters shall prophesy, and your young men shall see visions, and your old men shall dream dreams." (Acts 2:16–17)

The gift of the Holy Spirit had wrought a great wonder in the hands of the apostles. There were some who said that they were full of new wine, but that could not be that new wine should be the cause of such miracles. And, therefore, Saint Peter speaks to those mockers, telling them that they were not drunken as they supposed, because it was but the ninth hour of the day. [It is] as if he should say [that] those who use drunkenness are not accustomed to be drunk so soon, much less then are they drunk, who never used drunkenness all their lifetime.

Now, having proved that it was not drunkenness, he shows what was the true cause thereof. And because some did doubt that after Christ's ascension the Holy Spirit should come upon them all, Saint Peter, to assure them of the truth, alleges authority out of the Scripture by the prophet Joel. Wherein we do see the apostle Peter does still continue to tread in the steps of his Master, Christ Jesus, withal He did prove all by the authority of the Scripture (Luke 4). Although they had the words of Christ, yet they did not think much to yield account of the doctrine by Scripture. Thus ought men to do also in these times, to prove all our matters by the Scriptures. And, therefore, Peter does cite a place out of the second chapter of the prophet Joel, verse 28, where is firstly a prophecy, secondly a promise of grace, and thirdly a great effect of this.

The prophet does begin with temporal things and end with spiritual things, for that is the use. And this we must learn to do, namely, not to rest in those worldly and temporal things, for the godly do not so much esteem of these things because they know that they are but vain. The second thing is this, that the outward benefits of God are signs of His love toward us. This also we ought to learn, for it is the cause that the children of God have such comfort within, in that they sue those benefits which God has given them to the glory of God.

Now, to the words: "And it shall be in the last days." Here Saint Peter does confirm the words of the prophet Joel which he had spoken before concerning things to come. *Question.* But when shall these things come to pass? *Answer.*

"In the last days." Saint Paul, in the fourth [chapter] to the Philippians, would have us to expel all cares out of our minds because it will not be long until Christ does come.[1] Also, we are taught to watch and pray, that we may be ready to meet Christ at His coming, and to be like to the servants that do wait for their masters. Third, we learn by this that we must look for no more messiahs or prophets, for there shall come no more until the end of the world. For we do know that Christ is the true prophet and Messiah, and therefore we must with patience expect His coming. This world may be compared to an old man; yea, it is like unto one who is very old, who lies bedridden[2] upon his bed, not able to turn any way, which is a trouble to all men and is able to help none. Such a one is this world, and we ought to think of this world as of an old man lying bedridden, which is troublesome to all and helps none, but notwithstanding this world shall [come] an end, though some think otherwise that the world is eternal.

Now we are come to the second part, which is the promise, in these words: "I will pour out my Spirit upon all flesh." Here the prophet does not say, "I will give" or "I will distribute," but he says, "I will pour out my Spirit," which is a word of great abundance and a word of effusion; not small drops, but great showers of the grace and Spirit of God shall be poured upon all His apostles. This promise is made [in] Isaiah 44:3: "I will pour water upon the thirsty and floods upon the dry ground." As the Lord does thus pour His gifts on His children, so He pours His curses on His enemies. All the effects of the Spirit are poured on us. The Lord does give unto His servants that which He does know most expedient for them and which shall be most for His glory and our great and everlasting comfort.

Another thing is here to be learned, namely, what is a certain note of the true church of Christ. The differences of the churches are not in the beauty but in the graces of God, for those who have the Spirit of God poured on them, those are the true church, for Christ says His kingdom is not of this world, but it is in you that are My elect.[3]

This Spirit shall be poured out. *Question.* Upon whom? *Answer.* "Upon all flesh." This is a blessed connection between the Spirit and the flesh. Here we learn what we are in ourselves, to wit, flesh, and like the flower of the field that soon passes and decays in a moment.[4]

---

1. Phil. 4:5–6.
2. The MS contains an archaic form of the word "bedridden"—namely, "bethred," or more commonly, "bedrid."
3. John 18:36.
4. Ps. 103:15.

Now we are come to the third, namely, to the effects, in these words: "Your young men shall see visions." By prophesying is meant foretelling what is to come. The gift of prophesying was given to the apostles, for many of them did prophesy. Visions do signify that appearance of God, as if he were awake, that is in <...>, yet they saw Him not with their bodily eyes. So that, by this he means that they should be like unto prophets. Some perhaps will say, "Why have not we them?" *Answer.* Because then it was the sign of the church of Christ.

Revelation 18:4

(Sermon 1)

"Come out of her, my people." (Rev. 18:4)

Now we are come to the reasons whereby one may be assured of his salvation.

The first reason is taken from faith, whereby one may be assured of life everlasting. And in this reason two things are to be proved.

The first is that faith is an infallible assurance of our salvation. This appears by places of Scripture. [In] Romans 4:20, Paul says, "Neither did he doubt the promise of God through unbelief, but was strengthened in the faith, being fully assured that he which had promised was able to perform it."[1] And doubtless in the same place he says, "Abraham was strong in faith being fully assured." Where he shows that it is a property of truth to assure, and by this the first point is evident.

The second point is that true faith is a particular assurance. That is proved thus. It is the property [of faith] to apprehend the promise of salvation, for faith[2] is nothing else but that whereby we apprehend Christ with His benefits, and that this is so appears by Scripture. [For example, in] John 6, our Savior proves that to eat the body of Christ and to believe Christ is all one. As the body has his[3] hand, mouth, and stomach to eat the corporal food, so has the soul his hand, mouth, and stomach to apply the spiritual food. So then, this is belonging to true faith to be assured of our salvation, and it is a true proportion of the same. Now we must see how true faith does apprehend the promises. It is done by an action of the mind when we do acknowledge that, and believe that, life belongs unto us by Christ. By this, therefore, it is manifest that faith is a particular assurance. The conclusion then follows that this true faith is an infallible and particular assurance of our salvation, that a man be assured of his salvation.

The second reason is that:

That which the Holy Ghost testifies unto us, that we must believe.

---

1. The citation is a slight abridgement of Romans 4:20–21.
2. The MS says "Christ" where "faith" was clearly intended.
3. Perkins employs the third-person masculine (his) instead of the third-person neuter (its).

But the Holy Ghost testifies unto us our adoption,
Therefore, we must believe.[4]

The first part is evident, then secondly approved by the [epistle to the] Romans, when Paul says, "For you have not received the spirit of bondage to fear again, but you have received the Spirit of adoption whereby we cry 'Abba Father.'"[5] It is evident, therefore, that this testimony of the Holy Spirit is an earnest testimony. The conclusion follows that we must in this life believe our adoption.

The third argument is that:

That which everyone prays for, that he must believe.
But everyone prays to be saved,
Therefore, everyone must believe his salvation.

That first appears [in] John 14:13,[6] where John's will is that whatsoever any man asks, he must be assured of it.

The fourth reason is that:

Whatsoever God commands in the gospel, that we both must and
    can believe,
But God commands all every[one] to believe,
Therefore, every man both must and can believe.

"Repent and believe the gospel" (Mark 1:15). To believe the gospel in that place is to believe that Christ died for him. John says the commandment of God is to believe that Christ died for him.[7] The conclusion then follows that everyone can and ought to believe his salvation. And thus much of the reasons.

Now, against those the papists object. First, that men are not assured of their faith, but that they do believe the articles of faith only. *Answer.* Howsoever some do believe only the articles of faith, yet some are fully assured of the faith, and thus ought everyone to be assured of their salvation by faith.

Secondly, they object that a man is not assured of his perseverance in grace. *Answer.* If a man be assured of his salvation, it must needs be that he shall always persevere in that grace, for he shall never be wholly overcome but only shall be troubled and vexed. Again, those which are ingrafted into the mystical

---

4. This text contains several syllogisms which have been formatted to make their logic clear. The manuscript does not format them in this manner, though this structure was clearly in the mind of the author.

5. Rom. 8:15.

6. The MS states "John 11:24." John 14:13 is clearly the intended reference.

7. 1 John 3:23.

body of Christ can never be cut off from Christ again. And to affirm this does bring in an illustration of baptism.[8]

Lastly, they object saying they grant we must believe our salvation, yet there must needs be some doubting and wavering. *Answer.* Whosoever does truly believe does by God's Spirit know that he does truly believe. Again, whereas they say that one cannot believe their salvation because they cannot repent [of] all their sins because some sins they know not, we answer [that] he which repents of his sins, both [his] known and unknown sins are forgiven. The conclusion then is that everyone ought to have a full and a particular assurance of our own salvation.

Thus much of the third point, namely, of the assurance of our salvation.

---

8. Perkins's point is that baptism would need to be repeated as a reentry into the faith if one could genuinely be severed and reunited to Christ repeatedly. Cf. Perkins, *Reformed Catholic*, RHB 7:32.

Revelation 18:4

(Sermon 2)

"Go out of her my people." (Rev. 18:4)

Now follows the 11th [point], touching the sacrifice of the Lord's Supper, which the papists call the sacrifice of the Mass.

A sacrifice is a sacred [or] solemn action by which a man offers some outward thing to God to please Him. Thus were the sacrifices in the Old Testament. Improperly the duties of any commandment are called sacrifices, but these are sacrifices only by resemblance. When we here speak of sacrifice, we must properly understand the first [sense of the word].

In handling this, we will show how far we are to consent and dissent.[1] Touching our consent, it is only in one thing, namely, to believe that the Lord's Supper may be truly called a sacrifice, and it may be so called for three causes. Firstly, because it is a commemoration of the real sacrifice of Christ upon the cross. Secondly, because every communicant does present himself a living and acceptable sacrifice to God. For as often as we receive the sacrament, so often do we <...> this notion. Thirdly, because of the end of the sacrifice, namely, for the giving of alms to the poor, and this has been a custom in the apostles' time. In former times the sacrifice has been called an oblation because of the alms given at the Lord's table. And for these three causes is the Lord's Supper called a sacrifice. And thus much of our consent.

The difference is that the Church of Rome makes the Lord's Supper to be a real sacrifice, and that the minister does offer the real body of Christ as an oblation for themselves. We, on the contrary, deny this, acknowledging no real oblation but only one through Christ, and that the oblation at the Lord's Supper is only spiritual. In outward [we] say that there is a spiritual sacrifice; the Church of Rome says, "be fed spiritual sacrifices, there is one real sacrifice." This difference is so great that the Church of Rome or our church must be no church.

First, to prove our doctrine, namely, that there is but one oblation upon the cross ever in the sacrament. The first proof [is] Hebrews 9:10,[2] "Christ offered himself not often but once." [Cf.] Hebrews 9:25, 10:10.

---

1. I.e., with respect to Roman Catholic doctrine.
2. Hebrews 9:28 appears to be the correct reference.

Objection. The papist expounds the text thus: the sacrifice of Christ for the substance is only one, but in regard of the manner there may be two or more. Christ made but one bloody [sacrifice] but many unbloody sacrifices. *Answer.* The author to the Hebrews takes for granted that the sacrifice of Christ is only bloody, for he knew not any unbloody sacrifice. His reason is set down as "man dies but once, and then comes to judgment."[3] So Christ offered Himself but once. Again, "without shedding of blood there is no remission of sins" (Heb. 9:22). So then, the unbloody sacrifice whereof they make their distinction is nowhere mentioned in the Scripture.

Secondly, if the sacrifice in the Lord's Supper be the same that was on the cross, it must either be a continuation or a repetition. The sacrifice on the cross was most perfect, and therefore there cannot be a continuation. If they say that it is a repetition, then they make that on the cross to be unperfect. Therefore, they can neither say a continuation nor a repetition.

Thirdly, to have a real sacrifice in the Lord's Supper is against the nature of a sacrament. The reason is because the end of the Lord's Supper is the commemoration of Christ. Now if it be a commemoration, it cannot be present, for the memory is of things absent. Again, the end of the Lord's Supper is to give Christ unto us with His benefits. Now, in a real sacrifice the case is quite contrary, for there the priest does give Christ unto God. Christ is not given to us, but we give Christ to God, which are quite contrary and cannot possibly stand.

Now, they say this sacrifice is not offered to make a satisfaction to God, but to apply the satisfaction made by Christ. But the former answer takes away this, for a sacrifice is no means to apply Christ to us. God gives Christ to us, and we receive Christ. The Holy Spirit makes a difference between Christ the high priest [and] the Levitical priests, which are many (Heb. 7:24–25). Christ was one alone in His own person. In the Old Testament there were many priests. In the New Testament there is only one, Christ alone, and none under Him, to supply His person. Now Christ, being one, there cannot be two priests in the New Testament, but the papists make more priests of the New Testament than in the Old.

Again, if any offer Christ to God, then a man must be a mediator to God for Christ. The Church of Rome says that there is indeed a priest which does offer Christ only as He was offered on the cross and differing only in the manner. Now, if it be true, then it must needs be that that priest be a mediator to God for the acceptation of Christ, which is most impossible. It is then most absurd to make any man a priest properly.

---

3. Heb. 9:27.

Now the arguments [by] which the Church of Rome proves these [things] are these.

[*Objection 1*.] Firstly, "And he is the priest of the living God, etc." (Gen. 14:18). Now they reason [that] this Melchizedek brought forth bread and wine, being a priest. *Answer.* Melchizedek indeed was a type of Christ, not in regard of the act of sacrificing but in regard of his person.[4] The resemblance between them both was this. First, Melchizedek was a priest, so was Christ. Melchizedek was a prince of righteousness, so was Christ. Melchizedek was without father and mother, so was Christ. Now then, it is a foolishness of the Church of Rome to say that Melchizedek was of the like of Christ in regard of the act of sacrificing. Secondly, when Melchizedek brought forth bread and wine, it was not for a sacrifice but to comfort Abraham. When it is said he was a priest of the high God, it is not meant because there he did offer oblation, because that he did [to] bless Abraham.

Objection 2. The Lord's Supper comes in the room of the Passover, but the person was a sacrifice, ergo it is a sacrifice. *Answer.* The Passover is called a sacrifice, not because it was sacrificed but by sacrificing he means killing. So, when it is said there was prepared a place to sacrifice, is meant a place to kill the Passover.[5] This [was] called then a sacrifice, not properly but because it was killed as a sacrifice was.

Objection [3]. "The prophet says there shall be a clean offering" (Mal. 1:11). *Answer.* This place must be understood of spiritual sacrifices, as said Saint Paul, that prayers be made with lifting up of pure hands.[6]

Objection [4]. "We have an altar of which" (Heb. 13:10). We have an altar. If there be an altar, then there must be a real priest. *Response.* There must not be understood any altar, but a spiritual altar as appears in the words following.

Objection [5]. When there is an alteration of the law, there must be a new covenant, etc., new priests and sacrifices, but in the New Testament there is so; therefore, there must be a new sacrifice. *Response.* All this may be granted, for Christ was not actually offered before the New Testament. But in regard of God, He was offered before the beginning of the world, but actually He was not offered before the New Testament.

---

4. The MS erroneously states "passion" instead of "person." See Perkins, *Reformed Catholic*, RHB 7:97.

5. Cf. Mark 14:12.

6. 1 Tim. 2:8.

Jude 3

(Sermon 1)

"Beloved when I gave all diligence to write unto you of the common salvation, it was needful for me to write unto you to exhort you that you should earnestly contend for the maintenance of the faith which was once given to the saints." (Jude 3)

Omitting the preface in this text, I come to the substance, which is an exhortation to faith, where by "faith" is meant the solemn doctrine delivered by the prophets. But now to the particular heads of this exhortation. The points which the apostle touches are three. First, that this faith is a precious treasure, and so much does every word in the text signify. The second is that the saints, that is, the church of God, is the keeper of this faith, and that is shown in these words, "given to the saints." The third point is the office of the church and every good member in the church, and that is to fight manfully for the faith. And of these in order.

Thus, first, that faith is a precious treasure, appears by the twofold use.[1] The first is that it comes from God [with] all things necessary for our salvation, and in this regard it excels all the learning and laws of man. And that appears in sundry particulars. For first, the laws of man reveal but part of the moral law, and no points of the gospel. Now this faith for which we are to fight reveals the moral law perfectly, and the gospel also wholly. Secondly, the law and learning of man know nothing of the cause or remedy of man's misery. Man's learning only knows it, not the cause of it. The faith reveals the first and perfect cause of man's misery and the remedy thereof. Thirdly, the laws of man speak only of temporal happiness in this life; this faith knows the everlasting happiness of the everlasting life, and this is the first use.

The second use is that this faith is the instrument of working all grace for everlasting life. And not the letters or bare syllables or the words said do this, but the doctrine of faith. And therefore, Paul calls it the power to salvation. And in regard of these two uses it is truly called a precious treasure.

---

1. Perkins gives three uses rather than two. This error also appears in the published version. Perkins, *Jude*, RHB 4:92.

The use of this is manifold. We learn, first, that we must be swift to hear this doctrine publicly delivered and embrace it with all willingness because it so pleased God to reveal it. Secondly, if the doctrine of true religion be a treasure, we must hide and treasure it in our hearts, for a treasure is not to be cast up and down at six and sevens,[2] but it must be laid up in the safest place. Now that is the heart. Thus did [say] David in the 119th Psalm, "I hid thy word in my heart."[3] And James, in his second chapter, says it must be rooted in our heart.[4] That this may be done, three things are necessary: firstly, to have care to know it; secondly, to remember it; [and] thirdly, to have our affections put upon it.

The third use is, if this be a treasure, it brings with it true wealth and honor and true pleasure, for that is the nature of a treasure. And to this end read the third [chapter] of Proverbs, from the 13th to the 18th verse.[5] And this is verified by experience in this our land, for we have had peace, wealth, and all earthly commodities, and we have been protected by the hand of God from all our enemies round about, he alone fighting for us. And whence proceed all those doctrines of true religion preached among us.

The second point is that the church of God is the keeper of this faith. In the 15th [verse] of [1] Timothy 3, the church is called "the ground and pillar of the truth."[6] And in the 1st [chapter] of Canticles, [verse] 7, the spouse demands of Christ where she shall find Him at noon day. Christ answers that He will be where the sheepfold[7] is, that is, where the good shepherds, the faithful ministers, keep the fold.[8] A register is known by the words that she keeps, and the church is known by the faith and doctrine. And this is the mark by which we know the popish religion not to be the true church, and the Turkish and atheists to be no religion. Seeing then that we are keepers, it stands us in hand to look to ourselves that we be not put out [of] office, and it [be] given to others which have better deserved it, and will bring forth better fruits than we have done.

Now, we shall do our office if we bring forth the fruits of our office, and that is the fruit of amendment of life, which if we do we shall be good stewards. Here in these words of the text, "once given to the saints," is to be considered a double circumstance of time. First, once given for all, that is, perfectly, never after to have any new giving. By this we learn that all revelations by visions, all traditions in matters of salvation, as purgatory, alms, masses, and prayers for

---

2. *At six and sevens*: put to risk.

3. Verse 11.

4. The intended reference is James 1:21. cf. Perkins, *Jude*, RHB 4:92.

5. Prov. 3:13–18.

6. 1 Tim. 3:15.

7. The MS states, "shiffold."

8. Song 1:7.

the dead, are diabolical, and only of the devil. Likewise, the supremacy of the pope and all other traditions of men in matters of salvation are diabolical and mere profanations of the wholesome doctrine of faith. The reason is because the true faith was but once given for all.

Secondly, in this circumstance, "once given," being so understood not by writing but given in the heart to show us that faith once given and wholly lost can never be recovered. This is to be understood not of a particular fall, as of Peter for denying his master, but of a general falling away. This serves to admonish all lest they fall wholly away. It is dangerous to fall by infirmity, but to fall away wholly is far more dangerous. And to take heed of this apostasy or falling away, we must take heed of declination in religion, for that is one step to apostasy (2 Peter 2:21). And it is to be feared that in these days of ours there is a much declining, for in former times true religion has been much more embraced than it is now. And that we may the more take heed of apostasy, we must beware of calling in question the grounds of our religion. For as Cyprian says, <...> <...> "Of holy things there must be no deliberation, but we must believe them without question."

The third point is the office of the church of God and every member, and that is to fight for the faith. It is not only the office of the magistrate or the minister, but every member of the church must fight. Neither is this fight by strength or bodily weapons, but they are spiritual duties with which we must arm ourselves. And to this fight there are four things necessary by which we must fight: (1) by doctrine, (2) by confession, (3) by example, [and] (4) by prayer.

First, by doctrine, because everyone, not only ministers but every particular man and woman, yea, every servant, must teach according to his gifts and in his calling. By confession, for that every [person] must confess and profess not only in the time of peace but in adversity, yea, to the face of the adversaries, this faith. By good example and good life, [as in the] 2nd [chapter] to the Philippians, [verse] 15, "shine as lights in the midst of a wicked nation."[9] By prayer, and therefore Christ in the gospel says, "Pray to God that he would daily send forth laborers to the vineyard."[10] And by all these four means must we all fight for the faith, not only the ministers but every member of the church of God.

---

9. Phil. 2:15.
10. Matt. 9:37–38; Luke 10:2.

Jude 4

(Sermon 2)

"For there are certain men crept in, which were before of old ordained to this condemnation: ungodly men they are which turn the grace of our God into wantonness, and deny God the only Lord Jesus Christ." (Jude 4)

In the former verse, the apostle sets down an exhortation to fight for the apostolic faith. In this verse he proceeds to confirm his exhortation by a reason drawn from the state of the enemies of this faith. The reason stands thus: there are certain men which live secretly among you, and which have crept in among you for nothing but to look to overthrow the apostolic doctrine. And, therefore, for these men's sake, it stands you in hand[1] to fight for the maintenance of it. And this reason concerns our church as much as it did the primitive church. For as in Saint Jude's time there were some which did secretly go about to subvert this doctrine, some likewise are there in our day now, both atheists and present professed papists, which creep in secretly into our Church of England, secretly laboring to undermine and overthrow our religion. And, therefore, it stands us likewise in hand to fight for the maintenance of this doctrine.

In this reason Saint Jude propounds a description of these wicked men which were crept into the congregation of God. He describes them by five things. First, by their hypocrisy in these words: "crept in." Secondly, by their estate before God in these words: "ordained to condemnation." Thirdly, by their religion in these words: "to ungodly men." Fourthly, by their doctrine in these: "turn the grace of God into wantonness." Fifthly, by their lives in these words: "deny God the only Lord Jesus Christ," for those words are to be understood of denying God by their lives. Of these in order.

First, they are described by their hypocrisy: "there are certain men crept in," that is, there are certain men who do insinuate themselves into your society. In which words the apostle lays two things to their charge. The first is that they pretend themselves to be servants of Christ, when indeed they were the very enemies of Christ, wherein we may see the policy of the devil, that when he can by no means overthrow this faith, he will cause wicked men to join themselves to the church and make themselves professors of this faith, that

---

1. *Stand in hand*: to make conducive to one's interests.

there they may take occasion to overthrow the same. This is set down [in] Matthew 13:25, where by a parable the devil's practice in sowing tares among wheat is set down. In the little house of God there was a Cain and a Canaan. In the little house of Christ there was a Judas, and in the excellentest church that ever was, there were heretics. For in Judas's time, who lived with the apostles, in the happiest age that ever was, yet we see that the worst heretic crept in among them. For the devil's practice is only to stir up atheists and secret papists, to subvert the true and apostolical faith.

[Use.] Where the apostle says there are some "crept in," we are first not to be offended thereat, neither therefore to separate ourselves from the church because such are crept in, but we must know that it is Satan's practice to cause such to creep in. But [we] must take heed we be not offended thereat, for the children of heaven might not be alone, but must be mingled with the Canaanites. Again, by this word, "crept in," we learn that they are not of the church of God. They are indeed in the church, but they are no members of the church.

The second thing that he lays to their charge in the words "crept in" is that they take upon them[selves] the office of teachers being not called. Wherein we learn that it is needful that they which teach publicly must first be called, then afterward teach, otherwise they creep in. That everyone must be called before he teaches appears by these reasons. First, it is the order that God has set down that teachers should be called. "How shall they preach unless they be sent?" (Rom. 10:15). "No man takes this honor unto himself but he that is called of God" (Heb. 5:4). Secondly, the ministry of the Word is God's ministry and not man's; therefore, the man that teaches must stand in God's name. Now, no man must be so bold with God as to stand in His name, or to speak His Word, unless God calls and appoints him to do it. Thirdly, he that teaches must maintain that which he teaches, and he that maintains it must have the government and protection of it, and he that has it must pray to God for it. Now, who can pray to God for it if he knows in his conscience that God has not called him to do it? And how shall he think to obtain his petition? For the people that hear cannot hear with comfort and profit unless they know that the teacher is called of God to teach. The which we see verified in a commonwealth, for if the governor be not called and lawfully set in his authority, who will obey? When then men enter into any office, either ecclesiastical or civil, if they enter by money or by favor of some man, they are not lawfully said to be called, but to creep in. Thus much of the first point, hypocrisy.

The second point is concerning their estate before God, in these words: "ordained to condemnation." The which concerns not so much the temporal estate as the estate before God. The sense of the words is this: of old [God] ordained this condemnation <...>[2] which were before enrolled, booked or billed, as in books of records to this condemnation. The word "condemnation" in the original signifies both judgment in this life and also condemnation in the life to come, which may very well agree to this sense, because those which are crept into the church, and trouble the church, shall in this life first be judged for troublers of the church, and thereto were first ordained, and consequently to that own condemnation in the second place. So, both significations of the word agree to this place: first, ordained to be judged for troubling the church, and consequently to condemnation in the second signification.

From this point we learn that God keeps records or books of all the actions of every particular man. The books and records of God are of three kinds. The first is a book of providence. "Thine eyes did see me when I was without form, for in thy book were all things written" (Ps. 139:16). In this book are all the hairs of our heads, and the sands of the sea, and the fall of every sparrow.[3] The second kind of book is the book of the last judgment. "And I saw the dead stand before God and the books were opened" (Rev. 20:12). The third kind is the book of life wherein is set down the name of every particular man that shall be saved. By these three books we are to understand the counsel and knowledge of God, for by His knowledge and counsel all things past from the beginning and which shall come before the end are as well known as if He should have them written of in a book.

The use of this is twofold. First, in regard of God there is no chance at all, for chance and [the] providence of God are quite contrary. Second use: that nothing comes to pass on earth without the decree of God, no, not the action of the wickedest man that is, for God, though He wills not the thing, yet He wills the being of the thing. Hence, we learn a special part of true religion, that as God before all worlds decreed the salvation of some, so He decreed the damnation and reprobation of others. For confirmation of this, look [at] 1 Peter 2:8, "Unto the which thing they were even ordained." First [epistle] of Thessalonians 5:9, "For God hath not appointed us unto wrath but to obtain salvation." [In] Romans 9 God is compared to the potter that makes the vessel, some to honor, others to dishonor, and unless God had decreed some to be saved [and] other[s] to be damned, that comparison cannot stand.[4] And in the same chapter to the Romans, "I have loved Jacob but hated Esau," that is, "in my counsel I have purposed to love the one and hate the other."[5]

---

2. This word is illegible because the MS is damaged. It appears to be "those," "men," or something similar.

3. Matt. 10:29–30.

4. Verse 21.

5. Verse 13.

Objection. If this be so, that in His own will [God] rejects some and chooses others, God deals unjustly to ordain man to their destruction. *Answer.* First, we must know that creatures must not create a law of justice to our Creator, who is justice itself and whose will is justice itself. For first, God wills a thing and then it is just. It is not first just and then God wills it, but He first willed it and then it is just because He willed it.

Secondly, though God chooses some and refuses others, yet He does it in most wise and just order, for herein God proceeds by degrees. The degrees are two: first, grace, [and] second, the riches of His grace. For the first, namely, grace simply, God gives it generally to all, and passes by none, but for the second, namely, the gifts of His grace, in regard of this He passes by some and gives them not to all. God then does not simply ordain a man to condemnation, but because he sins. He does not first ordain him to damnation, but leaves him to his sin, and sinning he deserves his condemnation, yet [God is] not moved by his sin, but his sin having relation to his condemnation.

Use. For that God of His own will chooses some [and] refuses others, it ought to move us to humble ourselves with fear and reverence before God and to use all the good means to work our salvation. "Thou standest by faith, be not high minded, but fear."[6] Secondly, if this be true, we must not be offended when we see wicked man oppugn and withstand the gospel of Christ. Thirdly, we see that those divines are far overshot that teach that [God] chooses all men by a universal and general election to salvation, and say that man himself is the cause of his reprobation, and man himself is the framer of his election. And this not only papists but other divines teach [it also]. But the Holy Spirit far refutes this opinion, teaching that they were of old accorded to damnation, not that they enroll themselves but were of old enrolled. And this universal election breeds a drowsy security in the hearts of men, when election is made so easy that every man that will may work his salvation.

"Which were of old ordained, etc." Here he first sets down the limit which was before all worlds. Secondly, the cause of God's decree, which is of Himself, not of the creature, because the decree was before any creature had any being. And, therefore, Paul says, "God loved Jacob [and] hated Esau before either of them had done either good or evil."[7] "As he has chosen us before the foundation of the world" (Eph. 1:4). And Christ Himself says [in] Matthew, "I thank thee heavenly father that thou hast hid these things from the wise and prudent of the world, and revealed them to babes. And this thou hast done because it was thy good pleasure."[8]

---

6. Rom. 11:20.
7. Rom. 9:11–13.
8. Matt. 11:25–26.

Jude 4

(Sermon 3)

"Ungodly men they are, etc." (Jude 4)

We have heard the seducers described by two things before: first, by their hypocrisy, [and], secondly, by their eternal estate before God. The third thing by which Jude describes them is their religion, and that in these words: "ungodly men they are." Ungodliness is a sin much spoken of yet not so much known. Therefore, it is requisite first to know what an ungodly man is, which shall appear by knowing what ungodliness is. It is a great and grievous sin, far greater than any of the seven deadly sins, so termed by the papists, for it is the mother sin of them all.

The greatness of it appears for that it is rooted in the heart. It is not so well discerned for that it is inward, not outward. It is a sin of the first table and of the first commandment of the first table. And as the first table is a greater commandment than the second, so this being a break of the first, it is a greater sin than those of the second, for the nature of this sin is to rob God of His honor.

Ungodliness has three main parts or properties. (1) It denies God honor, which is due to Him. (2) It gives honor due to God to other things than God. (3) It gives to God sometimes His honor due to Him, but not in due manner.

For the first, ungodliness denies God of His honor due to Him [in] three ways. First, it makes the ungodly man bar God of His honor by ignorance, in not acknowledging the Godhead and the power thereof as the power of God, the mercy of God, the justice of God, the providence of God, and the presence of God. "The fool has said in his heart there is no God" (Ps. 14);[1] that is, [he] denies in his heart the power, providence, mercy, justice, and presence of God. And in this is the nature of the wicked, that though their conscience accuses them and warns them there is a god, yet their hearts do not acknowledge the form and properties of the Godhead.

Second, ungodliness denies God of His honor by keeping back the ungodly man from subjecting his conscience to the law and commandment of God, and [he] denies subjection. "They say also unto God, 'Depart from us, for we desire not this knowledge of thy ways'" (Job 21:14). But to this Christ Himself finds an

---

1. Verse 1.

answer. "Moreover, those mine enemies, which would not that I should reign over them, bring hither and slay them before me" (Luke 19:27).

Third, ungodliness denies God of His honor due to Him by holding back the ungodly man's heart from praying to God. "They call not upon the Lord" (Ps. 14:4). And that is the property of an ungodly man never to pray to God, and herein they differ not from swine and brute beasts, which receive all things and never look from whence they came.

The second property: ungodliness gives honor due to God to some other. Thus men do when they set their love, joy, and heart upon some other thing more than upon God. For the honor of God is to have the heart and the affections thereof. Therefore, the covetous man is called in the Scripture an idolatrous man because his heart is more upon his riches than upon God. So, the devil is called a god because men make him their god by setting their heart and delight more upon sinning, that comes from the devil, than upon God. And, therefore, 2 Timothy says, "Men shall be lovers of their pleasures more than God."[2] In a word, he that sets his heart upon anything more than God, he gives the honor due to God to some other thing.

The third property is to give to God honor due to Him, but not in due manner. It is not enough to be godly outwardly and make an outward profession, but he must be inwardly affected, for God must have the worship of the heart. In a word, then, this sin of ungodliness is that mother sin of all. For in this epistle many sins are reckoned up, yet Jude begins with this, purposely after hypocrisy and their estate before God, to show that this is the mother of all that are rehearsed. All the chapter (Rom. 1) consists of a rehearsal of the sins of the Gentiles, and the mother sin of all is a profane and ungodly heart. When Abraham was in the land of Gerar, he would not confess Sarah to be his wife (Gen. 20). Being demanded the cause, he answered, because he thought the fear of God was not in that place, and therefore they would not stick to kill him,[3] showing that where an ungodly heart is, he will not stick to commit any sin.

Use. This being so grievous a sin, and the mother sin of many more, and the more dangerous because spiritual, we are taught to labor to see and discern this sin in our hearts, and from our hearts to bewail the same above all other. But some will say, "We are not tainted with this sin." I answer: it is a common sin. We indeed join ourselves in holy exercises, we hear the Word, we receive the sacraments, and we have the form of outward obedience because the prince's law commands so much. But there are many that want the power of religion and godliness. Some have very secure hearts, they never think of their sin,

---

2. 2 Tim. 3:4.
3. Verses 10–11.

never of the judgment for it, never think to give an account for their sin, never think of hellfire, and therefore never humble themselves inwardly, because they perform outward obedience. But though we have the form of obedience, yet the cares of the world fill and possess the heart, [so] that they will not suffer the power of God to enter. Again, many have the power of religion, yet they cannot brook to have the conscience brought in subjection to every law of God, and therefore many fail in the heart and single eye. Therefore, we must labor to see this sin of ungodliness in our heart and to bewail it. And if we cannot see it, there worse is our case and the more ungodly we [are], for sure it is we have it because it was bred in our bones.

Secondly,[4] we are here taught to exercise ourselves to godliness, and that we may do this we must prepare ourselves before and make a good beginning. Now for to begin well we must acknowledge God's justice to us, God's providence to us, God's mercy to us, and His power. For when the Galatians knew not, they served them which were no gods.[5] Secondly, that we may exercise ourselves in this holiness, we must worship God in our spirit, and this is right godliness, the other is hypocrisy. *Question.* How shall one worship in soul? *Answer.* This worship stands in two things:

> Faith
> Actions of faith

First, faith is that whereby we generally believe the whole Word of God, both New and Old Testaments. Now, especially we believe God's mercy in the forgiveness of sins, God's providence in all things, and God's presence in all places, and this is spiritual worship.

The second thing, that is, the actions of faith, is twofold:

> Subjection
> Elevation or lifting of the heart

Subjection is in three respects. Firstly, to God's judgment, that is when by grace we call ourselves to an account for our sins and entreat mercy for the forgiveness of them. The second subjection is a subjection to His Word, to the law both of the first and second table, when we suffer all our consciences to be ruled by His laws. The third subjection is to the good pleasure of God, as when we rest in God's good will, though it be against our good will. And by these three kinds of subjection do we worship God.

The second action of faith is elevation or lifting up of our souls to God. That is done for two causes. First, to ask God's graces. Secondly, to give Him thanks

---

4. I.e., second use. Cf. Perkins, *Jude*, RHB 4:100.

5. Gal. 4:8.

for all His blessings received. To conclude then: to persuade us to exercise this godliness, Paul says, "Godliness is great gain" (1 Tim. 6:6). That is, he that worships God aright, he shall want nothing that he can think either in this life or in the life to come. If, therefore, a man will be rich, let him but be a godly man and worship God aright. He shall presently have great gain. In a word, then, for us which have had the Word of God preached among us, which has been denied to many nations, what must we do [is] as Paul to Titus tells us that we must learn to deny ungodliness, because we have received the grace of God.[6]

---

6. Titus 2:12.

Jude 4

(Sermon 4)

"Which turn the grace of our God into wantonness." (Jude 4)

We have heard the three first points whereby the seducers are described. Now follows the fourth point in these words: "which turn the grace of God into wantonness." In this point of the description two things [are] to be considered: firstly, the vice here condemned, [and,] secondly, the virtue contrary to this vice.

For the vice, that it may the better appear, let us see the meaning of these words: "which turn the grace of God into wantonness." By "grace," here we are to understand that which before was understood by faith, namely, the doctrine of the gospel. The doctrine is so called "grace" in Titus 2:11–12, "The grace of God that brings salvation unto all men hath appeared and teaches us that we should deny ungodliness, etc." This teaching grace in that place is nothing else but doctrine of remission of sins, and this is called grace because it is the mere grace and mercy of God.

"Into wantonness." By wantonness properly is meant that sin whereby men addict themselves to incontinency and unlawful pleasures of the flesh. But here it must needs be taken now generally for a profane liberty of sinning, not for the particular sin of inconstancy.

"Turn the grace, etc." "Turn," that is, put the grace of God out of his[1] place and apply it to a coarse end. Now, this misapplying of the grace of God is not only in practice but also in doctrine and teaching. As we see, these seducers did misapply the grace of God in teaching. These seducers Saint Peter describes almost in the same words as they are here set down: "There shall be false teachers among you, which privately shall bring in damnable heresies, even denying the Lord, etc." (2 Peter 2:1).

Of these seducers in ancient times we read of many, as Simon Magus and his disciples. Also, the disciples of Basilides[2] and innumerable others, which teach the liberty of sin because of God's mercy, which is nothing else than to

---

1. I.e., its.

2. Basilides was an early Gnostic (second century), who claimed to have inherited his teaching from Matthew. Cf. Perkins, *Jude*, RHB 4:102n129.

turn the grace of God into wantonness. And this old and ancient sin, the devil in this our age has again renewed. And that is in four sorts of men.

The first kind are the libertines of this age, men that are enemies to the law of God, teaching us that because we are under grace, therefore we are not under the obedience of the law, but that the law is abolished.

The second kind of men which in this age turn the grace of God into wantonness are Anabaptists, who because they find in Scripture that God has promised plenty of grace, they teach that all magistracy and civil jurisdiction is unlawful.

The third kind are the professed papists and the present Church of Rome with their religion which does turn the grace of God into wantonness, which is manifest by this. God has given to His church the power of the keys to open and to shut. The Roman religion has converted this power of the keys and made it first an instrument of profaneness, for by this power of the keys the Roman Church has set up a new priesthood of forgiving sins and offers sacrifice to this priest.[3] Secondly, this their power of the keys is an instrument of injustice, when by the power of the keys they stir up rebellions and seditions. Thirdly, it is an instrument of all covetousness, for by the power of the keys they sell pardons, and thereby the pope does daily enrich himself. And if there were nothing else, yet this one practice of the Church of Rome proves they turn the grace of God into wantonness. No man that holds this Roman religion is any whit the better for it, but the more <…> it only shows <…> <…> them in their sin. And, first, it makes them gross hypocrites, for this religion is nothing but a ceremonial and bodily worship which appears among other [of] their ceremonies [as much as] in this one. Religion requires fasting; therefore, they command fasting from flesh, yet they give liberty to use in the fasting the strongest wine and strongest spices that are. And what fasting can this be but ceremonial fasting? Secondly, this religion makes them proud, for they teach that man by his works may merit heaven and by his sufferings may satisfy for his sins. Thirdly, this religion makes man secure, for it teaches that men may [by] the power of the keys have a full pardon for their sins if they are [to] pay the money requested, and though they fail in payment, yet it teaches that they may make amends in purgatory. Fourthly, it makes a man in temptation to be desperate. Lastly, it renews the old sins of old heresies. It makes them to turn the grace of God into wantonness, which appears as in other things so in this one, that it forbids marriage, yet it tolerates fornication by the maintaining of these stewes.[4] And this to turn the grace of God into wantonness.

---

3. Probably intended to read "by this priest." Cf. Perkins, *Jude*, RHB 4:103.
4. *Stewe*: brothel.

The fourth kind of men which turn the grace of God into wantonness are among us, carnal and formal Protestants. First, many turn God's grace to wantonness by election and dispute thus: "If I be predestined to salvation, I shall be saved; if not, I shall be damned. Live I as I can, God's decree cannot be altered." Secondly, many abuse the mercy and longsuffering of God, for because God is merciful, they defer their repentance while they are young till they are old,[5] and they plead for themselves, "young saints, old devils" and "at what time however a sinner repents, God will put his wickedness out of His remembrance, etc." And thus, the longsuffering of God is abused, and so His grace is turned into wantonness. Thirdly, many under the pretense of brotherly love do break out into all excess of sin, misspending and lavishing those riches which God has given them, in gaming and revelry, and [not] keeping good fellowship, and all under pretense of love. Again, fourthly, many turn the grace of God into wantonness in keeping no Sabbath. And for their excuse they say they are not bound to the Jewish Sabbath, and therefore will make no difference of time and so keep no Sabbath at all. Lastly, some because they have grace given them, sin willingly, and say, "Let us sin that grace may abound."[6] But these and all the most turn the grace of God into wantonness. Thus much of the vice.

Now, in a word, of the virtue. The virtue, contrary to the vice forbidden herein, is to make a holy use of the grace of God. This is done when the grace of God is applied to the right end. The end why God gave His grace is that we should be thankful to Him and testify this thankfulness by our obedience. That this is true appears, first, by the testimony of Scripture. "We being delivered out of the hands of our enemies should serve him without fear" (Luke 1:74). Romans 6, the whole chapter, especially the 15th, 16th, [and] 17th verses, "What then, shall we sin? etc." "For the grace of God that brings salvation unto all men has appeared" (Titus 2:11).

Secondly, this appears by all points of [the] gospel and newness of life. For the chief end of election is that we might be holy. Likewise, the chief end of vocation is holiness, and therefore Paul says to the Romans, "You are called [to] be holy."[7] The end of sanctification is to free man from the corruption of our sins. The end of justification is to free man from the guilt of those sins. The end of faith is to purify the heart. The end of love is to keep man to keep the commandments.

---

5. Pages 165–66 in the MS are torn out. This sheet of the book was evidently removed before the sermon was recorded. The text reads continuously from page 164 to 167.

6. Rom. 6:1.

7. Rom. 1:7.

Thirdly, Christ is a mediator, and that by two ways:

Merit
Efficacy or virtue

Now, Christ by His virtue and efficacy does as well forgive sin as by His merit He does kill sin. And, therefore, if we have grace by His merit and not forgiveness by His efficacy, what avails it? Therefore, having the first, let us be thankful for it, that we may have the second.

The use then of this second point is that we, having been partakers of the grace of God, our duty is to make use of the same grace. The principal use (as we said before) is to be thankful to God by our obedience. And, therefore, Paul says, "I beseech you brethren by the mercies of God, to present yourselves as an acceptable sacrifice to God."[8] Where the ground of his exhortation is the grace of God. If we believe God to be our Father and Christ our Redeemer, we do it by grace. Let us, therefore, for this grace, show ourselves thankful by our obedience: to God that we may seem His children, to Christ that it may appear that we are redeemed. He that is delivered out of prison and set at liberty, if he desires again to lay in the dungeon, he must needs be accounted a mad man. Likewise, we being delivered by grace from all our sins and the guilt thereof, if we do now desire again to lay in the dungeon of our sins, are we to be accounted less mad? Now, the chief way to escape this dungeon and prison of our sins from which we are freed is to show ourselves thankful to God by our obedience for delivering us.[9]

---

8. Rom. 12:1.

9. Bottom of the page: *verte tria folia* (Latin): "Turn the three leaves."

Jude 4

(Sermon 5)

"Which turn the grace of God into wantonness, and deny God the only Lord, and our Lord Jesus Christ." (Jude 4)

We have begun to speak of the fourth point whereby those seducers are described, namely, by their doctrine in turning the grace of God into wantonness. We have shown the meaning of the words. Now follows another point to be considered in this point, and that is in these words: "Turn the grace of *our* God" and not only the grace of God.[1] For [the] better understanding of this circumstance, three things are to be considered: (1) how God comes to be our God; (2) what you must do that God be our God; [and] (3) what benefit we have by God's being our God.

For the first, it is answered, God comes to be our God not by any merit of ours but by the free and gracious covenant of God, the covenant of the gospel, revealing our remission of sins and everlasting life by Christ. [In] Jeremiah, 31st chapter, God makes a new covenant with the Israelites, and in the 33rd verse the tenor of the covenant is set down, which is this: "I will put my law in their inward parts, and I will be their God and they shall be my people." And upon this ground the whole church of God says, "God is our God."

For the second point, what we must do that God may be our God, the answer is that we must make covenant with God. Now, as in every covenant there is a twofold consent, namely, of either party, so in this covenant with God there must be a double consent: one consent on God's part that He will be our God, [and] one consent on our part that we will be His people. For the first consent, God propounds His consent generally in His written Word and more particularly in the ministry of His Word and sacraments. For God, giving to us His Word and sealing it with His sacraments, does as really give consent to us to be our God as if He should speak from heaven. Having then the Word and ministry, we have God's consent in the covenant. Now, there remains a second consent, that is ours, that we take God to be our God. Our covenant has two degrees. One degree is outward in outward profession, where man receives the outward seals of God's covenant, namely, His Word and sacraments. And to

---

1. Emphasis original.

do this is something, for hereby we are distinguished from Turks, but this not sufficient. And, therefore, there is a second degree in our consent, and that is the consent of the heart unto God. Now this consent of the heart is when these three things are performed. First, when with bitterness we bewail our sins. Secondly, when we care to do the will of God and reconcile ourselves to the same. Thirdly, when we purpose in our hearts never to sin again. And when we do thus, our covenant with God, that He shall be our God and we His people, will be for authentical, as any bargain between man and man.

For the third point, what benefit we have by having God to be our God. It is answered that, first, it is the foundation of all our comfort. In the 41st [chapter] of Isaiah, God lays down singular comforts for His children, and the main foundation of all is this: "I am your God."[2] Christ in His <...> agony had this comfort, crying, "My God, My God" (Matt. 27:46). David in the same words (Ps. 30).[3] "My God, my God, my God, why hast thou forsaken me?" (Ps. 22:1). David also, when he looked for nothing by death, comforts himself in that he had a God who kills and makes alive, brings down to the ground and raises up (1 Sam. 2:6). We are then here taught to labor every day to use all good means to have this grounded in our heart: that God is our God. For when friends, health, wealth, and all things forsake us, this is the ground and foundation of our comfort: to have God [as] our God. So is it the foundation of all unfeigned obedience. The whole [of] Psalm 95 is a psalm of obedience, and the 7th verse is a ground of the whole psalm, where he says, "For he is our God and we his people, etc." The 50th Psalm, likewise, is an exhortation to obedience to God's Word. And the 7th verse is a ground of all: "Hear, O my people, for I am God, even thy God." And indeed, whosoever is persuaded that God is his God, he cannot willingly sin, for the ground of all spiritual worship is grounded upon this. And thus much of the first point, namely, the doctrine of the seducers in this word: "Turn the grace of God into wantonness."

The fifth and last thing whereby those seducers are described is their lives and manners, in these words: "Deny God, the only Lord and our Lord Jesus Christ." In these words, there may seem some difficulty in the translation of these words: "God the Lord, and our Lord Jesus Christ." For some think these words to be meant both of God the Father and God the Son: God the Father in these words, "God the Lord," [and] God the Son in these words, "And the Lord Jesus Christ." But they seem to me to be understood only of God the Son, and that for these reasons. (1) Because the tenor of the words do apply all that is spoken to Christ, and not to God the Father. (2) Because Saint Peter uses the

---

2. Verse 10.
3. Verse 2.

same words almost, in the same sense, "denying him that has bought them" (2 Peter 2:1).[4] So, the meaning is they deny God the only Lord, that is the ruler, even the Lord Jesus Christ.

And thus much for the words, now to the matter.

In this point two things are to be considered. First, the fault and sin of those seducers, that is, in denying of Christ. The second thing is a description of Christ, describing Him to be God, the only Lord and our Lord Jesus Christ, which is done to <...> the former, namely, their sin. For the first, to deny Christ is to renounce Christ, and as much as in men lies to make the death of Christ of no effect. And this denial of Christ does presuppose the redemption of Christ. *Objection.* Those seducers are said before to be preordained to condemnation, and secondly are said to deny the redemption of Christ. Now, if they were redeemed by Christ, how could they be preordained to condemnation? *Answer.* These were redeemed by Christ, but not in the decree of God. But they are redeemed in their own judgment. For we do and ought to believe that every Christian man is redeemed, so then in regard of the judgment of the church and in regard of their own judgment and profession. So they profess so much by their outward appearance, they are said to be redeemed, <...> of God's decree.

The second thing in this point is the aggravating of their sin by the description of Christ. He says barely they denied Christ, but Him that was our Lord Christ. He describes Him by three titles. First, "the Lord," that is, the ruler and governor of all things in heaven and earth, for so much the original word signifies. The second title is the "only" Lord. This expresses and manifests the divinity, that there is but one God. Neither is it added to exclude the Father or the Holy Spirit, but it excludes the devil, the world, and the flesh, which many men make their god. The third title is "our" Lord and Savior, etc. Christ is our Lord [in] two ways; first, in regard that God before all beginning gave to Him the rule of His church, [and,] secondly, He is our Lord by the right of redemption.

In this last point, two things may be asserted. First, how these men denied Christ. *Answer.* They deny Him not absolutely with their lips, for then the church would perceive them, and then they could not have been said to have crept in. But they denied Christ by their licentious living. And this is common in this land, to profess Christ with the lips and deny Him in their lives. Every Christian confesses Christ at the Lord's Table, yet in their lives they despise Him, and instead of calling upon His name, profane His name, some by

---

4. The original erroneously cited verse 7.

swearing, some by gaming, and many by minding nothing but worldly things. And [they] think it curious preciseness to obey and profess Christ in our lives.

The second question is in what respect these denied Christ. *Answer*. In two respects: firstly, in respect of His lordship, [and,] secondly, in respect of His Godhead. For the first, they denied Him in regard of His lordship, for when Christ redeemed them to be His people and He their lord, they deny Him to be their Lord. The devil shall be their lord. They will not Jesus Christ to rule over them, but they acknowledge Christ to be their Savior, to carry their sins, but their ruler He shall not be. Secondly, they deny Him in regard of His Godhead. For that they could well afford with the merit of Christ, but they put away the power of His Godhead. They cannot abide the virtue of the death of Christ, which is to subdue the corruptions of their nature. They make account of the merit but not of the efficacy. We must then learn to make Christ not only our Savior but our Lord. We must not only acknowledge His merit but His efficacy, for if He be our Savior and not Lord, He is no Savior. "Come unto me all you that are laden, and I will ease you" (Matt. 11:28). Here He gives comfort to all generally, yet He strains[5] His speech in the next words: "Take my yoke on you, etc.," teaching us that though God has great afford of comforts, yet it is only for them that will take the yoke of Christ, not for them that deny He shall be their Lord and rule over them. For unless we will take His yoke, we shall have none of His comfort.

---

5. *Strains*: restrains.

Jude 5

(Sermon 6)

"I will therefore put you in remembrance, forasmuch as you once knew this, how that the Lord, after that he had delivered the people out of Egypt, destroyed them afterward which believed not." (Jude 5)

These words depend upon the former verse as an answer to an objection. The objection is not set down but may be gathered out of the words. The objection is this is. *Objection.* Those seducers had professed Christ; therefore, there was no danger. *Answer.* The answer to this reaches from this 5th verse to the end of the 20th verse. The form of the answer is this:

> All such persons as give to themselves liberty of sinning shall
> be destroyed,
> But those seducers give to themselves liberty of sinning, etc.
> They shall be destroyed.[1]

And, therefore, seeing their end is destruction, there was great danger, though they had professed Christ.

So this answer consists of two parts or propositions. First, such as give to themselves liberty of sinning, their end is destruction. This is plainly shown in the 5th, 6th, and 7th verses. The second part is [that] these seducers give to themselves liberty of sinning. This is set down from the beginning of the 8th verse to the end of the 20th. For the first, namely, such as give themselves the liberty of sinning, though it be not plainly expressed in many words, yet there is a particular proof of it set down by three examples. The first is the destruction of the Israelites in the 5th verse. [The] second is the fall of the angels in the 6th verse. [The] third is the overthrow of Sodom and Gomorrah in the 7th verse. And by these three does he confirm his argument.

In this 5th verse, two things are set down. First, a preface, in these words: "I will therefore put you in remembrance, for as much as you once knew this." And, secondly, the first example, namely, the destruction of the Israelites.

For the preface, it seems to prevent an objection which might be made, after this sort: "Tell us what we know not, this we know already." Now this he

---

1. The syllogism is not formatted in this way in the manuscript.

prevents, saying, "I will put you in remembrance, etc." The preface concerns three points. First, the practice of the apostles in these words: "I will put you in remembrance." [The] second point is the properties of the church, which one property is knowledge of the church in these words: "for as much as you know, etc." The third point is the infallible knowledge of the church, which is also the second property of the church, in these words: "you once knew, etc." Of these in order.

The first is the practice of the church, in which we learn what is the office of all teachers, and that is not only to teach things not known but also to revive them, for knowledge often lays dead in the mind, and therefore it ought to be stirred up again. "Wherefore I will not be negligent to put you always in remembrance of things that you have knowledge" (2 Peter 1:12). Here we learn two things. First, hearers must not be offended if they hear the same things often repeated, for it is the office of the minister not only to teach but to remember them of that which he has taught. Secondly, such hearers as have knowledge must not be offended if they hear nothing but that which they know already, because the minister's duty is to remember them of such things as they know.

[The] second point is the properties of the church. The first property is the knowledge of the Scriptures, to know the histories of the Bible and the examples in the Scripture. Thus did Timothy, who, as he said of himself, was from his childhood instructed in the Scripture.[2] This is far otherwise in these days, for now men plead for themselves ignorance and think it a good excuse. Because the knowledge of the Scriptures concerns the ministers only (say they), they have nothing to do with the Scripture and profess this ignorance. But they which profess this, profess this ignorance, profess that they are not belonging to Christ. For it is the property of the saints of Christ to have knowledge.

The third point, which is the second property of the church, is in these words: "once knew, etc." The saints of God, as they have knowledge of Scripture, so they have certain and infallible and unchangeable knowledge. By this we may judge of those in these days which hold no religion, that they are not belonging to Christ, but are atheists. Here we learn our duty, which is to hold one religion certainly. And that which we know we must know, we must know it once, not twice, and know it certainly and <...> many question of the alteration of it. And thus much of the preface.

Now follows the reason. The first part is set down by three examples. The first example [is] in this verse, of the Israelites who willingly sinning against God were destroyed. "Yet they presumed obstinately to go up, etc." (Num. 14:44–45). In this example [are] three things to be considered. First, who

---

2. 2 Tim. 3:15.

they were that were destroyed. That is set down in these words: "delivered the people." Secondly, at what time they were destroyed. That was after He had delivered them out of Egypt. Thirdly, what was the cause of their destruction. That was because of their unbelief, in these words: "destroyed them which believed not." Of these in order.

For the first, who they were. It is answered: the people, that is, the posterity of Abraham, Isaac, and Jacob, and the twelve patriarchs, the Israelites, the chosen people of God, who had privileges above all the nations of the earth besides, which had given them the Word, the sacraments, and all other worthy means and blessings of God. "Which are the Israelites to whom pertain the adoption, and the glory, and the covenant, and the giving of the law, and the service of God, etc." (Rom. 9:4). By this we are taught that no outward privileges or means of salvation are effectual, but fruitless when they are not used in the right use. For their efficacy consists in the use (Rom. 2:25; Gal. 6:15). And Paul, though he had many privileges, yet he counted all loss in comparison of Christ (Phil. 3:7). This must admonish us not to content ourselves with the outward means of salvation and think it sufficient if we be once baptized and often receive the sacraments. But we must labor to use them aright, for when they are out of their right use, they make to our further condemnation. We must use them, therefore, aright in faith and repentance.

The second thing is the time when they were destroyed. That is answered: after their delivery out of Egypt. Where we see [that] after blessings received of God, if man goes forward in sin, then judgment follows, yea, though they be the chosen children of God, as we see in this example. And to show this the <…> of the whole book of Judges is namely that after blessings received, judgment follows sin. After the days of Solomon, Jeroboam, and after him Rehoboam, falls to idolatry, for which sin they were punished almost four hundred years. Jacob said to God that if He would but hand him food and raiment, that then he would pay all his vows to God, but God bestowed not only food and raiment but many great blessings. And because Jacob forgot his vow, God accounted it a sin. And for that sin he was punished, in that Dinah was deflowered. We in England have received many blessings; we have been delivered out of Egypt from the pope and the Church of Rome, unto unspeakable blessings. Yet it is a general fault in this land that there is less love to God and His Word than was thirty years ago, and therefore we may be sure that if we continue in this, that after such blessings as God has bestowed upon us, there will great judgments follow.

The third point is the cause for which they are punished. That is answered: for their unbelief, because they believed not the Word of God. Three sundry points [are] to be considered.[3]

[The] first is wherein did not they believe God. *Answer*. God had promised them four hundred years before to guide them into the land of Canaan which He had given them. God had promised protection in their journey. God had confirmed His promises by sundry miracles. Now their unbelief was in this: that they believed not that God would bring to this land.

The second point is why God destroyed them for their unbelief and not for other sins, as their rebellion and their disobedience and their murmuring against God. *Answer*. This is answered because unbelief was the main sin of all their other sins, for the disobedience and the murmuring came from this: that they did not believe God. Secondly, this sin of unbelief does in a more special manner deny God of His honor, and therefore for it more than the others He destroyed them. Moses, though he did not want this obedience, yet because he did but alike fail in it, he was barred out of the land of Canaan. He might not go into it, only see it.

[Use.] Herein we learn that which is taught [in] Hebrews 3:12–13, to labor that we have not our hearts hardened through unbelief. Secondly, we learn to exercise ourselves in faith concerning God's mercy and His promises. Caleb and Joshua, because they rested in the promises of God, they were brought into the land of Canaan, and so we if we rest in the promises of God and mercy of God, we shall with Caleb and Joshua be brought to that heavenly Canaan, the kingdom of heaven. Thirdly, we learn obedience. "Harden not your hearts, etc." (Ps. 95:8). This is slenderly preached in these days, for whereas we should yield obedience to God with our belief, we instead thereof, when God punishes us for our sins, we lay the fault of our punishment upon witches and think some had bewitched us. But those men do bewitch themselves, and their own unbelief is the witch, no other witch. We must then learn in such a case not to lay the fault of our punishment upon witches but must lay it upon our sins and look to them. We are taught further to judge of sin not in our own judgment, for this sin of unbelief in our judgment is no sin because it lurks in the heart. But we must judge of sin by the law of God.

---

3. The third point—namely, "what was this destruction?"—is missing from this manuscript. Cf. Perkins, *Jude*, RHB 4:112.

Jude 5

(Sermon 7)

"Destroyed them afterward which believed not." (Jude 5)

In the example of the Israelites there were three things propounded: first, who was destroyed; secondly, at what time; thirdly, for what cause. Concerning the two[1] first we have thoroughly spoken. Of the third, namely, their unbelief the cause, we have begun to speak. Of that something remains to be spoken.

Firstly, it seems the Holy Spirit speaks generally that He destroyed all the people of the Israelites for their unbelief, but we are not to understand it generally, but particularly with an exception, which exception [is] set down [in] Numbers 14:37–38. Now by this exception we learn that God in His justice and anger remembers His mercy and forgives. Punishing the Israelites, He mingles His mercy with His anger in saving the younger sort, all under seventeen years of age, though they did not believe. And, therefore, we learn that, when God does exercise us with temptations, to pray to Him that He will not wholly abandon and forsake us.

Again, where it is said they were destroyed for their unbelief, a doubt may be moved,[2] that it was a point of injustice in God to punish them for unbelief because they repented for it (Num. 14:40). *Answer.* It was a feigned and counterfeit repentance, and their confession of unbelief was counterfeit, which appears because they still disobeyed God. For God commands them to turn back to the wilderness of Arabia, but they would not. By this we see the nature of man is to feign and counterfeit repentance. The which is seen in men when God visits them with sickness, for then they say that if they can recover, they will lead a new life, but when they are recovered, they neither change heart nor life. By this we are taught always to suspect our hearts, lest we have in them feigned and counterfeit repentance. Again, by their unbelief we are all taught particularly to take heed of unbelief, that we do not feignedly repent for it.

Now, that we may do this we will show how we may repent unfeignedly for our unbelief. First, we must lay aside the common persuasion of the goodness of our faith, and as we do this so we must labor to discern in our own hearts

______

1. The MS states "three," which appears to be a typographical error.
2. *Moved*: removed.

the secret sin of unbelief. That we may the better discern this sin of unbelief, we will propound particular signs by which we may know it.

The first [sign is] when we do not believe that presence of God which is seen ordinarily when we are ashamed to speak many things in the presence of men which we both do and speak in the presence of God. And the presence of man keeps us in more awe than the presence of God, and this is a proof that we do not believe the presence of God. Again, this is proved because we do not believe the particular providence of God as we should, or not believe it at all. First, when we have health, wealth, friends, etc., we think ourselves happy, but when we want[3] them, we are filled with sorrow. When we have this pledge, then we are well, but when the means are gone, then we are sorrowful, so that we are like to the usurer[4] which will not trust the man himself but will trust his hand.

[The] second sign of unbelief is this: when a friend promises in adversity that he will help us, we are comforted, but in the promising of God we are not comforted.[5]

[The] third sign [is] when we dare not believe the lordship of God, that He is able to destroy both body and soul. This appears because many will bestow all their care to live a civil life, and unblamable before man, yet will not stick to commit any sin secretly.

[The] fourth sign is that we do not believe the mercy of God in pardoning our sins. For when temptation and adversity come, we find much despair and doubt of ourselves, as Job spoke many impatient things against God, as that He would kill him and he was the mark at which He shot it.[6]

[The] fifth sign to discern our unbelief is when we believe not the agony and passion of Christ, as when we remember that Christ was crucified and suffered for us and do not fight and crucify ourselves. We do not believe the agony and suffering of Christ, because our sins were the spears that pierced His side and that made Him sweat drops of blood. And if we believe this passion of Christ, it would not make to lift up our hands and exalt ourselves, but to hold down our heads and pull down our peacock feathers.

[The] sixth sign [is] that we do not believe that we descended and rose with Christ, which is proved because in this life all our care is upon earth and earthly things, which would not be if we ascended with Christ, for then should our mind be where He is,[7] and that is in heaven and heavenly things.

---

3. *Want*: lack.

4. *Usurer*: one who loans money for interest.

5. The MS erroneously reads, "we are not promised." Cf. Perkins, *Jude*, RHB 4:115.

6. Job 16:11–13.

7. Col. 3:1–2.

[The] seventh sign is that we do not believe the last judgment, which is proved because we are not affrighted with the fear and terror of it. We live as securely as if there should never be any judgment.

[The] eighth and last sign [is] that we do not believe our own death, which is proved because man delays the amendment of their life until the last gasp. And the cause of this is unbelief where they think not, be they ever so old, that they shall live yet, still live longer.

The second thing which we must do to repent unfeignedly is to mourn for our unbelief, for it is a point of grace to mourn according to the man in the gospel, "Lord I believe; help my unbelief."[8] And the disciples, "Lord, increase our faith."[9]

Thirdly, we must acquaint ourselves in all the promises of the gospel. Promises are of two sorts:

> main promises
> dependent of them

Main promises are pardon of our sins and promise of everlasting life. Dependent promises are promises of good success if we do as God would have us.

Fourthly, we must put our confidence in the promises of God. We must build and settle our hearts upon them. As the earth hangs most strangely in the midst without any prompt, only by the virtue of the Word of God, so must we stay our hearts in the promises of God, and our hearts must hang, without any prompt, only upon those promises.

Thus much of the first example, the Israelites.

---

8. Mark 9:24.
9. Luke 17:5.

Jude 6

(Sermon 8)

"The angels also which kept not their first estate, but left their own habitation, he hath reserved in everlasting chains under darkness unto the judgment of the great day." (Jude 6)

We have spoken before of the first example, namely, the Israelites. Now follows the second example, namely, of the angels in this verse. In this example [there are] three things to be considered: (1) the persons punished, namely, the angels; (2) the sin or fall of the angels, in these words: "which kept not their first estate, but left their own habitation"; [and] (3) the punishment of the angels, in these words: "he has reserved in everlasting chains under darkness."

For the first, the angels are the persons punished. Sundry things are to be considered. First, that it pleases the Holy Spirit to make choice of the angels, because by creation they are the most excellent creatures. Manna is called the bread of angels (Ps. 78:25), and Paul says if he had the tongue of man and angels,[1] not as though angels did eat manna or that they had tongues, but if they had tongues, they should have the excellentest tongues. By this we learn that the excellency of the creature cannot escape the punishment of God and even <…> the more for His excellency.

We apply this unto our lives thus. In these days among us we have many good means as of schools and learned men, and there are among us many to whom we may say, as the woman of Tekoa said to David, "They are angels of God."[2] Now, they and all must learn not, therefore, to put up to live as we list, but be taught by this fearful example of the angels to submit ourselves to the obedience of God. Secondly, in that the angels are the persons punished, we learn that the angels are substances (though invisible), not mere qualities, but living substances, having soul and understanding, for else could they not sin, neither be capable of punishment. For qualities can neither sin nor receive any punishment. If any say that because they are punished, they are bodily substances, I answer, it is sufficient if they be spiritual substances because the punishment is spiritual. By this we learn that the seducers are deceived which

---

1. 1 Cor. 13:1.
2. 2 Sam. 14:17.

think the angels nothing else but motions. Also, many Anabaptists are deceived which think the angels nothing else but good and bad success.

"The angels, etc." The name of "angels" signifies messengers. It is a name of office. Their office was in heaven to tend upon the will of God, and upon this office they are all called messengers, for the name signifies not the nature but the office. And in this regard of office, they must be our examples. We, living in this world, must be like the angels, conformable and obedient to the will of God. And, for this cause, we pray in the second petition: "Thy will be done as it is in heaven."[3]

This name given to the evil angels teaches us that they are justly punished because their office was to do the will of God, which they did not. Again, where it is said, "the angels kept not their estate," there is a distinction of angels. Some left their beginnings, some stood in their beginnings, being then two sorts of angels. This is to be understood not of all angels but only those that fell. And Saint Luke makes a higher distinction of angels, saying, "angels elected of God,"[4] which if there be any elected, there are also some condemned. If any ask the cause of this distinction, I answer, there is no cause of this distinction known to man, only to God it is known, no reason of man can be given. It stands only in the will of God. And of this distinction we are all to stand amazed at the Word of God herein.

Thus much of the persons.

The second point is the sin or fall of the angels in these words: "which kept neither beginning, etc." In this fall of the angels three things [are] to be considered: (1) the cause of the fall, (2) the parts of the fall, [and] (3) the measure of the fall.

For the first, the cause is set down in these words: "which kept not their first estate, etc." Where the Holy Spirit expressly shows that the angels themselves were the cause of the fall, which is manifested thus: either God, or man, or themselves, were the cause. But [it was] neither God nor man, so [it was] themselves. Proved thus: not God, because God punishes them for their fall, which were a great injustice in God to punish them for it and be the cause Himself.

Objection. God did foresee the angels' fall. Now a man that foresees another man's danger, and does not prevent it, is to be blamed. Therefore, God is to be blamed for the fall of the angels. *Answer.* He that foresees any evil to come and does not prevent it is accessary to it if he be bound to prevent it. God did

---

3. Matt. 6:10.
4. 1 Tim. 5:21. The term comes from Paul, not Luke.

foresee and foreknow this fall, yet He is not to be blamed, because He was not bound to prevent it.

Objection 2. God did not confirm the angels in His grace, and they, being not confirmed, fell. And, therefore, God <…> cause because He did not confirm them. *Answer.* God gave grace to the angels, but He did not confirm them in it, yet is not God in fact [the cause]. For God gave them power to persevere in that which was good, but He gave them not the perseverance itself. He gave power of willing perseverance, but He gave them not the will itself. Secondly, man is not the cause of the fall, because they fell before man was. *Objection.* A good tree cannot bring forth bad fruit. Angels were created good; therefore, they could not fall. *Answer.* A tree remaining good cannot bring forth bad fruit, so those angels if they had not fallen could not have done anything worthy of punishment.

Thus much of the cause of the fall.

Now we come to the parts. The parts of the fall are two. First, the fall from their beginning in these words: "which kept not their first estate." Second, the fall from their habitation, in these words: "but left their own habitation."

For the first, "kept not their first estate." These words are expounded [in] John 8:44, "he hath been a murder from the beginning and abode not in the truth," which words are all one with these. For by this truth is meant the image of God in righteousness and holiness, as is expounded [in] Ephesians 4:24. And it is well called truth, because this righteousness and holiness has no hypocrisy in it but is truth itself. So then, the first part of the fall is that they put away the true image of God, namely, righteousness and true holiness.

The second part of the fall is that they left their habitation. Some would think this but a small matter, but it is a great sin. For God first made both the angels and men most excellent places in which He would testify to them His presence and in which they should serve Him. The place of the angels was heaven; the place of man was paradise. After this place was lost, the place was the house of the patriarchs; after it, the temple; after it, the congregation of Christ; and after this life, heaven. By leaving their habitation, the angels left two things: firstly, the presence of God; secondly, their own calling.

And thus much of the parts of the fall.

The third thing is the measure of their fall, namely, how far forth they fell. The words signify that they fell quite [far] and forsook God and heaven wholly, not in part. *Objection.* If the angels falling fell wholly without redemption, then who shall be saved? For if not the angels, then much less the faithful [who are] not comparable to the angels in righteousness. *Answer.* There is a difference between the grace of nature and the grace above nature. The angels, when they were created, had a will, but it was changeable. The faithful will cannot be changed. God gave to all His creatures a freedom of will to will that which was good. The angels and Adam wanted[5] the will to persevere; they had only the power of it, not the will itself. The faithful have not only the power but the will itself. "I will put my fear in their hearts, that they shall not depart from me" (Jer. 32:40). By grace, then, it is not with the faithful as it was with the angels and with Adam, that they must either stand or fall. For by grace, they have the power to persevere.

Use. The angels left their beginning and fell by leaving the image of God. We must, therefore, use all means to have this image restored in our hearts. To do this we must labor to have a good conscience and to have a subjection and obedience to the will of God, and take example herein by the angels. And although our beginning be with the angels' beginning already lost, namely, the image of God, righteousness and holiness, yet we have a second beginning which we must take heed to. So, we are born and baptized in true faith, and we can say more than former nations that we have been baptized in true religion. Now, we must take heed by the angels that we hold this, our second beginning, that we hold this our faith in which we were baptized, and never lose this second beginning lest, with the angels, we be condemned.

---

5. *Wanted*: lacked.

Jude 6

(Sermon 9)

"But left their own habitation, he hath reserved in everlasting chains under darkness unto the judgment of the great day." (Jude 6)

We have spoken of the two uses of the fall of the angels. The third use is that no place of Scripture does set down any particular sin as the first offense of the angels. The Holy Spirit only sets it down generally. *Objection.* The Scriptures should be sufficient to resolve all doubts in religion whatsoever. Now there is a great doubt what was the first offense of the angels, and therefore how is the Scripture a sufficient judge in controversies? *Answer.* We must not think the Scriptures a judge to determine all controversies (for these are immeasurable), but it is so penned that is can sufficiently resolve the conscience of any man of all things which concern his salvation. Now this question does not any whit tend to the salvation of any of our souls.

Fourth Use. Where the angels left the habitation, we are taught to seek our habitations. Some will say, what is our new habitation? *Answer.* God assigned to the angels and to Adam their habitations, not an earthly paradise but a heavenly place, heaven itself. Christ tells His disciples that in His Father's house there are many dwelling places and that He goes to prepare them a place (John 14:2). Though our dwelling house be in heaven, yet the gates of this house are not in heaven but on earth, for all places on earth on which God's people worship Him are the very doors and gates of heaven and the suburbs thereof. In Genesis 28, Jacob in his vision saw the presence of God, and in that place built him an altar which, in the 17th verse, he calls the gates of heaven.[1] So now, seeing what our habitation is, many uses follow.

First, we must always labor that we be found worthy to enter into that habitation which is our dwelling place, heaven. And that we may be worthy, we must walk in the way of repentance and obedience. We must take up Christ's cross and deny ourselves.

Second, we are taught always to have care to join ourselves to the assemblies of the church of God, where God is worshiped, because those assemblies are the doors and suburbs, and therefore though we be not in heaven, yet we

---

1. The MS erroneously attributes this vision to Abraham rather than Jacob.

are near, even at the door. In this regard David desired to be a doorkeeper in the house of God. And Joseph left king Pharaoh's house to join the church of God.

Third, in that heaven is our habitation, we are taught to cast our joy not on earth by houses and lands, for they are but tents for pilgrims, but on our heavenly habitation. Cain was ruler of a whole city, yet for all that, for all his houses and lands, he was called but a vagabond because he had no care to join himself to the congregation of the faithful and to dwell in that house and heavenly habitation. Therefore, our heart must be where our true habitation is.

Fifth Use. We are taught every day to prepare ourselves for death. For here all habitations are but tents, and therefore we must prepare ourselves for that true habitation prepared of God. And, therefore, men are not too much to be grieved for the death of their friends, for the faithful go to a most happy habitation, and therefore, though we cannot at the first enter in, yet we must press to the doors and leave friends, parents, country, yea, and our own lives if we cannot otherwise.

Last Use. The angels by creation were the children of God. Their office was to serve and tend upon God. Now, they by leaving this fell. Where we are taught that, seeing we as well as the angels have callings, we must not leave our callings but must walk worthily of them.

Thus much of the second part of the fall.

Now follows the last part, the punishment of the angels in these words: "he hath reserved in everlasting chains under darkness unto the judgment of the great day." Here the punishment is set down by two degrees. (1) Their custody in these words: "he has reserved in everlasting chains under darkness." (2) Their full punishment in these words: "the judgment of the last day."

Touching the first, their custody consists in two things: (1) reserved in chains [and] (2) reserved under darkness. By chains here two things are meant. First, that the power of God does restrain the power of the devil (Rev. 20:1–2). Secondly, by chains is meant the angels' guiltiness, for guiltiness is nothing but binding the angels to destruction. For God, after the fall of the angels, delivers them up to destruction, and as God does this, so they in their consciences acknowledge this to be done for their offenses, for their conscience tells them that they are bound, and this, their own consciences, are the chains.

[Use.] By this we are taught to take heed of an evil conscience and to labor for a good conscience which may excuse, not accuse. For evil consciences are the everlasting consciences, binding us to everlasting destruction. Second, we learn by this that the most excellent liberty in the world is to do the will of God. Men think it liberty to sin, but that brings these chains. The only liberty is to keep a good conscience, and in a good conscience to serve God.

It is added, "everlasting chains," where we see the angels shall stand eternally guilty, never to be released, nor have any hope of redemption. Herein mark the love of God. Angels, the most excellent creatures, falling, are never redeemed. Man falls, yet God grants him a redeemer. Angels once bound can never be loosed. Men, though they be bound, yet the chains are not eternal, but may be loosed. And this ought to stir up all men to thankfulness, for we can never be sufficiently thankful to God for this His so great mercy.

Thus much of the first part, "reserved in everlasting chains."

Now follows the second part of their custody in these words: "under darkness." By darkness we are to understand the anger and wrath of God and the want of His favor. *Objection.* It seems they are not altogether out of the favor of God, because they have the grace of God. They have the grace of God because they have faith. They have faith because they believe, as the very devils themselves believe. *Answer.* They believe, yet they have not faith by the grace of illumination, but they have this faith by the virtue of that natural understanding since their creation, before they fell. They are not, since their fall, indeed with any grace. Now that this darkness is the wrath of God, we are here taught to seek the favor of God and to place our joy and delight in it, and we must say with David, "Lord, show us the light of thy countenance."[2] That we may <...> some hope of the favor of God.

Thus much of the second point, the custody, and thus much of the first degree of the punishment.

Now follows the second degree in these words: "reserved unto the judgment of the great day," that is, reserved or kept under that condemnation by which they shall be condemned and judged in the great day. Mark here that the angels are not as yet come to the full punishment; therefore, the evil spirit says to Christ in the gospel, "Why art thou come to torment us before our time?"[3] Now mark further the Holy Spirit smites all men with a further fear in the next words, "great day," that is, the last day, which is called great day because in that day the great works of God shall be brought to pass.

First, in that day, by the sound of the trumpet all men shall be called to judgment.

Second, in that day, all the works, and all the intents, both good and bad, of every man shall be revealed (Eccl. 12:14).

Third, in that day, God shall give sentence to both good and bad: salvation to the good, damnation to the bad.

---

2. Ps. 4:6.
3. Matt. 8:29.

Fourth, He shall reward all generally: the faithful with life eternal, the infidels with everlasting fire.

Fifth, in that day, Christ shall give up His kingdom to His father. Then shall all civil and ecclesiastical government cease. Christ Himself gives up His kingdom. He Himself must cease to reign, as He is Mediator, yet as He is God He shall reign forever.

Jude 7

(Sermon 10)

"As Sodom and Gomorrah and the cities about them, which in like manner as they did committed [fornication], and followed strange flesh, are set forth for an example, and suffer the vengeance of eternal fire." (Jude 7)

Here follows the third example, namely, of Sodom and Gomorrah, which is the first part of a comparison or similitude, for so the first word "as" signifies. The latter part of this similitude is set down in the eighth and ninth verses. In this third example [are] three things to be considered: (1) the people destroyed, (2) the sin for which they were destroyed, and (3) the punishment for the first. The people were the Israelites.[1] For the second, the sin was the committing of fornication. For the third, the punishment was the suffering of the vengeance of God.

Concerning the first, the people were the cities of Sodom and Gomorrah, and the neighbor cities adjoining which are not here named but in Deuteronomy 29:23 are set down to be Admah and Zeboim. In this first point, sundry things [are] to be considered.

First, he notes the cities themselves, which he does to signify a universal destruction of all things and persons. This does Peter make plain, saying that Sodom and Gomorrah were turned into ashes.[2] Where we learn that the cities and nations, not subject to God, shall be utterly and totally destroyed, but God's people, though they be destroyed, yet they shall not be utterly and wholly destroyed. Yet, therefore, in regard of this we are not to harden ourselves but to humble ourselves to God.

Second, when the cities themselves are destroyed, there are the children destroyed for the sin of their parents, and herein mark the secret judgment of God. *Objection.* But this is injustice in God. *Answer.* First, children and infants are creatures of God, God is Lord of their life, and therefore [there is] no injustice in God. Second, children are, after a sort, a part of their parents, and therefore with temporal punishment He may punish the children being

---

1. This is a transcription error. The people were the inhabitants of Sodom and Gomorrah, as he goes on to specify. Cf. Perkins, *Jude*, RHB 4:127.

2. 2 Peter 2:6.

to be considered as they are part of the parents. Third, the infants are subject to original sin, and therefore if it please God, He may punish the children with the father with everlasting condemnation. If they had no sin at all, then indeed it were injustice, but being tainted with original sin, He might instead condemn them.

Third, in that Sodom and Gomorrah is destroyed we have an example of vengeance. God calls the Jews, princes of Sodom, and the people, people of Gomorrah (Isa. 1:10), yet after, in the 18th verse, He tells them that though their sins were as crimson, they shall be made as white as snow, [and] though they were red as scarlet, they shall [be] as wool. Lay those two places together and see how His mercy matches His judgment. He saves a people which, by His own witness, [were] as great sinners as Sodom and Gomorrah (Isa. 1:10), yet [He] condemns Sodom and Gomorrah as appears in this text. God vouchsafes mercy to them that are the vessels of the devil. "If any purge himself from these he shall be a vessel to honor" (2 Tim. 2:21). "God granted mercy to wicked Manasseh."[3] This teaches us all not to be discouraged from turning to God, considering that God is so merciful that He will show His mercy to those that are very hellhounds, to those that are as wicked as the people of Sodom and Gomorrah condemned in hell. For if a man will use the means, mercy is to be found, and therefore let all consider this and not refuse the means.

Fourth, the same day that Sodom and Gomorrah were destroyed, Lot was delivered.[4] *Question.* How came this to pass? *Answer.* The Lord sent His angels to fetch out Lot out of the city, which shows us that, though God seems to have forgotten us, yet in [the] time of our need He will never fail His own children. The Israelites thought that God had forgotten His promise that He would deliver them, yet the same night that the 430 years were expired they were delivered.[5]

It is added, "the cities about," that is, the two adjoining cities, Admah and Zeboim, were destroyed. The reason is because they also had sinned in fornication as Sodom and Gomorrah had done. Hence, we learn not to fashion ourselves to the manners and customs of the world, for here the lesser cities, Admah and Zeboim, though they might do as the great cities Sodom and Gomorrah did, but they also tasted of their punishment. We must, therefore, follow the example of Lot, who though he lived with them, yet he abhorred their manners. Though he communicated with them, yet he communicated not with their sins.

Thus much of the first part: the persons punished.

---

3. 2 Chron. 33:12–13.
4. Gen. 19:15–26.
5. Ex. 12:51.

Now follows the second part, the sin, in these words: "committed [fornication] and followed strange flesh." The first sin they committed is fornication. In this sin these points are to be considered: firstly, the occasion of the sin; secondly, the cause of the sin; [and,] thirdly, the measure of the sin.

For the first, the occasion, look [at] Genesis 13:10, "Before Sodom and Gomorrah were destroyed, they were rich cities: they were as the garden of the Lord." Now upon this plenty of all things follows the sin.

For the second, the cause of the sin, they are these. The first is pride. The second is fullness of bread, that is, spending time in eating and drinking. [The] third is abundance of idleness, which comes by reason of peace. [The] fourth is unmercifulness toward the poor. And these four does Ezekiel set down to be the beginning of their sin.[6] There may be a fifth cause [to] be added, and that is want of instruction, taken out of Genesis 19:14, "When Lot told his sons in law that God would destroy the city, he seemed to them as if he had mocked."

And thus much of the second cause of their sin.

Now follows the measure of the sin, that is, that they gave themselves over to commit fornication. It is said in the third [chapter] of Isaiah, [verse] 9, that the Israelites did declare their sins as Sodom and hid them not, and addicted themselves wholly to sin. By this, sundry instructions [are] to be learned.

First, by these destructions we may take a view of these latter times. It may be said of the iniquity of these times that it passes the iniquity of Sodom, which is showed thus: by Sodom spiritually is to be understood the Church of Rome, as is Revelation 11:8. Now this Church of Rome matches Sodom, nay, it is a schoolmaster of Sodom and teaches Sodom. For it takes away matrimony and allows stewes.[7] And what is this but to be as Sodom, or rather to pass Sodom in fornication. And, therefore, we must take heed how we communicate with this Sodom. "As it was in the days of Lot, they ate and drank," and, "After these examples shall it be in the day when the Son of Man shall be revealed" (Luke 17:28, 30).

By this place we learn that these last times are like the times of Sodom and Gomorrah.[8] For [while there was] one Sodom and one Gomorrah in the Old Testament, there are now many Sodoms and many Gomorrahs. "Whosoever shall not receive your words, it shall be easier for Sodom and Gomorrah at the last day than for them" (Matt. 10:14–15).[9] Where we see that it is a greater sin

---

6. Ezek. 16:51–52.

7. *Stewe*: brothel.

8. The MS is missing the leaf containing pages 199–200; however, the text reads continuously from page 198 to page 201. This leaf was evidently missing before the present sermon was transcribed.

9. The original erroneously cited verse 13.

not to obey the doctrine of Christ brought into the church than to commit the sin of Sodom and Gomorrah. In these days, indeed, many receive the Word outwardly, but how few do embrace it inwardly? They only desire to live civilly before man.

Secondly, in that fornication is the sin for which they were punished, we learn to fly [from] fornication. And that for this reason, because the curse and vengeance of God is set upon them in this example. Job 31:12, speaking of fornication, says, "This is a fire that shall devour to destruction." "Neither fornicators, idolators, nor adulterers shall inherit the kingdom of heaven" (1 Cor. 6:9). And there are other reasons set down to fly this fornication: (1) because our bodies are God's bodies (1 Cor. 6:13), (2) our bodies must be raised again (1 Cor. 6:14), (3) our bodies are members of Christ (1 Cor. 6:15), (4) our bodies are the temples of the Holy Ghost (1 Cor. 6:19), [and] (5) our bodies are bought and are not our own (1 Cor. 6:20).

Of this we have an example in Joseph, who, having the fear of God in his heart, said, "How can I do this great wickedness and so sin against God?" (Gen. 39:9).

Thirdly, in that Sodom and Gomorrah were destroyed for fornication, mark the horrible vengeance of God for this sin. For this sin of fornication they were utterly destroyed. It is, therefore, to be wished that in these days the punishment of whoredom might be no less than death, for it far exceeds theft. The thief hurts some few, whom he injures. The fornicator hurts whole families, towns, and kingdoms. As we see here, whole cities were destroyed for it.

Thus much of the second part: their sin.

Now follows the third part, the punishment, in these words: "suffer the vengeance of eternal fire." In this punishment three things [are] to be considered. First, the matter, that is, eternal fire. Second, the time when they were punished, that is, when they are at the height of their sins. Third, the use of the punishment.

[Regarding] the first, the matter, we are not to understand any bodily fire like unto our fire, but by "fire" is to be understood the most fearful apprehension of the horrible wrath of God, and that both in soul and body.

For the second, the time, it was when they were at the height of their sins. God indeed is slow to wrath, but He does make recompense for His slowness with the greatness of His punishment.

For the third, the use. This is an example to the whole world of God's judgment, and by this we are taught that God's judgments are real sermons: not sermons vocal, which preach in word, but which teach in deed and in effect. For by this example of the destruction of Sodom He preached and showed His judgment ever since.

Jude 8

(Sermon 11)

"Likewise, notwithstanding these dreamers also defile the flesh, and despise government, and speak evil of them that are in authority." (Jude 8)

We heard in the 5th verse how the apostle Jude, from the 4th verse to the 20th, goes about to prove that the end of these seducers is destruction, by this reason: they which take unto themselves liberty of sinning, their end is destruction. The major [premise] is proved in the 5th, 6th, [and] 7th verses by three several examples. The second part of the reason is proved in this 8th verse and in the verses following to the end of the 20th.

In this 8th verse, three things [are] to be considered. Firstly, the apostle sets down two sins of the seducers. The first is that they defile the flesh. The second is that they contemn[1] magistracy. Secondly, he sets down the foundation of their sins in this word, "dreamers," so that the dreaming was the fountain and cause of their sin. Thirdly, he sets down the manner of their sinning in these words: "likewise, notwithstanding." The manner of their sinning is set down two ways. First, as Sodom and Gomorrah sinned, so these seducers sinned. Secondly, though these seducers heard of God's judgment against Sodom and Gomorrah, yet they as the men of Sodom and Gomorrah defile the flesh.

Thus much of the substance of this verse.

In the handling of it, we will consider first the fountain of the sins, secondly the sinners themselves. For the first, the fountain is that they are dreamers wherein first, we consider their sleep, secondly their dreams. Their sleeping was spiritual, and they [were] deluded by their sleep. As in the bodily sleep the senses are all benumbed, so in the spiritual sleep the will lies all benumbed and never affected with God's promises. They were eating and drinking till the flood came (Matt. 24).[2] *Dives* fared deliciously every day; he never thought of the fear of hell until he felt it.[3]

Sleep is threefold. First, natural, in which a man lives naturally in sin till God awakes him. "Awake you that sleeps" (Eph. 5:14). [The] second kind of

---

1. *Contemn*: show contempt.

2. Verse 38.

3. Dives (Latin: rich) is the name traditionally given to the rich man in Jesus's parable (Luke 16:19–31).

sleep is properly the remnant of natural sleep. "I sleep but my heart wakes" (Cant. 5:2).[4] This sleep is in the children of God. Their heart will never suffer them to sleep a dead sleep. [The] third kind of sleep is set down [in] Ephesians 4:18–19, where there is no fear of evil, and the heart [is] past feeling, then we sin with <…>, having increased our natural sleep. And such sleep as were these seducers.

Thus [much] of the first part: they sleep in sin. The second part follows, sleepers deluded by dreams. By dream we meant false imaginations. There is the rich man's dream of his happiness, as though nothing else had remained for him (Luke 12:19). "Then said thou art rich, etc." (Rev. 3:17). And such are our dreams by nature, which unless God gives us grace to prevent, they will bring damnation upon body and soul. This befell the learned Pharisee. He dreamed falsely of his estate before God (Luke 18).[5]

Use. By this we see why so few are sorrowful for their sins. The cause is because men are commonly sleepers and deluded by the false imaginations of their dreams, and the devil takes of every one of them his advantage. One sort says thus, they are unlearned and therefore God will excuse them, though they live and die like the beasts in ignorance. Another says thus, they have lived thus long and yet they never felt any cross of God upon them for their sin but prospered in all things. Therefore, they dream that they are in the favor of God. Others, having great learning, never reform their lives. They dream that God, who has given them learning, will also give them grace. Others again live most wickedly, dreaming with [the] slothful servant that their Master will not yet come,[6] and therefore give themselves to all kind of wickedness that the world cries shame on them. To be short, the common dream of most men is, they esteem not of the body of Christ, but take it for some dream. They take the promises of Christ for dreams, and that in the very elect in some sort. For when it was told Sarah that she should have a child in her old age, she laughed and took it but for a dream. And that is expressed in the 12th Psalm. They were as in a dream when the Lord delivered them out of Babylon,[7] and that was the dream of Peter, that he doubted whether he was out of prison or not.[8] And, therefore, as we repeat our bodily dreams after we awake out of sleep, so it were much more to be wished that we would call to mind and repeat our spiritual dreams, that we might repent us for them. For as long as these strong imaginations and dreams are in our hearts, God cannot enter.

---

4. Song 5:2.
5. Verses 10–11. The MS erroneously cites Luke 19.
6. Matt. 25:14–30.
7. Ps. 126:1.
8. Acts 12:9.

If these spiritual dreams be the cause of so many sins, we will use the exhortation of Saint Paul, "Awake you that sleepest" (Eph. 5:14). Therefore, that we may awake out of our dreamful sleep, we must consider the means. The first means is the consideration of the infinite justice of God against sin. The second means is the consideration of the greatness of our sins, and the number of them, like unto the sands of the sea. Thirdly, we must every day and hour look for an evil day, knowing that as we shall die, so we shall stand before God. And as bodily death leaves us, so spiritual death shall find us. Fourthly, we must remember the solemn vow which we made in baptism. The fifth means is the consideration of Christ's death for our sins, and His passion, which made Him say, "My God, my God, why hast Thou forsaken me?" Sixthly, that of Saint Paul must move us: "The day is come and the sun is up, therefore walk worthy of the children of light."[9] And thus a man may perceive himself to be awakened, as when the mind does discover the corruption of the heart, and when he mourns for his sin and cries unto God for grace, then he is in part awakened, for these are the works of grace.

Now follows the third duty; [that is,] we must seek the contrary virtue: wakefulness and sobriety. Which that we may do, we must observe and mark our own sins with what sin we are most usually undertaken. For the devil will take his advantage. He will not infect every man with the same sin, but every man with that wherein he is most delighted.

Use 2. Again, every day we must look for an evil day, we must not flatter ourselves, "peace, peace,"[10] for then destruction hangs over us.

Use 3. We must think every day the last day, that when our Master comes, He may find us waking.

Use 4. Lastly, seeing by nature we are all dreamers, and deluded in our dreams, we must labor that the Word of God dwell in our hearts plentifully. For man's heart is deceitful, and his natural reason <...> dreams.

---

9. Rom. 13:12; Eph. 5:8.
10. Cf. Jer. 6:14; 8:11.

Jude 8
(Sermon 12)

"Likewise, notwithstanding these dreamers also defile the flesh, and despise government, and speak evil of them that are in authority." (Jude 8)

We have spoken of the fountain of the sins of those seducers. Now we come to the sins themselves, two whereof are set down in this verse. The first sin is that they "defile the flesh," [and] the second is that they "despise government."

Touching the first: "they defile their flesh." The meaning is that they defile or abuse their bodies by committing fornication. Of this sin we spoke in the 7th verse; therefore, here we will only repeat this again, that if this fornication be the sin of Sodom, then it is all our duties to keep our bodies in chastity. "I beseech you brethren, by the mercies of Christ (says Saint Paul), give up your bodies a living sacrifice, holy, acceptable unto God" (Rom. 12:1).

Concerning the second sin, it is set down in these words: "despise government." The sin is contempt of authority. This sin Jude sets down by two branches. Firstly, by their doctrine or opinion, in these words: "despise magistracy." Secondly, by their practice, in these words: "speak evil of them that are in authority." For the first, "despise government," that is, refuse, put down, and put away from them all civil government. Now, seeing these seducers put away government, we see they themselves were not under government, for then they could not put it away. *Objection.* This cannot be. They must (will they, nil they) be under government, for magistrates will keep them under. *Answer.* The next words, their practice, namely, that they speak evil of those that are in authority, shows it, for though they be kept under, yet they cease not to revile them that are in authority. But first, of their doctrine and opinion, then of their practice. Touching the first, their opinion in that they despise government, three things are to be considered: first, what is government; secondly, upon what grounds these seducers refuse government; [and,] thirdly, upon what grounds Jude reprimands them for refusing government.

Touching the first, what government is, we must understand that government is of two sorts:

Human

Divine

This divine government is an absolute power of life and death. This power is in the Father, the Son, and in the Holy Spirit, but the administration of it is committed only to the Son. But this government is not here meant, for if they had denied divine government, then they had denied God, and then could they not have made a show of religion as they did. This then is meant only of human government and civil dominion, as when man is set over man. Now this civil government is a state of superiority consisting in the power to command and in the power of the sword. It is called a state of superiority. This appears [in] Romans 13:1, "Let every soul be subject to the higher power." It is further added, "consisting in the power of commanding and the power of the sword." By the power of commanding is to be understood the power of making laws. By the power of the sword is meant, first, the power of arrestment; secondly, the power of imprisonment; thirdly, the power of putting to death; [and,] fourthly, the power of making war.

Here we see a difference between this civil power and the power of ministers. First, because the minister has no power in himself; the power of civil government is in the magistrate himself. Secondly, the civil magistrate has the power of the sword, to death by violence. But the minister must not; he must only deal by persuasions and exhortations. Thirdly, we here see a difference between this power and power in families and schools because governors of families and schools cannot put to death, but these governors may. *Question.* How far does this civil government extend? *Answer.* It extends itself in all causes and all things of man, either of the church or commonwealth. For the church, "The king when he was set upon his throne, he must do all the ordinances, that is, he must see them done, etc." (Deut. 17),[1] [that is,] "cause them to be done." And this did Josiah when he commanded the people to keep the Passover and caused his people to keep the covenant.

Yet there are two things to be remembered. First, civil government does not in the same sort rule causes ecclesiastical and civil, but after this manner. Civil causes belong to the magistrate both for the execution and also for the ordering of them. Ecclesiastical causes belong to the magistrate, but only for the ordering of them. The execution of them belongs only to the ministers. [The] second [thing] to be remembered is that there are things of God and things of man. Things of God, as His Word, sacraments, and articles of faith, and these belong to the minister and not to [the] magistrate, but the magistrate's power extends itself to all things of man. Yet thus it extends itself to his body and his goods, but it extends not itself to his soul, for that is God's. Government is of three

---

1. Verses 18–19.

sorts: (1) of a multitude, that is, popular; (2) of a town; [and] (3) of one man. Of these three, the first, namely, popular government, is here meant.

This much of the first point: what government is.

Now to the second [point]: upon what ground these seducers despise government. For we may assure ourselves they had some arguments upon which they grounded, and their arguments some Anabaptists in these days do allege, they and many, especially four.

First, they deny authority by this argument: subjection came in by sin; therefore, Christ taking away sin took away subjection also. [The] major [premise] is proved, because before the fall of man the lordship of God was only over fishes and other creatures, not over man, and after the fall then came man to be in subjection. *Answer.* Subjection is of two sorts. One is servile subjection as of a slave to his master. The second is civil subjection, as when one man is over another for his own good or for the common good. Now servile subjection came in by the fall, but civil subjection, which is here meant, was before the fall, as appears by Paul to Timothy, saying because the woman was taken out of the man, therefore she must be subject to the man.[2]

Second, every believer in this life is in the kingdom of heaven. But in the kingdom of heaven there is no civil government, there [is] only Christ's governance, so to all believers all civil government ceases. *Answer.* There are two kinds of government. One [is] spiritual, that is, in the heart inwardly, and in regard of this there is no difference between king and subject, lord and master. But there is another government, that is, civil, and having the king rule his subject and the lord his servant. And according to these two kinds of government, every Christian takes upon him two persons: one as he is a civil member in the commonwealth and so he acknowledges civil government, but as he is a member in the kingdom of heaven so he acknowledges no government. Indeed, if he were a member of the kingdom of heaven only and not of the commonwealth, then he might refuse civil government. But being members of both, he is bound to be subject to both.

Third, civil government is full of cruelty, and magistrates by the use of the sword, killing the body, can also kill the soul because they give not liberty to repent. *Answer.* The malefactor that is condemned and will not be turned to repentance at the fear of present death, it is not likely that ever he will repent, if he lives. But howsoever, God says that a malefactor must die to cut off the devil, and [with] good reason. For when the malefactor dies, there is but one person and one soul destroyed, but if he should live there were danger of his infecting many hundred souls.

---

2. 1 Tim. 2:12.

Fourth, they plead liberty, grounding upon Saint Paul's words, "stand thus in your liberty."[3] Now this government <...>[4] liberty, say they. And to confirm their liberty they allege places of Scripture. First, "Owe nothing to any man" (Rom. 13).[5] Now, therefore, they will not owe subjection. *Answer.* But that is meant of civil things as money and such things, but love and such things are not meant. Also, they allege "kings' children are free" (Matt. 17).[6] *Answer.* That He speaks of Himself, who was heir to the crown.

Fifth, they allege that of the Corinthians, "you are bought with a price, be not servants of men."[7] *Answer.* That is to be understood, be not subject to men as your absolute and sovereign Lord, and do not serve man for God.

Lastly, they object that they must live so as that they cannot be governed by magistrates. *Answer.* Indeed, we should live so. But no man does live so, and therefore in that regard we have need of magistracy.

---

3. Gal. 5:1.
4. The MS is damaged here such that this word is illegible.
5. Verse 8.
6. Verse 26.
7. 1 Cor. 7:23.

Jude 8

(Sermon 13)

"Likewise notwithstanding these dreamers also detest the flesh, and despise government, and speak evil of them that are in authority." (Jude 8)

In the opinion and doctrine of these seducers we have considered three things: (1) what government is [and] (2) upon what ground these seducers despise government. Of those before. Now we come to the third thing, namely, upon what ground Saint Jude reproves these seducers.

The ground upon which he reprehends them is this: civil magistracy is a solemn ordinance of God, and it is the absolute will of God that every person shall be subject to rule and magistracy. "Let every soul be subject to the higher powers" (Rom. 13:1). "Every soul," that is, every person without exception. The higher powers are those that are set over us. Mark them further in the same chapter: "You must be subject not because of wrath only, but also for conscience sake" (v. 5). Now, this conscience is not in regard of government itself but in regard of God's commandment which binds every man to be subject, and this is the ground upon which he reproves them. Further, Christ, taking upon Himself man's nature, takes upon Him also all these conditions [of] our nature. He subjects Himself to Pontius Pilate, to arraignment, to condemnation, to execution itself. Paul also subjects himself to Caesar: "and he said he is bound to judgment under Caesar" (Acts 25).[1]

Objection. But this may seem to be contradicted by Scripture. "Behold this day have I set thee over nations, and over kingdoms to pluck up, and to root out, and to destroy and throw down, to build, and to plant" (Jer. 1:10). So it seems the ministers are not subject to civil government. *Answer.* Jeremiah is set over nations, but not by the use of the sword, but by preaching. And by preaching he plucks up and roots out, destroys, and throws down. And that is the meaning.

Objection. "Kings shall come and serve and minister to the church" (Isa. 60:10). So, kings and princes are subject to the ministers. *Answer.* In the church there are the things of God and the persons. Now here is not meant that kings

---

1. Verse 10.

shall serve the persons in the church, but the things of God in the church, that is, the ordinances of God: His Word and sacraments.

Objection. Princes and rulers are sheep; the ministers are shepherds. Now the sheep are under these shepherds and at their command. *Answer.* In the minister two [things are] to be considered: (1) their persons [and] (2) their ministry. Now in regard of their persons, all ministers are subject to their princes, but in regard of the ministry, all princes and rulers are subject to it. And yet, thus that the minister teaches the Word aright, otherwise they are not subject to it, but have authority to reform it. But as long as it is practiced aright, they are to be subject to the ministry itself, things, not to the persons. The baron, earl, or duke must obey the base sergeant, not for himself or his person but for the prince's sake whose person he represents. So the best man, be he baron, earl, duke, or prince must obey the base minister, [as regards] things, not for his own sake yet for God's sake whose person he represents. Yet [it is] always to be remembered that this subjection is to the Word being practiced aright, for otherwise princes have power to order it and see it preached aright. And [in] this regard princes are called shepherds. "He says to Cyrus, thou art my shepherd, etc." (Isa. 44:28).

Use [1]. By this we see the great wickedness of sundry persons of this age. First, herein we see the wickedness of the bishop of Rome, for he usurps to himself supremacy over all princes of the earth, whereas he himself should be subject to his own emperor. For "every soul must be subject" (Rom. 13) and, therefore, if he has a soul, he must be subject to the emperor. He answers [in] that place, but every soul be subject, that is, says he, every soul to whom subjection belongs. He grounds [this] upon 2 Chronicles 26, [where] Uzziah the king is deprived of his kingdom by Azariah the high priest. *Answer.* Read the 20th verse of the same chapter [and] you shall find that the priest only by admonition caused him to depart and did not by force thrust him out of his kingdom. Again, they object, 2 Chronicles 23, where Jehoiada the priest put down Athaliah the queen and set up Joash in the kingdom.[2] *Answer.* This is answered two ways. First, Jehoiada was the next to the king,[3] and yet not he alone but all the states of the land agreed by general counsel to depose the queen. Secondly, Jehoiada the priest did not give Joash the kingdom but only helped him to the profession of his right, for he was the right heir to the crown.

Use 2. If everyone must be subject, then we gather that the immunity of the clergy from the authority of magistrates is a wicked immunity and almost rebellion. But some will say magistrates owe them this privilege. But that respects

---

2. Verses 1–20.

3. I.e., next in line of succession to the crown.

them not, for it is the law of nature and of God to be subject, and therefore the bounty of man cannot exempt them from that which God commands.

Use 3. The Roman bishop has usurped power of freeing subjects from their oath made to their princes. And this is damnable because the law of God does flatly command this subjection in conscience.

Use 4. We are here taught what to think of popish religion, namely, that it is a religion forever to be abolished. And that for this reason, true religion teaches especially two things: (1) to fear God [and] (2) to honor our prince. This popish religion does neither of these, so [it is] to be abolished for that. First, it only pretends the honor of God. It does not honor Him indeed, which appears because it fails in the second, namely, in honoring the prince. For it robs kings of their honor, as we heard before.

Use 5. By this doctrine we are taught that all wandering persons and beggars passing from place to place are the very plague of all commonwealths, for they live neither under magistrate nor minister, and therefore they put away government.

Use 6. Lastly, by this we see that their oath to the bishop of Rome is a most wicked oath, for everyone is bound to be subject to civil magistrates. Now the oath to the bishop of Rome takes away and usurps this authority.

Thus much of the opinion, now to the practice.

The practice is set down in these words: "speak evil of them that are in authority." Their practice is, when they cannot put down magistracy, then they speak evilly of it. In the practice we will consider: (1) the sin itself [and] (2) how the apostle does amplify it in this verse and in the beginning of the next. Touching the sin itself, it is speaking evilly of the magistrates. This is a great sin. "Curse not the king, no not in thy thought" (Eccl. 10:20). This is so great a sin that Paul says, "receive not an accusation against an elder under two or three witnesses" (1 Tim. 5).[4] By this then we see the greatness of <...>.[5]

Use. By this we may see as in a glass the sins of this day. For now common table talk is to speak of the doings of kings and doctrine of ministers. *Objection.* Paul calls the high priest a painted wall, therefore we have an example. *Answer.* Paul himself answers that he knew him not a high priest. Not that he knew him not, but because he knew him not by his doings, that is, he was no true ruler; he was an infidel and usurper.

Use 2. If one may not speak evil of magistrates, then a private man has no warrant to put another private man to death. [In] 1 Samuel 24, David was to succeed Saul in his kingdom. Saul therefore sought to kill him. Yet David,

---

4. Verse 19.

5. The MS is damaged here such that this word is illegible.

finding him asleep, could have killed him, but his heart smote him. Here we see what manner of persons those are that are sent from other nations privately to suck away the heart blood of our dread sovereign, the anointed of the Lord. It is manifest that these are the very vessels of the devil and that they have no spark of godliness in them, for this horrible sin is against the law of nature. Here we are taught our duty, that is, to speak well of magistrates. For they are the Lord's deputies and, therefore, we must pray for them. Nebuchadnezzar, though a heathen and wicked king, yet the people were commanded to pray for him.

And thus much of the sin itself.

Jude 8–9

(Sermon 14)

"And speak evil of them that are in authority. Yet Michael the archangel, when he strove against the devil, etc." (Jude 8–9)

In the practice of the seducers, we considered two things: firstly, the sin itself; secondly, how the apostle Jude sets down the greatness of it. Of the sin itself we spoke before. Now we come to the second [point] to show how Jude does amplify the fact.

First, he begins in the end of this 8th verse, and then in the verse following. In this verse he begins in these words, "speak evil of them that are in authority," that is, according to the original, speak evil of majesties, or dignities, or honors, that is, to rail on persons placed in dignity, honor, or majesty, that is, princes. The reasons stand thus: they speak evil of those persons on whom God has bestowed honor, dignity, or majesty, and therefore they do ill because they dishonor them whom God has honored. Princes are here called dignities or honors or majesties for two causes.

First, because it has pleased God to communicate to them His own title and has placed them in His own room. God stands in the assembly of gods; He judges among gods (Ps. 82:1). That is, God is present in the congregation of judges, and judges are called "gods" in regard of civil government, and in that regard they are in God's room and are His deputies. And this is proved: "They are called gods because the commandment of God is given to them" (John 10:35); "Jehoshaphat said to the judges, 'take heed what you do, for you execute not the judgment of man but of God, and he will be with you in judgment'" (2 Chron. 19:6). And this is the first cause for which magistrates are called dignitaries.

The second cause why they are called honors, majesties, or dignities is because it pleases God to bestow upon princes and magistrates His especial grace, though not always for sanctification, yet for government, for He furnishes them not only with majesty but also with wisdom, courage, valor, and all things belonging to magistracy. "God gave to Saul, when he was made king, another heart" (1 Sam. 10:9), though not in regard of sanctification. "After the anointing of David, the Spirit of God came upon him" (1 Sam. 16:13). "God gave part of the Spirit of Moses to the elders of Israel" (Num. 11:17).[1] And this is the second reason.

And thus, we see the dignity of magistrates is no small dignity. For what greater dignity than for man to stand in the room of God and be as God.

Doctrine 1. In that they are called dignities and majesties and honors, we learn that it is not unlawful for princes and magistrates to maintain a glorious pomp before man (as gorgeous apparel, stately buildings, troops of men), because their authority is outward, and therefore for authorizing of it, it is lawful to use outward pomp. King Agrippa and Bernice came forth "with great pomp," and the Holy Spirit does not there condemn their pomp but allows of it (Acts 25:23).[2]

Doctrine 2. Seeing they are thus called magistrates and therefore bound in especial manner to honor God because God honors them, and therefore they are bound to honor God again. Now, God is honored when true religion and virtue is honored, and therefore magistrates are bound to honor true religion and virtue.

Doctrine 3. In that they are so called, we learn that princes and magistrates are bound to execute all justice without particularity or bribery, because God places them in His room. This was Jehoshaphat's lesson (2 Chron. 19:6), and this was Moses's lesson in Deuteronomy: "You execute God's judgment, go fear God."[3]

Doctrine 4. Seeing magistrates are in God's room, we are to obey them as God Himself. They are as gods, and therefore when they command, we are to obey. So the son his father, the servant his master, [so also] the commonwealth's man is bound to obey his civil magistrate as God.

Doctrine 5. Lastly, in that they are thus called, we learn that it is not unlawful for subjects to give to their princes titles of "majesty" and "grace." For "majesty" the Holy Spirit here commands them by the same title. Now, it is also lawful to give them [the] title of "grace" because they are here called glories, because God gives them especial graces. And, therefore, they may call them graces as well as glories, because He calls them glories for their graces.

Thus of the 8th verse.

Now of the 9th verse: "Yet, Michael the archangel when he strove against the devil, etc." In these words is contained a second reason whereby he sets down the greatness of the sin of the seducers for railing on magistrates. The reason is taken from a comparison from the greater to the lesser after this manner:

---

1. The original erroneously cited verse 7.
2. The original erroneously cited verse 33.
3. Deut. 1:17.

The angel, yea Michael the archangel, durst not be so bold as to rail
    on the devil.
But these seducers most inferior to the angel do rail on those which
    are in authority who are much better than the devil.
So their fault must needs be greater.

Question. Whence had Jude this history of the contention between Michael and the devil? *Answer.* The substance of this is in Scripture. There is set down the death of Moses and how God buried him (Deut. 34:5). Yet the contention for his body is nowhere set down in Scripture, only the substance of it is set down in the forenamed place.

Question. Wherein had Jude his contention between the devil and Michael? *Answer.* Either out of some book then extant among the Jews and not now extant among us, or else he had it by tradition, for sundry things we have through the hands of the Jews which were never recorded in writings. As, for example, 2 Timothy 3:8, there is Jannes and Jambres named, which withstood Moses. Now, he finds not these men named in any place of Scripture, and therefore he had it either out of some book then extant and not now, or he had it by tradition.

Here popish doctors object thus. *Objection.* The written Word of God is not perfect, but there are two parts of Scripture: (1) written Word, and this is the Bible, [and] (2) things not written, but tradition, things delivered from hand to hand. Now, the written Word is not sufficient of itself but must have help from tradition. It is proved by this [place] of Jude, who records a thing wherein the written word fails and has help from the unwritten, namely, tradition. *Answer.* We must know that this their doctrine is of the devil, for we are to hold that canonical Scripture is perfect and all sufficient and needs no supply made by tradition. For proof, we must know this: everything takes its perfection from the end, for if it be sufficient in the end, it is all sufficient, though it wants in some things. Now, the end of Scripture is God's glory and the salvation of the people. But the written sacred Word, the Bible, is perfect in this end, for it delivers doctrine sufficient to advance the glory of God and save the soul of any man. That this is the end of the Scripture is proved: "These things are written that you might believe, etc." (John 20:31) and "Whatsoever is written, was written for our learning" (Rom. 15:4).

By this we see the doctrine of [the] Roman Church and that which they allege for themselves, as that there are many things both in the New Testament set down of the Jews which in the Old Testament is nowhere set down, as for this, the example of Michael, which shows with the <...>. I say we see this their doctrine is false, for we answer that it is true that there are many true things passing from hand to hand, and yet are nowhere written, but that is not the question. But the question is whether any tradition be unwritten that is necessary to the salvation of the soul. Indeed, this of the archangel is a true history and has an excellent use, but it does not pertain to the salvation of the soul, and so it makes not the Scripture imperfect.

Objection. But they object farther a place of Scripture out of the Romans, that Scripture must be expanded by the rule of faith. Now, say they, this rule of faith is not in the Scripture, but the rule of faith is the consent of all Catholics, and so the Scripture is imperfect because it has not the end of faith. *Answer.* The rule of faith is not the consent of all Catholics, but it is the sentence and judgment which Catholics propound and gather out of plain places of Scripture concerning faith and love.

Objection. Secondly, they say again that canonical Scripture is the undoubted Word of God, and to believe this is a matter of salvation, but we can never believe this but by the tradition of the church. And, therefore, they conclude that the written Word is insufficient for salvation and needs tradition. *Answer.* This is false that we cannot believe the Scripture to be the Word of God but by the tradition of the church, which will appear thus. First, let us consider this ground: every act has certain principles which, being taken away, the act falls, which prove all things and cannot be proved itself. As the carpenter grounds upon the straightness of his lines, and never calls that into question, so this art of divinity has its ground and principles which cannot be denied. The first ground and principle in divinity is that the written Word is the undoubted Word of God. Upon this then it follows that we are to believe the Scripture to be the Word of God without the tradition of the church.

The second ground: in divine things faith is first, and then follows knowledge, which is gotten by experience and reason. That is, as soon as we know what is God's will, we first assent with faith, then after follows the knowledge. I mean knowledge gotten by experience and reason. But in human things, first comes knowledge, then faith, as that fire is hot, first he knows it, then after believes it because he finds it by experience. But it is otherwise in divinity. As God tells Abraham he shall have a son, Abraham first gives his assent and believes it, though against hope, and after he knows it. "If any will do the will of the father, then he shall know of the doctrine, whether it be of God, or whether I speak of myself" (John 7:17).[4]

If this be so, then Scripture says thus, "thus saith the Lord." Then when we hear the Scripture say thus, we must not first go and hear the church and

---

4. The second half of this verse is unclear in the MS, but it is evident that Perkins cites the entire verse from the Geneva Bible.

first believe it, and after believe this Word of God. For that is to dishonor God, attributing to the creature more than the Creator. But we must first believe the Word of God. [We are to do this on] three grounds. We know Scripture to be Scripture by Scripture, not by the tradition of the church, for who that craves it, shall find the end, the Author, and the use of it, to be most excellent. We are then still to reverence this Scripture and hold it to be perfect, that is, perfect in its end, perfect in its author, [and] perfect in its use. And in defense of this doctrine, we are to stand and die.

Exodus 22:18

(Sermon 1)

"Thou shalt not suffer a witch to live." (Ex. 22:18)

These words contain in them one of the judicial laws of Moses touching the punishment of witchcraft. We <have chosen to entreat of this argument>[1] in particular, especially for these causes: first, because of the <rife> and <common practice of> witchcraft; secondly, <there are> all sorts of <men who hold that witchcraft is nothing else but a mere illusion. Many who are> learned hold this opinion that <witches are nothing but> persons deluded of the devil.

In this Scripture <are two things to be considered:> first, what witchcraft is; secondly, what punishment is due <the witch.>

Concerning the first, it is a matter of great difficulty, <because there are> diverse and sundry opinions <touching this point.> So that we may <properly and> thoroughly <define witchcraft, we must first put> forth the nature of it <as it is delivered in the books of the Old and New Testaments and> by the opinion of learned <and godly men.>

[2]<…> practice of witchcraft <…> be defined <as a wicked art, serving for the working of wonders, by the assistance of the devil, so far forth as God shall in justice permit.>

It is called an art <because it is commonly so called and esteemed among men. For as in all good and lawful arts,> there are to be performed certain <rules and practices, so witchcraft has certain superstitious grounds and principles whereupon it stands.>

…[3]

<…> the beginning he tempted Eve, he <enclosed within it> many sins. Among others [it] brought them <the sin of> discontentment[4] of the state of

---

1. Much of the content is missing from the MS because the page is torn and faded. The content has been supplied from *Damned Art of Witchcraft*, RHB 9:307–11.

2. It is difficult to ascertain from the published version how this sentence is to be completed.

3. Approximately one third of the page is missing. Presumably, it contains a condensed version of *Damned Art of Witchcraft*, RHB 9:309–11.

4. The MS states, "discontentation." This term has been changed to "discontentment" throughout this volume.

man. And this act <is> derived <from> them unto all men. It stands itself in many things.

First, in outward estate either in regard of poverty being upon man or <in want of> honor. This is one cause of discontentment in men, that they may help and relieve themselves. This we might show <by> examples of some men, who are servants of Satan, who not content with their state have for this cause learned and put in practice witchcraft.

The <second> cause of this sin is curiosity, when men are not content with that portion of inward gifts which God has given them as <wit,> learning, understanding, and such like. This <has> made men to practice witchcraft, that they might work wonders.

It is added: by the assistance of the devil, to put a difference between all holy and divine arts, and this. In a lawful art, the work-maker, if he is skillful in this art, can exercise and practice it without the aid and help of another. But there is not the like reason in this <art of witchcraft.> It is impossible that any witch <…> in practice witchcraft without the devil's efficiency. But here we are to <see that> a witch can work <…> <…> <…> assistance.

To understand this <we are to proceed to a further point:> that there are two kinds of <wonders: true and plain>.[5]

<A true wonder> is done simply <either above or against the power of nature, and it is properly called a miracle>. [For example, in] Exodus 14:21, "The Lord caused the sea to run back by a strong east wind all the night and made the sea dry land."[6] [It is] a wonder above nature that the east wind should <move the waters and> let it be dry ground, for it is both against <…> <…> nature of the sea and the wind. Indeed, the wind <…> <…> in the sea by making the water <…> <…>.[7] There is no wind that has the power to <part the waters> to be dry ground. And, therefore, it is a miracle <of God.>

What is over and against nature <is> only proper to God, <and not to any creature> whatsoever, nor to the devil. Therefore, as <in the beginning> God made all things alone in the world, so <it is> only proper to God to change and abolish the <order of nature established at creation.> A miracle is a part of the creation, no <…> <…> in the world which any part of the creation <…> <…>.[8] Therefore, to work miracles belongs to God alone.

---

5. Much of the content is missing from the MS because the page is torn and faded. The content has been supplied from *Damned Art of Witchcraft*, RHB 9:312–13.

6. The original erroneously cited Exodus 11:2.

7. It is difficult to ascertain from the published version how this sentence is to be completed.

8. It is difficult to ascertain from the published version how this sentence is to be completed.

Exodus 22:18

(Sermon 2)

"Thou shalt not suffer a witch to live." (Ex. 2:18)

We have heard the definition opened in part only, the last clause left unhandled, which is so far as God in mercy permits <witchcraft. I add it,>[1] first, to show that God permits witchcraft. The causes why <He> does so are, first, to prove His own children whether they will believe in Him or cleave to the devil. The <…> false prophets and wonders shall be wrought to prove <whether> God's children will believe in Him or not (Deut. 13:3). Secondly, He permits it to punish the wickedness of men, for oft the punishment <of one is> another (2 Thess. 2:11). It is there set down because they <followed> not the true religion and obeyed it not; therefore, they <believed lies>. And in these days, He suffers wicked men to be <rife among those who> will not believe nor make account of religion.

Second, <this last clause is> added to show that the devil can so do that which God permits <him> and no more. This appears [in] Exodus 8, <where Moses and Aaron set> down the rod and turned it into a serpent <and the magicians of Egypt> by God's permission and of <power> of devil <did the same. But when He turned the dust of the land into lice,> they could not turn them. And <they themselves gave the true reason thereof, saying "That this> was the finger of God." [In] 1 Kings <22:22,> Satan says he will be the lying spirits in the mouth of Ahab's prophets, and so by God's permission went out. [In] Mark <5:12–13,> they could not go into the swine till Christ had permitted them, and Christ cast them out by His word.

Thus much of the description of witchcraft.

The second point <is> the ground of the practices of witchcraft, which is <a league> or covenant between the witch and the devil [by] which they mutually bind themselves together. This <…> <…> foundation of witchcraft, and it is evident and [a] doctrine proved first by Scripture, Psalm 58:3,[2] wherein are set down two points. First, that the <work of a charm> was able to stay the

---

1. Much of the content is missing from the MS because the page is torn and faded. The content has been supplied from *Damned Art of Witchcraft*, RHB 9:322–24.

2. The MS states Psalm 35:30. This Scripture reference does not exist.

adder from stinging. <Second, it is set> down the ground of his enchantment. The <foundation> is nothing else than the fellowship and agreement which is between the devil and the enchanter. Therefore, in the fourth [chapter] of Matthew, the devil says "all these will be given thee," where he offers to make a compact and covenant with Christ.[3] The devil is ready on his part to make covenant with men [and] here wanted [no]thing but the consent of Christ.

Question. Why can witches bring many things to pass by the help of the devil which other men cannot do? *Answer.* It is no great learning nor efficacy that he has of his mouth, but having made a league with the devil, by virtue thereof, the devil appears in the likeness of <…>.

The covenant of the devil is of two sorts: an express or a secret covenant. The first by express and solemn words on both parts, but what it is better <set down> in the writings of men than in the Scripture.

Thus much of the grounds of witchcraft.

Thirdly, of the kinds <of witchcraft.>[4] It is either divining witchcraft <or that which is> in working and practice. First, of the <…> it is to be remembered that> neither of them can be done without <a league with the devil.>

Divination is a part of witchcraft, whereby men reveal strange things either past, present, or to come by the help of the devil. First of it in general.

Objection. How comes it to pass that the devil can foretell them? *Answer.* There are sundry ways whereby he is permitted to do this.

First, by the Old and New Testaments, wherein are prophecies set down. By this the devil is able to reveal strange things, for the devil learns and understands the Bible better than we. Alexander, before he made war with Darius, consulted with an oracle, namely, the devil, <touching> the issue of his war. The devil's answer was that he would be conqueror, and upon that he made war, and <conquered> the emperor as the devil had said. And this he did by the Old Testament (Dan. 8).[5] This [is] there set down in particular of Alexander, otherwise he could not have done it.

Secondly, the cause is that he knows the causes of all the compositions of natural things which men never knew.

Thirdly, he can do this because he is present in all places at consultations and meeting of men made manifest by speech. He by this can foreknow that which shall <be done.>

---

3. Matt. 4:9.

4. Much of the content is missing from the MS because the page is torn. The content has been supplied from *Damned Art of Witchcraft*, RHB 9:329–30.

5. In the published edition, the citation is Daniel 11:3.

Fourthly, he can do it by putting into men's minds wicked <purposes>, and so labor with them till he has brought things to pass. By this means he foretells that which he means to <effect>.

<Fifthly, he> does it by reason of his speed by which he can <convey himself through> the world in short times, and so by this his agility <he can> bring strange things from place to place.

Sixthly, God uses the devil oft times to bring to pass His judgments. And these being revealed [to the devil], he can tell [of] them. [In] 1 Samuel <28:19>, "Tomorrow thou shalt be with me <and the Lord shall give the host of Israel into the hands of the Philistines>." Because God had delivered Saul in regard of <His good spirit, the> devil being appointed the instrument <to work his overthrow, hereupon he was able to foretell> the particular time.[6]

---

6. Cf. *Damned Art of Witchcraft*, RHB 9:331.

Exodus 22:18

(Sermon 3)

"Thou shalt not suffer a witch to live." (Ex. 22:18)

We have heard the grounds of the practices of witchcraft. Now we are to speak of the sorts of it, for it is either in revealing of strange things or it is that which is called unlawful divination. We have heard besides how the devil is able to discover these strange things. We are now to speak of the sorts of this divination, which is either in means or without means.

First, of that which is done by means. And it is either by such means as are altogether the true creatures of God or by means altogether forged. Of the first there are four parts.

The first is wrought by the flying of birds aloft or below, on the right hand or on the left. And by the noise which they made, they did divine either good or bad success. This kind is forbidden [in] Deuteronomy 18:10–11.

The second is done by the entrails of beasts. [In] Ezekiel 21, the king of Babylon, by the signs in the liver of the sacrifices, guessed what should be the success of his wars.

Objection. Why are both those kinds condemned by Scripture? *Answer.* Because they are not the signs of good or bad success. For God did not in the creation set down that these should be the signs of any such thing, neither did He make any such appointment since their creation. And, therefore, they are signs only diabolical and <…> of the devil. And, therefore, the divination <…> <…>[1] diabolical.

And here we may <judge> of certain usual fond divinations among us, as when a man finds a <piece of> iron, it is a sign of good success. And when a man takes a journey and a hare crosses in the way, that he thinks is a sign of great ill luck and so breaks off his journey for that time. And when a man's ear tingles, he thinks some man talks of him. And when the salt falls toward him, he divines some such thing. But all these fears are superstitious, for they have no force neither in the order in nature nor in God's Word, and therefore the divination thereof is fond and superstitious. And they are of this kind, though

---

1. Much of the content is missing from the MS because the page is torn. The content has been supplied from *Damned Art of Witchcraft*, RHB 9:333–35.

not so gross and palpable as the others, for in no case can they be warranted, and therefore we must abstain from using of them.

The third kind of divination is by the stars <and> called astrology. [In] Deuteronomy 18:10–11,[2] all the devilish arts are there set down, and this is one of them, divination by the stars.

Objection. The stars are causes of many things that come to pass. *Answer.* They are so, but they are only common and general causes and not particular causes of particular events. Now a man cannot know any particular event by the general causes only without <knowing> the particular cause. The common cause brings not forth the particular effect but only helps the particular cause; therefore, by these cannot particular effects be known and foretold. And, therefore, we cannot divine things to come by them unless we can judge the disposition of particular causes [in] the general, which we cannot do.

This divining therefore is forged. Therefore, it <is to be> numbered among wicked acts, for that it is nothing but dotages of man's brain. For lawful arts are set down by rules which are gathered by experience. Now the rules of this art all stand of no experience, for the same constitution of all the stars never comes twice and therefore there can be no experience of them. Again, no man can know every particular star nor the virtue of any one.

Objection. The star has many effects in the inferior creature; therefore, there may be a note of them. *Answer.* Indeed, they have many operations, yet it does not follow that thereof there may be an art, for it is not possible that a man should know the virtue of every particular star.

---

2. The original erroneously cited verse 19.

"You have heard that it was said of old time, 'Thou shalt not commit adultery,' etc." (Matt. 5:27)

In this verse and in the verse following, Christ goes about to reform the seventh commandment to its proper use and meaning. As before He lays down the false exposition which the scribes and Pharisees gave to it, which is in the 27th verse, "You have heard that it was said of old time thou shalt not commit adultery." Secondly, He gives the new meaning and proper sense in the 28th verse, and so forward.

"You have heard that it was said old time, or of old teachers." These words are a preface laid down before the commandment. "You have heard," that is, "you My hearers have often heard the scribes and Pharisees teach that this was the meaning of the seventh commandment." Hence, we may observe two things: [first,] that the scribes and Pharisees using it in expounding the commandment are here reproved by our Savior, Christ. Secondly, that it is not lawful to teach having no surer ground than antiquity to build upon, which the papists often do.

"Thou shalt not commit adultery." These words are the words of the Holy Spirit wherein the seventh commandment is laid down, yet they are not to be taken in another sense than the words import. And that we may the better see how they expound them, we will see what adultery here mentioned is. Adultery is the breach of wedlock, some one of the breakers whereof are at the least either married or espoused. It is [called] a breach of wedlock to show that property which is belonging to this sin, [namely,] to dissolve the knot of marriage. Idolatry, though it be a great and grievous sin, condemned in the two first commandments of the first table, yet herein it comes short of this sin. Of any, whether man or woman, this is added to take away the laws of some countries, which give a privilege to the man, [namely, that] though he abuses himself with a single party, yet he commits not adultery, though he sins.

Thirdly, "espoused" is added though the marriage is yet unfinished. "There shall not be a whore of the daughters of Israel, neither a whore keeper of the sons of Israel" (Deut. 23:17). The Pharisees expound this commandment, taking it only for bodily adultery, making it no larger. We see then the words are the words of the Holy Spirit, but the sense is the sense of the Pharisees.

Uses. There we may see the straightness of the Pharisees in cleaving to the words but changing the sense. Thus the atheists and the papists do so in the institution of the sacrament, "This is my body." This must admonish us not only to stand upon the words but to labor for the sense. Whereas the Lord does namely condemn this sin, and these false teachers do so, we may learn that this is a great and grievous sin. Paul says, "He is an infidel that provides not for his family."[1] And if that be so, then he is worse than an infidel that does disperse and send [away] his family. Wedlock is the seminary of the church and commonwealth.

Since then we see adultery being the breach of wedlock, it is also the breach of the church of God and commonwealth. Secondly, the adulterer takes away his neighbor's chastity, which in no wise can be called again.

Thirdly, he makes his own house a stewe.[2] For in his abusing his neighbor, his neighbor does so unto him again, as we may see in David, who dealing thus with Uriah, also one [of] his sons did see to his, by the just judgment of God.[3] No adulterer can enter into the kingdom of heaven.[4] He may indeed repent, but he ceases then to be an adulterer. Here then, this being so, it was to be wished that seeing it is a more grievous sin than theft that it were punished with death as theft is.

Thus much of the exposition of the scribes and Pharisees.

"But I say unto you." He speaks as a lawgiver and a prophet who is able to give the true meaning of His own law.

"Whosoever looks upon a woman to lust after her has committed adultery with her." The words may be taken two ways, either *by* looking lusts or *in* looking lusts. Here are two things set down. First, the occasion of adultery, which is looking upon a woman to lust after her. Secondly, that inward adultery is here condemned.

For the first, looking upon a woman simply is not sin, but it may be an occasion to praise God, as the Queen of Sheba did when she by looking upon Solomon took occasion thereby to praise God.[5] Here then the idle and curious looking is condemned. Idle looking is when they have no occasion to look. Curious looking is when they look because they will look. In the sixth [chapter] of Genesis, the sons of God saw the daughters of men,[6] where this very action of looking upon them is condemned. In Genesis 39:7, Potiphar's wife cast her

---

1. 1 Tim. 5:8.
2. *Stewe*: brothel.
3. 2 Sam. 11, 13, 16.
4. 1 Cor. 6:9.
5. 1 Kings 10:6–9.
6. Gen. 6:2.

eyes upon Joseph, which cast of her eyes was the beginning of her naughtiness. So David, walking upon his house, cast his eyes upon Bathsheba, which was the beginning of his adultery. And seeing this is so, we ought all to take heed as at all times, so especially in the public assembly when we come to hear the Word of God. David prays [to] the Lord that He would keep his eyes from beholding vanity (Ps. 119:37). And Job, in his 31st chapter, made a covenant with his eyes.[7]

And so, as these are made the occasions of adultery and so condemned, here it follows that many other occasions also by proportion are condemned, as books of love, and unchaste talk and songs. Secondly, all plays and comedies wherein the vanity and light and unchaste behavior is set forth to the eyes. Thirdly, light attire of women whereby men are made to behold them with a light and idle eye. Fourthly, the mixed dancing of men and women. Fifthly, all idle company is here condemned. "Evil company corrupts good manners" (1 Cor. 15).[8] And such is all company which is not warranted either by the general or particular calling. Sixthly, the pampering of the body with meat and drink. And this was the very sin of Sodom. Seventh, idleness when we are not employed in some lawful calling.

Hence then we see that no man is able to excuse himself from his motives to sin. We must then with Job lay our hands over our mouths and humble ourselves and acknowledge this sin,[9] and as we must do so, so also ever hereafter take heed of this and the like.

---

7. Verse 1.
8. Verse 33.
9. Job 40:4.

Isaiah 50:4

"The Lord God has given me a tongue of the learned that I should know."
(Isa. 50:4)

The main question handled is concerning outward worship of conscience. We have reduced it to eight heads. The [first] is invocation. Of this we have spoken before. The second head is the preaching of the Word. Of this at this time. The questions touching this are of two sorts: (1) concerning teachers [and] (2) concerning hearers. Questions which concern the teachers we will defer to their proper place and come to the questions concerning hearers.[1]

The first question of conscience concerning hearers is how a man may profitably, and to his comfort and salvation, hear the Word of the preacher. That this is a necessary question appears [in] Luke 8:18, "Take heed therefore how you hear, etc." *Answer.* For answering this we must know that for profitable hearing, three things are necessary: (1) a preparation before, (2) a right disposition in hearing, [and] (3) a right practice after.

Touching the first preparation, how we should prepare ourselves, it requires sundry directions.

The first direction is that we must be swift to hear. "Wherefore let every man be swift to hear, etc." (James 1:19). In this commandment of Saint James, we are enjoined to remove from us all hindrances that may <hinder>[2] the hearing. These hindrances and the remedies thereof we will set down.

The first impediment is presumption, when a hearer presumes in his own knowledge in teaching. The remedy of this Saint James sets down: "Be slow to speak" (James 1:19). And in the third chapter, first verse, he expounds himself: "My brethren, be not many masters, etc." That is, do not presume on your own stability of teaching. "If any man will be wise, let him be a fool" (1 Cor. 3:18). So then, in a word, we learn to be willing to learn of our inferiors. [In] 2 Kings 5, Naaman was willing to be healed of his leprosy by Elisha.

The second impediment is troubled and disordered[3] affections, especially unabashed anger either against their teacher or any other. This is commonly

---

1. See Perkins's *Calling of the Ministry*, RHB 10:195–280; and *Art of Prophesying*, RHB 10:281–356.
2. This term is supplied from *Whole Treatise of Cases of Conscience*, RHB 8:271.
3. The MS states, "misordered."

verified, for let that hearer conceive but an ill opinion of their teacher, he hardly professes. The remedy of this Saint James gives in the next word: "Be slow to wrath" (James 1:19). For <...> anger causes a man to cast off all care of doing any good thing.

The third impediment is the superfluity of maliciousness, that is, the abundance of sins and corruptions which the hearers have in their heart and life. This maliciousness has three branches. [The] first branch is hardness of heart set down [in] Matthew 13 in the parable of the seeds. [The] second branch is the cares of the world set down in the same place of Matthew (v. 22), there called the thorns which grow up, and choke, etc. The third branch is the itching ear. "But having your ears itching shall after their own lusts gather a heap of teachers" (2 Tim. 4:3). This itching ear is when a man desires to have no other doctrine than that which shall please his nature. And those are the three branches.

The remedy of this impediment is set down [in] James 1:21: "Lay apart all superfluity of maliciousness." That is, we must break off the sins and corruptions of our heart. "Break up your fallow ground, and sow not among the thorns" (Jer. 4:4). [In] Exodus 19:10, God commands the Israelites three days before to sanctify themselves, that is, to cut off their corruptions. The second remedy of maliciousness is set down [in] James 1:21: "Receive with meekness the word." And this much of the direction.

The second direction in the preparation is to lift up our hearts in prayer to God before we come, for although we have outward ears, <...> we cannot hear, unless we have God's grace enabling the heart to understand that which we hear, for the understanding heart is the hearing heart.

The third direction is that the hearer must always sit himself in the presence of God. "Cornelius saith to Peter we are all present before God to hear all things commanded of God" (Acts 10:33).

Thus much of preparation.

The second thing is disposition in hearing. Touching this, two rules [are] to be considered.

First, when the Word is delivered, the hearer must hear with judgment. "Believe not every spirit, but try the spirits, whether they are of God" (1 John 4:1). "Try all things and keep that which is good" (1 Thess. 5:21). Now there are three kinds of judgment: (1) a private judgment of any private man, (2) a judgment of the prophets and ministers, [and] (3) the judgment of God. And those three judgments are subject to the other in order: the private judgment of a man is subject to the judgment of the minister, and the judgment of the minister is subject to the judgment of God.

Upon this rule two things follow. First, though everyone has a private judgment, yet no private man is to censure his teacher, not but that they may be censored, for their judgment is subject to the judgment of God. Second, that the hearer is not to propound to himself any doctrine but that which is either plainly set down in the Word or has been taught by the minister. And the not keeping of this rule has been the cause of many schisms.

The second rule in the disposition is that we must come to be deeply rooted. This is set down in the parable of the soils (Matt. 13). Not only the unlearned but the learned and wise in the world is to care that this Word is not only taught for knowledge but also for the deeper rooting of the Word in our hearts. For this better and deeper rooting, four things are required. First, that the hearer knows and understand it. [The] second is set down [in] Hebrews 4:2, "The word which they heard profited not because it was not mixed with faith." Where we say that the second thing is that it must be mixed with faith. This faith must, first, be generally to believe the doctrine delivered, and, secondly, we must have a care to apply the Word which was heard. The third thing required for our ingrafting is that we must be well affected by the Word. For an example of this we have Josiah, who when he heard the law, his heart melted.[4] The fourth thing for ingrafting is that the Word must dwell in the hearers, and therefore Paul says to the Colossians, "Let the word dwell in you."[5] Now the Word dwells where it abides and takes place.

The third and last thing in profitable hearing is a right practice after the hearing it; that is, the doctrine so delivered must be laid in the heart. "I hid the word in my heart" (Ps. 119:11). [The] second duty in practice after is to meditate of that which was delivered with prayer unto God. [In] Leviticus 11, those beasts which were clove-footed and chewed the cud were admitted both [to] be eaten and to be offered in sacrifice. By chewing the cud, many divines think [is] meant sacred meditation. So then, as those beasts in chewing the cud do fetch up again what they have eaten, so must we fetch up again to our minds that which we have heard. The third duty is that every teacher labor to have an experience in himself of the Word which he hears, that he may say it is good by experience: "Taste you and see, etc." (Ps. 34:8).[6] The fourth duty is examination. "I have considered my ways" (Ps. 119:59). The fifth, and last, is obedience to it, that when occasion so rises we may put in practice.

---

4. 2 Kings 22:19.
5. Col. 3:16.
6. The MS erroneously states Psalm 54:8.

Matthew 23:37–38[1]

"Jerusalem, Jerusalem, which killest the prophets, and stonest them that are sent to thee, how often would I have gathered thy children together as the hen gathereth her chickens under her wings and you would not. Behold your habitation shall be, etc." (Matt. 23:37–38)

This chapter contains the substance of a sermon that Christ made to the Jews at Jerusalem. From the 1st verse to this 37th verse contains that which He spoke against the teachers of Jerusalem, namely, the scribes and Pharisees. In this verse and to the end of the chapter is set down an invective against Jerusalem itself and all its inhabitants. In these words two things are to be considered. First, that sin and rebellion of the Jews in this 37th verse. [The] second is the punishment of the sin in the 38th verse: "Behold your habitation, etc."

For the first, the sin; in it three things are to be considered. First, the place and persons wherein and in whom this rebellion is, that is, Jerusalem [is] the place and the inhabitants are the persons, contained in these words: "Jerusalem, Jerusalem." [The] second is the degree of the rebellion in these words: "which killest the prophets, etc." [The] third is the manner and form of the rebellion in these words: "How often would I have gathered, etc." That is, "I would have gathered you together, but you would not." The punishment is set down in the 38th verse, of which we will speak in its place.

First Part: The Place and Persons
For the first, the place and persons are here [said] to be Jerusalem and the inhabitants thereof, which was a city of God honored with more privileges than all the cities of the world besides. In the ninth chapter of Romans, verse 4, the privileges are set down. Firstly, that they are true Israelites, that is, that they came of the seed of Abram, Isaac, and Jacob. Secondly, that pertinent to them, adoption, that is, that they were inwardly called to be God's children. Thirdly, that the glory of God belongs to them, whereby glory is meant that mercy seat, which is the testimony of God's presence. Fourthly, that to them belongs the covenant, that is, the covenant of the two tables [of the law]. Fifthly, that

---

1. This sermon of the late 1590s became the introduction to Perkins's *Treatise on God's Free Grace and Man's Free Will*, RHB 6:391–95.

the giving of the law belongs to them. Sixthly, that the public worship of God belongs to them. Seventhly, that the promises pertain to them. And in Micah 4:2 there is an eighth privilege noted, that is, "that the law shall go forth of Zion, and the word of the Lord from Jerusalem." And yet, for all these privileges, He complained of them for rebellion. Neither is this the first time that He accused them of it, for in Isaiah 5:4 He compared it to a vineyard, in that which He had husbanded. So much, that in the fourth verse He asks what He should do to that vineyard which He has not done, and [of] which He complains that when He looked for ripe grapes, it brought forth wild grapes.

Doctrine 1

Hence, we learn, firstly, that whereas God bestows [the] greatest mercies, there oftentimes is the greatest wickedness and rebellion, as we see here written in the example of Jerusalem. Now that which is herein said of Jerusalem may be said of us, for within these forty years,[2] the Lord has blessed us with many mercies, both temporal and spiritual, than ever He did any land, yet we are not thankful for it, but wicked [imitators] of Jerusalem, giving not that care of serving of God, accounting it <...> <...> but preciseness, and therefore <...> there may be no excuse for us in England, that we may [not] behold our sins.

Doctrine 2

Secondly, hence we gather that God's assistance is not bound to any place or persons, for if ever any had the assistance of God bound unto it, it had been Jerusalem, but this had not as we see by this place. This, believes the Church of Rome, goes about to <...> for which they allude. *Objection.* "The priests' lips should preserve knowledge, etc." (Mal. 2:7). Whence they gather that the priests' lips hand a promise to preserve knowledge, and therefore God's assistance is bound to the priests. *Response.* But I answer that that is not a promise, but a commandment. "The lips *should*," that is, they *must* preserve knowledge.

Objection. Again, they allege Matthew 23:2, "The scribes sit in Moses' chair."[3] *Response.* I answer that by Moses' chair is not meant the seat of Moses, but the doctrine of Moses, taught and expounded, not the place.

Objection. Again, they object [with] John 16:13, "The Spirit of God shall lead you into all truth." So they cannot err. *Answer.* This was not directed to all believers nor to all ministers but only to the chosen apostles, and apostolic

---

2. I.e., since the beginning of the reign of Elizabeth in 1558, which dates this sermon circa 1598. Perkins often refers to the duration of Elizabeth's reign in his writings and sermons as a time in which England had enjoyed the preaching of sound doctrine but had made inadequate use of God's provision.

3. The original erroneously cited Matthew 25:2.

authority, yet does it not belong to [the] church at all times and in every respect, but only when they follow in the work of their apostleship. We must then believe that God does not annex the assistance of His Spirit to any place or persons whatsoever. Hence then appears that it is false that a counsel assembled cannot err. Secondly, hence appears that it is false that the pope of Rome when he sits in his consistory cannot err, as the Church of Rome affirms, that though as he is a man he may err, yet as he is in that place he cannot err. Thirdly, hence appears that succession of ministers in a place is not a note of the church.

Doctrine 3

For the place, where He doubles it, "Jerusalem, Jerusalem," He signifies that He does three things. First, that He holds it a wonder and an incredible thing that Jerusalem should rebel. Second, He testifies His exceeding detestation and loathing of this sin. Thirdly, (1) it serves to stir up the Jews and us by them, to loath their rebellion, and to take a warning by it to detest unthankfulness (the reason is because of rebellion); [and] (2) detestable sins follow: falsehood [and] injustice. By how much, therefore those two are to be avoided, [since] by so much that man's rebellion against God [is] to be detested, because it is always accompanied with these two.

And thus much of the first part: the place and persons.

Second Part: The Degree of the Sin

The second part is the degree of the sin, with the words "which killest the prophets, etc." In Psalm 1:1, three degrees of rebellion are set down. First, to walk in the counsel of the wicked. Second, to stand in the ways of sinners. Third, and greatest, to sit in the scorner's seat. This third and greatest sin is Jerusalem's sin and may be termed desperate rebellion. In this degree are three things set down: (1) impenitency, (2) a sacrilegious and profane contempt of God's salvation, [and] (3) cruelty, yea, a custom in cruelty, for so much the word imports, which are "killing" and "stoning," which note a continuance of the same. That this sin may better appear two questions are to be handled.

Question 1. How can this city, having such mercies of God, grow up to that height of iniquity? *Answer.* In every actual sin are four things to be considered: (1) the thought when it first comes in his mind; (2) the guiltiness of the fault; (3) the punishment of the act, which is two, death of body and soul; [and] (4) a blot imprinted in the soul of him that sins, which blot is a proneness to commit the same and an increasing of the natural corruption in the same or greater sins. As we find by experience in Adam, who after he had but once sinned, the blot thereof was so imprinted in him that it made not only himself but also all his posterity prone to the same and greater sins. For as it is the nature of a drunken man, the more he drinks the more his thirst[4] increases, so by sinning increases sin. *Answer.* So then to answer, by this means it is that this city came to that height of sin, namely, by the custom of sinning. Further, by the consideration of this, we are to take care how we sin against God, for besides the punishment of the sin, the blot thereof is set in our souls, by which we in daily sin alienate ourselves from God.

Question 2. Seeing this city grew to such a height of sin, how could it be called the city of God? *Answer.* Though the greatest part were hypocrites, yet there were some true Christians as Joseph, Elizabeth, and others. Now, the better part for the most part signifies the name and not the greater part, and so it was called the city of God soundly. It being a reputed city of God, He had not forsaken Jerusalem as yet, though it had forsaken Him. And, therefore, as a wife that commits adultery remains a reputed wife till their bill of divorce be given, so Jerusalem was called the city of God, being not yet forsaken of Him.

Whence we learn not to give our rash judgment of any man, for we know not whether God will forsake them, though they forsake Him. Also, firstly, in that Jerusalem is come to this height of sin, we see the proneness of our nature to sin against God, and therefore we must be acquainted with our nature and labor to cut off all occasions of sin. Secondly, by this city we may have a view of the city of Rome, for Jerusalem is a true <...> of Rome. Thirdly, by the example of Jerusalem we are taught to profess ourselves the children of God, for you shall be seen to have peace (Isa. 2:4). Fourthly, if Jerusalem is blamed for killing the prophets, we must look <...> by to submit ourselves to the ministry of the prophets. Fifthly, we are taught not to be discouraged though we be afflicted and persecuted, for God's children may assure themselves that in His good time God will undo all.

---

4. The MS states, "dright."

Chapter 7

Funeral Sermon for William Perkins

In late 1602, the bodily remains of William Perkins were interred at Great St. Andrew's Church at the expense of Christ's College.[1] These two neighboring locations represent the extraordinarily broad scope of Perkins's ministry. At St. Andrew's he ministered as a popular preacher, pastor, and author, while at Christ's he served as a fellow, teacher, and academic theologian. Perkins's funeral sermon was delivered by James Montagu,[2] master of Sidney-Sussex College and future bishop of Winchester.[3] Perkins and Montagu had been close friends, Montagu also serving as one of the trustees of Perkins's will (see Introduction). Michael Foster,[4] a student at Corpus Christi College, was present at the funeral and wrote down Montagu's sermon in his notebook.[5]

The sermon bears the marks of Montagu's Christ's College education, of which Perkins's instruction was a significant part. It employs Ramist methodology and clearly reflects Perkins's preaching priorities—namely, delivering clear biblical exposition according to the theological parameters of the Reformed tradition while drawing out doctrines and uses for the edification of all.[6]

---

1. Michael Jinkins, "Perkins, William (1558–1602)," in *Oxford Dictionary of National Biography* (Oxford: Oxford University Press, 2004), accessed August 29, 2016, http://www.oxforddnb.com/view/article/21973.

2. For more on Montagu, see the brief biographical sketch in the introduction to this volume.

3. Thomas Fuller, *The Holy State* (Cambridge: Roger Daniel for John Williams, 1642), 92; Thomas Fuller, *Abel Redevivus: or, The Dead Yet Speaking; The Lives and Deaths of the Modern Divines* (London: Thomas Brudenell for John Stafford, 1651), 439; Samuel Clark, *The Marrow of Ecclesiastical History, Contained in the Lives of One Hundred Forty-Eight Fathers, Schoolmen, First Reformers, and Modern Divines Which Have Flourished in the Church since Christ's Time to This Present Age* (London: Printed for T. V. and are to be sold by William Roybould at the Unicorn in Pauls-Church-yard, 1654), 852; Benjamin Brook, *The Lives of the Puritans* (London: James Black, 1813), 2:134.

4. Michael Foster (fl. 1598–1608) was a native of Norfolk who would return there to serve in ordained ministry at Snoring and Kelling. At the time of Perkins's death, he had recently graduated BA at Corpus Christi College. Venn, *Alumni Cantabrigienses*, pt. 1, vol. 2, p. 162.

5. British Library, Collections from Several Sermons, Harley MS 976, "Montigu—obitum Perkins. Josh: 1:2," ff. 2r–5r.

6. See William Perkins, *Art of Prophesying*, RHB 10:281–356. On Perkins's approach to

Montagu likens England's loss of Perkins to Israel's loss of Moses and considers the prospect of God raising up successors to continue Perkins's legacy just as He raised up Joshua to succeed Moses. Beyond expressing appreciation for Perkins's abilities and achievements, Montagu describes the manner of his death, which has long been a point of biographical interest. Montagu exhibits an apologetic concern, held in common with Perkins's earliest biographer, that Perkins's dying prayers for God's mercy were not driven by despair but by dependance on God's grace even through the course of a particularly slow and painful process of dying, during which he lost almost all ability to speak.[7] In the face of the ignominy of death, Montagu highlights the believer's triumphant position over death by virtue of union with Christ and the believer's certain future by means of Christ's resurrection.

Montagu ends his sermon on an ominous note, portraying a possible future for England akin to the time of Israel's exile, when its enemies would mock its once glorious status now in ruin. Evidently, Montagu shared the same fear as Samuel Ward, another of Perkins's proteges and later master of Sidney Sussex College, that the loss of Perkins might mark a dramatic decline in the good estate of Cambridge University. On the day of Perkins's death, Ward wrote in his diary: "God knows his death is likely to be an irreconcilable loss and a great judgment to the university, seeing there is none to supply his place."[8] Montagu echoes this concern while hoping and praying that God would raise up another Joshua among them and that a rich Cambridge tradition of Reformed preaching, piety, and evangelism would continue.

Indeed, Perkins was to become the fountainhead of a rich Puritan succession,[9] and he is often described as "the father of Puritanism" for good reason.[10] However, the unfolding of events in the seventeenth century would have given Montagu and Ward reason to believe that their pessimistic expectation of God's judgment had come to pass. The succeeding decades would

---

biblical exposition, see Andrew S. Ballitch, *The Gloss and the Text: William Perkins on Interpreting Scripture* (Bellingham: Lexham Press, 2020).

7. Cf. Fuller, *Holy State*, 91. Samuel Ward's diary entry on the day of Perkins's death witnesses to this reality: "In his sickness, being in great extremity by reason of the stone, he was most quiet and patient, and when it was motioned unto him as he was putting out his hand, what he wanted, he answered, 'Nothing but mercy.'" M. M. Knappen, ed., *Two Elizabethan Puritan Diaries by Richard Rogers and Samuel Ward* (Gloucester: Peter Smith, 1966), 130.

8. Knappen, *Two Elizabethan Puritan Diaries*, 130.

9. See Paul R. Schaefer Jr., *The Spiritual Brotherhood: Cambridge Puritans and the Nature of Christian Piety* (Grand Rapids: Reformation Heritage Books, 2011).

10. J. I. Packer, "An Anglican to Remember. William Perkins: Puritan Popularizer," in *Pilgrims, Warriors, and Servants: Puritan Wisdom for Today's Church*, St. Antholin Lectures Volume 1: 1990–2000, ed. Lee Gatiss (London: Latimer Trust, 2010), 145.

witness the rise of Arminian and Laudian influences within the Church of England,[11] a brutal civil war, and a marked departure from Perkins's Reformed theological heritage.

11. See Nicholas Tyacke, *Anti-Calvinists: The Rise of English Arminianism c. 1590–1640* (Clarendon Press: Oxford, 1987). Cf. H. C. Porter, *Reformation and Reaction in Tudor Cambridge* (Cambridge: Cambridge University Press, 1958), 414–29. However, it is important to recognize that Reformed theology maintained a presence in the established Church of England. See Stephen Hampton, *Grace and Conformity: The Reformed Conformist Tradition and the Early Stuart Church of England* (Oxford: Oxford University Press, 2021); Stephen Hampton, *Anti-Arminians: The Anglican Reformed Tradition from Charles II to George I* (Oxford: Oxford University Press, 2008).

On the Occasion of the Death of William Perkins

James Montagu[1]

"Moses my servant is dead, now therefore arise Joshua, and go over the Jordan, etc." (Josh. 1:2).

These words are the words of God at the death of His servant Moses, which are not unfitly applied to His worthy servant of God who departed.

In these words are considered two things:

1. Publication of Moses's death: "Moses my servant is dead."
2. Vocation of Joshua to succeed his place: "Now therefore arise."

In the publication we must consider the words: (1) the proper name of "Moses"; (2) the title or epithet given to him, "my servant"; [and] (3) the issue of all flesh, "he is dead."

In the vocation we may also note three things:

1. Joshua must arise.
2. That he must not only arise, but that he must go to Jordan.
3. Not only proceed so, but he must go into the land [of] Canaan and possess it.

First, that I may not omit anything[2] which may seem pertinent to the matter, let us consider the circumstance of time when these words were spoken to Joshua. They were of not presently after his departure, but thirty days after his death (Deut. 34).[3]

It was a custom [among] most of the Jews, that if a private person died, they should solemnize his death seven days after. [We have an] example in Job's friends, who lamented over him for seven days; also, in the men of Jabesh Gilead who lamented Saul's death seven days.[4] For Saul, by reason of his death, was no better than a private man, and therefore [he] had no public farewell.

---

1. The original states: "Montigu—obitum Perkins."
2. The original includes a double negative: "that I may not omit nothing which may."
3. In the margin: *Sepaltura disserit,* "Discusses the burial."
4. 1 Sam. 31:11–13.

Now for a more public person there was allotted a month for the solemnizing of the farewell, as we see in Moses and Aaron.[5] The reasons why they had so much time allotted:

First, the embalming of their body. So, Jacob was kept forty days for the reason of the tempering of the oil in that hot country.[6] But in <...> and other colder countries it might be effected in thirty days.

[The] second reason [was] for the assembly of the friends together for the solemnizing of their farewells, and to feast after the long time of mourning, as may appear in the death of Samuel,[7] as also in the farewell of Abner[8] and in the raising of the ruler's daughter in the New Testament.[9]

Third, the last reason was that some solemn song, or funeral verses, might be made, as at marriages there were songs of praise of them that were married; so, at the farewell lamentations, as in the lamentations of Jeremiah (2 Chron. 35:25).[10]

These were the three reasons why the funerals of noble men were so long deferred by reason of embalming to preserve them from corruption, whose lives they so <...>. Secondly, to preserve their name, and that was by the assembly of their friends and kinsfolk together. Thirdly, for the consolation of the living by hymns and songs in praise of the deceased.

The two things in general which are to be considered are what God says of Moses: "my servant is dead."[11] It is the testimony of God to set forth the manner and death of His servants (though ever so dear to Him) in few words. This we see in Abraham, whose story fills thirteen chapters,[12] and two or three verses serve for his death.[13] So [too] in [the cases of] Jacob,[14] Isaac,[15] and David.[16]

The reason of this is twofold <...> why God briefly set down the death of the faithful, and why He would not as well set down the conflicts and combats they have with Satan at the hour of death, as He did the like rather in their lifetimes, as the strife of Jacob which he had for the well.[17]

---

5. Num. 20:29; Deut. 34:8.

6. Gen. 50:1–3.

7. 1 Sam. 25:1.

8. 2 Sam. 3:31–39.

9. Mark 5:38–43.

10. The original erroneously cited 2 Chronicles 31:22.

11. In the margin: *Deus suorum obitq- denotata,* "God denotes the deaths of His [servants]."

12. Gen. 12–25.

13. Gen. 25:8–10.

14. Gen. 49:33.

15. Gen. 35:28–29.

16. 1 Kings 2:10–11.

17. Gen. 32:24–32.

The first reason [is] to let us all understand that the things which He registers in His book is the life of man, and not his death.[18] For without all doubt as a man is in his life, so shall he be at his death. For *qualis vita, finis ita.*[19] And if he has lived in holy conversation, he cannot but die in the fear of God.

The second reason is to cross the corruption by nature, that is,[20] to exceed in the praise of the dead; therefore, God, so moderately here, has set forth His own example in saying little or nothing of the death of His servants.

Now, therefore, seeing the public solemnity of the funeral of <…> persons is so commendable and warranted by Holy Scripture, so that [we are to] be moderate, and [that] without excuse.

It is fit at this time to speak of this saint of God. For his personal and private life, I say nothing. His especial skill in tongues[21] and sciences I pass over. Only I will speak of him as a public person, and that in three respects:

1. His preaching and doctrine
2. His writings
3. His life and conversation

And these three had the coherence, dependance, and sequel one of the other, as none which had read his writings but should hear his preaching, and none saw his life but read a lively comment of the both. Great was his knowledge, and singular was his conscience, his mind understanding rare knowledge of Christian religion. No man read his writings but professed in[22] the store of [his] knowledge. No man knew his life but had[23] in him a wise and holy conversation.

His skill was singular in these two things:

1. In handling a common place
2. In private conference

For the first, he would have laid down whatsoever the matter required soundly and plainly, distinguishing most naturally, observing[24] most acutely, answering most soundly, considering most directly and thoroughly as any of his time.

---

18. In the margin: *quia vitam cuspicit,* "He looks to the life."
19. "As is the life, so is its end."
20. The original states: *id est* (Latin).
21. That is, languages.
22. To?
23. Witnessed?
24. This word is obscure in the original, but it appears to be "observing."

And God has given him a wonderful gift, a peaceable nature. And as his conscience did suffer him to conceal any corruption in any person whatsoever,[25] but he did it in such sort as he gave offense to none but sought to win all. As to the deed. And here appears great knowledge and zeal, want[26] of vain affection [or] desire of the applause of the people. Yet God gave him a most noble name, his books never any of them content with a single impression, but every [one] of them published twice at the least, some of them every year newly imprinted, and translated into other tongues. And as I hear two <…> out this <…>.

This may issue in brief to have spoken of his life, because I will not break any rule of moderation by excess. And for his death it was as his life, to wit, a continual death. I omit divers passionate speeches and only observe two: that he desired continually the prayers of God's saints and children. Secondly, that God gave him obedience to his cross and patience to endure it. And thirdly and lastly, mercy.

For being asked at any time what he wanted, his answer was ever "God's mercy." His speeches were not many, for God had taken away from him the use of his tongue, so that he could not say distinctly [nor] utter his words by reason of the <…> of his mouth fallen down. But his hands and heart were often lifted up to heaven, where I leave him with God and the blessed company of angels. If David bewailed the death of his natural son, Absalom,[27] much more the sons of this prophet ought to lament him who was the father of prophets, yea, the only prophet of our time. If David did mourn for Saul who sought his life,[28] much more we for him who sought to raise us from the death fire and [to] the life of righteousness, and enriched our souls with such doctrine out of the sacred Word of God. And as God said of Jeroboam, "he was a man which caused Israel to sin,"[29] so on the contrary point I may say of him, that he was a man which caused the people of England to honor the Lord.

Now to the publication of the death of Moses. First, for his title, "my servant."[30] I observe here that God, when He calls him by his proper name again and again, it was for the modesty of Moses. For he, being a most meek, mild, and modest man, never named himself in all his writings.[31] Second, it is also spoken in the third person, likewise arguing his modesty. Lastly, in the writings of his three books, there are named institutes with his governance, and

---

25. That is, to bear with the faults of others.

26. *Want*: lack.

27. 2 Sam. 18:33.

28. 2 Sam. 1:17–27.

29. 1 Kings 14:16; cf. 15:34; 16:2, 19, 26; 22:52.

30. In the margin: Doctrine.

31. In the margin: Moses's *modestia*.

yet Moses did in modesty avoid vainglory. Now, God as He had before showed it, gives him his proper name.

Observe this, that in the genealogy of the kings,[32] three kings' genealogies were not mentioned at all.[33] In the story of the rich man in John's gospel, the poor man only had his name, to wit, Lazarus, for the honor of the one and the dishonor of the other.[34] Judas, after such time as he had betrayed Christ, was not named any more Judas Iscariot, but Judas the betrayer of Christ.[35] Jeroboam [was] not called by his own name, but [was known as] he that made Israel to sin.[36] Ahab [was] not [known] by his name, but [as] he that wrought wickedness in the sight of the Lord.[37] So God almost never named any in the Scriptures but for honor's sake. As <…> <…> say, *honoris causa nomino*.[38]

Secondly, Moses is not only called by his name, but that [by] his title, "my servant." And he is called God's servant for three reasons.[39]

First, for the cause that some thought that he was dead, and that for two reasons: (1) for his infidelity [and] (2) because he entered not into Canaan. Now, God testifies the contrary, not that he was His servant only in his life but also in his death: "Moses my servant is dead."

The second reason why he was called God's servant: God might have said of him that for his life and death he was another Noah, walking uprightly before God and defended by God as Noah in the ark.[40] Or He might have named him Enoch, being translated as he was.[41] Or He might have graved[42] him with the title of a king, having the conduct of his people out of the land of Egypt thus far toward the land of Canaan.[43] But He calls him only "Moses my servant." For if He had called him by any of the other names, as Noah, Enoch, a king, etc., then all these titles had been past and buried in oblivion. Only this title of the servant of God is perpetual.

The third reason he was called a servant only [was] because this was the highest title given to any under the law. The dearest children and prophets of God were called but servants. But now under the gospel we have the title of

---

32. In the margin: *Nomina plen[um]que honoris causa in ponetur.*
33. This reference is unclear.
34. Luke 16:20–31.
35. E.g., Matt. 27:3; John 18:5.
36. See references above.
37. 2 Kings 17:11.
38. "I only name him to do him honor." A classical phrase used by Cicero.
39. In the margin: *Rat: 3: quare appellat.*, "Three reasons for his address."
40. Gen. 6:9; 7:17–24.
41. Gen. 5:24.
42. *Graved*: engraved, stamped upon.
43. Ex. 12:31–Deut. 34.

sons.[44] Here we note that as God enlarges His benefits, so He enlarges the name of the receivers. God from the beginning [was] called the "Creator of heaven and earth,"[45] until Abraham's time when He was called "the father of Abraham, Isaac, and Jacob,"[46] until the time they were brought out of the land of Egypt and then He was called "the God that brought thee out of the land of Egypt,"[47] until the time of the delivery out of the captivity of Babylon and then He was called "the God that brought them out of a far country." But when Christ came, He was called "the Father of the Lord Jesus Christ."[48] And Christ by Jacob was called Shiloh;[49] by David, "the Messiah";[50] and now by us, "the Son of God." As also were the <…> (for the Holy Spirit has no epithet under the law) called them prophets and servants of God, until the coming of Christ and then He calls them His friends,[51] and afterward His apostles called them the sons of God.[52]

Only in a word the use thereof. Seeing there is no man but esteem highly of his style and title, and it is a thing that most men strive much after, let us learn to get us such a title as to be accounted the sons of God. For this is a sure title that shall never fail us. And here withal have the saints of God in former times accounted themselves highly graced. If any man takes from an emperor the least part of his life or title, it is made so heavy a matter that nothing but death can satisfy for such an offense. And should not we much more value and esteem the title of being servants of God? We shall consider which <…> where we <…> <…>. For the names of Alexander, Caesar, Nero, and Pompey, etc., and in those less famous (and as for their souls, we hope well of them), but what is now become of their names?

Now "Moses my servant," what is become of him?[53] He is dead. The reasons why he[54] is affirmatively set down that he is dead is twofold:

1. Moses went up, as usually he was wont to do, to the mount to speak with God, and for making the people doubt whether he was dead or not.

2. They inquired after him but could not find him dead.

---

44. In the margin: *Nos non servii, sed filii*, "No longer slaves, but sons."

45. Gen. 14:19.

46. Ex. 3:6.

47. Ex. 20:2.

48. Rom. 15:6.

49. Gen. 49:10.

50. Ps. 110:1; Matt. 22:42–45.

51. John 15:15.

52. Gal. 4:6; 1 John 3:2.

53. This line is an allusion to Exodus 32:1. In the margin: *Moses mortuus dicit quare*, "He says why Moses died."

54. It?

The reason of this was for that his body being left, they, being given to superstition, might easily have been driven to commit idolatry in worshiping his body whom they greatly loved and remembered in his life. Hence was it that Elijah was diligently sought after, but not found, being taken up, etc.[55] So that here God speaks it out of all controversy, and to take away all doubting, "Moses my servant is dead."

Observe here also that when any of the brave servants of God in the Old Testament have been departed, though they were never so noble, yet leave all their titles, [for] they are dead.[56] So was it said of Abraham, Isaac, and Jacob: "They lived thus long and died." But in the New Testament there is no such thing mentioned as death. As in the beginning of Matthew, Abraham begat Isaac, Isaac begat Jacob, etc., and no mention [is] made of death in all their lives. Let us come to particular persons, and we shall see this verified. Our Savior Christ, though the story of His death is first set down at large in every particular by the four evangelists, yet three of these vary the epitaph, as He gave up the ghost, etc., [and] avoid saying He was dead. It is said of Stephen in the Acts that, when he had thus said, he slept.[57] Our Savior Christ put this out of all controversy in the raising of Jairus's daughter. They all said she was dead, but He said no, but she sleeps.[58] Not that He disagreed from them in matter and substance, but in the manner and style of speaking. The apostle Paul, writing to the Thessalonians and Corinthians, both these reason the rising of Christ, infers all: "We which are alive shall not weep [for] them that are asleep";[59] "We shall not all sleep, but we shall all be changed."[60] Here we see the title of death carefully avoided by the apostles' <…> <…>, as we see the same in their writings. And as this is the style and phrase and manner of the Scriptures, for there is in it a further matter to be considered than the bare avoiding of the same phrase. For a man living and dying in Christ cannot properly be said to be dead, for there is in every man a twofold union in Christ:

Natural
Spiritual

A man dying, the natural union between the body and the soul is dissolved. But the spiritual union between our souls and bodies in Christ is absolute and indissoluble. So that in Christ neither in life nor death can we be severed from

---

55. 2 Kings 2:17.
56. In the margin: Doctrine.
57. Acts 7:60.
58. Mark 5:39.
59. 1 Thess. 4:13.
60. 1 Cor. 15:51.

Him, as He is our head. Here is a transformation of the terms but no dissolution of the union. As when He was alive His body was united to His soul, so being dead our bodies are united to the soul in Christ. I make it plain by a familiar example. A man takes corn and puts it into the ground. If it rots, it never rises again. But if it dies, it has power to arise again. So, the body is sown in hope, as the apostle says,[61] and by a spiritual instinct the body is united in Christ to the soul, giving a spiritual kind of life.

Now for the use hereof.[62] All men must labor then for this union in Christ, because it is never dissolved, and hereby the body is still in hope to have the fruition of the soul again.[63] Hence also is it plain that the bodies of the damned rise again by no virtue of Christ as Savior, but only by the power of Christ the Judge.[64] But it is contrary with the righteous. For it is an axiom [that] the cause of the correlation being first, the grounds can never fail.

A man is called the servant of God. It is a bond of relation and is correlative to God <...> as alone or <...>. Now if the Lord, which is cause of this correlation, never fail, [then] it is impossible for us being [thus] grounded to fail.[65] The same is the ground of relation in Christ of the Father. If the Father, which is the cause, be not dead, it is impossible for the Son to cease to be His Son.

And thus much for his point, "Moses my servant is dead." A word or two now of the succession of Joshua into his office. "Now therefore arise Joshua, etc." This word "arise" has two uses in the Scripture:

1. When a man is called by God to any function.

2. When a man has been in long sorrow and lamentation, he is bidden in the Scriptures to arise, and both these in one [are] expressed.[66]

Note here the mercy of God in this charge. "Moses is dead, therefore Joshua arise." Aaron is gone; his son Eleazar succeeds him in his room.[67] David is gone; Solomon succeeds him in his kingdom.[68] And thus we see it fall out in the tenor of the Old Testament.

---

61. 1 Cor. 15:42–44.

62. In the margin: *Usus unio in xpto desiderada*, "Use: Desire for union with Christ."

63. This point appears to rest on the Aristotelian distinction between the formal and material cause and the notion that the form of the body is in the soul. Thus, the Christian's soul persists beyond death by means of union with Christ and thereby also retains the form of the body even while the matter of the body is dissolved in death. The form of the soul comes into material fullness ("fruition") once again by means of the resurrection.

64. In the margin: *Quomodo resuscitat impiis*, "How He raises the ungodly."

65. In the margin: *Pater et filii fuit correlata*, "Father and sons were correlated."

66. The Latin marginal note is illegible.

67. Num. 20:25–29.

68. 1 Kings 2:10–12.

In the New Testament also presently upon the <…> of them, the apostles succeeded. So through the whole Scripture, one special member goes out [and] another is raised up in his room.

Uses.[69] Now, therefore, if we would know when God deals in judgment [and] when in mercy with His people, such is a golden rule: either in raising up of another special member in his room whom He has taken from us, thereby showing His great mercy, or His judgment in taking away of Moses and not raising up Joshua in his stand. We see His mercy verified in divers examples of the Scripture in this kind. No sooner I say, Aaron is dead, but Eleazar is priest in his stead. David was no sooner dead, nay, in his lifetime, [but] Solomon sat on his throne. After Jesus Christ, afterward His apostles. His judgment also when he took away Joshua.[70]

So, God threatens to take away the angel in the Revelation, and what before the church [was] nothing but desolation. So that if God raises up none or one work, that is judgment. How has God dealt with us of this land these forty years and more, no sooner are gone but another rises up, as I could insist in divers particulars, but I leave the same to your consideration.

Next consider that when as God bids Joshua arise, and that three times, it argues his backwardness and unwillingness. Secondly, we see that though the ministry of God be Joshua's, yet it is our nature to be loath to arise. And the reason hereof is that they are prisoners of their own imbecility and weakness.

For if they should be willing, and offer to intrude themselves, as too many <…> are nowadays, what argues it but arrogance, and too much confidence in their own strength, but when it comes to trial, then they are found the weakest of all, and most backward in their performance of their duties. But Joshua thought it a point of modesty and good manners to stay God's leisure, which ought to invite us in all modesty to be imitators of his example, being to be called to any vocation, especially to the ministry.

When God commanded Moses to go to Pharaoh, and he sought to excuse himself by pleading the slowness of his tongue and want of eloquence, and therefore desired God that he would send another, we read not that he was condemned or checked of God for his excuse and backwardness at the first to go on God's errand.[71] So Jeremiah alleged his imbecility till God touched his tongue in coals from His altar.[72] And hence also, Joshua at the last arose and went to possess the land. And as he was to arise upon the vocation of God, so he showed them in the possession of the land. That he went not for honor and

---

69. In the margin: *Usus. Judicionem dei considerare*, "Use: Consideration of God's judgment."
70. In the margin: Judgment.
71. In the margin: *Piorum modestia*, "The modesty of the pious."
72. Isa. 6:6–7. This reference is to the prophet Isaiah, not Jeremiah.

ambition, because he would not till God had three times commanded him. For look likewise into the history after he had entered into the land of Canaan and won it, yet he would not have one <...> for his own possession (although he might lawfully have challenged it all) till the Israelites gave it [to] him. And this he did rather because [of] the twelve spies that before went to Canaan to search the land, only Caleb and Joshua told them that the people were but bread for them. The other ten told them that they were too strong.[73]

Now lest the people should have objected and said he before told them to encourage them to set on, and so to purchase him a kingdom in the land of Canaan, he therefore avoiding all ambition and vain glory begs his own possession of the Israelites in the land of which he himself (by God's assistance) had won. And this is the duty of every faithful magistrate and teacher, that being raised by God's word to their place and calling, they should propound [not] their own glory but God's honor, to be the scope of all in their actions and enterprises. But we see that contrary among us, being raised to place[s] of authority we will be sure to get of the bread of governance which serves sweet and pleasant to the taste. And in our places we propound our own sake, so that God's glory is least of all thought upon us. I would urge this, that magistrates and men of higher place and office in this town may so far intend God's glory and His church's good that whereas God has taken away a Moses, they may command or at the least by reward send forth a faithful Joshua in his room. That men, passing by this place where so worthy a man had before taught, seeing it not again supplied, might justly exclaim and say to the shame both of the university, to one and us all: "This was the house of God, but now it is laid waste, etc."[74]

Finis.

---

73. Num. 13:26–14:9.

74. An allusion to biblical prophecies of judgment: Isa. 5:9; Jer. 12:10–11; 33:10; Matt. 23:38; etc.

Perkins's Preface,
Exposition of the Lord's Prayer (1592)

Perkins's publication of his lectures on the Lord's Prayer (1592) was motivated by their unauthorized publication in the same year. The following notice was prefixed to Perkins's authorized edition of the work.[1]

An advertisement to the Reader

Good Reader, there was a book of late published in London under this title, *Perkins upon the Lord's Prayer*.[2] In it I have double injury: first, it was published without my knowledge or consent; and, secondly, the book is faulty both in the matter and manner of writing.

In the matter, these things are not well set down.

1. The commandment of prayer, very easy to be kept (3.b).
2. Prayer is the restoration of the gospel (7.b).
3. The three first petitions concern God's glory; the latter three the means of God's glory (1.b).
4. God's name taken for His deity and not for His attributes or titles (15.b).
5. A man must pray for the day of his death (26.a).
6. Repentance is sufficient not only to bring a true faith but also to renew it (34.a).
7. A lesson in the Lord's Prayer taken out of popery (45.a).
8. The doctrine of satisfaction for sin is a most vile doctrine (52.b).
9. God and the devil agree in the manner of temptation (61.b).
10. God offers men the occasion to sin (62.a).

---

1. William Perkins, *An Exposition of the Lord's Prayer, in the Way of Catechising Serving for Ignorant People. By W. Perkins* (London: Robert Bourne & John Porter, 1592), 3v–4v.

2. *Perkins upon the Lords Praier: By Order of Catechising, Devided into Three Parts the First Is the Commandements: The Second, the Creed and the Third, the Doctrine of the Lords Praier* (London: R. Bourne, 1592).

Likewise, the manner of writing has other faults.

1. In the middle of the Lord's Prayer there is placed a discourse of the Lord's Supper.
2. The end of the Lord's Prayer is not expounded at all but frivolously.
3. There are very many places which have no common reason in them, as:
   i. God's angels do His will in countenance (39.b).
   ii. Our daily bread is communicating bread (45.b).
   iii. To walk before God in the truth of the satisfaction of God's justice (51.a).
   iv. To purge a clear conscience (51.b).
   v. The pages 65, 66, [and] 67 are so penned as the reader cannot know what was my meaning.

Now, considering [that in] this ungodly practice Christian and well-disposed people are much abused, to omit the injury done to myself, I thought it my duty to make a redress by publishing this treatise according as the points therein were delivered. Otherwise, I was not willing to have set down anything in the way of exposition of the Lord's Prayer, because it is already sufficiently performed by others.

Perkins's Sermons on Jude 3–4:
Three Sources Compared

The following chart sets the Tomlin and Hutton transcriptions of Perkins's sermons on Jude 3–4 against the text published by his posthumous editors. Annotations and footnotes have been removed here but can be found in the Tomlin and Hutton texts published in this volume and in Taylor's published version (RHB 4:91–108).

Thomas Taylor	James Tomlin	Hutton MS
		[**Sermon 1**] Jude 3, *"Beloved when I gave all diligence to write unto you of the common salvation, it was needful for me to write unto you to exhort you that you should earnestly contend for the maintenance of the faith which was once given to the saints."*
		Omitting the preface in this text, I come to the substance, which is an exhortation to faith, where by "faith" is meant the solemn doctrine delivered by the prophets. But now to the particular heads of this exhortation. The points which the apostle touches are three. First, that this faith is a precious treasure, and so much does every word

Thomas Taylor	James Tomlin	Hutton MS
		in the text signify. The second is that the saints, that is, the church of God, is the keeper of this faith, and that is shown in these words, "given to the saints." The third point is the office of the church and every good member in the church, and that is to fight manfully for the faith. And of these in order.
The Use Thus we have shown in part that faith is a most precious treasure, beset with many enemies against whom we must always contend, which we shall yet more clearly see in beholding the use of this treasure, which is twofold.		Thus first, that faith is a precious treasure, appears by the twofold use.
First, to reveal from God unto man all things needful unto salvation concerning doctrine or manners, wherein it excels all man's learning. For, first, all the laws and learning of men reveal the moral law only in part, and mingle it with superstitions and ceremonies, but they reveal no part of the gospel. Only this doctrine of faith reveals in the full perfection both the law and gospel.		The first is that it comes from God [with] all things necessary for our salvation, and in this regard it excels all the learning and laws of man. And that appears in sundry particulars. For first, the laws of man reveal but part of the moral law, and no points of the gospel. Now this faith for which we are to fight reveals the moral law perfectly, and the gospel also wholly.

Thomas Taylor	James Tomlin	Hutton MS
Secondly, the laws and learning of men know nothing (much less reveal) of man's misery, neither the cause nor the remedy thereof. But this doctrine of faith knows and reveals both; namely, the first cause to be the sin of our first parents, and the proper and perfect remedy to be the death of Christ.		Secondly, the law and learning of man know nothing of the cause or remedy of man's misery. Man's learning only knows it, not the cause of it. The faith reveals the first and perfect cause of man's misery and the remedy thereof.
Thirdly, men's laws and learning speak at large of temporal happiness, but know nothing of eternal. But this doctrine not only knows the true happiness of men but teaches and describes the ready way thereunto.		Thirdly, the laws of man speak only of temporal happiness in this life; this faith knows the everlasting happiness of the everlasting life, and this is the first use.
The second use of this doctrine of faith is that it is a most perfect instrument of the Holy Ghost for the working of all graces in the hearts of men. I mean not the letters and syllables, but the doctrine of the prophets and apostles taught and believed. Paul calls it the "power of God to salvation." And Christ Himself says that His Word "is Spirit and life," that is, the instrument of the Spirit whereby life eternal is procured.		The second use is that this faith is the instrument of working all grace for everlasting life. And not the letters or bare syllables or the words said do this, but the doctrine of faith. And therefore, Paul calls it the power to salvation. And in regard of these two uses it is truly called a precious treasure.

Thomas Taylor	James Tomlin	Hutton MS
For which two notable uses it is a most precious treasure. Whence we learn, first, to be "swift to hear" this doctrine taught in the public ministry, because in it God opens His treasure to dispense the same unto us (James 1:19). Secondly, it being a precious treasure we must hide the same in the coffers of our hearts: "I have hid thy word in my heart" (Ps. 119:11). It must be an "engrafted word" in them (James 1:21).	Then if it be a precious treasure, then we must be "swift to hear," as the apostle James says, and "slow to wrath." We must cheerfully hear the same and be very greedy to receive the prize and profit thereof. Again, if it be a treasure, we must hide it in our hearts, for a treasure, we know, is not fit to be cast up and down, but it must have a fit place to be hid in, and the place and secret chamber and coffer wherein this treasure must be [is] in our hearts, so that we are happy if we can say with David, "I have hid thy word in my heart that I might not sin against thee" (Ps. 119).	The use of this is manifold. We learn, first, that we must be swift to hear this doctrine publicly delivered and embrace it with all willingness because it so pleased God to reveal it. Secondly, if the doctrine of true religion be a treasure, we must hide and treasure it in our hearts, for a treasure is not to be cast up and down at six and sevens, but it must be laid up in the safest place. Now that is the heart. Thus did [say] David in the 119th Psalm, "I hid thy word in my heart." And James, in his second chapter, says it must be rooted in our heart.
And this duty we practice,	We shall hide [it] in our heart by these three means:	That this may be done three things are necessary.
first, when we have care to know it;	1. When we have a care to embrace it and hear it preached.	Firstly, to have care to know it.
secondly, to remember it;	2. To remember it daily to lay it up and meditate on it.	Secondly, to remember it.
thirdly, when we set the affections of our hearts upon it, as men do upon their treasures.	3. When we apply all our affections to it, and put in practice in our lives and conversations.	Thirdly, to save our affections but upon it.
Thirdly, if it be the treasure of the church, then it brings to the possessors of it, wealth, honor,	If it be a treasure, it must bring true honor and delight, prosperity, riches; even so does this treasure.	The third use is, if this be a treasure, it brings with it true wealth and honor and true pleasure, for that

Thomas Taylor	James Tomlin	Hutton MS
and pleasure, as other treasures do. For as the house of Obed-Edom was blessed for the ark, so is that heart which holds true wisdom within it (Prov. 3:13–14). We in this land have good experience of this truth, who by God's blessing have above forty years enjoyed wealth, peace, honor, and above all, God's protection. And whence have these flowed but from the true faith and religion set down in the prophets and apostles, maintained and defended amongst us? Which if we would have continued, we must also continue to hold and effect this truth as a treasure unto the end.	While the ark was in the house of Obed-Edom, he prospered, and all his family. To this end, he does exhort the paint[ing of] wisdom before our eyes, which wisdom is nothing but the Word of God, saying, "It is better than gold, or precious stone" (Prov. 3:14). And truly this treasure makes this our land flow over with prosperity and peace, for forty years of true faith is the cause of so many heavenly, spiritual, earthly, and temporal blessings. Let us, therefore, having the same, keep it secretly in our hearts, that our profit and joy (as the prophet says [in] Psalm 4) might be full. Then shall our wealth still increase.	is the nature of a treasure. And to this end read the third [chapter] of Proverbs, from the 13th to the 18th verse. And this is verified by experience in this our land, for we have had peace, wealth, and all earthly commodities, and we have been protected by the hand of God from all our enemies round about, he alone fighting for us. And whence proceed all those doctrines of true religion preached among us.

Head 2: The saints are keepers of the treasure

Thomas Taylor	James Tomlin	Hutton MS
The second point or head of the exhortation is that the saints are the keepers of this treasure of faith, to whom it "was once given."	Now, the second point is this, namely, that the saints only are keep[er]s of this faith.	The second point is that the church of God is the keeper of this faith.
Whence we may learn, first, that it is an infallible note of the true church of God to keep, maintain, and defend the wholesome doctrine of religion, delivered by the prophets and apostles. It was noted	First, [it] is a notable mark to know that true church of God by. And by this we may discern that true church from the counterfeit, [namely], that the true servants of God they have their part	In the 15th [verse] of [1] Timothy 3, the church is called "the ground and pillar of the truth." And in the 1st [chapter] of Canticles, [verse] 7, the spouse demands of Christ where she shall find Him at

Thomas Taylor	James Tomlin	Hutton MS

to be the chief preroga-
tive of the Jews, that to
them the "oracles of God
were committed" (Rom.
3:2). Hence the church
is called the "ground and
pillar" of truth, because
in her public ministry she
maintains and preserves
the same (1 Tim. 3:15).
She asks Christ where she
shall be sure of Him, and
not miss of finding Him
in her necessity. He makes
answer: she shall be sure
of Him in the "tents of
shepherds" (Song 3:7).
Whence may be truly
concluded that neither are
the assemblies of Turks
nor heretics the churches
of God, because they
fight against the truth.
Neither is the Church of
Rome a true church of
God, because the truth of
doctrine is for substance
reversed amongst them.

chiefly and principally
in this treasure of God
their Father. This was
the chiefest honor of the
Jews above the Gentiles,
above all other nations,
which they kept: the ark,
the law, the statutes, the
excellent treasures of
God (Rom. 3). So, this is
now our credit, our joy,
our comfort, our honor.
"Come to the tents of the
shepherds, my spouse, my
love, where I am" (Song
1:7), says the bridegroom
Christ Jesus to His sister
and spouse, the church.
And by this we maintain
the wholesome doctrine
of the prophets and apos-
tles in very substance.
So are we keepers of the
faith.

noon day. Christ answers
that He will be where the
sheepfold is, that is, where
the good shepherds, the
faithful ministers, keep
the fold. A register is
known by the words that
she keeps, and the church
is known by the faith and
doctrine. And this is the
mark by which we know
the popish religion not to
be the true church, and
the Turkish and atheists
to be no religion.

As also we may be con-
firmed that our churches
are the true churches of
Christ by this infallible
note: a register is known
by its records. So our
church is known to be
God's register, because
it keeps faithfully the
records of the prophets
and apostles. Secondly,
that it stands us in hand
to whom this treasure
is now committed, so

Second, in that we are
keepers of this heavenly
treasure, we must learn
two doctrines. First, to
praise and magnify the
name of God, acknowl-
edging His fatherly love to
us above all other nations.
"He hath not dealt so with
every nation." Second, it
stands us upon (seeing we
are stewards and keep[er]
s of the treasure) to be so
diligent in keeping and

Seeing then that we are
keepers, it stands us in
hand to look to ourselves
that we be not put out
[of] office, and it [be]
given to others which
have better deserved it,
and will bring forth bet-
ter fruits than we have
done. Now, we shall do
our office if we bring forth
the fruits of our office,
and that is the fruit of
amendment of life, which

Thomas Taylor	James Tomlin	Hutton MS
faithfully to keep it, that it be not taken from us and given to others who will keep it better; which we shall do by making this use of it, that we bring forth the fruits of it in amendment of life, else our unthankfulness shall justly bereave us of it.	using the same, that we may never be displaced, and others put in our room. For that is the office of a keeper, to be daily circumspect and daily exercised in keeping the same.	if we do we shall be good stewards.
Concerning that circumstance in the text "once given" and not often, it may bear a double sense. First, it was given (as we say) once for all, that is, perfectly, sufficiently, as never after needing any alteration or addition. Whence we note, first, that all revelations in matter of salvation and religion given since are frivolous and superstitious, for there is but one edition of true faith, and no other edition of revelation besides or without the Word; such as the papists have devised to confirm their purgatory, prayer, and alms for the dead, mass, etc., seeing all necessary doctrine to salvation was once given perfectly. Secondly, that all church traditions in matter of religion and doctrine of salvation are mere profanations of true doctrine, and argue it to be imperfect; as those of	"Once given to the saints." God gives His faith once. This "once" may be understood two ways. First, once for all, that He never needs to give it any more to the saints, wherein we learn divers necessary and wholesome instructions. The chief whereof is that there is no alteration of the divine words of God, and that all the visions, all the precepts and traditions of man in matters of religion, more than the Word of God has or allows, are mere superstition and idolatry, yea are all vain and frivolous additions of the brain of man. And to such there is heavy sentence pronounced: "Whosoever shall add anything, etc." (Rev. 22). Wherein we see the pureness and perfection of the Word of God in its own nature, but which we are so blockish that we	Here in these words of the text, "once given to the saints," is to be considered a double circumstance of time. First, once given for all, that is, perfectly, never after to have any new giving. By this we learn that all revelations by visions, all traditions in matters of salvation, as purgatory, alms, masses, and prayers for the dead, are diabolical, and only of the devil. Likewise, the supremacy of the pope and all other traditions of men in matters of salvation are diabolical and mere profanations of the wholesome doctrine of faith. The reason is because the true faith was but once given for all.

Thomas Taylor	James Tomlin	Hutton MS
the mass, of receiving the communion in one kind, of the pope's supremacy, of works of satisfaction, and many more.	cannot well understand the same.	

Secondly, it may be thus understood, "once given to the saints," that is, not in writing but in the hearts of the saints, when they are truly enlightened; and therefore if after enlightening it be quite lost, it is not given the second time, and consequently cannot be recovered. "If a man who hath been once enlightened and tasted of the good word of God, fall away, it is impossible that he should be renewed again by repentance" (Heb. 6:4). From which we must learn to beware of apostasy and falling from the faith, yea, and all steps and degrees leading thereunto, as of declining from our grounds of religion. For better had it been for us never to have known the way of truth than after the knowledge of it to forsake the holy commandment (2 Peter 2:22). Which is the more to be remembered, because religion has been more cherished than now it is, and the declining from it

Again, it may be understood "once for all" in regard of God's [grace], that that it being once lost it will never be received again (Heb. 6). But it is not meant of some frailness and weakness whereby man may revolt from the same for a time and give occasion of offense, but of such revolting and backsliding as is of willful stubbornness and unbelief, whereby we make a shipwreck of faith. First, this serves, therefore, to admonish us to take heed of apostasy and backsliding from this faith which now we embrace, for this is so dangerous that, once it being lost, it can never be recovered again. Second, not only so, but also to take heed even of the least declination and sliding in religion, which is a means of the former, and a first step and degree to apostasy. Third, we are forewarned [in] 2 Peter 2 not to call in question and deliberate and doubt of the ground of our religion,

Secondly, in this circumstance, "once given," being so understood not by writing but given in the heart to show us that faith once given and wholly lost can never be recovered. This is to be understood not of a particular fall, as of Peter for denying his master, but of a general falling away. This serves to admonish all lest they fall wholly away. It is dangerous to fall by infirmity, but to fall away wholly is far more dangerous. And to take heed of this apostasy or falling away, we must take heed of declination in religion, for that is one step to apostasy (2 Peter 2:21). And it is to be feared that in these days of ours there is a much declining, for in former times true religion has been much more embraced than it is now. And that we may the more take heed of apostasy, we must beware of calling in question the grounds of our religion. For as Cyprian says, <...> <...> "Of holy things there

Thomas Taylor	James Tomlin	Hutton MS
a great deal less. If it be asked, how may we prevent apostasy? I answer, never call any ground into question. Here Cyprian's rule is to be learned, that divine matters admit no deliberation.	but hold it steadfastly. James says, "A wavering minded man, (meaning [in] matters of religion) is as a ship tossed up and down with waves." And the doubt and deliberation concerning the grounds of our religion is dangerous and is a second step to apostasy. Fourth, we are charged to be continually exercised in the Scriptures, that we may become strong men in Christ, that no illusions, no persuasions of the enemy, the papists, or anything for life and death may be able to remove us from the faith once received. And, therefore, "Search the Scriptures," says Christ (John 5). "His delight is the law of the Lord and thus is he exercised day and night," which is continually said the Psalms (Ps. 1). This is a means to be freed from the former evils.	must be no deliberation, but we must believe them without question."

Head 3: The office of the church is to fight for the treasure

Thomas Taylor	James Tomlin	Hutton MS
The third point of the exhortation is the office of the church of God and every member of it, and that is to maintain, yea, to "fight for the maintenance" of this treasure. And this is not a bodily	The third point of the true church is to fight manfully for the faith once received. The persons that fight are the saints: all Christians in general. The battle that they must fight is specifically not by	The third point is the office of the church of God and every member, and that is to fight for the faith. It is not only the office of the magistrate or the minister, but every member of the church

Thomas Taylor	James Tomlin	Hutton MS
fight by strength of arm or bow, but a spiritual fight by spiritual duties, which every member of the church must take up, and namely by four duties.	sword, bill, and mattock, but by the shield of faith, the helmet and buckler of constancy. The enemies against whom [they must fight] are the wicked deceivers spoken in the next verse and in our times antichrists.	must fight. Neither is this fight by strength or bodily weapons, but they are spiritual duties with which we must arm ourselves.
	The manner how we must fight is diverse. We must fight by: 1. doctrine, 2. confession, 3. example, 4. prayer.	And to this fight there are four things necessary by which we must fight: (1) by doctrine, (2) by confession, (3) by example, [and] (4) by prayer.
First, by doctrine, for every man in his place and calling must be a prophet and must teach all under him. The father must teach the children, the master his servants, and thus keep out Satan and all satanic doctrines.	First, by doctrine or obedience, everyone in his calling and place is a prophet, [and] is commanded to teach not only those committed to his charge, as children and his family, but among others [to] teach and defend the grounds of religion against whosoever. "Your sons and daughters shall prophesy" (Joel 2). And this belongs principally to masters and superiors. Their servants must teach their masters also in the Word of life.	First, by doctrine, because everyone, not only ministers but every particular man and woman, yea, every servant, must teach according to his gifts and in his calling.
Secondly, by confession, every man being called must stand against the gates of hell by constant witnessing of the truth. Sanctify God in your	Second, one must confess and profess the true faith always before all persons and in all places. "He that is ashamed of me (says Christ) before men,	By confession, for that every [person] must confess and profess not only in the time of peace but in adversity, yea, to the face

Thomas Taylor	James Tomlin	Hutton MS
hearts, and be "ready always to give an account of the hope that is in you" (1 Peter 3:15).	him will I be ashamed of in the kingdom of heaven." "Hold out (says Paul) your faith before all persons in humility of heart." And this confession is needful, if place so requires, in the people of God that they must not be afraid to profess the truth before princes, before tyrants. "I will confess your name before kings. I will sing of thee among the nations," says David (Ps. 57).	of the adversaries, this faith.
Thirdly, by example of a good and unblameable life, suitable to the doctrine. This makes men "shine as lights" in the world (Phil. 2:15).	Third, we must fight for the maintenance of our religion by prayer. "Pray to the Father (says Christ to His disciples and so to all Christians) that he will thrust forth laborers into the harvest" (Matt. 11).	By good example and good life, [as in the] 2nd [chapter] to the Philippians, [verse] 15, "shine as lights in the midst of a wicked nation."
Fourthly, by prayer, that the Lord would send forth laborers into His harvest to withstand all false doctrines and heresies, so that the faith and religion wherewith He has honored us these many years may be maintained unto us and continued unto ours forever.	Fourth, we must not only profess ourselves to be Christians, but we manifest the same by our good example and pattern of life, "that men seeing our good works (may be more encouraged, etc.) and glorify our Father who is in heaven." "That we may shine as stars in the sky." Then shall our doctrine and manner and conversation of life be acceptable to God and liked and praised of others. Let us, therefore, fight with Rome	By prayer, and therefore Christ in the gospel says, "Pray to God that he would daily send forth laborers to the vineyard." And by all these four means must we all fight for the faith, not only the ministers but every member of the church of God.

Thomas Taylor	James Tomlin	Hutton MS

| | and antichrists whosoever for the maintenance of the pure treasure of God's truth. Let the death hold it out, that we may be accounted good stewards. | |

Part 2
The Exhortation
(vv. 3–23)

2. Confirmed by the State of the Church (v. 4)

| "For there are certain men crept in, which were of old before ordained to this condemnation: ungodly men they are which turn the grace of our God into wantonness; and deny God the only Lord and our Lord Jesus Christ" (v. 4). | Jude 4, *"For there are certain men crept in which were before of old ordained to this condemnation: ungodly men they are, which turn the grace of our God into wantonness, and deny God the one Lord and our Lord Jesus."* | [**Sermon 2**] Jude 4, *"For there are certain men crept in, which were before of old ordained to this condemnation: ungodly men they are which turn the grace of our God into wantonness, and deny God the only Lord Jesus Christ."* |

| Here the apostle proceeds to confirm his exhortation by a reason drawn from the state of the church in his time, and it is thus briefly framed: there are certain men which secretly seek to undermine and overthrow the faith, therefore you ought the more earnestly to contend for it. | In this verse is propounded the whole sum of the epistle, wherein he confirms his exhortation in the former verse by a reason taken from the condition of the adversary against whom they should fight. And this concerns us now as well as yourselves to whom Jude wrote in those days, for now there are secret enemies without, like men going among the sheep in lamb's clothing, but within are ravening wolves seeking cunningly | In the former verse, the apostle sets down an exhortation to fight for the apostolic faith. In this verse he proceeds to confirm his exhortation by a reason drawn from the state of the enemies of this faith. The reason stands thus: there are certain men which live secretly among you, and which have crept in among you for nothing but to look to overthrow the apostolic doctrine. And, therefore, for these men's sake, it stands you |

Thomas Taylor	James Tomlin	Hutton MS
	and secretly to undermine the true doctrine and religion which here in England we profess.	in hand to fight for the maintenance of it.
		And this reason concerns our church as much as it did the primitive church. For as in Saint Jude's time there were some which did secretly go about to subvert this doctrine, some likewise are there in our day now, both atheists and present professed papists, which creep in secretly into our Church of England, secretly laboring to undermine and overthrow our religion. And, therefore, it stands us likewise in hand to fight for the maintenance of this doctrine.
And that these adversaries lurking amongst them might the better be descried, he describes them by five several adjuncts: first, by their hypocrisy in "creeping in"; secondly, by their estate before God, "they are of old ordained to this condemnation"; thirdly, by their religion, "ungodly men they are"; fourthly, by their doctrine, "they turn the grace of our God into wantonness"; fifthly, by their lives, "they deny the only Lord."	The reason is set forth by a description of these men. They are described by their: 1. Hypocrisy: "certain men crept in." 2. Eternal condition: "ordained to this, etc." 3. Religion: "ungodly men they are." 4. Doctrine: "turn the grace of God, etc." 5. Lives: "deny the Lord God and our Lord, etc."	In this reason Saint Jude propounds a description of these wicked men which were crept into the congregation of God. He describes them by five things. First, by their hypocrisy in these words: "crept in." Secondly, by their estate before God in these words: "ordained to condemnation." Thirdly, by their religion in these words: "to ungodly men." Fourthly, by their doctrine in these: "turn the grace of God into wantonness." Fifthly, by their lives in these words: "deny

Thomas Taylor	James Tomlin	Hutton MS
		God the only Lord Jesus Christ," for those words are to be understood of denying God by their lives. Of these in order.

Adjunct 1

Thomas Taylor	James Tomlin	Hutton MS
For the first, "There are certain men crept in." That is, there are men who secretly have insinuated themselves into your societies, professing themselves to be teachers of the true faith, but are indeed the destroyers and disturbers of it. In which words two sins are laid to their charge.	First, their hypocrisy is seen in this, that they cunningly winded themselves into the fellowship of God's people, making a show of zeal to God, when thereby they sought nothing else but [to] undermine and (if it could be possible) to deface the same.	First, they are described by their hypocrisy: "there are certain men crept in," that is, there are certain men who do insinuate themselves into your society.
First, that they cunningly joined themselves unto the church, pretending themselves to be the servants of Christ and of the church, and yet were enemies to both. Here mark the subtlety of Satan who causes profane men to join themselves to the societies of the saints, that by this means mingling his instruments with the members of the church, he may by degrees corrupt the faith and overthrow the church. The parable shows that wheresoever the good husbandman sows his good seeds, this malicious man scatters his tares (Matt. 13:25). In Abraham's house shall be an Ishmael; in Isaac's, an	Under their hypocrisy here lays two things to their charge: first, their dissimulation; second, their usurpation. Their dissimulation in that they made a show of religion, under a color of society, with the righteous, to overthrow the same (Matt. 13:25). Wherein we see the crafti[ness] of Satan together with his malice, that he raises up enemies of all sorts, as in the primitive church, <…>, atheists, wicked men mingled with the godly that he might overthrow their faith (this is <…> and will be not the end of the word), his subtleness and timing joined	In which words the apostle lays two things to their charge. The first is that they pretend themselves to be servants of Christ, when indeed they were the very enemies of Christ, wherein we may see the policy of the devil, that when he can by no means overthrow this faith, he will cause wicked men to join themselves to the church and make themselves professors of this faith, that there they may take occasion to overthrow the same. This is set down [in] Matthew 13:25, where by a parable the devil's practice in sowing tares among wheat is set down. In the little house of God there was

Thomas Taylor	James Tomlin	Hutton MS
Esau; in the ark, a cursed Ham; in Christ's family, a Judas. In the primitive church the devil raised up of all sorts of heretics [in] great numbers. In our own church the devil stirs up daily troops of atheists and papists, to the corrupting and depraving of true faith and religion.	together with his malice against the righteous.	a Cain and a Canaan. In the little house of Christ there was a Judas, and in the excellentest church that ever was, there were heretics. For in Judas's time, who lived with the apostles, in the happiest age that ever was, yet we see that the worst heretic crept in among them. For the devil's practice is only to stir up atheists and secret papists, to subvert the true and apostolical faith.
The Use. First, we must not take offence when we see ungodly men in the church, much less cut ourselves from it by separation, but rather conceive of the policy of Satan who for the hindrance of the faith thrusts them in. When the Israelites entered into the land of Canaan they must not dwell alone but be mingled with the Canaanites, the enemies of the church, lest the land being too much dispeopled, wild beasts should prevail and devour the people of God. So the Lord (ordering the malice of Satan to the good of the church) suffers seducers in the church both to exercise the faith and patience of His, as also to prevent	But let us not be offended when we see this in the true church of God, that the wicked are here mingled with the godly, for it must be so in this life in the church militant, which by daily exercise and daily strife, by doctrine and life, which I said before, the faith of His people might be put in use for their trial. And we must know this, that the wicked persons and seducers are nothing else but instruments the devil uses to supplant true religion. Although the papists affirm that they be members of church, they be members of Satan, dead members annoying all the whole body.	[Use.] Where the apostle says there are some "crept in," we are first not to be offended thereat, neither therefore to separate ourselves from the church because such are crept in, but we must know that it is Satan's practice to cause such to creep in. But [we] must take heed we be not offended thereat, for the children of heaven might not be alone, but must be mingled with the Canaanites. Again, by this word, "crept in," we learn that they are not of the church of God. They are indeed in the church, but they are no members of the church.

Thomas Taylor	James Tomlin	Hutton MS
greater dangers, which they might in their secure condition fall into. Secondly, hence we see that such hypocrites as these are, though they are in the church, yet they are not of it. They are no members of that body (as the Romish church teaches) for they only "creep" into it. The second fault that is laid to their charge is that they are intruders, thrusting themselves into the office of teaching, not being called thereto, but "creep" into the calling. Whence we note that it is most necessary that those who are to teach publicly in the church should be first called thereunto.	Again, they set down by their hypocrisy, usurping of office, and function of the ministry, they thrust themselves into public government, and teaching of the church, and so they pester and fill the church with a most damnable doctrine, giving instead of wine, vinegar to the people; instead of nutmeg, gall; instead of honey, poison; and so they think by bring[ing] strife in the church, to overturn the whole ground of pure religion. Mark herein a further degree of Satan's subtlety, thinking if he can dissolve the head, the whole body will be dead. And, therefore, in setting over them in authority such seducers they will quickly be led away unto error, usurping their authority, thrusting themselves into the bosom of the church without any calling thereunto, which none can lawfully do but those that are called unto the ministry. And so, no calling, no preaching, and that for these reasons.	The second thing that he lays to their charge in the words "crept in" is that they take upon them[selves] the office of teachers being not called. Wherein we learn that it is needful that they which teach publicly must first be called, then afterward teach, otherwise they creep in. That everyone must be called before he teaches appears by these reasons.
Reasons. First, besides the avoiding of this sin of	First, because the minister is not his own, but the	First, it is the order that God has set down that

Thomas Taylor	James Tomlin	Hutton MS
creeping into the church, it is the order that God has set in the same: "that he that is to teach should first be sent" (Rom. 10:14). And, "No man taketh this honor," (that is, lawfully) to himself, "except he be called as Aaron was."	messenger of God, and an ambassador must come in the name of his prince, so must God's ambassadors. And how should they go in the name of their prince, the high and mighty God, to take upon them such a weighty office unless they be sent and are made with gifts and graces answerable thereto?	teachers should be called. "How shall they preach unless they be sent?" (Rom. 10:15). "No man takes this honor unto himself but he that is called of God" (Heb. 5:4).
Secondly, the ministry is God's and not man's because the minister stands in God's room and speaks in His name, which he can never do truly unless God send him and depute him in His stead.	Second, he that teaches publicly must defend what he teaches and, therefore, he must pray to God for the assistance of His Spirit, which none can presume to crave, neither can he have any assurance in his conscience that he shall obtain, unless he is called unto that weighty office.	Secondly, the ministry of the Word is God's ministry and not man's; therefore, the man that teaches must stand in God's name. Now, no man must be so bold with God as to stand in His name, or to speak His Word, unless God calls and appoints him to do it.
Thirdly, the minister must maintain that which he teaches, unto which he had need (as in all the parts of his calling) of God's special protection. For the which he must be always instant in prayer, which he can never be assured of, if he is not persuaded of the truth of his calling.	Third, the people must account him as God's own messenger, and that the word which he speaks is from God, which they cannot do unless they acknowledge that he has a calling thereto. Neither is he God's messenger if he has no calling thereto.	Thirdly, he that teaches must maintain that which he teaches, and he that maintains it must have the government and protection of it, and he that has it must pray to God for it.
Fourthly, the people cannot hear with comfort and profit, if they be	Therefore, to know who are usurpers of high offices, civil and	Now, who can pray to God for it if he knows in his conscience that God

Thomas Taylor	James Tomlin	Hutton MS
not persuaded that God has called the teacher to instruct them: "How can they hear, etc." (Rom. 10:14). This truth extends itself also to all other offices as well civil as ecclesiastical; all which are to be wielded and executed by men lawfully called unto the same. All entrance then into any office in church or commonwealth by money, favor of men, or any unlawful means, is intrusion; and such are not called of God but are to be ranged among these seducers who creep into places and come not in by God's call or approbation.	ecclesiastical, which creep into the office, they are these sorts: (1) they that have no calling thereunto, (2) they that procure it by friendship, [and] (3) [they that procure it] by money. All these and most of this sort are said to creep into their office, and they are such as commonly by their doctrine or their lives do annoy God's flock.	has not called him to do it? And how shall he think to obtain his petition? For the people that hear cannot hear with comfort and profit unless they know that the teacher is called of God to teach. The which we see verified in a commonwealth, for if the governor be not called and lawfully set in his authority, who will obey? When then men enter into any office, either ecclesiastical or civil, if they enter by money or by favor of some man, they are not lawfully said to be called, but to creep in. Thus much of the first point, hypocrisy.
Adjunct 2 The second adjunct whereby the seducers are described is their estate before God, being "men of old ordained to this condemnation." That is, they were before all times, locked, enrolled, or billed unto condemnation, even as though their names had been set down in a book.	**The Second Point** Their eternal estate and condition before God: "which were of old ordained to this condemnation." The plain meaning hereof is this: which were before all times before the foundation of the earth was laid registers billed or enrolled to this judgment, namely, to trouble the church and so consequently to procure their own damnation.	The second point is concerning their estate before God, in these words: "ordained to condemnation." The which concerns not so much the temporal estate as the estate before God. The sense of the words is this: of old [God] ordained this condemnation <...> which were before enrolled, booked or billed, as in books of records to this condemnation.
By "condemnation" is meant judgment, as the particle "this" does plainly	In these words is set down the eternal estate of those men, that they are written	The word "condemnation" in the original signifies both judgment

Thomas Taylor	James Tomlin	Hutton MS
show, which makes this the plain meaning: they were of old ordained to this judgment in this life, to try, exercise, and molest the church of God, and so consequently to procure unto themselves at length their own just condemnation.	in God's book [and] what manner of men they should be.	in this life and also condemnation in the life to come, which may very well agree to this sense, because those which are crept into the church, and trouble the church, shall in this life first be judged for troublers of the church, and thereto were first ordained, and consequently to that own condemnation in the second place. So, both significations of the word agree to this place: first, ordained to be judged for troubling the church, and consequently to condemnation in the second signification.
In which words we are taught, first, that God keeps His books of registry and records, in which all things are set down, the persons, behaviors, and eternal estate of all men; which books are of three sorts. First, the book of His providence, containing all particulars of things past, present, and to come, in which the Lord saw the members of David when he was yet unformed (Ps. 139:16). In the same book, "the number of the hairs of our heads," and "the falling of sparrows to the ground," are recorded.	To prove this the Scripture is plentiful. 1. There are some that be books of the providence of God, as says the psalmist, "In thy book were all things written of thee which were in time accomplished" (Ps. 139). 2. Other books that the Scripture mentions which be books of God's judgments (Dan. 9; Rev. 22). 3. There are some called books of records, or books of men's names (Phil. 4:3). Our Savior said, "Rejoice rather that your names are	From this point we learn that God keeps records or books of all the actions of every particular man. The books and records of God are of three kinds. The first is a book of providence. "Thine eyes did see me when I was without form, for in thy book were all things written" (Ps. 139:16). In this book are all the hairs of our heads, and the sands of the sea, and the fall of every sparrow. The second kind of book is the book of the last judgment. "And I saw the dead stand before God and the books were opened" (Rev.

Thomas Taylor	James Tomlin	Hutton MS
The second book is of the last judgment, in which the persons and sins of all men all enrolled. "The thrones were set up, the ancients of days did sit: thousand thousands ministered unto him, and ten thousand thousands stood before him: the judgment was set, and the books opened" (Dan. 7:9–10). "I saw all great and small stand before God; and the books were opened, and another book was opened" (Rev. 20:12). The third is "the book of life," in which are written the names of those who are to be saved. Paul says of Clement and his other fellow laborers that "their names were written in the book of life" (Phil. 4:3). Now by these books we may not grossly conceive material books, such as men note what they would remember in, but the counsel, election, providence, pleasure, and knowledge of God, wherein all these things are so certainly set down, as if any man should write them in a book.	written in the books of life" (Luke 10).	20:12). The third kind is the book of life wherein is set down the name of every particular man that shall be saved.
	But we must not imagine that there are any material books wherein He should inscribe with pen and ink, but as in all the course of the Scripture, the Holy Spirit speaks metaphorically according to our sense, as when He says, "The Lord walked in the garden at the cool of the day" (Gen. 6), and in the delivering of the Israelites from the bondage in Egypt "with a mighty hand and an outstretched arm." And in Exodus, Moses saw His back part, as though God was a man like us in substance and matter. But by these metaphors, taken from man, our dull and senseless nature may be more effectually drawn to consideration of the thing that is spoken of.	By these three books we are to understand the counsel and knowledge of God, for by His knowledge and counsel all things past from the beginning and which shall come before the end are as well known as if He should have them written of in a book.
Out of which we note two things.	Then, the lesson we learn out of this [is] God's knowledge and understanding of all things	The use of this is twofold.

Thomas Taylor	James Tomlin	Hutton MS
	indicating and disposing thereof, which the Scripture calls by the name of a steward who writes all things in a book are many.	
First, that in regard of God there is no chance neither any event by it. In regard of men indeed who know not the causes of things, many chances may be, but God's providence and chance are contrary, He having all things written before Him with their causes.	First, we learn that in regard of God there is no chance, fate, or fortune (as the heathen <…> on) but everything is done by His will. And this is the foolishness of man, that when anything good or ill come to them, the cause whereof is hidden from, they ascribe it presently to fortune and never look up to God that sent the same.	First, in regard of God there is no chance at all, for chance and [the] providence of God are quite contrary.
Secondly, that nothing comes to pass without the decree of God, no not the wicked actions of men. Which God not only foresees but decrees, for this Jude insinuates, saying, "they were ordained to this judgment." And even that which is against the will of God comes not to pass without His will, God willing the being of that which He wills not to effect, and though He esteems not evil to be good, yet He accounts it good that evil should be.	Second, there is nothing [that] comes to pass but by the will and ordination of God. Yea, even that which is done against His will, yet it is His will that it should be so. So it is true He wills the thing that is evil, and yet He wills it not, for He wills not the action or thing itself, but He wills the being thereof.	Second use: that nothing comes to pass on earth without the decree of God, no, not the action of the wickedest man that is, for God, though He wills not the thing, yet He wills the being of the thing.
Further, where he says, "ordained of old to this condemnation," we learn	Here we are to consider a little a special point of religion concerning	Hence, we learn a special part of true religion, that as God before all worlds

Thomas Taylor	James Tomlin	Hutton MS
that as God has before all worlds decreed the electing of some to salvation, so He has decreed the refusal and rejecting of others to condemnation. Many were disobedient, unto the which "they were even ordained" (1 Peter 2:8). "God hath not ordained you to wrath, but to obtain salvation through Christ" (1 Thess. 5:9), showing that some are ordained to wrath, who are not to obtain salvation through Christ. God is compared to a potter, framing vessels of "honor" and "dishonor," vessels of mercy and vessels of wrath (Rom. 9:22). In the same place, "I have loved Jacob, and hated Esau"; that is, I have decreed so to do. For the whole chapter speaks of God's counsel and unchangeable decree.	election and reprobation, that God has from the beginning of the world ordained some to be vessels [of] wrath and some to be vessels of honor. Concerning eternal reprobation, we find it proved by the Scripture in many places. "God hath not ordained you to wrath" (1 Peter 3:8). Romans 1:28; 9:22; 2 Thessalonians 2:12; 1 Timothy 2:20; 2 Peter 2:12. If in the foresaid place of Paul (Rom. 9:22), where God is compared to a potter who makes some vessels of the selfsame mold to be vile and contemptable for dishonor, others to be vessels meet for the table, even so says He, "I have loved Jacob and hated Esau," that is, "in My everlasting decree and counsel."	decreed the salvation of some, so He decreed the damnation and reprobation of others. For confirmation of this, look [at] 1 Peter 2:8, "Unto the which thing they were even ordained." First [epistle] of Thessalonians 5:9, "For God hath not appointed us unto wrath but to obtain salvation." [In] Romans 9 God is compared to the potter that makes the vessel, some to honor, others to dishonor, and unless God had decreed some to be saved [and] other[s] to be damned, that comparison cannot stand. And in the same chapter to the Romans, "I have loved Jacob but hated Esau," that is, "in my counsel I have purposed to love the one and hate the other."
Objection. If this be so (will some say) then God deals unjustly, that absolutely ordains some men to condemnation and perdition.	*Objection*: Then, if it be so that God does from all eternity refuse some as well as choose some others, then He deals unjustly in that simply He ordains some to salvation and others to damnation absolutely.	*Objection*. If this be so, that in His own will [God] rejects some and chooses others, God deals unjustly to ordain man to their destruction.
Answer. We must know that we are creatures, and may not presume to	*Answer*. We must not adjudicate and prescribe any justice or injustice to	*Answer*: First, we must know that creatures must not create a law of justice

Thomas Taylor	James Tomlin	Hutton MS
prescribe a law of justice to the Creator, whose will is justice itself (whatsoever we may conceive) and makes the things willed good because it is willed, and not willed because it is good.	our Creator. "Shall we, the vessel, say to the potter, 'why hast thou made me thus?'" Because that our judgments are altogether corrupt, we must give care to the will of God. For He, being high and mighty, and all the scope of salvation and reprobation in His knowledge, therefore He knowing what their estate will be before they be conceived, and seeing He is not the cause thereof anyway, how should it be accorded injustice in Him?	to our Creator, who is justice itself and whose will is justice itself. For first, God wills a thing and then it is just. It is not first just and then God wills it, but He first willed it and then it is just because He willed it.
Secondly, though God refuse and reject men, yet He does it in [a] most wise order and just proceeding, in these two degrees. First, He vouchsafes to some men the riches of His grace tending to life everlasting, which special abundant grace He denies to some others passing by them, who being left of Him unto themselves fall into sin. Secondly, for sin God decrees judgment and condemnation, so as He does not simply and absolutely ordain His creature to hell, but in regard of sin; not that sin is a cause of the decree moving Him unto it, but that He decrees not	Further, secondly, God refuses men in order. He observes degrees. He vouchsafes His grace to all, but He vouchsafes the riches of His grace to some. And in that regard, He passes by some part of mankind and leaves them to themselves in His justice, and then they sin, and then consequently for sin their condemnation is just. For He ordains not condemnation simply, but *præcedente causa*, and therefore sin before is not the cause of damnation. And so, God, being the Creator and Potter, who will argue Him of injustice in doing with His own what He will?	Secondly, though God chooses some and refuses others, yet He does it in most wise and just order, for herein God proceeds by degrees. The degrees are two: first, grace, [and] second, the riches of His grace. For the first, namely, grace simply, God gives it generally to all, and passes by none, but for the second, namely, the gifts of His grace, in regard of this He passes by some and gives them not to all. God then does not simply ordain a man to condemnation, but because he sins. He does not first ordain him to damnation, but leaves him to his sin, and sinning he deserves his

Thomas Taylor	James Tomlin	Hutton MS
condemnation without respect of sin and relation unto it; which speech we need not fear to speak, because the Holy Ghost so speaks.		condemnation, yet [God is] not moved by his sin, but his sin having relation to his condemnation.
The Use. First, if some men be passed by of God, we must humble ourselves under His mighty hand, and with fear and trembling work our salvation. "Some are cut off, thou standest by faith, be not high minded but fear" (Rom. 11:20).	Then, we must make a double use of the same. First, we are taught to humble ourselves under the hand of God and go on in the course of our salvation with fear and trembling as the apostle says, "Be [not high minded but fear]" (Rom. 11).	Use. For that God of His own will chooses some [and] refuses others, it ought to move us to humble ourselves with fear and reverence before God and to use all the good means to work our salvation. "Thou standest by faith, be not high minded, but fear."
Secondly, we may not be offended when we see the gospel not received, yea, hated of men, and the professors of it persecuted, for many are of old ordained to be underminers of the truth even to this condemnation, which by disobedience they hasten upon themselves. "If the gospel be hid to any, it is to them that perish."	Secondly, we must not be offended when we hear or see the gospel of Christ oppugned and resisted by the wicked, because they all are not appointed to be the heirs of salvation with Christ.	Secondly, if this be true, we must not be offended when we see wicked man oppugn and withstand the gospel of Christ.
Thirdly, many divines overshoot themselves, that seek to obscure or overthrow this doctrine of reprobation, teaching that God for His part elects all, and that man himself is the cause of reprobation, so as man is either the savior or damner of		Thirdly, we see that those divines are far overshot that teach that [God] chooses all men by a universal and general election to salvation, and say that man himself is the cause of his reprobation, and man himself is the framer of

Thomas Taylor	James Tomlin	Hutton MS
himself by receiving or refusing grace offered; whereas the Scripture speaks otherwise, and here teaches us that some men were enrolled to certain judgment by God before all worlds.		his election. And this not only papists but other divines teach [it also]. But the Holy Spirit far refutes this opinion, teaching that they were of old accorded to damnation, not that they enroll themselves but were of old enrolled.
The darkening of this doctrine breeds security of spirit, wherein grace is made so large and salvation so easy that if men will they may be saved; whereas our doctrine leads to the fear of God and a care to walk as in His presence continually.	*Objection.* But again, this seems to breed security in the hearts of man. If election and reprobation of everyone is set down by God before their conception, then it may seem hard on God's side. They may say that God is the cause thereof, and if a man ever so strive in the way of religion, if he be ordained to destruction, all is nothing, and if a man is ever so lewd, if he be willed to salvation, he shall be saved. *Answer.* I deny that, for (firstly) it is not possible that the godly should be at all times so void of God's Spirit to be so vain and wicked as once to think of any such thing; although their frailties often break forth, yet [they] have the power by God's Spirit with the same to arise again. But the wicked are contrarily so prone to wickedness only, it is a death to them to do	And this universal election breeds a drowsy security in the hearts of men, when election is made so easy that every man that will may work his salvation.

Thomas Taylor	James Tomlin	Hutton MS
	good because they have not the Spirit of sanctification which works faith in them, as the godly have. And, therefore, without the Spirit, and without faith wrought in them by the Spirit, they cannot possibly have any sense of God's love to them, and so they cannot follow that which is acceptable. And thereupon they fall into sin, and so consequently for sin they are condemned. So, the one is as naturally prone to sin, as the other is by God's Spirit to holiness. Secondly, again (to make it more clear and to confound those papists that would have God to be the cause of the salvation and damnation of all) it cannot be so, for God places all in a particular church, where His Word, will, and sacraments are indifferently offered to all. All are made partakers of His grace. They may take the water and refuse the fire, they may believe and be saved, [or] they may be obstinate and condemned. Now then, God offering His grace to all, He would not the death of the sinner. And in another place, "O, that	

Thomas Taylor	James Tomlin	Hutton MS
	my people would have obeyed my voice. All my prophets have I sent to turn them to me but they would not." And in another place, this is the speech of the Israelites to God's prophet: "We will not walk in thy ways; we will not come into it" (Jer. 5). Now, if man will not receive God's grace when it is offered unto him, the fault is in himself, and who will say otherwise but that he is worthy of his condemnation? Offer a sick man health, and if he would not gladly receive the means being offered, he is worthy to be sick still. Alas, we are all sick of one disease. Shall we despise to be saved? Shall we refuse to be partakers of health by the publishing of the gospel? When Christ cried, "Come to me you that are weary laden, I will ease you," will we not come? We are worthy by our judgment to have our burden redoubled upon us if we refuse such comfortable tidings. Third, and here appears the wisdom of the Holy Spirit in that He shows men as well of destruction as salvation to deter and drive them from sin.	

Thomas Taylor	James Tomlin	Hutton MS
	For if salvation should be made so general abounding to all, and yet God should be full of mercy, where should then His justice appear? So, He must be a God of justice as well as of mercy, and His justice must also be manifested to keep the godly in awe and to <…> them from sin, as also if it will profit no way <…> to make the wicked inexcusable, who neither will be bended to obedience with mercy, nor yet by justice [be] deterred from sin. And, therefore, He tells them of their condition.	
Lastly, in that it is added they were "preordained of old," note, first, the time of the rejection of some men, namely, before all worlds. Secondly, the proper cause of the decree of God, which must needs be in Himself, because it was before the creature was. Before "they had done good or evil" (Rom. 9:11); that is, before He considered of their good or evil in His decree, He decreed to "love the one, and hate the other." So whom He chooses, He chooses in Himself (Eph. 1:9), not informing His judgment, nor framing His counsels	"Of old times," which is before the foundation of heaven and earth were laid. Now the proper and true cause of God's decrees is not of the creature, but of Himself, because His counsel was before the creature was made when His eternal counsel has registered every man's estate before the world was made. "I have loved Jacob and hated Esau" (Rom. 9:13), namely, before they were conceived. He tells them that they are chosen in God to be heirs with Him together with His Son of His glory (Eph. 1). And so much briefly concerning	"Which were of old ordained, etc." Here he first sets down the limit which was before all worlds. Secondly, the cause of God's decree, which is of Himself, not of the creature, because the decree was before any creature had any being. And, therefore, Paul says, "God loved Jacob [and] hated Esau before either of them had done either good or evil." "As he has chosen us before the foundation of the world" (Eph. 1:4). And Christ Himself says [in] Matthew, "I thank thee heavenly father that thou hast hid these things from

Thomas Taylor	James Tomlin	Hutton MS
as man does from outward respects, He goes not out of Himself for any motive to choose or refuse, but "because his good pleasure was such" (Matt. 11:26). This confutes the popish error, which affirms that God did decree according to His foresight of faith or infidelity, the saving of some and refusing of others. But this cannot stand, seeing God's decree is in order and time before the creature, which being the latter cannot be the cause of the former.	this doctrine in which occasion offered itself to our meditation in this text.	the wise and prudent of the world, and revealed them to babes. And this thou hast done because it was thy good pleasure."
		[Sermon 3] Jude 4, *"Ungodly men they are, etc"* We have heard the seducers described by two things before: first, by their hypocrisy, [and], secondly, by their eternal estate before God.
Adjunct 3 The third adjunct or property of these seducers is their want of religion: "Ungodly men they are."	**The Third Point.** The third reason is taken from their religion, or rather their want of religion, in these words, "ungodly men they are."	The third thing by which Jude describes them is their religion, and that in these words: "ungodly men they are."
Ungodliness is a sin much spoken of but not so well known, and therefore it is requisite to show the nature of it, that we may know who an ungodly man is; the rather because	Ungodliness is a sin much spoken of but not so well known. Therefore, we will set it down as briefly but substantially as we can. It is a grievous sin, a capital offense, a mother sin of	Ungodliness is a sin much spoken of yet not so much known. Therefore, it is requisite first to know what an ungodly man is, which shall appear by knowing what ungodliness is. It is a great and

Thomas Taylor	James Tomlin	Hutton MS
it is a grievous sin, much greater than any of the seven deadly sins of the papists, being the ground of them all. Secondly, because it is rooted in the bottom of the heart, and cannot be so easily discerned as others, though as dangerous as any. Thirdly, because it is a sin more spiritual against the first commandment of the first table, directed against God Himself, robbing Him of His due honor.	all, even of those seven deadly sins, as the papists and also the old ethnics as Horace, etc., have averred of. It is grounded and rooted in the bottom of the heart, so it is a secret sin, because it is not discerned of man, such a hypocritical and subtle sin it is. It is a spiritual sin, for it is not only against the second table but principally against the first. It respects God and not man, for it is such a sin that it seeks to rob God of His true honor and worship due to Him.	grievous sin, far greater than any of the seven deadly sins, so termed by the papists, for it is the mother sin of them all. The greatness of it appears for that it is rooted in the heart. It is not so well discerned for that it is inward, not outward. It is a sin of the first table and of the first commandment of the first table. And as the first table is a greater commandment than the second, so this being a break of the first, it is a greater sin than those of the second, for the nature of this sin is to rob God of His honor.
For the clear knowledge of which, consider three main parts or properties of ungodliness.	Ungodliness has three main properties: (1) it denies the honor due unto God, (2) it gives that which is due to God to others, and (3) it gives God due honor but not in a due manner.	Ungodliness has three main parts or properties. (1) It denies God honor, which is due to Him. (2) It gives honor due to God to other things than God. (3) It gives to God sometimes His honor due to Him, but not in due manner.
First, that it denies God the honor due unto Him, and that three ways. First, by ignorance it causes the ungodly man to rob Him of His honor, in that he acknowledges not the Godhead, but in his heart he inwardly denies the providence, the presence,	For the first, it causes the ungodly men by not acknowledging God and the Godhead, which is to deny His excellent attributes as mercy, justice, wisdom, and providence, when occasion is offered. "The fool has said in his heart there is no god"	For the first, ungodliness denies God of His honor due to Him [in] three ways. First, it makes the ungodly man bar God of His honor by ignorance, in not acknowledging the Godhead and the power thereof as the power of God, the mercy of God,

Thomas Taylor	James Tomlin	Hutton MS
the justice, mercy, power, and the other attributes of God. "The thought of the heart of the fool" (that is, of every ungodly man) "is that there is no God" (Ps. 14:1). Not that in conscience he is not convinced of the contrary, but by reason of his wicked heart, upon occasion offered, he is willing to acknowledge none.	(Ps. 14:1), that is, the wicked who in their heart acknowledge not the grace and providence of God.	the justice of God, the providence of God, and the presence of God. "The fool has said in his heart there is no God" (Ps. 14); that is, [he] denies in his heart the power, providence, mercy, justice, and presence of God. And in this is the nature of the wicked, that though their conscience accuses them and warns them there is a god, yet their hearts do not acknowledge the form and properties of the Godhead.
Secondly, by not subjecting the conscience and life to the written will and Word of God, but rejecting and renouncing subjection thereunto. Thus Job brings in the ungodly man, saying to the Almighty, "Depart from us, we will have none of thy ways"; which is too outrageous to be the speech of the tongue, but of the heart casting off the Lord's yoke. To whom the King shall say: "Those mine enemies that would not have me to reign over them, bring them hither and slay them before me" (Luke 19:27).	The second way is by not subjecting his conscience, heart, will, and affections to the written Word of God. Such as are disobedient and study such as say, "We will not walk in your ways, depart from us" (Job 21:14). We will not suffer every will to be yoked to God's law, libertas quoniam placam. We will live as we list. The Jews say, "We will not have this man to rule over us" (Luke 19). But says Christ, "Bring these my enemies (such traitors) and slay them before my face."	Second, ungodliness denies God of His honor by keeping back the ungodly man from subjecting his conscience to the law and commandment of God, and [he] denies subjection. "They say also unto God, 'Depart from us, for we desire not this knowledge of thy ways'" (Job 21:14). But to this Christ Himself finds an answer. "Moreover, those mine enemies, which would not that I should reign over them, bring hither and slay them before me" (Luke 19:27).
Thirdly, by not lifting up the heart by invocation of	Third, when they lift not up their [hearts] by	Third, ungodliness denies God of His honor due to

Thomas Taylor	James Tomlin	Hutton MS
God for blessings needful, and in thanksgiving for benefits received. The property of the ungodly man is that "he calleth not upon God" (Ps. 14:4). This point of atheism makes a man like a beast, which looks not up from whence his food falls.	invocation, neither pray to Him for such things they lack, or give some thanks for such benefits which they have received. This property is set upon three heads. "He calls not upon God, which is brutish and swinish behavior, to receive with all greediness the mast under the trees, and never look up from where they come" (Ps. 14:4). *Brutum.*	Him by holding back the ungodly man's heart from praying to God. "They call not upon the Lord" (Ps. 14:4). And that is the property of an ungodly man never to pray to God, and herein they differ not from swine and brute beasts, which receive all things and never look from whence they came.
The second property of ungodliness, to attribute and give this honor, which it denies God, unto something else than God, as when the ungodly man sets his love, joy, fear, or any other affection upon anything besides God. Thus the covetous man becomes an idolater. And in the last times men shall be lovers of pleasures more than of God (2 Tim. 3:4).	The second property is to take away the honor of the Creator and give [it] to the creature, which is when a man displaces and dispossesses himself of God's honor and sets all his will and affection on some other adjunct. Therefore, the covetous man is called an idolater because he makes the eyes his god, and instead of Him sets up an idol in his heart. So says Paul, "Men in the last times shall be lovers of pleasures more than of God" (2 Tim. 3). And this sin is far too manifest in these our days.	The second property: ungodliness gives honor due to God to some other. Thus men do when they set their love, joy, and heart upon some other thing more than upon God. For the honor of God is to have the heart and the affections thereof. Therefore, the covetous man is called in the Scripture an idolatrous man because his heart is more upon his riches than upon God. So, the devil is called a god because men make him their god by setting their heart and delight more upon sinning, that comes from the devil, than upon God. And, therefore, 2 Timothy says, "Men shall be lovers of their pleasures more than God." In a word, he that sets his heart upon anything more than God,

Thomas Taylor	James Tomlin	Hutton MS

Hutton MS: he gives the honor due to God to some other thing.

Thomas Taylor: The third property of it is, when it gives God His due honor, to deny Him the true manner, which causes the ungodly man to content himself with a form and show of godliness, outwardly bearing himself as godly, but inwardly wants the power of it [2 Tim. 3:5]. The heart is not single but full of fraud, doubting, and deceit before God, who looks into it, and delights not with the approaching of the lips, when the heart is removed. By which we see the practice of the ungodly man, sundry ways robbing God of His due honor, which one sin entertained, breeds and nourishes sins of all sorts. And so much we are given to understand in the placing of it here, as the first sin of the seducers producing a great number of sins more, noted in them through the epistle; neither can any other be looked for but that the life should be plentiful in all sins, where the heart is possessed of this ungodliness. The Gentiles acknowledged not God, and therefore He gave them up to "vile

James Tomlin: TThird, the last kind is more secret than the two former, for all the sin lies hidden in the heart, and by the outward appearance they seem to be very religious but yet their hearts are full of sin. This is a hypocritical sin. It has godliness in show but not the power of godliness. They have a double-eye and a double-heart, and our Savior admonishes all His to beware of the leaven of the Pharisees, namely, their double-heart, and exhorts [us] to have a single eye. Therefore, ungodliness is an inborn sin of the heart which seeks to deprive God of His honor. It is a dangerous sin, for if the heart be once tainted therewith, the whole body will sin when occasion is offered. This sin comes from the heart. The profane heart is the cause of this sin. The Jews knowing God would not know Him (Rom. 1). Abraham said, "There is no fear of God in this place" (Gen. 13), and consequently he thought that all manner of ungodliness reigned in that place. Now, that [un]godliness is a sin

Hutton MS: The third property is to give to God honor due to Him, but not in due manner. It is not enough to be godly outwardly and make an outward profession, but he must be inwardly affected, for God must have the worship of the heart. In a word, then, this sin of ungodliness is that mother sin of all. For in this epistle many sins are reckoned up, yet Jude begins with this, purposely after hypocrisy and their estate before God, to show that this is the mother of all that are rehearsed. All the chapter (Rom. 1) consists of a rehearsal of the sins of the Gentiles, and the mother sin of all is a profane and ungodly heart. When Abraham was in the land of Gerar, he would not confess Sarah to be his wife (Gen. 20). Being demanded the cause, he answered, because he thought the fear of God was not in that place, and therefore they would not stick to kill him, showing that where an ungodly heart is, he will not stick to commit any sin.

Thomas Taylor	James Tomlin	Hutton MS

affections" (Rom. 1:26), and this was the ground of all those sins reckoned there, above twenty in number (vv. 29–31). Abraham thought not amiss that he might easily be slain for Sarah his wife (whom therefore he durst not confess) if the "fear of God" were not in Abimelech's court (Gen. 20:11), giving us to know that where the fear of God is not in the heart, there is no bones made of any sin in the life, no not of murder itself.

especially against [God], besides the testimonies, the notation or name thereof tells us plainly.

Use 1. We are hence taught to spy out in ourselves this hidden and secret sin, and heartily to bewail it above all other sins as the mother sin of the rest. But some say, we are not tainted with this sin, we abhor to be counted ungodly. Answer. It is too common a sin among all sorts. We have indeed an outward form of godliness. We come to hear the Word, to pray, to receive the sacraments, but the most want the power of it in their hearts. For, first, the laws bind our outward man to this outward form, but the hearts of men remain secure, seldom thinking of their sin and damnable

The use that we are to make of it is: First, by how much more secret it is, by so much the more must we labor by prayer, and endeavor in ourselves daily to discern the same in ourselves, for it [is] a sin subject to all, even the godly in some manner. And when we have found it, to bewail the same, and crave pardon, and to pray for God's Spirit to aid us, that we might daily fight against it, to keep it under. We are liars if we say this sin be not rife in these days, even among us professing Christianity. We may flatter ourselves that we follow some exercises, we are conversant in God's Word, we receive

Use. This being so grievous a sin, and the mother sin of many more, and the more dangerous because spiritual, we are taught to labor to see and discern this sin in our hearts, and from our hearts to bewail the same above all other. But some will say, "We are not tainted with this sin." I answer: it is a common sin. We indeed join ourselves in holy exercises, we hear the Word, we receive the sacraments, and we have the form of outward obedience because the prince's law commands so much. But there are many that want the power of religion and godliness. Some have very secure hearts, they never

Thomas Taylor	James Tomlin	Hutton MS

Thomas Taylor

estate by it, and seldom sorrowing for the same, and saying, "What have we done?" Secondly, many have the form of godliness, whose hearts are filled with the cares of this life, which choke up the power of godliness, and will not suffer it to seat itself there, seeing the love of the world and the love of God cannot stand together. Thirdly, many having this form cannot abide to subject their hearts and lives unto the laws of God; yea, they would exempt their speeches and affections from such strictness, and count it too much preciseness. These are all fruits of the ungodly heart, of which the fewer we can see in ourselves the more they be, and the more to be bewailed.

Use 2. Further, hence we are to take out that lesson which the apostle teaches, to exercise ourselves unto godliness (1 Tim. 4:7), for if ungodliness be such a mother sin, we must endeavor ourselves to the contrary. For which purpose, we must, first, prepare ourselves thereunto (else we shall fail in

James Tomlin

the sacraments, but what of it? Let us look to our lives; let us look into our hearts. For the political laws of the law bind us to outward obedience. Some never call themselves to account for their sin, but still lay in the cradle of security. Some are filled with the things of this world, neglecting their soul's health. Many are in subjection to the form of worship, but few to the substance. They cannot break to have themselves and all their actions squared by God's law. So more need have we to beware this sin in ourselves and others.

Second, we must follow the rule of Saint Paul (1 Tim. 4), namely, to exercise ourselves no more in the works of darkness but to be clothed with the armor of light [and] to exercise our hearts in the duties of godliness by two means of ways. First, we must prepare ourselves to make a good beginning

Hutton MS

think of their sin, never of the judgment for it, never think to give an account for their sin, never think of hellfire, and therefore never humble themselves inwardly, because they perform outward obedience. But though we have the form of obedience, yet the cares of the world fill and possess the heart, [so] that they will not suffer the power of God to enter. Again, many have the power of religion, yet they cannot brook to have the conscience brought in subjection to every law of God, and therefore many fail in the heart and single eye. Therefore, we must labor to see this sin of ungodliness in our heart and to bewail it. And if we cannot see it, there worse is our case and the more ungodly we [are], for sure it is we have it because it was bred in our bones.

Secondly, we are here taught to exercise ourselves to godliness, and that we may do this we must prepare ourselves before and make a good beginning. Now for to begin well we must acknowledge God's justice to us, God's providence to us, God's mercy to us, and His power. For when the

Thomas Taylor	James Tomlin	Hutton MS
the whole exercise) by learning to acknowledge God's providence, presence, mercy, and justice in everything. When the Galatians "knew not" God, they worshipped them which by nature were no gods (Gal. 4:8). No godliness can stand with the ignorance of God, neither can it be exercised in particular actions unless we behold Him thus in the particulars. Secondly, to this exercise of godliness we must, first, inwardly worship God in our spirits, souls, hearts, and affections, not in lips only, speeches, and outward actions: "For the right worshippers, worship him in spirit and truth" [John 4:23]. Paul "served God in his spirit" [Rom. 1:9].	and proceeding. Therefore, we must learn first to acknowledge God's providence over all things, whereunto knowledge must first be enjoined. The Gentiles, they knew not God, or they could not acknowledge the true God. And so consequently, instead of the true God, they worshipped idols. Then, where there is not knowledge, there is no acknowledgment; and where there is [no] confession, there is no godliness. Second, we must [worship] God in Spirit and truth as Christ says. Romans 1, "To worship God in my spirit," says [this] chapter, [verse] 9, [meaning] when a man by grace can worship God in soul and outward affection. [Ramist structural chart see p. 147]	Galatians knew not, they served them which were no gods. Secondly, that we may exercise ourselves in this holiness, we must worship God in our spirit, and this is right godliness, the other is hypocrisy.
Question. How shall a man do this? Answer. True inward worship stands in two things: first, in faith; secondly, in the actions of faith.	First, seeing we speak of God here contrary to the sin afore spoken of, in this inward worship which belongs to Him especially is twofold, namely, (1) faith [and] (2) the actions of faith.	*Question.* How shall one worship in soul? *Answer.* This worship stands in two things: 1. Faith. 2. Actions of faith.
Faith is that whereby a man generally believes	Faith in God is chiefly divided into three heads:	First, faith is that whereby we generally believe the

Thomas Taylor	James Tomlin	Hutton MS
the whole Word of God, containing the law and the gospel, to be the truth of God itself, and particularly concerning himself three things: first, God's mercy in the forgiving of his own sins; secondly, His presence in all his actions; thirdly, His providence over all events good or bad that befall him.	We must believe and be steadfastly assured of (1) His mercy in forgiving and forbearing us for ourselves; (2) His providence in His fatherly care and protection over us, even over our bodies in feeding and clothing us, etc.; [and] (3) His presence, wheresoever we be He sees us and whatsoever we do. He is ready, therefore, to hear us when we pray unto Him, and of this must we be always assured. The first serves to comfort us and encourage us to ask pardon in the sight of our sins. His providence ought to move us to thanksgiving. His presence serves to comfort us in the good duties in our calling. Yet though we merit not, yet He sees us and forgets us not, but for His mercy's sake rewards us. Second, it serves to deter and provoke us from sin to well doing, seeing he is everywhere always to see our doings. He is altivides, He is θεός ἀπὸ τὸ θεείν because He sees and rewards the wicked according to his evil.	whole Word of God, both New and Old Testaments. Now, especially we believe God's mercy in the forgiveness of sins, God's providence in all things, and God's presence in all places, and this is spiritual worship.

Thomas Taylor	James Tomlin	Hutton MS
The actions of faith are two: first, subjection of the heart unto God in three respects.	Second, the actions of faith are twofold.	The second thing, that is, the actions of faith, is twofold: 1. Subjection. 2. Elevation, or lifting up the heart. Subjection is in three respects.
First, to God's judgment, that seeing He passes sentence against our sins, we also should call ourselves to account for them, confess them, condemn ourselves for them, and entreat for mercy. Secondly, to His Word and laws of both tables by hearty and conscionable obedience, willingly taking up His yoke and suffering ourselves to be directed by all His laws. Thirdly, to the good pleasure of God known by the event, whether sickness or health, want or abundance, in departing from our own wills, and patiently, yea, thankfully submitting them unto His blessed will.	[First,] subjection, which is three[fold]. (1) A subjection to His judgments, which is when we by grace are subject before Him, in the sight of our sins accusing ourselves, and for Christ's sake craving pardon for the same. (2) A willing subjection of the heart and affection to the will of God in His written Word by obedience, when we do lay up to our profit the Word of God, the means of salvation, in our hearts, bringing forth the fruits thereof. (3) When we submit ourselves to God's pleasure. And this His pleasure concerning us is not known till the event of it, when we submit our wills to God's will in all things, though they be contrary to our wills and expectation, as Abraham (Gen. 12 and 22). And these be true examples of a humble subjection of a Christian.	Firstly, to God's judgment, that is when by grace we call ourselves to an account for our sins and entreat mercy for the forgiveness of them. The second subjection is a subjection to His Word, to the law both of the first and second table, when we suffer all our consciences to be ruled by His laws. The third subjection is to the good pleasure of God, as when we rest in God's good will, though it be against our good will. And by these three kinds of subjection do we worship God.
The second action of faith is the elevation or lifting up of the heart unto God	The second fruit of faith is elevation: lifting up the heart to God to ask	The second action of faith is elevation or lifting up of our souls to God. That

Thomas Taylor	James Tomlin	Hutton MS
incessantly, both in suing for His grace and aid in the seasonable supply of our necessities, as also in blessing Him for blessings received. In these stand the practice of the true worship of God in the spirit, which is true godliness, unto which we may be incited by these reasons.	such as we need in body or soul, and to give Him thanks for the benefits we have received. And this is true worship due to God. This is true godliness. The reasons why we should thus follow after godliness are principally three, set down by the apostle Saint Paul.	is done for two causes. First, to ask God's graces. Secondly, to give Him thanks for all His blessings received.
First, because this godliness has the promise of this life and the life to come (1 Tim. 4:8), that is, the godly man has title to all blessings of all kinds. Secondly, godliness is great gain (1 Tim. 6:6). Every man affects gain, but if any man would attain it, let him be godly. Men are often crossed in the world, and things succeed not with them, they are not prospered in their callings and duties of it, and seeing no reason of it, marvel why they should not thrive as well as others; whereas indeed being ungodly men they want that which should bring in their gain. Thirdly, let the consideration of the last judgment joined with the dissolution of heaven and earth move us hereunto: "Seeing all these things shall be dissolved, what manner	(1) "Godliness is great gain" (1 Tim. 6). If we will thrive here on earth and live an acceptable and a good life, if we will be rich and full of worldly wealth, let us *ascultare pietatē*. (2) "It has the promises of this life and a better life." Because then if we follow after godliness, we shall not only be rich, but rich in God. We shall obtain His favor and love, which is better than riches, yea, and lastly everlasting felicity in Christ. (3) "Concerning the last judgment, when all things must be dissolved" (2 Peter 3). Now, because we know not the hour of this dissolution, let us *colere pietatē*, "be godly," and then shall we be taught to wait for His coming and then shall we live soberly and justly in this present evil world, to	To conclude then: to persuade us to exercise this godliness, Paul says, "Godliness is great gain" (1 Tim. 6:6). That is, he that worships God aright, he shall want nothing that he can think either in this life or in the life to come. If, therefore, a man will be rich, let him but be a godly man and worship God aright. He shall presently have great gain. In a word, then, for us which have had the Word of God preached among us, which has been denied to many nations, what must we do [is] as Paul to Titus tells us that we must learn to deny ungodliness, because we have received the grace of God.

Thomas Taylor	James Tomlin	Hutton MS
of persons ought we to be in holy conversation and godliness?" (2 Peter 3:11). As though he had said, seeing nothing else shall stand us in stead but godliness, how are we to frame ourselves to the practice of it? Fourthly, the appearing of grace teaches us to deny all ungodliness, and to live godlily in this present world (Titus 2:12). If this is the end of the gospel's appearing, and we have been they to whom it has appeared with peace and prosperity above forty years, how can we be but inexcusable and speechless before God if we remain untaught in this duty but continue still in the ways of ungodliness?	be heirs of an everlasting kingdom. Amen.	
Adjunct 4 The fourth adjunct whereby the seducers are described is their doctrine, in these words: "they turn the grace of God to wantonness."	**Proceed to the fourth point.** *"Which turn the grace of our God into wantonness."* [Jude 4]	[**Sermon 4**] Jude 4, "Which turn the grace of our God into wantonness." We have heard the three first points whereby the seducers are described. Now follows the fourth point in these words: "which turn the grace of God into wantonness."
In which consider two points: first, the sin or vice here condemned; secondly, the	This has two points: (1) the vice here condemned [and] (2) the	In this point of the description two things [are] to be considered: firstly, the vice here

Thomas Taylor	James Tomlin	Hutton MS
duty or contrary virtue commanded.	virtue contrary to the vice commanded.	condemned, [and,] secondly, the virtue contrary to this vice. For the vice, that it may the better appear, let us see the meaning of these words: "which turn the grace of God into wantonness."

The Vice Condemned
Before we can know the former, we must search out the meaning of the words. And, first, by "grace" is meant the doctrine of the gospel, called in the former verse by the name of "faith." So it is called [in] Titus 2:11, "The grace of God hath appeared, teaching us, etc.," because it teaches us that remission of sins and life everlasting are obtained only by the mere grace of God in Christ.

First, we must know the meaning of this word "grace." By it is understood the grace of God to salvation to every believer, namely, that gospel of Christ Jesus, because it is the doctrine of grace for the remission of sins by Christ, by which we are made heirs of glory.

By "grace," here we are to understand that which before was understood by faith, namely, the doctrine of the gospel. The doctrine is so called "grace" in Titus 2:11–12, "The grace of God that brings salvation unto all men hath appeared and teaches us that we should deny ungodliness, etc." This teaching grace in that place is nothing else but doctrine of remission of sins, and this is called grace because it is the mere grace and mercy of God.

By "wantonness" is properly understood that sin whereby men addict themselves wholly to intemperance, incontinency, and unlawful pleasures. But here it must be taken generally for a licentious profane kind of living and liberty of sinning.

Second, by the word "wantonness" is no[t] meant the particular sin, [but] a provocation to the lust of the flesh, the sum of incontinency (Rom. 7). But it seems to be taken more generally, as namely a free liberty to sin against God when a man gives himself liberty and license to sin.

"Into wantonness." By wantonness properly is meant that sin whereby men addict themselves to incontinency and unlawful pleasures of the flesh. But here it must needs be taken now generally for a profane liberty of sinning, not for the particular sin of inconstancy.

Thomas Taylor	James Tomlin	Hutton MS
"Turn," that is, they displace the grace of God, applying it from a right to a wrong end, and that not only in practice of life but in propounding of doctrine tending thereunto. As though he had more plainly said that whereas the doctrine of grace in the gospel teaches men free justification by faith in Christ without the works of the law, these men pervert this gracious doctrine and teach that therefore men may live as they list, and so themselves do also. By which same sin such seducers are elsewhere noted in the Scripture. Some gathered from Paul's doctrine the same liberty, saying, "Why do we not then evil that good may come of it?" (Rom. 3:8). And some such are mentioned, who beguiled divers with wantonness through the lusts of the flesh, "promising unto them liberty" (2 Peter 2:19).	Third, this vocable "turn" signifies in the original very forcibly, as namely to displace the grace of God, to misconstrue the word and the doctrines of the whole Scripture according to their own fancies, so that it may be most pleasing to their lust. As namely, seeing God, to the comfort and encouragement of His children, in well doing does make a large treatise, even whereof His mercy, and thereupon, seeing He is so merciful, these deceivers presume with confidence to give themselves liberty and will to sin against God, as some gathered from Paul's doctrine, "to do good that evil might come thereon" (Rom. 3:8). Peter (from whom as by the doctrine and manner of phrase it appears Jude gathered this example) said as here, "Men under pretense of godliness crept in, teaching men to live according to their lusts" (2 Peter).	"Turn the grace, etc." "Turn," that is, put the grace of God out of his place and apply it to a coarse end. Now, this misapplying of the grace of God is not only in practice but also in doctrine and teaching. As we see, these seducers did misapply the grace of God in teaching. These seducers Saint Peter describes almost in the same words as they are here set down: "There shall be false teachers among you, which privately shall bring in damnable heresies, even denying the Lord, etc." (2 Peter 2:1).
Ecclesiastical histories mention many such who sprung up after the apostles' days, as the Libertines, Simon Magus and his disciples, who taught that men might lawfully commit fornication. So	And Christ's name has been generally used in the old ages. Simon Magus and his disciples taught men that they might lawfully commit fornication and adultery, which is most abominable. The	Of these seducers in ancient times we read of many, as Simon Magus and his disciples. Also, the disciples of Basilides and innumerable others, which teach the liberty of sin because of God's

Thomas Taylor	James Tomlin	Hutton MS
also the disciples of Basilides, Eunomius, and the Gnostics, heretics who taught that men might live as they list, seeing how such liberty was procured them, being freed from being under the law any longer. Which sin died not with those cursed heretics, but the devil has in these last days revived it, especially in four sorts of men.	Gnostics also, as Eusebius, etc., taught the people to sin grossly against God, against the first and second table. And now, in these flourishing times of the gospel, this sin dies not, but is renewed again afresh, especially in [the following] sort of men.	mercy, which is nothing else than to turn the grace of God into wantonness. And this old and ancient sin, the devil in this our age has again renewed. And that is in four sorts of men.
First, the Libertines of this age, who hold with the former, that being under grace we are free from the obedience of the law.	First, the libertines of this age teach men to be enemies to the law of grace, because we are under grace (say they) and the law can take no hold of us. We are not so bound to keep the law but live as we list. We owe no obedience thereto, seeing Christ for us has fulfilled it.	The first kind are the libertines of this age, men that are enemies to the law of God, teaching us that because we are under grace, therefore we are not under the obedience of the law, but that the law is abolished.
Secondly, the Anabaptists, who (upon the consideration of abundant grace and peace in the New Testament, and of the liberty obtained by Christ) teach that civil jurisdiction and magistracy is unlawful, as also to make war, and to take an oath before a magistrate; which sort of men are not so well known here as in other churches, but are dangerous enemies (wheresoever) both to the grace of God and good of	Second, the Anabaptists who because they find it written in God's Word, "I will pour out my Spirit upon all flesh" (Joel 2), "Plenty of grace shall be as long as the moon endures" (Ps. 92), therefore they make the magistracy to be void and that there need be no oaths, etc. And thus, they play upon God's grace, presuming to give liberty to have all masters, whereas if this were not,	The second kind of men which in this age turn the grace of God into wantonness are Anabaptists, who because they find in Scripture that God has promised plenty of grace, they teach that all magistracy and civil jurisdiction is unlawful.

Thomas Taylor	James Tomlin	Hutton MS
man, for where the civil sword does cease, there can no society stand in safety.	there could be no society among us.	

Thomas Taylor	James Tomlin	Hutton MS
Thirdly, another kind of Libertines are the papists and the popish church with the whole Roman religion, themselves being open enemies unto the grace of God, and their whole religion turning it into wantonness and liberty of sinning, and that divers ways. First, God having of His grace given unto the church a power of the keys to open and shut heaven, that religion has turned it into an instrument, first, of profaneness, in setting up a new priesthood to absolve and loose men's sins properly, in offering a sacrifice for the quick and the dead, so abolishing the sacrifice of Christ. Secondly, of injustice, for by it they depose kings and princes, they free subjects from their allegiance, they stir them up and encourage them to conspiracies, rebellions, and maintain in other states, factions, civil wars, and seductions, and all by virtue of their power. Thirdly, of horrible covetousness, for by it they sell pardons for thousands of years, the	Third, the present Roman Church [first] is an enemy to Christian liberty, and they turn God's grace into wantonness. For God has given a gift to His ministers for the profit of His church by the keys, and they add them as a means of profaneness and covetousness. For by that they set up a new priesthood and sacrifice. They offer every day sacrifice for the sins of the people. And so, they seek to abolish the sacrifice of Christ Jesus, who once for all offered His body for the ransom of many. Secondly, by the same he challenges rights over all nations. All princes and people must be in subjection to him. They must kneel down, and kiss his toes, and lead his horses in his progress. Thirdly, again (to pass many others) he makes the keys to be means of vice and filthiness, for thereby he sells pardon at their pleasure, and this their licentious liberty is most abominable.	The third kind are the professed papists and the present Church of Rome with their religion which does turn the grace of God into wantonness, which is manifest by this. God has given to His church the power of the keys to open and to shut. The Roman religion has converted this power of the keys and made it first an instrument of profaneness, for by this power of the keys the Roman Church has set up a new priesthood of forgiving sins and offers sacrifice to this priest. Secondly, this their power of the keys is an instrument of injustice, when by the power of the keys they stir up rebellions and seditions. Thirdly, it is an instrument of all covetousness, for by the power of the keys they sell pardons, and thereby the pope does daily enrich himself. And if there were nothing else, yet this one practice of the Church of Rome proves they turn the grace of God into wantonness. No man that holds this Roman religion is any

Thomas Taylor	James Tomlin	Hutton MS

Thomas Taylor

which sales have brought to the Church of Rome the third part of the revenues of all Europe; which one practice, if there were no more, proves plainly that that church turns the grace of God to the liberty of sin.

Secondly, their whole religion is a corrupted religion, and makes the receivers of it the children of Satan more than before. For, first, it makes men hypocrites, requiring nothing but an external, bodily, and ceremonial worship, without any inward power of it. As in fasting, it requires only a show of it, as to abstain from flesh and white meats, but they may use most delicate fishes, the strongest wines, and sweetest spices. And in other parts of their religion is no less hypocritical. Secondly, it makes men proud and arrogant, teaching the freedom of will unto good, if the Holy Ghost do but a little help it, that a man can merit by his works, that he can satisfy God's justice by suffering for sin, yea, that he can perform some works of supererogation. Who can hold these points

James Tomlin

Second, again, their religion is most wicked, for it serves wholly to nourish sin and uncleanness, and makes both carnal and sensible libertines. And all their service to God is but a bodily and corporal service, as (1) in fasting they must eat no flesh and white meat, but spiced wine, etc., they do account lawful, and of this sort is their ceremonial religion. (2) It makes men proud and insolent that they may by their good works merit salvation. (3) It makes them presumptuous, for they affirm that they have of nature free will to do of themselves what good they will by the light help of the Spirit, whereas the very will is of God. (4) That they can fully satisfy God's wrath by their own suffering for their sins, whereas indeed there is no name in heaven or earth whereby we can be saved but by Christ Jesus.

Hutton MS

whit the better for it, but the more <…> it only shows <…> <…> them in their sin.

And, first, it makes them gross hypocrites, for this religion is nothing but a ceremonial and bodily worship which appears among other [of] their ceremonies [as much as] in this one. Religion requires fasting; therefore, they command fasting from flesh, yet they give liberty to use in the fasting the strongest wine and strongest spices that are. And what fasting can this be but ceremonial fasting? Secondly, this religion makes them proud, for they teach that man by his works may merit heaven and by his sufferings may satisfy for his sins. Thirdly, this religion makes man secure, for it teaches that men may [by] the power of the keys have a full pardon for their sins if they are [to] pay the money requested, and though they fail in payment, yet it teaches that they may make amends in purgatory.

Thomas Taylor	James Tomlin	Hutton MS

Thomas Taylor

and be humble? Thirdly, it makes men secure, teaching that they may have full pardon of all their sins by the power of their keys for money, and that though they have no merits of their own, they may buy the merits of other men; yea, although in their death they fail of repentance, yet for some money they may be eased in purgatory. What shall any rich man now care how he live or die, seeing all shall be well with him for a little money? Fourthly, it makes men in their distress desperate, teaching that no man can be assured of his salvation without some revelation. Fifthly, it revives the old sin of these seducers, teaching that divers men and women may not marry, that were adultery, and yet openly tolerating stewes and uncleanness. Which what is it else but to maintain wantonness? Whereby the chief teachers of that church witness themselves the right succession, not of the apostles (as they pretend) but of these seducers and other wicked heretics old and new.

James Tomlin

(5) Most notoriously, by their damnable doctrine, they say that all authority of life and death eternal is in the pope's hand, and that if they die, not having repented for their sins, they may go into purgatory, and therefore [by] a little bodily purification they may earn eternal life. (6) The pope tolerates communion stews and harlots, flat forbidden in the seventh commandment, and in all the law. (8) Again, their religion makes a man, when he is ready to give up the ghost, despair that then they are ready to fly to God. For they doubt whether they shall be saved or not, whereas the godly, they are sure and certain of their salvation. And though when a Christian gave Machiavellian (a chief doctrine among the papists) counsel: flee to God to hope on Him, and cast away all merit, etc. "Yea (said he desperately), you may tell me now of this, but tell not any of the rest of my brethren." And therefore, we see the very end of their doctrine, that desperately and despairingly they end their lives. (9) A most palpable note whereby they turn God's grace into wantonness

Hutton MS

Fourthly, it makes a man in temptation to be desperate. Lastly, it renews the old sins of old heresies. It makes them to turn the grace of God into wantonness, which appears as in other things so in this one, that it forbids marriage, yet it tolerates fornication by the maintaining of these stewes. And this to turn the grace of God into wantonness.

Thomas Taylor	James Tomlin	Hutton MS
	is this: that they bind certain degrees of men to continency to abstain from matrimony, and so some that have not the gift of continence fall into the most filthy sin, to the great dishonor of God.	
The fourth sort of Libertines are carnal and formal Protestants, who first turn the counsel of God's election into wantonness by reasoning thus: if I am elected to salvation, I shall be saved, let me live as I will; or if not, I cannot be saved do what I will or can, because God's counsels are unchangeable; and thus conclude to spend their days in all wantonness.	The fourth sort of those that abuse the grace of God are among ourselves, and especially in five sorts of persons. First, they that turn the decree of God concerning eternal election and reprobation into a sin saying that if they be ordained to salvation, they shall be [saved], and contrarily those that be predestinated to confusion shall be confused, and so they promise liberty of living unto themselves.	The fourth kind of men which turn the grace of God into wantonness are among us, carnal and formal Protestants. First, many turn God's grace to wantonness by election and dispute thus: "If I be predestined to salvation, I shall be saved; if not, I shall be damned. Live I as I can, God's decree cannot be altered."
Secondly, they turn the mercy of God into wantonness, thus reasoning in their hearts: because God is merciful, therefore I will defer my repentance as yet, for at whatsoever time a sinner repents, God will put away all his sins out of His remembrance. What, young saints, old devils? Thus the timely acceptance of God's mercy offered is become a reproach. Besides many more, who,	Second, youth who being young and lusty, strong of body, and wanton, do defer the time of their repentance till they be old, gathering from the place of Isaiah, "At what time soever a sinner repents, etc., he shall be saved." And if they say, "If we can but an hour before our death repent it is sufficient," and so they promise themselves to sinning, abusing the long-suffering of God. The	Secondly, many abuse the mercy and longsuffering of God, for because God is merciful, they defer their repentance while they are young till they are old, and they plead for themselves, "young saints, old devils" and "at what time however a sinner repents, God will put his wickedness out of His remembrance, etc." And thus, the longsuffering of God is abused, and so

Thomas Taylor	James Tomlin	Hutton MS
because the Lord defers punishment, set their hearts to do evil.	preacher says, "Because God defers his plagues they will go on in their wickedness," but cries to them, saying, "Remember thy creator in the days of thy youth" (Eccl. 12).	His grace is turned into wantonness.
Thirdly, others under pretence of brotherly love, misspend all that they have in wantonness, riot, excess, company keeping, gaming, to the beggaring of themselves and undoing of their own families, unto which they ought to show their love in the first place.	A third sort are such prodigal epicures of this world, which are of [three] sorts. (1) Such as be too prodigal in spending the blessing of God on others, either for praise of men or in sign of love. (2) Such as spend away their substance in gaming. (3) Such as make away all by riotness excess of wantonness in eating and drinking like filthy gluttons whose belly is their God, and so at length come to beggary or thievery.	Thirdly, many under the pretense of brotherly love do break out into all excess of sin, misspending and lavishing those riches which God has given them, in gaming and revelry, and [not] keeping good fellowship, and all under pretense of love.
Fourthly, others under pretext that the Jewish Sabbath is abrogated, and that Christ has brought such liberty as has abolished distinctions of times, take liberty to keep no Sabbath at all, whence many tradesmen will do what they list on this day, and dispatch those businesses which they can find no time for in the weekdays.	Fourth, profane and worldly persons such as make no difference of days, and will indeed keep no Sabbath (I mean spiritual rest upon the Sabbath) but turn the Sabbath, which should be a day of holiness, to profaneness in speeches and actions by unlawful pleasures and delights.	Again, fourthly, many turn the grace of God into wantonness in keeping no Sabbath. And for their excuse they say they are not bound to the Jewish Sabbath, and therefore will make no difference of time and so keep no Sabbath at all.

Thomas Taylor	James Tomlin	Hutton MS
Fifthly, some because they would humble themselves, commit divers sins and continue in others. These say in themselves, let us continue in sin that grace may abound. All these sorts of men turn the grace of God into wantonness, and practice the vice here condemned.	Fifth, a last sort are such as mock the ground of religion: sin and wickedness such as the apostle speaks of, "who do evil that good may ensue." Those all, which we have spoken of, do most palpably translate the grace of God [and] make it the ground of their sin.	Lastly, some because they have grace given them, sin willingly, and say, "Let us sin that grace may abound." But these and all the most turn the grace of God into wantonness. Thus much of the vice.

The Virtue Commanded

Thomas Taylor	James Tomlin	Hutton MS
The second thing to be considered is the contrary virtue, and that is to make a godly and holy use of the grace of God, and to apply it to the right end for which God vouchsafes it unto us, to wit, that we might be thankful unto Him, and testify the same in obedience to all His laws.	Thus far have we spoken of the vice forbidden. Now comes the second part of this point to be spoken, namely, the virtue that we must do contrary to the former vice. Which is that we make a good use of the grace of God any ways bestowed upon us, which we shall do if we apply it to a good end. The end of God's grace is that we might be thankful to God for the same, which is proved by these reasons.	Now, in a word, of the virtue. The virtue, contrary to the vice forbidden herein, is to make a holy use of the grace of God. This is done when the grace of God is applied to the right end. The end why God gave His grace is that we should be thankful to Him and testify this thankfulness by our obedience.
Which appears, first, by testimony of Scripture: "We are delivered out of the hands of our spiritual enemies, to serve him in holiness and righteousness" (Luke 1:74–75). "We are under grace, therefore let us give up the members of our bodies, weapons of righteousness" (Rom. 6:16).	First, by the Scriptures, "He delivered us from our enemies, wherefore? That we might serve him in holiness all the days of our life." Romans 6:10. "The grace of God hath appeared teaching us to deny the works of the flesh and to live righteously and soberly in this present evil world" (Titus 2).	That this is true appears, first, by the testimony of Scripture. "We being delivered out of the hands of our enemies should serve him without fear" (Luke 1:74). Romans 6, the whole chapter, especially the 15th, 16th, [and] 17th verses, "What then, shall we sin? etc." "For the grace of God that

Thomas Taylor	James Tomlin	Hutton MS
"The grace of God hath appeared, teaching us to deny ungodliness" (Titus 2:11).		brings salvation unto all men has appeared" (Titus 2:11).
Secondly, the end of all God's grace is that we should be furthered in holiness of life. We are elected that we might be holy; the end of our calling is that we may be saints; justification frees from punishment of sin; sanctification from corruption and sin itself; faith purifies the heart; love contains us in obedience; he that has hope purges himself; and so of all other graces.	Second, the end of our election is that we might be holy. The end of our calling was that we might be holy. "As I am holy," says Christ, "so be you holy." Sanctification, the end of it [is] to free us from bondage. Faith purifies the heart. Hope to purify the affections. The end of love to make men obedient to the command.	Secondly, this appears by all points of [the] gospel and newness of life. For the chief end of election is that we might be holy. Likewise, the chief end of vocation is holiness, and therefore Paul says to the Romans, "You are called [to] be holy." The end of sanctification is to free man from the corruption of our sins. The end of justification is to free man from the guilt of those sins. The end of faith is to purify the heart. The end of love is to keep man to keep the commandments.
Thirdly, Christ is a Mediator two ways: first, by merit to procure life and work our salvation; secondly, by efficacy, that is, whereby His death is powerful to cause us to die to sin, and His resurrection to raise us from the grave of sin to a new life. And He is no Mediator by His merit to those who are destitute of this efficacy.	Third, another reason may be drawn from our Savior. He is a mediator between God and us, first, by the merit of His death and passion to forgive our sin [and] to reconcile us again; second, by the efficacy of His resurrection, namely, to raise us from sin to holiness in Him. The end and scope of all is to allure us, first, to thankfulness; second, to be obedient and holy in our vocations; third, to move us to amendment of life.	Thirdly, Christ is a mediator and that by two ways: 1. Merit. 2. Efficacy or virtue. Now, Christ by His virtue and efficacy does as well forgive sin as by His merit He does kill sin. And, therefore, if we have grace by His merit and not forgiveness by His efficacy, what avails it? Therefore, having the first, let us be thankful for it, that we may have the second.

Thomas Taylor	James Tomlin	Hutton MS

The Use. We have in this land been many years partakers of this grace of God. Our duty then is to make a holy use of it, and walk thankfully before God. "I beseech you by the mercies of God" (which he had in the former chapter mentioned) "that ye give up yourselves a holy sacrifice to God" (Rom. 12:1). No more forcible argument can be urged to stir up men to thankful obedience than this, for if God's mercy in Christ cannot move, what will? Let this then persuade us likewise. If we believe God to be our Father, that is a great grace. Let this grace move us to walk as children before Him. Let the grace of our redemption move us to walk as redeemed ones, rescued out of such captivity wherein we were enthralled to sin and Satan, seeing it were a madness to return to such bondage again. If Christ is dead for us, let that grace move us to die to sin. If He being risen again sits at God's right hand that we might sit there with Him, let that grace move us to walk as those that are risen with Him, and have our conversation in heaven, seeking (even

Therefore, with Paul we must learn this doctrine: in all things to submit ourselves to God's Word, "I beseech you by the mercy of God, offer up your bodies and souls as an acceptable sacrifice to God."

Fourth, another end is that we take heed we sin no more, that we may hold our bodies and souls in awe before Him, endeavoring to walk before Him unblameably. Therefore, to conclude, the sum of all is thankfulness, obedience. And the one must show forth the other: our thankfulness must [be] showed to Him throughout the whole course of our lives by walking in His precepts. *Res essentiales.*

The use then of this second point is that we, having been partakers of the grace of God, our duty is to make use of the same grace. The principal use (as we said before) is to be thankful to God by our obedience. And, therefore, Paul says, "I beseech you brethren by the mercies of God, to present yourselves as an acceptable sacrifice to God." Where the ground of his exhortation is the grace of God. If we believe God to be our Father and Christ our Redeemer, we do it by grace. Let us, therefore, for this grace, show ourselves thankful by our obedience: to God that we may seem His children, to Christ that it may appear that we are redeemed. He that is delivered out of prison and set at liberty, if he desires again to lay in the dungeon, he must needs be accounted a mad man. Likewise, we being delivered by grace from all our sins and the guilt thereof, if we do now desire again to lay in the dungeon of our sins, are we to be accounted less mad? Now, the chief way to escape this dungeon and prison of our sins from which we are freed is to show ourselves

Thomas Taylor	James Tomlin	Hutton MS
while we are below) the things that are above; and so of the rest.		thankful to God by our obedience for delivering us.

[**Sermon 5**] Jude 4, *"Which turn the grace of God into wantonness, and deny God the only Lord, and our Lord Jesus Christ."*

We have begun to speak of the fourth point whereby those seducers are described, namely, by their doctrine in turning the grace of God into wantonness. We have shown the meaning of the words.

Thomas Taylor	James Tomlin	Hutton MS
Further, the apostle, to make those seducers more odious, says not simply they turn the grace of God but "of our God" into wantonness, which notes the indignity of their act, in which consider these things.	Now more nearly to the text ("the grace of our God"). Out of these words a notable point of doctrine, the several parts whereof are three: (1) how God comes to be our God, (2) what we ought to do to have God to be our God, [and] (3) the weight and moment of this ground, in that we have God the God of heaven to be our God.	Now follows another point to be considered in this point, and that is in these words: "Turn the grace of our God" and not only the grace of God. For [the] better understanding of this circumstance, three things are to be considered: (1) how God comes to be our God; (2) what you must do that God be our God; [and] (3) what benefit we have by God's being our God.
	For the first ground, we must know that God became our God not by any desert of us but by His gracious covenant made unto us in His gospel, wherein He publishes	For the first, it is answered, God comes to be our God not by any merit of ours but by the free and gracious covenant of God, the covenant of the gospel,

Thomas Taylor	James Tomlin	Hutton MS

First, by what means God becomes "our God"; and that is not by any merit of ours but by means of the gracious covenant propounded in the gospel, promising pardon and remission of sin in and by Christ. This is called the "new covenant" which the Lord contracts with His people, where writing His law in their inward parts, He becomes their God, and they His people (Jer. 31:33).

Secondly, what must we do to say truly and in assurance that God is our God? Answer. We must for our parts make a covenant with Him, unto which is required a consent on either party. First, on God's part, that He will be our God, which we shall find, not in any revelation besides the Scriptures, but generally in the Word, and more specially in the ministry of the gospel and administration of the sacraments, annexed as seals unto the covenant; in which God does as surely covenant with us as if He should from heaven speak unto us. Secondly, on our part is required consent, of which there be two degrees. First, when

remission of sins and mercy and grace through Christ Jesus. He says to the Israelites, "I will make a new covenant" (Jer. 31), and He sets down the tenor of the covenant, "I will write my law in their hearts. And they shall be my people and I will be their God" (verse 33). And of this covenant between Him and us, He is said to be our God.

Second, now the covenant standing thus on His side, we must learn what we must do on our part, that this covenant may be kept, that God may be our God. We must also make a league and covenant with God, for in every covenant there is a double consent, a mutual consent of both parties. And in this regard, on our side God will be our God. Now His covenant is specified in His Word. The dispensation of the gospel is as sure a bond as if He Himself should now speak to us from heaven. The second consent is of us, which consent, if it be mutual, there be two degrees of the same. First, outward in profession when we profess the

revealing our remission of sins and everlasting life by Christ. [In] Jeremiah, 31st chapter, God makes a new covenant with the Israelites, and in the 33rd verse the tenor of the covenant is set down, which is this: "I will put my law in their inward parts, and I will be their God and they shall be my people." And upon this ground the whole church of God says, "God is our God."

For the second point, what we must do that God may be our God, the answer is that we must make covenant with God. Now, as in every covenant there is a twofold consent, namely, of either party, so in this covenant with God there must be a double consent: one consent on God's part that He will be our God, [and] one consent on our part that we will be His people. For the first consent, God propounds His consent generally in His written Word and more particularly in the ministry of His Word and sacraments. For God, giving to us His Word and sealing it with His sacraments, does as really give consent to us to be our

Thomas Taylor	James Tomlin	Hutton MS
we make an outward profession of faith, hear the Word, receive the sacraments, baptism and the Lord's Supper, which serve to distinguish us from Jews, Turks, etc. This is somewhat but not sufficient to make God our God, seeing it is common to the very hypocrites themselves.	worship of God by receiving the seals of our faith as the sacraments. And this the hypocrite may do. Therefore, this outward degree is somewhat [of value], but it is not sufficient but only distinguishes them in show from Turks, etc.	God as if He should speak from heaven. Having then the Word and ministry, we have God's consent in the covenant. Now, there remains a second consent, that is ours, that we take God to be our God. Our covenant has two degrees. One degree is outward in outward profession, where man receives the outward seals of God's covenant, namely, His Word and sacraments. And to do this is something, for hereby we are distinguished from Turks, but this not sufficient.
Secondly, seeing he is not a Jew which is one outwardly, but which is a Jew within, there is required in our consent a further degree, which stands in an inward consent of the heart whereby a man takes God for his God. Which is then begun when, first, a man acknowledges and bewails his sins; secondly, when he endeavors to be reconciled to God; thirdly, when he purposes never to sin again.	But the second degree is needful, which is inward. This mutual consent is [three]fold. (1) When a man does by grace acknowledge himself to be a miserable sinner, a vile wretch in the sight of God. (2) When he humbles himself before God in the consideration thereof, laying open his nakedness and seeking by all means to be reconciled to God. (3) When he promises and strives with himself never to commit the same again and endeavors by all means possible to live in obedience and holiness before him.	And, therefore, there is a second degree in our consent, and that is the consent of the heart unto God. Now this consent of the heart is when these three things are performed. First, when with bitterness we bewail our sins. Secondly, when we care to do the will of God and reconcile ourselves to the same. Thirdly, when we purpose in our hearts never to sin again. And when we do thus, our covenant with God, that He shall be our God and we His people, will be for authentical, as

Thomas Taylor	James Tomlin	Hutton MS

| | | any bargain between man and man. |

When this covenant is thus concluded by consent of both parties, a man may safely and truly say that God is his God.

Thus is the covenant mutually consented, and thus God vouchsafes to be called our God when by grace we walk obediently before Him. And thus is the virtue of the covenant, [namely, that] we may call Him our God.

Now seeing we know these things, our duty is to labor to be settled and assured in our conscience that God is our God. For, first, in this assurance is the foundation of all true comfort. All the promises of God are hereupon grounded and herein accomplished, that God is our God. "Be not afraid, I am thy God" (Isa. 41:10). Yea, Christ being upon the cross, having the pangs of hell upon Him, herein stayed Himself: "My God, my God" (Ps. 22:1). So David, being ready to be stoned to death, "comforted himself in the Lord his God" (1 Sam. 30:6).

The third thing is the benefit of this league. To say truly, by the virtue of the covenant, that God is our God is the greatest comfort that a mortal man can have in this life. This was or might have been the greatest joy of Israel: "I am thy God." "I am the Lord thy God" (Ex. 20). And to the comfort of His church, God always rehearses this ground: "I am the God of Abraham, Isaac, and Jacob." And our Savior Christ, when the agony and passion was in the greatest measure upon Him, stayed His manhood in this saying: "My God! My God! Why hast thou forsaken me?" David in all afflictions stayed himself on his God: "O my God, I cry unto thee daily." And David, being in a narrow strait, stayed himself assuredly in God's protection, saying, "My

For the third point, what benefit we have by having God to be our God. It is answered that, first, it is the foundation of all our comfort. In the 41st [chapter] of Isaiah, God lays down singular comforts for His children, and the main foundation of all is this: "I am your God." Christ in His <…> agony had this comfort, crying, "My God, My God" (Matt. 27:46). David in the same words (Ps. 30). "My God, my God, my God, why hast thou forsaken me?" (Ps. 22:1). David also, when he looked for nothing by death, comforts himself in that he had a God who kills and makes alive, brings down to the ground and raises up (1 Sam. 2:6).

Thomas Taylor	James Tomlin	Hutton MS
	God is at hand to deliver us." Yea, this the foundation of our comfort, that by the virtue of this covenant our bodies at the last day shall arise to be glorified with God in heaven. The use of this doctrine is twofold: First, this is a good ground of faith, namely, to provoke us always to engraft the knowledge hereof in our hearts, and also never to doubt and distrust a whit of His help in things we go about, or His mercy when we are in misery, sickness, or danger, but always rely on Him to our comfort: "He is my God, therefore will he have a care for me."	
And not only is it the foundation of all our comfort in this life, but of our happiness after death itself, being the ground of those two main articles of our faith: the resurrection of the body and the immortality of the soul. For by virtue of this covenant alone shall we rise again after death to life, glory, and immortality; as Christ Himself disputing against the Sadducees, from hence proves the resurrection, in that "God is the God of Abraham, Isaac, and Jacob."		We are then here taught to labor every day to use all good means to have this grounded in our heart: that God is our God. For when friends, health, wealth, and all things forsake us, this is the ground and foundation of our comfort: to have God [as] our God.
Secondly, it is the ground of all obedience. The prophet, exhorting men thereunto, uses this as a reason: "For he is the Lord our God, and we are the people of his hands" (Ps. 95:7). The preface of the moral law, enforcing obedience, lays the same ground: "For I am the Lord thy God which	Second, this is a notable ground of obedience. "He is our God, we are the sheep of his pasture" (Ps. 95). The whole scope of the 50th Psalm is to assure the Israelites that God is their God, and so that they should walk obediently and uprightly before Him. And if we be thus persuaded and	So is it the foundation of all unfeigned obedience. The whole [of] Psalm 95 is a psalm of obedience, and the 7th verse is a ground of the whole psalm, where he says, "For he is our God and we his people, etc." The 50th Psalm, likewise, is an exhortation to obedience to God's Word. And the

Thomas Taylor	James Tomlin	Hutton MS
brought thee out of the land of Egypt." See also Psalm 50:7. And whosoever is truly persuaded that God is his God, cannot but obey Him.	have this grounded in our heart, it is impossible that we should sin again against God. David confessing of himself, "I have put my trust in thee O Lord" (Ps. 31), and the ground thereof follows, "I said thou art my God." So that the ground of all spiritual worship is this: to be assured of exceeding mercy and fatherly providence of God to sinners in vouchsafing to be called their God. Thus much for the fourth point.	7th verse is a ground of all: "Hear, O my people, for I am God, even thy God." And indeed, whosoever is persuaded that God is his God, he cannot willingly sin, for the ground of all spiritual worship is grounded upon this. And thus much of the first point, namely, the doctrine of the seducers in this word: "Turn the grace of God into wantonness."
Adjunct 5 The fifth property of these seducers is "that they deny God the only Lord, and our Lord Jesus Christ." Thus are they described by their manners.	**The Fifth Point** *"And deny God the only Lord and our Lord Jesus Christ."* The last point in this verse of these seducers are their manners, which is set down by their sin in denying not only God but Christ Jesus the redeemer of mankind.	The fifth and last thing whereby those seducers are described is their lives and manners, in these words: "Deny God, the only Lord and our Lord Jesus Christ."
The translators of this epistle were (as it seems) of [the] opinion that these words are properly spoken of God the Father and of God the Son also. But by the tenor of the words in the original, it seems that they are all to be understood of Christ, and not of the Father, and are thus to be read: "Which	Here we must consider the meaning of the text, namely, the true and significant meaning of the words, namely, these, "God the only Lord and our Lord Jesus Christ." There are sundry opinions hereof. Some read it thus: "God the Lord, etc." Others: "God the only ruler, which is Jesus Christ."	In these words, there may seem some difficulty in the translation of these words: "God the Lord, and our Lord Jesus Christ." For some think these words to be meant both of God the Father and God the Son: God the Father in these words, "God the Lord," [and] God the Son in

Thomas Taylor	James Tomlin	Hutton MS
deny that only Ruler who is God and our Lord Jesus Christ." Again, the tenor of the words, being borrowed from the Epistle of Peter, may thence be rightly expounded. Now Peter speaking of the same sin of these seducers, applies it only to be a denial of Christ: "they deny the Lord that bought them" (2 Peter 2:1). In the words then consider two things: first, the sin here condemned, namely, "to deny Jesus Christ"; secondly, a description of Christ.	Others have: "The Lord God, etc." But as the variety hereof, in sense they come all together, and because this epistle was borrowed from Peter, as it is evident by the style and phrase, and these words are, "Who denied the Lord who bought them" (2 Peter 3), and so I hold that the most significant, that by the "Lord and our Lord Jesus Christ" is nothing but a synonym of words given to Christ our Lord to the excellency of His office of mediatorship, which they deny. And, therefore, I read it thus (as it is in effect), "and deny God the only ruler which is our Lord Jesus Christ."	these words, "And the Lord Jesus Christ." But they seem to me to be understood only of God the Son, and that for these reasons. (1) Because the tenor of the words do apply all that is spoken to Christ, and not to God the Father. (2) Because Saint Peter uses the same words almost, in the same sense, "denying him that has bought them" (2 Peter 2:1). So, the meaning is they deny God the only Lord, that is the ruler, even the Lord Jesus Christ. And thus much for the words, now to the matter.
	The meaning of the word "deny." To deny Christ is in this place to renounce Christ, to forsake Him in their deeds, and to make His death void as much as in them lays. We must understand these words to receive their ground from the redemption of Christ, which office of His they denied, that is renounced and acknowledged not. *Objection.* But here rests an objection: how should they be redeemed by Christ and yet ordained to judgment?	
For the first, "to deny Jesus Christ" is to renounce and forsake Christ, and so much as in a man lies to make His death void and of none effect. Now because this denial presupposes a redemption (as Peter mentions: "they denying the Lord that bought them"), this question is to be cleared: how these men being reprobates, can be said to be redeemed by Christ? Answer. We		In this point two things are to be considered. First, the fault and sin of those seducers, that is, in denying of Christ. The second thing is a description of Christ, describing Him to be God, the only Lord and our Lord Jesus Christ, which is done to <…> the former, namely, their sin. For the first, to deny Christ is to renounce Christ, and as much as in men lies to make the death of Christ of no

Thomas Taylor	James Tomlin	Hutton MS

must not think that they were in God's decree ever redeemed, for then had they been saved. "He doing whatsoever he willeth" (Ps. 115:30). But it is to be meant in regard of themselves and other men, for both in their own conceit and judgment they were redeemed as also in the judgment of others, who are to be led by the rule of charity in passing their judgment upon men, and to account of them as redeemed, leaving all secret judgments to God.

Answer. We must know that they were [not] redeemed, neither was the blood of Christ shed for them, neither have they any part therein, namely, by the decree and will of God. For whatsoever He wills in grace that He <…>, and says that He does, and so because Peter said they "denied him that bought them," we must know that they were bought by the counsel and decree of God. And it is our part to judge every one redeemed of God, although they be utter enemies for those reasons, expressed before in the catechism concerning imputation. And indeed, all that profess Christ we must judge for the redeemed in regard of their profession. These professed Christians were but yet denied Him by their deeds. As they denied Him to be their only ruler but they acknowledge Him to be the redeemer as appears [in] Titus 3. And that they are redeemed by Him and yet they do derogate much from the godhead of Christ.

effect. And this denial of Christ does presuppose the redemption of Christ. Objection. Those seducers are said before to be preordained to condemnation, and secondly are said to deny the redemption of Christ. Now, if they were redeemed by Christ, how could they be preordained to condemnation? Answer. These were redeemed by Christ, but not in the decree of God. But they are redeemed in their own judgment. For we do and ought to believe that every Christian man is redeemed, so then in regard of the judgment of the church and in regard of their own judgment and profession. So they profess so much by their outward appearance, they are said to be redeemed, <…> of God's decree.

Secondly, the description of Christ by three

To make their sin more odious he adds very

The second thing in this point is the aggravating of

Thomas Taylor	James Tomlin	Hutton MS
things: first, that He is a Ruler, yea, an only Ruler, a "Lord" and Ruler over all things in general, in heaven, earth, and hell, and more specially a "Lord" over His elect only. And in that He is said to be an only Ruler, it must not be meant as excluding the Father and Holy Ghost, but all false gods and false christs, as the Father is called the only God (John 17:3), for all outward actions of the Trinity are common to all the persons. Secondly, that He is "God," which is a notable place against all Arians to prove the Godhead of Christ. Thirdly, He is said to be "our Lord." Ours in two respects especially: first, of the free donation of His Father, who gave to Him a people to be Lord and King over before all worlds; secondly, in regard of His work of redemption which He wrought for them who were of the Father given unto Him.	excellent titles to Him whom they denied, as namely (1) that [He] is our ruler and governor, so much the word "Lord" signifies, [and] (2) in that it is said "the only Lord," which serves to put a difference between all idol gods. In the same is not excluded the Holy Spirit, but all three also are included and comprehended in the word "Lord," for all the actions done by one person are mutually done by one Godhead, "only ruler which is Christ." This is an excellent place to prove the Godhead of Christ, in that He is called "the only ruler," which He is called in respect of His church, which He is head of. And He governs it in two manners of ways. First, by His death before all times a lamb slain from the beginning of the world, He is Lord over the church. Second, by the right of redemption, in that He took upon Him the nature of man to be abased in all things and according to His manhood to suffer death for the redemption of sinners, and thus may He rightly challenge superiority and lordship over His church which thus He redeemed.	their sin by the description of Christ. He says barely they denied Christ, but Him that was our Lord Christ. He describes Him by three titles. First, "the Lord," that is, the ruler and governor of all things in heaven and earth, for so much the original word signifies. The second title is the "only" Lord. This expresses and manifests the divinity, that there is but one God. Neither is it added to exclude the Father or the Holy Spirit, but it excludes the devil, the world, and the flesh, which many men make their god. The third title is "our" Lord and Savior, etc. Christ is our Lord [in] two ways; first, in regard that God before all beginning gave to Him the rule of His church, [and,] secondly, He is our Lord by the right of redemption.

Thomas Taylor	James Tomlin	Hutton MS
Out of that which has been here said, we may note these two points. First, how these seducers deny Christ; namely, not openly and plainly, for then the church should have espied them, neither in word nor speech, for in word they professed Him, but in their deeds denied Him, living after their own lusts and encouraging others in the same course (Titus 1:16).	But, first, let us look further into their sin, how they may be said and wherein to deny Christ Jesus. First, they deny Him secretly and inwardly in their hearts by not acknowledging Him to be Lord and ruler over. [Ramist structural chart, see p. 156]	In this last point, two things may be asserted. First, how these men denied Christ. *Answer.* They deny Him not absolutely with their lips, for then the church would perceive them, and then they could not have been said to have crept in. But they denied Christ by their licentious living. And this is common in this land, to profess Christ with the lips and deny Him in their lives. Every Christian confesses Christ at the Lord's Table, yet in their lives they despise Him, and instead of calling upon His name, profane His name, some by swearing, some by gaming, and many by minding nothing but worldly things. And [they] think it curious preciseness to obey and profess Christ in our lives.
And this sin is revived and renewed in this our age, wherein too many outwardly and in word profess Christ, come to the Word and sacraments, but covertly and in their deeds deny Him, whose lives are very full of Epicurism and earthliness, and mouths filled with blasphemies and reproaches against true	They deny him, first, concerning His lordship, for they will be content to be accounted His servants and that they were redeemed by Him. But they cannot brook Him to be their Lord to rule them, and thus they wear his livery but they will not be His servants.	The second question is in what respect these denied Christ. *Answer.* In two respects: firstly, in respect of His lordship, [and,] secondly, in respect of His Godhead. For the first, they denied Him in regard of His lordship, for when Christ redeemed them to be His people and He their lord, they deny Him to be their Lord. The

Thomas Taylor	James Tomlin	Hutton MS
obedience, which of them is counted too much niceness and preciseness. These are the disciples of the old heretics, whom (without repentance) the like fearful judgments await, which befell them.		devil shall be their lord. They will not Jesus Christ to rule over them, but they acknowledge Christ to be their Savior, to carry their sins, but their ruler He shall not be.
Secondly, we may observe in what regards they deny Christ; namely, first, in regard of His Godhead by withstanding the means of that power of Christ whereby (having redeemed them) He would sanctify their hearts to obedience. The merit of His redemption is welcome to them, but they will [have] none of the efficacy of it, which sanctifies and renews the inner man, subdues sin, and quickens the life of God in them. Secondly, in regard of His Lordship by denying Him obedience, which as to a Lord is due unto Him. A Redeemer they would have Him, but not a Lord. So every man would have portion in Christ's redemption, but their lusts must be their lords, and they servants to sin and Satan. But these be "those enemies that will not he should reign over them, who shall be brought and slain before him" [Luke 19:27]. Our	Secondly, they deny the power of His Godhead by which He is their Lord by His Spirit to write His laws in their hearts. And this they refuse. They would have Christ to redeem them, but they will not have Him their Lord. They will make His death of endless merit, able to blot out all their sins, and yet they cannot away Him to be their teacher, to be taught by Him, and so they make Christ a packhorse to carry away their sins. Thus, they will have His death, but they will none of the merit and efficacy of His death. Much like to the old Pharisees, "We will not have this man to rule over us." But what says He, therefore, "Bring these mine enemies, and slay them before my face." "If you would presume to apply My death to yourselves, and yet disdain to have Me your Lord and ruler, your teacher, and your master, I will none	Secondly, they deny Him in regard of His Godhead. For that they could well afford with the merit of Christ, but they put away the power of His Godhead. They cannot abide the virtue of the death of Christ, which is to subdue the corruptions of their nature. They make account of the merit but not of the efficacy. We must then learn to make Christ not only our Savior but our Lord. We must not only acknowledge His merit but His efficacy, for if He be our Savior and not Lord, He is no Savior. "Come unto me all you that are laden, and I will ease you" (Matt. 11:28). Here He gives comfort to all generally, yet He strains His speech in the next words: "Take my yoke on you, etc.," teaching us that though God has great afford of comforts, yet it is only for them that will take the yoke of Christ, not for them that deny He shall

Thomas Taylor	James Tomlin	Hutton MS
part then is (if ever we would find comfort in Christ) to make Him our Lord. His counsel is that those that are laden should come unto Him for ease, but the next words are "take my yoke upon thee" [Matt. 11:29]. And if we would have Him our justification, let Him become also our sanctification.	of you, I will not own you to be My servant, neither have you any part or portion in Mine inheritance, neither have you any profit by My death and passion."	be their Lord and rule over them. For unless we will take His yoke, we shall have none of His comfort.
	Now to the second point, which is outward, wherein they show themselves to be enemies to Christ Jesus, namely, in their deeds and conversation, in that they give themselves liberty to sin, to do what they list, yet worship Him and come to His table, and make fain show of religion. And yet, in their lives and deeds they deny Him and behave themselves as subtle thieves to get away the hearts of the people by giving themselves liberty to their own lusts. And all their worship is nothing but from their teeth and outward, and this lip service they give to Him only.	
	Now, to make an application of both these together, these are sins very general among	

Thomas Taylor	James Tomlin	Hutton MS
	Christians. For they will obey the form but none of the substance, they will come to the church and they be conversant in God's service, and yet when they are absent, they be extortioners, drunkards, idolaters, etc. And thus, they embrace Christ, but yet they refuse Him as their lives and conversations plainly testify. "If you love me keep my commandments." But they will love Christ, and yet they will none of His precepts. They will not have Him to be their Lord and ruler. We are taught, therefore, the contrary: to acknowledge Christ Jesus to be our Lord and ruler, and to show forth the same by being obedient unto Him, to be taught by Him to hold Him as our Savior, so our Lord equal with God in the deity. "Come to me (says He) all ye that are weary and laden, and I will refresh you" (Matt. 11). But how not as these adversaries take Him as a redeemer but will do nothing in sign of His love and thankfulness they owe to Him, says He in the next verse, "Take up my cross and follow me or else I know you	

Thomas Taylor	James Tomlin	Hutton MS
	not. I own you, depart ye cursed." These Christ teaches of, others shall allege, "Lord have we not taught in thy name?" "No, depart from me." And this shall be their portion. Let us, therefore, both honor Him [as] a father, obey Him as a prince, fight under His banner as faithful soldiers to their captain against the world, sin, Satan, and authorities. As loving and good servants, submit ourselves willingly to His precepts as godly people, under their minister be content to be taught by hunger and thirst for His Word of salvation of our souls. Then shall we at last be imputed worthy of His kingdom, to which He brings us for His mercy's sake. Amen.	

Catalog of Editions of Perkins's Works

Perkins's works have previously been cataloged by Breward, who compiled a list of all known editions published in Britain and in Europe, including editions in English, Latin, Dutch, German, Spanish, French, Czech, Hungarian, Irish, and Welsh.[1] The following list updates and vastly extends Breward's, distinguishing significant differences between editions and including a more complete set of bibliographic data.[2] Given our focus on the early modern publication of Perkins's works, it does not include editions of works by Perkins published after 1750 (of which there are few in any case).

In what follows, individual imprints, editions, revisions, and translations of a discrete work have been grouped together. Where two or more treatises were bound together, that imprint is listed under both titles. In cases where a treatise consists of a set of shorter pamphlets (e.g., *Estate of a Christian*), these are itemized. Individual printings of pamphlets and sections of longer works are also listed. English imprints included in works volumes are indicated in grey text and indexed to that volume's listing. All of Perkins's works are listed in order of shorthand title, and references are provided to their reprinting in the recent RHB edition (10 vols., 2012–2020). A shorthand Latin title is also provided for works that originally appeared in Latin, though they are listed under their English title.

Works in English are indexed according to their English Short Title Catalogue (ESTC) or Wing Catalogue (Wing) references.[3] In the case of the

---

1. Ian Breward, ed., *The Works of William Perkins* (Appleford: Sutton Courtney Press, 1970), 613–32.

2. A shortcoming of Breward's catalogue is that he did not distinguish between different editions of individual works—for example, Perkins's three progressively revised and expanded editions of *Armilla Aurea / A Golden Chain*, or even Robert Hill's dialogical reframing of the work (see below). He also excludes bibliographic data which is of potential historical import in the service of brevity.

3. English Short Title Catalogue, British Library, http://estc.bl.uk/. The ESTC integrates and updates both the Short Title Catalogue (STC) covering 1475–1640 and the Wing catalogue (Wing) covering 1641–1700. Alfred W. Pollard and Gilbert R. Redgrave, *A Short-Title Catalogue of Books Printed in England, Scotland, & Ireland and of English Books Printed Abroad, 1475–1640*, 2nd ed. (London: Bibliographic Society, 1976–1991); Donald G. Wing, ed., *Short-Title Catalogue*

occasional work that lacks an ESTC or Wing reference, it is indexed by its "ESTC Citation Number" (ESTC Cit.).[4] Books published outside Britain are indexed according to their Universal Short Title Catalogue (USTC) references.[5] Bibliographic details have also been gathered from a range of other secondary sources and from the present researcher's findings, including viewing physical or digitized editions.[6]

As such, this list is intended to be nonspeculative. It does not include list works on the basis of deductive logic alone (e.g., the editions before a listed "fifth edition"), or suggest potentially lost editions on the basis of Stationers' Company entries,[7] but only catalogs works for which there is evidence of their actual publication. The cataloging of early modern books is still a work in progress, and the present list will doubtless need to be supplemented in the future, as indeed catalogues such as ESTC and USTC are works perpetually in a state of progress.[8]

---

of Books Printed in England, Scotland, Ireland, Wales, and British America, and of English Books Printed in Other Countries, 1641–1700, 2nd ed., 4 vols. (New York: Modern Language Association of America, 1972–1994).

4. Priority has been given to ESTC references because it is freely accessible online. However, the print editions of STC and Wing have also been consulted. Blayney briefly explains "why STC is far from obsolete, why ESTC still has a long way to go, and why USTC is never likely to surpass those 'rival' sources at doing what they were designed to do best." Peter W. M. Blayney, "If It Looks like a Register…," *The Library: The Transactions of the Bibliographical Society* 20, no. 2 (2019): 235.

5. Universal Short Title Catalogue, University of St. Andrews, https://www.ustc.ac.uk/.

6. Breward, *Works of William Perkins*, 613–32; M. A. Shaaber, *Check-List of Works of British Authors Printed Abroad, in Languages Other than English to 1641* (New York: Bibliographical Society of America, 1975), 134–35. For Dutch language editions, see Cornelis W. Schoneveld, *Intertraffic of the Mind: Studies in Seventeenth-Century Anglo-Dutch Translation with a Checklist of Books Translated from English into Dutch, 1600–1700* (Leiden: Brill, 1983), 220–26; J. van der Haar, *From Abbadie to Young: A Bibliography of English, Most Puritan Works, Translated i/t Dutch Language* (Veenendaal: Uitgeverij Kool B. V., 1980), 1:96–108; W. J. op 't Hof, *Engelse pietistische geschriften in het Nederlands, 1598–1622*, Monografieën Gereformeerd piëtisme (Rotterdam: Lindenberg, 1987). For German language editions, see Edgar C. McKenzie, *A Catalog of British Devotional and Religious Books in German Translation from the Reformation to 1750* (Berlin: De Gruyter, 2016), 320–37. For Hungarian language editions, see Klára Koltay, "Two Hundred Years of English Puritan Books in Hungary," *Angol filológiai tanulmányok* [Hungarian studies in English] 20 (1989): 61–62.

7. For an approach to lost books based on Stationers' Register data, see Alexandra Hill, *Lost Books and Printing in London, 1557–1640: An Analysis of the Stationers' Company Register*, Library of the Written Word 68 (Leiden: Brill, 2018). Blayney is more pessimistic about the number of nonextant works listed in the Stationers' Registers that were ever printed ("If It Looks like a Register…," 235). There are multiple examples in this catalogue of Perkins's works. For example, on May 2, 1608, William Welby registered to publish two editions each of Perkins's *Four Godly Treatises* and an English translation of *De Memoria* (Arber 3:376); however, there is no evidence that either was ever published.

8. See Stephen Tabor, "ESTC and the Bibliographical Community," *The Library: The Transactions of the Bibliographical Society* 8, no. 4 (2007): 367–86.

This catalogue also integrates data from Abner's transcription of the *Registers of the Company of Stationers, 1554–1640* (Arber).[9] The Stationers' Company was authorized by royal charter to regulate the English publishing industry.[10] The main significance of the registration of titles with the Stationers' Company for this catalogue is that it can help determine publication dates or the order of publication of titles published in the same year. This data is also supplemented with the dates of dedicatory material from the start of volumes whenever they include such dates, whether by Perkins or one of his editors. Perkins wrote more dedications and forewords than this catalogue makes notes of, typically of the "to the reader" variety; however, these have been noted only where they include dates. All dates are according to the "new style," meaning that old-style dates (that is, where the end of the year was taken as Lady Day, March 25) have been updated where necessary.

Most of the listed editions published in Britain are available in digital format on Early English Books Online (EEBO).[11] Many titles, both published in Britain and Europe, are available for free download online via gateways such as Post Reformation Digital Library (PRDL)[12] and a growing number of online digital repositories.

Antidicsonus and *Artificiosa Memoria* [RHB 6:475–506; 6:507–21]
> G. P. Cantabrigiensis, *Antidisconus Accessit Libellus in Quo Dilucide Explicatur Impia Dicsoni Artificiosa Memoria.*
>
> 1. London: Henry Middleton, 1584. [ESTC 19064]

Case of Conscience [RHB 8:595–638]
> *A Case of Conscience, the Greatest That Ever Was; How a Man May Knowe Whether He Be the Child of God or No. Resolved by the Worde of God. Whereunto Is Added a Briefe Discourse, Taken out of Hier. Zanchius.*
>
> 1. London: by Thomas Orwin, for Thomas Man and John Porter, 1592. [ESTC 19665]

---

9. Edward Arber, ed., *A Transcript of the Registers of the Company of Stationers of London, 1554–1640 AD*, 5 vols. (London: privately printed, 1875–1894). The data from this work has been made available online at Stationers' Register, https://stationersregister.online/. However, this was still in its beta phase of development at the time of publication and only retrieved incomplete results.

10. See especially Peter W. M. Blayney, *The Stationers Company and the Printers of London, 1501–1557*, 2 vols. (Cambridge: Cambridge University Press, 2013).

11. Early English Books Online, University of Michigan, https://about.proquest.com/en/products-services/eebo.

12. Post-Reformation Digital Library, Janius Institute for Digital Reformation Research, Calvin Theological Seminary, www.prdl.org.

2. London: Printed by Robert Robinson, for Thomas Man and John Porter, 1592. [ESTC 19665.5]

3. Edinburgh: Printed by Robert Waldegrave, printer to the Kings Majestie, 1592. [ESTC 19666][13]

4. London: Printed [by Adam Islip] for John Legat, 1595. [ESTC 19667]

5. [Bound together: *Estate of a Christian, Case of Conscience, Lord's Prayer, Grain of Mustard Seed*]. London: Printed by the widow Orwin [and Felix Kingston] for John Porter, 1597. [ESTC 19712]

6. In [*Works*]. [Cambridge]: Printed by John Legat, printer to the Universitie of Cambridge, 1600. [ESTC 19646].

7. In *Works*. Cambridge: Printed by John Legat, printer to the Universitie of Cambridge, 1603. [ESTC 19647]

8. In *Works*. Cambridge: Printed by John Legat, printer to the Universitie of Cambridge, 1605. [ESTC 19648]

9. In *Works*, vol. 1. Cambridge: Printed by John Legate, printer to the Universitie of Cambridge, 1608. [ESTC 19649]

10. In *Works*, vol. 1. Cambridge: Printed by John Legate, 1612. [ESTC 19650]

11. In *Works*, vol. 1. London: Printed by John Legatt, 1616. [ESTC 19651]

12. In *Works*, vol. 1. London: Printed by John Legatt, 1626. [ESTC 19652]

13. In *Works*, vol. 1. London: Printed by John Legatt, and are to be sold by James Boler, George Lathum, John Grismond, Robert Milbourne, and John Bellamie, 1631. [ESTC 19652.5]

14. In *Works*, vol. 1. London: Printed by John Legatt, and are to be sold by Iames Boler, George Lathum, John Grismond, Robert Milbourne, and John Bellamie, 1631. [ESTC 19653.5]

15. In *Works*, vol. 1. London: Printed by John Legatt, 1635. [ESTC 19654]

Stationers' entries: to Thomas Man, January 27, 1592 [Arber 2:602]; half to Leonard Green, August 4, 1608 [Arber 3:387]; John Legat to John Legat [Jr.], January 2, 1621 [Arber 4:45]; Thomas Man's share to Paul Man and Jonas Man, May 3, 1624 [Arber 4:117]; Paul and Jonas Man's share to Leonard Green, July 29, 1628 [Arber 4:201]; [Jonas Man's share] to Benjamin Fisher, July 6, 1629 [Arber 4:215]; Fisher's share to Robert Young, March 27, 1637 [Arber 4:378].

Dutch

Een geval der Conscientie verclarende de swaerste questie die daar is: namelijck hoe yemandt weeten of kennen sal, of hy een Kindt Gods is. [trans. Vincent Meusevoet]

1. Amsterdam: Jan Evertsz II Cloppenburgh, 1613. [USTC 1507088]

2. In *Verscheyden theologische wercken*. Haarlem: Adriaen I Roman for Jan Evertsz II Cloppenburgh, 1614. [USTC 1012617]

---

13. Breward claims that the actual printer was "Eliot's Court Press" (*Works*, 615).

Christ Crucified [RHB 9:1–22]

A Declaration of the True Manner of Knowing Christ Crucified.

1. [Cambridge]: Printed by John Legate, printer to the Universitie of Cambridge, 1596. [ESTC 19685]

2. [Cambridge]: Printed by John Legat, printer to the Universitie of Cambridge, 1597.

3. [Bound with *Salve* & *Discourse of Conscience*]. Cambridge: Printed by John Legat, printer to the Universitie of Cambridge, 1597. [ESTC 19686, bound in 19743].

4. In [*Works*]. [Cambridge]: Printed by John Legat, printer to the Universitie of Cambridge, 1600. [ESTC 19646].

5. In *Works*. Cambridge: Printed by John Legat, printer to the Universitie of Cambridge, 1603. [ESTC 19647]

6. In *Works*. Cambridge: Printed by John Legat, printer to the Universitie of Cambridge, 1605. [ESTC 19648]

7. In *Works*, vol. 1. Cambridge: Printed by John Legate, printer to the Universitie of Cambridge, 1608. [ESTC 19649]

8. London: By John Legate, printer to the Universitie of Cambridge, 1611. And are to be sold in Pauls Churchyard at the signe of the Crowne by Simon Waterson. [ESTC 19686.5]

9. In *Works*, vol. 1. Cambridge: Printed by John Legate, 1612. [ESTC 19650]

10. London: By John Legatt, printer to the Universitie of Cambridge, 1615. [ESTC 19687]

11. In *Works*, vol. 1. London: Printed by John Legatt, 1616. [ESTC 19651]

12. London: Printed by John Legatt, dwelling in Little-Wood-streete, 1621. [ESTC 19687.5]

13. London: Printed by John Legatt, dwelling in Little-Wood-streete, 1625. [ESTC 19687.7]

14. In *Works*, vol. 1. London: Printed by John Legatt, 1626. [ESTC 19652]

15. In *Works*, vol. 1. London: Printed by John Legatt, and are to be sold by James Boler, George Lathum, John Grismond, Robert Milbourne, and John Bellamie, 1631. [ESTC 19652.5]

16. In *Works*, vol. 1. London: Printed by John Legatt, and are to be sold by Iames Boler, George Lathum, John Grismond, Robert Milbourne, and John Bellamie, 1631. [ESTC 19653.5]

17. In *Works*, vol. 1. London: Printed by John Legatt, 1635. [ESTC 19654]

18. London: Printed by John Legatt, [c. 1638]. [ESTC 19687a]

Dedication (Perkins): January 5, 1596.

Stationers' entry: to John Legat, January 19, 1596 [Arber 3:57].

Dutch

Verclaringe van de rechte maniere om te kennen Christum den ghekruysten. [trans. Vincent Meusevoet]

1. Leiden: Jan Bouwensz, for Laurens Jacobsz (Amsterdam), 1599. [USTC 424322]
2. Amsterdam: Volraedt Gaubisch for Laurens Jacobsz, 1601. [USTC 1548964]
3. Amsterdam: s.n., [1601]. [USTC 1525721]
4. Amsterdam: Jan Evertsz II Cloppenburgh, 1604. [USTC 1021416]
5. Haarlem: Aegidius Roman for Jan Evertsz Cloppenburgh, 1608. [USTC 1010822]
6. Amsterdam: Jan Evertsz II Cloppenburgh, 1623. [USTC 1016496]
7. Amsterdam: for Jillis Kok, 1653.
8. Amsterdam: for Jillis Kok, 1657.
9. In *Alle de Werken*, Amsterdam: J. von Someren, 1659–1663.

German

Nothwendiger, und gründlicher Bericht, deß Frommen, Hoch- und Wolgelehrten Herrn, Guilielmi Perkinsii Angli, Von der heylsamen, und seligmachenden Erkanotnüß Jesu Christi unsers Heylands: Ihm, unserm Herrn Jesu Christi, und seinem wahrhafftigen. [trans. Johann Ulrich]

1. Oppenheim: durch Hieronymus Galler, in verlegung Levinus Hulsius (widow of), 1610. [USTC 2054768]

Combat [RHB 1:71–165]

Satans Sophistrie Answered by Our Saviour Christ, and in Divers Sermons Further Manifested by That Worthy Man Maister William Perkins. To Which Is Added, a Comfort for the Feeble Minded: Wherein Is Set Downe the Temptations of a Christian. [ed. Robert Hill]

1. London: Printed by Richard Field for E. Edgar and are to be sold [by C. Burby] at the signe of the Swan in Paules Churchyard, 1604. [ESTC 19747.5]
2. London: Printed by Richard Field for E. Edgar and are to be sold [by C. Burby] at the signe of the Swanne in Paules Churchyard, 1604. [ESTC 19747.7]

Revised Edition

The Combat betweene Christ and the Divell Displayed: or A Commentarie upon the Temptations of Christ: Preached in Cambridge by That Reverend and Judicious Divine M. William Perkins. The Second Edition, Much Enlarged by a More Perfect Copie, at the Request of M. Perkins Executors, by Tho. Pierson Preacher of Gods Word. Hereunto Is Prefixed an Analysis or Generall View of This Combat: And a

Twofolde Table Added: One of Places of Scripture; the Other of Speciall Points to Be Observed.

1. London: Printed by Melchisedech Bradwood for E. Edgar and are to be sold [by Cuthbert Burby] in Pauls Churchyard at the signe of the Swan, 1606. [ESTC 19748]

2. In *Works*, vol. 3. Cambridge: Printed by Cantrell Legge, printer to the Universitie of Cambridge, 1609. [ESTC 19649]

3. In *Works*, vol. 3. Cambridge: Printed by Cantrell Legge, printer to the Universitie of Cambridge, 1613. [ESTC 19650]

4. In *Works*, vol. 3. Cambridge: Printed by Cantrell Legge, printer to the Universitie of Cambridge, 1618. [ESTC 19651]

5. In *Works*, vol. 3. London: Printed by John Legatt, and are to be sold by James Boler, George Lathum, John Grismond, Robert Milbourne, and John Bellamie, 1631. [ESTC 19652.5]

6. In *Works*, vol. 3. London: Printed by John Haviland, 1631. [ESTC 19653a]

7. In *Works*, vol. 3. London: Printed by John Haviland, for James Boler, 1631. [ESTC 19653b]

8. In *Works*, vol. 3. London: Printed by John Haviland, and are to be sold by Iames Boler, George Lathum, John Grismond, Robert Milbourne, and John Bellamie, 1631. [ESTC 19653b.5]

Dedication (Hill): January 12, 1604; (Pierson): June 25, 1606.

Stationers' entries: to Eliazar Edgar, August 15, 1603 [Arber 3:248]; to John Hodges, April 19, 1613 [Arber 3:520]; to Samuel Macham, December 7, 1613 [Arber 3:538]; …James Boler's half to the Stationers' Company Master & Wardens in trust for Boler's children, September 7, 1638 [Arber 4:436].

Dutch

De Sophisterie des Sathans, beantwoort door onsen Heere Jesum Christum. [trans. Vincent Meusevoet]

1. Haarlem: Aegidius Roman for Jan Evertsz II Cloppenburgh, 1605. [USTC 1020939]

2. Amsterdam: for Jan Evertsz II Cloppenburgh, 1610. [USTC 1012566]

De Strijdt Tusschen Christum en den Duyvell.

1. In *Alle de Werken*, Amsterdam: J. von Someren, 1659–1663.

Creed [RHB 5:1–416]

An Exposition of the Symbole or Creed of the Apostles, according to the Tenour of the Scriptures, and the Consent of Orthodoxe Fathers of the Church. By William Perkins.

1. Cambridge: Printed by John Legatt, printer to the Universitie of Cambridge, 1595. And are to be solde [by R. Bankworth] at the signe of the Sunne in Pauls Churchyard in London, [1595]. [ESTC 19703]

Revised Edition

An Exposition of the Symbole or Creede of the Apostles, according to the Tenour of the Scriptures, and the Consent of Orthodoxe Fathers of the Church: Revewed and Corrected by William Perkins.

1. Cambridge: Printed by John Legat, printer to the Universitie of Cambridge, 1596. [ESTC 19704]

2. Cambridge: John Legate, 1596.

3. Cambridge: Printed by John Legate, printer to the Universitie of Cambridge, 1597. [ESTC 19705]

4. In [*Works*]. [Cambridge]: Printed by John Legat, printer to the Universitie of Cambridge, 1600. [ESTC 19646].

5. In *Works*. Cambridge: Printed by John Legat, printer to the Universitie of Cambridge, 1603. [ESTC 19647]

6. In *Works*. Cambridge: Printed by John Legat, printer to the Universitie of Cambridge, 1605. [ESTC 19648]

7. In *Works*, vol. 1. Cambridge: Printed by John Legate, printer to the Universitie of Cambridge, 1608. [ESTC 19649]

8. London: By John Legate, printer to the Universitie of Cambridge, 1611. And are to be solde in Pauls Churchyard at the signe of the crowne by Simon Waterson. [ESTC 19705.4]

9. In *Works*, vol. 1. Cambridge: Printed by John Legate, 1612. [ESTC 19650]

10. London: Printed by John Legatt, Printer to the Universitie of Cambridge, 1616. [ESTC 19705.7]

11. In *Works*, vol. 1. London: Printed by John Legatt, 1616. [ESTC 19651]

12. In *Works*, vol. 1. London: Printed by John Legatt, 1626. [ESTC 19652]

13. London: [Printed] by John Legatt, and are to be sold by Simon Waterson, at the signe of the Crowne in Pauls-church yard, 1631. [ESTC 19706]

14. In *Works*, vol. 1. London: Printed by John Legatt, and are to be sold by James Boler, George Lathum, John Grismond, Robert Milbourne, and John Bellamie, 1631. [ESTC 19652.5]

15. In *Works*, vol. 1. London: Printed by John Legatt, and are to be sold by Iames Boler, George Lathum, John Grismond, Robert Milbourne, and John Bellamie, 1631. [ESTC 19653.5]

16. In *Works*, vol. 1. London: Printed by John Legatt, 1635. [ESTC 19654]

Dedication (Perkins): April 2, 1595.

Stationers' entries: to John Legat, April 24, 1595 [Arber 2:296]; to John Legat [Jr.], January 2, 1621 [Arber 4:45].

Latin
Symbolum Apostolicum
  1. In *Catechesis*. Hanau: Wilhelm Antonius, 1608. [USTC 2014551]
  2. In *Catechesis*. Genevae: P. Aubertus, 1611. [USTC 6702940]

Dutch
Eene grondige ende clare uytlegginghe over de t'waelf artyckelen des christelycken gheloofs. [trans. Vincent Meusevoet]
  1. Amsterdam: Laurens Jacobsz, 1603. [USTC 1019273]
  2. Amsterdam: Jan Evertsz II Cloppenburgh, 1605. [USTC 1012497]
  3. Amsterdam: Jan Evertsz II Cloppenburgh, 1610. [USTC 1012542]
  4. Amsterdam: Jan Evertsz II Cloppenburgh, 1611. [USTC 1012489]
  5. In *Opera Theologica*. Amsterdam: Jan Evertsz II Cloppenburgh, 1615. [USTC 1032964]
  6. Amsterdam: Johannes van Someren, 1659.

German
Symbolum: Das ist, Gründtliche und außführliche Erklährung deß Apostolischen Glaubens Bekandtnus, Durch...H. Wilhelmum Perkinsum, anfänglich in Englischer Spraach beschrieben, und jetzt auß dem Niderländischen ins Hochteutsch bracht, Durch Johannem Heupolium. [trans. Johann Heupel]
  1. Hanau: Wilhelm Antonius, 1603. [USTC 2104798]
  2. In *Catechismus*. Basel: Jacob Trew, 1606. [USTC 2066455]

Eine gründtliche und klare Außlegung über die zwölff Articul deß Christlichen Glaubens [trans. Johann Heupel].
  1. In *Catechismus*. Basel: Jacob Trew, 1606. [USTC 2066455]
  2. In *Catechismus*. Hanau: Wilhelm Anton, 1607. [USTC 2105736]

Damned Art [RHB 9:293–403]
A Discourse of the Damned Art of Witchcraft; So Farre Forth as It Is Revealed in the Scriptures, and Manifest by True Experience. Framed and Delivered by M. William Perkins, in His Ordinarie Course of Preaching, and Now Published by Tho. Pickering Batchelour of Divinitie and Minister of Finchingfield in Essex. Whereunto Is Adjoyned a Twofold Table; One of the Order and Heades of the Treatise; Another

of the Texts of Scripture Explaned, or Vindicated from the Corrupt Interpretation of t he Adversarie. [ed. Thomas Pickering]

1. Cambridge: Printed by Cantrel Legge, printer to the Universitie of Cambridge, 1608. [ESTC 19697]

2. Cambridge: Printed by Cantrel Legge, printer to the Universitie of Cambridge, 1609.

3. In *Works*, vol. 3. Cambridge: Printed by Cantrell Legge, printer to the Universitie of Cambridge, 1609. [ESTC 19649]

4. Cambridge: Printed by Cantrel Legge, printer to the Universitie of Cambridge, 1610. [ESTC 19698]

5. In *Works*, vol. 3. Cambridge: Printed by Cantrell Legge, printer to the Universitie of Cambridge, 1613. [ESTC 19650]

6. In *Works*, vol. 3. Cambridge: Printed by Cantrell Legge, printer to the Universitie of Cambridge, 1618. [ESTC 19651]

7. In *Works*, vol. 3. London: Printed by John Legatt, and are to be sold by James Boler, George Lathum, John Grismond, Robert Milbourne, and John Bellamie, 1631. [ESTC 19652.5]

8. In *Works*, vol. 3. London: Printed by John Haviland, 1631. [ESTC 19653a]

9. In *Works*, vol. 3. London: Printed by John Haviland, for James Boler, 1631. [ESTC 19653b]

10. In *Works*, vol. 3. London: Printed by John Haviland, and are to be sold by Iames Boler, George Lathum, John Grismond, Robert Milbourne, and John Bellamie, 1631. [ESTC 19653b.5]

11. London: Printed by James Boler, 1631.

Dedication (Pickering): October 26, 1608.

Stationers' entries: [to Cantrell Legge]; [half] to James Boler, June 1, 1629 [Arber 4:212]; Boler's half to the Stationers' Company Master & Wardens in trust for Boler's children, September 7, 1638 [Arber 4:436].

Latin

Βασκανολογια, hoc est Tractatio De Nefaria Arte Venefica, Quatenus S. Scripturis Explicatur [et] Veritas Eius Quotidianâ Experientiâ Comprobatur: Subiecto Rerum Indice , Auctore Guilielmo Perkinso; Interprete Thoma Draxo, SS. Theologiae Baccalaureo. [trans. Thomas Draxe]

1. Hanoviae: Guilielmum Antonium, 1610. [USTC 2106771]

Dutch

Tractaet vande ongodlijcke toover-const.

1. Amsterdam: Jan Evertsz II Cloppenburgh, 1611. [USTC 1012553]

2. In *Vijf Tractaten*. Amsterdam: Jan Evertsz II Cloppenburgh, 1611. [USTC 1012552]

3. In *Alle de Werken*. Amsterdam: J. von Someren, 1659–1663.

De Memoria and *Admonitiuncula* [RHB 6:523–40; 6:541–58]

G. P. Cantabrigiensis, *Libellus de Memoria Verissimaque Bene Recordandi Scientia. Huc Accessit Eiusdem Admonitiuncula ad A. Dicsonum de Artificiosae Memoriae, Quam Publice Profitetur, Vanitate.*

1. London: Robert Waldegrave, 1584. [ESTC 19065]

Stationers' entries: [to Robert Waldegrave?]; to William Welby, May 2, 1608 [Arber III: 376].

Death's Knell [pseudonymous]

Deaths Knell: or, The Sicke Mans Passing-Bell: Summoning All Sicke Consciences to Pr[e]pare Themselves for the Comming of the Grea[t] Day of Doome, Lest Mercies Gate Be Shut Against Them: Fit for All Those That Desire to Arrive at the Heavenly Jerusalem. Whereunto Are Adde Prayers Fit for Housholders. [pseudonymous]

1. Ninth edition. London: [By G. Purslowe] for M. Trundle, and are to be [sold] at her shop in Smith-field, 1628. [ESTC 19684]

2. Tenth edition. London: T. Cotes a. R. C[otes] f. M. Trundle, 1629. [ESTC 19684.1]

3. Eleventh edition. London: Printed [by T. Cotes?] for John Wright and are to be sold at his shop without Newgate at the signe of the Bible, 1629. [ESTC 19684.2]

4. Sixteenth edition. London: [Printed] for John Wright, and are to be so[ld] at his shop without Newgate, 1637. [ESTC 19684.7]

5. Tenth Edition. London: Printed for F. Coles, T. Vere, W. Gilbertson, and J. Wright, 1664.

6. Thirteenth Edition. Glasgow: Printed by Robert Sanders, 1705.

Stationers' entry: listed in the estate of Margaret Trundle, June 2, 1629 [Arber 4:213].

Discourse of Conscience [RHB 8:1–94]

A Discourse of Conscience: Wherein Is Set Downe the Nature, Properties, and Differences Thereof: As Also the Way to Get and Keepe Good Conscience.

1. [Cambridge]: Printed by John Legate, printer to the Universitie of Cambridge, 1596. [ESTC 19696]

2. [Bound with *Salve* & *Christ Crucified*]. Cambridge: Printed by John Legat, printer to the Universitie of Cambridge, 1597) [= ESTC 19646 in ESTC 19743].

3. In [*Works*]. [Cambridge]: Printed by John Legat, printer to the Universitie of Cambridge, 1600. [ESTC 19646].

4. In *Works*. Cambridge: Printed by John Legat, printer to the Universitie of Cambridge, 1603. [ESTC 19647]

5. In *Works*. Cambridge: Printed by John Legat, printer to the Universitie of Cambridge, 1605. [ESTC 19648]

6. In *Works*, vol. 1. Cambridge: Printed by John Legate, printer to the Universitie of Cambridge, 1608. [ESTC 19649]

7. In *Works*, vol. 1. Cambridge: Printed by John Legate, 1612. [ESTC 19650]

8. In *Works*, vol. 1. London: Printed by John Legatt, 1616. [ESTC 19651]

9. In *Works*, vol. 1. London: Printed by John Legatt, 1626. [ESTC 19652]

10. In *Works*, vol. 1. London: Printed by John Legatt, and are to be sold by James Boler, George Lathum, John Grismond, Robert Milbourne, and John Bellamie, 1631. [ESTC 19652.5]

11. In *Works*, vol. 1. London: Printed by John Legatt, and are to be sold by Iames Boler, George Lathum, John Grismond, Robert Milbourne, and John Bellamie, 1631. [ESTC 19653.5]

12. In *Works*, vol. 1. London: Printed by John Legatt, 1635. [ESTC 19654]

Dedication (Perkins): June 14, 1596.

Stationers' entries: John Legat to John Legat [Jr.], January 2, 1621 [Arber 4:46].

Latin

Anatomia Sacra Humanae Conscientiae, Guilielmi Perkinsii Angli, Doctrina, Iudicio, Candore Praestantiss. Theologi: Qua Ipsius Natura, Proprietates, ac Differentiae Dextre Poduntur, cum Curandi Conservandiq[ue] Genuina Methodo.

1. Basel: Ludwig König (I), 1603. [USTC 2039738]

2. Basel: Ludwig König (I), 1604. [USTC 2104961]

Dutch

Een excellent tractaet van de conscientie. [trans. Vincent Meusevoet]

1. Haarlem: Gillis Rooman, 1598. [USTC 424040]

2. Amsterdam: Jan Evertsz II Cloppenburgh, 1598.

3. Leiden: Christoffel Guyot for Laurens Jacobsz, 1602. [USTC 1514770]

4. Amsterdam: Jan Evertsz II Cloppenburgh, 1604. [USTC 1021414]

5. Amsterdam: Jan Evertsz II Cloppenburgh, 1608. [USTC 1022124]

6. Amsterdam: Jan Evertsz II Cloppenburgh, 1614. [USTC 1012532]

7. Amsterdam: A.v. Blanken, 1651.

8. In *Alle de Werken*. Amsterdam: J. von Someren, 1659–1663.

French

Notables Considerations Touchant la Conscience Humaine [trans. Simon Goulart]

   1. Geneva: P. and J. Chouët, 1607.

Czech

Anatomia conscientiae. Aneb pobožné rozbírání a vysvětlení svědomí lidského [trans. Jan Regius].

   1. Prague: Karel Karlsperk, 1620.

End of the World [RHB 6:445–74]

A Fruitful Dialogue concerning the End of the World.

   1. In *Four Treatises*. London: J. Wolfe for R. Watkins, 1587. [ESTC 19721.3]

   2. In *Works*, vol. 3. Cambridge: Printed by Cantrell Legge, printer to the Universitie of Cambridge, 1609. [ESTC 19649]

   3. In *Works*, vol. 3. Cambridge: Printed by Cantrell Legge, printer to the Universitie of Cambridge, 1613. [ESTC 19650]

   4. In *Works*, vol. 3. Cambridge: Printed by Cantrell Legge, printer to the Universitie of Cambridge, 1618. [ESTC 19651]

   5. In *Works*, vol. 3. London: Printed by John Legatt, and are to be sold by James Boler, George Lathum, John Grismond, Robert Milbourne, and John Bellamie, 1631. [ESTC 19652.5]

   6. In *Works*, vol. 3. London: Printed by John Haviland, 1631. [ESTC 19653a]

   7. In *Works*, vol. 3. London: Printed by John Haviland, for James Boler, 1631. [ESTC 19653b]

   8. In *Works*, vol. 3. London: Printed by John Haviland, and are to be sold by Iames Boler, George Lathum, John Grismond, Robert Milbourne, and John Bellamie, 1631. [ESTC 19653b.5]

Dutch

Een vruchtbare t'samensprekinghe van het eynde des wereldts. [trans. Vincent Meusevoet]

   1. Amsterdam: Jan Evertsz II Cloppenburgh, 1613. [USTC 1012619]

   2. In *Verscheyden theologische wercken*. Haarlem: Adriaen I Roman for Jan Evertsz II Cloppenburgh, 1614. [USTC 1012617]

   3. In *Alle de Werken*. Amsterdam: J. von Someren, 1659–1663.

Estate of a Christian[14] [RHB 8:441–594]

1. How far a reprobate
2. How far the elect
3. Dialogue
4. Religion of Rome
5. Conflict
6. Applying God's word
7. Consolations
8. Spiritual desertions

> *A Treatise Tending unto a Declaration whether a Man Be in the Estate of Damnation or in the Estate of Grace: And if He Be in the First, How He May in Time Come out of It: If in the Second, How He Maie Discerne It, and Persevere in the Same to the End. The Points That Are Handled Are Set Downe in the Page Following.* [n.b. this edition contains treatises 1–7]
>
> 1. London: [Printed] by R. Robinson, for T. Gubbin and I. Porter, 1590. [ESTC 19752]
>
> 2. London: [Printed] by R. Robinson, for T. Gubbin and I. Porter, 1590. [ESTC 19752.3]
>
> 3. London: [Printed] by R. Robinson, for T. Gubbin and I. Porter, [1590?]. [ESTC 19752.5]

Dedication (Perkins): November 24, 1589.

Stationers' entries: [see entries for *Four Treatises*, which likely apply here]; half to Leonard Green, August 4, 1608 [Arber 3:387]; John Legat to John Legat [Jr.], January 2, 1621 [Arber 4:45].

Revised Edition

> *A Treatise Tending unto a Declaration, whether a Man Be in the Estate of Damnation, or in the Estate of Grace: and if He Be in the First, Howe Hee May in Time Come out of It: If in the Second, How He May Discerne It, and Persever in the Same to the End. Revewed and Corrected by the Author. The Poynts That Are Handled Are Set Downe in the Page Following.* [n.b. this and subsequent editions contain all eight treatises]
>
> 1. London: [Printed] by Thomas Orwin for John Porter and Thomas Gubbin, 1591. [ESTC 19753]
>
> 2. London: [Printed] by Thomas Orwin for John Porter and Thomas Gubbin, 1592. [ESTC 19753.5]
>
> 3. London: Printed by the widdow Orwin for John Porter and John Legate [Cambridge], 1595. [ESTC 19754]

---

14. Modern scholars have referred to this work by a variety of shorthand titles, but early modern publishers referred to it as *The Estate of a Christian*, or similar (e.g., Arber 4:45; cf. 3:387).

4. London: [Printed] by the widdow Orwin for John Porter and John Legate, 1595. [ESTC 19754.3]

5. [Bound together: *Estate of a Christian, Case of Conscience, Lord's Prayer, Grain of Mustard Seed*]. London: Printed by the widow Orwin [and Felix Kingston] for John Porter, 1597. [ESTC 19712]

6. [London]: Printed for John Porter and John Legat, 1600. [ESTC 19754.7]

7. In [*Works*]. [Cambridge]: Printed by John Legat, printer to the Universitie of Cambridge, 1600. [ESTC 19646].

8. In *Works*. Cambridge: Printed by John Legat, printer to the Universitie of Cambridge, 1603. [ESTC 19647]

9. In *Works*. Cambridge: Printed by John Legat, printer to the Universitie of Cambridge, 1605. [ESTC 19648]

10. [Cambridge]: Printed for Leonard Greene, 1608. [ESTC 19755]

11. In *Works*, vol. 1. Cambridge: Printed by John Legate, printer to the Universitie of Cambridge, 1608. [ESTC 19649]

12. In *Works*, vol. 1. Cambridge: Printed by John Legate, 1612. [ESTC 19650]

13. London: [Printed] by John Legatt, 1614. [ESTC Cit. S504330]

14. In *Works*, vol. 1. London: Printed by John Legatt, 1616. [ESTC 19651]

15. London: [Printed] by John Legat and are to be sold by Arthur Johnson, 1619. [ESTC 19756]

16. London: Printed by William Jones for T. Pavier and are to be sold at his shop in Juie Lane, 1623. [ESTC 19676.5]

17. In *Works*, vol. 1. London: Printed by John Legatt, 1626. [ESTC 19652]

18. In *Works*, vol. 1. London: Printed by John Legatt and are to be sold by James Boler, George Lathum, John Grismond, Robert Milbourne, and John Bellamie, 1631. [ESTC 19652.5]

19. In *Works*, vol. 1. London: Printed by John Legatt and are to be sold by Iames Boler, George Lathum, John Grismond, Robert Milbourne, and John Bellamie, 1631. [ESTC 19653.5]

20. In *Works*, vol. 1. London: Printed by John Legatt, 1635. [ESTC 19654]

Stationers' entry: half to Leonard Green, August 4, 1608 [Arber 3:387]; …Thomas Pavier to Edward Brewster and Robert Birde, August 4, 1626 [Arber 4:164].

Dutch

Een Verhandeling (van acht deelen), Strekkende tot verklaringe, of yemant zy in den staat der verdoemenis… [trans. Vincent Meusevoet]

1. In *Alle de Werken*. Amsterdam: J. von Someren, 1659–1663.

Translations of Individual Treatises

1. *How Far a Reprobate May Go in the Christian Religion*

First work in *Guilielmi Perkinsii Theses, oder Schlußrede, in welchen klärlich angezeiget wirt, wie weit ein Mensch in der Erkandtnüß, und Bekandtnüß deß h. Evangelii kommen, und fortschreiten möge, und nichts destoweniger in der Zahl der Gottlosen und Verworffenen seyn könne. Item, Ein schöner trostreicher und nützlicher Tractat, wie das h. göttliche Wort zu eines jedlichen Menschen Seele sol applicirt und zugeeygnet werden. Verdeutschet durch Iohan. Huldericum Textorem.* [trans. Johann Ulrich]

   1. Oppenheim: H. Galler for L. Hulsius, 1610. [USTC 2054525]

36 Voorstellingen thoonende hoe verre yemandt kan komen in de belijdenisse des H. Euangelij nochtans bevonden worden in 't getal der godloosen ende verworpenen. [trans. Johannes Wallebius]

   1. In *Vijf Tractaten*. Amsterdam: Jan Evertsz II Cloppenburgh, 1611. [USTC 1012552]

   2. In *Opera Theologica*. Amsterdam: Jan Evertsz II Cloppenburgh, 1615. [USTC 1032964]

   3. Amsterdam: [Printed] for Jillis Kok, 1650.

   4. Amsterdam: [Printed] for Jillis Kok, 1655.

2. *The Estate of a True Christian in This Life*

Latin

Curriculum Hominis Christiani: Sive Status et Progressus Eius in Hac Vita Descriptus Aphōrisikōs in Quo Explicatur, Quotis Gradibus, Quantoque Intervallo in Pietatis Negotio Homines Electi Possint [et] Soleantreprobos Excedere [et] Superare, Authore Guil. [trans. Thomas Draxe]

   1. Oppenheim: Hieronymi Galleri for Levini Hulsius, 1615.

Dutch

De standt eens christen mensches in desen leven. [trans. Vincent Meusevoet]

   1. Amsterdam: G. Guyot (Leiden) for L. Jacobsz, 1601. [USTC 1011390]

   2. Amsterdam: Laurens Jacobsz, 1603. [USTC 1021413]

   3. Amsterdam: [Printed] for Jan Evertsz II Cloppenburgh, 1607. [USTC 1012487]

   4. Amsterdam: [Printed] for Jan Evertsz II Cloppenburgh, 1612. [USTC 1020934]

   5. Amsterdam: Jillis Kok, 1656.

3. *A Dialogue to the Same Purpose*

Dutch

Een Dialogue oft T'samensprekinghe vanden staet van een Christen mensche. Vergadert door M.Perkins, uyt de lieflicke ende wel-smakende Schriften van M.Tindal, ende Bradfert. [trans. Willem Teelinck]

   1. Middleburch: A. Vande Vivere, 1617.
   2. Amsterdam: Jan Evertsz II Cloppenburgh, 1619.
   3. Middleburg: A. Vande Vivere, 1642.
   4. Amsterdam: Baltus De Wild, 1655.
   5. Amsterdam: J. Kok, 1657.

German

Dialogus: oder Gesprech des…Herrn Guilielmi Perkinsi: Von dem Stande eines waren Christen in diesem Leben…Mit beygefügten Motiven, oder bewegenden Ursachen, warumb man sich des waren Christenthum befleißigen solle. Auß dem Englischen ins Hochteutsch…übersetzet durch Bernhardum Nicaeum Ancumanum [trans. Bernhardus Nicaeus Ancumanus].

   1. Emden: Helwig Kallenbach, 1664.

4. *How a Reprobate May Perform All the Religion of the Church of Rome*

Dutch

Hoe een verworpenen volbrengen kan den gantzen Godsdienst der Roomze Kerke.

   1. [In *Alle de Werken*. Amsterdam: J. von Someren, 1659–1663].

5. *The Conflicts of Satan with a Christian*

Dutch

De aenvechtingen des sathans: eene tsamensprekinge, begrijpende den strijt tusschen den sathan ende den christen mensche. [trans. Vincent Meusevoet]

   1. Leiden: Christoffel Guyot for L. Jacobsz, 1601. [USTC 1011389]
   2. Amsterdam: Laurens Jacobsz, 1603. [USTC 1012500]
   3. Amsterdam: Jan Evertsz Cloppenburch, 1605.
   4. Enkhuizen: Jasper Tournay for Jan Evertsz Cloppenburch, 1607. [USTC 1012287]
   5. Amsterdam: Jan Evertsz Cloppenburch, 1610.
   6. Amsterdam: Jan Evertsz Cloppenburch, 1612. [USTC 1549034]
   7. Amsterdam: [Printed] for Jillis Kok, 1653.
   8. Amsterdam: [Printed] for Jillis Kok, 1656.

German

Ein ernstliches Gespräch, zwischen einem Christen und dem Satan.

   1. In *Ein nützliches und lehrreiches Büchlein.* Oppenheim: Friederich Hulsius, 1610. [USTC 2067549]

   2. In *Drey nützliches und lehrreiches Büchlein.* Frankfurt, 1660.

   3. In *Drey nützliches und lehrreiches Büchlein.* Bern: Georg Sonnleitner, 1666.

6. *How the Word of God Is to Be Applied Aright to Troubled Consciences*

Voorstellingen van de rechte wijse…op welck een Mensch sal weeten Gods Heyligh Woort tot sijner saligheyt sich toe te passen.

   1. In *Vijf Tractaten.* Amsterdam: Jan Evertsz II Cloppenburgh, 1611. [USTC 1012552]

   2. Amsterdam: J. Kok, 1653.

   3. Amsterdam: J. Kok, 1656.

Second work in *Guilielmi Perkinsii Theses, oder Schlußrede, in welchen klärlich angezeiget wirt, wie weit ein Mensch in der Erkandtnüß, und Bekandtnüß deß h. Evangelii kommen, und fortschreiten möge, und nichts destoweniger in der Zahl der Gottlosen und Verworffenen seyn könne. Item, Ein schöner trostreicher und nützlicher Tractat, wie das h. göttliche Wort zu eines jedlichen Menschen Seele sol applicirt und zugeeygnet werden. Verdeutschet durch Iohan. Huldericum Textorem.* [trans. Johann Ulrich]

   1. Oppenheim: H. Galler for L. Hulsius, 1610. [USTC 2054525]

7. *Consolations for the Troubled Consciences of Weak Christians*

Dutch

Vertroostinghe voor beroerde conscientien van boetveerdighe sondaren. [trans. Vincent Meusevoet]

   1. Amsterdam: Jan Bouwensz for Laurens Jacobsz, 1599. [USTC 424324]

   2. Amsterdam: Volraedt Gaubisch for Laurens Jacobsz, 1601. [USTC 1514766]

   3. Amsterdam: Jan Evertsz II Cloppenburgh, 1604. [USTC 1021415]

   4. Haarlem: G. Rooman for J. E. Cloppenburch, 1608. [USTC 1022128]

   5. Amsterdam: Jan Evertsz II Cloppenburgh, 1620. [USTC 1020935]

   6. Amsterdam: A. den Blanken, 1651.

   7. Amsterdam: Jillis Kok, 1653.

   8. Amsterdam: Jillis Kok, 1656.

German

Ein Trostreiches Gespräch H. Guilielmi Perkinsi: Allen Zu viel erschreckten, und zweiffelhafftigen Gewissen, gantz nutzlich zu läsen: Verteutscht durch Wolgang Meyern, Dienern deß Worts Gottes inn Basel. [trans. Wolfgang Meyer]

   1. Basel: Johann Schröter and Konrad Foillet, 1608. [USTC 2027843]

Ein liebliches und trostreiches Gespräch [trans. Johann Ulrich]

   1. Bern: Georg Sonnleitner, 1665.

Ein liebliches und trostreiches Gespräch zwischen einem Prediger und Christen [trans. Johann Ulrich]

   1. In *Zwey lehr- und trostreiche.* Bern: Georg Sonnleitner, 1665.

   2. In *Zwey lehr- und trostreiche.* Bern: Georg Sonnleitner, 1669.

8. *A Declaration of Certain Spiritual Desertions*

Dutch

Een Verklaringe van eenige Geestelijke Verlaatingen.

   1. [In *Alle de Werken.* Amsterdam: J. von Someren, 1659–1663].

German

Gründtliche Erklärnge etlicher geistlichen Verlassungen Gottes. [trans. Johann Ulrich]

   1. In *Zwey lehr- und trostreiche Stücke.* Oppenheim: Friederich Hulsius, 1610. [USTC 2080581]

Etlicher geistlicher Verlassungen, alle träge und schläfferige Evangelische damit zu erschrecken.

   1. In *Drey nützliche und lehrreiche Büchlein.* Frankfurt, 1660.

   2. In *Drey nützliche und lehrreiche Büchlein.* Bern, 1666.

Czech

O opuštěni Božim. [trans. Jiřík Oeconomus]

   1. Prague: Daniel Sedlčanský, 1610.

Hungarian

Kettős kereszt, Es Késértet alatt nyögő Keresztyén embernek lelki orvoslasa, Az az: Első A 'Satan keserteti ellen való Lelki Fegyver, Es Masodik, Egy Lelki Tanitó, és egy gyengélkedő Keresztyén között való gyönyörüséges Beszélgetés; Mellyet amaz b.e. Perkinsus Villyám Angliai nyelven irott, és abból Deák nyelvre fordittatott múnkájából, Istene dicsössére s' Nemzete javára Magyarra forditott. [trans. Debreczeni T. István]

   1. Debreczenben: István Toltesi, 1685.

Exhortation [RHB 9:79–122]

First work in: *M. Perkins, His Exhortation to Repentance, out of Zephaniah: Preached in 2. Sermons in Sturbridge Faire. Together with Two Treatises of the Duties and Dignitie of the Ministrie: Delivered Publiquely in the Universitie of Cambridge. With a Preface Præfixed Touching the Publishing of All Such Workes of His as Are to Be Expected: With a Catalogue of All the Perticulers of Them, Diligently Perused and Published, by a Preacher of the Word.* [ed. William Crashawe, bound with *Ministry*]

   1. London: Imprinted by T. C[reede]. for William Welby and are to bee sold at his shop in Pauls Churchyard, at the signe of the Grey-hound, 1605. [ESTC 19706.5]

A Faithfull and Plaine Exposition upon the Two First Verses of the Second Chapter of Zephaniah: By That Late Reverend Preacher of Gods Word, Maister Perkins. Containing a Powerfull Exhortation to Repentance: As Also the Manner How Men in Repentance Are to Search Themselves. Preached at Sturbridge Faire, in the Field; Taken from His Mouth: And Afterwards Diligently Perused; and Now Published for the Common Good. By a Preacher of the Word. With a Preface Prefixed, Touching the Publishing of M. Perkins His Workes. And a Catalogue of All Such Particulars Thereof, as Are to Be Expected. [ed. William Crashawe]

   1. [London: G. Snowdon for W. Welby, 1605.] [titlepage missing] [ESTC 19706.7]

   2. [Third Impression]. London: Printed by Thomas Creede for William Welby and are to be sold at his shop at the signe of the Greyhound in Paules Churchyard, 1606. [ESTC 19707]

   3. [Fourth Impression]. At London: Printed by Thomas Creede for William Welby, 1607. [ESTC 19707.5]

   4. [Fifth Impression]. At London: Printed by Thomas Creede for William Welby, 1609. [ESTC 19708]

   5. In *Works*, vol. 3. Cambridge: Printed by Cantrell Legge, printer to the Universitie of Cambridge, 1609. [ESTC 19649]

   6. In *Works*, vol. 3. Cambridge: Printed by Cantrell Legge, printer to the Universitie of Cambridge, 1613. [ESTC 19650]

   7. In *Works*, vol. 3. Cambridge: Printed by Cantrell Legge, printer to the Universitie of Cambridge, 1618. [ESTC 19651]

   8. In *Works*, vol. 3. London: Printed by John Legatt and are to be sold by James Boler, George Lathum, John Grismond, Robert Milbourne, and John Bellamie, 1631. [ESTC 19652.5]

9. In *Works*, vol. 3. London: Printed by John Haviland, 1631. [ESTC 19653a]

10. In *Works*, vol. 3. London: Printed by John Haviland for James Boler, 1631. [ESTC 19653b]

11. In *Works*, vol. 3. London: Printed by John Haviland and are to be sold by Iames Boler, George Lathum, John Grismond, Robert Milbourne, and John Bellamie, 1631. [ESTC 19653b.5]

Stationers' entries: to William Welby, December 7, 1604 [Arber 3:278]; to Michael Baker, October 1, 1610 [Arber 3:444]; …possibly included in Snodham's assignment to William Stansby, February 23, 1626 [Arber 4:153]; to John Haviland, July 30, 1630 [Arber 4:238]; Haviland and John Wright, September 4, 1638 [Arber 4:431].

Dutch

Eene Vermaninghe tot boetveerdigheydt uyt Zephania. [trans. Vincent Meusevoet]

1. Amsterdam: [Printed] for Jan Evertsz II Cloppenburgh, 1610. [USTC 1012535]

2. Amsterdam: Jillis Kok, 1658.

3. In *Alle de Werken*. Amsterdam: J. von Someren, 1659–1663.

Forged Catholicism / Problema [RHB 7:169–410]

Guilielmi Perkinsi Problema de Romanæ Fidei Ementito Catholicismo. Estq́[ue] Antidotum contra Thesaurum Catholicum Iodoci Coccij. Et Propaideiæ [sic] Iuventutis in Lectione Omnium Patrum. Editum Post Mortem Authoris Operâ & Studio Samuelis Wardi. [ed. Samuel Ward]

1. Cantabrigiæ: Ex officina Ioannis Legat, 1604. Extant Londini apud Simonem Waterson in Coemeterio D. Pauli ad insigne Coronæ. [ESTC 19734]

2. Hanau: Wilhelm Antonius, 1604. [USTC 2078910]

3. Hanau: Wilhelm Antonius, 1611. [USTC 2120154]

English

William Perkins His Probleme of the Forged Catholicisme, or Universalitie of the Romish Religion.

1. In *Works*, vol. 2. Cambridge: Printed by John Legate, printer to the Universitie of Cambridge, 1608. [ESTC 19649]

2. In *Works*, vol. 2. Cambridge: Printed by John Legate, 1613. [ESTC 19650]

3. In *Works*, vol. 2. Cambridge: Printed by John Legate, 1617. [ESTC 19651]

4. In *Works*, vol. 2. London: Printed by John Legatt and are to be sold by James Boler, George Lathum, John Grismond, Robert Milbourne, and John Bellamie, 1631. [ESTC 19652.5]

5. In *Works*, vol. 2. London: Printed by John Legatt, 1631. [ESTC 19653]

Stationers' entries: English translation to Master Burbie, Felix Kingston, and Martin Clerke, December 5, 1607 [Arber 3:334]; to John Legat, January 29, 1607 [Arber 3:338]; to John Legat [Jr.], January 2, 1621 [Arber 4:46].

Dutch

Problema dat is: Een voor-stellinghe van het valsch voor gheven des pausdoms dat het roomsche gheloof het alghemeyne gheloof zijn soude.

1. Amsterdam: Jan Evertsz II Cloppenburgh, 1609. [USTC 1012539]

2. In *Opera Theologica*. Amsterdam: Jan Evertsz II Cloppenburgh, 1615. [USTC 1032964]

3. Amsterdam: Johannes van Someren, 1659.

Foundation [RHB 5:481–509]

The Foundation of Christian Religion Gathered into Six Principles. And It Is to Bee Learned of Ignorant People, That They May Be Fit to Heare Sermons with Profite, and Receive the Lord's Supper with Comfort.

1. London: T. Orwin for J. Porter, 1590. [ESTC 19709]

2. [London?]: Printed by Thomas Orwin for John Porter, 1591. [ESTC 19710]

3. [London?]: Printed for Thomas Gubbins and John Porter, 1592. [ESTC 19710.5]

4. At London: Printed [by John Orwin] for John Porter and John Legat, 1595. [ESTC 19711]

5. London: Printed by the widow Orwin [and Felix Kingston] for John Porter, [Thomas Man, Ralph Jackson, and Hugh Burwell, Cambridge], 1597. [ESTC 19712]

6. In [*Works*]. [Cambridge]: Printed by John Legat, printer to the Universitie of Cambridge, 1600. [ESTC 19646].

7. Cambridge: Printed [by John Legat] for John Porter, 1601. [ESTC 19713]

8. In *Works*. Cambridge: Printed by John Legat, printer to the Universitie of Cambridge, 1603. [ESTC 19647]

9. [Cambridge: J. Legat] Printed for John Porter, 1604. [ESTC 19713.5]

10. In *Works*. Cambridge: Printed by John Legat, printer to the Universitie of Cambridge, 1605. [ESTC 19648]

11. [London?]: Printed for John Porter, 1606. [ESTC 19714]

12. Cambridge: John Legate, 1608. [ESTC 19715]

13. In *Works*, vol. 1. Cambridge: Printed by John Legate, printer to the Universitie of Cambridge, 1608. [ESTC 19649]

14. In *Works*, vol. 1. Cambridge: Printed by John Legate, 1612. [ESTC 19650]

15. London: [Printed] by John Legatt, printer to the Universitie of Cambridge, 1615. [ESTC 19715a]

16. [London]: [Printed] by John Legatt, printer to the Universitie of Cambridge, 1616. [ESTC 19715a.5]

17. In *Works*, vol. 1. London: Printed by John Legatt, 1616. [ESTC 19651]

18. London: [Printed] by John Legatt, printer to the Universitie of Cambridge, 1617. [ESTC 19716]

19. London: [Printed] by John Legatt, printer to the Universitie of Cambridge, 1618. [ESTC 19717]

20. In *Works*, vol. 1. London: Printed by John Legatt, 1626. [ESTC 19652]

21. London: Printed by John Legatt, 1627. [ESTC 19717.5]

22. London: Printed by John Legatt and are to bee sold by Robert Allott at the signe of the Beare in Pauls Churchyard, 1629. [ESTC 19718]

23. London: Printed by John Legatt and are to bee sold by Robert Allot at the signe of the Beare in Pauls Churchyard, 1632. [ESTC 19718.5]

24. London: Printed by John Legatt and are to be sold by Robert Allot at the signe of the Beare in Pauls Churchyard, 1633. [ESTC 19719]

25. London: Printed by John Legatt and are to bee sold by Robert Allott at the signe of the Beare in Pauls Churchyard, 1635. [ESTC 19719.7]

26. In *Works*, vol. 1. London: Printed by John Legatt and are to be sold by James Boler, George Lathum, John Grismond, Robert Milbourne, and John Bellamie, 1631. [ESTC 19652.5]

27. In *Works*, vol. 1. London: Printed by John Legatt and are to be sold by Iames Boler, George Lathum, John Grismond, Robert Milbourne, and John Bellamie, 1631. [ESTC 19653.5]

28. In *Works*, vol. 1. London: Printed by John Legatt, 1635. [ESTC 19654]

29. London: Printed by John Legatt and are to bee sold by M. Allot at the signe of the Beare in Pauls churchyard, 1636. [ESTC 19720]

30. London: Printed by John Legatt and are to bee sold at the signe of the Beare in Pauls Churchyard, 1638. [ESTC 19721]

31. London: Printed by John Legatte and are to bee sold at the signe of the Beare in Pauls Curch-yard, 1641. [Wing P1563]

32. [Cambridge: s.n.], 1642. [Wing P1564]

33. London: Printed by John Legat and are to be sold at the signe of the Beare, Pauls Churchyard, 1642. [Wing P1564A]

34. London: Printed by John Legatt and are to bee sold at the signe of the Beare, Pauls Churchyard, 1642. [ESTC Cit. R472955]

35. London: Printed by John Legat and are to be sold at the signe of the Bear in Paules Churchyard, 1645. [Wing P1564B]

36. London: [Printed] by John Legat, 1646. [Wing P1564C]

37. London: Printed by John Legatt, 1647. [Wing P1565]

38. London: Printed by John Legatt and are to be sold by Richard Tomlins at the sign of the Sun and Bible in Pie-corner, 1654. [Wing P1566A]

39. London: Printed by John Field and are to be sold by John Williams, at the Crown in S. Pauls Churchyard, and George Sawbridge at the Bible on Ludgate-hill, 1660. [Wing P1566B]

40. London: Printed by John Field, and are to be sold by George Sawbridge at the Bible on Ludgate-hill, 1661. [Wing P1566C]

41. London: Printed by John Streater and are to be sold by George Sawbridge living at the Bible on Ludgate-hill, 1671. [Wing P1567]

42. n.p., 1672.

43. London: Printed for George Sawbridge at the Bible on Ludgate hill and John Williams at the Crowne in St Pauls Churchyard, 1677. [Wing P1568]

44. Boston in New-England: Printed by Samuel Green and sold by Mary Avery near the Blue Anchor in Boston, 1682. [Wing P1569]

45. London: Printed for H. Sawbridge at the Bible on Ludgate Hill, 1682. [Wing P1568A]

46. s.l.: s.n., 1688. [Wing P1570]

47. n.p.: 1690.

48. London: [s.n.], Printed in the Year 1723. [ESTC Cit. T121302]

Stationers' entries: half to Leonard Green, August 4, 1608 [Arber 3:387]; John Legat to John Legat [Jr.], January 2, 1621 [Arber 4:45]

Supplementary

John Robinson, *An Appendix to Mr. Perkins His Six Principles of Christian Religion.*

   1. [Amsterdam: successors of G. Thorp, 1635.] [ESTC 21107.5]

   2. [Amsterdam: successors of G. Thorp,] Printed 1636. [ESTC 21107.5]

   3. [London]: Printed in the yeere 1641. [Wing R1691]

John Robinson, *A Briefe Catechisme concerning Church-Governemnt. By That Reverend Divine Mr. John Robinson, and May Fitly Be Adjoyned to Mr. Perkins Six Principles as an Appendix Thereto.*

   1. London: [s.n.], printed in the yeare 1642. [Wing R1693]

John Robinson, *An Appendix to Mr. Perkins His Six Principles of Christian Religion. Touching the More Solemn Fellowship of Christians, (the Church of God) as Being a Divine Institution. Very Fit and Necessary to Be Learned by All Sorts of People, in These Perilous Times.*

   1. London: Printed by J. L. for N. Bourn and are to be sold at his shop at the south entrance of the Royal Exchange in Cornhill, 1656. [Wing R1692]

Charles Broxholme, *The Good Old Way: or, Perkins Improved, in a Plain Exposition and Sound Application of Those Depths of Divinity Briefly Comprized in His Six Principles: By That Late Painful and Faithful Minister of the Gospel, Charles Broxolme in Darby-shire.*

1. London: Printed for John Rothwel and Thomas Maxey and sold at the Bear and Fountain in Cheap-side and near Baynards-Castle in Thames-street, 1653. [Wing B5217]
2. London: Printed for John Rothwel and T. Maxey and sold at the Bear and Fountain in Cheap-side and by Joseph Barber at the Lamb in the new buildings [in Pauls Churchyard], 1653. [Wing B5217A]
3. London: Printed for John Rothwel at the Fountaon in Gold-smiths-Row Cheap side, 1657. [Wing B5218]

James Bacon, *A Plaine & Profitable Catechisme Whereunto Is Added a Sermon Preached upon Exod.23.2. By That Reverend and Judicious Divine Mr James Bacon, Late Minister of Burgate in Suffolke. Now First Published by His Son in Law H. W.* ("A Practical Catechisme, Introductory to a Large Exposition of Reverend Mr Perkins, His Catechism" [p. 1])

1. Oxford: Printed by W. Hall for R. Davis, 1660. [Wing B344]

John Wallis, *Tractatus Grammatico-Physicus de Loquela Sive Sonorum Formatione. Cui Subjungitur Johannis Podensteiner Clavis Linguæ Anglicanæ Juxta cum Guilielmi Perkins Tractatu Anglico de Fundamento Religionis Christianæ.* [supplement to Perkins]

1. Hamburg: Sumtibus viduæ Gotfried Schultzen, bibliopolæ Hamburgensis, 1688. [Wing P1570]

Latin

Fundamenta Religionis Christianae,

1. n.p., 1603.
2. Hamburg: G. Schultzen, 1688.

Dutch

De catechismus ofte somma van de gheheele christelijcke religie in ses fondamenten t'samen ghestelt.

1. Amsterdam: Jan Evertsz II Cloppenburgh, 1609. [USTC 1514805]
2. Amsterdam: s.n., 1610. [USTC 1540714]
3. In *Opera Theologica.* Amsterdam: Jan Evertsz II Cloppenburgh, 1615. [USTC 1032964]
4. Amsterdam: Johannes van Someren, 1659.

German

*Catechismus Oder Summa Christlicher Lehre, Das ist, Außführliche Erklärung
der Hauptstücke Christlicher Religion, als nämlich der Artickel des Christlichen
Glaubens, der heiligen Tauffe und Abendmals Christi, der heiligen zehen Gebott
und Gebets des Herrn.* [trans. Johan Heupel].

    1. Hanau: Wilhelm Antonius, 1607. [USTC 2105736]

*Catechismus Des Hochgelehrten, Frommen, und Berümbten Herren, Guilielmi
Perkinsi[i], Weiland Dieners der Kirchen Christi Engelland: In welchem Anfenglich
Sechs veste Gründe und Fundament der gantzen Religion…gelegt sind; Demnach
aber alle und jede Ha.* [trans. Wolfgang Meyer]

    1. Basel: Jakob Trew, 1606. [USTC 2066455]

*Catechismus Oder Summa Christlicher Lehre, Das ist, Außführliche Erklärung
der Hauptstücke Christlicher Religion, als nämlich der Artickel des Christlichen
Glaubens, der heiligen Tauffe und Abendmals Christi, der heiligen zehen Gebott
und Gebets des Herrn.*

Contents: *Foundation, Creed,* & *Armilla Aurea,* chs. 19–30.

    1. Hanau: Wilhelm Anton, 1606.

    2. Hanau: Wilhelm Antonius, 1607. [USTC 2105736]

Der Grund der Christlichen Religion.

    1. Leipzig: Johann Heinrich, 1692

    2. Leipzig: Johann Heinrich, 1694.

Irish

*The Christian Doctrine, or the Foundation of Christian Religion, Gathered into
Six Principles. Necessarie for Every Man to Learn. Translated into Irish by Godfrey
Daniel, Master in the Arts. And Also Brief and Plain Rules for the Reading of the
Irish Tongue.* = *An teagasg Críosttuide, nó Fundameint an chreidim Críosttuide.*

    1. Dublin: [Printed] by Will. Bladen, 1652. [Wing P1561]

Welsh

*The Foundation of Christian Religion. Gathered into Six Principles, by Mr. William
Perkins. Translated into Welsh. Whereto Also Is Added the Welsh Alphabet, for the
Instruction of the Unlearned in That Language. By E. R. Sail crefydd gristnogawl
wedi ei rhannu yn chewch o rannau new Wyddorion, o waith W. P. Wedi ei gyfia-
ethu. Ir iath gymráec at osod allan. Drwy ddymuniad E. R.*

    1. London: Printed by Richard Constable for George Calvert and are to be
        sold at his shop at the sign of the Half-Moon in Waltings-street, 1649.
        [Wing P1566]

Four Treatises
1. End of the world
2. How far a reprobate
3. Conflict
4. Applying God's Word

Foure Godly Treatises; Very Necessary to Be Considered of All Christians. The First Is concerning the Ende of the Worlde. The Seconde Sheweth How Farre a Wicked Man and a Reprobate May Goe in the Profession of the Gospell. The Third Is of the Conflicts of Sathan with the Christian. The Fourth, of the Right Applying of Gods Word to the Conscience.

   1. London: J. Wolfe for R. Watkins, 1587. [ESTC 19721.3]

Stationers' entries: to Richard Watkins and John Porter, October 19, 1587 [Arber 2:476]; to William Welby, May 2, 1608 [Arber 3:376].

Foure Treatises Necessarie to Be Considered of All Christians. The First Sheweth, How Farre a Wicked Man May Goe in Christianitie. The Second, of the Conflicts of Sathan with the Christian. The Third That a Papist Cannot Go beyond a Reprobate. The Fourth How the Elect May Goe beyond All Reprobates.

   1. London: T. Orwin for J. Porter [of Cambridge] and T. Gubbin, 1588. [ESTC 19721.5]

Stationers' entry: to John Porter and Thomas Gubbin, August 21, 1588 [Arber 2:496].

Galatians [RHB 2:1–394]
A Commentarie or Exposition, upon the Five First Chapters of the Epistle to the Galatians: Penned by the Godly, Learned, and Judiciall Divine, Mr. W. Perkins. Now Published for the Benefit of the Church, and Continued with a Supplement upon the Sixt Chapter, by Rafe Cudwort Bachelour of Divinitie. [ed., Ralph Cudworth]

   1. Cambridge: Printed by John Legat, printer to the Universitie of Cambridge, 1604. [ESTC 19680]

   2. London: [Printed] by John Legatt, printer to the Universitie of Cambridge, 1617. [ESTC 19681]

   3. In *Works*, vol. 2. Cambridge: Printed by John Legate, printer to the Universitie of Cambridge, 1608. [ESTC 19649]

   4. In *Works*, vol. 2. Cambridge: Printed by John Legate, 1613. [ESTC 19650]

   5. In *Works*, vol. 2. Cambridge: Printed by John Legate, 1617. [ESTC 19651]

   6. In *Works*, vol. 2. London: Printed by John Legatt and are to be sold by James Boler, George Lathum, John Grismond, Robert Milbourne, and John Bellamie, 1631. [ESTC 19652.5]

   7. In *Works*, vol. 2. London: Printed by John Legatt, 1631. [ESTC 19653]

Dedication (Cudworth): August 10, 1604.

Stationers' entries: to John Legat and Simon Waterson, February 23, 1607 [Arber 3:340]; Legat's share [half] to John Legat [Jr.], January 2, 1621 [Arber 4:46]; Waterson's share [half] to John Waterson, August 19, 1635 [Arber 4:346].

Latin
Baptismus [Galatians 3:26–28]
1. In *Catechesis*. Hanau: Wilhelm Antonius, 1608. [USTC 2014551]
2. In *Catechesis*. Genevae: P. Aubertus, 1611. [USTC 6702940]

Dutch
Wtlegginghe ende grondige verclaringe, op den sendt-brief des apostels Pauli tot den Galaten. [trans. Vincent Meusevoet]
1. Enkhuizen: Jasper Tournay for Jan Evertsz II Cloppenburgh, 1607. [USTC 1025734]
2. In *Opera Theologica*. Amsterdam: Jan Evertsz II Cloppenburgh, 1615. [USTC 1032964]

Over den Zendbrief aan de Galaters.
1. In *Geleerde en Godzalige Uytleggingen*. Amsterdam: Johannes van Someren, 1662.

God's Free Grace [RHB 6:385–443]
A Treatise of Gods Free Grace, and Mans Free Will.
1. [Cambridge?]: Printed by John Legat, printer to the Universitie of Cambridge, and are to be sold at the signe of the Crowne in Pauls churchyard by Simon Waterson, 1601. [ESTC 19750]
2. In *Works*. Cambridge: Printed by John Legat, printer to the Universitie of Cambridge, 1603. [ESTC 19647]
3. In *Works*. Cambridge: Printed by John Legat, printer to the Universitie of Cambridge, 1605. [ESTC 19648]
4. In *Works*, vol. 1. Cambridge: Printed by John Legate, printer to the Universitie of Cambridge, 1608. [ESTC 19649]
5. In *Works*, vol. 1. Cambridge: Printed by John Legate, 1612. [ESTC 19650]
6. In *Works*, vol. 1. London: Printed by John Legatt, 1616. [ESTC 19651]
7. In *Works*, vol. 1. London: Printed by John Legatt, 1626. [ESTC 19652]
8. In *Works*, vol. 1. London: Printed by John Legatt and are to be sold by James Boler, George Lathum, John Grismond, Robert Milbourne, and John Bellamie, 1631. [ESTC 19652.5]
9. In *Works*, vol. 1. London: Printed by John Legatt and are to be sold by Iames Boler, George Lathum, John Grismond, Robert Milbourne, and John Bellamie, 1631. [ESTC 19653.5]

10. In *Works*, vol. 1. London: Printed by John Legatt, 1635. [ESTC 19654]

Stationers' entries: John Legat to John Legat [Jr.], January 2, 1621 [Arber 4:46].

Latin
De Libera Dei Gratia, [et] Libero Hominis Arbitrio, Solida [et] Succincta Tractatio, Nunc Recens ex Lingua Anglica in Latinam Conversa, Opera [et] Studio Wolfgangi Mayeri in Evangeli. [trans. Wolfgang Meyer]

   1. Oppenheim: Levinus Hulsius (widow of) [et] Hieronymus Galler, 1610. [USTC 2041574]

Dutch
Een tractaet van de vrye genaede Gods, ende vrye wille des menschen.

   1. Leiden: Henrick van Haestens for Jan Jansz Orlers, Andries Clouck, and Jean Maire, 1611. [USTC 1011608]

   2. In *Vijf Tractaten.* Amsterdam: Jan Evertsz II Cloppenburgh, 1611. [USTC 1012552]

   3. Haarlem: Adriaen I Roman for Jan Evertsz Cloppenburgh, 1613. [USTC 1012618]

Golden Chain / Armilla Aurea [RHB 6:1–272]

First Latin Edition
Armilla Aurea, Id Est, Miranda Series Causarum et Salutis & Damnationis Iuxta Verbum Dei: Eius Synopsin Continet Annexa Tabula.

   1. Cantabrigiæ: Ex officina Johannis Legatt, 1590. [ESTC 19655]

Second Latin Edition
Armilla Aurea, Id Est, Theologiae Descriptio Mirandam Seriem Causarum & Salutis & Damnationis Iuxta Verbum Desproponens: Eius Synopsin Continet Annexa ad Finem Tabula / Accessit Practica Th. Bezæ Pro Consolandis Afflictis Conscientijs. Editio Secunda.

   1. Cantabrigiæ: Ex officina Johannis Legatt, extant Londini apud Abrahamum Kitson, ad insigne solis in Cæmiterio D. Pauli, 1591. [ESTC 19655a]

First English Edition
A Golden Chaine, or the Description of Theologie, Containing the Order of the Causes of Saluation and Damnation, according to Gods Worde. A Viewe of the Order Wherof, Is to Be Seene in the Table Annexed. Written in Latin by William Perkins, and Translated by an Other. Hereunto Is Adioyned the Order Which M. Theodore Beza Used in Comforting Troubled Consciences. [trans. Robert Hill]

1. At London: Printed by Edward Alde and are to be sold by Edward White at the little north doore of S. Paules Church at the signe of the Gunne, 1591. [ESTC 19657]

2. Printed by John Legate, printer to the Universitie of Cambridge, and are to be sold [by A. Kitson] at the signe of the Sunne in Paules Churchyard in London, 1591. [ESTC 19658]

3. At London: Printed by Edward Alde and are to be sold by Edward White at the little north doore of S. Paules Church at the signe of the Gunne, 1592. [ESTC 19660]

4. Edinburgh: Printed by Robert Waldegrave, printer to the Kings Majestie, 1592. [ESTC 19661]

Third Latin Edition

Armilla Aurea Id Est, Theologiæ Descriptio Mirandam Seriem Causarum & Salutis & Damnationis Iuxta Verbum Dei Proponens: Eius Synopsim Continet Annexa Tabula. Editio Tertia Recognita & Aucta. Accessit Practica Th. Bezæ Pro Consolandis Afflicits Conscientiis.

1. Cantabrigiæ: Ex officina Johannis Legatt. Extant Londini apud Abrahamum Kitson, ad insigne Solis in Camiserio D. Pauli, 1592. [ESTC 19656]

2. Cantabrigiæ: Ex officina Johannis Legatt. Extant Londini apud Abrahamum Kitson, ad insigne Solis in Camiserio D. Pauli, 1592. [ESTC 19656.5]

Gvl. Perkinsi Angli Armilla Aurea: Sive Theologiae Descriptio, Mirandam Seriem Causarum Salutis & Damnationis Hominum, Juxta Verbum Dei, Exponens. Adiectis Iteratâ Istâ Editione Tabulis Methodicis Accessit Etiam ad Finem Practica Theod. Bezae, Pro Conscientiis Affictis Consolandis.

1. Basel: per Konrad von Waldkirch, 1594. [USTC 661116]

2. Basel: per Konrad von Waldkirch, 1596. [USTC 613125]

3. Basel: per Konrad von Waldkirch, 1598. [USTC 661117]

4. Basel: per Konrad von Waldkirch, 1599. [USTC 661118]

5. Basel: per Konrad von Waldkirch, 1614. [USTC 2142982]

Second English Edition

A Golden Chaine, or the Description of Theologie, Containing the Order of the Causes of Salvation and Damnation, according to Gods Word. A View Whereof, Is to Be Seene in the Table Annexed. Written in Latine, and Translated by R. H. Hereunto Is Adjoyned the Order Which M Theodore Beza Used in Comforting Afflicted Consciences. The Second Edition, Much Enlarged, with a Table at the Ende. [trans. Robert Hill]

1. [Cambridge]: Printed by John Legate, printer to the Universitie of Cambridge, 1592. [ESTC 19661.5 / 19659]

2. [London]: Printed by [Adam Islip for] John Legat, printer to the Universitie of Cambridge, 1595. [ESTC 19662]

3. [London]: Printed by [J. Orwin for] John Legate, printer to the Universitie of Cambridge, 1597. [ESTC 19663]

4. In [*Works*]. [Cambridge]: Printed by John Legat, printer to the Universitie of Cambridge, 1600. [ESTC 19646].

5. In *Works*. Cambridge: Printed by John Legat, printer to the Universitie of Cambridge, 1603. [ESTC 19647]

6. In *Works*. Cambridge: Printed by John Legat, printer to the Universitie of Cambridge, 1605. [ESTC 19648]

7. In *Works*, vol. 1. Cambridge: Printed by John Legate, printer to the Universitie of Cambridge, 1608. [ESTC 19649]

8. In *Works*, vol. 1. Cambridge: Printed by John Legate, 1612. [ESTC 19650]

9. In *Works*, vol. 1. London: Printed by John Legatt, 1616. [ESTC 19651]

10. In *Works*, vol. 1. London: Printed by John Legatt, 1626. [ESTC 19652]

11. In *Works*, vol. 1. London: Printed by John Legatt and are to be sold by James Boler, George Lathum, John Grismond, Robert Milbourne, and John Bellamie, 1631. [ESTC 19652.5]

12. In *Works*, vol. 1. London: Printed by John Legatt and are to be sold by Iames Boler, George Lathum, John Grismond, Robert Milbourne, and John Bellamie, 1631. [ESTC 19653.5]

13. In *Works*, vol. 1. London: Printed by John Legatt, 1635. [ESTC 19654]

Dedications (Perkins): January 20, 1590 [*Armilla Aurea*]; April 18, 1591 [*A Golden Chain*]; (Hill): July 23, 1592 [*A Golden Chain*]; (Perkins): July 23, 1592 [*A Golden Chain*].

Stationers' entries: to Thomas Newman and Thomas Gubbin, September 1, 1590 [Arber 2:561]; to John Legat by commandment of the bishop of London, for Latin and English translation, July 27, 1592 [Arber 2:618]; to Thomas Man for English translation, June 4, 1604 [Arber 3:264]; to John Legat [Jr.], January 2, 1621 [Arber 4:45]

Dialogical Versions

A Comfort for the Feeble Minded. Wherein Is Set Downe That Spirituall Combat Which Is Betwixt a Christian and Satan. Written Shortly by the Former Author, and Made in Forme of a Dialogue by R. H. for the Benefite of Such as Are Exercised with Temptations. [ed. Robert Hill] [a dialogical adaption of *A Golden Chain*, chs. 40–44, 48, 58; diagram from end of *Two Treatises 2.Combat*].

1. London: Printed for E. E[dgar], 1604. In *Satans Sophistrie Answered…* London: Printed by Richard Field for E. Edgar, 1604. [ESTC 19747.5]

2. London: Printed for E. E[dgar], 1604. In *Satans Sophistrie Answered…* London: Printed by Richard Field for E. Edgar, 1604. [ESTC 19747.7]

A Golden Chaine, or the Description of Theologie. Containing the Order of the Causes of Salvation and Damnation, according to Gods Word, a View Whereof Is to Be Seene in the Table Annexed. Written in Latine by That Man of God, M. William Perkins, Translated into English by Robert Hill, and by Him Now Drawne into Familiar Questions and Answers, without Another Addition to the Booke. Examine and Judge. [ed. Robert Hill]

1. London: [Printed] by John Legatte, printer to the Universitie of Cambridge, and are to be sold at his house in Trinitie lane, [1612]. [ESTC 19664]

2. London: Printed by John Legatt, dwelling in Little-Wood-streete, 1621. [ESTC 19664.5]

Dutch

De gulden keten, ofte, eene beschrijvinghe van de gantsche theologie. [trans. Phillippum Ruyl]

1. Amsterdam: Gillis Rooman for Jan Evertsz Cloppenburch, 1606. [USTC 1010799]

2. Amsterdam: Jan Evertsz II Cloppenburgh, 1610. [USTC 1021111]

3. In *Opera Theologica.* Amsterdam: Jan Evertsz II Cloppenburgh, 1615. [USTC 1032964]

4. Amsterdam: Samuel Imbrechts, 1651.

5. Amsterdam: Samuel Imbrechts, 1654.

6. Amsterdam: Samuel Imbrechts, 1657.

7. Amsterdam: Johannes van Someren, 1659.

Selections and Abridgements

Richard Marsal, *Fifteen Considerations, Stirring Us Up to the Watchfulnesse of These Dangerous Times. With, Fourteen Directions to Every Godly Christian, Who Is Desirous to Go out to Fight the Lords Battles against Antichrist. Also, Thirteen Principles of Religion; by Mr. Perkins: By Way of Question and Answer. Shewing, What Necessitie There Is for All That Are for Reformation, and Are Desirous to Venture Life, Fortune and Estate, for Religion, King, Parliament, Laws, Liberties; against Those Who (If They Prevail) Will Blot Out Religion, and Utterly Destroy Us All. Published by Richard Marsal Minister of Gods Word. Published by Authority, and Printed with Order.* [selected points from *A Golden Chain*]

1. London: Printed by Bernard Alsop, 1645. [Wing M723]

2. London: Printed by Bernard Alsop, 1647 [i.e., 1646]. [Wing M724]

XXIX. Directions and Considerations, Stirring Us Up to Watchfulnesse, Where Every Christian May Get Armour in These Dangerous Times, to Fight against Antichrist, and His Adherents. With Thirteen Principles of Religion, by M. Perkins: By Way of Question and Answer. Shewing, What Necessitie There Is for All That Are for Reformation, and Are Desirous to Venture Life Fortune and Estate, for Religion,

King, Parliament, Laws and Liberties; against Those Who (if They Prevail) Will Blot Out Religion, and Utterly Destroy Us All. Published by Richard Marsal Minister of Gods Word. Set Forth by Authority, and Printed with Order. [selected points extracted from *A Golden Chain*]

   1. London: Printed by Bernard Alsop, 1647 [i.e., 1646]. [Wing M724]

The Whole Duty of Man, Containing a Practical Table of the Ten Commandments: Wherein the Sins Forbidden, and the Duties Commanded, or Implied, Are Clearly Discovered.
Contents: *A Golden Chain*, chs. 19–30 [abridged]

   1. London: Printed for William Miller at the Gilded Acorn in S. Paul's Churchyard, near the little north door, 1674. [Wing P1573]

Latin
Decalogus
Contents: *Armilla Aurea*, chs. 19–30.

   1. In *Catechesis*. Hanau: Wilhelm Antonius, 1608. [USTC 2014551]
   2. In *Catechesis*. Genevae: P. Aubertus, 1611. [USTC 6702940]

Dutch
Eene grondige uytlegginghe der thien gheboden Gods. [trans. Vincent Meusevoet]
Contents: *Armilla Aurea*, chs. 19–30.

   1. Amsterdam: Laurens Jacobsz, 1603. [USTC 1019275]
   2. Amsterdam: Jan Evertsz II Cloppenburgh, 1605. [USTC 1012471]
   3. Amsterdam: Jan Evertsz II Cloppenburgh, 1605. [USTC 1012497]
   4. Amsterdam: Jan Evertsz II Cloppenburgh, 1610. [USTC 1012542]

German
Gründliche Erklärung der zehen Gebott Gottes [trans. Johann Heupel]
Contents: *Armilla Aurea*, chs. 19–30.

   1. In *Christliche und griindliche Erhliirunge der Zehen Gebott und Ge bets dess Herren*. Hanau: G. Antonius, 1604.

Gründliche Erklärung der zehen Gebott Gottes [with *Erklärunge des Gebetts deß Herren*]. [trans. Johann Heupel]
Contents: *Armilla Aurea*, chs. 19–30; *Lord's Prayer*.

   1. In *Catechismus*. Hanau: Wilhelm Anton, 1607. [USTC 2105736]
   2. In *Catechismus*. Basel: Jacob Trew, 1606. [USTC 2066455]

Grain of Mustard Seed [RHB 8:639–58]

A Graine of Musterd-Seed, or, the Least Measure of Grace That Is or Can Be Effectuall to Salvation.

1. London: Printed by Thomas Creed for Raphe Jackson and Hugh Burwell, 1597. [ESTC 19724.5]

2. [Bound together: *Estate of a Christian, Case of Conscience, Lord's Prayer, Grain of Mustard Seed*]. London: Printed by the widow Orwin [and Felix Kingston] for John Porter, 1597. [ESTC 19712]

3. In [*Works*]. [Cambridge]: Printed by John Legat, printer to the Universitie of Cambridge, 1600. [ESTC 19646].

Revised

A Graine of Musterd-Seede or, the Least Measure of Grace That Is or Can Be Effectuall to Salvation. Corrected and Amended by W. Perkins.

1. [Cambridge]: Printed by John Legat, printer to the Universitie of Cambridge, and are to be sold in Pauls Churchyard at the signe of the Crowne by Simon Waterson, 1603. [ESTC 19724.7]

2. In *Works*. Cambridge: Printed by John Legat, printer to the Universitie of Cambridge, 1603. [ESTC 19647]

3. In *Works*. Cambridge: Printed by John Legat, printer to the Universitie of Cambridge, 1605. [ESTC 19648]

4. At London: Printed [by Adam Islip] for Cuthbert Burbie, 1607. [ESTC 19724.9]

5. In *Works*, vol. 1. Cambridge: Printed by John Legate, printer to the Universitie of Cambridge, 1608. [ESTC 19649]

6. London: [Printed] by John Legate, printer to the Universitie of Cambridge, and are to be sold in Pauls Churchyard at the signe of the Crowne by Simon Waterson, 1611. [ESTC 19725]

7. In *Works*, vol. 1. Cambridge: Printed by John Legate, 1612. [ESTC 19650]

8. London: [Printed] by John Legatt, printer to the University of Cambridge, 1615. [ESTC 19726]

9. In *Works*, vol. 1. London: Printed by John Legatt, 1616. [ESTC 19651]

10. J. Legatt, 1620.

11. London: Printed by John Legatt, dwelling in Little-Wood-streete, 1621. [ESTC 19726.5]

12. London: Printed by J[ohn] L[egat], dwelling in Little-Wood-streete, 1625. [ESTC 19726.7]

13. In *Works*, vol. 1. London: Printed by John Legatt, 1626. [ESTC 19652]

14. J. Legatt, 1630.

15. In *Works*, vol. 1. London: Printed by John Legatt and are to be sold by James Boler, George Lathum, John Grismond, Robert Milbourne, and John Bellamie, 1631. [ESTC 19652.5]

16. In *Works*, vol. 1. London: Printed by John Legatt and are to be sold by Iames Boler, George Lathum, John Grismond, Robert Milbourne, and John Bellamie, 1631. [ESTC 19653.5]

17. In *Works*, vol. 1. London: Printed by John Legatt, 1635. [ESTC 19654]

18. London: Printed by John Legatt, [c. 1638]. [ESTC 19727]

19. Newcastle: Printed and sold by John White, [1750?]. [ESTC Cit. T203922]

Stationers' entries: to Ralph Jackson, February 7, 1597 [Arber 3:80]; to Cuthbert Burby, April 27, 1602 [Arber 3:205]; to William Welby, October 16, 1609 [Arber 3:420]; to Thomas Snodham, March 2, 1618 [Arber 3:621]; John Legat to John Legat [Jr.], January 2, 1621 [Arber 4:46]; Snodham to William Stansby, February 23, 1626 [Arber 4:153]; to John Haviland, July 30, 1630 [Arber 4:238]; Haviland and John Wright, September 4, 1638 [Arber 4:431].

Dutch

Van het Cleene Mostaertzaeden. [trans. Vincent Meusevoet]

1. In *Vijf Tractaten*. Amsterdam: Jan Evertsz II Cloppenburgh, 1611. [USTC 1012552]

2. Amsterdam: J. Kok, 1656.

3. Amsterdam: J. Kok, 1657.

4. In *Alle de Werken*. Amsterdam: J. von Someren, 1659–1663.

German

Das geistliche Senffkömlein, oder die aller kleineste Maß der Gnaden Gottes, welche zum Heyl und Seligkeit deß Menschen gnugsam seyn mag. [trans. Johann Ulrich]

1. In *Zwey lehr- und trostreiche Stücke*. Oppenheim: Friedrich Hulsius, 1610. [USTC 2080581]

2. In *Zwey lehr- und trostreiche Stücke*. Bern: Georg Sonnleitner, 1665.

3. In *Zwey lehr- und trostreiche Stücke*. Bern: Georg Sonnleitner, 1669.

Harmony / Harmoniae [RHB 1:1–70]

Specimen Digesti, sive Harmoniae Bibliorum Veteris et Novi Testamenti.

1. Cantabrigiae: Ex officina Johannis Legat, 1598. [ESTC 19749]

Dedication (Perkins): December 31, 1597.

Stationers' entries: to John Legat, March 17, 1598 [Arber 3:106]; (English and Latin) to John Legat [Jr.], January 2, 1621 [Arber 4:46].

Specimen Digesti, Sive Harmoniae Bibliorum Veteris et Novi Testamenti, Auctore Guilielmo Perkinso Anglo, SStae Theologiae D.

   1. Hanau: Wilhelm Antonius, 1602. [USTC 2078490]

   2. Hanau: G. Anton, 1614.

Harmonie: ofte Cort begrijp des Ouden ende Nieuwen Testaments.

   1. Amsterdam: Gerrit Hendricxsz van Breughel for Jan Evertsz Cloppenburgh, 1611. [USTC 1032810]

   2. Amsterdam, 1611, in *Breede Uytlegginge*, Amsterdam, 1612.

English
A Digest or Harmonie of the Bookes of the Old and New Testament.

   1. In *Works*, vol. 2. Cambridge: Printed by John Legate, printer to the Universitie of Cambridge, 1608. [ESTC 19649]

   2. In *Works*, vol. 2. Cambridge: Printed by John Legate, 1613. [ESTC 19650]

   3. In *Works*, vol. 2. Cambridge: Printed by John Legate, 1617. [ESTC 19651]

   4. In *Works*, vol. 2. London: Printed by John Legatt and are to be sold by James Boler, George Lathum, John Grismond, Robert Milbourne, and John Bellamie, 1631. [ESTC 19652.5]

   5. In *Works*, vol. 2. London: Printed by John Legatt, 1631. [ESTC 19653]

Dutch
Hermonie ofte Cort Begrijp des Ouden en Nieuwen Testaments. [trans. J Pannelius]

   1. Amsterdam: Jan Evertsz II Cloppenburgh, 1611.

   2. Someren, 1662.

Hebrews [RHB 3:1–411]

The Practice of Faith, Set Down at Large in the XIth Chapter to the Hebrews and Briefly Described in the 6 Verses Following. [unauthorized]

   1. n.p. [1602/3]. [not extant]

A Cloud of Faithfull Witnesses, Leading to the Heavenly Canaan: Or a Commentarie upon the 11. Chapter to the Hebrewes, Preached in Cambridge by That Godly, and Judicious Divine, M. William Perkins. Long Expected and Desired; and Therefore Published at the Request of His Executours, by Will. Crashawe, and Tho. Pierson, Preachers of Gods Word: Who Heard Him Preach It, and Wrote It from His Mouth. [ed. William Crashawe and Thomas Pierson].

   1. At London: Printed by Humfrey Lownes for Leo. Greene, 1607. [ESTC 19677.5]

   2. At London: Printed by Humfrey Lownes for Leo. Greene, 1608. [ESTC 19678]

3. In *Works*, vol. 3. Cambridge: Printed by Cantrell Legge, printer to the Universitie of Cambridge, 1609. [ESTC 19649]

4. [London]: Printed for Leonard Greene, 1613. [ESTC Cit. S479404]

5. In *Works*, vol. 3. Cambridge: Printed by Cantrell Legge, printer to the Universitie of Cambridge, 1613. [ESTC 19650]

6. In *Works*, vol. 3. Cambridge: Printed by Cantrell Legge, printer to the Universitie of Cambridge, 1618. [ESTC 19651]

7. London: Printed by William Stansby for Henry Fetherstone and John Parker, 1622. [ESTC 19679]

8. In *Works*, vol. 3. London: Printed by John Legatt and are to be sold by James Boler, George Lathum, John Grismond, Robert Milbourne, and John Bellamie, 1631. [ESTC 19652.5]

9. In *Works*, vol. 3. London: Printed by John Haviland, 1631. [ESTC 19653a]

10. In *Works*, vol. 3. London: Printed by John Haviland for James Boler, 1631. [ESTC 19653b]

11. In *Works*, vol. 3. London: Printed by John Haviland and are to be sold by Iames Boler, George Lathum, John Grismond, Robert Milbourne, and John Bellamie, 1631. [ESTC 19653b.5]

Stationers' entries: to William Cotton, November 12, 1602 [Arber 3:221]; to Leonard Green, June 12, 1607 [Arber 3:353]; to Walter Burre and Leonard Greene, October 3, 1610. [Arber 3:445]; Burre's half to Henry Fetherstone and John Parker, November 2, 1618 [Arber 3:635]; Fetherstone's share to Parker, April 3, 1626 [Arber 4:158]; Green's half to Master Boler, December 13, 1629 [Arber 4:223]; Parker's share to John Haviland and John Wright, September 4, 1638 [Arber 4:433]; Boler's half to the Stationers' Company Master & Wardens in trust for Boler's children, September 7, 1638 [Arber 4:436].

Dutch

First work in: *Breede uytlegginge ende grondighe verclaringhe over het elfste capittel van den brief des apostels Pauli tot den Hebreen. Ten tweeden, over den gheheelen sendt-brief des apostels Jude.* [trans. Vincent Meusevoet]

1. Amsterdam: Gerrit Hendricxsz van Breughel for Jan Evertsz Cloppenburgh, 1612. [USTC 1032808]

Een wolke van getrouwe getuygen, leydende na 't hemelze Canaan. Ofte Een uytlegginge over 't elfde capittel tot den Hebreen.

1. Gedrukt in 't onzes Heeren, 1662. [USTC 1540712]

Over het elfde Capittel aan de Hebreen.

1. In *Geleerde en Godzalige Uytleggingen*. Amsterdam: Johannes van Someren, 1662.

Hepieíkeia [RHB 10:357–98]

Hepieíkeia: or, A Treatise of Christian Equitie and Moderation. Delivered Publikely in Lectures by M. W. Perkins, and Now Published by the Consent of His Assignes in Cambridge by a Preacher of the Word. [ed. William Crashawe]

1. [Cambridge]: Printed by John Legat, printer to the Universitie of Cambridge, and are to be sold in Pauls Churchyard at the signe of the Crowne by Simon Waterson, 1604. [ESTC 19699]

2. In *Works*, vol. 2. Cambridge: Printed by John Legate, printer to the Universitie of Cambridge, 1608. [ESTC 19649]

3. In *Works*, vol. 2. Cambridge: Printed by John Legate, 1613. [ESTC 19650]

4. In *Works*, vol. 2. Cambridge: Printed by John Legate, 1617. [ESTC 19651]

5. In *Works*, vol. 2. London: Printed by John Legatt and are to be sold by James Boler, George Lathum, John Grismond, Robert Milbourne, and John Bellamie, 1631. [ESTC 19652.5]

6. In *Works*, vol. 2. London: Printed by John Legatt, 1631. [ESTC 19653]

Dedication (Crashawe): September 10, 1603.

Stationers' entries: to John Legat and Simon Waterson, February 23, 1607 [Arber 3:340]; John Legat's share [half] to John Legat [Jr.], January 2, 1621 [Arber 4:46]; Waterson's share [half] to John Waterson, August 19, 1635 [Arber 4:346].

Dutch

Een tractaet van de christelycke billickheyt.

1. Amsterdam: Jan Evertsz Cloppenburgh, 1613, in *Verscheyden theologische wercken*, Haarlem: Adriaen I Roman for Jan Evertsz II Cloppenburgh, 1614. [USTC 1012617]

2. In *Alle de Werken*. Amsterdam: J. von Someren, 1659–1663.

How to Live [RHB 10:1–29]

How to Live, and That Well: In All Estates and Times, Specially When Helps and Comforts Faile.

1. [Cambridge]: Printed by John Legat, printer to the Universitie of Cambridge, and are to be sold at the Crowne in Pauls Churchyard by Simon Waterson, 1601. [ESTC 19728]

2. [Cambridge]: Printed by John Legat, printer to the Universitie of Cambridge, and are to be sold in Pauls Churchyard at the signe of the Crowne by Simon Waterson [London], 1603. [ESTC 19728.5]

3. In *Works*. Cambridge: Printed by John Legat, printer to the Universitie of Cambridge, 1603. [ESTC 19647]

4. In *Works*. Cambridge: Printed by John Legat, printer to the Universitie of Cambridge, 1605. [ESTC 19648]

5. [Cambridge]: Printed by John Legat, printer to the Universitie of Cambridge…and are to be sold in Pauls Churchyard…by Simon Waterson, 1607. [ESTC 19728.5+]

6. In *Works*, vol. 1. Cambridge: Printed by John Legate, printer to the Universitie of Cambridge, 1608. [ESTC 19649]

7. London: [Printed] by John Legat, printer to the Universitie of Cambridge, and are to be sold in Pauls churchyard at the signe of the Crowne by Simon Waterson, 1611. [ESTC 19729]

8. London: [Printed] by John Legatt, printer to the Universitie of Cambridge, 1615. [ESTC 19730]

9. In *Works*, vol. 1. London: Printed by John Legatt, 1616. [ESTC 19651]

10. London: Printed by John Legatt, dwelling in Little-Wood-streete, 1621. [ESTC 19730.3]

11. London: J. Legat, 1625. [ESTC 19730.5]

12. In *Works*, vol. 1. London: Printed by John Legatt, 1626. [ESTC 19652]

13. In *Works*, vol. 1. London: Printed by John Legatt and are to be sold by James Boler, George Lathum, John Grismond, Robert Milbourne, and John Bellamie, 1631. [ESTC 19652.5]

14. In *Works*, vol. 1. London: Printed by John Legatt and are to be sold by Iames Boler, George Lathum, John Grismond, Robert Milbourne, and John Bellamie, 1631. [ESTC 19653.5]

15. In *Works*, vol. 1. London: Printed by John Legatt, 1635. [ESTC 19654]

16. London: Printed by John Legatt, 1638. [ESTC 19730.7]

Stationers' entries: to John Legat, December 7, 1601 [Arber 3:197]; to John Legat [Jr.], January 2, 1621 [Arber 4:45].

In *A Garden of Spiritual Flowers*. [excerpts]

1. [various editions between 1609 and 1687, see below]

Latin

EYZΩIA: Hoc est ee Bene Beateque Vivendi Ratione Tractatus, Auctore Guilielmo Perkinso Theologo Anglo. Latinus e Belgico Aactus a I. H. [trans. I. H.]

1. Hanoviae: G. Antonium, 1603. [USTC 2091714]

Dutch

Hoemen leven sal, ende dat wel: wanneer hulpe ende troost ontbreeckt. [trans. Vincent Meusevoet]

1. Leiden: Christoffel Guyot for Laurens Jacobsz, 1602. [USTC 1016140]

2. Amsterdam: Jan Evertsz II Cloppenburgh, 1606. [USTC 1012523]

3. Amsterdam: Jan Evertsz II Cloppenburgh, 1610. [USTC 1012522]

4. Amsterdam: Jan Evertsz II Cloppenburgh, 1624. [USTC 1020932]

5. In *Alle de Werken*. Amsterdam: J. von Someren, 1659–1663.

German

Rechte edle Kunst wohl und christlich zu leben…ubversetzt durch Wolgang Mayern. [trans. Wolfgang Mayer]

1. Oppenheim: H. Galler, 1610.

First work in: *Recht Lebens- und Sterbens Kunst.* [trans. Lucas Stockle]

1. Helmstedt: P. Zeising, 1680.

2. Frankfurt: P. Zeising, 1684.

Hungarian

Az Ember Eletenek Bódogúl való Igazgatasanak módgyáról. Es ismét Patika Szerzámos Bolt. Melyben sok-fele halaloknak nemei és természeti: Es az Bódogúl valo meghalásnak igaz módgya: világosan tanittatik. Wilhelmus Perkinsus, Angliai Theologus által. Deákból Magyarra fordittatot Iratosi T. János Pap által. [trans. Iratosi T. János]

1. Lőcse: Brever Lőrintz, 1637.

2. Lőcse: Brever Lőrintz, 1641.

3. Lőcse: Brever Lőrintz, 1651.

Idolatry [RHB 7:411–514]

A Warning against the Idolatrie of the Last Times. And an Instruction Touching Religious, or Divine Worship.

1. [Cambridge]: Printed by John Legat, printer to the Universitie of Cambridge, 1601. [ESTC 19763.5]

2. [Cambridge]: Printed by John Legat, printer to the Universitie of Cambridge, and are to be sold at the signe of the Crowne in Pauls Churchyard [, London,] by Simon Waterson, [1601]. [ESTC 19764]

3. In *Works*. Cambridge: Printed by John Legat, printer to the Universitie of Cambridge, 1603. [ESTC 19647]

4. In *Works*, vol. 1. Cambridge: Printed by John Legate, printer to the Universitie of Cambridge, 1608. [ESTC 19649]

5. In *Works*, vol. 1. Cambridge: Printed by John Legate, 1612. [ESTC 19650]

6. In *Works*, vol. 1. London: Printed by John Legatt, 1616. [ESTC 19651]

7. In *Works*, vol. 1. London: Printed by John Legatt, 1626. [ESTC 19652]

8. In *Works*, vol. 1. London: Printed by John Legatt and are to be sold by James Boler, George Lathum, John Grismond, Robert Milbourne, and John Bellamie, 1631. [ESTC 19652.5]

9. In *Works*, vol. 1. London: Printed by John Legatt and are to be sold by Iames Boler, George Lathum, John Grismond, Robert Milbourne, and John Bellamie, 1631. [ESTC 19653.5]

10. In *Works*, vol. 1. London: Printed by John Legatt, 1635. [ESTC 19654]

Stationers' entries: to John Legat, December 7, 1601 [Arber 3:197]; to John Legat [Jr.], January 2, 1621 [Arber 4:46].

Latin

De Idololatria Postremi Huius Temporis Tractatio, Nunc Recens ex Lingua Anglica in Latinam Conversa Opera [et] Studio Wolgangi Mayeri SS. Theol. D. [trans. Wolfgang Meyer]

1. Oppenheim: Levinus Hulsius (widow of) [et] Hieronymus Galler, 1616. [USTC 2030142]

Dutch

Waarschouwing teeghen de afgoodery in de laaste tyden. [trans. Vincent Meusevoet]

1. Amsterdam: Jan Evertsz Cloppenburgh, 1604.

2. In *Opera Theologica*. Amsterdam: Jan Evertsz II Cloppenburgh, 1615. [USTC 1032964]

3. Amsterdam: Amsterdam: Johannes van Someren, 1659.

Imaginations [RHB 9:181–252]

A Treatise of Mans Imaginations. Shewing His Natural Evill Thoughts: His Want of Good Thoughts: The Way to Reforme Them. Framed and Preached by M. Wil. Perkins. [ed. Thomas Pierson]

1. Cambridge: Printed by John Legat, printer to the Universitie of Cambridge, and are to be sold in Pauls churchyard at the signe of the Crowne by Simon Waterson, 1607. [ESTC 19751]

2. In *Works*, vol. 2. Cambridge: Printed by John Legate, printer to the Universitie of Cambridge, 1608. [ESTC 19649]

3. In *Works*, vol. 2. Cambridge: Printed by John Legate, 1613. [ESTC 19650]

4. In *Works*, vol. 2. Cambridge: Printed by John Legate, 1617. [ESTC 19651]

5. In *Works*, vol. 2. London: Printed by John Legatt and are to be sold by James Boler, George Lathum, John Grismond, Robert Milbourne, and John Bellamie, 1631. [ESTC 19652.5]

6. In *Works*, vol. 2. London: Printed by John Legatt, 1631. [ESTC 19653]

Dedication (Pierson): August 20, 1606.

Stationers' entries: to John Legat and Simon Waterson, February 23, 1607 [Arber 3:340]; John Legat's share [half] to John Legat [Jr.], January 2, 1621 [Arber 4:46]; Waterson's share [half] to John Waterson, August 19, 1635 [Arber 4:346].

Dutch

Een tractaet van de inbeeldinghe des mensches.

1. Haarlem: Adriaen I Roman for Jan Evertsz Cloppenburgh, 1613. [USTC 1012618]

2. in *Verscheyden theologische wercken.* Haarlem: Adriaen I Roman for Jan Evertsz II Cloppenburgh, 1614. [USTC 1012617]

3. In *Alle de Werken.* Amsterdam: J. von Someren, 1659–1663.

German

Tractätlein von des Menschen natürlichen Gedancken. [Bound with John Down-ame's *Christian Warfare*]

1. Cassel: Johann Inebrand, 1667.

2. Cassel: F. Hertzog for J. Ingebrand, 1668.

3. Cassel: F. Hertzog for J. Ingebrand, 1674.

Jude [RHB 4:1–285]

A Godlie and Learned Exposition upon the Whole Epistle of Jude, Containing Threescore and Six Sermons: Preached in Cambridge by That Reverend and Faithfull Man of God, Master William Perkins; and Now, at the Request of His Executors, Published by Thomas Taylor, Preacher of Gods Word. Wherunto Is Prefixed a Large Analysis, Containing the Summe and Order of the Whole Book, according to the Authors Owne Method. To Which Are Further Added Foure Briefe Tables, to Direct the Reader in the Finding, of Either; 1. Common Places of Religion. 2. More Generall Doctrines. 3. Questions Determined. 4. Places of Scripture, Either Expounded, or Cleered from Corruption. [ed. Thomas Taylor]

1. London: [Printed] by Felix Kyngston for Thomas Man, 1606. [ESTC 19724]

2. London: Printed by Felix Kyngston for Thomas Man, dwelling in Pater noster row, at the signe of the Talbot, 1606. [ESTC 19724.3]

3. In *Works*, vol. 3. Cambridge: Printed by Cantrell Legge, printer to the Universitie of Cambridge, 1609. [ESTC 19649]

4. In *Works*, vol. 3. Cambridge: Printed by Cantrell Legge, printer to the Universitie of Cambridge, 1613. [ESTC 19650]

5. In *Works*, vol. 3. Cambridge: Printed by Cantrell Legge, printer to the Universitie of Cambridge, 1618. [ESTC 19651]

6. In *Works*, vol. 3. London: Printed by John Legatt and are to be sold by James Boler, George Lathum, John Grismond, Robert Milbourne, and John Bella-mie, 1631. [ESTC 19652.5]

7. In *Works*, vol. 3. London: Printed by John Haviland, 1631. [ESTC 19653a]

8. In *Works*, vol. 3. London: Printed by John Haviland for James Boler, 1631. [ESTC 19653b]

9. In *Works*, vol. 3. London: Printed by John Haviland and are to be sold by Iames Boler, George Lathum, John Grismond, Robert Milbourne, and John Bellamie, 1631. [ESTC 19653b.5]

Stationers' entries: [Thomas Man] to Paul Man and Jonas Man, May 3, 1624 [Arber 4:117]; Jonas Man's share to Benjamin Fisher, July 6, 1629 [Arber 4:215]; Thomas, Paul, and Jonas Man's share in Perkins's works to Benjamin Fisher and Widow Man, August 12, 1635 [Arber 4:344]; Fisher's share to Robert Young, March 27, 1637 [Arber 4:378].

Dutch

Een geleerde en godtvruchtige verklaringhe over den zendbrief Jude. [trans. Vincent Meusevoet]

1. Amsterdam: J. E. Cloppenburch, 1611.

Second work in: *Breede uytlegginge ende grondighe verclaringhe over het elfste capittel van den brief des apostels Pauli tot den Hebreen. Ten tweeden, over den gheheelen sendt-brief des apostels Jude.* [trans. Vincent Meusevoet]

1. Amsterdam: Gerrit Hendricxsz van Breughel for Jan Evertsz Cloppenburgh, 1612. [USTC 1032808]

Over den Zendbrief Jude.

1. In *Geleerde en Godzalige Uytleggingen.* Amsterdam, 1662.

Lord's Prayer [RHB 5:417–79]

M. Perkins upon the Lordes Praier: By Order of Catechising, Devided into Three Partes. The First Is, the Commandements: The Second, the Creede: And the Thirde, the Doctrine of Praier, as It Is Written Mat. 6.9 Verse. [unauthorized edition]

1. London: Printed by R. B[ourne]. and are to be solde by Edward White at the little north doore of Pauls at the signe of the Gun, 1592. [ESTC 19699.5]

An Exposition of the Lords Prayer, in the Way of Catechising Serving for Ignorant People. By W. Perkins. [revised]

1. London: Printed by Robert Bourne and John Porter, 1592. [ESTC 19700]

2. London: Printed by [J. Wolfe for] Robert Bourne and John Porter, 1593. [ESTC 19700.5]

3. Edinburgh: Printed by Robert Waldegrave, printer to the Kings Majestie, 1593. [ESTC 19701]

Second Edition

*An Exposition of the Lords Prayer: In the Way of Catechising Serving for Ignorant
People. Hereunto Are Adjoined the Praiers of Paule, Taken out of His Epistles. By
W. Perkins.*

1. London: Printed [by Adam Islip] for John Legat, 1595. [ESTC 19702a /
   19702]

2. London: Printed by the Widow Orwin for John Porter and Ralph Jackson,
   1596. [ESTC 19702a.5]

3. [Bound together: *Estate of a Christian, Case of Conscience, Lord's Prayer,
   Grain of Mustard Seed*]. London: Printed by the widow Orwin [and Felix
   Kingston] for John Porter, 1597. [ESTC 19712]

4. In [*Works*]. [Cambridge]: Printed by John Legat, printer to the Universitie of
   Cambridge, 1600. [ESTC 19646].

5. In *Works*. Cambridge: Printed by John Legat, printer to the Universitie of
   Cambridge, 1603. [ESTC 19647]

6. In *Works*. Cambridge: Printed by John Legat, printer to the Universitie of
   Cambridge, 1605. [ESTC 19648]

7. In *Works*, vol. 1. Cambridge: Printed by John Legate, printer to the Universitie of Cambridge, 1608. [ESTC 19649]

8. In *Works*, vol. 1. Cambridge: Printed by John Legate, 1612. [ESTC 19650]

9. In *Works*, vol. 1. London: Printed by John Legatt, 1616. [ESTC 19651]

10. In *Works*, vol. 1. London: Printed by John Legatt, 1626. [ESTC 19652]

11. In *Works*, vol. 1. London: Printed by John Legatt and are to be sold by James
    Boler, George Lathum, John Grismond, Robert Milbourne, and John Bella-
    mie, 1631. [ESTC 19652.5]

12. In *Works*, vol. 1. London: Printed by John Legatt and are to be sold by Iames
    Boler, George Lathum, John Grismond, Robert Milbourne, and John Bella-
    mie, 1631. [ESTC 19653.5]

13. In *Works*, vol. 1. London: Printed by John Legatt, 1635. [ESTC 19654]

Stationers' entries: to Roberte Bourne, January 4, 1592 [Arber 2:601]; to John Porter
and Robert Bourne, March 1, 1592 [Arber 2:604]; to Felix Kingston, June 25, 1599,
"A booke in Welshe being parkins vppon the lordes praier" [Arber 3:145]; half to
Leonard Green, August 4, 1608 [Arber 3: 386]; John Legat to John Legat [Jr.],
January 2, 1621 [Arber 4:45].

Latin

Oratio Dominica.

1. In *Catechesis*. Hanau: Wilhelm Antonius, 1608. [USTC 2014551]

2. In *Catechesis*. Genevae: P. Aubertus, 1611. [USTC 6702940]

Dutch

Een Uvtlegginghe des Ghebedt des Heeren. [trans. Vincent Meusevoet]

1. Amsterdam: J. E. Cloppenburch, 1603.

2. Amsterdam: J. E. Cloppenburch, 1605.

3. in *Catechismus.* Basel: Jacob Trew, 1606. [USTC 2066455]

4. in *Catechismus.* Hanau: Wilhelm Anton, 1606.

5. in Catechismus. Hanau: Wilhelm Anton, 1607. [USTC 2105736]

6. Amsterdam: J. E. Cloppenburch, 1610.

7. Amsterdam: J. E. Cloppenburch, 1615.

8. Amsterdam: Johannes van Someren, 1659.

Eene uutlegginghe des ghebedts des Heeren, dienende om slechte luyden te onderwijsen. [trans. Vincent Meusevoet]

1. Amsterdam: Laurens Jacobsz, 1603. [USTC 1019277]

2. Amsterdam: Jan Evertsz II Cloppenburgh, 1605. [USTC 1012493]

3. Amsterdam: Jan Evertsz II Cloppenburgh, 1610. [USTC 1012541]

Korte Ulvtlegginghe over de Ghebeden des…Pauli. [trans. Vincent Meusevoet]
Contents: prayers of Paul from appendix of *Lord's Prayer.*

1. Amsterdam: Jan Evertsz II Cloppenburgh, 1605.

2. Amsterdam: J. Kok, 1654.

3. Amsterdam: J. Kok, 1657.

German

Gründtliche Erklärung der zehen Gebott Gottes.

1. In *Catechismus.* Basel: Jacob Trew, 1606. [USTC 2066455]

2. In *Catechismus.* Hanau: Wilhelm Anton, 1606.

3. In Catechismus. Hanau: Wilhelm Anton, 1607. [USTC 2105736]

Erklärunge deß Gebetts deß Herren [with *Erklärunge der Gebotten Gottes*]. [trans. Johann Heupel]

1. In *Christliche und griindliche Erhliirunge der Zehen Gebott und Ge bets dess Herren.* Hanau: G. Antonius, 1604.

Welsh

Agoriad Bvrr ar Weddi'r Argylwydd.

1. n.p., 1677.

Lyers

First work in: *Foure Great Lyers, Striving Who Shall Win the Silver Whetstone. Also, a Resolution to the Countri-Man, Proving Is Utterly Unlawfull to Buye or Use Our Yeerly Prognostications. Written by W. P.*

  1. At London: Printed by Robert Waldegrave, 1585. [ESTC 19721.7]

Manner & Order / *De Praedestinationis* [RHB 6:273–384]

De Praedestinationis Modo et Ordine: Et de Amplitudine Gratiae Divinae Christiana & Perspicua Disceptatio.

  1. Cantabrigiae: ex officina Johannis Legat, 1598. [ESTC 19682]

De Praedestinationis Modo et Ordine: Et de Amplitudine Gratiae Divinae Christiana et Perspicua Disceptatio. Per Guilhelmum Perkinsium. Theologum Anglum.

  1. Basel: Konrad von Waldkirch, 1599. [USTC 628757]

  2. Hanoviae, 1603.

  3. Basel: Konrad von Waldkirch, 1603. [USTC 2091713]

  4. Basel: Konrad von Waldkirch, 1613. [USTC 2145891]

English

A Christian and Plaine Treatise of the Manner and Order of Predestination, and of the Largenes of Gods Grace. First Written in Latine by That Reverend and Faithfull Servant of God, Master William Perkins, Late Preacher of the Word in Cambridge. And Carefully Translated into English by Francis Cacot, and Thomas Tuke. [trans. Francis Cacot and Thomas Tuke]

  1. At London: Printed [by F. Kingston] for William Welby and Martin Clarke, 1606. [ESTC 19683]

  2. In *Works*, vol. 2. Cambridge: Printed by John Legate, printer to the Universitie of Cambridge, 1608. [ESTC 19649]

  3. In *Works*, vol. 2. Cambridge: Printed by John Legate, 1613. [ESTC 19650]

  4. In *Works*, vol. 2. Cambridge: Printed by John Legate, 1617. [ESTC 19651]

  5. In *Works*, vol. 2. London: Printed by John Legatt and are to be sold by James Boler, George Lathum, John Grismond, Robert Milbourne, and John Bellamie, 1631. [ESTC 19652.5]

  6. In *Works*, vol. 2. London: Printed by John Legatt, 1631. [ESTC 19653]

Dedication (Cacott and Tuke): February 19, 1605.

Stationers' entries: for English translation to William Welby and Martyn Clerke, August 12, 1606 [Arber 3:327]; Clerk's interest passed to Cuthbert Burby, November 10, 1606 [Arber 3:332]; all assigned to John Legat, January 29, 1607 [Arber 3:338]; to John Legat [Jr.], January 2, 1621 [Arber 4:46].

Dutch

Een tractaet, christelijck ende duydelijck verhandelende de maniere ende het ver-
volgh der predestinatie Gods. [trans. Phillippum Ruyl]

  1. Amsterdam: Jan Evertsz II Cloppenburgh, 1609. [USTC 1012536]

  2. In *Opera Theologica.* Amsterdam: Jan Evertsz II Cloppenburgh, 1615.
     [USTC 1032964]

  3. Amsterdam: Jan Evertsz II Cloppenburgh, 1659.

Ministry [RHB 10:195–280]
1. Job
2. Isaiah

> *Of the Calling of the Ministerie Two Treatises, Discribing the Duties and Dignities*
> *of That Calling. Delivered Publickly in the Universitie of Cambridge, by Maister*
> *Perkins. Taken Then from His Mouth, and Now Dilligently Perused and Published,*
> *by a Preacher of the Word With a Preface Prefixed Touching the Publishing of*
> *Maister Perkins His Workes, & a Catalogue of All Such Particulars Thereof, as Are*
> *to Bee Expected.* [ed. William Crashawe]

  1. London: by I. R[oberts]. for Willliam [*sic*] Welby and are to be sold at
     his shop in Paules-Churchyard, at the signe of the Grayhound, 1605.
     [ESTC 19733]

Second work in: *M. Perkins, His Exhortation to Repentance, out of Zephaniah:*
Preached in 2. Sermons in Sturbridge Faire. Together with Two Treatises of the
Duties and Dignitie of the Ministrie: Delivered Publiquely in the Universitie of
Cambridge. With a Preface Præfixed Touching the Publishing of All Such Workes
of His as Are to Be Expected: With a Catalogue of All the Perticulers of Them, Dili-
gently Perused and Published, by a Preacher of the Word. [ed. William Crashawe;
bound with *Exhortation*]

  1. London: Imprinted by T. C[reede]. for William Welby and are to bee sold
     at his shop in Pauls Churchyard, at the signe of the Grey-hound, 1605.
     [ESTC 19706.5]

Third Impression:
Of the Calling of the Ministerie, Two Treatises. Describing the Duties and Dignities
of That Calling. Delivered Publikely in the Universitie of Cambridge, by Maister
Perkins. Taken Then from His Mouth, and Now Dilligently Perused and Published,
by a Preacher of the Word. [ed. William Crashawe]

  1. London: Printed by Thomas Creede for William Welby and are to be sold
     at his shop at the signe of the Grey-hound in Paules Churchyard, 1606.
     [ESTC 19733a]

2. In *Works*, vol. 3. Cambridge: Printed by Cantrell Legge, printer to the Universitie of Cambridge, 1609. [ESTC 19649]

3. In *Works*, vol. 3. Cambridge: Printed by Cantrell Legge, printer to the Universitie of Cambridge, 1613. [ESTC 19650]

4. In *Works*, vol. 3. Cambridge: Printed by Cantrell Legge, printer to the Universitie of Cambridge, 1618. [ESTC 19651]

5. In *Works*, vol. 3. London: Printed by John Legatt and are to be sold by James Boler, George Lathum, John Grismond, Robert Milbourne, and John Bellamie, 1631. [ESTC 19652.5]

6. In *Works*, vol. 3. London: Printed by John Haviland, 1631. [ESTC 19653a]

7. In *Works*, vol. 3. London: Printed by John Haviland for James Boler, 1631. [ESTC 19653b]

8. In *Works*, vol. 3. London: Printed by John Haviland and are to be sold by Iames Boler, George Lathum, John Grismond, Robert Milbourne, and John Bellamie, 1631. [ESTC 19653b.5]

Stationers' entries: William Welby, January 22, 1605 [Arber 3:280]; to Michael Baker, October 1, 1610 [Arber 3:444].

Dutch

Twee tractaten van de ampten ende waerdicheden des heylighen dienstes: de konst van het propheteren; de kragt des gebeds. [trans. Vincent Meusevoet]

1. Amsterdam: Jan Evertsz II Cloppenburgh, 1610.

2. In *Alle de Werken.* Amsterdam: J. von Someren, 1659–1663.

Mount [RHB 1:167–734]

The Reformation of Covetousnesse. Written upon the 6. Chapter of Mathew, from the 19. Verse to the Ende of the Said Chapter. By William Perkins.

1. London: [By T. Creede] for Nicholas Ling and John Newbery, 1603. [ESTC 19735.6]

Stationers' entries: to Thomas Bushell, November 23, 1602 [Arber 3:222]; …Nicholas Linge to John Smethwick, November 19, 1607 [Arber 3:365].

A Godly and Learned Exposition of Christs Sermon in the Mount: Preached in Cambridge by That Reverend and Judicious Divine M. William Perkins. Published at the Request of His Exequutors by Th. Pierson Preacher of Gods Word. Whereunto Is Adjoyned a Twofold Table: One, of Speciall Points Here Handled; the Other, of Choise Places of Scripture Here Quoted. [ed. Thomas Pierson]

1. [Cambridge]: [Pr]inted by Thomas Brooke and Cantrell Legge, printers to the Universitie Cambridge, 1608. [ESTC 19722]

2. In *Works*, vol. 3. Cambridge: Printed by Cantrell Legge, printer to the Universitie of Cambridge, 1609. [ESTC 19649]

3. Printed by Cantrell Legge, Printer to the Universitie of Cambridge, 1611. [ESTC 19723]

4. In *Works*, vol. 3. Cambridge: Printed by Cantrell Legge, printer to the Universitie of Cambridge, 1613. [ESTC 19650]

5. In *Works*, vol. 3. Cambridge: Printed by Cantrell Legge, printer to the Universitie of Cambridge, 1618. [ESTC 19651]

6. In *Works*, vol. 3. London: Printed by John Legatt and are to be sold by James Boler, George Lathum, John Grismond, Robert Milbourne, and John Bellamie, 1631. [ESTC 19652.5]

7. In *Works*, vol. 3. London: Printed by John Haviland, 1631. [ESTC 19653a]

8. In *Works*, vol. 3. London: Printed by John Haviland for James Boler, 1631. [ESTC 19653b]

9. In *Works*, vol. 3. London: Printed by John Haviland and are to be sold by Iames Boler, George Lathum, John Grismond, Robert Milbourne, and John Bellamie, 1631. [ESTC 19653b.5]

Dedication (Pierson): May 1608.

Stationers' entries: to Cuthbert Burby, April 2, 1604 [Arber 3:259]; to Cantrell Legge, June 14, 1608 [Arber 3:381]; [part?] to William Welby, October 16, 1609 [Arber 3:421]; to Thomas Snodham, March 2, 1618 [Arber 3:621]; to William Stansby, February 23, 1626 [Arber 4:153]; Legge's share to James Boler, June 1, 1629 [Arber 4:212]; Stansby's share to John Haviland, July 30, 1630 [Arber 4:238]; Haviland and John Wright, September 4, 1638 [Arber 4:431]; Boler's share (i.e., one third) to the Stationers' Company Master & Wardens in trust for Boler's children, September 7, 1638 [Arber 4:435].

Latin
Seronmis [sic] Christi in Monte,
1. n.p., 1603.

Dutch
Eene godtsalighe ende geleerde uytlegginghe der predicatie Christi op den bergh. [trans. Vincent Meusevoet]

1. In *Opera Theologica*. Amsterdam: Jan Evertsz II Cloppenburgh, 1615. [USTC 1032964]

2. Amsterdam: Baltus De Wild, 1650. [USTC 1014094]

Over 't Vijfde, zefte en zevende Capittel van Mattheus.

1. In *Geleerde en Godzalige Uytleggingen*. Amsterdam, 1662.

De Kragt des Gebeds. Over Matth. 7. 7. ["The Power of Prayer"] [trans. Vincent Meusevoet]

1. Amsterdam: J. Kok, 1657.

Teghen de giericheyt. Gheschreven opt seste capittel Matthei, vant negenthiende vers tot het eynde des voorseyden capittels. [trans. Vincent Meusevoet] [= *The Reformation of Covetousness* (unauthorized), 1603]

1. Amsterdam: Jan Evertsz II Cloppenburgh, 1604. [USTC 1514779]
2. Amsterdam: Jan Evertsz II Cloppenburgh, 1604. [USTC 1022126]
3. Amsterdam: Jan Evertsz II Cloppenburgh, 1605. [USTC 1021412]
4. Amsterdam: Jan Evertsz II Cloppenburgh, 1616. [USTC 1012540]
5. In *Alle de Werken*. Amsterdam: J. von Someren, 1659–1663.

Nova et Expedita [pseudonymous]

[no author], *Nova et Expedita via Comparandæ Linguæ Latinæ*

1. [London]: Ex officina Iohannis Legatt, florentissimæ Academiæ Cantabrigiensis typographi, [c. 1590]. [ESTC 24695a.5]

Nova et Expedita via Comparandæ Linguæ Latinæ. Authore Guilielmo Perkinso, Olim Cantabrigiensis. Jam Recèns in Usum Studio Sorum Edita. [pseudonymous]

1. London: Thomas Harper, 1644. [Wing P1571]

Oeconomie [RHB 10:109–94]

Christian Oeconomie: or, A Short Survey of the Right Manner of Erecting and Ordering a Familie, according to the Scriptures. First Written in Latine by the Author M. W. Perkins, and Now Set forth in the Vulgar Tongue, for More Common Use and Benefit, by Tho. Pickering Bachelar of Diuinitie. [ed. Thomas Pickering]

1. At London: Imprinted by Felix Kyngston and are to be sold by Edmund Weauer, 1609. [ESTC 19677]
2. At London: Imprinted by Felix Kyngston, 1609. [ESTC 19677.3]
3. In *Works*, vol. 3. Cambridge: Printed by Cantrell Legge, printer to the Universitie of Cambridge, 1609. [ESTC 19649]
4. In *Works*, vol. 3. Cambridge: Printed by Cantrell Legge, printer to the Universitie of Cambridge, 1613. [ESTC 19650]
5. In *Works*, vol. 3. Cambridge: Printed by Cantrell Legge, printer to the Universitie of Cambridge, 1618. [ESTC 19651]
6. In *Works*, vol. 3. London: Printed by John Legatt and are to be sold by James Boler, George Lathum, John Grismond, Robert Milbourne, and John Bellamie, 1631. [ESTC 19652.5]
7. In *Works*, vol. 3. London: Printed by John Haviland, 1631. [ESTC 19653a]
8. In *Works*, vol. 3. London: Printed by John Haviland for James Boler, 1631. [ESTC 19653b]

9. In *Works*, vol. 3. London: Printed by John Haviland and are to be sold by
Iames Boler, George Lathum, John Grismond, Robert Milbourne, and John
Bellamie, 1631. [ESTC 19653b.5]

Stationers' entries: to Master W. Cotton and Leonard Green, June 2, 1609 [Arber
3:411]; …William Leake's half to William Barrett, February 16, 1616 [Arber 3:603];
Barrett's share to John Parker, April 30, 1626 [Arber 4:158]; …Cantrell Legge's share
to James Boler, June 1, 1629 [Arber 4:212]; Leonard Green's share to James Boler,
December 13, 1629 [Arber 4:223]; Parker's share to John Haviland and John Wright,
September 4, 1638 [Arber 4:433]; Coler's share to the Stationer Company's Master &
Wardens in trust for Boler's children, September 7, 1638 [Arber 4:436].

Dutch

De christelyke huys-regeringe. [trans. Vincent Meusevoet]

1. In *Verscheyden theologische wercken*. Haarlem: Adriaen I Roman for Jan
Evertsz II Cloppenburgh, 1614. [USTC 1012617]

2. In *Alle de Werken*. Amsterdam: J. von Someren, 1659–1663.

Prognostications [RHB 9:405–38]

Second work in: *Foure Great Lyers, Striving Who Shall Win the Silver Whetstone.
Also, a Resolution to the Countri-Man, Proving Is Utterly Unlawfull to Buye or Use
Our Yeerly Prognostications. Written by W. P.*

1. At London: Printed by Robert Waldegrave, 1585. [ESTC 19721.7]

*A Resolution to the Countri-Man, Proving Is Utterly Unlawfull to Buye or Use Our
Yeerly Prognostications. Written by W. P.*

1. In *Works*, vol. 3. Cambridge: Printed by Cantrell Legge, printer to the Universitie of Cambridge, 1609. [ESTC 19649]

2. In *Works*, vol. 3. Cambridge: Printed by Cantrell Legge, printer to the Universitie of Cambridge, 1613. [ESTC 19650]

3. In *Works*, vol. 3. Cambridge: Printed by Cantrell Legge, printer to the Universitie of Cambridge, 1618. [ESTC 19651]

4. In *Works*, vol. 3. London: Printed by John Legatt and are to be sold by James
Boler, George Lathum, John Grismond, Robert Milbourne, and John Bellamie, 1631. [ESTC 19652.5]

5. In *Works*, vol. 3. London: Printed by John Haviland, 1631. [ESTC 19653a]

6. In *Works*, vol. 3. London: Printed by John Haviland for James Boler, 1631.
[ESTC 19653b]

7. In *Works*, vol. 3. London: Printed by John Haviland and are to be sold by
Iames Boler, George Lathum, John Grismond, Robert Milbourne, and John
Bellamie, 1631. [ESTC 19653b.5]

Dutch

Onderrichtinghe van het mis-bruycken der prognosticatien. [trans. Vincent
Meusevoet]

1. Amsterdam: Jan Evertsz II Cloppenburgh, 1613. [USTC 1012620]

2. In *Verscheyden theologische wercken.* Haarlem: Adriaen I Roman for Jan
   Evertsz II Cloppenburgh, 1614. [USTC 1012617]

Prophesying / Prophetica [RHB 10:280–356]

Prophetica, Sive de Sacra et Unica Ratione Concionandi Tractatus.

1. Cambridge: Ex officina Johannis Legatt, celeberrimæ Academiæ Cantabrigiensis typographi, 1592. [ESTC 19735]

Second Revised Edition

*Prophetica, Sive de Sacra et Unica Ratione Concionandi Tractatus. Editio Secunda
Auctior & Correctior ab Authore Facta.*

1. [Cambridge]: Ex officina Iohannis Legate, celeberrimæ Academiæ Cantabrigiensis typographi, 1592. [ESTC 19735.2]

*Prophetica; Sive de Sacra et Unica Ratione Concionandi, Tractatus, Auctore
Guilielmo Perkinso Anglo Cantabrigiensi, SStae Theologiae D.*

1. Hanau: Wilhelm Antonius, 1602. [USTC 2065461]

*Prophetica Sive de Sacra et Unica Concionandi Ratione Tractatus Nervosiss.,…
Conscriptus a Praestantiß. Viro Guilielmo Perkinsio Cantabrig. Anglo…Theologo
Cui Adiuncta est Pia, Perspicua, [et] Brevis Disceptatio, de Tribus Summe Contro-
versis Hodie*

1. Basel: per Konrad von Waldkirch, 1602. [USTC 2078580]

English

*The Arte of Prophecying, or, A Treatise concerning the Sacred and Onely True Man-
ner and Methode of Preaching First Written in Latine by Master William Perkins;
and Now Faithfully Translated into English (for That It Containeth Many Worthie Things Fit for the Knowledge of Men of All Degrees) by Thomas Tuke.* [trans.
Thomas Tuke]

1. London: [Printed] by Felix Kyngston for E. E. and are to be sold in Pauls
   Churchyard at the signe of the Swan, 1607. [ESTC 19735.4]

2. In *Works*, vol. 2. Cambridge: Printed by John Legate, printer to the Universitie of Cambridge, 1608. [ESTC 19649]

3. In *Works*, vol. 2. Cambridge: Printed by John Legate, 1613. [ESTC 19650]

4. In *Works*, vol. 2. Cambridge: Printed by John Legate, 1617. [ESTC 19651]

5. In *Works*, vol. 2. London: Printed by John Legatt and are to be sold by James Boler, George Lathum, John Grismond, Robert Milbourne, and John Bellamie, 1631. [ESTC 19652.5]

6. In *Works*, vol. 2. London: Printed by John Legatt, 1631. [ESTC 19653]

Dedications (Perkins): December 12, 1592; (Tuke): January 1, 1606.

Stationers' entries: English translation to Cuthbert Burby and Eleazar Edgar, December 10, 1606 [Arber 3:334]; to John Legat, January 29, 1607 [Arber 3:338]; to John Legat [Jr.], January 2, 1621 [Arber 4:46].

Dutch

Prophetica, dat is, een heerliick Tractaet von de heylige ende eeninghe maniere vom Predicken.

1. Amsterdam: s.n., 1605. [USTC 1506215]

2. Amsterdam: Jan Evertsz II Cloppenburgh, 1606. [USTC 1020937]

3. Amsterdam: Jan Evertsz II Cloppenburgh, 1609. [USTC 1012568]

4. In *Alle de Werken*. Amsterdam: J. von Someren, 1659–1663.

Reformed Catholic [RHB 7:1–167]

A Reformed Catholike: or, A Declaration Shewing How Neere We May Come to the Present Church of Rome in Sundrie Points of Religion: And Wherein We Must for Ever Depart from Them: With an Advertisement to All Favourers of the Romane Religion, Shewing That the Said Religion Is against the Catholike Principles and Grounds of the Catechisme.

1. [Cambridge]: Printed by John Legat, printer to the Universitie of Cambridge, 1597. [ESTC 19735.8]

2. [Cambridge]: Printed by John Legat, printer to the Universitie of Cambridge, 1598. [ESTC 19736]

3. In [*Works*]. [Cambridge]: Printed by John Legat, printer to the Universitie of Cambridge, 1600. [ESTC 19646].

4. In *Works*. Cambridge: Printed by John Legat, printer to the Universitie of Cambridge, 1603. [ESTC 19647]

5. Cambridge: Printed by John Legat, printer to the Universitie of Cambridge, and are to be sold at the signe of the crowne in Pauls Churchyard by Simon Waterson, 1604. [ESTC 19737]

6. In *Works*. Cambridge: Printed by John Legat, printer to the Universitie of Cambridge, 1605. [ESTC 19648]

7. In *Works*, vol. 1. Cambridge: Printed by John Legate, printer to the Universitie of Cambridge, 1608. [ESTC 19649]

8. London: [Printed] by John Legatte, printer to the Universitie of Cambridge, and are to be sold in Pauls Churchyard at the signe of the Crowne by Simon Waterson, 1611. [ESTC 19738]

9. In *Works*, vol. 1. Cambridge: Printed by John Legate, 1612. [ESTC 19650]

10. In *Works*, vol. 1. London: Printed by John Legatt, 1616. [ESTC 19651]

11. London: [Printed] by John Legat, printer to the Universitie of Cambridge, 1619. [ESTC 19739]

12. In *Works*, vol. 1. London: Printed by John Legatt, 1626. [ESTC 19652]

13. London: Printed by John Legatt, 1634. [ESTC 19740]

14. In *Works*, vol. 1. London: Printed by John Legatt and are to be sold by James Boler, George Lathum, John Grismond, Robert Milbourne, and John Bellamie, 1631. [ESTC 19652.5]

15. In *Works*, vol. 1. London: Printed by John Legatt and are to be sold by Iames Boler, George Lathum, John Grismond, Robert Milbourne, and John Bellamie, 1631. [ESTC 19653.5]

16. In *Works*, vol. 1. London: Printed by John Legatt, 1635. [ESTC 19654]

Dedication (Perkins): June 28, 1597.

Stationers' entries: to John Legat, August 1, 1597 [Arber 3:88]; to John Legat [Jr.], January 2, 1621 [Arber 4:46].

Latin

Catholicus Reformatus: Hoc est, Expositio Et Declaratio, Quae Ostendit Quatenus Ecclesiae ex Dei Verbo Reformatae in Multis ac Diversis Religionis Capitibus cum Ecclesia Rom. Qualis ea Hodie Est, Consentiunt, ac in Quibus ac Quatenus ab ea Dissentiunt, ad.

1. Hanau: Wilhelm Antonius, 1601. [USTC 2026168]

2. Hanau: Wilhelm Antonius, 1603. [USTC 2132924]

3. Hanau: Wilhelm Antonius, 1604.

4. Hanau: Wilhelm Antonius, 1608. [USTC 2040732]

Dutch

De ghereformeerde catholyck. Dat is: Een verklaringe van d'overeen-stemminge ende t'verschil tusschen de gereformeerde ende roomsche Kercke. [trans. Everard Boot]

1. Middelburg: Richard Schilders, 1604. [USTC 1514776]

2. Enkhuizen: Jan Jansz Camerling, 1633. [USTC 1010263]

3. Amsterdam: Johannes van Someren, 1659.

De ghereformeerde catholyck. Dat is: Een verklaringe van d'overeen-stemminge ende t'verschil tusschen de gereformeerde ende roomsche Kercke. [trans. Vincent Meusevoet]

1. Amsterdam: Jan Evertsz II Cloppenburgh, 1605. [USTC 1012492]

2. In *Opera Theologica*. Amsterdam: Jan Evertsz II Cloppenburgh, 1615. [USTC 1032964]

Een heerlijck ende zeer schoon tractaet van het avondtmael. [trans. G. Van Breen]
Contents: *Reformed Catholic*, chs. 10–11.

1. Amsterdam: Jan Evertsz II Cloppenburgh, 1613. [USTC 1012622]

2. In *Verscheyden theologische wercken*. Haarlem: Adriaen I Roman for Jan Evertsz II Cloppenburgh, 1614. [USTC 1012617]

German

Der Catholische Reformierte Christ: Das ist, Richtige Erklerung und bericht, wie nahe oder ferne die Kirchen, so auß und nach Gottes wort reformiert oder verbessert sind, in vilen und unterschiedlichen Religionspuncten, mit der Römischen Kirchen… [trans. Johann Heidfeld]

1. Herborn: [Christoph Corvinus], 1602. [USTC 2052411]

2. Herborn: Christoph Rab, 1602.

3. Herborn: …, 1608.

4. Herborn: …, 1618.

Der Catholische Glaub.

1. Newstadt an der Hardt: N. Schrammen, 1606.

Spanish

Catholico reformado. O una declaracion que muestra quanto nos podamos. Conformar con la Iglesia Romana, tal, qual es el dia de hoy, en diversos puntos de la religion: y en que puntos devamos nunca jamas convenir, sino para siempre apartarnos della. Yten, un aviso à los afficionados à la Iglesia Romana, que muestra la dicha religion Romana ser contra los Catholicos rudimentos y fundamentos del catecismo. Compuesto por Guillermo Perquino licenciado en sancta theologia, y trasladado en Romance castellano por Guillermo Massan gentil-hombre, y à su costa imprimido. [trans. Guillermo Massan]

1. [London]: En casa de Ricardo del campo [Richard Field], 1599. [ESTC 19741]

2. Amsterdam: en casa de Jacob Pietersz Wachter, 1624. [USTC 5026317]

3. Amsterdam: en casa de Jacob Pietersz Wachter, 1624. [USTC 1019803]

French

Le Catholique Reformé.

1. Lyon: Pour François Le Febure, 1602.

2. Lyon: Pour François Le Febure, 1607.

Hungarian

Catholicus Reformatus, Az az, Egynehány vetélködes ala vettetet hitnek agazati-nak magyarázattya, mely meg mutattya, az igaz Keresztyén Anyaszentegyháznak menyben eggyezni köllyön, az Romai Anyaszentegyházzal, menyben tüle külöm-bözni, és menyben soha véle nem eggyezni. Adattatot ez melle rövid intes, az Romai valláson lévekhöz, melyben meg mutattatik az ő vallasok ellenközőnek lenni, az igaz közönseges keresztyeni vallassal, és az hitnek fondamentomaval. Mely irattatot először Angliai nyelven Guilielmus Perkinsus Anglus által. Az után fordittatot His-paniai nyelvre, Guilielmus Massanustól. Harmadszor déákul, egy fő, böles, tudos embertul. Mostan immár Magyarra fordittatot: Ketskemeti C. János Vngvari Praedikátor által. [trans. Kecskeméti C. János].

1. n.p., 1620.

Revelation [RHB 4:287–626]

Lectures upon the Three First Chapters of the Revelation: Preached in Cambridge Anno Dom. 1595. by Master William Perkins, and Now Published for the Benefite of This Church, by Robert Hill Bachelor in Divinitie. To Which Is Added an Excellent Sermon, Penned at the Request of That Noble and Wise Councellor, Ambrose, Earle of Warwicke: in Which Is Proved That Rome Is Babylon, and That Babylon Is Fallen. [ed. Robert Hill]

1. London: Printed by Richard Field for Cuthbert Burbie and are to be sold at his shop in Paules Churchyard at the signe of the Swan, 1604. [ESTC 19731]

Second Edition

A Godly and Learned Exposition or Commentarie upon the Three First Chapters of the Revelation. Preached in Cambridge by That Reverend and Judicious Divine, Maister William Perkins, Ann. Dom. 1595. First Published for the Benefit of Gods Church, by Robert Hill, Bachelor of Divinitie. The Second Edition Revised and Enlarged after a More Perfect Copie, at the Request of M. Perkins Executors, by Thomas Pierson, Preacher of Gods Word. Hereunto Is Prefixed an Analysis of the Vision in These Three Chapters: And a Twofold Table Added; One of Places of Scripture: The Other of Speciall Points to Bee Observed. [ed. Thomas Pierson]

1. London: Printed by Adam Islip for Cuthbert Burbie and are to be sold at his shop in Paules Churchyard at the signe of the Swan, 1606. [ESTC 19732]

Third Edition

A Godly and Learned Exposition or Commentarie upon the Three First Chapters of the Revelation. Preached in Cambridge by That Reverend and Judicious Divine, Maister William Perkins, Ann. Dom. 1595. First Published for the Benefit of Gods Church, by Robert Hill, Bachelor of Divinitie. The Third Edition, Revised and Enlarged after a More Perfect Copie, at the Request of M. Perkins Executors, by Thomas Pierson, Preacher of Gods Word. Hereunto Is Prefixed an Analysis of the Vision in These Three Chapters: And A Twofold Table Added; One of Places of Scripture: The Other of Speciall Points to Bee Observed. [ed. Thomas Pierson]

1. London: Printed by Adam Islip for Cuthbert Burbie and are to bee sold at his shop in Paules Churchyard at the signe of the Swan, 1607. [ESTC 19732a]

2. In *Works*, vol. 3. Cambridge: Printed by Cantrell Legge, printer to the Universitie of Cambridge, 1609. [ESTC 19649]

3. In *Works*, vol. 3. Cambridge: Printed by Cantrell Legge, printer to the Universitie of Cambridge, 1613. [ESTC 19650]

4. In *Works*, vol. 3. Cambridge: Printed by Cantrell Legge, printer to the Universitie of Cambridge, 1618. [ESTC 19651]

5. In *Works*, vol. 3. London: Printed by John Legatt and are to be sold by James Boler, George Lathum, John Grismond, Robert Milbourne, and John Bellamie, 1631. [ESTC 19652.5]

6. In *Works*, vol. 3. London: Printed by John Haviland, 1631. [ESTC 19653a]

7. In *Works*, vol. 3. London: Printed by John Haviland for James Boler, 1631. [ESTC 19653b]

8. In *Works*, vol. 3. London: Printed by John Haviland and are to be sold by Iames Boler, George Lathum, John Grismond, Robert Milbourne, and John Bellamie, 1631. [ESTC 19653b.5]

Stationers' entries: to Cuthbert Burby, March 21, 1604 [Arber 3:255]; to William Welby, October 16, 1609 [Arber 3:420]; to Master Snodham, March 2, 1618 [Arber 3:621]; to William Stansby, February 23, 1626 [Arber 4:153]; to John Haviland, July 30, 1630 [Arber 4:238]; Haviland and John Wright, September 4, 1638 [Arber 4:431].

Dutch

Een uyt-nemend tractaet vervaetende de lessen, uytlegghende de drie eerste capittelen der Openbaringhe Iohannis. [trans. Vincent Meusevoet]

1. Amsterdam: Jan Evertsz II Cloppenburgh, 1610. [USTC 1020954]

2. Amsterdam: Jan Evertsz II Cloppenburgh, 1640.

Over de drei eerste Capittelen van de Openbaringe Joannis.

1. In *Geleerde en Godzalige Uytleggingen.* Amsterdam, 1662.

Salve [RHB 10:399–458]

A Salve for a Sicke Man, or, A Treatise Containing the Nature, Differences, and Kindes of Death; as Also the Right Manner of Dying Well. And It May Serve for Spirituall Instruction to 1. Mariners When They Goe to Sea. 2. Souldiers When They Goe to Battell. 3. Women When They Travell of Child.

1. [Cambridge]: Printed by John Legate, printer to the Universitie of Cambridge, 1595. [ESTC 19742]

2. [Cambridge]: Printed by John Legate, printer to the Universitie of Cambridge, 1595. [ESTC 19742.5]

3. [Bound with *Christ Crucified* & *Discourse of Conscience*]. Cambridge: Printed by John Legat, printer to the Universitie of Cambridge, 1597. [ESTC 19743].

4. [Cambridge]: Printed by John Legate, printer to the Universitie of Cambridge, 1600. [ESTC 19743.3]

5. In [*Works*]. [Cambridge]: Printed by John Legat, printer to the Universitie of Cambridge, 1600. [ESTC 19646]

6. [Cambridge]: Printed by John Legat, printer to the Universitie of Cambridge, and are to be sold in Pauls Churchyard at the signe of the Crowne by Simon Waterson, 1603. [ESTC 19743.5]

7. In *Works*. Cambridge: Printed by John Legat, printer to the Universitie of Cambridge, 1603. [ESTC 19647]

8. In *Works*. Cambridge: Printed by John Legat, printer to the Universitie of Cambridge, 1605. [ESTC 19648]

9. Cambridge: Printed by John Legat printer to the Univertsiie [*sic*] of Cambridge…and are to be sold in Pauls Churchyard…by Simon Waterson, 1607. [ESTC 19743.5+]

10. In *Works*, vol. 1. Cambridge: Printed by John Legate, printer to the Universitie of Cambridge, 1608. [ESTC 19649]

11. J. Legatt, [1610?].

12. London: by John Legat, printer to the Universitie of Cambridge, and are to be sold in Pauls churchyard at the signe of the Crowne by Simon Waterson, 1611. [ESTC 19745]

13. In *Works*, vol. 1. Cambridge: Printed by John Legate, 1612. [ESTC 19650]

14. London: [Printed] by John Legatt, printer to the Universitie of Cambridge, 1615. [ESTC 19746]

15. In *Works*, vol. 1. London: Printed by John Legatt, 1616. [ESTC 19651]

16. London: Printed by John Legatt, dwelling in Little-Wood-streete, 1621. [ESTC 19746.3]

17. London: Printed by John Legatt, dwelling in Little-Wood-streete, 1625. [ESTC 19746.7]

18. In *Works*, vol. 1. London: Printed by John Legatt, 1626. [ESTC 19652]

19. London: Printed by John Legatt, dwelling in Little-Wood-streete, 1632.
    [ESTC 19747]

20. In *Works*, vol. 1. London: Printed by John Legatt and are to be sold by James
    Boler, George Lathum, John Grismond, Robert Milbourne, and John Bella-
    mie, 1631. [ESTC 19652.5]

21. In *Works*, vol. 1. London: Printed by John Legatt and are to be sold by Iames
    Boler, George Lathum, John Grismond, Robert Milbourne, and John Bella-
    mie, 1631. [ESTC 19653.5]

22. In *Works*, vol. 1. London: Printed by John Legatt, 1635. [ESTC 19654]

23. London: by John Legatt, [c. 1638]. [ESTC 19747.3 / 19744]

Stationers' entries: to John Legat, October 6, 1595 [Arber 3:49]; to John Legat [Jr.],
January 2, 1621 [Arber 4:45].

Latin
*Myrothecium: Hoc Est, de Natura Diversisque Mortis Generibus: Et de Ratione
Bene, Feliciterque Moriendi, Tractatus, Auctore Guilelmo Perkinso Theologo Anglo.
Latinus e Belgico Factus a C. B. Ecclesiae Belgicae, Quae Est Hanoviae, Ministro.*

  1. Hanau: Wilhelm Antonius, 1603. [USTC 2104758]

Dutch
*Salve voor een sieck mensche, ofte een tractaet vervatende de natuere, onderschey-
dentheden, ende soorten des doots.* [trans. Vincent Meusevoet]

  1. Leiden: Jan Bouwensz for Laurens Jacobsz, 1599. [USTC 424325]

  2. Amsterdam: [Printed] for Laurens Jacobsz, 1602. [USTC 1010481]

  3. Amsterdam: Jan Evertsz II Cloppenburgh, 1604. [USTC 1012498]

  4. Amsterdam: Jan Evertsz II Cloppenburgh, 1607.

  5. Haarlem: Aegidius Roman for Jan Evertsz Cloppenburgh, 1608.
     [USTC 1022117]

  6. Amsterdam: Jan Evertsz II Cloppenburgh, 1620. [USTC 1012533]

  7. In *Alle de Werken*. Amsterdam: J. von Someren, 1659–1663.

German
ΕΥΘΑΝΑΣΙΑ: die recht edle Kunst wol zu sterben. [trans. Jacob Mayern]

  1. Basel: L. Konig, 1605.

Second work in: *Recht Lebens-und Sterbens Kunst.* [trans. Lucas Stockle]

  1. Helmstet: P. Zeising, 1680.

Artzney wider die Furcht und Schrekken des zeitlichen Todes, und wie ein Christ recht Lust und Begierde zu demselben bekommen möge. [trans. Lucas Stockle]

1. Frankfurt and Helmstadt: P. Zeising, 1684.
2. n.p., 1700.

French

La Manière de bien et heureusement mourir.

1. Geneve: J. Chouët, 1604.
2. In *Remèdes contre le mal-reiglé mespris, l'oubliance et la trop grande apprehension de la mort.* Paris: J. Chouët, 1604.

Hungarian

Patika Szerszamos Bolt. Az az sokfele halaloknak termeszetekről, es azoknak nemeiről. Es ismet Az jól és bódogul való meg halásnak módgyáról való tanitás. Iratot. Wilhelmus Perkinsus, Angliai Theologus által. Magyar nyelvre Fordittatot, Iratosi T. János, Thoronyai Praedikátor által. [trans. Iratosi T. János]

1. Lőcse: Brever Lőrintz, 1637.
2. Lőcse: Brever Lőrintz, 1651.

Tongue [RHB 9:253–91]

A Direction for the Governement of the Tongue, according to Gods Worde.

1. Cambridge: Printed by John Legate, printer to the Universitie of Cambridge, and are to be solde by Abraham Kitson at the signe of the Sunne in Pauls Churchyard in London, 1593. [ESTC 19688]
2. Edinburgh: Printed by Robert Waldegrave, printer to the Kings Majestie, 1593. [ESTC 19689]
3. Cambridge: John Legate, printer to the University of Cambridge, and to be sold by R. Bankworth in London, 1595. [ESTC 19760.5 / 19759]
4. [London: Printed by R. Field for] John Legat, printer to the University of Cambridge, 1597. [ESTC 19761]
5. Edinburgh: Robert Waldegrave, [1597?].
6. Cambridge: Printed by John Legate, printer to the Universitie of Cambridge, 1600. [ESTC 19689.5]
7. In [*Works*]. [Cambridge]: Printed by John Legat, printer to the Universitie of Cambridge, 1600. [ESTC 19646].
8. [London]: Printed by John Legat, printer to the Universitie of Cambridge, and are to be sold in Pauls churchyard at the signe of the Crowne by Simon Waterson, 1603. [ESTC 19690]
9. In *Works*. Cambridge: Printed by John Legat, printer to the Universitie of Cambridge, 1603. [ESTC 19647]

10. In *Works*. Cambridge: Printed by John Legat, printer to the Universitie of Cambridge, 1605. [ESTC 19648]

11. In *Works*, vol. 1. Cambridge: Printed by John Legate, printer to the Universitie of Cambridge, 1608. [ESTC 19649]

12. London: [Printed] by John Legate, printer to the Uniuersitie of Cambridge, and are to be sold in Pauls Churchyard at the signe of the Crowne by Simon Waterson, 1611. [ESTC 19691]

13. In *Works*, vol. 1. Cambridge: Printed by John Legate, 1612. [ESTC 19650]

14. London: [Printed] by John Legatt, printer to the Uniuersity of Cambridge, 1615. [ESTC 19692]

15. In *Works*, vol. 1. London: Printed by John Legatt, 1616. [ESTC 19651]

16. London: Printed by John Legatt, dwelling in Little-Wood-streete, 1621. [ESTC 19693]

17. London: Printed by John Legatt, dwelling in Little-Wood-streete, 1625. [ESTC 19693.5]

18. In *Works*, vol. 1. London: Printed by John Legatt, 1626. [ESTC 19652]

19. In *Works*, vol. 1. London: Printed by John Legatt and are to be sold by James Boler, George Lathum, John Grismond, Robert Milbourne, and John Bellamie, 1631. [ESTC 19652.5]

20. In *Works*, vol. 1. London: Printed by John Legatt and are to be sold by Iames Boler, George Lathum, John Grismond, Robert Milbourne, and John Bellamie, 1631. [ESTC 19653.5]

21. London: Printed by John Legatt, dwelling in Little-Wood-streete, 1632. [ESTC 19694]

22. Edinburgh: Printed by John Wreittoun, 1634. [ESTC 19695]

23. In *Works*, vol. 1. London: Printed by John Legatt, 1635. [ESTC 19654]

24. London: John Legatt, [c. 1638]. [ESTC 19684.5]

25. London: Printed by John Legatt, [c. 1638]. [ESTC 19694.5]

Dedication (Perkins): December 12, 1592.

Stationers' entries: to John Legat, February 14, 1593 [Arber 2:626]; to John Legat [Jr.], January 2, 1621 [Arber 4:45].

Latin

Lex Linguae, Seu Linguae Componendae Praescriptum, Verbo Dei Consentaneum, Autore Guilielmo Perkinso…et Interprete Thoma Draxo. [trans. Thomas Draxe]

1. Oppenheim: Levinus Hulsius (widow of) [et] Hieronymus Galler, 1613. [USTC 2016335]

Licentiati, Tractatus Vere Aureus, de Linguae Regimine, Iuxta Dei Verbum Latinitate Donatus a Thoma Draxo… [trans. by Thomas Draxe]

    1. Hanau: Wilhelm Antonius (heirs of), 1614. [USTC 2029534]

Dutch

Eene onderwijsinghe voordraghende hoe men de tonge behoort te regeeren na den woorde Gods. [trans. Vincent Meusevoet]

    1. Amsterdam: Laurens Jacobsz, 1600. [USTC 425092]

    2. Amsterdam: Laurens Jacobsz, 1603. [USTC 1012495]

    3. Amsterdam: Jan Evertsz II Cloppenburgh, 1607. [USTC 1012494]

    4. Amsterdam: Jan Evertsz II Cloppenburgh, 1614. [USTC 1020936]

    5. Amsterdam: J. Kok, 1654.

    6. Amsterdam: J. Kok, 1657.

    7. In *Alle de Werken.* Amsterdam: J. von Someren, 1659–1663.

German

Zungenleitter das ist, Ein edler und herzlicher Unterricht, wie man die Zunge zu Gottes Ehre, deß Nechsten und eines jeglichen selbst eygenen Nutzen recht brauchen könne und solle, Erstlich Beschrieben in Englischer Spraache von Herrn Guilielmo Perkinso. [trans. Heinrich Sprüngli]

    1. Oppenheim: Levinus Hulsius (widow of) and Hieronymus Galler, 1616. [USTC 2056180]

Zungenleiter…auß dem Lateinischen Exemplar verteutschet durch Heinrich Sprüngli…

    1. Zurich: Georg Hamberger, 1623.

Czech

Traktát velmi platný a užitečný o správě jazyka, nejprve v englickém jazyku vedle slova Božího sebraný od Vilhelma Perkynsa. [trans. Simeon Valecius]

    1. Prague: Matěj Pardubský, 1616.

True Gain [RHB 9:23–78]

The True Gaine: More in Worth Then All the Goods in the World.

    1. [Cambridge]: Printed by John Legat, printer to the Universitie of Cambridge, 1601. [ESTC 19757]

    2. [Cambridge]: Printed by John Legat, printer to the Universitie of Cambridge, and are to be sold at the signe of the Crowne in Pauls Churchyard by Simon Waterson, 1601. [ESTC 19757.5] [Issued with *Idolatry*, ESTC 19764].

    3. In *Works.* Cambridge: Printed by John Legat, printer to the Universitie of Cambridge, 1603. [ESTC 19647]

4. In *Works*. Cambridge: Printed by John Legat, printer to the Universitie of Cambridge, 1605. [ESTC 19648]

5. In *Works*, vol. 1. Cambridge: Printed by John Legate, printer to the Universitie of Cambridge, 1608. [ESTC 19649]

6. In *Works*, vol. 1. Cambridge: Printed by John Legate, 1612. [ESTC 19650]

7. In *Works*, vol. 1. London: Printed by John Legatt, 1616. [ESTC 19651]

8. In *Works*, vol. 1. London: Printed by John Legatt, 1626. [ESTC 19652]

9. In *Works*, vol. 1. London: Printed by John Legatt and are to be sold by James Boler, George Lathum, John Grismond, Robert Milbourne, and John Bellamie, 1631. [ESTC 19652.5]

10. In *Works*, vol. 1. London: Printed by John Legatt and are to be sold by Iames Boler, George Lathum, John Grismond, Robert Milbourne, and John Bellamie, 1631. [ESTC 19653.5]

11. In *Works*, vol. 1. London: Printed by John Legatt, 1635. [ESTC 19654]

Dedication (Perkins): January 20, 1601.

Stationers' entries: to John Legat, December 7, 1601 [Arber 3:197]; to John Legat [Jr.], January 2, 1621 [Arber 4:46].

Dutch

Het ware gewin, waerdiger dan alle de goederen die inde werelt zijn. [trans. Vincent Meusevoet]

1. Amsterdam: Herman de Buck for Laurens Jacobsz, 1601. [USTC 1010480]

2. Amsterdam: Jan Evertsz II Cloppenburgh, 1604. [USTC 1022118]

3. Amsterdam: Jan Evertsz II Cloppenburgh, 1604. [USTC 1012499]

4. Amsterdam: Jan Evertsz II Cloppenburgh, 1606.

5. Amsterdam: Jan Evertsz II Cloppenburgh, 1616. [USTC 1016497]

6. In *Alle de Werken*. Amsterdam: J. von Someren, 1659–1663.

Two Treatises [RHB 9:123–80]

1. Repentance

2. Combat

Two Treatises. I. Of the Nature and Practise of Repentance. II. Of the Combat of the Flesh and Spirit.

1. Cambridge: Printed by John Legate, printer to the Universitie of Cambridge, and are to be sold [by Abraham Kitson] at the signe of the Sunne in Paules Churchyard in London, 1593. [ESTC 19758]

2. Cambridge: Printed by John Legate, printer to the Universitie of Cambridge, and are to be sold at the Signe of the Sunne in Pauls Churchyard in London, 1595. [ESTC 19760]

3. Cambridge: Printed by John Legate, printer to the Universitie of Cambridge, and are to be sold [by R. Bankworth] at the signe of the Sunne in Pauls Churchyard in London, 1595. [ESTC 19760.5]

Second Edition

Two Treatises. I. Of the Nature and Practise of Repentance. II. Of the Combat of the Flesh and Spirit. Second Edition Corrected.

1. [London]: Printed by [Richard Field for] John Legate, printer to the Universitie of Cambridge, 1597. [ESTC 19761]

2. [London]: Printed by John Legate, printer to the Universitie of Cambridge, 1600. [ESTC 19761.1]

3. In [*Works*]. [Cambridge]: Printed by John Legat, printer to the Universitie of Cambridge, 1600. [ESTC 19646].

4. In *Works*. Cambridge: Printed by John Legat, printer to the Universitie of Cambridge, 1603. [ESTC 19647]

5. In *Works*. Cambridge: Printed by John Legat, printer to the Universitie of Cambridge, 1605. [ESTC 19648]

6. In *Works*, vol. 1. Cambridge: Printed by John Legate, printer to the Universitie of Cambridge, 1608. [ESTC 19649]

7. London: [Printed] by John Legat, printer to the Universitie of Cambridge, and are to be sold in Pauls Churchyard at the signe of the Crowne by Simon Waterson, 1611. [ESTC 19761.3]

8. In *Works*, vol. 1. Cambridge: Printed by John Legate, 1612. [ESTC 19650]

Corrected

Two Treatises. 1. Of the Nature and Practise of Repentance. 2. Of the Combate of the Flesh and Spirit. Fifth Edition Corrected.

1. London: [Printed] by John Legatt, printer to the University of Cambridge, 1615. [ESTC 19761.5]

2. In *Works*, vol. 1. London: Printed by John Legatt, 1616. [ESTC 19651]

3. London: [Printed] by John Legatt, printer to the Universitie of Cambridge, 1619. [ESTC 19761.7]

4. Cambridge: J. Legatt, 1621. [ESTC 19761]

5. London: Printed by John Legatt, dwelling in Little-Wood-streete, 1621. [ESTC 19761.9]

6. London: Printed by John Legatt, dwelling in Little-Wood-streete, 1625. [ESTC 19762.5]

7. In *Works*, vol. 1. London: Printed by John Legatt, 1626. [ESTC 19652]

8. In *Works*, vol. 1. London: Printed by John Legatt and are to be sold by James Boler, George Lathum, John Grismond, Robert Milbourne, and John Bellamie, 1631. [ESTC 19652.5]

9. In *Works*, vol. 1. London: Printed by John Legatt and are to be sold by Iames Boler, George Lathum, John Grismond, Robert Milbourne, and John Bellamie, 1631. [ESTC 19653.5]

10. Cambridge: J. Legatt, 1632. [ESTC 19763]

11. In *Works*, vol. 1. London: Printed by John Legatt, 1635. [ESTC 19654]

12. London: Printed by John Legatt, [c. 1638]. [ESTC 19763.3]

Dedication (Perkins): November 13, 1593.

Stationers' entries: to John Legat, November 29, 1593 [Arber 2:640]; to John Legat [Jr.], January 2, 1621 [Arber 4:45].

Latin

Metanoiologia, Id Est Erudita & Salutaris Tractatio de Natura et Praxi Resipiscentiae in Libri Calce Adiectus Est Indiculus Rerum Praecipuarum. [trans. Thomas Draxe]

1. Openheim: H. Galleri for L. Hulsii, 1615.

Dutch

Twee tractaten. 1. Van de natuere ende t'betrachten der boetveerdichheyt. 2. Van den strijt des vleeschs ende des gheests. [trans. Vincent Meusevoet]

1. Amsterdam: L. Jacobsz, 1599. [USTC 424323]

2. [Leiden]: [Printed] by Christoffel Guyot for Laurens Jacobsz, 1601. [USTC 1548965]

3. Amsterdam: Jan Evertsz II Cloppenburgh, 1604. [USTC 1012496]

4. Haarlem: Aegidius Roman for Jan Evertsz II Cloppenburgh (Amsterdam), 1608. [USTC 1010826]

5. Amsterdam: Dirck Cornelisz Troost for Jan Evertsz II Cloppenburgh, 1610. [USTC 1012534]

6. Amsterdam: Johannes van Someren, 1622.

7. In *Alle de Werken*. Amsterdam: J. von Someren, 1659–1663.

German

Der Streit und Kampff deß Fleisches und deß Geistes. [trans. Johann Ulrich]

1. In *Ein nützliches und lehrreiches Büchlein*. Oppenheim: Friederich Hulsius, 1610. [USTC 2067549]

2. In *Drey nützliche und lehrreiche Büchlein*. Frankfurt, 1660.

3. In *Drey nützliche und lehrreiche Büchlein*. Bern, 1666.

Czech

Traktát trojí krátký, ku potěšení zarmoucených kajících lidí. Translated by Simeon Valecius.

    1. Prague: Matěj Pardubský, 1612.

    2. Prague: Matěj Pardubský, 1613.

    3. Prague: Matěj Pardubský, 1616.

Vocations [RHB 10:31–107]

    A Treatise of the Vocations, or, Callings of Men, with the Sorts and Kinds of Them, and the Right Use Thereof. Written by Mr. W. Perkins. [ed. Thomas Pickering]

    1. Cambridge: Printed by John Legat, printer to the Universitie of Cambridge, and are to be sold in Pauls Churchyard at the signe of the Crowne by Simon Waterson, 1603. [ESTC 19751.5]

    2. In *Works*. Cambridge: Printed by John Legat, printer to the Universitie of Cambridge, 1603. [ESTC 19647]

    3. In *Works*. Cambridge: Printed by John Legat, printer to the Universitie of Cambridge, 1605. [ESTC 19648]

    4. In *Works*, vol. 1. Cambridge: Printed by John Legate, printer to the Universitie of Cambridge, 1608. [ESTC 19649]

    5. In *Works*, vol. 1. Cambridge: Printed by John Legate, 1612. [ESTC 19650]

    6. In *Works*, vol. 1. London: Printed by John Legatt, 1616. [ESTC 19651]

    7. In *Works*, vol. 1. London: Printed by John Legatt, 1626. [ESTC 19652]

    8. In *Works*, vol. 1. London: Printed by John Legatt and are to be sold by James Boler, George Lathum, John Grismond, Robert Milbourne, and John Bellamie, 1631. [ESTC 19652.5]

    9. In *Works*, vol. 1. London: Printed by John Legatt and are to be sold by Iames Boler, George Lathum, John Grismond, Robert Milbourne, and John Bellamie, 1631. [ESTC 19653.5]

    10. In *Works*, vol. 1. London: Printed by John Legatt, 1635. [ESTC 19654]

Dedication (Pickering): February 16, 1602.

Stationers' entries: John Legat to John Legat [Jr.], January 2, 1621 [Arber 4:46].

Dutch

Een tractaet vande beroepinghen der menschen. [trans. Vincent Meusevoet]

    1. Haarlem: Aegidius Roman for Jan Evertsz II Cloppenburgh [Amsterdam], 1605. [USTC 1020940]

    2. Amsterdam: [Printed] for Jan Evertsz II Cloppenburgh, 1610. [USTC 1012567]

    3. In *Alle de Werken*. Amsterdam: J. von Someren, 1659-63.

Whole Cases [RHB 8:95–440]

The First Part of the Cases of Conscience. Wherein Specially, Three Maine Questions concerning Man, Simply Considered in Himselfe, Are Propounded and Resolved, according to the Word of God. Taught and Delivered, by M. William Perkins in His Holy-Day Lectures, by Himselfe Revised before His Death, and Now Published for the Benefit of the Church. [ed. Thomas Pickering]

  1. Cambridge: Printed by John Legat, printer to the Universitie of Cambridge, and are to be sold in Pauls Churchyard at the signe of the Crowne by Simon Waterson, [1604]. [ESTC 19668]

The Whole Treatise of the Cases of Conscience, Distinguished into Three Bookes: The First Whereof Is Revised and Corrected in Sundrie Places, and the Other Two Annexed. Taught and Delivered by M. W. Perkins in His Holy-Day Lectures, Carefully Examined by His Owne Briefes and Now Published Together for the Common Good, by T. Pickering Bachelour of Divinitie. Whereunto Is Adjoyned a Twofold Table: One of the Heads and Number of the Questions Propounded and Resolved; Another of the Principall Texts of Scripture Which Are Either Explained, or Vindicated from Corrupt Interpretation. [ed. Thomas Pickering]

  1. Cambridge: Printed by John Legat, printer to the Universitie of Cambridge, and are to be sold in Pauls Churchyard at the signe of the Crowne by Simon Waterson, [1606]. [ESTC 19669]

  2. Cambridge: Printed by John Legat, printer to the Universitie of Cambridge, and are to be sold in Pauls Churchyard [, London,] at the signe of the Crowne by Simon Waterson, 1608. [ESTC 19670]

  3. In *Works*, vol. 2. Cambridge: Printed by John Legate, printer to the Universitie of Cambridge, 1608. [ESTC 19649]

  4. Cambridge: Printed by John Legat, printer to the Universitie of Cambridge, 1609.

  5. London: [Printed] by John Legat, printer to the Universitie of Cambridge, and are to be sold in Pauls Churchyard at the signe of the Crowne by Simon Waterson, 1611. [ESTC 19671]

  6. J. Legatt, 1613.

  7. In *Works*, vol. 2. Cambridge: Printed by John Legate, 1613. [ESTC 19650]

  8. London: [Printed] by John Legatt, printer to the Universitie of Cambridge, and are to be sold in Paules churchyard at the signe of the Crowne by Simon Waterson, 1614. [ESTC 19671.5]

  9. London: Printed by John Legatt, printer to the Universitie of Cambridge, 1617. [ESTC Cit. S124299]

  10. In *Works*, vol. 2. Cambridge: Printed by John Legate, 1617. [ESTC 19651]

  11. London: [Printed] by John Legatt, printer to the Universitie of Cambridge, 1619. [ESTC 19672]

12. London: Printed by John Legatt and are to be sold by Simon Waterson at the signe of the Crowne in Pauls Churchyard, 1628. [ESTC 19673]

13. In *Works*, vol. 2. London: Printed by John Legatt and are to be sold by James Boler, George Lathum, John Grismond, Robert Milbourne, and John Bellamie, 1631. [ESTC 19652.5]

14. In *Works*, vol. 2. London: Printed by John Legatt, 1631. [ESTC 19653]

15. London: Printed by John Legatt and are to be sold by Simon Waterson at the signe of the Crowne in Pauls Churchyard, 1632. [ESTC 19674]

16. London: Printed by John Legatt and are to bee sold by John Waterson at the signe of the Crowne in Pauls Churchyard, 1635. [ESTC 18675]

17. London: Printed by John Legatt and are to bee sold by John Waterson at the signe of the Crowne in Pauls Churchyard, 1636. [ESTC 19676]

18. London: Printed by John Legatt and are to be sold at the sign of the Crowne in Pauls Churchyard, 1642. [ESTC P1574]

19. London: Printed by J. L. and are to be sold by Thomas Pierrepont at the sign of the Sun in Paules-Churchyard, 1651. [ESTC P1575]

Dedications (Pickering): June 28, 1604; November 20, 1606.

Stationers' entries: to John Legat and Simon Waterson, February 23, 1607 [Arber 3:340]; John Legat's share [half] to John Legat [Jr.], January 2, 1621 [Arber 4:45]; Legge's tables in vol. 3 to James Boler, June 1, 1629 [Arber 4:212]; Waterson's share [half] to John Waterson, August 19, 1635 [Arber 4:346].

Latin

Aureæ Casuum Conscientiae Decisiones: Tribus Libris Comprehensæ, Primo Nunc Recens ex Lingua Anglica in Latinam Conversæ, [et] cum Reliquis Eiusdem Authoris Scriptis Diligenter Collatæ, ac Magna Acceßione Locup. [trans. Wolfgang Mayer]

1. Basel: Heinrich Waldkirch and Johann Jakob Genath (the Elder), 1608. [USTC 2079946]

2. Basel: Heinrich Waldkirch and Johann Jakob Genath (the Elder), 1609. [USTC 2080188]

3. Basel: Konrad von Waldkirch, 1609. [USTC 2119298]

4. Basil: Heinrich Waldkirch and Johann Jakob Genath (the Elder), 1609. [USTC 2067160]

De Casibus Conscientiae Libri III: In Festorum Dierum Praelectionibus Anglice Traditi [et] Propositi, Nunc Vero Latinitate Donati a Thoma Draxo… [ed. Thomas Draxe]

1. Hanau: Wilhelm Antonius, 1609. [USTC 2132871]

*Aurearum Decisionum Casuum Conscientiae…, Primo Nunc Recensadiectus, [et]
ad Reliqua Eiusdem Authoris Scripta Recensitus…Opera [et] Studio Wolgangi
Mayeri Teil: Liber 2: De Homine, qua schetikōs ad Deum af.* [trans. Wolfgang
Meyer]

 1. Basel: Johann Jakob Genath (the Elder), 1609. [USTC 2002047]

*Ethica Christiana, Id Est, Aurearum Decisionum Casuum Conscientiae, Opera
[et] Studio Wolgangi Mayeri Teil: Liber 3: De Homine ad Hominem Comparate
Considerato: Quo eaae Quaestiones, Quae ex Consideratione Virtutum Emergunt,
Pertra.* [trans. Wolfgang Meyer]

 1. Basel: Konrad von Waldkirch, 1609. [USTC 2106272]

Dutch

Een tractaet van de ghevallen der conscientie, vervat in drie boecken. [trans. Vincent Meusevoet]

 1. Harlem: Gillis Rooman for Jan Evertsz Cloppenburgh, 1608. [USTC
    1548966]
 2. Amsterdam: Jan Evertsz Cloppenburgh, 1618.
 3. Utrecht: [Printed] for Lucas Simonsz de Vries, 1648.
 4. Amsterdam: [Printed] for Abraham Jeuriansen van-Blacken, 1651.
 5. In *Alle de Werken*. Amsterdam: J. von Someren, 1659–1663.

German

Casus Conscientiae, Das ist: Gewissens-Spiegel. [trans. Henrich Sprüngli]

 1. Basel: J. J. Genath, 1640.

*Kurtz unnd gründliche Erörterung etlicher wichtigen Fragen von der Bekanntnuß
deß seeligmachenden Glaubens an Jesum Christum vor den Feinden der Warheit:
darinn auch gehandelt wirdt von der Flucht zur Verfolgungszeit…in das Teutsche
ubersetzt durch Heinrich Springli.* [trans. Heinrich Springli]

Contents: *Whole Treatise*, bk. 2, ch. 12.

 1. Zurich: Georg Hamberger, 1623.

*Gewissens-Spiegel darinn zuersehen allerley Zufälle des menschlichen Gewissens,
durch welche dasselbe mag angefochten werden. Sammt beygefügter gründlicher
Lehre, wie man sich in alle dieselbige zu richten habe.* [trans. T. D.]

 1. Helmstädt: P. Zeising, 1690.
 2. Helmstädt: P. Zeising, 1700.

Hungarian

*Ama Szent Iras feitegetesben hatalmas és igen tudos Doctornak G. Perkinsus-
nak A'Lelki-isméretnek akadékiról irott drága szép tanitásának első könyvében,
az akarmi okbol meg-félemlet és rettegö lelki esméretnek megvigasztalására és
gyógitására, le-tött istenes orvoslási.* [trans. Tsepregi Turkovitz Mihaly Colosvari
Lakos]

Contents: *First book of the Cases of Conscience*

> 1. Amsterdam: Jánsonius Janos által Tsepregi Turkovitz Mihaly költségével,
>   1648. [USTC 1019804]

Works

> [Bound together: *Salve, Christ Crucified & Discourse of Conscience*].

> 1. Cambridge: Printed by John Legat, printer to the Universitie of Cambridge,
>   1597. [ESTC 19743]

> [Bound together: *Estate of a Christian, Case of Conscience, Lord's Prayer, Grain
> of Mustard Seed*].

> 1. London: Printed by the widow Orwin [and Felix Kingston] for John Porter,
>   1597. [ESTC 19712]

[***Works***] [no titlepage]

> Contents: (1) *Golden Chain*, (2) *Creed*, (3) *Lord's Prayer*, (4) *Estate of a Christian*,
> (5) *Case of Conscience*, (6) *Tongue*, (7) *Two Treatises*, (8) *Salve*, (9) *Christ Cruci-
> fied*, (10) *Discourse of Conscience*, (11) *Reformed Catholic*, (12) *Foundation*,
> (13) *Grain of Mustard Seed*.

> 1. [Cambridge]: Printed by John Legat, printer to the Universitie of Cambridge,
>   1600. [ESTC 19646].

*The works of That Famous and Worthie Minister of Christ, in the Universitie of
Cambridge, M. W. Perkins: Gathered into One Volume, and Newly Corrected
according to His Owne Copies. With Distinct Chapters, and Contents of Every
Booke, and a Generall Table of the Whole.*

Contents: (1) *Golden Chain*, (2) *Creed*, (3) *Lord's Prayer*, (4) *Estate of a Christian*,
(5) *Case of Conscience*, (6) *Tongue*, (7) *Two Treatises*, (8) *How to Live*, (9) *Salve*,
(10) *Discourse of Conscience*, (11) *Reformed Catholic*, (12) *Christ Crucified*,
(13) *Foundation*, (14) *Grain of Mustard Seed*, (15) *True Gain*, (16) *Idolatry*,
(17) *God's Free Grace*, (18) *Vocations*.

> 1. Cambridge: Printed by John Legat, printer to the Universitie of Cambridge,
>   1603. [ESTC 19647]

Corrected Edition [1 Volume]

The Works of That Famous and Worthie Minister of Christ, in the Universitie of Cambridge, M. W. Perkins: Gathered into One Volume, and Newly Corrected according to His Owne Copies. With Distinct Chapters, and Contents of Every Booke, and a Generall Table of the Whole.

Contents: (1) *Golden Chain*, (2) *Creed*, (3) *Lord's Prayer*, (4) *Estate of a Christian*, (5) *Case of Conscience*, (6) *Tongue*, (7) *Two Treatises*, (8) *How to Live*, (9) *Salve*, (10) *Discourse of Conscience*, (11) *Reformed Catholic*, (12) *Christ Crucified*, (13) *Foundation*, (14) *Grain of Mustard Seed*, (15) *True Gain*, (16) *Idolatry*, (17) *God's Free Grace*, (18) *Vocations*.

1. Cambridge: Printed by John Legat, printer to the Universitie of Cambridge, and are to be sold [by S. Waterson] at the signe of the Crowne in Pauls Churchyard, [1605]. [ESTC 19648]

Second Edition [3 Volumes]

<u>Volume 1</u>

The Workes of That Famous and Worthie Minister of Christ, in the Universitie of Cambridge, M. William Perkins. The First Volume. Newly Corrected according to His Owne Copies. With Distinct Chapters, and Contents of Euery Booke, and a Brief Table of the Whole, of the Matter, and Questions in Controversie Therein Handled.

Contents: (1) *Golden Chain*, (2) *Creed*, (3) *Lord's Prayer*, (4) *Estate of a Christian*, (5) *Case of Conscience*, (6) *Tongue*, (7) *Two Treatises*, (8) *How to Live*, (9) *Salve*, (10) *Discourse of Conscience*, (11) *Reformed Catholic*, (12) *Christ Crucified*, (13) *Foundation*, (14) *Grain of Mustard Seed*, (15) *True Gain*, (16) *Idolatry*, (17) *God's Free Grace*, (18) *Vocations*.

1. Cambridge: Printed by John Legate, printer to the Universitie of Cambridge, and are to be sold at the signe of the Crowne by Simon Waterson, 1608. [ESTC 19649]

2. Cambridge: Printed by John Legate, 1612. [ESTC 19650]

3. London: Printed by John Legatt, 1616. [ESTC 19651]

4. London: Printed by John Legatt, 1626. [ESTC 19652]

<u>Volume 2</u>

The Workes of That Famous and Worthie Minister of Christ, in the Universitie of Cambridge, M. William Perkins. The Second Volume. Newly Corrected according to His Owne Copies. With Distinct Chapters, and Contents of Every Booke Prefixed: And Two Tables of the Whole Adjoined; One of the Matters, and Questions: The Other of Choice Places of Scripture. [ed. Thomas Pickering]

Contents: (1) *Whole Cases*, (2) *Galatians*, (3) *Hepieíkeia*, (4) *Imaginations*, (5) *Forged Catholicism*, (6) *Manner & Order*, (7) *Prophesying*, (8) *Harmony*.

1. Cambridge: Printed by John Legate, printer to the Universitie of Cambridge, and are to be sold at the signe of the Crowne by Simon Waterson, 1608. [ESTC 19649]

2. Cambridge: Printed by John Legate, 1613. [ESTC 19650]

3. Cambridge: Printed by John Legate, 1617. [ESTC 19651]

<u>Volume 3</u>

The Workes of That Famous and Worthie Minister of Christ, in the Universitie of Cambridge, M. W. Perkins. The Third and Last Volume. Newly Corrected and Amended, Containing His Learned Expositions of Sundrie Choise Places of Scripture, with Some Little Tractates. The Particulars Whereof Thou Maist See in the Next Page, with the Order of Their Placing. Hereof Is Adjoined a Two-Fold Table; One of the Chiefe Points and Questions, the Other of Choice Places of Scripture. [ed. Thomas Pierson]

Contents: (1) *Mount* (Cambridge: Cantrell Legge), (2) *Hebrews* (Printed for Leonard Greene), (3) *Revelation* (Printed for the widow Burbie), (4) *Combat* (Printed for E. Edgar), (5) *Exhortation* (Printed for W. Welbie), (6) *Ministry* (Printed for W. Welbie), (7) *End of the World* (Printed for W. Welbie), (8) *Jude* (Printed for Thomas Man), (9) *Damned Art* (Printed by Cantrell Legge), (10) *Prognostications* (Printed by Cantrell Legge), (11) *Oeconomie* (Printed for Leonard Greene, and Felix Kingston).

1. Cambridge: Printed by Cantrell Legge, printer to the Universitie of Cambridge, 1609. [ESTC 19649]

2. Cambridge: Printed by Cantrell Legge, printer to the Universitie of Cambridge, 1613. [ESTC 19650]

3. Cambridge: Printed by Cantrell Legge, printer to the Universitie of Cambridge, 1618. [ESTC 19651]

Corrected Edition [3 Volumes]

<u>Volume 1</u>

The Whole Works of That Famous and Worthy Minister of Christ in the Universitie of Cambridge, M. William Perkins, in Three Volumes. The First Volume. Newly Corrected according to His Owne Copies. With Distinct Chapters and Contents of Every Booke Prefixed, and Two Tables of the Whole Adjoyned, One of the Matter and Questions, the Other of Choice Places of Scripture.

Contents: [as above].

1. London: Printed by John Legatt and are to be sold by James Boler, George Lathum, John Grismond, Robert Milbourne, and John Bellamie, 1631. [ESTC 19652.5]

2. London: Printed by John Legatt and are to be sold by Iames Boler, George Lathum, John Grismond, Robert Milbourne, and John Bellamie, 1631. [ESTC 19653.5]

3. London: Printed by John Legatt, 1635. [ESTC 19654]

Volume 2

The Whole Works of That Famous and Worthy Minister of Christ in the Universitie of Cambridge, M. William Perkins, in Three Volumes. The Second Volume. Newly Corrected according to His Owne Copies. With Distinct Chapters and Contents of Every Booke Prefixed, and Two Tables of the Whole Adjoyned, One of the Matter and Questions, the Other of Choice Places of Scripture. [ed. Thomas Pickering]

Contents: [as above].

1. London: Printed by John Legatt and are to be sold by James Boler, George Lathum, John Grismond, Robert Milbourne, and John Bellamie, 1631. [ESTC 19652.5]
2. London: Printed by John Legatt, 1631. [ESTC 19653]

Volume 3

The Whole Works of That Famous and Worthy Minister of Christ in the Universitie of Cambridge, M. William Perkins. The Third and Last Volume. Containing His Learned Expositions of Sundry Choice Places of Scripture, with Some Little Tractates. The Particulars Whereof Thou Mayest See in the Next Page, with the Order of Their Placing. Hereto Is Adjoyned a Two-Fold Table, One of the Chiefe Points and Questions, the Other of Choice Places of Scripture. [ed. Thomas Pierson]

Contents: Contents: (1) *Mount* (London: John Haviland), (2) *Hebrews* (London: John Haviland), (3) *Revelation* (London: John Haviland), (4) *Combat* (London, 1631), (5) *Exhortation* (London: John Haviland), (6) *Ministry* (London: John Haviland), (7) *End of the World* (London: John Haviland), (8) *Jude* (Printed by the Assignees of Thomas Man, etc.), (9) *Damned Art* (London: James Boler), (10) *Prognostications* (London: James Boler), (11) *Oeconomie* (London: James Boler).

1. London: Printed by John Legatt and are to be sold by James Boler, George Lathum, John Grismond, Robert Milbourne, and John Bellamie, 1631. [ESTC 19652.5]
2. London: Printed by John Haviland, 1631. [ESTC 19653a]
3. London: Printed by John Haviland for James Boler, 1631. [ESTC 19653b]
4. London: Printed by John Haviland and are to be sold by James Boler, George Lathum, John Grismond, Robert Milbourne, and John Bellamie, 1631. [ESTC 19653b.5]

An Abridgement of the Whole Body of Divinity Extracted from the Learned Works of That Ever-Famous and Reverend Divine, Mr. William Perkins / by Tho. Nicols.

1. London: Printed by W. B. for William Hope at the blue Anchor, on the Northside of the Royal Enchange, 1654. [Wing P1560]

Latin

Opuscula Theologica Varia: Multiplici Doctrina [et] Consolatione Cumulatissima; Indicem Tractatuum in Hoc Libro Contentorum, Aversa Indicat Pagina, ex Anglico in Latinam Linguam Translata a Thoma Draxo. [trans. Thomas Draxe]

Contents: (1) *Spiritual Disertions*, (2) *Estate of a Christian: 5. Dialogue*, (3) *Estate of a Christian: 7. Consolations*, (4) *Grain of Mustard Seed*, (7) *Estate of a Christian: 6. Applying God's Word*, (8) *Estate of a Christian: 1. How Far a Reprobate*, (9) *Estate of a Christian: 4. Religion of Rome* [abridged], (10) *Christ Crucified*, (10) *Two Treatises: 2. Combat*, (11) *Foundation* [abridged].

    1. Hanau: Wilhelm Antonius, 1608. [USTC 2079733]

Guilielmi Perkinsi Anglo-Britanni, Viri Clarissimi, Opera Theologica. [Volume 1]

Contents: (1) *Armilla Aurea*, (2) *De Praedestinationis*, (3) *Prophetica*, (4) *Problema*, (5) *Reformed Catholic*, (6) *Foundation*, (7) *God's Free Grace*, (8) *Opuscula Theologica Varia* [cf. above], (9) *Damned Art*, (10) *Discourse of Conscience*, (11) *Whole Cases*, (12) *How to Live*, (13) *Salve*, (14) *Harmoniae*.

    1. Genève: Pierre Chouët et Jacques Chouët, 1611. [USTC 6702897]

    2. Genève: Pierre Chouët et Jacques Chouët, 1611. [USTC 6702932]

    3. Geneva: Pierre Chouët et Jacques Chouët, 1618. [USTC 6700678]

    4. Genève: Pierre Chouët et Jacques Chouët, 1619.

    5. Genève: Pierre Chouët et Jacques Chouët, 1624.

    6. Genève: Pierre Chouët et Jacques Chouët, 1628.

    7. Geneva: Pierre Chouët et Jacques Chouët, 1658.

    8. Geneva: Pierre Chouët et Jacques Chouët, 1668.

Guilielmi Perkinsi Anglo-Britanni, Viri Clarissimi, Operum Omnium Theologica Coram Quae Extant. [Volume 2]

Contents: (1) *Ministry*, (2) *Combat*, (3) *Mount*, (3) *Estate of a Christian: 2. How Far the Elect*, (4) *Estate of a Christian: 3. Dialogue*, (5) *Galatians*, (6) *Prognostication*, (7) *Exhortation*, (8) *End of the World*, (9) *True Gain*, (10) *Epieikia*, (11) *Estate of a Christian: 2. How Far the Elect* [repeated], (12) *Two Treatises: 1. Repentance* (13) *Tongue*, (14) *Case of Conscience*, (15) *Imaginations*, (16) *Idolatry*, (14) *Hebrews*, (15) *Oeconomia*, (16) *Estate of a Christian: 4. Religion of Rome*, (17) *Jude*, (18) *Revelation*.

    1. Geneva: Pierre Chouët et Jacques Chouët, 1618. [USTC 6700678]

    2. Geneva: Pierre Chouët et Jacques Chouët, 1624.

    3. Geneva: Pierre Chouët et Jacques Chouët, 1628.

    4. Geneva: Pierre Chouët et Jacques Chouët, 1658.

    5. Geneva: Pierre Chouët et Jacques Chouët, 1668.

Catechesis: In Qua Initio Sex Firma [et] Immota Totius Religionis Christianae Iacta Sunt Fundamenta…Deinde Omnia [et] Singula Christianae Religionis Capita… commentario illustrata. [trans. Johann Lotichius]

Contents: (1) *Foundation,* (2) *Creed,* (3) Baptism [*Galatians, 3:26–28*] and Lord's Supper [*Reformed Catholic,* chs. 10–11], (4) Decalogue [*Armilla Aurea,* chs. 19–30] and *Lord's Prayer.*

1. Hanau: Wilhelm Antonius, 1608. [USTC 2014551]
2. Genevae: P. Aubertus, 1611. [USTC 6702940]

Dutch

Vijf Tractaten, van Meester Wilhelmum Perkinsum. Namentlijck, I. Van de vrye ghenaede Godes, ende de vrye wille des Mensches. 2. Van het cleene Mostaert-zaedeken. 3. Van de graeden der belijdenisse des H. Euangeliums, tot welcke oock de Verworpenen connen comen. 4. Van de maniere hoe een Mensch sich Gods heylighe woordt ter zalicheydt sal toe-eyghenen. 5. Van de schrickelicke Tooverye.

Contents: (1) *God's Free Grace,* (2) *Grain of Mustard Seed,* (3) *Estate of a Christian: 1. How Far a Reprobate,* (4) *Estate of a Christian: 6. Applying God's Word,* (5) *Damned Art.*

1. Amsterdam: Jan Evertsz II Cloppenburgh, 1611. [USTC 1012552]

Een seer uytnemende tractaet ende verhandelinghe der H. sacramenten des Nieuwen-verbondts ofte Testaments.

Contents: Sacraments [*Galatians 3:26–28; Reformed Catholic,* chs. 10–11].

1. Amsterdam: Jan Evertsz II Cloppenburgh, 1613. [USTC 1012621]
2. In *Opera Theologica.* Amsterdam: Jan Evertsz II Cloppenburgh, 1615. [USTC 1032964]
3. Amsterdam: Jan Evertsz II Cloppenburgh, 1659.
4. In *Verscheyden theologische wercken.* Haarlem: Adriaen I Roman for Jan Evertsz II Cloppenburgh, 1614. [USTC 1012617]

Verscheyden theologische wercken Wilh. Perkinsi. Vervatende zeer profijtelijcke, leersame ende morale schriften,…Wt de Engelsche in onse Nederl. tale over-gheset, door Vinc. Meusevoet. [trans. Vincent Meusevoet]

Contents: (1) *Oeconomie,* (2) *Equity,* (3) *Case of Conscience,* (4) *Imaginations,* (5) *End of the World,* (6) *Prognostications,* (7) Baptism [*Galatians 3:26–28*], (8) Lord's Supper [*Reformed Catholic,* chs. 10–11].

1. Haarlem: Adriaen I Roman for Jan Evertsz II Cloppenburgh, 1614. [USTC 1012617]

Opera theologica dat is De theologische wercken M. Wilhelmi Perkinsi. Vervatende verscheiden leersame ende troosteleyke tractaeten ende uytleggingen.

Contents: (1) *Creed*, (2) Decalogue [*Armilla Aurea*, chs. 19–30], (3) *Lord's Prayer*, (4) *Foundation*, (5) Sacraments [*Galatians 3:26–28*; *Reformed Catholic*, chs. 10–11], (6) *Golden Chain*, (7) *Manner & Order*, (8) *Estate of a Christian: 1. How Far a Reprobate*, (9) *God's Free Grace*, (10) *Reformed Catholic*, (11) *Forged Catholicism*, (12) *Idolatry*, (13) *Galatians*, (14) *Mount*.

    1. Amsterdam: Jan Evertsz II Cloppenburgh, 1615. [USTC 1032964]

Alle de Werken (3 vols.). [trans. P. Heringa, Vincent Meusevoet, Hendrick Uylenbroeck, etc.]

    1. Amsterdam: J. van Someren, 1659–1662.

    2. Amsterdam: J. von Someren, 1659–1663.

Geleerde en Godzalige Uytleggingen. [trans. Hendrick Uylenbroeck]

Contents: (1) Sermon on the Mount, (2) Galatians, (3) Hebrews 11, (4) Jude, (5) Revelation.

    1. Amsterdam: Johannes van Someren, 1662.

Sommighe regulen, welcke aenwijsen, hoe men een christelick ende godsalich leven leyden sal. ghetrocken uyt de schriften van W. Perkins ende Otho Casm. ["Rules for how one should lead a Christian and godly life. Drawn from the writings of William Perkins and Otto Casmann"]

    1. Breda: Isaac Schilders, 1615. [USTC 1019208]

Urim et thummin, dat is: Lichten en volmaaktheden. Bestaande in een korte en heerlijke beschrijvinghe van de voornaamste stukken der christelijke godts-dienst en oeffeninghen inde god-zaligheidt. [trans. Peter de Lang] [a compilation of material from Perkins]

    1. Amsterdam: Petrum De Lange for Abraham de Wees and Baltus De Wild, 1658.

German

Catechismus des hochgelehrten, frommen und berümbten Herren Guilielmi Perkinsi.… Auß Englischer Sprach in die Teutsche gebracht: In welchem anfenglisch Sechs veste Gründe und Fundament der gantzen Religion, als ein kurtze Introduction…gelegt sind: demnach aber alle und jedes Hauptstück des Catechismi, als die zehen Gebott, das Gebett Christi, der Apostolisch Glaub und beyde Sacrament des Tauffs und Herrn Nachtmals, außführlich erkläret werden.… in den Truck verfertiget durch Wolgang Mayem [ed. Wolfgang Mayer; trans. Wolfgang Mayer and Johann Heupel]

Contents: (1) *Foundation*; (2) Ten Commandments [*Golden Chain*, chs. 19–30], (3) *Lord's Prayer*; (4) *Creed* (5) Sacraments [*Reformed Catholic*, chs. 10–11].

  1. Basel: Jacob Trew, 1606.

  2. Hanau: Wilhelm Anton, 1606.

Gründliche Erklerung Der Lehre von den H. Sacramenten, der H. Tauff unnd Abendmals unsers lieben Herrn Jesu Christi, Nach anleitung H. Göttlicher Schrift, durch…Guilielmum Perkinsum, In Engelländischer Spraach beschrieben: Jetz aber auß dem Niderländ.

Contents: *Reformed Catholic*, chs. 10–11; *Galatians 3:26–28*.

  1. Hanau: Wilhelm Antonius, 1607. [USTC 2092693]

  2. Hanau: W. Anton, 1644.

Catechismus oder Summa Christlicher Lehre, das ist, außführliche Erklärung der Hauptstücke christlicher Religion, als nämlich der Articul des christlichen Glaubens, der heiligen Tauffe und Abendmahls Christi, der heiligen zehen Gebott und Gebets des Herrn…. auß Niderländischer Sprach ins Hochteutsch bracht durch Johan Heupein [trans. Johann Heupel]

  1. Hanau: Wilhelm Anton, 1607.

Drey nützliche und lehrreiche Büchlein, Guilielmi Perkinsii. Gründliche Erklärung, 1. etlicher geistlicher Verlassungen, alle träge und schläfferige Evangelische damit zu erschrecken… 2. Ein ernstliches Gespräch zwischen einem Christen und dem Satan. 3 Der Streit und Kampff deß Fleisches und deß Geistes…verteutschet, und auffs new Aufgelegt. [trans. Johann Ulrich]

Contents: (1) *Estate of a Christian: 8. Spiritual Desertions*, (2) *Estate of a Christian: 5. Conflict*, (3) *Two Treatises: 2. Combat*.

  1. Frankfurt, 1660.

  2. Bern: Georg Sonnleitner, 1666.

Ein nützliches und lehrreiches Büchlein Guilielmi Perkinsi, darinnen zufinden 1. Ein ernstliches Gespräch, zwischen einem Christen und dem Satan. 2. Der Streit und Kampff des Fleisches und deß Geistes…. verdeutschet durch Iohan Huldericum Textor. [trans. Johann Ulrich]

Contents: (1) *Estate of a Christian: 5. Conflict*, (2) *Two Treatises: 2. Combat*.

  1. Oppenheim: Friederich Hulsius, 1610. [USTC 2067549]

Zwey lehr- und trostreiche Stück[e] Guilielmi Perkinsii, 1. Das geistliche Senffkömlein, oder die aller kleineste Maß der Gnaden Gottes, welche zum Heyl und Seligkeit deß Menschen gnugsam seyn mag. 2. Gründtliche Erklärung etlicher geistlichen

Verlassungen Gottes… verteutschet durch Iohan Huldericum Textorem. [trans. Johann Ulrich]

Contents: (1) *Grain of Mustard Seed* (2) *Estate of a Christian: 8. Spiritual Desertions.*

  1. Oppenheim: Friederich Hulsius, 1610. [USTC 2080581]

Zwey lehr- und trostreiche Tractätlein Guilielmi Perkinsii 1. Ein liebliches und trostreiches Gespräch zwischen einem Prediger und Christen, darinnen einem betrübten, bußfertigen Sünder kreffdger Trost zugebracht wird…2. Das geisdiche Senffkömlein, oder die allerkleineste Maß der Gnade Gottes, welche zum Heil und zur Seligkeit des Menschen genügsam seyn mag. Allen betrübten…Seelen zum Trost…verteutschet, und auffs new auffgelegt.

Contents: (1) *Estate of a Christian: 7. Consolations,* (2) *Grain of Mustard Seed.*

  1. Bern: Georg Sonnleitner, 1665.

  2. Bern: Georg Sonnleitner, 1669.

Welsh

Cyfarwydd-deb i'r anghyfarwydd, sef, llyfr yu cynnwys, 1. Angoriad byrr ar weddi 'r arglwydd 2. Ymiddidanion rhwng y carwr ar cymro. 3. Ymddiddanion rhwng Crist a'r Publican, rhwng C'rist a'r Pharisæad, a rhwng Crist a'r Credadyn ammheus, fef Canwyll Crist. 4. Amryw reolan duwiol: Y cwbl i gyfarwyddo pobl, pa fodd i chwilio 'r serythyrau er lefadriw Heneidiau: a pha fodd I ddyfod at Frist i gael iechydwriaeth dragwyddol: a pha fodd i weddro yn 'ol ewyllys Duw, i gael grás a thrus are dd oddiwrtho ef, a pha fodd I fyw' ir sanctardd yn y byd presennol. [trans. Robert Holant]

  1. London: Thomas Dawks, 1677. [Wing P1561A]

Garden

A Garden of Spirituall Flowers. Planted by Ri. Ro. Will. Per. Ri. Gree. M. M. and Geo. Web. The Fift Time Imprinted. [contains: Perkins, "Directions How to Live Well, and to Die Well"]

  1. [Fifth Imprint]. London: Printed [by W. White] for T. Pauier and are to be sold at his shop entering into the Exchange, 1609. [ESTC 21205]

A Garden of Spirituall Flowers. Planted by Ri. Ro. Will. Per. Ri. Gree. M.M. and Geo. Web. I Part.

  1. London: Printed by W. White for T. Pauier and are to be sold at his shop entering into the Exchange, 1609. [21204.7]

  2. London: Printed by T. Snodham for T. Pauier, dwelling at the signe of the Catte and Parrets neare the Exchange, 1613. [ESTC 21207.3]

  3. London: Printed by W. White for T. Pauier and are to be sold in Iuie Lane, 1616. [ESTC 21207.5]

4. London: Printed by I. D[awson]. for E. B[rewster]. and Robert Bird and are to be sold at his shop in Cheap-side at the signe of the Bible, 1628. [ESTC 21210.3]

A Garden of Spirituall Flowers. 2 Part. Yeelding a Sweet Smelling Sauour in the Nosthrils of Each True-Hearted Christian.

1. London: Printed by T. S[nodham]. for T. Pauier, dwelling at the signe of the Catte and Parrets neare the Exchange, 1612. [ESTC 21213.1]

2. London: Printed by T. S[nodham]. for T. Pauier, dwelling at the signe of the Catte and Parrets neare the Exchange, 1613. [ESTC 21213.2]

3. London: Printed by T. S. for T. Puuier [*sic*], dwelling in Ivie Lane, 1617. [ESTC 21213.4]

4. London: Printed by T. S[nodham]. for T. Pauier, dwelling in Ivie Lane, 1619. [ESTC 21213.5]

5. London: Printed by T. S[nodham]. for T. Pauier, dwelling in Ivie Lane, 1622. [ESTC 21213.7]

6. London: Printed by T. S. for T. Pauier, dwelling in Ivie Lane, 1625. [ESTC 21213.8]

7. London: Printed by T. C[otes]. for Robert Bird, at the signe of the Bible in Cheapside, 1629. [ESTC 21213.9]

Revised Edition

A Garden of Spirituall Flowers. Planted by Ri. Ro. Will. Per. Ri. Gree. M. M. and Geo. Web. Corrected and Inlarged. 1. Part.

1. London: Printed by T. B[rudenell]. for R. Bird, dwelling at the signe of the Bible in Cheapside, 1630. [21210.5]

2. London: Printed by I. B[eale]. for R. Bird, dwelling at the signe of the Bible in St. Laurencelane, 1631. [ESTC 21211]

3. London: Printed by R. B[adger]. for Robert Bird, and are to be sold at his shop at the signe of the Bible in St. Lawrance lane, 1632. [ESTC 21212]

A Garden of Spirituall Flowers. Planted by Ri. Ro. Will Per. Ri. Green M. M. and Geo. Web. Corrected and Inlarged. 2. Parts.

1. London: [Printed by T. B. for John Wright, dwelling in the Old-Bailey], 1643. [R1825aA]

A Garden of Spiritual Flowers· Planted by Ri. Ro. Will. Per. Ri. Green. M. M. and Geo. Web. Corrected and Enlarged. In Two Parts.

1. London: Printed by R. I. for J. Wright, next door to the Globe in Little-Brittain, 1667.

2. London: Printed for George Conyers, at the Golden Ring on Ludgate-Hill, 1687.

Publishers of Perkins (approximate dates active)
Thomas Man (1578–1624), Cuthbert Burby (1562–1607), Henry Middleton (1567–1587), Robert Waldegrave (1578–1603), Nicholas Linge (1580–1607), Simon Waterstone (1584–1635), Thomas Orwin (1587–1593), Thomas Newman (1587–1593), John Porter (1587–1607), Thomas Gubbin (1587–1619), John Legat (1588–1621), William Leake (1592–1634), Walter Burre (1597–1621), William Stansby (1597–1639), Felix Kyngston (1597–1640), John Smethwick (1597–1640), Thomas Bushell (1599–1617), Eleazar Edgar (1600–1613), Thomas Pavier (1600–1625), John Hodges (1601–1625), Thomas Snodham (1603–1625), William Welby (1604–1618), Martin Clerke (1606–1611), Samuel Machan (1606–1615), Leonard Greene (1606–1630), William Barrett (1607–1624), Cantrell Legge (1607–1628), Jonas Man (1607–1635), Henry Fetherstone (1608–1627), Michael Baker (1610–1611), John Parker (1617–1638), John Haviland (1621–1640), Benjamin Fisher (1621–1637), Paul Man (1622–1635), John Legat Jr. (1621–1640), James Boler (1624–1634), John Wright Jr. (1634–1640). [Arber 5:216–77]

Scripture Index

Revelation (*continued*)

14:8	45–71
14:9–11	70
17:1–6	50
17:5	47
17:9	50
17:9–11	66
17:18	52
18:2	57, 61
18:3	68
18:4	228–33
18:11–19	61
18:21	61
19:3	61
19:19	63
20:1–2	265
20:12	141, 239
22:18	136

Subject Index